WOLFGANG GOETHE

WOLFGANG GOETHE

BY

GEORG BRANDES

Authorized Translation From the Danish

BY

ALLEN W. PORTERFIELD

NEW YORK
CROWN PUBLISHERS
1936

CONTENTS

VOLUME I

CONTENTS

CONTENTS

CONTENTS

Volume II

CONTENTS

CONTENTS

CONTENTS

CONTENTS.

TRANSLATOR'S NOTE

THE first draft of this translation was made at Copenhagen between November 1, 1916, and May 1, 1917. The second edition of "Wolfang Goethe" had appeared just before my arrival in Denmark in September, 1916. At Dr. Brandes's own request, this and not the first or unrevised edition was translated. The contract with the author was signed at his home, 27 Strandboulevard, Copenhagen, on March 20, 1917. While the translation was in progress, I corresponded with a number of American publishers who welcomed the idea of bringing out the work in this country and England.

Then came April 6, 1917. From August, 1917, until July, 1919, I was with the colors, in the United States, France, and Germany. During this period the manuscript was shelved awaiting the return to the arts of peace. Then came the backwash from the war. During these years of demobilization, retrospect, and reconstruction, years in which I was attached to the staff of the New York *Evening Post,* the translation was subjected to a complete revision. I made it my avocation, rewriting chapter after chapter, as opportunity offered.

Then came the German translation: 1922. This proved interesting and helpful. The German translators have deleted a number of remarks which were unfavorable: these I have retained. They have added a number of illuminating observations

not found in the Danish; these I have inserted, for
they are manifestly emendations by the author.
They were obliged, one would think, to go direct
to Goethe's German in the matter of quotations.
In the majority of instances they have. This has
made it easier, for Dr. Brandes is a foe of notes
and references. It was, consequently, at times
nearly impossible to locate a sentence from Goethe's
voluminous works. There were, this being the
case, a few passages in my original manuscript
which were translations of translations. There are
none in this

The sole changes I have felt at liberty to make
have to do with paragraphing, the substitution of
sectional divisions for chapter headings (there are
one hundred and forty chapters in the original
Danish), and the form or type in which the quotations appear. The notes on Scandinavian writers
have been added in the belief that they would make
the work more easily intelligible to the English-
speaking world. My objective, all told, has been
nothing more pretentious than to give an accurate
and idiomatic reproduction of the biography as it
was written. It is not fiction; I have consequently
not felt that it was my privilege to lift it up to any
great extent. It is science; I have therefore regarded it as my inescapable duty not to let it down
at all.

I owe a debt that is not small to Dr. Robert
Herndon Fife, Executive Officer of the German
Department of Columbia University, who went
through the translation and made a number of sug-
gestions of which I have taken full advantage. Miss
Virginia Lee Bowen read the proof with what

Goethe himself might have called *ein sonnenhaftes Auge*. My obligation to her for this is real. It also gives me unqualified pleasure merely to indicate the debt I owe my wife, Elsie de V. Porterfield, who did the better half of the mute, inglorious work that went into the Copenhagen draft. Without her reassurance, "Wolfgang Goethe" would never have been translated by me. With her partnership, all this writing, all this translating, recalls such memories as one carries away from intimate association with good literature itself.

A. W. P.

Randolph-Macon Woman's College,
July 5, 1923.

xii PREFACE TO THE SECOND EDITION

back to the history of his soul and dissolved in psychology.

In other words, the portrayal in this study runs along after the fashion of life itself, or it runs as

Was Goethe

PREFACE TO THE SECOND EDITION

The original feature of this book lies in the fact that, so far as the author knows, it is the first attempt to develop, without regard to the material connection of final and complete achievements, Goethe's personality from the cell up. It bears the same relation to the prevailing treatises on Goethe's life and works that his own treatise on botany bears to that of Linné: there are no rubrics.

This book does not contain a special section on Goethe as a lyric writer, nor does it contain one on Goethe as a naturalist or a dramatist or a philosopher or a manager of a theatre. Nor is there one separate and comprehensive section on *Götz* or *Iphigenie* or *Wilhelm Meister*. And—strange as it may seem—there is no isolated section on *Faust*.

The poetic outlines and fragments are portrayed just as they arise in the poet's fancy. In case they were elaborated or revised, the results are given at the point where they belong in the history of Goethe's development. Scientific conjectures with their corresponding experiments are discussed, each for itself, just as it engaged the investigator's mind, each in that stage of the development of Goethe's mind in which the hypothesis moves from unconscious life to consciousness. There are no rubrics. As with his poetic constructions and creations, his scientific discoveries and hypotheses are also traced back to the history of his soul and dissolved in psychology.

In other words, the portrayal in this study runs along after the fashion of life itself; or it runs as does the bronze until it becomes plastic in the form of the statue.

There is an intentional omission of easy and everyday *resumés* such as readers are accustomed to and, it would seem, take to with docility. There are no judgments on the man and his deeds which drive the conclusions through and clinch them for all time on the other side. No such plebeian questions as the following are raised: Was Goethe good? Was Goethe religious? Was Goethe national? Was Goethe inspired? Was he a snob? Was he an idealist, or a realist, or a pessimist, or an optimist? Was he warm? Was he cold? Was he philanthropic? Was he misanthropic?

All such questions—questions born of faith in rubrics and definitions and overlooking the fact that the life of a man, and particularly that of a genius, is a changeable, variable affair, rich in all manner of development—are rendered, it is to be hoped, superfluous by a presentation which, through the process of remelting, has dissolved them and deposited the answers in the hot, running stream. And this stream, congealed in time, becomes a plastic whole.

INTRODUCTION

NOTHING can seem more superfluous than the publication of still another book on Goethe, a great many more having already been written on him than he himself produced with all his diligence. It must be borne in mind, however, that one does not do this for Goethe's sake but for one's own sake: It is done with the idea of assembling the impressions that have come down from a mind studied interest in which has been a lifelong affair.

Goethe was the greatest poet of the last three centuries. But it is not the poet alone in him that fascinates and captivates. For the mere poetic factor in its complete isolation has perchance been somewhat overestimated in our day excluding as it does at times neither mental indigence nor spiritual immaturity and rudeness. It is Goethe as a natural and spiritual force, and as a profoundly human and magnificent personality, that one studies out of necessity and with satisfaction.

His mind had its limitations just as his character had its defects; yet we are justified in calling him the incarnation of humanity at its loftiest. To his mind nothing was foreign. He was more superbly endowed than any of his predecessors for several centuries back; he was more epoch-making than any of his contemporaries: he was more highly gifted than his successors. He was a type and a model by virtue of his many-sidedness and because of the complete fullness of his nature—a nature that was in itself a combination of pronounced contrasts.

Goethe is among minds what the Pacific Ocean is among the waters of the earth. The peaceful or Pacific Ocean is at once the largest and the deepest. In reality only a small part of it is pacific. To the north and south of this narrow belt the Pacific Ocean is tossed about by local winds and trade winds, it has its currents and its counter currents, its warm streams and its cold. It has earthquake waves, too, which are unlike those of any other great body of water. It is even so with Goethe in that he is the greatest and deepest of creative minds known to modern times. There is also in his life and lifework a broad, peaceful zone while all the rest is quiet and storm, warm streams and cold streams, currents and counter currents, and earthquake waves as well.

Wherever the German language is spoken Goethe enjoys undisputed renown. After a relatively long period, during which he was misunderstood and wrongly interpreted, he has become the national Germanic god. He is equally admired as a poet, as a scientist, as a philosopher, and as a man. The names of Luther, Lessing and Schiller, of Mozart, Beethoven and Wagner, even those of Kant and Schopenhauer, indeed even those of Frederick the Great and Bismarck cannot compete with Goethe's. He is in one person for Germany what Leonardo da Vinci, Michael Angelo and Galileo are for Italy, Molière, Racine and Voltaire for France, Shakespeare, Newton and Darwin for England, Linné,[1]

---

[1] Carolus Linæus (Karl von Linné) was born in 1707 and died in 1778. Though he journeyed to Lapland and resided for a while

Tegnér [2] and Berzelius [3] for Sweden: the comprehensive expression of the country's enduring glory and highest culture. For Europe and America he should typify not merely the deepest and broadest poetic phenomenon but also the most superbly endowed human being in general that has concerned himself with literature since the days of the Renaissance.

When one examines his actual standing, however, in the non-Germanic reading world, the picture becomes at times somewhat different. The well-nigh uniform admiration which, in German-speaking countries, his least important works have enjoyed along with his best, combined with the idolatry that accompanies every note from his hand and every

in the Netherlands, he is associated with the University of Upsala, where he was professor of botany from 1741 until his death. He is best known for his founding of the "Linnæan" system in botany. It was artificial as contrasted with the later system developed by Jussieu and his followers. Linné divided the entire plant world into twenty-four classes largely according to the number of styles or stigmas or stamens. It had very little value from the scientific point of view, though it was useful in its day in that it gave a key to botanical nomenclature.   —TRANSLATOR.

[2] Esaias Tegnér (1782-1846) was not a prolific writer. His collected works were published at Stockholm, 1876, in two volumes. His posthumous works appeared at Stockholm, 1873-1874, in three volumes. He is best known for his "Frithjofs Saga" (1825) based upon the old Norse saga of like name. It is one of the most famous romances in Scandinavian literature. His literary career began in 1808 with "War Songs for the Militia of Scania." He was elected bishop of Weixö in 1824. But his fame rests entirely, and securely, on his "Frithjof's Saga." It has been translated into the leading languages of the world.   —TRANSLATOR.

[3] Baron Johan Jacob Berzelius (1779-1848), aside from introducing a new nomenclature in chemistry, discovered selenium, thorium and cerium. He first exhibited calcium, barium, strontium, columbium, cilicium and zirconium as elements. He did a great deal by way of perfecting the atomic theory after Dalton. His textbook on chemistry (1820-1828) was translated into all European languages. Goethe became personally acquainted with him while at Karlsbad, in what was then Bohemia.
                                   —TRANSLATOR.

sentence that is ascribed to him, has had a challenging effect, while *Goethe-Philologie,* so justified in Germany, has tended to discourage. Erudite terrorism, which considers it an act of presumption to refuse to pay attention to, indeed even to show admiration for, every single line by Goethe has goaded non-Germanic readers and investigators on to a type of criticism in which good grace plays a very subordinate rôle. In France and England, for example, the two countries that represent the highest scientific and artistic refinement of today, dissatisfaction with Goethe the man is not infrequently expressed while depreciatory judgments on his works are by no means uncommon. The French and English agree, though grudgingly, that Goethe is a personality of the first rank, but they do not stop here. At his poetic creations they level a species of criticism which is not to be considered unreasonable simply because it is sharp.

In France indifference and misjudgment, admiration and misunderstanding, have a much longer history than correct interpretation, which, even to this day, has by no means won a secure place for itself. Eduard Rod's book, 1898, replete as it is with information and acumen, is born of the ill-will that persists.

From the very first, when Goethe was known in France only as the author of *Werther,* he was admired by the sentimentalists but looked at askance by the followers of Voltaire (just as in Germany he was held in but slight esteem by Lessing and Nicolai). He was also regarded as a perverter of youth by the pious who were unable to see anything in the book but a challenge to suicide. Later, when

Werther began to enjoy more intelligent recognition, it was still this work of Goethe's younger days that constituted the chief obstacle in the way of an entirely fair appreciation. For nearly eight lustrums the public either would not or could not see in him anything other than the author of this sentimental little novel. And for a long while, even during the days of Madame de Staël, this frenzied poet of passion, conducting himself as a perfectly proper, indeed even distinguished official, was an object of actual amazement to Frenchmen who came to Weimar on a casual visit.

The French regarded *Götz* as the direct outgrowth of the theories of the predecessors of the Romantic School, that is to say, of the writers who balked at and fought against Classicism. The older generation consequently decried Goethe's dramas as formless and worthless. Likewise in his lyrics the French were slow to see anything but the romantic and supernatural elements that found unquestioned favor with the Romanticists — fairy kings, mermaids and sorcerers.

For years and years, *Faust* was looked upon as a work of unrelieved negation. Even so highly gifted an individual as Benjamin Constant, who knew Germany well, found *Faust* immoral, flat, sterile, and distinctly inferior to *Candide* with which it had been compared. Madame de Staël's opinion of Part I is, all the world knows, even more amusing: "Whether the drama is a phantom of poetic madness or of rationalistic *Weltschmerz* is momentarily indeterminable. We can only hope that there will be no repetition of this species of literary creation." There was no danger.

In extenuation of French critical opinion we should not forget that the judgments pronounced on Goethe by Germany's leading men at the time of the publication of the *Faustfragment* were no less unfavorable. Neither Schiller nor A. W. Schlegel showed enthusiasm of any sort. From Schiller's circle came the scornful taunt that Gretchen was portrayed like a "goose." Körner, Schiller's most intimate friend, complained of the doggerel (*Bänkelsängerton*). Tieck could not understand what a man to whom the spirit of the earth had been revealed was trying to do with the wretched Mephistopheles. Huber had such a vague idea as to the meaning of Faust's monologue that he came to the conclusion that there must be something cryptic about it, intelligible only to the initiated critic.

In France the attacks that appeared after 1870 were motivated by patriotism. The French thought that they would be striking victorious Germany a mortal blow if they could in some way belittle the personality of that particular German who was regarded as the pride of the nation. They read Goethe with very unfavorable eyes. The younger Dumas wrote all manner of malicious fiddle-faddle about him. The French took serious offense at the laconic way in which the elderly Goethe referred to his youthful indebtedness to French literature as contrasted with the profuse references that were derogatory in spirit. They were repelled by his circumstantiality as a narrator and by his inability to compose a greater whole, a weakness that characterizes his entire literary output. Moreover, the neo-Christian and neo-Catholic movement in France took serious exception to the lack of Christian spirit in Goethe's writings as well as to that trait of the author which commentators and others have long been pleased to call his egoism, his selfishness.

In England the grudge against Goethe since the days of Carlyle and Lewes, and in America, since Emerson, has been motivated by the study of the moral side of life. There are phases of Goethe's character that jar the Englishman's conception of a gentleman. There is, for example, the way in which Goethe exposed the amiable Kestner and his wife Charlotte to public curiosity when he published his *Werther,* with its caricature of Albert, even though Albert and Kestner by no means coincided.

But the chief grievance that has found firm lodgement in modern England against Goethe is the one that concerns itself with the purely artistic in his lifework. In England great wonderment is expressed at the small number of actual masterpieces revealed by close scrutiny of Goethe's enormous output. An inordinate proportion of space is taken up with topical and occasional poems, heavy and stupid comedies and farces, incompleted plans, pure fragments, epigrams on persons or events now forgotten, inanimate allegories, and heaps of scientific material piled up in order to prove some impossible theory such as the woefully unsuccessful *Farbenlehre.* The masterpieces are relatively few, say the British, because, with the exception of a short period, Goethe never applied himself unreservedly to his true vocation—to the writing of poetry. He allowed business to sap him of his strength. For ten long years, and these the very best for a poet, from his twenty-seventh to his thirty-seventh, he gives up poetic activity entirely and dedicates himself to the wearisome affairs of statecraft in Weimar. During all this time he writes practically nothing but poetry for set occasions. Hence the lack of unity in his more pretentious works. He let them lie too long; they are as a rule heterogeneously or poorly constructed. He constantly took them up anew and revised them, or he worked new pieces into them, or he continued them after he had half forgotten the original plan.

Götz von Berlichingen exists in three different forms, not counting detached scenes. *Iphigenie* was revised five times. *Wilhelm Meisters Lehrjahre* lay so long that it was finally completed after a plan that differed entirely from the original one; two versions exist. *Wilhelm Meisters Wanderjahre* was elaborated according to no plan whatsoever; it is a mere compilation. And finally we come to his main work, *Faust,* which was outlined and laid aside, and then taken up again and then laid aside again and taken up again, so that its composition extends over a period of sixty years. It is consequently difficult to say how many Fausts there are in *Faust;* one there certainly is not. The entire work contains a series of geological strata, and these strata lie at times as they do when a great mass of material tumbles over—in one confused and conglomerate pile.

Hence it is that Goethe is called an experimenter. His basic misfortune lay in the fact that he had no great literary tradition back of him which could support him and show him the way; that he either wanted to or had to create, experimentally, modern German literature. This explains his intense sensitiveness to impressions from a great variety of sources.

First we note those from France, from the eighteenth century drama in Alexandrines. He wrote *Die Laune des Verliebten* and *Die Mitschuldigen.* Then under Herder's influence he became acquainted with Shakespeare, and felt the effects of the sentimentality of Rousseau and Ossian; his *Götz* is modeled after Shakespeare, while *Werther* grew out of Rousseau. Later he fell into pseudo-classicism, imitated the Greek tragedy in *Iphigenie,* wrote *Hermann und Dorothea,* an idyl on a pseudo-Greek scale, copied Propertius and Catullus in the *Römische Elegien,* imitated Martial in the *Venezianische Epigramme,* turned back to Racine and translated two tragedies of Voltaire. And last of all, influenced by Oriental poetry, he reproduced Hafis and Saadi.

Dowden has asked: What is his style? And Dowden has replied: Shall we say it is French-English-Greek-Roman-Persian-German?

The fact, however, that Goethe's works are modeled after so many different sorts of styles is not in itself necessarily objectionable. I know that in my own experience, the first time I stood on St. Mark's Place in Venice, directly opposite the old Doges' Palace, that miracle of Moorish-Gothic style which rests on a series of short, Greek columns, surmounted by Gothic arches, which in turn support the massive wall of red and white marble blocks—I know that the one word that immediately leaped to my lips as I stood there was: *Goethe.*

I was impressed with the number of worlds—Antique, Gothic, Oriental—that were here united into a harmonious whole. And standing before this amazing architectural pile, my thoughts quite naturally reverted to that great spirit who reared a similar edifice in the world of poetry. Revelling in the beauties of the Strassburg Cathedral, he created the Gothic Gretchen; inspired by the Antique, he created the Greek women Iphigenie and Helena. He poetized the Italian Eleanore, the Dutch Clärchen, the Persian Suleika and then grouped these diverse incarnations of the spirit of different times and different lands as so many statues around the pediment of his own life monument.

The objection that Goethe was neither able to follow a traditional German style nor to create one has precious little weight. Who would dare say that the modern genius, with an undisputed right to seek his nourishment from the cultures of the earth, shall be born exclusively of national custom and shall tread only those ways that the national artists of times past have opened up? When a man of this rank is so constituted that from the very first the historic art forms lie before him like an open book, should he not be permitted to take from them anything and everything that coincides and harmonizes with his nature? When Goethe studies and lauds Boileau (read the letter to his sister Cornelia from Leipzig in which he places Boileau above Tasso), then Herder and the writers whom Herder cultivated, Euripides and Hafis for example, it is he himself in all of these disguises who transforms everything which, as an apprentice, he had appropriated.

That hoary and rustic conception concerning independence and originality is so stupid! Even when Goethe was a young man people understood by an "original" person one who is peculiar, odd; and by a "genius" one who (apparently) owes no man anything. To that sort of originality Goethe refers when he has Mephistopheles reply to the student, who was so proud of his independence, with the stinging words: *Original! Fahr hin in deiner Pracht!* If originality could be acquired in that fashion then he would be a genius who walks on his head and gesticulates with his feet.

An artist, it is said, follows his own infallible instinct and is not an experimenter. Few artists have had more instinct than Goethe; yet he simply kept on experimenting. Who will say that an artist must not experiment? Within the past five centuries there has been no greater artist than Leonardo da Vinci; and no one ever experimented more than he. With his mind's surprising many-sidedness he anticipates Goethe; in his infallibility he even surpasses him. And yet he constantly designed artistic and technical plans, posited ingenious scientific conjectures—and very rarely carried them out.

The question will not down: What is Goethe and what can he be today for non-Germanic peoples, for the very considerable minority of contemporaneous, spiritually enlightened individuals devoid of national and religious prejudices and speaking a language that was not his? What is to be the attitude toward Goethe of those who do not cherish that unbounded piety for him which is the inevitable consequence of national and linguistic fellowship but who are attracted to substantial greatness and have no fear for the slight and yet necessary exertion without which it is absolutely impossible to come into intimate association with him?

For most so-called educated men and women in each non-Germanic nation Goethe is only a name. There are to be sure quite a few who have read this and that by him without being genuinely impressed by what they have read or feeling sincerely grateful to the author for having written it. It is to this latter class that one should try to explain the real significance of Goethe. For these people he is not easily accessible; the language in which he wrote is not theirs, his being is a fortress and not an open town, and he lived in an age poles removed from the present. Goethe never rode in a railway train, he never sailed on a steamship. He read by a tallow lamp and wrote with a goose quill. Born but five years before Holberg's death, he was a contemporary of Voltaire in the first part of his life and of Byron in the second.

Outside of Germany one can hear otherwise quite intelligent individuals condemn the modern study of Goethe and characterize it as a matter of pure affectation. One can hear both trained and untrained men say that it is wholly abnormal for people of our day to pretend that they read *Wilhelm Meisters Lehrjahre* or *Die Wahlverwandtschaften* with pleasure. These works, critics of this sort contend, were once entertaining, perhaps even of absorbing interest, whereas now they have only historical value. Still less importance is attached to Goethe's letters.

It is true that a great number of human beings, especially, it may be, in the Scandinavian countries, merely affect or pretend to be admirers of Goethe;

that it is difficult for a modern young non-Germanic man or woman to wade through some of Goethe's epic and dramatic works; and finally, that the perusal of Goethe's letters is for the great majority a work of supererogation. Not only *Die Wanderjahre* and the second part of *Faust* but even *Werther* must now appear antiquated to youthful readers. Yet in the majority of instances one is richly rewarded for cracking the historic shell and forcing one's way into the human or poetic kernel. Indeed in many instances the fruit in question has no shell; it is all meat.

A half-grown boy or girl can read *Götz von Berlichingen* with genuine satisfaction. It is about the best introduction that could be selected for a boy, for aside from being a humorous and vivid portrayal of human beings it is replete with tumultous accounts of brave deeds, zeal for liberty, passionate love, melodrama and resounding words. *Egmont* is a happy introduction for a young man or a mature young woman. One finds here no longer the pathos that characterizes *Götz*,—that pathos which, strange to say, Kierkegaard [4] missed in Goethe's works. By virtue of the poet's steady control of the situation, the characters now stand out clear, calm, and unforgetable.

The first part of *Faust* widens the horizon for

---

[4] Sören Aabye Kierkegaard (1813-1855), perhaps the greatest prose writer Denmark has ever known, was brought up in an intensely religious atmosphere. He spent his life fighting for the principles of Christianity. His later years were embittered by his violent quarrel with the State Church of Denmark which he claimed had the form but not the substance. It was as an outspoken opponent of Rasmus Nielsen, Kirkegaard's faithful disciple, that Brandes made his debut in literature.

—TRANSLATOR.

Goethe's real greatness. The aim of the titular character is a definitive understanding and exhaustive enjoyment of the universe. A single scene, such as the walk on Easter Morning, with its highly colored pictures of life, the vivaciousness of the conception of nature, the melodious diction, and the depth, seriousness, and bitterness of the insight into human nature, contains the most exalted ideas thus far found in modern poetry.

These works give the young mind such a rich booty that a desire is awakened for more. In this way the reader soon becomes sufficiently versed in Goethe to apply himself to the *Gedichte,* possibly the most admirable part of Goethe's manifold achievement.

One will do best to begin with the *Balladen* which, containing as they do, an epic element, offer no particular difficulty. It is advisable to proceed from the quite simple ballads such as *Der Sänger* and *Der Fischer* to the profound ones such as *Der Gott und die Bajadere* and *Die Braut von Korinth.* After these the shorter philosophic works can be taken up, such as *Prometheus, Ganymed, Mahomets Gesang,* and after very little exertion one can read the poems descriptive of nature, or the love songs, or the table songs.

The poems that reveal Goethe's indisputable mastery within a self-imposed boundary open up a view into his personal life of feeling and thought with all its wholesomeness and fullness. He can be as simple as a folksong or he can present an entire philosophy in a brief poem. The inner richness of his being makes it impossible for even a short stanza to be empty. It is here that we derive an idea as to the real magnitude of his being.   He can be playful and graceful, rich and jovial, aglow with an inner fire, impetuously defiant, jocose, wise, sublime.

It is easy in this way to get an impression of Goethe's greatness; and having reached this point, it becomes a source of unaffected joy to see him disguise himself now as a Roman, now as a Persian. A study of the *Römische Elegien* or the *West-Oestlicher Divan* reveals the vastness of Goethe's thirst for knowledge, his longing for ever greater and ever-widening fields; furthermore, one responds with keener pleasure to the increasingly facile play of poetic expression.

Having reached this point it is possible to steep one's self in the boundless store of apothegms in verse and prose which Goethe bequeathed to the world. It is a veritable gold mine of wisdom and experience pertaining unto things of this life. The older one becomes, the more nourishment one will find for his mind and the more material for new deliberation. Even where these apothegms are less effective because of the thought contained in them than because of their lapidary style, even here, in their brevity, they have an amazing power.

After this it is possible to take up Goethe's life, his *Dichtung und Wahrheit*. This is one of the great books of the nineteenth century. It is Goethe's attempt to explain himself. It is, however, not simply the unique explanation of the genesis of a genius that admits of no imitation; it is a very educative work on general principles. Goethe's life, his conversations (which are often excellent though not always wholly reliable), and the best of his letters are writings from which those of the younger generation who wish to be autodidactic—many never will—can learn a great deal concerning simple but important characteristics such as strict, thorough-going order, constant attention to the guiding call of one's own nature and the power that follows there-from, and finally to the development of a keen recep-tivity and many-sided humanity.

Goethe had his very definite limitations. He was a cunctator; and he was not a heroic character, de-spite the fact that he was a real man. But one can-not expect the characteristics of a Garibaldi in a Goethe any more than in a Shakespeare. Goethe remains the great model in many spiritual fields.

When one has seen how distinctly personal his entire poetic activity is, that is to say, how little actual material there is in his work, one is at once struck by the lack of self-reflection. One never meets Goethe's mere self in his works. Smaller minds picture themselves; Goethe never. He never lost himself in self-contemplation. He never wished to live from his own blood. He invariably sought his nourishment outside of himself. He is concrete even when he is lyrical. It is from him that we learn to abhor chimeras and to hold fast to realities.

That is one point. Another lesson that we can learn from Goethe is never to go scurrying around after the material goods of this life; never to seek mere personal development, but to revere that which germinates and grows unaided within us. It is from Goethe that we learn never to seek any nourishment other than that which suits us, that which we can digest and assimilate.

It is wonderful when we stop to think how little of this world Goethe ever felt a desire to see. He never saw America, though it interested him greatly. He never saw Paris, he never saw London, he never saw St. Petersburg, he never saw Vienna. Only one single time did he catch a fleeting glimpse of Berlin. He flourished like a green bay tree in a town of 6,200 inhabitants.

If he passionately longed for Rome and studied Italy from north to south, Sicily included, it was because there came a time in his life when the sight of the monuments of antiquity and of the art works of the Renaissance was an actual essential to his inner progress. Nothing ever attracted him which was not necessary to his inner development.

Sparing of the nature within him, he understood the nature without. Because everything in him was quiet growth, peaceful unfolding, slow formation, and complete transformation, he understood growth, transformation, metamorphosis in the natural world and came in time to make far-reaching discoveries in botany, osteology, and geology. In one single field of natural science he made a grave error, an error which he never abandoned, just as he made mistakes at times as poet in the domain of the epic and the drama. But he went as far in science as he could in his rôle of nature-loving and nature-grasping seer. What could not be seen or foreboded or conjectured eluded his range of power. But who can now see as he saw!

Take, by way of illustration, a field that has only subordinate significance for his fame, such as the criticism of art; read his little treatise on Leonardo da Vinci's *Last Supper*. This is the first explanation we have of the renowned painting appreciated and explained by virtue of the seer's eye which he had in a matchless degree, the eye that analyzes and synthesizes at the same time.

There have lived, to be sure, more accomplished poets than Goethe; he was perfect only in his shorter works. The larger ones he worked over so completely that the one text confuses the other, or he let them lie until the spirit came over him again, took them up anew, gave the new an artistic connection with the old, and struggled with it all so long that it acquired a new motivation or became loggy, diffuse, inconsequential. But what is good is superior to anything that has been written within recent centuries. Greater though Goethe was than any poet that mighty France has produced, he was greater as a mind than as a poet. As a human being in general, he was greater than his life-work because of the example he set as to how one should live.

His influence on his people is immeasurable, incalculable, overwhelming, despite the fact that he has not been able to fashion his people after his own model. If Germany at this moment is one of the most powerful countries on the earth, Goethe has had his part as a teacher and educator in this development. If, on the other hand, Germany in its power has fallen a hopeless prey to arrogance and haughtiness, it simply means a defection from Goethe.

He was a picture in miniature of the producing, classifying, preserving power of the universe. He produced and understood with equal certainty; he had an equal amount of imagination and reason. He never sought to know himself but to grasp nature. Self-reflection was foreign to him, self-development was everything. He protected his self-development with an instinct of self-preservation that was at once his wise counselor and unerring guide. He was a creator within the creation, a reason within all-reason, a nature within nature, just as we speak of a state within a state. He was, too, within himself a whole and complete civilization.

WOLFGANG GOETHE

VOLUME I

WOLFGANG GOETHE

CHAPTER I

FRANKFORT-ON-THE-MAIN—PARENTS—CHILD-HOOD AND COUNT THORANC—GRETCHEN

FRANKFORT-ON-THE-MAIN, where Johann Wolfgang Goethe was born on the 28th of August, 1749, was, by reason of its location and history, a sort of metropolis, so ancient as to have been the site of one of Charlemagne's royal palaces. In 843 it became the capital of the East Franconian Empire, that is to say, of Germany. It remained an Imperial Free City until the thirteenth century. At the time of the Reformation, in 1536, it became the permanent place of election of the German emperors. The city preserved its independence and privileges until the middle of the eighteenth century. Frankfort was an aristocratic Republic with walls, towers, and gates, within which the self-sufficient citizens, isolated from the surrounding world, were governed by a few old patrician families who kept an eye ever single to venerable traditions. Measured by modern standards, Frankfort, at the time of Goethe's birth, was only a small place with about 33,000 inhabitants, but it was a prosperous commercial centre where the merchants' fairs, immensely attractive to foreigners, were held twice a year. It was a pious, formal, conventional, old-fashioned city, wholly capable of taking care of itself and solicitous always lest the citizen of good family escape. Lying midway between North Germany and South Germany, though much more akin to the South than to the North, it was here that North German intelligence and pedantry flourished along side of South German lack of restraint, joy in living, and love of colors, manifested especially during the coronation festivities following the various imperial elections.

Of these the ever-alert boy had heard long before he saw them, for there was, as Goethe himself says in his autobiography, no Frankfort citizen of mature years who did not look upon the coronation festivities as the red letter days in his life. Goethe's great uncle Von Loen had described in detail the coronation of Charles VII in 1742. That of Francis I in 1745 had likewise been magnificent and had won the hearts of the people because of the unquestioned marital love between the Emperor and Maria Theresa. The coronation of Joseph II as Roman King in 1764, which had so completely captivated the fancy of Wolfgang, then fourteen years old, was a delight to all the senses. The mere arrival in the city of the Electors, each accompanied by an enormous retinue, was an occasion of matchless splendor. Even the coachmen and postillions, Goethe says, looked as though they came from another country, indeed from another world. There was so much to look at and point at and explain that one never came to one's self. The eye roamed over gorgeously adorned doublets, gold embroidered mantles, huge tall feather hats. The ear was filled with the peal of bells from the steeples and tones of the organ from the cathedral. Fountains gushed forth red wine and white wine. A fatted ox was roasted on a great spit over a coal fire.

Dignified on workdays, on holidays the city fairly revelled in exhibitions of splendor and luxury. Its inhabitants were a people who, living in a milder climate than that of North Germany, were of a lighter temper and a warmer nature, a people whose sensuousness was naïve and whose intelligence never became unnatural. In contrast to Berlin, Hamburg and Königsberg as spiritual centres, Frankfort lay south of the wine-line—that line which draws the boundary between the cities in which the joy of life grows and those into which the joy of life has to be imported.

The contrast between Goethe himself and his predecessors in German literature from the North is most pronounced. Gottsched was rational, Klopstock was supramundane, Lessing was all intelligence, all Enlightenment without grounding in the appreciation of nature or history. Herder, who attacks Enlightenment and continually speaks of the unconscious, the natural cause and the mystery is, in his innermost being, devoid of substantial appreciation of his immediate surroundings. Herder had no definite and distinct relation to the physical world and consequently no eye for painting and sculpture. It is no wonder, then, that he felt so ill at ease on Italian soil and that he became more and more irritated with increasing age by those very characters in Goethe's works in whom Goethe implants a sound

and strong, sensuous realism.   In short, these writers from the North manifested at all times a marked
tendency toward moralizing, accompanied by vastly
more reason than imagination.

The lighter, more pliant, more frivolous Wieland,
who incidentally did not lack grace, is, as a South
German, more of a sexual being than any of the
above-mentioned Northerners.   Kant, the great
critical philosopher, comes from Königsberg; Schelling, the philosopher of nature, whose ideas not
infrequently appeal to and coincide with Goethe's
own ideas, hails, like Wieland, from South Germany.

In Frankfort, as in Goethe, northern and southern
Germany met and formed a unity which, as Hehn
has said, reminds one of an agate: half gray, half
white.   The town continued to remain a central
point long after Goethe's birth, for in the nineteenth
century it became the first seat of the German Confederation and later (1848) of the first German
Reichstag.

Goethe left Frankfort in 1775; he was then
twenty-six years old.   Though he soon felt socially
at home in Weimar, where he spent the last fifty-six
years of his life, he never became entirely acclimated
to Weimar.   He felt rather as though he were banished to a land where the sky is grayer, the sun paler,
the air colder—a land without grapes.

II

It is impossible to explain the origin of genius;
and yet we find certain fundamental traits of
Goethe's make-up in his ancestors, as he himself has

roguishly told us in a little poem, the following lines
of which have been quoted time out of mind:

> Vom Vater hab' ich die Statur,
> Des Lebens ernstes Führen,
> Von Mütterchen die Frohnatur
> Die Lust zu fabuliren.

Goethe seems to owe to his father, Johann Caspar Goethe (1710-1782) the orderliness that was
characteristic of his personal conduct as well as of
his literary and scientific papers, the systematic element in his existence, the discipline at first forced
upon him and later self-imposed. Without this, his
ingenuity along various diverging lines and his inborn defiance of rules would not have allowed him
to become the conscientious and diligent worker that
he was. It was the poet, the artist, in him that
sketched all sorts of plans and let them lie unfinished for decades—*paresseux avec délices,* as Figaro
says of himself in Beaumarchais; it was the man of
order and system in him that induced him to complete fragments in large numbers and to subject the
first sketch to infinite revision.

Goethe's father was thirty-nine years old, his
mother eighteen, when he was born. The contrast
in the natures of the parents was strengthened still
further by the difference in their ages, and equalized
in the son in such a way that the personality of his
mother became the stronger and the one that stood
in the more intimate relation to Middle Germany.

The father was a lawyer; he had studied at Giessen and Strassburg. For the latter city he had an
especial regard and eventually sent his son there.
But of far greater significance for the son's future

was the fact that his father had lived for a while
in Italy, and longest in Rome. The journey to Italy,
from which he returned in 1740, was the great event
in his life. The entrance hall to the house was
adorned with Roman views in copper engravings.
When still at a tender age, the son had seen, inside
and out, day after day, the Piazza del Popolo, the
Coliseum, San Angelo, the Piazza of St. Peter's,
and St. Peter's itself. The otherwise laconic father
described in detail these buildings and places. He
had a pronounced preference for the Italian language, which he taught to his wife and later to his
son and daughter. Being a collector, like his son,
he had brought back from Italy a small collection of
species of marble and other natural curiosities. He
devoted a great deal of time to slowly, carefully
and methodically writing up the description of his
Italian journey, in Italian, with the help of an
Italian teacher, and copying it off in numerous pam-
phlets. Having, too, a by no means ordinary voice,
his wife was obliged to accompany the old gentleman in the singing of Italian arias and melodies.
He could also play the flute and the lute.

Johann Caspar Goethe, who in 1742 had received
the title of *Kaiserlicher Rat,* touchily and for very
inconclusive reasons, retired from all public activity
and spent his remaining days as a domestic tyrant.
Martinet that he was on general principles, his wife
never breathed freely, never came to herself, until
death removed him after she had spent a number
of years nursing him.

Goethe's father was not a man of mean characteristics. He possessed endurance, persistence, zeal
for learning and teaching, and marked conscien-

tiousness. He was strict with himself and others and had marked ability to do without those things that are ordinarily called necessities. It is plain that some of these traits were inherited by the son. The most conspicuous contrast to his son lay in an utter lack of imagination.

In 1776 he suffered a stroke of apoplexy and was from then on an humbled soul; in 1779 he began to lose his memory; in 1781 he had another stroke which paralyzed him. He died in 1782—and his death evoked not one word of lament from his son.

Strong pedant that he was, he had watched with a firm hand and an unloving disposition over the instruction and education of his children. In many ways, Goethe's education resembles that of John Stuart Mill half a century later. As a mere child, the father had had Wolfgang taught Latin, Greek, French, English, Italian, Hebrew, geography and history, as well as the basic principles of various natural sciences. The boy was obliged to write down his conversations with his comrades or his father; he had to make an outline of the sermons he heard on Sundays; and he had to write poetry on various themes as an exercise in metrics and rhyming.

The father was equally exacting as a teacher and a householder. Time and again did the son have to suffer from the old gentleman's penuriousness, so that loans from his comrades and friends constituted the only way out. When, for example, he published at his own expense, in company with Merck, his first more pretentious work, *Gottfried von Berlichingen,* the father flatly refused to render him any sort of financial aid. Johann Casper Goethe treated his son somewhat as Frederick William I, a generation earlier, had treated the Great King, at that time Prince. The sternness, irrational and intolerable, was little inclined to instil in the two great men a feeling of filial piety, though it had its good effect. The precocious boy could well stand excessive hemming-in, and his poetic nature, independent as it was and rebellious at the very thought of restraint, became so much the more powerful because it had been subjected to severe discipline.

Whereas the father descended from German working men (his grandfather came to Frankfort as a tailor's apprentice and acquired considerable wealth; his great-grandfather had been a smith), the poet's mother, Katharina Elizabeth Textor (1731-1808), called *Frau Rat,* or by her pet name *Frau Aja,* came of an aristocratic family. The poet's maternal ancestors, in several branches, had been teachers, lawyers, and distinguished officials. Frau Aja's father was Frankfort's highest official, City Governor (*Stadtschultheiss*) and Chairman of the fourteen Councillors (*Schöppen*). These councillors not only controlled the city but occupied its highest tribunals. The City Governor, chosen for life, was Frankfort's juridical head. The name Textor had been latinized; it was originally Weber.

Frau Aja was a brunette with dark brown eyes, tall and well formed, healthy and unaffected, natural and extremely vivacious, with a fund of good humor and jolly good mood that simply would not be influenced by any sort of adversity, warm of heart and free of care, a true daughter of the Rhineland. Her ears had always been accustomed to the music of the Main; the dialect of Frankfort had always been her language. There had not been instilled

into her the more refined manners of exclusive society, though she had received a good education in
the public schools and possessed that broad culture
which makes one frank and free in all conditions
of life even when in the presence of superiors. She
was not simply natural, she was nature itself. She
was not simply fanciful and endowed with marked
ability as a narrator; she had also a clear understanding and precocious experience. As a result of
her cheerful piety and determination to get the best
out of everything, she had created for herself a
philosophy of life which never forsook her. The
God whom she had found in the Old Testament was,
as her son says, an unchangeable family God. She
felt that the unhappiness of a great many people
was of their own making; their lives were bitter
because they themselves had made them so. She
felt impelled to know the good and the bad sides
of life, to feel its strength and to have confidence in
herself. In one place she says: "One should enjoy
the small pleasures of life and not strive after the
great ones. I brook no thorns; I merely reach out
after the smaller joys. If the door is low I bow.
If the stone can be pushed out of the way, I do so;
if it is too heavy, I walk around it. In this way I
find every day something that delights me."

She was easily inspired. Vivacious conversation
was her chief pleasure; association with great men
enraptured her. Like her son she was rich in comparisons and was an exceptionally good inventor and
narrator of stories. With brilliant self-character-
ization she once wrote to Frau von Stein: "I have
a gift of making everyone, utterly regardless of
rank, age or sex, happy on leaving me. I like people

very much, a fact which old and young appreciate.
I go through the world without demands, and that
pleases the sons and daughters of the earth. I
preach to no one. I always try to find the good
points in people and leave the bad ones to Him
who created mankind and who best knows how to
smooth off the sharp corners. In this way I keep
myself well, happy and contented." She was entirely without sentimentality, though she always
wore her heart on her sleeve.

That the son, from childhood on, played comedies, took an interest in the theatre, the art of acting,
and the writing of dramas, was due to the mother's
influence. She nourished a burning passion for the
theatre, had the very best of judgment concerning
everything theatrical, and constantly received actors
into her home. The son's sanguinity is also to be
traced back to the mother, she being indeed even
more sanguine than he. She had a few adages
which are highly characteristic of her personality
and partly of his. One was: "Experience creates
hope." Another was: "Learn to live and live to
learn." There was no cowardice in her character.
She preserved, resultantly, her equanimity even
during the war times through which she lived, when
foolish and depressing rumors were daily buzzing
about her ears. Like her son, she saw to it that
she was neither disturbed nor downcast. Her calm
was dear to her. Love of rest was a chief feature
of her character. She avoided strong, violent impressions, had a pronounced dislike for anything disquieting or exciting, was utterly indifferent to newspaper headlines on political events, demanded of
her servants that they should not relate anything

painful or disagreeable that had taken place in her
own home or in that of her neighbors.   She was,
moreover, of a very active nature, rid herself quickly
of all difficulties, and invariably removed the most
disagreeable one first.

That her life, however, was not smooth and easy
is seen from the fact that of her children only
Wolfgang and Cornelia lived.   In 1755 she lost her
second daughter, then one year old, in 1759 a six-
year-old son, Wolfgang's playmate, for whom he
took down lessons and stories but at whose death
he shed not one single tear.   Shortly thereafter there
died another little daughter, two and a half years
old, and a few years later (1760) the youngest son.
The attempt has been made to explain all of these
deaths as due to various diseases introduced into
Frankfort when the troops were mobilized there.
But who knows the real cause?   With a single exception, Goethe's own children, two boys and two
girls, died when quite young.   These deaths have
been ascribed to the fact that the maternal grandfather was addicted to drink and that indeed the
grandparents on both sides of the house were inordinate lovers of wine.   In each of the above cases
the explanation is eminently unsatisfactory.   There
were in all probability germs of disease in the family
such as one frequently finds in families that produce
geniuses.

III

Goethe was only seven years old when the Seven
Years War broke out with the invasion of Silesia
by Frederick the Great in 1756.   Not only in Germany itself but in neighboring states as well two

parties arose, one for, one against Frederick the Great. Goethe's grandfather, who, as a Councillor of Frankfort, had carried the imperial canopy over Francis I at his coronation and had received a great gold chain with the picture of the Empress, sided with Austria. Some of his daughters and sons-in-law did likewise. Goethe's father, who had been made a *Rat* by Charles VII, the rival emperor, remained loyal to Prussia. Consequently the family gatherings on Sunday were soon disturbed. Discussions arose, hostilities became frequent, painful scenes ensued.

In 1755 the same thing happened to the little boy that happened to the great Voltaire. The earthquake in Lisbon had shaken his firm faith in a good God. A year later his faith was shaken in another direction. He had always been taught that this or that which was agreed upon as being proper and befitting should be done, not for its own sake, but for the sake of the people. Otherwise what would people think! What would they say to this? The boy had genuine reverence for that enigmatic concept, *Die Leute.* He had imagined that this *Volk* would understand and appreciate impartially. Now he saw that the opposite was true. Great merits such as those of Frederick the Great were belittled and derided, indisputable accomplishments such as his were abused and distorted, not by the rabble, but by such otherwise judicious men as his grandfather and his uncles. He lost his faith in the people's sense of justice.

On New Year's Day, 1759, just as the father had re-arranged and renovated the house in the *Hirschgraben,* the French soldiers were billeted upon him.

It was particularly exasperating to him to have no less an individual than the personal representative of the King of France, *le lieutenant du roy,* Count Thoranc, who was an officer in charge of rents, reclamatior and claims. It was his business to settle disputes between the troops and the citizens and to adjust all financial matters. The Count was a French nobleman, born at Castle Mouans near Grasse in the Provence. He was tall, slender, serious by nature, with fiery black eyes and dignified bearing, a passionate lover of art, a zealous collector of paintings, extremely polite and considerate withal, though stern when offended.

Goethe's father was beside himself with wrath when he saw his house, in which every single object was arranged with a scrupulous pedantry, exposed to the arbitrariness of an unwelcome stranger. Since, too, the old gentleman was a friend of Prussia he naturally hated the French. He consequently and immediately placed himself on a war footing with the *Königsleutenant,* never exchanging a word with him, though he spoke French quite well. Goethe's mother, who could speak Italian but not French, had to begin at once to learn it, transacting business in the meanwhile with the Count through an interpreter, Herr Diene, the adaptable and intelligent neighbor across the street.

The Count, according to Goethe, was flattered at the trouble to which the mother of the family subjected herself at her age—she was then twenty-eight and from Goethe's point of view rather old, and since there was something cheerful and spiritual in the Count's bearing, there soon arose the very best of feeling between him on the one hand and

Goethe's mother and the interpreter on the other. Though there came times when the Count was melancholy, shut himself in and saw no one, once these spells were over, he was again the same gentle, lighthearted, vivacious Frenchman. He remained in Frankfort for more than three years. He seems to have left the Goethe house in the summer of 1761 and Frankfort temporarily in June of the same year. He returned to Frankfort for a month in January-February 1763. Young Goethe passed in and out at his door, became his favorite and received from him his first impression of French character and point of view.[1]

The alert youth came, however, in contact not simply with one prominent Frenchman; he received a general introduction to French customs and usages. For the benefit of the soldiers quartered in Frankfort, a company of French actors had come to the city. Every evening they played tragedies of Racine or less renowned writers, comedies of Molière, Destouches, Marivaux, La Chaussée, Diderot, and Palissot. Goethe, having received a free ticket of admission to the theatre from his influential grandfather, spent all of his evenings there. At first he enjoyed the action without being able to understand what was being said. In this way he trained his ear so thoroughly that in course of time he could not only understand French but speak and write it

[1] Is it possible that the intelligent and amiable French official, who lived in the same house, made absolutely no impression on the young mother who could not help but compare him with her own querulous, suspicious, disagreeable, domineering, pedantic husband? I have been told in France that a package of letters from Goethe's mother to Count Thoranc was found at Castle Mouans about ten years ago. My authority is the well known French author Léon Blum, but it is possible that he has been misinformed.

fairly well. Of inestimable value to him in this
connection was the acquaintance of a small French
boy of his own age who belonged to the company.

IV

In his autobiography Goethe has interwoven with
his account of the coronation festivities the story of
his first captivation by a young woman. He has
portrayed with the art of a great master this youthful love affair, which must have made a profound
impression upon him in view of the fact that he
identified the object of his juvenile enthusiasm and
yearning with the heroine of *Faust,* at least so far
as the name is concerned, for he named the heroine
of *Faust* after the girl with whom he as a mere boy
had fallen in love.

Goethe tells how he made the acquaintance, on
the streets and in the alleys of Frankfort, of a number of boys of equal age, or a little older, primarily
by reason of the fame that he enjoyed because of
his skill at writing verses. Thus he became familiar
with a circle of young people who belonged to the
lower middle class and in comparison with whom
he was relatively wealthy and decidedly aristocratic.
The others made their way through life as copyists
for lawyers, tutors to small children, messengers for
merchants, or errand boys for brokers. They held
their frugal meetings on Sundays and holidays, and
amused themselves, after the fashion of half-grown
boys, with all sorts of hoaxes. They induced Goethe
to send to a slightly conceited young chap a declaration of love, in verse, somewhat like the one that

Shakespeare's Malvolio sends to Olivia. They also persuaded him to write the answer.

At one of their gatherings he met for the first time a young girl, Gretchen by name, who served the company with wine. Goethe does not say where (it was in the unpretentious inn *Zum Puppenschenkelchen* where she was a waitress). She was "of unusual, and if we take her surroundings into consideration, of incredible beauty."

Goethe has given the figure an extraordinary freshness, good sense, and in view of her immature adorer, a chaste and restrained bearing. From the time of the first meeting her figure haunts him incessantly. If he has no hope of seeing her soon, he goes to church solely on her account, where, during the long Protestant services, he can look at her to his heart's content, though he does not dare offer her his company when she leaves. That her form is associated with the Church seems even now to anticipate *Faust*.

On the occasion of that jocular mystification, the fourteen-year-old boy, suddenly finding it his duty to affect the woman's rôle, wrote down everything that he would have liked to have Gretchen write to him, and thereby mystified himself no less than another. Gretchen, sitting by the window, rose from her spinning wheel—a reference which, like that to the church, is evidently premonitory of *Faust*. She gives him sisterly, reasonable advice, reads through his works, and when he characterizes it as the acme of happiness if one who esteemed and adored her could receive just such a letter from her, she signs it half in jest. In ecstasy he wishes to embrace her. "No kissing," she says, "that is so common; but love me, if that be possible." He worships her; he presses his lips against her hands.

He portrays her bearing and gestures. She either sat by the spinning wheel or she assumed some other position that was becoming to her. She clasped her hands around her crossed arms, supported herself against the edge of the table and listened attentively while in this position. She gave no one her hand; she could not endure being touched. Only at times she sat down by the side of Wolfgang, especially when he wrote or read aloud, and then it might happen that she confidingly leaned her arm against his shoulder or looked on the book or paper. Once she kissed him on the forehead. That is the unique caress he is supposed to have received from her.

So tenderly has Goethe as a man of sixty years delineated this situation. In actuality it could hardly have been so delicate and incorporeal. For this is unquestionably the relation to which the seventeen-year-old Wolfgang refers, when, on October 1, 1766, he writes from Leipzig to his friend Moors concerning his affair with Kätchen Schönkopf; he says that he could win this girl's good will only with his heart and his character: "I need no presents in order to preserve her good favor and I now look down with eyes of scorn on the exertions with which I formerly won the favor of a W." That goes to show that the fair Gretchen in Frankfort was just as susceptible to the joy created by an attractive present as is the Gretchen in *Faust*. "W" means in all probability *Wagnerin* just as the "S" of the letter means *Schönköpfin*.

However visionary and unreal the affair may

have been on the part of the fourteen-year-old boy,
it came to a sudden and tragic end and neither party
was really to blame. In his autobiography Goethe
does not even go so far as to ascribe guilt to Gretchen's cousins. In all probability, however, Gretchen was more guilty than Goethe himself admits.
A young man of the circle, Johann Adolf Wagner
by name, had induced Wolfgang to give him a letter
of introduction to his grandfather, the influential
Textor, as a result of which the young man in question received a position as an officer of justice. In
this capacity he became guilty of such serious of-
fenses as swindling, forgery, false bonds, and falsification of wills. In the resultant lawsuit even the
boy Goethe was cross-examined by a friend of the
family to whom the case had been entrusted by the
magistrate. The examiner was greatly grieved, for
he desired above all to shield his guiltless friends.
The outcome of the entire hurry-scurry was that
Wolfgang was removed from the dubious society
into which he had been drawn while Gretchen was
banished from Frankfort and sent home.

Yet her picture hovered before his mind for
quite a while; it was evidently interwoven with the
Friederike Brion episode when Goethe conceived
Gretchen's delightful figure in *Faust*. On the other
hand, the hubbub into which Goethe was dragged
through his alliance with the Frankfort Gretchen
was undeniably the immediate inspiration of his first
bitter comedy entitled *Die Mitschuldigen*. He himself says in his autobiography: "As a result of my
affair with Gretchen and through its indirect consequences, I gained, when still quite young, an insight
into the mysterious forces that are undermining

middle-class society." He adds that out of that sort of experience he planned several dramas of which only *Die Mitschuldigen* was completed.

But it was not until nearly nineteen years of his life had elapsed that young Goethe could complete such a work, evincing as it does almost disagreeable maturity and pessimism. He first passes through various stages. However great his skill in verse-making when quite young, we have, aside from some congratulatory rhymes, no other poetry from Goethe's childhood except the *Gedanken über Jesu Christi Höllenfahrt,* published in 1766. This is a denunciatory speech by Christ, in well constructed and carefully rhymed strophes, delivered to the doomed in Hell. It is a quite baroque introduction to Goethe's poetic activity, for it reveals, in a thoroughly impersonal fashion, the influence of the then dominating Klopstock and his school.

CHAPTER II

Leipzig—First Collection of Poems—*Die Mitschuldigen:* A Drama

Johann Casper Goethe sent his son Wolfgang, when only sixteen, to the University of Leipzig to study law. Wolfgang would have much preferred Göttingen, where the science of languages and antiquities flourished, and though he adapted himself to his father's determination, he studied at Leipzig only what pleased him.

The main thing in the young man's development just then, however, was not the fact that he went to this place or to that, but that he escaped from the city of his birth and was placed in entirely new surroundings. The Germans have, incidentally, in contrast to the Scandinavians, French and English, the excellent arrangement by which the young student rarely spends his entire time at just one university, but avails himself of the opportunities offered by several. In case the first that he attends is not wholly to his liking, he quickly selects another that seems to offer greater advantages for his particular development.

Goethe attended lectures on jurisprudence, though without either substantial pleasure or enduring profit, on history, physics and Latin literature; he studied under those professors who represented æsthetics, Clodius for example, and Gottsched and

Gellert on literature. But he wrote burlesques on
Clodius, saw only the comic side of Gottsched, whose
influence after all on German literature had been
profound, and never came into a really intimate
relation with Gellert, who, half frivolous, half pietistic, could not completely win the young Goethe's
heart, despite the fact that he had influenced him
more or less, as can be seen in his first little dramatic attempt, *Die Laune des Verliebten*.

Young Wolfgang learned indeed more from the
city than from its university. Away from home for
the first time on his own responsibility, in absolute
freedom, lord over his own time, with no stern
father to dog his steps, he drew abundant nourishment from the life and art of Leipzig, then so
cultured. Among his slightly older friends, E. W.
Behrisch seems to have meant the most to him.
Behrisch was broadminded and affable, and keenly
appreciative of the ventures of the youthful genius.
He won the confidence which Goethe just then so
badly needed; and when Behrisch left Leipzig in
order to accept a position as tutor to a young German prince, he wrote three odes to him, the third
and best of which contains deeply emotional expressions concerning the grief natural to an over-sensi-
tive mind:

> Sei gefühllos!
> Ein leichtbewegtes Herz
> Ist ein elend Gut
> Auf der wankenden Erde.
>
> .   .   .   .   .
>
> Tod ist Trennung!
> Dreifacher Tod
> Trennung ohne Hoffnung
> Wiederzusehen.

In Leipzig, Goethe laid the foundation not only for his literary but for his artistic education as well. It is in Leipzig that he is initiated, not simply into the cultivation of plastic art, which follows him his whole life long, but into the striving after talented dilettantism in drawing and sketching. He achieves, as a matter of fact, passing excellence as a plastic artist, though he did not fully realize that his efforts in this direction were merely those of a dilettant until fully twenty years later. He frequents the home of the engraver Stock in order to learn the art of engraving; he is also a steady guest in the home of the painter Adam Friedrich Oeser, under whose guidance he learns how to draw accurately and gracefully. Oeser in turn, who had been a close personal friend of Winckelmann, introduces him into the general history of art. It was in Oeser's home that Winckelmann had written the work that marks a distinct epoch in Germany, *Gedanken über die Nachahung der griechischen Werke*. Oeser himself, be it said, was not a mere blind follower of Winckelmann; he cherished, to be sure, a genuine reverence for the antique, but as a painter he was partly Italian and partly French and had moreover been influenced by Rembrandt. There is hardly any doubt but that it was in Oeser's home that Goethe conceived the initial regard for Winckelmann which inspired him, even in old age, to write a very good book in his honor.

It was in Leipzig that he read him for the first time, and whoever has read Winckelmann as a young man will readily understand what a strong, though abstract, enthusiasm for Grecian antiquity was instilled in the then untested and inexperienced mind.

The effect on Goethe was not seen until much later. But Winckelmann's statement that the special characteristic of Greek masterpieces is a noble and quiet greatness made a lasting impression upon Goethe's inmost being, especially since Lessing, of whose *Laokoon* he had at the same time made a thorough study, proclaimed the fact that noble simplicity and calm grandeur constituted the ideal of the ancients. To Oeser's daughter Goethe writes in 1769: "He who treads the *simple* way, let him tread it and be silent. Humility and circumspection are the most essential prerequisites for every step on this way which finally gives its due reward. This I owe to your dear father." *Laokoon* delighted him partly because of the sharpness of its reasoning and the clarity of its idea. Here was a book with a unilateral straightforwardness, of which the young reader had hitherto been unaware, that stamped once for all descriptive poetry and emotionally programmatic art as erroneous methods of procedure. As the entire literate world now knows, Lessing was merely attempting to draw a clear and unmistakable line of demarcation between the field and function of poetry on the one hand and those of plastic art on the other.

The book delighted him all the more by reason of its pleasing attitude toward beauty. It banished the ugly (Death portrayed as a skeleton, the Devil with hideous grimaces) from the field of plastic art, wherein the appeal is to the intuition, and relegated it (as an element in universal harmony) to the realm of poetry, wherein the appeal is to the imag-

ination. It was as if young Goethe himself had
said that Death was a genius with inverted torch,
hardly to be differentiated from sleep, and not a
skeleton with rattling bones. Owing to a peculiar
shyness, young Wolfgang had become acquainted
with such men as Gottsched and Gellert, but not
with Lessing who had been in Leipzig for a while.

That Goethe did not allow himself to be led
blindly along by the theories of *Laokoon* is proved
by the fact that he undertook a journey to Dresden
in order to see its rich and beautiful collection of
paintings. Despite his intensive study of ancient
sculpture, he did not permit himself time in Dresden
for even a brief visit to that part of the gallery.
He saw only hurriedly the Italian paintings and that
for the genuinely Goethean reason that he was un-
familiar, at first hand, with the landscapes and
people portrayed in them. But he studied Dutch
paintings to his heart's satisfaction, notwithstanding
the fact that Lessing had scornfully and unreasonably disposed of them by calling them painters of
dirt (*Kotmaler*).

Since his father had instilled in him a profound
hatred of hotels, he rented a room in the home of
relatives of one of his Leipzig comrades, a shoemaker by trade and an excellent character at heart.
He became so thoroughly taken up with Dutch
paintings that he saw with Dutch eyes. The home
of the shoemaker was to him an Ostade by day and
a Schalcken by night.

Externally a complete change came over the
young man while in Leipzig, which he later, in
Faust, called "a little Paris." He doffed his old-
fashioned, home-spun clothing, such as he had worn

in Frankfort, and dressed himself with great care and good taste. It was especially in Professor Böhme's home that he learned to set a real value on polite and polished manners. Frau Böhme took a maternal interest in him; she taught him much that was æsthetically valuable.

The chief event, however, in the emotional life of the temperamental young student was that he fell violently in love. The object of his affectionate interest was Käthchen Schönkopf, daughter of a wine-dealer at whose house he was accustomed to take his midday meal. She was an attractive young girl of the middle class, amiable, correct and certainly not unresponsive to his homage. But he became a prey to intolerable jealousy, suffered extreme torture and made her miserable at the same time. She loved him passionately. As late as 1770, he writes to her from Frankfort: "You know that so long as I have known you I have lived only as a part of you." The relation between the two ran through various stages of sensitiveness and mutual dissatisfaction until the young lady preferred a wooer of less dissimilar tastes and more serious intentions. They parted as friends and there is both emotion and grace in the letters Goethe wrote her after the breach.

Here, as in Frankfort, Goethe was a regular attendant at the theatre where he became personally acquainted with several prominent actors who gave him an insight into the nature of the stage. He was also initiated, chiefly by Behrisch, into the frivolous life of the city. Unattached as he was, he participated in various youthful dissipations with disquieting results to his health. He had for a long

while been extremely nervous, inclined to hypochondria, and had suffered from indigestion caused
by the unaccustomed food and the heavy Merseburg
beer (as an older man he attributed it to coffee,
which he always disliked). Completely overcome
by jealousy, "whimsical as a child cutting teeth,"
he was doubly susceptible to a life of frivolity. He
woke up one night with a hemorrhage, hovered for
days between life and death, and in course of time
suffered from a tumor on the neck so that he had
to be sent back home to Frankfort, an unwelcome
convalescent—so far as his father was concerned.
As to the exact nature of his illness, physicians such
as Möbius, Freund, B. Fränkel and Kirstein, have
endeavored to reach some definite conclusion, but
no two of them agree.

II

The first collection of Goethe's poetry that we
possess was written during his stay in Leipzig, under
the title *Annette*. The poems were copied by Behrisch in 1767; Goethe was then eighteen years old.
Anna Katharina Schönkopf, the titular Annette, a
trifle older than Goethe, was the daughter of the
wine dealer with whom the young genius, together
with a number of his comrades, was accustomed to
take his midday meal. She had inspired the poems
and to her they are dedicated.

These small bits of verse are highly characteristic
of Goethe's earliest artistic period. Rococo through
and through, they are entirely devoid of juvenile
sensibility and pathos. They remind us much more
of Wieland than of Klopstock; they stand infinitely

nearer to French than to German. They sing of
erotics, pleasure, friendship, and virtue after the
fashion of the eighteenth century before Rousseau
had opened the sluices of bombast and declamation.

After all, had not the boy's education been half
French? Count Thoranc, the leader of the troup of
French actors at Frankfort, the theatre of Molière
and his successors at Leipzig had all helped to fill
his mind and soul with French rococo culture. Also,
in order to perfect himself in the French language,
and thereby please his father, he wrote from time
to time poems and letters to h.s sister and others,
in a French that is far from excellent. There was
to be sure in his epistolary style a youthful jollity
that is quite German; there was, too, at times something affected and decidedly sentimental, as in the
odes to Behrisch or in the letters to Auguste Stolberg. But when he wishes to be really creative, he
returns to rococo forms, as in these poems.

The problem in eroticism demanding solution at
this point is as follows: How shall the lover take
his girl by surprise in order to get her into his
power? It is merely a question of catching her off
her guard and then consoling her; she must not be
taken by storm or frightened. To that end he tells
a little story (*Ziblis*) about how the girl fled from
a horned sylvan god that was pursuing her, and
how she allowed herself to be captured without
resistance by a young man who first defended her
and then caressed her.

The question is raised whether love always requires that the girl yield. In another short story
entitled *Lyde* the negative answer is given. Amin
succeeded in seducing Lyde and at first his rapture

was intense.   But in course of time he grew weary
of reiterated enjoyment and endeavored to get rid
of the girl decently and in order.   He pretended
that he had to go on a journey and commended her
to his friend who was to act as her guide and consoler.   She neither felt nor manifested the slightest
tinge of regret and seized the proffered opportunity
with avidity.   She became fervent; the friend became bold.

We are regaled first of all in the two stories with
extended advice as to the most expeditious method
of capturing coy young women.   In the spirit of
youthful frivolity, and with a goodly measure of
charm, Goethe shows us, alternately in prose and
verse, that the way to proceed is first to strike up
a friendship; then it is relatively easy to go over
to a kiss and a caress.   But the pursuer must remember that he is always exposed to the danger
of the girl's slipping away at the last moment.
Then he explains how, with the help of Amor, she
may be aroused and eventually befooled.

As counterpieces, there are two stories in verse.
Triumph der Tugend bears a striking similarity to
the two concerning Cupid's triumph.   The familiar
devices employed in the game of seduction re-occur,
with this difference: At the close the girl appeals to
the man's better nature, expounds the embrace as a
quite serious affair, and brings it about that he
retires.

And finally, in the humorous *Pygmalion*, the
Greek legend is exploited in the flippant spirit of
the eighteenth century.   Pygmalion was a naïve
dunderhead who had never pressed a woman to his
bosom and consequently fell in love with a statue.

A friend extricated him from this ridiculous situation by securing him a girl of real flesh and warm
blood. But unsophisticated as he was, he proceeded
forthwith to marry her. Amor punished him for
his persistent abstinence by giving him a wife.

All of this is youthful without being exactly jejune; it is buoyant and ingenious without an excess
of emotional excitement. It is in short fetching.
And it betrays a surprising equanimity for so young
a mind.

In the little collection called *Leipziger Lieder-
buch,* as in *Annette,* there is very little display of
passion either of love or jealousy; but there is an
abundance of measure and moderation, levity and
sensuousness, wit and mirth, and here and there a
bit of precocious common-place. The poet gives
sober counsel:

> Du junger Mann, du junge Frau!
> Lebt nicht zu treu, nicht zu genau
> In enger Ehe!
> Die Eifersucht quält manches Haus
> Und trägt am Ende doch nichts aus
> Als doppelt Wehe.

He reveals too for so young a man a remarkable
familiarity with the nature of women:

> Das Mädchen wünscht von Jugend auf
> Sich hochgeehrt zu sehen.
> Sie ziehrt sich klein und wächst herauf
> In Pracht und Assembleen.
> Der Stolz verjagt die Triebe
> Der Wollust und der Liebe.

In the poem entitled *Der wahre Genuss,* the development of which is as natural as can be, he has

portrayed all the joy he experienced from his association with Käthchen Schönkopf. We read, in the
Anacreontic style of the eighteenth century:

> Für nichts besorgt als meine Freude,
> Für mich nur schön zu sein bemüht,
> Wollüstig nur an meiner Seite,
> Und sittsam wenn die Welt sie sieht;
> Dass unsrer Glück die Zeit nicht schade,
> Räumt sie kein Recht aus Schwachheit ein,
> Und ihre Gunst bleibt immer Gnade,
> Und ich muss immer dankbar sein.

In the verses from this period there breaks
through every now and then a plain, simple, straightforward tone. There is, for example, the cordial
greetings to his mother—that good mother whom
he otherwise never in his whole life squarely com-
pensated for the immense affection she had showered
upon him.

> Grüss mir die Mutter, sprich, sie soll verzeihen,
> Dass ich sie niemals grüssen liess, sag' ihr,
> Dass, was sie weiss, dass ich sie ehre. Sag's
> Dass nie mein kindlich Herz, von Liebe voll
> Die Schuldigkeit vergisst, und ehe soll
> Die Liebe nicht erkalten, eh ich selbst
> Erkalte.

In the poem entitled *Unbeständigkeit,* written in
bright, rippling verses, the youth lays bare his flickering, flippant erotic nature. He lies in the babbling
brook with outstretched arms, presses each oncom-
ing wave lovingly to his breast, the one after the
other with alternate longing. He plays the rôle
of brother to his fellows. He informs them that
should they ever be deceived, they should remember

that it is just as sweet to kiss the second as it was to kiss the first.

The Greco-Roman apparatus is frequently preserved. In *Die Spröde* there appears a Thyrsis, in *Die Bekehrte* a Damon, in *Die schöne Nacht* a fresh nature-sense penetrates the Roman mythology in a way that augurs quite well:

> *Luna* bricht die Nacht der Eichen,
> Zephirs melden ihren Lauf,
> Und die Birken streun mit Neigen
> Ihr den süssten Weihrauch auf.

We have a delightful bit of rococo in *Die Brautnacht:* It begins

> Im Schlafgemach, entfernt vom Feste,
> Sitzt Amor dir getreu, und bebt,
> Dass nicht die List muthwill'ger Gäste
> Des Brautbetts Frieden untergräbt.

It closes:

> Schnell hilft dir Amor sie entkleiden,
> Und ist nicht halb so schnell als du;
> Dann hält er schalkhaft und bescheiden
> Sich fest die beiden Augen zu.

That sounds like a charming text to a painting by Fragonard.

Goethe's first dramatic attempt, *Die Laune des Verliebten,* a paraphrasing of the scenes of jealousy between himself and Kätchen Schönkopf with the addition of the parallel scenes between the other couple, Johann Adam Horn and Constance Breitkopf, is written in a similar though less excellent style.

The tiny drama is a pastoral in Alexandrines, that

is to say, in that unhappy metre into which the Germans, and after them their Northern neighbors, transformed the sprightly French Alexandrine verse. Lacking rhythmical sense for the undulating, alternating element in this verse, they substituted for it the tiresome iambic hexameter with the cæsura in the middle. It is the metre that Holberg introduced into Denmark with his *Peder Paars*.[5]

The action takes place between young ladies and gentlemen with Greco-French names: Eridon and Lamon, Amine and Eglé. They play the flute and the shawm. Lambs with bright red ribbons about their necks would look quite well in their immediate vicinity. In their hands they should have the shepherd's crook with bow attached. The playlet would have adapted itself very well to illustrations by Boucher, who died, incidentally, the year before it was written.

III

Vastly different, however, is the drama that directly followed, *Die Mitschuldigen*. Its similarity is to be found only in the purely external, in that it is also written in the metre that the Germans call Alexandrine. But this drama is a picture of reality, of society, born of pessimism incorrigible, inharmonious throughout, inspired by a flippancy which in its essence is compounded of forbearing, tolerant

---

[5] Ludvig Holberg (1684-1754) wrote his comic epic entitled *Peder Paars* in 1719. It is a satire on the artificial poetry of Classicism with its "Lusiads" and "Henriads" and other creations in imitation of Homer. These are typical verses:

> Ved Lilien paa Mark nu lignes maa en Qvinde;
> Hun ei arbeide vil, ei meere sye og spinde.

—TRANSLATOR.

contempt for human beings. In the leading character, Wolfgang—he was not yet twenty years old
—apparently desires to lampoon himself and his
foibles. Alceste, a well-to-do young man, pays violent court to a young woman. She is kindly disposed
to him, but married and settled, though unhappily.
In this character who, like Kätchen Schönkopf, is
the daughter of an innkeeper, he portrays at once
feminine amiability and feminine weakness. Irre-
vocably bent on securing a husband, she stoops to
a wretched, characterless person so soon as it becomes evident to her that all of her more prominent
suitors are making her only left-handed proposals.

After a few years of absence, Alceste has returned to the town where the subsequent action
takes place; he is received into the inn owned by
Sophie's father. On finding her married to Söller,
a reveller and a gambler, he feels his old yearnings
reappear. He has lived there for a considerable
time without coming nearer her. Finally, as Söller
is planning an evening at a masquerade, Alceste
inveigles Sophie into a nocturnal rendezvous. With
a modicum of reluctance she yields. But on that
very same night her husband decides to rob Alceste.
The father (an imitation, by the way, of the inquisitive host in Lessing's *Minna von Barnhelm*) sneaks
up into Alceste's room in order to pry into a letter
that Alceste had received on that afternoon. In
this way all of the characters find themselves in the
same room on the same night. Alceste and Sophie
keep their tryst, and indeed quite tenderly, but owing to Sophie's relative reserve the affair ends without substantial results. Söller, convinced of his
marital misfortune and intending to use this as a

foil in case of detection, steals a comfortable sum of money from Alceste's strong box.

When, on the next morning, the young cavalier misses his money, the very money he had planned to spend on Sophie, she at once suspects her father. Was not his wax taper found in the young man's room? The father in turn suspects the daughter so soon as he learns of her visit to the room and immediately conveys his suspicion to Alceste, whose reasoning is natural, if unkind, in that he concludes that if Sophie has really taken the money she has no right to boast of her virtue and stir up trouble. But when he treats her in accordance with his ugly conjecture, he offends her and does her an injustice. At last he comes to see that no one other than the reprobate Söller is the thief. When Söller, however, makes it plain that Alceste's treatment of him is no better than his own treatment of the well-to-do young man, the leading character realizes that what the situation demands is forbearance and indulgence.

The diminutive, and unsatisfactory, drama is constructed with considerable dramatic ability. It is evident that the author had written it after attending many dramatic performances and reading many plays. The form is genuine but old-fashioned, not only by reason of its numerous monologues and asides but also because these asides are at times answered—one would fancy they were supposed to be inaudible—by the person hidden behind the scenes. And several times, as in the case of the German romanticists later on, the spectators have something to say from the stalls.

We have the drama in three redactions, the first of which begins with the second act. The second

complete redaction, likewise from 1769, is the freshest and boldest, filled as it is with blunt, Molièresque
expressions, which were afterwards deleted, along
with such brusque remarks as the following, made
by Alceste to Söller:

Er lässt der jungen Frau das kalte Bett allein.

In the revised edition this is changed so as to read

Er lässt die junge Frau zur Winterzeit allein.

In both of the complete editions there are quite
a few allusions to contemporary events. In the
first, as also later in *Stella,* reference is made to the
Corsican Paoli's conflict with the French, the unrest
in Poland, Turkey's declaration of war against Russia, and the comet, seen in October, 1768. In the
second edition, written in the following year, there
is an allusion to America's trouble with England
and the sale of soldiers by German princes that
followed, to the illness of Frederick the Great and
other events. The drama was in short a photo-
graph of his own affairs as well as those of the
surrounding world.

CHAPTER III

BROKEN in health and weak of courage, the
young man returned to his ancestral home in Frankfort to recuperate under his mother's loving treatment. She rejoiced at the thought of having her
son with her again; she had missed him so much;
she was soon to lose him again; and from then on
she was to see him with depressing infrequency.
His sister Cornelia likewise was glad to have him
home. For three years uninterruptedly she had
been obliged to bear her father's sternness and in-
consistency all alone. Now he aired his dissatisfaction on his son who had returned from the
university without having taken his law examina-
tions, without even a thorough grounding in law,
and in addition to all of this so exhausted from
illness that he had to be treated leniently.

Young Wolfgang remained in Frankfort from
the autumn of 1768 to the spring of 1770. From
the very first he felt terribly ill at ease. He longed
for Leipzig, especially for Oeser's home and all
that Oeser had meant to him: love for an ideal of
beauty and sound judgment as to artistic values. In
Frankfort he suffered "a famine of good taste."
In perpetual feud with his father, he tried to find
consolation in general reading. He took up Wie-

land whose *Agathon* and *Musarion* glorified a sort of Hellenism and whose style was that very same erotic rococo which had won him, heart and soul, in Leipzig. Following out the spirit of Wieland he struck up a love affair with one of Cornelia's friends, Charitas Meixner from Worms. She was a few months older than Cornelia, had been married in the same year, and like her died, 1777, in childbed.

In the year 1768 she was eighteen years old. Even when she was but sixteen, Goethe had doted on her and, after the fashion of youth, unable to keep his affair to himself, told his friends all about it. In a letter to Augustin Trapp, dated June 2, 1766, he writes, in his French:

O vous savez trop, que Worms me tient au coeur. Vous connaissez ma passion pour la belle Charitas que vous l'avez crue le plus fort motif de m'amener à Vous écrire en me donnant par Stern le doux espoir de me faire entendre des nouvelles qui touchent de plus près votre charmante nièce.

> Ecrivez moi! Que fait l'enfant autant aimé
> Se souvient-il de moi? Ou m'a il oublié?
> Ah ne me cachez rien, qu'il m'élève ou m'accable,
> Un poignard de sa main me serait agréable.

It is surprising that Goethe, perhaps because *Kind* in German is neuter gender, fancies that in French one must use *il* in referring to a girl; and the combination *m'a il* leaves a distinctly bad taste in the mouth. The long prose sentence is a model of stylistic awkwardness, though there can be no doubt as to the warmth of the inspiration. And now, over two years having elapsed and the fair Charitas having become more mature by that much, the attraction returned in reënforced form.

Rich in contrasts as young Goethe's nature was,
his illness called forth at the same time a decided
inclination to piety and mysticism. He studied
chemistry and cabala, alchemy and magic; he
thought that a pietistic physician had saved his life
by some cryptic, miraculous method; he sought after
miracles; he was inclined to believe in them, like
his Faust after him. He steeped himself in Arnold's
history of the church and heretics, a book in which
the sanctimonious historian explains the weaknesses
of human kind as manifestations of diabolic inter-
ference.

He came especially under the immediate influence of that particular one of his mother's friends
whom she admired the most and revered without
qualification, Fräulein Susanna Katharina von Klettenberg (1723-1774). Frau Aja, bright and cheerful as she was, had a pronounced inclination toward
something higher than drab daily life and housekeeping; this more exalted occupation she found in
the piety that was preached and practiced by her
friend, at whose bedside she sat, steadfast and deeply
moved, in the hour of death.

Susanna von Klettenberg was delicately formed
and well developed, and had a cordial, natural disposition, which was all the more prepossessing in her
case since she herself came of a distinguished family
and associated with prominent people. She was
always carefully dressed despite the Moravian simplicity of her costumes. She had been influenced by
the leading Pietists, Spener and Francke, though she
invariably spoke with noticeable reservation of
Count Zinzendorf, the real founder of the Moravian Society. She must have made an unusual

impression because of her purity of heart and innocence; she must have been endowed with a goodly
measure of genial and captivating superiority. It
was under her influence that young Wolfgang wrote,
in his sixteenth year, in the pious dialect of that
time, the poem on Christ's descent into Hell. This
situation explains, too, the inscription: *Auf Verlangen entworfen.* It was also obviously under her
influence that the twenty-year-old Wolfgang, after
a violent recurrence of his illness, attended (1769)
the Moravian Synod at Marienborn where he was,
however, almost repelled by what he saw.

In a warm letter of August 26, 1770, Wolfgang
reports to Susanna von Klettenberg, in a tone of
youthful freedom, concerning his association with
the pious people of the neighborhood. He writes:
"I really applied myself to them in an attempt to
appreciate them, but it seems as if it was not to be:
I could not live with them on the right sort of
footing. They are so thoroughly tiresome that my
vivacity could not stand them. They are exclusively
a people of mediocre intelligence, who thought their
first rational thought with their first religious experience, and they fancy that this is everything, for
beyond religion they know nothing." He finds
them vain, churchly, and punctilious.

It is plain that by this time Goethe has been freed;
his feelings are no longer those of his adolescent
days. Constant reading of the Bible had not merely
opened his eyes to the Oriental way of feeling and
Oriental brilliancy of color (as is revealed even in
his old age in the *West-Oestlicher Divan*) ; it had
given him also that living interest in religious problems such as appears in the, after all, half rational-

istic essays from his youth entitled *Brief des Pastors*
and *Zwo Biblische Fragen*.   At any rate, the influence of Susanna von Klettenberg on Goethe's being
was so strong that he felt impelled to portray her
in his great novel, where, as is well known, she is
immortalized in *Die Bekenntnisse einer schönen
Seele*.

That the subject was deserving of Goethe's profound interest, is beyond all doubt.   But the letters
on which the portrayal of her is based are lost.
Goethe most likely destroyed them, just as in all
probability he destroyed the letters on which the
first part of *Werther* is based and to which this part
really owes its undying freshness.   So far as the
notes from Susanna von Klettenberg's own hand are
concerned, and the notes of her conversation that
Goethe may have had at his disposal, these are also
lost.   And we must say that the *Reliquien* left by
her and published by J. M. Lappenberg in 1849
(on the hundredth anniversary of Goethe's birth)
do not justify her renown.   Her moral and religious
treatises on friendship, Christian friendship, steadfastness in friendship, undignified flirting with
friends, on Heaven and divine joy,—all are thoroughly tiresome, pious tracts.   Her letters, few in
number, are in general the letters of a Protestant
nun.   Her poems, which are nearly all hymns to
Jesus, possess but little poetic worth.   The best of
them, and the only secular one, is the poem *An die
Spindel*.   She prefers the spinning wheel to the
brush.   That individual who no longer values splendor and beauty, who does not even care about praise,
does not feel impelled to reproduce such things.
She prefers the spinning wheel to the pen.   What

should she do with the symbols of thought? She thinks more quickly without them. The last verses run:

> Komm, Spindel, komm, ich kann nicht müssig sitzen,
> Das Nichtsthun ist mir Qual und Tod,
> Sollt ich mit feiner Arbeit mich erhitzen,
> Das machte mir die Augen roth.
>
> Doch Bücher! Ja, die hätt' ich bald vergessen,
> Sehr wichtig dem, der sie für nöthig hält;
> Die Mäuse wollen meine fressen,
> Da hab' ich sie in Schrank gestellt.
>
> Komm, Spindel, komm, froh soll die Hand dich lenken,
> Du lässt mir Kopf und Herze frei;
> Empfindungsvoll kann ich da fühlend denken,
> Das Andre ist doch Narrethei.

So she is done with all things secular; she will abandon books and eschew paintings. It has been impossible for me to derive a single grain of nourishment from what she wrote; but she lives for all time as a transfigured being in and by virtue of Goethe's art.

II

Goethe was suddenly torn loose from all the things which in reality accorded so little with his deeper nature: pietistic brooding, magical whims, mystical experiments, and flirtations with pretty girls, including the one from Worms. In 1770, his father sent him to Strassburg, where he himself had been a student. It was a piece of genuine good fortune for Wolfgang: He was once more liberated from the narrowness of Imperial Frankfort, and

placed in a city where the essential characteristics
of two great nations met. He was to live for a
while in a city that was at once French and German; in a city with an old Germanic past and new
French present.

Just as in Leipzig, he soon made the acquaintance
of a number of older and younger men; his table
companions were all excellent and interesting personalities. There was one man nearly fifty years
old, Justice Salzmann, a thoughtful individual of
good taste, well fitted to become the confidant of a
young genius with big ideas in his head and acute
pangs in his heart. There was the mystic and physician Jung-Stilling who, by reason of his sound learning and genuine piety, was quite instructive to a
youth of Goethe's type. Moreover, he took it upon
himself to defend Goethe with vigor and no little
audacity when he saw others casting supercilious
glances at him because of his wig and other slight
eccentricities of dress. And there was the valiant
Lerse, whose name has been preserved and whose
character has been immortalized in *Götz von Berlichingen*. But the most important of all the acquaintances the young Goethe made was that of
Johann Gottfried Herder.

Herder was then physically ill and spiritually dejected. He was suffering from a fistula in one of his
eyes. In order to remove it it was found necessary
to give the tear duct a natural outlet through the
nose. To do this an incision in the lacrymatory
sack and presumably a piercing of the nose bone had
to be undergone. Convalescence was to be a matter of three weeks.

Herder had come to Strassburg in September

1770. In the spring of 1771 he writes, after repeated and unsuccessful operations, that instead of
one incision and one boring through the nose there
had been twenty incisions and two hundred dressings
of the wound, while the three weeks of convalescence
had been extended to six months. And after all this
pain, annoyance and expense, the eye was worse than
when he first arrived.

On his arrival Herder had given up his position
with the Prince of Eutin. As the Prince's travelling
companion, he had stayed for a while in Darmstadt,
where he had made the acquaintance of Caroline
Flachsland, who later became his wife. Her parents
were dead and she was living, under economic pressure, in the home of her inconsiderate brother-in-
law. Though herself destined to become in course
of time eccentric, gloomy, and ill tempered, she was
then tall, blue-eyed, of a childlike cheerfulness, and
a transcendental enthusiast withal. She cherished
a reverential love for the serious scholar whose disposition was not as happy as one would have expected from a man of his age, though there was no
doubt as to the genuineness of his affection for her.
He felt, however, that his position was far too uncertain for him to ask her to become formally engaged to him. And since he wrote to her not infrequently, in accordance with his custom, in the
tone of a seasoned schoolmaster, didactically and
sarcastically, she would have broken off her relation
to him with small regret. She was indeed won over
only with difficulty, and as the result of infinite beseeching and promising on his part.

Herder was despondent; he found Strassburg detestable; he visited no one. But the fame which he

enjoyed even at that time was drawing young men
to him. Two or three of these came to see him
almost every day. One of these was Wolfgang
Goethe, then twenty-one years of age. Herder
was twenty-six; but he had already accomplished so
much. In Königsberg Kant had drawn his attention
to Rousseau. He ardently dedicated himself to the
paradox that man is good by nature but spoiled by
civilization; he accepted with equal zeal the idea of
a return to nature. This coincided perfectly with
the influence he had previously received from another of his fellow-townsmen, Hamann, whose position as a prophet impressed him, and in whose
muddy writings he had found the sentence that
poetry is the mother tongue of mankind, and that
its origin was coeval with the origin of language
itself.

By virtue of the Germanic admiration for the
dark as being at once the deep, he was celebrated
by young talents as a seer and a magician. It must
in truth be conceded that he fought Enlightenment
to the benefit of belief in Christian revelation, which
the young thinkers had cast aside as a worn out
doctrine. People had become heartily tired of Enlightenment. That which was bathed in light no
longer satisfied the coming generation, yearning as
it then was for the mysterious in which the tangible
has its roots. Hamann had taught Herder that the
roots of poetry and language are intertwined; the
original language was set down as an imitation of
toneful and restless nature. Language was something that had grown naturally; it had evolved; it
was not the product of speculation. Nor was poetry
the creation of a few highly cultured private per-

sons; it was not the work of a few clever people. It was a world gift, a folk gift.

From Königsberg Herder went to Riga, whence he sailed for France. He remained in France half a year, six weeks of which were spent in Paris. He became acquainted there with such leading and brilliant intellects as d'Alembert, Barthélemy, and Diderot. He was especially captivated by the latter. Herder saw in him at once the modern Plato and the modern Terence. Diderot in turn was ultra-enthusiastic about the natural, and about natural morals. If Goethe was later influenced by Diderot as well as by Rousseau, it was Herder, whose critical writings had even then made him famous, that pointed the way.

Sick, dejected, at loggerheads with his sweetheart, full of seething ideas that were after all mature to a certain degree, already accustomed to admiration, Herder accepted the visits of Wolfgang with complete lack of ecstasy. He was poles removed from seeing genius in him, and never said a word in any of his letters, either in those to Caroline Flachsland or in those to Merck, about the studious young man who visited him as a rule every morning and every evening, and sometimes stayed with him the whole day. Not until March 1772, when Caroline made the acquaintance of Wolfgang, did Herder write her a few lines concerning him:

Goethe is really a good fellow, though exceedingly light-headed and sparrowish, for which I have frankly reproached him. He was at times the only one who visited me during my imprisonment in Strassburg, and I believe I can say without any self-praise that I left some impressions on him that will prove fruitful in the days to come.

Imagine for a minute these two men standing face to face in the little room in Herder's hotel! Herder, with his powdered hair in round curls, oval face, big clerical nose, under his black, heavy eyebrows, a pair of coal black eyes, one of which is red and inflamed; his dress is black, worn, home-made; over it he wears a thin black silk mantle the ends of which he has stuck in his pockets.

Opposite him stands Wolfgang Goethe, an elegantly clad youth, with his receding forehead, his hair smooth and combed straight back, ending in a little pig-tail, his pointed, seeking nose, his longish face with the beautiful mouth, his charming brown eyes with their penetrating glance—a questioning, yearning, overflowing universe in eternal unrest.

He reminds his associates of a sparrow or a woodpecker; he is always hopping about, liable to cry out at any moment, and inclined to mystifications and practical jokes. Jung-Stilling portrays his first impression of him. He has large clear eyes, a magnificent forehead and beautiful form; he entered the room rather dauntlessly and assumed the leadership without first trying to see whether he could gain it or not; he almost rolled his eyes inside out at the individual at whom he chanced to be looking. A few years later Jung-Stilling pictures him as he appeared in Elberfeld: "He dances around the table, makes faces, and conducts himself so oddly and childishly that the people in Elberfeld doubt whether he is entirely sane."

There was something youthfully presumptuous in him. He was accustomed to being coddled and was considered by many as being a sort of prodigy. And

now he met in the distempered and peevish Herder,
for the first time in his life, a being whose superiority expressed itself in mockery. Goethe tells him
about his collection of seals and is laughed at. Herder treats him like a schoolboy. Goethe says nothing
about his many distracting occupations, his studies
in chemistry and anatomy, and his mystic-cabalistic
investigations. Herder pokes fun at Wolfgang's
Latin Classics, beautifully bound and carefully arranged but unread. He taunts him by saying that
all the Latin he knows he has learned from Spinoza
—a fact which shows how early in life Goethe
busied himself with that thinker who was destined
later to have a decisive influence upon his life and
works. On the occasion of a loan of some books
Herder plays fast and loose with Goethe's name:

Der von Göttern du stammst, von Gothen oder vom Kothe,
Goethe, sende sie mir!

Goethe speaks of this with bitterness. We dislike puns on our names as much as we dislike having
our names forgotten.

Young Wolfgang had admired Herder's equanimity during the various operations, all of which were
extremely painful, though not one word of complaint was ever heard from the immortal patient.
He felt humiliated by his elder's superior bearing;
yet he was inspired; Herder's great characteristics,
his intuitive insight and abundant information,
worked on him like magic.

It was perfectly natural that Herder, repelled as
he was by his own youthful conceits in Goethe, just
as Goethe eighteen years later saw, to his displeasure, his own juvenile exaggerations reappear in

Schiller, should treat Goethe as a mere boy. He was living now "in that cave of loneliness where the soul is stamped and the character confirmed." It was not less natural that Goethe thought he had met the Sun whose Planet he was called to be. He felt like Jacob wrestling with the angel of the Lord.

Herder was not content simply to give him new ideas concerning the nature of poetry and language; he completely transformed his inner being. Spiritually Goethe stood, as is well known, under the supremacy of French rococo. Herder's own development had been French to the extent that he was profoundly influenced by the worshippers of nature, by Rousseau and Diderot. But when he conceived of them as the opposites of old Gallicism, he felt that he was in sharp national contrast to what is French, that is to say, to rococo. French literature appeared to him old and aristocratic, artificial and barren. Its criticism was negative; it sought after mere correctness. Its philosophy was flat and inadequate. Even Lessing, despite the fact that he was a disciple of Diderot, had felt opposed to French.

Goethe drank in these opinions and soon found himself in a complete mental right-about-face. His very stay in Alsace, which was half French, did much to Germanicize him. He was vexed when his comrades derided him because of his imperfect French. He and his companions tried to return to German brusqueness of expression. And while the two passionate daughters of his dancing teacher were quarreling with each other as to which one should have the beautiful young man, he fell in love with the German preacher's daughter out at Sesenheim.

Intimidated by Herder's superior irony, he never dared show him *Die Mitschuldigen;* just as little did it occur to him to show Herder the beautiful lyric poems he had begun to write. But what Herder taught him intoxicated him. Though Herder's own poetry was of no special value, and though he wrote of his love affairs in high-flown, Klopstockian phraseology, his all-embracing critical mind could correctly appraise a species of poetry that was poles removed from his own—folk poetry in all of its forms.

He was not the real modern discoverer of folk poetry. Before he had been enraptured by it, Percy's collection of Old English and Scottish Ballads had appeared. But Herder is the first man who, by reason of his knowledge of comparative literature, could unite the folk poetry of all nations in one study. In 1778 and 1779, his first edition of ingenious translations appeared. It contained ballads from Greenland, Lapland, and Esthonia, songs from Livonia and Lithuania, collected on the spot, lays from Tartary and Vandalia, Sicilian rhymes and Spanish romances, French, English, and Scottish ballads, lyrics from Shakespeare's dramas, songs from Ossian, for the genuineness of which he naïvely broke a lance, Eddie songs and Bardic poems, German songs from the Empire as well as from Switzerland, and even plays from barbarian nations. To the regret of Caroline Flachsland, he lost his liking for Klopstock, praised Ossian at the expense of his contemporary Gerstenberg, and valued a song from Lapland more highly in the original than in Ewald von Kleist's imitation.

Herder invariably proceeded from the artificial

and over-cultivated to the simple and naïve; he always placed that which grows above that which is grown. It is he who introduces Goethe to Northern folk poetry: He translates the Danish ballad, *Jeg lagde mit Hoved til Elverhoj,* and the ballad on the daughter of the king of the elves, entitled *Hr. Olaf, han rider.* From the latter Goethe derives his idea of the king of the elves. We see this appropriation in *Der Erlkönig,* which of course should be *Der Elfenkönig.* That Herder was not exactly a master of Danish is shown by the following verses:

> Die Fischlein schwammen in heller Flut
> Mit ihren Feinden spielend.

That is supposed to be a reproduction of:

> Alle smaa Fiske i Floden svam,
> De leged med deres Finne.

Finne is confused with *Fjende,* the former meaning "fins," the latter "enemies."

For Goethe this is the hour of fructification. Herder did not believe that he was capable of genuine inspiration; Goethe will show him. He roams about on foot through Alsace and collects twelve unknown folk songs just as God made them. They are for Herder, for Herder and no one else. He will not permit even his most intimate comrades to copy them; but young girls who have found favor in his eyes shall learn to sing them according to the old melodies.

What such songs were destined to mean for Goethe's poetry is readily seen by comparing *Röschen auf der Heide* and Goethe's *Heidenröslein.* The first two stanzas contain almost exactly the

same words; in the third a few lines have been
changed, but the change is a stylistic modification
by a facile hand.

Folk song:

> Es sah ein Knab' ein Röslein stehn,
> Röslein auf der Heiden,
> Sah, es war so frisch und schön,
> Und blieb stehn es anzusehn
> Und stand in süssen Freuden—
> Röslein, Röslein, Röslein roth,
> Röslein auf der Heiden.

Goethe:

> Sah ein Knab' ein Röslein stehn,
> Röslein auf der Heiden,
> War so jung und morgenschön,
> Lief er schnell es nah zu sehn,
> Sah's mit vielen Freuden.
> Röslein, Röslein, Röslein roth,
> Röslein auf der Heiden.

What Goethe appropriates in this way, he invariably revises but little, though sufficiently. Such
is the case with his *Nähe des Geliebten,* taken from
Friederike Brun, and the two Suleika songs, taken
from Marianne von Willemer. Let us, however,
not overlook the vast difference between this naïve
poetry and the old-fashioned, precocious lyrics of
his youth. Rococo no longer exists for him.

Macpherson's publication of the so-called songs
of Ossian more than anything else drew Herder's
attention to ancient folk poetry. The same thing
happened to him that happened to nearly all of
his contemporaries: the melodies of this artificial
nightingale sounded genuine. *Ossian* was first made
accessible to the Germans through the crack-brained

translation by Denis. Herder was ultra-enthusiastic over the *authentic* Ossian—as if there had really been one. As everybody now knows, Macpherson had given his work the semblance of ancient poetry by the skillful use of some old Irish and Scottish songs. He was a genuine poet who delighted in appearing as a poetic mystifier.

This Bardic poetry, which was fresher than Klopstock's, was a somewhat strained expression for exalted feelings, melancholy longings and memories, more modern than antique, altogether an affected and hazy temperamental art. But this Aeolian harp music awakened, somewhat as did Lamartine's later in France, the long since exsiccated appreciation for natural poetry. Herder infected Goethe with his inspiration for Ossian. It gripped him as it was to grip Bonaparte twenty years later who ranked Ossian even higher than Homer.

Goethe translated, very freely, a long selection of Ossian — Colma's, Ryno's, and Alpin's lyric-dramatic outbreak—in emotional prose. This he thoroughly revised and touched up and incorporated some of it in the second part of *Werther's Leiden*, which thus came to stand under the star of Ossian just as the sturdier and more wholesome first part stood under the star of Homer. The section beginning with *Stern der dämmernden Nacht!* harmonizes beautifully with Werther's infinite melancholy at the thought of approaching separation. The last words, not found in the original translation, which are read by Werther with tearful eyes, run as follows:

The tree speaks: Why wakest thou me, air of Spring? Thou lovest and sayest: I bedew with drops from Heaven!

But the time of my withering is near; near is the storm that carries my leaves along with it. To-morrow the wanderer will come; he will come who saw me in my beauty; his eyes will seek me far over the fields; but he will seek me in vain.

It is remarkable what a short span of time lies between the poems published under the collective title of *Annette,* and these translations after Ossian that sound so full and rich. If we compare the short piece written under the rubric of *Darthulas Grabgesang* with the Danish rendering of F. L. Mynster, Goethe's power and naturalness become at once apparent.

CHAPTER IV

RELATION TO SHAKESPEARE — RELATION TO GOTHIC STYLE—RELATION TO GREEK ANTIQUITY—RELATION TO THE OLD TESTAMENT

IT was also Herder who introduced Goethe to Shakespeare and elicited the young man's ebullient enthusiasm. Goethe had, to be sure, read the great Britisher while still in Leipzig, both in the original and in Wieland's prose translation. There is no doubt at all but that he was mightily impressed; but he studied Shakespeare at that time in the spirit and after the fashion of a foreigner.

Now he is carried away by him. He himself tells us that the junior club in Strassburg took upon itself the task of speaking in Shakespearean phraseology, in the style of Mercutio and the clowns. We have the best evidence of his jejune study in his address on Shakespeare's birthday, 1772. At this time Goethe cannot even spell the Englishman's name; he Germanicizes it. The title reads *Zum Schäkespears Tag*. But he cries out with bold familiarity: "Schäkespear, my friend, if you were still among us, I could live nowhere except with you. How willingly would I play the subordinate rôle of Py-

86

lades if you were Orestes!" His inspiration has now
become so thoroughly German that it is simply the
obverse side of his contempt for French. In con-
tradistinction to the French, he praises the tragic
art of the Greeks and the drama of Shakespeare,
which is "a beautiful cabinet of curiosities wherein
the history of the world passes in review before
our eyes." His address *Zum Schäkespears Tag*
is nothing more nor less than an outburst of immature enthusiasm, sincerely felt, and yet after all only
an echo of Herder's erudition. It is fresh and
warm; that is its sole virtue. It reveals precious
little originality and is, so far as the theme is concerned, remarkably devoid of thought. Goethe
cries Nature! Nature! Shakespeare's characters
are nature, a thing of dismay to the lax and inexperienced. The young Wolfgang confesses openly
that he has thought very little about Shakespeare
and, truth to tell, feels and imagines rather than
thinks. What he especially owes to Shakespeare is
the fact that he has liberated coming poets from the
nefarious restraint of rules. Since he has read
Shakespeare the unity of place seems to him painfully prison-like, while the unities of time and action
are simply onerous fetters on the imagination. He
has leaped out into unmeasured space and become
conscious for the first time in his life that he has
hands and feet.

And then there follows, *à la* Herder, a general
diatribe against the French drama. The Greek
drama, accepted by the French as their model, was
unapproachable; it would be easier for a Marquis
to imitate Alcibiades than for Corneille to follow
Sophocles.

The Greeks receive the young orator's inspired homage. He says rather beautifully and simply:

First as an intermezzo in divine service, then with solemn political application, the tragedy presented a few great actions of their ancestors to the people with the pure simplicity of perfection, and aroused whole and complete sensations in their souls, for the people themselves, as a nation, were great and complete. And in what sort of souls! In Greek souls! I cannot say just what that means but I feel it and for the sake of brevity I simply refer to Sophocles and Homer and Theocritus who have taught me to feel it.

All French tragedies are parodies. This is said by Goethe who, in this case, babbles according to Lessing's unjust judgments, and who, thirty years later, translates Voltaire's *Mahomet* and *Tancred*.

Shakespeare, on the contrary, creates real men and real women. He vied with Prometheus, formed human beings after the fashion of Prometheus, only on a colossal scale, so that they are occasionally misunderstood. But Goethe cries out: Nothing is so much nature as Shakespeare's men and women.

The French are once more hauled over the coals. All French dramatists, and the Germans who have been infected by them, even Wieland (through whom Goethe first became acquainted with Shakespeare) have, in comparison with the great Englishman, reaped but little honor. Voltaire is especially attacked. Voltaire, who always made a profession of calumniating majesties [he did, as everybody knows, everything but that], has likewise conducted himself as a genuine Thersites. "If I were Ulysses his back would smart under my sceptre."

Goethe hardly suspected then that in 1805, in the notes to Diderot's *Rameaus Neffe,* he would

praise Voltaire as the cleverest of all French writers
and ascribe to him forty-five grand characteristics.

II

In the essay on German architecture, entitled
Von Deutscher Baukunst, the reader is wellnigh
inundated with a stream of juvenile inspiration and
acute jingoism. It is really a hymn in praise of
Erwin von Steinbach, the architect of the Strassburg
Cathedral. It was written in the autumn of 1772.
And here also, the rococo that once filled Goethe's
soul is overcome, this time by Gothic.

The young man, manifestly under Herder's influence, who, be it noted, had but the faintest sort
of appreciation of plastic art, was profoundly moved
by the Cathedral. He had not simply examined it
carefully from the sidewalk; he had not simply
climbed the tower like so many visitors after him,
including Jens Baggesen;[6] he had not merely looked
at it. He had studied the very plans and drawings so carefully that he divined details of architecture that were never completed, such as the four
minor towers with the larger one in the centre. And
yet this essay contains virtually nothing bearing on
the real spirit of Gothic.

The treatise reveals a strong and reassuring feeling for the fact that the home of Gothic is the
North, where the art of the South will always seem

[6] Jens Baggesen (1764-1826) started on his first journey to
Germany in 1789. From Strassburg he went to Switzerland where
he became intimately associated with Lavater. Brandes refers to
his climbing the cathedral tower merely by way of showing his
willingness to do anything—once. His admiration for Immanuel
Kant was so great, for a while, that he adopted the name of
"Jens Immanuel Baggesen."   —TRANSLATOR.

out of place.   It gives a clean-cut impression of the
unity of the Cathedral, a point which had given rise
to heated debate on the part of some who contended
that its unity was strained and broken by the excess
of decorations.   It elevated the very term *Gothik* to
a place of honor and dignity where it had formerly
been a word of scorn and abuse.

Inseparable from the noble passion of the monograph is, however, a great deal of national flag-
waving.   Herder had indoctrinated Goethe with a
nationalism which in a few years was to appear foreign to his disciple.   He pours out his heart in detestation of the art of the Romance peoples; nor
does even Greek come off any better in so far as it
fails to meet German requirements.

He declaims, and with reason, against the Made-
leine Church in Paris with its pseudo-Greek columns,
the building of which had been begun about twelve
years previously.   He had never seen the Made-
leine—it was then far from completion and Goethe
never was in Paris—but he disliked it *à priori*.
Rodin, who understands Gothic cathedrals infinitely
better than Goethe, dislikes it even more cordially.
No man who appreciates art at all can prefer it to
Notre Dame in Paris.   Goethe does not go so far
that he, after the fashion of Rodin, would prefer
the Gothic Cathedral to the Parthenon.   Had it
fallen to his lot, as had been the case with Renan,
to stand on the Acropolis, he would have been able
to offer up his own prayer to Pallas Athene.   Each
of the two types of architecture, Antique and Gothic,
is dependent upon climatic conditions.   Gothic
arises in dark and foggy countries. Its towers pointing to heaven, its naves and cross aisles, excavated

from the depths as it were, arise out of the necessity of seeking light up above the clouds and catch it in the corners, or of gently lighting up the falling shades. Antique art, on the contrary, with its smooth upper surfaces, its sharp corners, and its scarcity of windows, is a daughter of blinding superfluous light which refuses to be caught, for that it is much too strong, and which disports itself unmercifully in the presence of any subtlety or dexterity, which it first reveals and then rejects.

At this stage of his development, Goethe did not sense the relativity of ideals. Nor did he realize that Gothic architecture was the expression of an intense religious feeling which had liberated itself from the Roman Church, otherwise he would hardly have been so hostile to this style later on. He did not understand that Gothic was an expression of the same imagination that resulted in the repeated Crusades of Louis the Pious, that it was the expression of the profundity and captiousness of the Scholastics, and of Mariolatry, which made piety an affair of sacred passion. Still less did he appreciate the fact that it was France that had taken the lead in this matter—France, the land where knighthood had especially flourished, and where the impulse to adventure, superinduced by the Crusades, had been especially vigorous. In its origin Gothic was, as is now generally known, entirely an art of northern France.

So little did Goethe even suspect all this that, in his newly awakened hatred of rococo, he had his Frenchman face the Cathedral of Strassburg, babble "Childishness," and point with pride to his *Dose à la Grecque.*

Goethe ridicules the Italians, the neo-French prophets who have a kind word for columns. Against columns as constituent parts of a modern structure he is intensely embittered. What he says against in-walled columns is true enough. But so far does the later worshipper of columns go in his aversion that he passionately scorns Bernini's beautiful colonnade in the front of St. Peter's, and triumphantly disposes of it by saying that the Roman plebeians, at least he has been told so, commit nuisance there. "It is Mother Nature," he says, "who causes this state of affairs. She despises the irrelevant and useless, so that you turn your eyes away and hold your nose in the presence of this miracle."

Of Gothic however he says: "That is German architecture, our architecture. The Italians cannot boast of an architecure that is really their own, and much less the French." The Italians have developed then no architecture of their own while the French are to admit that such originali,y as they appear to have is really German.

Let us notice, in parenthesis, the young author's delight in blunt, vulgar expressions. This style, he feels, he has learned from Shakespeare; it is anti-French first of all, and then it is German. But let us not be deceived by the poem written at the time, *So ist der Held, der mir gefällt*:

> Hoch ist sein Tritt, fest ist sein Schritt,
> Γ ller Deutschen Füsse gleiten nit.

Nor by the verses:

> Wieland soll nicht mehr mit seinesgleichen
> Edlen Mut von eurer Brust verscheuchen.

This is meant merely as a parody on Georg Jacobi's view point.

He had latterly written (February 16, 1770) to an acquaintance in Leipzig regarding Wieland:

To depict the character, the moods of this man, is not our affair. Of great men no one should speak except him who is himself so great that he can survey, that he can look over, the great men in question.

On February 20, 1770, he wrote to another acquaintance:

After Oeser and Shakespeare, Wieland is the only man whom I can look upon as my real teacher. Others had shown me where I was wrong; he showed me what was right, and how to do things right.

Wieland is then still precious in his sight; but he is not destined long to remain so.

So long as Gothic style harmonizes with Goethe's frame of mind, unbiased critical appreciation is impossible for him. But even in this preliminary Gothic period Goethe creates works that tower high up above the general level of world literature. It is not simply his *Gottfried von Berlichingen* that is Gothic; his pre-Weimarian *Faust* belongs in the same category. In a narrow, high-arched Gothic room Faust sits at his desk; the cathedral in which Gretchen hears the voice of the evil spirit is Gothic. In these oldest scenes of *Faust,* in the Gretchen tragedy, Goethe ascends to regions inaccessible to contemporary weapons of attack.

But the young genius has not yet quite reached that point; he has merely laid the foundation for it.

He still cultivates force with a sanctimonious vengeance; he expresses himself in a quite violent way;
he fishes for energetic phrases such as we find in the
letter to Herder where he says: "We two must hold
together, for the world is so full of shysters
(*Scheisskerle*)." In *Gottfried,* inspired by Herder,
Elizabeth says:

Charity is indeed a noble virtue; but it is the exclusive
privilege of strong souls. People who are charitable because they cannot help it are no better than people who
cannot retain their urine.

Such is the outcome of the naturalism which in
the case of young Wolfgang follows in the wake
of his supposed Shakespearean style, his visionary
enthusiasm for Gothic, and his Teutomania.

III

Herder himself, however, drove the youthful
genius into the arms of that particular people who
were to prove the most dangerous to his excessive
nationalism, and his predilection for Gothic art—
the Greeks of long ago. It was Herder who first
showed him their real greatness; he introduced his
disciple to them in a way that was quite different
from the one Wieland had employed in his flippant
Musarion and other works of a similar nature.
In these works by Wieland a stoic is made to look
askance when a pretty young woman exposes her
bosom or legs. Nor does Herder follow the method
of Winckelmann, who had talked to Goethe about
statues while Herder discusses poetry.
In accordance with his fundamental way of look-

ing at ancient things, Herder imbued Goethe with
the error that Homer, who was in actuality the aristocratic court poet of his time, was primitive folk
poetry.   Now he saw the Homeric heroes before
him like "freely wading storks."   And for a long
while the Greeks remain the favorite theme both
of his thoughts and of his representations.

In Wetzlar (as the beginning of *Werther* shows)
the Greeks constitute his sole study. He busies himself with Socrates, whom he thinks of portraying
as "a great man he would gladly press to his heart
out of the enthusiasm of love." Of him he reads
in Plato and Xenophon: "If I were Alcibiades for
just one day and one night, I would gladly die."
(Strange that Sören Kierkegaard,[7] seventy years
later, felt that he was likewise related to Alcibiades).   Here is something which comes from Hamann *via* Herder: the study of Socrates.

The zealous and studious youth feels drawn to
Theocritus, to Anacreon, to Pindar; he translates
and imitates the difficult but clever poets. While
reading Pindar he becomes conscious of the fullness
of his own being.

He writes to Herder: "The good spirit has at
last allowed me to discover the reason for my
woodpecker-like nature. It was made plain to me
on reading Pindar's ἐπικρατεῖν δύνασθαι (able to

---

[7] It is easy—and not easy—to see why Kierkegaard felt related
in spirit to Alcibiades. The Athenian general's self-will and un-
bridled insolence could hardly be said to have been duplicated in
the Danish defender of the Christian religion. Nor was Kierkegaard ever accused of profanation. Quite the contrary. But his
troubles with the spiritual authorities, his belief in his mission to
set his people right, his unquestioned talents, his capriciousness
and the bitterness of his declining years resemble to a marked degree those of his alleged affinity in the days of Socrates.
                                                —Translator.

overcome)." He feels like one of the victors in
the Olympic games of whom Pindar sings: "When
you boldly stand in your chariot and four young
horses plunge along wildly and disorderly in your
reins, you direct their strength, pull in the horse
that runs too far out, whip down the one that rears,
chase, lead, and turn them, strike them with the
whip, hold them back, urge them on, until at last
all sixteen feet bear you along, keeping perfect
step, to your goal—that is mastership, ἐπικρατεῖν,
virtuosoship."

He begins to feel that he is lord of his fiery and
powerful talents. Up to the present he had merely
sauntered around and looked about; he had never
taken definite hold. To take hold, to grip fast
(*drein greifen, packen*) becomes for him at present
the essential characteristic of all immortal excellence. Herder had told him that with him sight,
seeing is everything. Wolfgang understands that
now; he will get a firm hold of things; he will grasp
them aright. Sight and view mean in reality the
relinquishing of claim to; they signify the standing
off at a distance; tangibility on the other hand is
truth: "Of what avail are a thousand eyes without
the feeling hand?"

Despite the visionary bombast of expression, we
do note from now on a more passionate inclination
toward the palpable in art; toward the plastic.
Goethe's being becomes more and more replete with
a careful sensing; with a sensuous imagination.

He translates Pindar's fifth Olympic ode; and we
detect traces of this occupation, of these studies, of
these confessions of artistic faith, in *Wanderers
Sturmlied* from the same period, that wild, spiritual

song sung while wandering in the rain and storm. It closes as follows:

Wenn die Räder rasselten Rad an Rad
Rasch um's Ziel weg,
Hoch flog siegdurchglühter Jünglinge Peitschenknall,
Und sich Staub wälzt,
Wie vom Gebirg, herab sich
Kieselwetter ins Thal wälzt,
Glühte deine Seel' Gefahren, Pindar!
Muth, Pindar!—glühte—

IV

Herder also taught Goethe to understand the spirit of Hebraic poetry. It was, to be sure, neither historic lore nor philosophic wisdom which Herder proclaimed; he was as rich in error as in poetic receptivity. He naïvely derived the myth of creation from Egypt and had no doubt at all but that it was older than the legendary Moses whom he regarded as a historical figure. Goethe reveals the influence of Herder in his essay entitled *Zwo biblische Fragen,* his juvenile attempt at Hebraic archæology, and to no less degree when he undertakes to translate the *Song of Solomon* into separate songs. A few years later, Herder himself published the *Song of Solomon* under the rubric *Lieder der Liebe.* It was in accordance with Herder's idea that Goethe divided the venerable poem into different sections, each consisting of independent parts.

In one of these sections, the young girl, awakened at night by a dream, begins a fruitless search for her lover. She wanders about near her house, out

on the streets of the city, through the market places
and squares, but all in vain:

> Mich trafen die umgehenden Wächter der Stadt,
> Schlugen mich, verwundeten mich,
> Nahmen mir den Schleier,
> Die Wächter der Mauern.

Sulamith replies to the chorus of women:

> Ich beschwöre euch, Töchter Jerusalems.
> Findet ihr meinen Freund,
> Wollt ihr ihm sagen,
> Dass ich vor Liebe krank bin.

They ask:

> Was ist dein Freund vor andern Freunden,
> Du schönste der Weiber?
> Was ist dein Freund vor andern Freunden,
> Dass du uns so beschwörest?

She says:

> Mein Freund ist weiss und rot,
> Auserkoren unter viel Tausenden.
> Sein Haupt ist das reinste Gold.
> Seine Haarlocken scharwz wie ein Rabe.

It was from this that Goethe derived the motif of
the beginning of the fifth act of *Egmont,* on which
he began to work soon thereafter. Clärchen, who
has let the titular hero in so frequently at night,
seeks him now in vain. She rushes through the
streets, and the citizens endeavor to persuade her
to go home by calling her attention to the fact that
Alba's patrol will soon appear. She implores these
same citizens to protect Egmont.

> *Zimmermeister:* What's the matter with you, girl!
> *Klärchen:* Can't you understand me?   I mean the Count!
> I mean Egmont!

Jetter: Don't mention his name! It is fatal.

Klärchen: Don't mention his name? How? Don't mention his name? Who doesn't mention his name on every occasion? Where hasn't his name been written? I have often read his name with all of its letters in these stars . . . Whenever people said: 'There comes Egmont! He is coming from Ghent!'—the inhabitants of the streets through which he had to pass considered themselves fortunate. And when you heard the sound of his horse's hoofs, everyone of you laid down his work and over the worried faces which appeared at the window there came a ray of joy and hope as if from the sun itself. Then you took your children in your arms, as you stood in the doorway, and explained to them that that was Egmont, the greatest of men, that it was he. . . .

This is the motif, transformed and developed, from the *Song of Solomon:* "My friend is chosen from out among ten thousand."

The many divergent examples from various spiritual fields show what aims and ideas the first meeting and association with Herder evoked in young Wolfgang's mind. The relation to Herder is indeed the first outstanding example of a beneficent encroachment, so to speak, of an advantageous impregnation. Anything that was foreign to Goethe's deeper nature, and that had been taken up in a purely imitative fashion, Teutomania for example, was at once and for all time discarded. Anything that narrowed Goethe's mind, such as his aversion to columns or his dislike of the antique on modern soil, was immediately put aside. Anything, on the other hand, that was over-defiant of rules, too fanciful, the trend toward Shakespeare, for example, was, despite all the admiration for it and recognition of it, completely and vigorously renounced when Goethe cast his lot with the spirit of the Greeks

as that was conceived at the close of the eighteenth
century. And even more so when he returned to
French classicism and, contrary to Schiller's wishes,
once more championed Voltaire, that particular
writer of tragedies who was held in so slight esteem
by Lessing, and indeed later by Goethe himself.

But, however much Goethe may have swung from
one spiritual tendency to another, the breath of
genuine inspiration that he received from Herder
remained with him forever. He was exceptionally
fortunate to know in his early youth a mind that
was so much more completely developed than his
own and so much more comprehensive. This is indeed an experience which everyone who hopes to
accomplish something unforgetable in the domain
of art must undergo. Even the genius needs a men-
tor; and no one needs to a greater degree than a
genius that particular sort of emancipation which
fructifies.

CHAPTER V

FRIEDERIKE BRION—THE LYRICS OF YOUTH

FOR the development of Goethe during his stay in Strassburg, his acquaintance with Friederike Brion was of hardly less significance than his association with Herder. She was a very young girl, the daughter of a preacher then stationed at a small village not far from Strassburg.

Friederike stands out in Goethe's life with the glory of springtime; the memories of her love encircle her head with ravishing charm. The poems addressed to her give irrefutable proof of her influence. They are quite superior to anything the young poet had previously written. Just what she was, and what the relation between her and her youthful admirer was, we know only from the sketch in the tenth and eleventh books of *Dichtung und Wahrheit*. This is known to all men as a famous portrayal; and it seems to adhere rigidly to reality, though it does not necessarily have to be entirely true to life. In the very title Goethe has warned us that he has reserved to himself the privilege of remodelling in poet's fashion; and the author, then more than sixty years old, no longer had, it would seem, an entirely clear picture of this tragic idyl of his early life. At any rate, when comment on the causes of the dissolution between the two seemed desirable, the elder Goethe took advantage of the

intervening time and insisted that certain incidents, the very ones we would expect him to recall
quite easily, were now effaced from his memory.
There is, for example, that last meeting between
the two, distressing for both, but more so for the
deserted than the deserter. Goethe expresses himself as follows: "In this affliction and confusion I
simply had to see Friederike once more. Those
were painful days *concerning which I no longer have
a distinct recollection.*"

Accompanied by a friend who knew the parson's
family in Sesenheim, Goethe rode, he tells us, out
to the rustic parsonage, in order to make the acquaintance of the family of which he had heard so
many kind things and which had been compared by
acquaintances of his to the vicar's family in Goldsmith's *The Vicar of Wakefield*. Goethe and his
friend had just been made familiar with Goldsmith's
story through Herder, who had translated it and
read it to them. Goethe disguised himself by dis-
shevelling his hair and donning the thread-bare garb
of a mendicant theological student.

There is no doubt but that our hero cherished
from his very childhood a fondness for playing comedy, for mystifying, for appearing incognito, for
wearing some sort of disguise. This coincides with
his love for the theatre and the illusion connected
therewith. It was not in accord with the best of
taste, however, for Goethe to indulge in this hobby
just here where he was to be introduced into a perfectly strange and quite hospitable family. The
buffoonery took vengeance on him, to be sure, when
he felt out of place because of his unattractive external appearance, though he was repaid for his

attempt when he later appeared as an elegantly dressed young man of the world and made a quite pronounced and favorable impression. The importance attached to all the uncomfortableness and confusion which arose from this first disguise—which was almost immediately followed by a second—is a trifle disconcerting. Hardly less disturbing to the reader, who wishes a straightforward, logical account of the events and persons, is the persistency with which the parallel is maintained and elaborated between this country home and that of *The Vicar of Wakefield*.

However keen Goethe's power of observation may have been, he always had a tendency to see that which he had read mirrored in that which he experienced. On this account his own Werther, who at the very beginning of the story begs his friend to remain forever silent about the books, cannot so much as see the girls drawing water from the well without being reminded of the age of Homer when the daughters of the king attended to this task; and Werther's own Charlotte cannot stand by the window and watch the rain fall during the thunderstorm without repeating the word: *Klopstock!*

The portrayal of Friederike is balmy and beautiful, charmingly shaded and finely executed. When she finally appears in the doorway, after they had waited for her for quite a while, "there arose in truth a star in that rural sky." And a star arose in Goethe's own life at the same moment. In French Alsace, where the town girls dressed in French fashion, Friederike dressed "German," that is to say, partly like a country lass and partly like a city girl. She wore a white bodice with a short white

skirt reaching to her ankles so that her dainty feet
were plainly visible. Her apron was of black taffeta.
Slender and nimble as if she bore no weight at all,
she stood there before him, her heavy braids of
blond hair hanging down her back and seeming almost too heavy for her fine neck. She looked dauntlessly about with her clear blue eyes while her fine
little nose pointed in space as though there weren't
a single care in the whole wide world. Her straw
hat hung on her arm—she was an open-air being.

In his portrayal of her Goethe remarks that there
are some women who look best in the drawing room,
while others appear to better advantage out of
doors. Friederike belonged to the latter class. The
charm of her bearing seemed to vie with the flower-
bedecked earth; her cheerful, vivacious face seemed
in perfect harmony with the blue sky above. She
had a beneficent effect upon all who came into her
presence.

She was never more beautiful than when she
moved about quickly on an elevated path where she
came into full view. She was most beautiful when
she ran. Just as the roe seems to fulfil its real purpose in life when it gaily scampers across the sprout-
ing grass, just so did she seem to reveal her real
character most distinctly when she fleetly ran down
across the meadow near to the edge in order to
fetch something she had forgotten, or to look for
something she had lost, or to call to a couple that
had dropped behind.

The great master has succeeded, as an old man,
in conjuring up a character that is like spring, like
the flowers of the field, like a folk melody. And
this character is rich in traits that seem to exclude

each other: there is reserve and there is vivacity, naïveté and self-consciousness, mirth and calm deliberation. This character seems like a blending into one of the atmosphere of a clear day, of a balmy evening, and of a warm summer night. With inimitable finesse, we are shown how this character, which needs a background of flowering fields and running brooks, which is at home among shrubs and foliage stirred by the wind, loses some of its attraction in Strassburg when surrounded by tapestried walls and mirrors and clocks and porcelain figures. And yet, Friederike, despite her country dress, which stands out in conspicuous contrast to the fashionable costumes of the city, is quite equal to the occasion, and moves about with unimpeachable grace.

There is a great deal more inner tenderness in Goethe's delineation of Friederike than in that of any of his former women friends.

The affair with Gretchen ends, as all the world knows, with a discordant note. When, in the Frankfort lawsuit, her name was found at the close of the love letter that Wolfgang had sketched as a joke, she said,—and that in a legal cross-examination: "I cannot deny that I saw him frequently and with pleasure. But I always looked upon him as a child; my affection for him was that of a sister. I have given him some good advice." The clever, fifteen-year-old boy was annoyed by this statement. The familiarities which she, his senior by nearly three years, was accustomed to allow herself in his presence became in time intolerable to Goethe. For, he contended, her naturally sulky and peevish disposition never made it possible for him to enjoy the same or similar privileges.

The affair with Käthchen Schönkopf also had its disagreeable features. If not in anything else, at least in the garrulity with which everything was repeated to the drill-master Behrisch. In a letter to Behrisch, dated November 7, 1767, we read:

The hand that now touches the paper in order to write to you, this lucky hand she pressed to her bosom. Oh Behrisch! There is poison in these kisses! Why must they be so sweet? You see, I am indebted to you for this eternal bliss. It was your advice; it was your suggestion. Such an hour! What are a thousand dull, worm-eaten, care-worn, murky, fretful evenings in comparison with this one hour! And this hour I owe to you; and I know of no one to whom I would rather owe it than to you. God bless you! I often pray for you when I am in Heaven, and I am there when she holds me in her arms.

When he later praises Käthchen as his sweetheart, he initiates the reader into his great good fortune through the medium of charming verses:

> Ich, der ich diese Kunst verstehe,
> Ich habe mir ein Kind erwählt,
> Dass uns zum Glück der schönsten Ehe
> Allein des Priesters Segen fehlt.

In his relation with Friederike there is, on the contrary, not the slightest touch of anything disagreeable; there is no uppishness, no arrogance; there is not the least bit of puppyism; there is no mere physical desire; there is a feeling as of a deep respiration which enriches the life of the soul, a feeling strong and deep, though not necessarily lasting. With some people, the permanence of an emotion depends by no means upon its depth.

The infatuated young student never has the least grievance against the adored of his heart. A certain reserve on his own part was quickly overcome. As we know, the daughter of the French dancing master had pronounced a curse on the first woman who should kiss him after she had been so favored. The validity of the superstition was of short duration. Goethe is content, in 1813, with the following impersonal, philosophic comment:

Such a youthful affection, cherished at haphazard, may be compared to a bomb thrown up into the sky at night-time. It rises rather evenly, reaches the stars, mingles with them, seems to dwell for a while among them, and then it suddenly shoots down over the same course by which it rose, and spreads destruction at the end of its journey.

But Goethe could not explain his flight from Friederike by logic; nor could he condone it by philosophy. In a series of faithless heroes—Adelbert, Clavigo, Fernando, Faust—he punished himself for his inconstancy. And yet just as he had written concerning the rock-spring, and concerning himself in *Mahomet's Gesang,* he is not to be detained by any flower that entwines itself about his knee.

II

Such was the Sensenheim episode in retrospect; its immediate effect had been to open his lips to unforgetable song. We hear at once the new tone, the Goethe tone as one comes to know it, which breaks forth, the tone that is like the ring of the sword Skraep: it can be distinguished from among a hundred:

Erwache, Friederike,
Vertreib die Nacht,
Die einer deiner Blicke
Zum Tage macht.

Der Vögel sanft Geflüster
Ruft liebevoll,
Dass mein geliebt Geschwister
Erwachen soll.

These are to be sure simple words, the introductory stanza to a serenade, a morning song. Nor
does the rhythm seem at all remarkable; it is exceedingly plain, and yet there is in it the full sounding, ringing arsis of a wonderful overture. There
is an inner richness, a fullness of melody in the
sound just as there is fullness in a strong, flavored
wine, or fullness in the song of the nightingale.

Enter in, for here is Spring! Spring itself! Here
is a picture like that of the wooded soil in the days
when the anemones begin to bloom; like that of the
forest when it buds anew; a scented air like that
of the first warm days of the year; a welling forth
of bubbling springs, the unimpeded flow of silver
brooks. These verses, in themselves mere words,
have the feel of the fresh silk of early foliage, or
the smoothness of sweet-scented blades of grass.

The full significance of the word Spring, of the
word Youth in the case of a poet who was then
twenty-one years of age and whose mother was
eighteen years old at his birth, the full connotation
of the word Genius, a genius whose poetic fount
was soon to gush forth and spread out like a mighty
stream, whose poetic foliage was soon to cast its
shadow over generations—all of this fills the reader's soul and leaps to his lips when he reads these
poems.

Without a shadow of ostentation, Wolfgang gives
expression to his melancholy upon separation from

Friederike whose figure hovers before him without ceasing:

> Ein grauer, trüber Morgen
> Bedeckt mein liebes Feld,
> Im Nebel tief verborgen
> Liegt um mich her die Welt.
> O, liebliche Friederike,
> Dürft ich nach dir zurück,
> In *einem* deiner Blicke
> Liegt Sonnenschein und Glück.
>
> Der Baum, in dessen Rinde
> Mein Nam' bei deinem steht,
> Wird bleich vom rauhen Winde,
> Der jede Lust verweht.
> Der Wiesen grüner Schimmer
> Wird trüb wie mein Gesicht,
> Sie sehen die Sonne nimmer,
> Und ich Friederiken nicht.

Concerning this tree, in which he had carved his name beneath that of Friederike, he writes on a tablet in the beech summer house that stood in the parson's garden the following verses. They contain the fire of youth, the reverence of love, and for the first time unqualified mastery from the point of view of stylistic terseness:

> Dem Himmel wachs' entgegen
> Der Baum, der Erde Stolz!
> Ihr Wetter, Stürm, und Regen,
> Verschont das heil'ge Holz!
> Und soll ein Nam' verderben,
> So nehmt die obern in Acht!
> Es mag der Dichter sterben,
> Der diesen Reim gemacht.

To be sure these poems do not contain the same amount of delightful melody, inexpressibly con-

densed and mysterious, which we find in the poems
written in Weimar about ten years later when
Goethe was living under the mild sceptre of Frau
von Stein. Think of such a little poem as *Aus dem
Zauberthal dort nieden,* not to mention *Uber allen
Gipfeln ist Ruh!* And yet, the Sesenheim poems
are charming because of their simplicity and freshness.

And what a wonderfully descriptive and musical
poem that is in which Goethe describes a journey to
Sesenheim in burning expectation of seeing his sweetheart again! Goethe had revised it twice before
it appeared in 1775. He subdued and smoothed
out the passionateness and gave the style a more
rhetorical swing. But the fourth stanza alone has
been improved thereby. The first two stanzas sound
far more genuine and their impression is far more
vivid in the first version, which transports by reason
of its artistic fullness and truth:

Es schlug mein Herz, geschwind zu Pferde!
Und fort! wild, wie ein Held zur Schlacht!
Der Abend wiegte schon die Erde,
Und an den Bergen hing die Nacht.
Schon stund im Nebelkleid die Eiche
Wie ein gethürmter Riese da,
Wo Finsternis aus dem Gesträuche
Mit hundert schwarzen Augen sah.

Der Mond von einem Wolkenhügel
Schien schläfrig aus dem Duft hervor.
Die Winde schwangen leise Flügel,
Umsausten schauerlich mein Ohr.
Die Nacht schuf tausend Ungeheuer—
Doch tausendfacher war mein Muth.
In meinen Adern welches Feuer!
In meinem Herzen welche Gluth!

In every visit to Sesenheim, whether brief or prolonged, the joy of meeting was ever tinged with sorrow at the prospect of eventual separation. And how the shadow deepened, as this prospect of a final leave-taking became a certainty! And yet how jubilant the young student was at heart so soon as the conviction grew that he not only loved but was loved in turn:

> Der Abschied, wie bedrängt, wie trübe!
> Aus deinen Blicken sprach dein Herz.
> In deinen Küssen welche Liebe!
> In deinen Augen welcher Schmerz!
> Du gingst, ich stund, and sah zur Erden,
> Und sah dir nach mit nassem Blick,
> Und doch, welch Glück, geliebt zu werden!
> Und lieben, Götter, welch ein Glück!

CHAPTER VI

THE LICENTIATE—THE PRACTICE OF LAW— JOURNALISM—THE SPIRITUAL REVOLUTION

THE father had desired that Wolfgang should take his doctorate in law at Strassburg; he became only a licentiate. When his doctoral dissertation was rejected, he contented himself with offering a number of Latin theses which he wished to defend. That his proffered monograph was refused was due to the simple fact that he had attacked orthodoxy. Concerning the dissertation itself, we know only what is contained in a letter written on August 7, 1771, by a medical student:

There is a student here by the name of Goethe from Frankfort-am-Main who, it is said, has studied quite diligently at Göttingen and Leipzig. This young man, who is quite puffed up over his store of knowledge, but chiefly by reason of a few undesirable traits he has got from M. Voltaire, wanted to present a thesis with the title: *Jesus autor et judex sacrorum.* In this thesis he contended, among other things, that Jesus Christ was not the author of our religion, but that a number of other wise men composed it in his name. The Christian religion, he avers, is merely a rational, political institution, etc. But the right people had the good grace to forbid the publication of his masterpiece. Thereupon he presented, in order to give palpable vent to his contempt, the simplest kinds of theses. One was: *The natural law is what nature has taught all creatures.* The authorities laughed at him and his case, and with that the affair was ended.

112

It is entirely correct that the title of Goethe's first thesis read: *Jus naturae est quod natura omnia animalia docuit.* He presented indeed no fewer than fifty-six theses with the juridicial and political postulates, one after another, with no thought of logical arrangement.

Some of them are quite conservative, Nos. 43 and 44 for example: *It is the duty of the Prince to make all laws: it is also his duty to interpret them.* Or take No. 53: *The death penalty should not be done away with.* Some of them are quite liberal and cautiously expressed, as No. 54: *Should the woman who kills her newly born child suffer the death penalty? There is no unity among the learned on this point.*

He had now, like Faust, the title of *Magister* and was called *Doctor* out of courtesy. *Heisse Magister, heisse Doctor gar.* But deep down in his soul jurisprudence had but little attraction for him. He cast about with big literary tasks; he wanted to write a *Cæsar,* a *Götz von Berlichingen,* a *Faust.*

He never got very far with his Cæsar. All that he really wrote was a few speeches soon to appear as paralipomena at the close of his *Epimenides,* and then separately. At this time he evidently felt entirely at one with Cæsar, though a little later in his contribution to Lavater's *Physiognomische Fragmente,* where he really interpreted the pictures rather than the people, he speaks with the utmost warmth of Brutus and disparagingly of the one reproduction of Cæsar. He finds therein a selfishness hard as iron and more than tyrannical. But of the other contour he writes: "How great, pure,

and good! Mighty and powerful without defiance.
Immovable and irresistible. Wise, effective, lifted
up above all things, feeling himself fortune's son,
considerate, expeditious—the incarnation of all human greatness." Nor was he as an older man
kindly disposed to Cæsar's murderers. Concerning
them he writes in verse: "They begrudged Cæsar
his empire without knowing how to govern it themselves." We will later see what prevented him
from elaborating this theme.

It is plain that Goethe was thinking of Herder
and himself when he has Sulla say of Cæsar: It is
distinctly uncomfortable when such a whelp grows
up by the side of you. You can see by his very
limbs that he will in time completely outgrow you.

Two excellent speeches are put in Cæsar's mouth.
The first: "You know that I soon grow tired of
everything, but most quickly of praise and indulgence. Yes, Servius, in order to become and remain
a real man, I hope that I may have, so long as I
live, great antagonists and honored enemies." The
second: "So long as I live the base shall tremble,
and they will not have a sufficient amount of courage left to rejoice at my grave."

Strangely enough, Napoleon asked Goethe in
1808 to write a *Cæsar* that would be superior to
Voltaire's *Death of Cæsar*. Little did he realize
that the poet himself had been interested in this very
theme almost forty years before.

II

In August 1771, Goethe left Strassburg, and on
his way to Frankfort sojourned for a short while

in Mannheim where, for the first time in his life, he saw casts of Roman sculpture. For him, as for Winckelmann and Lessing, they represented the very apex of Greek art. He saw *Laokoon, The Apollo of Belvedere,* and *The Venus of Medici.* These, as well as various antique busts, made a profound impression upon him. It was from these casts that his conception of Hellenic sculpture was first acquired, long before he went to Italy. That there was a significant difference between Roman art and Greek art he neither felt nor knew.

Immediately upon his arrival in Frankfort he submitted his application to practice law, that is to say, to become counsel for the defense in private cases. His petition was granted and he appeared before the bar in several cases, in which the pleas have been preserved. We see how ardently he takes his client's case to heart, how youthful and pugnacious is the tone he adopts, and how every defense in his hands takes on the form of an indictment. He uses the strongest, frequently the very gruffest expressions. Clever he really is not; but he expresses himself in such picturesque comparisons, in such striking phrases, that one feels that back of the lawyer stands the poet. For example, he declares: "The cloak of untruth has been thoroughly perforated," or, "The raven abuses the jackdaw for being black," or, "If the highly praised building lot turns out to be only a body of water frozen over, the building which is erected on it will sink into its grave at the first wind of spring—a piece of genuine good fortune for the builder that he had not erected unto himself on this spot any columns of glory."

Goethe's first opponent was likewise not sparing in his use of words of gruff censure. The tribunal rebuked him as well as Wolfgang for transgressing the limits of dignity. Goethe accepted the reproof in good part and his tone became more moderate in the following suits. Yet we can see that he is vexed at the pedantry of professional men. Even in *Werther* the hero complains bitterly of the pedantry of his superior officer, the Ambassador, who is constantly correcting his language: "One always finds a better word, a cleaner particle." Goethe was thinking here partly of himself and partly of his model, young Jerusalem and the latter's disagreement with the Brunswick Ambassador.

III

In a letter from this same Jerusalem we read a number of things that are not exactly complimentary to Goethe: "During my day he was a ladies' man in Leipzig; now he has become also a newspaper scribbler in Frankfort."

On his arrival in Frankfort Goethe fell in with a circle of lively young men who, like himself, stood under Herder's leadership and who had decided to take over the redaction of an old paper called the *Frankfurter Gelehrte Anzeigen,* in order to make propaganda for their views and to start a vigorous protest against everything in German literature which they regarded as puffed up, harmful, hypocritical, flat, and stupid. There were the two brothers Schlosser, one of whom was soon to become Goethe's brother-in-law by marrying his sister Cornelia. Schlosser incidentally made her exceed-

ingly unhappy—through no desire on his own part.
There was Höpfner, professor of law at Giessen,
to whom Goethe introduced himself under the guise
of an unknown student of law, thus repeating his
conduct in Sesenheim, and there was Johann Heinrich Merck who, next to Herder, exercised the greatest influence on the development of Goethe's talents
during these first years and whom Goethe has immortalized as the sharp critic of his life and works.
It was Merck whom he selected as the model of the
biting, witty, cynical characters in his early productions, Mephisto in *Faust* and Carlos in *Clavigo*.

It must be said just here that Merck, as a con-
versationalist, employed expressions that were undoubtedly much more fresh and bold than those
which we find in his writings; from his many published letters no one would ever suspect that he had
pedagogical ability coupled with uncompromising
wit.

Merck was an extremely versatile individual who
wasted his talents in dilettantism. He was born at
Darmstadt in 1741 and was accordingly eight years
older than Goethe and vastly superior to him in
practical experience and worldly wisdom. He had
decided ability both as a merchant and as an author.
He won the applause of such contemporaries as
Herder, Wieland, Karl August, and the Duchess of
Weimar. Admitted to the very best circles, he
was at once regarded and treated as a friend and
brother. His knowledge was sound; in English
literature he was perfectly at home; he had translated not a little from English. French was to him
a second mother-tongue. His young wife, whom
he passionately loved from the very first, was a

French woman from Switzerland. To her he never spoke or wrote anything but French. He was moreover an excellent calculator and a prompt, firm, business man, though fortune at last deserted him completely.

More remarkable than his knowledge was his critical ability, sharp and yet reliable as it invariably was. Wieland said of him jestingly: "Haziness does not protect against, illusions do not exist in the presence of, his damnable perspicacity." As a critic of art he was stern and fearless though he won the good will of all by his fine feeling and charming modesty. This is also Dalberg's judgment. Wieland says somewhere concerning him, that it could never occur to a healthy human being to appeal to a higher tribunal than Merck (unless Merck happened to be so out of humor that his criticism reflected disgust and rancor). So far as Goethe is concerned, he was decidedly dependent upon Merck's opinion. He never forgot Merck's critical estimates of his works. Years later in his autobiography he records how it was Merck who first gave him the courage to publish *Götz,* and how his first expression concerning *Werther,* "well, that is rather pretty," brought the young author to despair, whereupon amends for the first opinion were made by a second, and how finally Merck, after having read *Clavigo,* reminded Goethe of his great aim by saying: "Such muck (*quark*) you must never write in the future; others can do that." Merck saw through the friends Wolfgang made in his naïveté, only to be quickly disappointed, such friends as Leuchsenring and the brothers Stolberg. Merck predicted Goethe's break with the latter and in-

spired him to write *Pater Brey* against the first. He
defined in these words Goethe's own poetic nature
before starting on his first journey to Switzerland:
"You try to give to the real a poetic form; others
try to make the so-called poetic real, and the result
is stupid trash." During his first visit to Weimar
he broke out once: "What the deuce can persuade
Wolfgang to stay here in Weimar bending and bow-
ing and scraping around the Court, bepraising others
or, what amounts to the same thing with me, having
himself praised by them. Can't he find anything
better to do?"

Such was the nature of the man who was the soul
of the new critical venture, which for a short time
was read by everybody in Germany who had intellectual interests. Lively correspondence and frequent meetings brought the collaborators together.
They met not simply with common interests, common ideals, common aims; they also discussed together the scientific and poetic phenomena of the
day. They were in complete harmony as to what
sort of judgment should be passed upon them.
Wolfgang kept the minutes of these meetings.

The articles were anonymous, a fact which later
made it quite difficult to ascribe to the various collaborators precisely what belonged to them. But
the articles were the product of more than one clever
mind, even though only one hand wielded the pen,
so that identification of each author is doubly difficult. This circumstance explains why the elder
Goethe included in his *Sämmtliche Schriften* one or
two articles which he in truth did not write, just
as he excluded one or two that he did write. Even
Wilhelm Scherer believed in his day that he de-

tected the pen of Goethe in a number of places where it can hardly be shown. The great Weimar edition of Goethe's works was the first to draw the line. It published, in small type, a number of articles which were, to be sure, written in the spirit of Goethe though it is quite safe to assume that he did not write them. There is, for example, the excellent little review of Dr. Münter's book on the conversion of Struensee, which Goethe thought he had written, and which in truth is so much like him. It is shown that in this book both the converted and the converter were insignificant, jejune human beings. And there is another Danish book which is mentioned in translation, Johannes Ewald's *Rolf Krage*.[8] Concerning it we have the laconic, pithy, and lucid, though not wholly warranted criticism expressed in these words:

Night, high treason, fratricide, incest and death, darkness, gruesomeness, the pain of love and the pain of death, so that we contemplate our journey home with a reverent, God preserve us!

Among these reviews there are several that deserve the closest attention of posterity, despite the fact that the books discussed have long since been hopelessly forgotten. There is, first of all, the critique of J. v. Sonnenfel's *Ueber Vaterlandsliebe*. It shows how great the spiritual independence of the young genius was, despite his susceptibility to Herder's teachings. We have seen Goethe captivated by all that is German at the expense of the

[8] Johannes Ewald (1743-1781) published his *Rolf Krage* in 1770. It is the first national tragedy of Danish literature. The work was based on Saxo's chronicles and is reminiscent of Klopstock. Rolf and Hother resemble the heroes of Kozebue and Iffland as much as they do those of the old Danish sagas.   —TRANSLATOR.

Romance nations; but this visionary enthusiasm did
not go so far that he, either in his youth or in his
mature years, forgot how much Germany lacked
from the point of view of a unified whole, of a real
fatherland.   Saturated as he is with the spirit of
eighteenth century cosmopolitanism, he does not feel
the loss of any such real fatherland; nor does he
regard it as something good.   On the contrary, he
derisively casts aside the then perpetual cries: "We
have no fatherland; we have no patriotism."   He
says:

When we find a place in the world where we can rest
with our belongings, a field that provides us with susten-
ance, a house in which to live, haven't we a fatherland? And
do not thousands upon thousands have that in every state?
And do they not live happy within this limit? Why all this
fruitless striving after a feeling that we neither can have nor
wish to have, which only in the case of certain peoples and
at certain times has been and is the result of many happily
coinciding circumstances?   Roman patriotism?   God preserve us from it as we would pray to be preserved from some
huge giant! We would find no chair to sit on, no bed to
lie in.

One is constrained to compare this outbreak with
the declaration by Goethe in 1806, when he experienced the formation of the Rhine Confederation
without the slightest bit of excitement.   He had
heard it said that a fatherland as a whole had been
lost on that occasion.   But he replied by saying that
no one had seen such a "whole," and that complaint about the loss of it seemed to him like affectation.   He felt in 1806 just as he felt in 1772.   It
was not until 1814, in *Epimenides*, that his heart
beat in unison with the Germany which had cast off
foreign dominion.

Another diverting and significant review is the one that tells of Goethe's first encounter with one of the Jacobi brothers. Professor Geheimrat Klotz, the antagonist whom Lessing had disarmed and ridiculed, had died in December 1771. A certain Hausen had, not long after Klotz's death, published his biography. It completely unveiled the mixture of skill and vulgarity with which Klotz, as editor of the magazine *Deutsche Bibliothek der schönen Wissenschaften,* had worked, with shameless self-advertisement, for insignificant confederates and with uncompromising insolence toward prominent men. One of Klotz's friends, all of whom now tried to get as far away from him as possible, was the delicate young lyric writer, Johann Georg Jacobi, who, in the form of a letter to a woman acquaintance, had had a defense published which amounted to a whining, pitiful self-glorification. He had promised the world to be good and noble; and good and noble he wished to continue to be. In anonymous letters someone doubted his love of virtue and his hostility to sin, but to doubt his character was impossible, however much this might be attempted by envy and calumniation.

Goethe had reviewed Jacobi's self-defense along with Hausen's biography. This was done boldly and directly:

Herr Jacobi and his good heart; the good heart and Herr Jacobi; a large part of the public is heartily sick of both. Couldn't he be an amiable poet without wishing to have himself loved everywhere and by everybody? Couldn't he be an honest man without all of these anxious protestations? . . . The content and nature of his declamation is most repellent to us. . . Would that Herr Jacobi might continue to be "the noble, warm friend of man, the wise and true

friend of virtue, and the stern enemy of sin" and leave the
rest of us in peace with his virtues!

That is a highly significant introduction to the
relation between Goethe and the two Jacobi
brothers, both of whom were from the very first
most repellent to him, though one of them became
his close friend, then felt deeply wounded by his
mocking criticism, and finally dedicated his *Woldemar* to him, a book which Goethe in the haughtiness
of youth had rightly scorned. The Jacobi brothers
occupy a very modest place in Goethe's life, though
he occupies a very important place in theirs, indeed,
even a definitive one in the case of Friedrich Heinrich, whose youth was essentially determined and
moulded by Goethe's. But his relation to Goethe,
despite all his personal friendliness, was merely one
of sharp contrasts—in so far as it is possible to
contrast a very great man with one who is, after
all, so insignificant and profoundly tiresome.

The third review deserving emphasis is that of
Gedichte von einem Polnischen Juden, though not
because of the poems themselves: they are at present
utterly unknown. The very title appealed to the
young reviewer, for it seemed to promise something
quite out of the ordinary—a high mettled soul, a
mind that goes deep, developed as it has been under
an alien and inhospitable sky. The preface contained, however, mere vapid self-complacency; and
in the verses themselves there was a deal of verdant commonplace which smacked neither of Juda-
ism nor of Poland. The reviewer then straightway
forgets his pitiable dilettant to whom he was supposed to draw attention, and gives instead a picture

of what is going on in his own mind. And with a
challenge to Germany's genius—expressed unfortunately in a diffuse and rickety style—he presents
us with a thought-provoking delineation of his own
character and his own expectations:

Let, O Genius of our Fatherland, a youth come forth
at once in all his glory, a youth who, full of the force and
buoyancy and mirth of younger years, will be the best fellow
of his circle . . . who will sing the most joyful song . . .
to whom the prettiest girl at the ball will gladly give her
hand— . . . whom the beautiful, clever, cheerful young
woman will try to catch by using all her charms . . . but
whose heart will proudly tear itself loose so soon as he sees
that his goddess is *only* beautiful, only clever, only cheerful . . . But let it be brought to light then, O Genius,
that it was not shallowness that gave rise to his uncertainty,
and let him find a girl who is worthy of him! . . . Truth
will be found in his poetry and living beauty as well, not
soap-bubble ideals such as are blown up in German songs by
the hundreds.

IV

In his father's house in Frankfort Goethe had a
confidante in his sister Cornelia. Distressed and
unhappy as she had been under her father's pedantic
tyranny, she was rejuvenated by association with
her brother and took part in his plans and under-
takings. In company with her he arranged the
Shakespeare celebration during which he delivered
the address of the occasion. He told her of the
suggestion he had received for a drama by reading
the memoirs of an old knight. It was her impatient
and kindly importunity that gave him no peace until
he had put on paper the ideas that filled him through-

out his stay in Frankfort and with which he now engaged her interest as well.

Die Geschichte Gottfriedens von Berlichingen mit der eisernen Hand is Goethe's first more pretentious work; it is written in his oldest style. The idea of this *Gottfried* goes back to Herder, whose Christian name the hero received, and further on back to the influence of Shakespeare, to which young Wolfgang was subjected through Herder during his Strassburg days. The influence of Herder—himself a disciple of Rousseau—is evident in the very opening scene.

Klopstock had devoted himself to German emotionalism; he had awakened a feeling for the exalted, though he saturated the minds of the people with the poetry of the chapel and other sanctimonious localities. Lessing had attacked the rigidly correct French tragedy by ·referring to Shakespeare. What he really did was to attack the Frenchmen's adherence to the rules in the name of the Aristotelian rules and to insist that Shakespeare upheld Aristotle as correctly interpreted. Herder had never proclaimed adherence to the rules and, as a student of Rousseau, was never satisfied with Enlightenment, the most basic element in Lessing's spiritual equipment. Where nothing in Lessing's whole make-up went beyond the limits of the eighteenth century, Herder prepared the way for the nineteenth century, thus coming into contact with the choicest minds of the new generation and incidentally leaving a strong impression upon them.

The youth of the day felt an especial need, first of all, of a deeper cultivation of the mind and thereby a more complete emancipation. In the old-fashioned, ill-governed, distintegrated Germany, youth felt under restraint, over-disciplined, but bedizzened socially to the point of unpleasant conspicuousness. On its wrists it wore society's manacles and over these lace cuffs. On youth's head there was a peruke and over this swayed and hovered obligatory fidelity and princely autocracy. Allmighty custom and usage bedaubed paint and powder on its face. With silk stockings on his legs, hat under his arm, and useless dress sword at his side, the rococo swain of that time, who knew how to bow and get about, was a finished product.

But his heart was yearning for something more. Enlightenment did not satisfy him. He yearned with tremendous vehemence for a revolution, not in the outer world, where he was fully aware of his omnipotence, but in the inner world where, at least in his own eyes, he was sovereign. Light and clarity no longer had their old appeal. He had a desire to find in some cryptic way the deep inner connection between the law of the natural life and the law of the spiritual life. The more the individual came to see his insignificance in society and the state, the more surely he felt that he was only a number, a taxpayer, a docile subject, just so much the more was he filled and carried away with the thought that he was a part of nature, of the infinitely great, a living spark in the flame of all-life, and as a citizen of the earth related to the spirit of the earth.

The individual had something divine in him; he had genius. This genius craved freedom from dogma in any form whether it pertained to life or art or science or religion. It made no difference, he would have none of this dogma with which the

devotees of Enlightenment had particularly concerned themselves. Everything that mankind had
heaped up in the course of centuries in the way of
limitations of freedom was the direct and diabolic
outcome of arbitrariness and iniquity. It became
a question of obeying one's genius, not some external law. Outside of the individual's genius, the
divine manifested itself in nature. It became therefore a question of following nature. Worship ever
brought nature to the fore.

Genuine poetry, which was the greatest thing in
life, was not the beautiful and abstract oratory that
had come over from the France of the seventeenth
century, but the poetry that was found in sublime
folk-poems, such as the Bible, in the folk-songs of
all nations, and in the poetry created by individuals
who, unhampered by the restraint of rules, had followed their own genius. There was Homer, by
way of illustration, and Ossian, and Shakespeare.
Shakespeare was great, not at all because he had
observed the Aristotelian rules, which the French
had misinterpreted, but because he had followed his
own endowed nature without regard to rules.

The preacher of these doctrines was Herder.
The youth that heard his message broke its manacles, washed its face clean of all powder and paint,
and took up into its soul abundant drafts of human
life and folk life. It hurled its periwig against the
wall and placed the crown of sovereign personality
on its head. It discarded, and that with vigor, the
blade of gallantry which heretofore had characterized the man of polite society, and waved the sceptre
of original genius in its hand. This revolution was

ushered in with storming violence; and as this violence was thought to have found final expression in
a poor specimen of a drama by Maximilian Klinger,
the name of the epoch arose therefrom: *Sturm und
Drang.*

CHAPTER VII

Gottfried von Berlichingen—NATURALISM OF STYLE—*Götz*

Die Historie Gottfriedens von Berlichingen mit der eisernen Hand, the first draught of *Götz,* was written in six weeks, without change of mood or flagging of energy. Goethe had read Götz von Berlichingen's autobiography in Strassburg. This collection of war anecdotes was written by the bold robber knight who had had his right hand shot off by a cannon ball during the war of the Bavarian Succession, and had had it replaced by a movable iron hand. The incident occurred in 1504. Götz was then twenty-four years old. The blunt, vivacious tone in these notes enraptured Goethe. That iron hand, which could wield the lance as well as the sword, became for the young poet a symbol of chivalric power and straightforward honesty. Its owner became for him the very incarnation of German honor. Götz appealed to him as the original personality that obeys his genius in calm defiance of all laws—those laws which are the subtle, juridical expression of injustice. As the Monk says of him, he is "the man whom the Princes fear and to whom the oppressed turn." He is the virile force in nature every act of which is a struggle for liberty. On this account all natural desires flourish in his presence. This accounts for the *Schwärmerei of* the Monk, Brother Martin, for him. Goethe had

Luther in mind. Luther's outbreak to Götz against the monkish vows is most significant:

Poverty, chastity and obedience, three vows, each one of which seems the most intolerable to nature; how intolerable then are all three of them together! . . . O Sir, what are the hardships of your life when compared with the misery of an order that damns the best impulses in us and by which we live, grow and prosper, and this out of a misunderstood zeal to get nearer to God!

There is a decidedly Protestant strain running throughout *Gottfried von Berlichingen.* The Monk expresses his desire for an active life of deeds and exploits, with danger and booty, for the freeman's life on the broad highway in the place of seclusion in the cell.

Then there is the heartfelt sigh of the Monk for the women of others, revealing in the case of the poet a more mature sensuousness than Luther's, with so little that was distinctly coarse and common. This yearning for the individually beautiful in woman appears in the very large part occupied by the siren Adelheid in the economy of the drama. That it was a strong desire is made obvious by the fact that even the demure Maria fears lest she may be taken by surprise by the passion which Weislingen fails to restrain when in her presence. She is afraid to live for a long time under the same roof with him: One has to be on one's guard against these men when their "paroxysms" come over them; it avails so little to appeal to their reason.

Götz is a nature, not an intelligence. He says in the last act:

They have mutilated me piece by piece: my hand, my liberty, my property, my good name. They have left me only the poorest part of my being, my head, and what is that without the rest!

Götz does not enjoy outward or personal prosperity; for that he is far too magnanimous. Sickingen says to him:

You always get the worst of it. The magnanimous individual is like the man who fed the fish from the bread of his own table and then, out of carelessness, fell into the pond and was drowned. The fish then ate the benefactor with the same relish that they had formerly eaten his benefactions and became fat and strong therefrom.

Goethe had to re-work his material not a little in order properly to transform the historical character that hovered before him. The historical Götz was fond of fighting; he struck for pleasure's sake, in order to measure his strength with that of others. Such was, for example, the *raison d'être* of his feud with Nuremberg. He evinces the fresh bloodthirstiness of a robber knight. In the first act the trooper says to Elizabeth:

Just as we rode out into the dusk, we saw a shepherd guarding his sheep. Five wolves fell upon the flock and attacked it most effectively. Luck to you, dear comrades! Luck at all hazards, and to us too! We were all much pleased at this good omen. And just then Weislingen came riding up with four servants.

The passage is taken from Götz's autobiography, with this difference: The speech in the autobiography refers to the capture of the Count of Waldeck.

Götz loves blood and booty. He requisitioned 18,000 guldens as a ransom for the Count of Waldeck. In Goethe's drama Elizabeth tells Gottfried's son the story of the tailor from Heilbronn, who was

such an excellent marksman that he took the first
prize at Cologne.   When the citizens of Cologne
refused to pay him what they owed him, Götz took
the matter in hand and the Cologne marksmen had
to give in.   That is the exploit.   What is omitted is
the fact that Götz and the tailor together took
twenty-three times as much as was originally due
them.   That is the booty.

Goethe embellishes to the highest degree Götz's
participation in the Peasants' War.   He has Götz
assume the leadership simply in order thereby to
prevent atrocities and to secure justice.   In reality
Götz made common cause with the bloodthirsty
rebels at first and then left them in the lurch; in
actuality he was imprisoned two years for this
breach and then set free under a 25,000 gulden bond
and with the assurance that he would never leave
his Castle Hornberg.   In his old age he became
inordinately pious.   During his last years he was
always surrounded by his village priest who, in return for an annual reward, took up his abode with
him as private confessor.

There is a great difference between the Götz who
dies in the priest's arms and Goethe's Gottfried who
dies with these words on his lips:

Poor woman!   I am leaving you in a degenerate world.
Don't forsake her, Lerse!   Lock your hearts more carefully
than your doors!   The age of dishonesty is coming; dishonesty enjoys freedom.   The good-for-nothing will rule
with cunning, and the brave man will fall into the net which
cowardice has placed in his path . . . O heavenly air, Liberty!   Liberty!   (He dies).

Elisabeth: Only up there, up there with you!   The world
is a prison.

Maria: Noble, noble man! Woe to the century that rejected you!
Lerse: Woe to posterity that misjudges you!

Goethe has done everything in his power to work himself into the language and customs of the sixteenth century; he made special investigations in order to be certain of the local color of that time; and he made a special effort to portray the romantically picturesque in the gipsy camp and in the secret tribunal. And yet, it is the favorite ideas of his own time that are glorified.

In the conversation between Gottfried and his little son, the father reveals practical knowledge of the thing at hand; the son reveals the useless book learning which is perfectly familiar with the definition but wholly ignorant of the thing itself, the brand of learning that is ascribed to Wagner in *Faust:*

Karl: I know something else.
Gottfried: What is it?
Karl: Jaxthausen is a village and a castle on the Jaxt and has belonged to the Lords of Berlichingen, personally and by right of inheritance, for the past two hundred years.
Götz: Do you know the Lords of Berlichingen?
Karl: (Looks at him fixedly).
Götz: (To himself.) He knows so much about books that he doesn't know his own father.—To whom does Jaxthausen belong?
Karl: Jaxthausen is a village and a castle on the Jaxt.
Götz: That isn't what I asked you. Thus do women educate their children, and would to God they alone did it this way! I knew all the paths, roads and ferries before I knew the names of the river, the castle and the village.

Gottfried is the original person, Karl the one spoiled by unreal education. The effeminate boy corresponds neither to the age's nor to young

Goethe's conception of manliness. The aunt's indulgent education is not responsible, but his own lack of naturalness. Gottfried says of him: "A hundred such aunts would not have kept me from riding the horses and sleeping in the stable." In reply to the question as to whether there will be a place for him in the world, his mother says:

No, my dear boy. Weak people do not fit into any place in the world; they would have to be vagabonds. On this account sensible women remain at home and effeminate fellows enter the monastery. When my husband starts on a journey, I am not the least bit afraid. If Karl went away, I would live in perpetual anxiety. He is safer in monastic garb that in that of a soldier.

The hero has at the beginning of the sixteenth century the ideals of peace and happiness of the closing eighteenth century. He is astonished at the blindness of the great men and the princes. In his utterances one notices the young poet's revolutionary temperament—which was soon to disappear. Gottfried says:

I have sympathy with master and subject. Woe, woe to the great man who builds on an excess of his esteem! Men's souls become stronger through oppression. But they see and hear not.

Georg: Would to God that all princes were blessed by their subjects as you!

Gottfried: If I only had many of them! I would never try to be happier than any single one of them, without making them happier. Now our Lords are a consuming fire which nourishes itself, without being satiated, on the happiness, number, blood and sweat of the subject.

When, at the close of the third act, Georg, Gottfried, and at last all cry out: "Long live Liberty!" Gottfried says:

When they (the great) come to have enough human heart
to taste the glory that comes from being a great man; when
they get so far that their country, well cultivated and blessed,
seems to them a paradise with their stiff, heavy, lonesome
gardens [Le Notre's]; when every farmer's round cheeks and
glad eyes and large families and peaceful prosperous country
are assured, and all dramas and all pictures seem to them
cold in comparison—then the neighbor will give his neighbor peace, because he himself is happy; then no one will try
to extend his boundaries. . . .

Georg: Will we ride horses then too?

Gottfried: The most restless head will find enough to do
. . . We will rid the forest of wolves and we will fetch
our quietly plowing neighbor a roast from the woods and in
pay for this we will eat soup with him. . . .

What is that but the cue taken from the exponent
of public welfare and world peace? With his noble
striving for these ideals Gottfried, who is looked
upon as a robber knight, stands out in sharp contrast to the entire legal fabric of that time, which
represents baseness brought into some sort of or-
derly coherence. This explains his exclamation in
the fourth act:

You call me a robber! God grant that your posterity may
be plundered and plucked to the last feather by honorable
civilian rogues, by friendly thieves and privileged criminals!

It is necessary to go to Schiller's *Räuber* to find a
repetition of that thought. Gottfried is nature and
genius, society is legal oppression and rogues' doings
within the law.

II

The naturalism of the style, its emphasis of the all-too-human, which disregards society, corresponds to the apotheosis of nature. In the later version Goethe toned this down more or less. The wild exaggeration is of a piece with the immaturity.

Elizabeth's disparaging statement concerning any-one who is charitable because it is impossible for him to be otherwise, has already been quoted.

The Bishop has asked Franz whether Weislingen is unhurt:

I said: He is well from the topmost point of his longest hair down to the nail on his little toe. I forgot that I recently had to trim your nails; but I did not tell him that for I did not wish to frighten him with an exception.

And yet the same Franz, who is so blunt and who has carried out an order in the way described, gives Goethe's conception of what makes a man a poet. He replies to Weislingen when the latter has become enraptured by Adelheid: "Beauty has made you a poet:"

I feel then at this moment what makes a poet—a full heart, entirely filled with just one feeling.

An idea as to the freedom of speech can be derived from the fact that in the third act, in a scene which incidentally has been preserved in *Götz*, two Imperial servants, who happen to be in a woods near a swamp, begin their conversation in the following way:

What are you doing? I have begged leave to go to the rear. Since that affair last evening my bowels have been so upset that I have to dismount every minute.

Gottfried's own answer to the foreign Captain is no less blunt. In the poem on the drama to Gotter, in 1772, one feels Goethe's delight in vulgar expressions:

> Und bring, da hast du meinen Dank,
> Mich vor die Weiblein ohn' Gestank.
> Musst all' die garstigen Worte lindern.
> Aus Scheisskerl Schurk, aus Arsch mach Hintern?

This is the same style that is later imitated in Schiller's *Räuber*. It speaks reluctantly of centuries, never of decades; it needs milleniums. Franz says, for example, when Adelheid chases him away at break of day:

Shall I leave! O that outweighs all the tortures of Hell simply to be able to enjoy Heaven's blessing for just one short moment. A *thousand* years are only a half a night. O how I hate day! O if we were only living in original night before the light was born, I would be one of the eternal gods, on your bosom, who in the brooding warmth of love lived in himself, and begot in one point the seeds for a *thousand* worlds, and would feel the joy of a *thousand* worlds in just one point.

Thus wrote Goethe when he was twenty-two years old. And even three years later he has Beaumarchais in *Clavigo* use, with regard to the inconstant *fiancé* of his sister, this cannibal-like outbreak: "My teeth are eager for his flesh and my palate thirsts for his blood." In the oldest edition we are even treated to the following:

O if I only had him beyond the sea! I would catch him, bind him to a post, tear his limbs off piece by piece, roast them right before his very eyes, eat of them and dish them up to you, women!

And even in a scene in *Faust* from the year 1773, entitled *Trüber Tag,* we find in the conversation in prose the convulsive passionateness, the wild outbreak of feeling, the ungoverned fustian, in which people of that day saw something Shakespearean. Exclamations, reiterations, execrations, superlatives! There is the grinding of greedy teeth. Infernal eyes are rolled around in their sockets. Save her, or woe be unto you; the most awful execrations upon you for *thousands* of years!

The style in *Gottfried* is as a whole the style of young Goethe. In just one single place it is formed entirely after Shakespeare's comedy. That is Liebetraut's speech on chess and his *concetti* on modesty.

> May I also mix you in, my gracious Lady?
> *Adelheid:* With modesty.
> With the modesty of a schoolboy? It blushes when it raises your fan. With the modesty of the courtier? For his lips your hand is Paradise, your lips are Heaven. The modesty of the bride is on your mouth and dares a downward movement to your bosom, where the modesty of the soldier quickly takes up a position and looks about for a *canapé.*

That is a study in style after the fashion of Rosalind and Beatrice and various Shakespearean clowns, —which did not turn out any too well and is therefore deleted, even in *Götz,* 1773.

III

Three different elements can be studied in the drama:

There is the historical element which is preëminently romantic, melodramatic—the punishment by the secret tribunal. Then there is the personal element; and finally the part that is the poet's free invention.

The personal element is the most important. Goethe has split himself into two different persons. In accord with his higher being, his yearning at this time, he is Götz, the bold nature hewn from a single block, who lives for justice and dies for freedom. In accord with his lower being, or more correctly according to the pangs of his own conscience, he is Weislingen, the faithless lover, the untrue friend, who is weak without maliciousness, bipartite and undependable in his bipartition.

He had, early in life, the swain's tendency to fall in love coupled with the genius's fear and dread of being tied down. For two years he loved Käthchen Schönkopf in Leipzig with restless passion and made the poor girl's life miserable through his jealousy over nothing. Then he left her and never felt at ease until the valiant, amiable girl, a year after his departure, became engaged to another man. But he felt the responsibility much more seriously for his flight from the preacher's charming daughter in Sesenheim, the gentlest and most unwary of the young women who loved him, and who, when he left her, was less alive than dead. · He erected a monument to her in Gottfried's sister Marie. He thought of himself in Weislingen's infidelity to her. When Goethe shortly thereafter was working at the Imperial Court at Wetzlar, his table companions called him by the pet name Götz; he alone was aware of the fact that he also deserved the name of the other leading character. He even asks Salzmann, October 1773, to send a copy of *Berlichingen* to Sesenheim and says: "Poor Friederike will feel somewhat consoled when she sees that the faithless lover is poisoned." In other words, he compares himself with Weislingen.

In Georg's relation to Götz there is something of Goethe's own visionary relation to Herder. He even uses in a letter to Herder from the middle of July 1772 the comparison that he, like Georg, is trying to wear the cuirass of the hero and that he will with time grow into it. For the figure of Elizabeth he used his own sprightly, doughty mother as a model. For Lerse's figure he used, with retention of both family name and baptismal name, his favorite Franz Lerse, a young Alsatian, his table companion in Strassburg, now immortalized.

The third element in this youthful work is the part that was wholly invented and therefore to a certain degree the loosest element in the drama, the entire Adelheid episode. As the poet himself in time fell in love with the great, bewitching coquette, this element gradually outgrew all the rest of the drama, and overshadowed it so completely that Goethe in *Götz* took it upon himself to curtail this motif unmercifully. The preponderance of the Adelheid figure disturbs the unity of the drama, veils its fundamental idea, and dissipates its interest. It is strongly executed, though it does not smack especially of reality.

Bielschowsky has expressed the opinion that Adelheid is drawn after the model of the uncommonly beautiful Henriette von Waldner, later Frau von Oberkirch. Adelheid's name, von Walldorf, is supposed to remind one of Frau von Oberkirch's name. But she was only sixteen years old in 1770. More-

over, there is no evidence that Goethe met her in
Strassburg. The assumption seems quite untenable.
A sixteen-year-old girl as a model for Adelheid!
Anyhow, the name never once occurs in Goethe's
life.

Franz portrays Adelheid as an enchantress:
"Heard of her beauty! That is as if you were to
say that you had seen music. It is impossible for
the tongue to portray one line of her perfections,
since the eye in her presence is no longer itself."
And when he describes her at the chess-table he gives
her the portrait of a Mona Lisa, only coarser, and
Germanic:

An exquisitely lowering line about her mouth and on her
cheeks. Half physiognomy. Half feeling. Seemed to be
threatening more than merely the ivory king. In the meantime nobility and friendship seemed to be sitting like a
majestic married couple on her black eyebrows, and ruling
with authority, and her dark hair waved like a splendid curtain over her queenly glory.

Adelheid, as a moving force, is the precise opposite of Götz: Pagan beauty, which is universal,
is contrasted with force and boldness, which is German. She reminds of Ariosto's Alcina, of Tasso's
Armida, and in this Old German world she amounts
to a Romance, sense-bewitching fairy.

She has heard so much of this "quintessence of
the masculine gender," as Weislingen is called, that
she feels drawn to him and is eager to conquer him.
She succeeds and for a time her expectations are not
disappointed. But she becomes tired of him, as
women do when they detect the effeminate trait in
a man. Adelbert has been shunted off his real
course because Gottfried's superiority pained him.

They had been educated together like two brothers. But undisciplined envy of Gottfried's superiority has induced Adelbert to desert him and ally himself with his enemies.

Adelheid has reckoned that hatred of his great antagonists will arouse all the manly characteristics in Weislingen. Instead of this, she sees him "whining like a sick poet, as melancholy as a healthy girl, as inactive as an old bachelor." She goads him on to combat with his vigorous rivals: "Victoria is a woman; she invariably throws herself into the arms of the bravest." When he finally tries to pull himself together, the nineteen-year-old Goethe puts this baroque, ill-fitting expression in her mouth: "I see in you an arisen, transfigured saint." The expression was destined to be deleted.

With Adelbert she is now done. Pitiable as he is, he becomes a burden to her, and she has him removed from her presence.

But she bewitches the page, Franz, whose youthful passion for her, though extremely sensual, is beautiful. She arouses the gipsy boy's coarse longing, and when she cries for help against him and is rescued by Franz von Sickingen, the second bridegroom of Maria, now deserted by Weislingen, he too is so overcome for a moment that he exclaims: "You were worth a throne." She rejects and sacrifices Franz for his sake. She has a tender affair with Karl, the heir to the throne. And when finally the executioner from the secret tribunal appears in her room, he is likewise overcome and offers to rescue her provided she will give him "what a man in the depth of night can demand of a woman." She acts as if she were submitting to him, gives him a thrust with a dagger, and is choked by his hands.

It was naturally unreasonable that a drama on Götz von Berlichingen should deal so largely with Adelheid. She divided, as has been circumstantially set forth, the action, robbed the drama of its equilibrium, and prevented it from revolving around a central point. It was then entirely proper for the young poet, urged on in all probability by Herder's unfavorable criticism, to force the beautiful sinner into the background and keep her within more narrow limits. Yet the Adelheid episode in the first sketch is fresher and more natural than in the recasted *Götz* of 1773, not to speak of the arrangement for the theatre of 1804. Formless as *Gottfried von Berlichingen* in general is, quickly and easily dashed off in youthful poetic frenzy, it stands as the outpouring of a fiery soul superior to all artistically better versions, in which there have been now deletions, now rewritings, now additions. The drama has lost in freshness and fullness what it gained in balance and taste. A few juvenilities have been removed; but this could have been done without such a thorough-going operation.

In this part of the work, Shakespeare's influence is especially noticeable. Adelheid is modelled after Shakespeare's Cleopatra. Weislingen stands between her and Marie just as Antonius stands between Cleopatra and Octavia. Both are married to the sister of their confederate; both have married in order to put the seal on the cessation of former hostilities; both desert the women to whom they are bound for the great temptress. And there is, moreover, another sort of Shakespearean situation

back of the drama where the brother appears as
the avenger of his sister on the faithless lover. The
triumvirate Laertes-Ophelia-Hamlet lies back of
Gottfried-Maria-Weislingen, just as it later on lies
back of Beaumarchais-Maria-Clavigo, and of Val-
entin-Gretchen-Faust.

As a matter of fact the frequency with which
Shakespearean situations are the models of scenes
in Goethe's works is quite conspicuous. Such is the
case at the close of *Clavigo* where the lover and
the brother meet at Maria's obsequies. Here is a
double reminder of the wrestling match between
Hamlet and Laertes over Ophelia's grave and the
contest between Romeo and Paris at Juliet's bier.

There is accordingly a grain of truth in Frederick
the Great's droll outbreak of embitterment against
Götz in his monograph on German literature. For
him the drama is a detestable imitation of Shakespeare's bad English drama.

*On peut pardonner à Shakespeare ces écarts bizarres; car
la naissance des arts n'est jamais le point de leur maturité.
Mais voilà encore un Götz de Berlichingen qui paraît sur la
scéne, imitation détestable de ces mauvaises pièces anglaises,
et le Parterre applaudait et demande avec enthousiasme la ré-
pétition de ces dégoûtantes platitudes.*

Back of this youthful work lies the idea that the
present has fallen from the heights on which the
past stood, a level where nature was of more avail
than art, boldness more than cunning, and the soundness and power of feeling more than so-called civilization, false and chlorotic as it is. These are
opinions which Goethe inherited, with Herder's
assistance, from Rousseau, and of which in the

North a number of Oehlenschläger's tragedies, following in the wake of *Götz,* have been the expression.

The recast of the original from the year 1773, for a long time the only one known, kept the spirit of the work unchanged; it simply fused the divergent scenes into a book drama, which had a tremendous success. In the latest version, however, from the year 1804, the sole one from which theatre goers know *Götz,* the spirit of the work is quite different. The great abbreviations were necessary and deserve no particular emphasis since they have nothing to do with the history of Goethe's development. With the alterations it is quite different. They show that the poet has since become a courtier, that he has been a minister, and that he has lived through the French Revolution with anguished horror. He has been a prince's friend and confidant for nearly one generation.

Everything, therefore, that was said in *Götz* against princes and courts, and a good deal of the enthusiasm for liberty, has been expunged. Götz's remark in the first act has disappeared: How we will hold our thumbs over the eyes of the princes! Likewise Sievers' remark: Would to God that we could get at the very life of the princes who draw the cap over our ears! Instead of this we have: A peasant is always as good as a rider, and perhaps even as good as a knight. In the dinner scene of the third act, the thrice repeated "Long live Liberty," is omitted. Likewise the place where Götz declares that the next to last of his words in the hour of death will be "Long live the Emperor!" and his very last words will be "Long live Liberty!"

The word *prince* is likewise deleted in Götz's speech: So long as there is no shortage of wine and fresh courage we will laugh at the imperiousness and intrigue of princes.

And it is well to note—parenthetically—that Mephisto's remark in the *Faust* of 1775 concerning the jewel-box runs as follows: I tell you there are things in that box that will win a *princess*. But in the publication of the poem in 1790 these are toned down to the painfully faint observation: I tell you there are things in that box that will win *another woman*.

In the second version of *Götz* for the theatre (for Goethe took up the work also in this new form again and again) the drama does not close with Götz's death and consequently not with the words "Heavenly air—Liberty, Liberty!" etc., but with the convening of the secret tribunal and the speech:

You who abhor outrages, you judges of the deep, work so long as night lasts! Yes, the day will come which will make you superfluous. Arise, thou day of the people, give them joy-bringing activity and let them as a pledge of *lawful* liberty in lustre from above dispose of power and righteousness!

In the various formations of *Götz* from the poet's youth the gipsies are treated sympathetically, as brave vagrants, malefactors of an innocent sort, for whom he, during his *Sturm und Drang* period, had more fellow-feeling than he had for correct plebeians. They steal, to be sure, a duck from a niggardly farmer, but that is justified vengeance; for he refused them a piece of bread; and they take care of Götz at the risk of their own lives so that he is forced to cry out in distress: "O Emperor, Emperor,

robbers are protecting thy children!" In the stage
version they have become bands of robbers, fraudu-
lent soothsayers, despicable rogues, who defend
Götz for purely selfish reasons since they need a
leader. And the gipsies' deceptive chiromancy gives
rise to an outbreak of theatrical sanctimoniousness
when Georg rejects them with wrath:

Away you ogres! Impudent brood of liars! I depend
upon God. What He decrees will happen. I pray to my
Saint; he will protect me. Saint George and his blessing!

Götz's relation to Georg has, on the whole, been
dragged down into the sentimental.

But this is not the place to dwell long on the
changes to which Goethe as *Excellenz* subjected his
youthful paean to liberty. When *Götz* appeared,
Goethe stood at one stroke as the spiritual leader
of Germany's youth. Herder, who had criticised
Gottfried, was the most eager to shower unreserved
praise on the "sole and eternal Götz." He exclaims
"God bless you a thousand times for having written
Götz!" The work appeared anonymously; but the
poet's name at once spread over Germany; never
had a work created such a sensation. For a long
time Klopstock and the entire thoroughly-German,
old-German party with him had ardently yearned to
see the great Germans of the past on the stage.
There they stood now in all their boldness and glory.
The coming generation had zealously craved and
longed for an art that would break with antiquated
rules and concern itself with affairs of outstanding
and general interest. Here was a superabundance
of love, bravery and freedom of speech. Even
Klopstock tried to come in touch with Goethe now.

Lavater did the same. Bürger and Voss, and the so-called *Hainbund* of which they were the leading spirits, approached him with enraptured admiration. He was suddenly proclaimed Germany's first author. That the old King, Frederick the Great, whose education had in actuality been French, expressed his wrathful disapproval of the drama, contending that it belonged to the very infancy of dramatic art, was of no particular consequence. It was a lonely voice from the past soon to be drowned out amid the storms of homage from the Germanic reading world.

CHAPTER VIII

CAESAR—*Mahomet*—*Prometheus*—*Prometheus*
AND *Faust*—*Götter, Helden und Wieland*—
Jahrmarktsfest—*Pater Brey*—*Satyros*

VIRTUALLY coeval with the idea of *Gottfried*,
several other dramatic plans arose in Goethe's mind.
Some of these he never even sketched; others never
advanced beyond the stage of brief fragments.
Among them were *Caesar, Mahomet* and *Prometheus*.

Of these three, *Caesar* was the oldest. As we
have already seen, the subject interested him while
he was in Strassburg. He wished to emphasize the
prominent features of Caesar's life just as he had
done in the case of Götz von Berlichingen. Caesar
had also rebelled against the existing order of government. He had likewise been a rebel and, in a
broad sense, a heretic after the fashion of heretics
about whom Goethe had read in Arnold's history.
His was the affair of a superior personality; he
was felled by mediocrities. Consequently, Goethe
espoused his cause and condemned his assassins.
But he soon saw that in order to give his drama
unity, as Shakespeare and Voltaire had done, he
would have to confine himself to his hero's death.
Trouble arose. A drama in which Brutus stood in
Caesar's light was quite contrary to the spirit of

149

the age and the environs in which Goethe then found
himself.   He could therefore only expect to see his
work condemned in the very circles he most wished
to please.

He writes therefore, June 1774, to Schönborn
saying that his *Caesar* will not please them (his
friends), for it was a time when even young, pious
German counts eulogized tyrannicide and thirsted
after tyrants' blood.   In the eighteenth book of
Dichtung und Wahrheit we have an account of a
visit which the Stolberg brothers paid Goethe while
he lived in Frankfort:

They had dined together only a few times when, flask
after flask of wine having been drunk, poetic hatred of tyrants began to manifest itself, and there was revealed a real
thirst for the blood of such monstrous men.   My father
shook his head.   My mother had hardly ever in her life
heard of tyrants.   She could do no more than recall pictures
of them in Gottfried's chronicle.   There was, for example,
King Cambyses who pierced the heart of the son through
with an arrow in his father's presence.   She went down to
the cellar, got a rare old wine, came back and placed the
bright red juice of the grape in cut glasses on the table and
said: There is some real tyrants' blood.   Drink it and be
merry, but don't talk about murder in this house!

And yet almost at the same time something in
Goethe began to speak to the advantage of Brutus.
In Lavater's *Physiognomische Fragmente* he wrote,
as above mentioned, in 1776, a eulogy on the appearance of Brutus in which individual expressions
likewise testify to enthusiasm for the original.   He
says, for example, that he was great in a world of
great men; that he exerted himself as do they who
meet with opposition, train themselves in opposition,

and do not fight fate but great men. He is depicted as a man who could endure no lord over him, nor could he himself be a lord, since he derived no pleasure from the thraldom of others.

Whether Goethe in time simply lost interest in the portrayal of the hated Caesar, or whether his sympathy became shaky, cannot be determined. We simply know that his drama on Caesar was never written.

II

The plan of *Mahomet* never advanced much farther than *Caesar*. This drama was likewise to set forth the struggle, victory, and death of an ingenious personality. More precisely, it was his initial idea to show how the great individual disseminates the divine that is in him, outwardly, so that he eventually comes in conflict with crude and raw surroundings, is obliged to adapt himself more or less to these, and is thereby debased and eventually undone.

As is known, nothing of this drama was ever written except the delightful hymn on the victorious course of genius, *Mahomets Gesang*. Originally, this was an alternating song between Ali and Fatima in honor of their master. It is the song of the spring that gradually swells into a mighty stream, carries everything along with it, and reflects everything in it as it flows. In its triumphant course, it receives brooks and tributary streams, grows from this unimpeded influx, gives a name to the country through which it runs and calls forth cities on its banks until, with fleets on its bosom and flags at its head as so many witnesses to its glory, it carries its

treasures, its brothers, its children, out to the great
Ocean, the Old Father, who awaits it with open
arms.

III

In 1773, Goethe began to study Spinoza. On
June 28, 1774, he said to Lavater that no one had
come so near to Jesus in his commitments on the
divine as had Spinoza. He had combatted the
Prophets, though he himself was a prophet. That
which, thanks to the influence of Herder and Hamann, had been a cherished belief on Goethe's part,
now become a settled conviction: God and the
World are one, like soul and body, and each individual human being is an expression of the world-
god. From this basic point of view he could not
fancy gods who were essentially different from himself, and who were superior to him. Nor could he
visualize happiness as consisting in subjection to the
gods; he could picture it only as being in harmony
with the divine cosmic whole.

With this idea in his mind he produced
Prometheus. Only two short acts were ever completed. But the monologue of Prometheus alone,
which Goethe included among his poems, is quite
sufficient to insure a poet immortality. The defiance
expressed in *Gottfried* has now become titanic. The
Titan who revels in power and self-esteem defies
the gods, even the god of gods. Everything that
Spinoza had taught, everything that Lessing had felt
without expressing it before he, to the consternation
of Jacobi (see Jacobi's treatise on Lessing's
Spinozism), professed this Prometheus, everything
that Ludwig Feuerbach later proclaimed is assem-

bled—or anticipated—in this youthful, beautiful, profound poem. A greater poem of rebellion has never been written. It is eternal. Each line is moulded for all time. Each line stands like so many letters of fire in the nocturnal sky of humankind. Few verses that have ever been written on this earth can be compared to it.

Prometheus arose from the feeling expressed in Goethe's little poem in which he makes such pleasure as we derive from nature and art dependent upon the creative ability:

> Was nützt die glühende Natur
> Vor deinen Augen dir?
> Was nützt dir das Gebildete
> Der Kunst ringsum dich her?
> Wenn liebevolle Schöpfungskraft
> Nicht deine Seele füllt,
> Und in den Fingerspitzen dir
> Nicht wieder bildend wird!

On this account, Prometheus occupies a happy position among the figures moulded by his hand.

The drama is laid out on a quite pretentious scale. It was to give an abbreviated picture of the whole of primitive life: the art of building, the origin of ownership, significance of the first death, and so on. The above mentioned, and truly marvelous monologue, *Bedecke deinen Himmel, Zeus!* with its dawn of the genius of youth, shows that while Goethe's contemporaries were striving after faith in a religion from without, he himself was diligently studying only the real and palpable with reverence and devotion, and was thereby coming to be a pious worshipper of nature as few before or after him.

Superficially viewed, the monolgue seems to contain only a denial of God:

> Who helped me against the Titans' arrogance?
> Who rescued me from death, from slavery?
> Has thou alone not done it all,
> Holy, glowing heart?

But that there lay no impiety back of this threat against Zeus is best seen from the poem *Ganymed,* which Goethe, in all probability, wrote soon after *Prometheus,* and which in his collection of poems he placed immediately after it. It seemed diametrically opposed in spirit, and yet it was close of kin. The two apparent contradictions really complement each other. Just as Prometheus is the one who despises Zeus, so is Ganymede the one whom Zeus loves and who loves him. The poems, then, are not contradictory but complementary. The god here is not the same as the god there. In *Prometheus* he is the tyrant, here he is the eternal Spring:

> How thou glowest upon me
> In the brightness of dawn
> O Spring, my beloved!
> With thousandfold joy of life
> There enters into my heart
> The sacred feeling of thy eternal warmth,
> Thou infinite beauty!

This beloved, this Zeus, is not man's conception of the Almighty, whom Goethe combatted in *Prometheus;* it is the creative power of All-Nature, thoroughly homogeneous with the impulse to create and the joy in creating which characterizes Prometheus.

But while Ganymede conceives of the fountain of

life and the fountain of joy as being outside of himself, yearns for its embrace and suffers dissolution
from his longing for this embrace, we detect in various places in *Prometheus* young Goethe's ability to
feel, in that moment when he no longer has any
yearning, the complete joy and fullness of existence.

The first place is where Prometheus, who has
created Pandora as a statue, says to her:

> O thou Pandora!
> Thou most sacred vessel for all gifts
> That are joy-bringing
> Under the wide heaven,
> Over the boundless earth
> Everything that refreshes me with the feeling of rapture,
> That in the shady coolness
> Has given me shelter,
> That the love of the sun ever gave me
> In the way of joy in Spring,
> That the warm waves of the sea
> Ever gave me in the way of tenderness
> When they lapped my breast,
> And whatever I have enjoyed in the way of pure heavenly
>   splendor
> And peace of soul,
> All that, all—my Pandora!

As is known, *Pandora* means "all gifts." She unites
for him all the gifts of existence in *one* being, in
one moment.

Fate, however, imparts life to the statues of
Prometheus. Pandora grows into a beautiful woman
who passes in and out of the master's workshop.
He converses with her regarding the joy of life.
She has known it, she says, as the purest happiness
in the kisses of her playfellows; she has known joy
when it lifted her feet from the earth, and taught

her to dance. She had also known pain when she
ran a thorn in her foot, or wept over a sheep she
had lost. Prometheus teaches that joy as well as
sorrow are dissolved during sleep. He asks
whether she realizes that there are many joys and
sorrows of which she knows nothing. Yes, she
says, her heart often longs for she does not know
what.

Then it is that Prometheus speaks these peculiar
and irritating words:

There is a moment which fulfills everything we have ever
longed for, dreamed of, hoped and feared. Pandora, it is
death.
Pandora: Death?
Prometheus: When, completely shaken from out of, and
in, the depths of your soul, you feel everything that ever
coursed through you, everything that has stormed your heart
to overflowing, and that has sought alleviation in grief . . .
when everything in you rings and quivers and quakes, and
you are no longer in control of your senses, so that you fancy
you are going to pass away, and everything about you sinks
into darkness, while you in your deep, innermost feelings
encompass a world—then man dies.
Pandora: O Father, let us die!

The first motif is interesting, for like many other
passages it shows how familiar young Goethe was
with the thought of one comprehensive feeling of
the glory of existence in *one* eternal moment. The
second motif is interesting, because it portrays natural death, not as the ebb from the fullness of life,
but as called forth by the excess of the feeling of
life itself, with a combining of everything that has
moved the heart to swell in *one* single moment, and
then be broken by this very fullness,—which is paradoxical but profound.

IV

Though not published until 1830, the drama *Prometheus*, which is a trifle older than the poem, belongs to the year 1773, or at the latest to the year 1774, and the last quotation becomes instructive when compared with Faust's wager with Mephistopheles in Part I of the tragedy, since Goethe did not formulate this wager until the year 1798-99: for the scene belongs among the last of Part I.

Judging from the conditions agreed upon, it is plainly Faust's idea that they can never be fulfilled. He regards the glory of the moment as wholly impossible of fulfillment; such an expression he can never make—and he consequently sets death as the penalty should all of this come to pass. Dissatisfied as he is, he feels all too deeply that it is impossible for the hour of absolute satisfaction ever to strike for him.

There is, to be sure, something ambiguous at this point. Faust conceives the satisfaction with the moment as a sign that man's constant striving, the very point wherein lies his deepest worth, would no longer exist for him, that life's supreme flame would be extinguished. That is what the following words, literally translated, mean: "If at any time I lie down in perfect ease upon my bed of sloth, then let all at once be over with me! If thou canst at any time by lying flatter me into making me feel satisfied with myself; if thou canst deceive me with enjoyment, so may that be my last day." But when Mephistopheles agrees and Faust gives him his hand, he adds what goes a great deal further: "If I ever say to the moment, tarry, pray, thou art so fair,

then thou canst put me in chains, then I will gladly
be ruined."—And this does not really come about
until Faust, old and blind, mistaking the rattling
of the spades of the Lemures, who are digging his
grave, for the rattling of the spades of masses of
people who are building a dam against the encroach-
ing sea—not until then, when, in his delusions, he
has visions of a free people on a free soil, does he
exclaim: "Now I may say to the moment: Tarry,
pray, thou art so fair!"

It is plain that Faust, in his last moments, has
by no means abandoned the expectations he cherished before entering upon the wager; by no means
has he laid himself down upon his couch of slothful
ease. It is in anticipation of the most exalted happiness of the future that he enjoys what is for him
the highest moment. And when the hour of death
strikes for him, it is the same sort of death of
which Prometheus spoke when he created Pandora:
When man in his inmost soul perceives in just one
moment every thing that has caused his heart to
swell so that in his feeling he spans a world—
then man dies.

There is a clearly perceptible difference, however,
between the genetic thought of *Prometheus* and that
of *Faust*. When Prometheus is conceived, Goethe
still believes in a Pandora, in a sacred vessel for all
the happiest gifts of life; and he believes that the
moment can be developed into such a vessel. Back
of the wager in Faust lies doubt as to the attainment
of happiness. We feel that the latter belongs to
riper years and more bitter experience. In order
to have written this, Goethe must have seen through
the nothingness of earthly joys. It is on this account

that Faust says in this connection that the red gold runs out of his hands as quicksilver, that the girl in his embrace is even now making coquettish eyes at the next man, that the beautiful meteor of honor merely appears in order to disappear, that the fruit of life rots before we pluck it.

There can, of course, be no doubt that Goethe, when he wrote the lines that introduce the acceptance of the wager knew that he would, and just how he would, have his Faust come out too short.—What could one expect, what could one imagine, would fill Faust's heart so that he would beg the moment to stay it being too fair to be allowed to fly away? However indigent our lives may be, we all know such moments, each varying according to our individual nature. One feels the greatest happiness in a festive mood, another on the finding of unexpected wealth, another on seeing a charming bit of natural scenery, another on enjoying the best of art, the most excellent of music, another on the satisfying of a long cherished ambition, another as a lover in the moment of confession and union. We could imagine Faust happy either when he found the woman who measured up to his ideals and enraptured him, or when he made some great discovery in natural science, or when he posited a new cosmic theory.

Goethe rejected all of these possibilities, which certainly must have passed before his inner eye, and devoted his undivided attention to one unique problem. Faust anticipates a future in which he has become a benefactor of mankind by presenting it with a piece of ground that will in itself serve as a constant protection against the sea. All of this is so different that he is no longer mindful of his youthful conviction concerning the slight value of indolent, secure happiness. And in his dying breath, consequently, he utters that immortal sentence: "He alone deserves life and liberty who has to gain them anew, day by day." But so deep, so persistent, despite the emendations in *Götz,* was the love of liberty in Goethe that, as a sage of eighty-two years, he laid down in these verses the sum total of his own wisdom, as well as that of his titular hero, pertaining to the joy of the eternal moment. That joy now consists with him in standing with a free people on a free soil and feeling that he himself has been the creator of this enviable condition.

In this we see a further development of the ideas with which the young disciple of Herder had lived. We detect in truth in various scenes of the original *Faust,* Part I, ideas that go back to the time of his ordination. When Faust turns to magic it is because of the aversion expressed in *Gottfried* to book knowledge as contrasted with that which comes from seeing and beholding. When the Earth Spirit reveals itself to Faust, who cannot even endure the sight, Goethe puts the creed of his own youth in the two expressions: Exalted Spirit, how near of kin do I feel myself to thee! And the reply: Thou resemblest the spirit thou comprehendest!

This last remark strikes Faust rather than Goethe; indeed it overwhelms Faust. Yet it contains a most substantial consolation. It is the good tidings for the lesser mind; the seeking mind is frequently absorbed in the subject of its study and adoration. This is the credo from the age of storming violence: The citizen of the earth is related to the spirit of the earth; he is a spark of the all-powerful flame.

V

The newly awakened strength and bold self-confidence in the young poet found expression in a series of short satirical works, the first of which is the little prologue to *Gottes neueste Offenbarungen,* a clever skit with Carl Friedrich Bahrdt as its objective. Bahrdt was a rationalist who had felt called to revise the New Testament. In the place of Luther's trenchant German he had substituted a flat, polished, modernized prose. The little professor sits at his desk writing when he and his much adorned wife are frightened by the tread of animals at the door. The four Evangelists and their followers enter: Matthew with the angel, Mark with the lion, Luke with the ox, and John with the eagle —a whole menagerie in fact. The professor's wife utters a piercing shriek.

Such mighty beards, such long robes, such intricate folds and such wild beasts terrify also Herr Bahrdt. He does not recognize his Evangelists, bedizzened and bedecked as they had been, in his version of them, when not wearing the costumes with which he had fitted them out. The Evangelists depart in disgust.

It is the same motif, with variations, that we have in the matchless farce entitled *Götter, Helden und Wieland,* Goethe's satirical masterpiece from his younger years. Here too an adapter is terrified on seeing gods and heroes, with whom he has played fast and loose, arrayed before him. It is about the cleverest bit of satire we have from Goethe's pen. Anyone who has had the good fortune to read it and enjoy it in his youth preserves the initial impression of it his whole life long.

If one reads Wieland's now forgotten *Alceste* with the thought of determining whether Goethe, in the arrogant uppishness of a young man, really did the opera an injustice one is forced to let Wieland act as his own attorney. The sole impression derived or derivable from his work is that of unmitigated insipidity. The dramolet, played in Weimar before Goethe's arrival, is nothing but a veritable Olympic contest of noble sentiments—the wife wishes to die for the husband, for example, but the husband declines the offer—in which there is not a single new or unforseen move and not a single unexpected or surprising observation. If one reads or sees Euripides's powerful drama one feels how modern, how far removed from Greek ethics, it is to have the husband prefer death and thereby spare the feelings of the wife. In fine, Wieland's play is a play of whining and virtue. It is singular, nevertheless, that it is the first attempt in German literature to modernize an antique theme as it was destined to be done in Goethe's *Iphigenie.*

Wieland's *Die Wahl des Herkules,* which Goethe ridiculed just as much as he ridiculed *Alceste,* is also a weak product. The demi-god stands in the middle, with Virtue and Vice at either side. It is inexpressibly vapid, and disingenuous in Wieland's mouth, to have Vice portrayed as an alluring woman whose seductive power consists solely in her ability to satisfy natural desires and at the sight of whom action of any sort is paralyzed, even though the action _ome from a Hercules! Here, too, Goethe's criticism did not go one step farther than was justified. And without his satire both of the bagatelles would have been buried long ago. And yet, it is probable that a few verses in *Herkules* gave the initial impulse to a few verses in *Faust:*

HERKULES

O Göttin, löse mir
Das Räthsel meines Herzens auf.
Zwey Seelen—ach, ich fühl es zu gewiss,—
Bekämpfen sich in meiner Brust
Mit gleicher Kraft: die bessre siegt, so lange
Du redest; aber kaum ergreift
Mich diese Zauberin mit ihren Blicken wieder,
So fühl' ich eine andere
In jeder Ader glühn, die wider Willen mich
In ihre Arme zieht.

Faust:

Du bist dir nur des einen Triebs bewusst
O lerne nie den andern kennen!
Zwei Seelen wohnen ach in meiner Brust.
Die eine will sich von der andern trennen.
Die eine hält in derber Liebeslust
Sich an die Welt mit klammernden Organen,
Die andre hebt gewaltsam sich vom Dust
Zu den Gefilden hoher Ahnen.

Götter, Helden und Wieland is opened by Mercury just as he is on the point of translating a group of shades to the lower world. He learns from Charon that Admet and Alceste are highly incensed at him. Likewise Euripides, who receives him on the yonder bank of the river where he abuses him roundly for what Wieland has said concerning him in his magazine entitled *Der teutsche Merkur.* Wie-

land has there praised his own *Alceste* at the expense
of Euripides's *Alkestis*. Mercury stoutly denies that
he has been in any way connected with the enterprise
that has usurped his name. Alceste, however, is
beside herself with wrath at the two "vapid, hag-
gard, pale little puppets" that are supposed to represent her and her husband.

Mercury's staff then conjures up Wieland as he
slumbers in the night. His shadow enters, in night-
cap, at the words: "Where is my dream leading
me?" The gods and heroes are presented to him:
"Are you Alceste, with that figure?" He had never
thought of her in that way. (Goethe has apparently
anticipated the stout figure of the Venus of Milo,
though the statue had not been discovered at the
time.) Mercury attacks Wieland who has misused
his name, and has treated the two exalted personages so shamefully. Wieland replies by saying that
he is under no obligations to pay respect to the
names of the heathen gods: "Our religion forbids
us recognize and worship any truth, greatness, divinity, or beauty outside of it. The names and
statues of your gods are therefore exposed and
mutilated." He assures him that he never once
thought of Mercury (or of the Greek Hermes)
when he gave the title to his journal. "No one
thinks anything at all of this; it is as if one said
Recueil, Portefeuille." In reply to Mercury's objection, "It is after all my name," he asks whether he
has not often seen his figure, with wings on the
head and feet, painted on snuff boxes, or in other
unheroic places.

In five literary epistles Wieland, with no appreciative conception of antiquity or of the value of

Euripides, had drawn attention to his portrayal of Admet and Alceste. Euripides replies energetically to his German critic, and Admet emphasizes the preëminence of the Greek poet, at the same time calling Wieland's attention to the fact that a man who was born when the Greeks defeated Xerxes, who moreover was a personal friend of Xenophon, and whose dramas were influential for an entire century, which can scarcely be said of Wieland's, perhaps knew more about conjuring up the shades of Admet and Alceste than a German poet with all his *delicatesse*. Euripides derides his German rivals: "There is a woman who wishes to die for her husband, a husband who wishes to die for his wife, a hero who tries to die for both, etc."

Wieland replies: "You talk in the manner of men from another world, the sounds of whose language I hear but whose meaning I do not grasp." The answer is droll: "We speak Greek." And not less droll is Euripides's remarks to Admet concerning Wieland: "You forget that he belongs to a sect which makes the dropsied, the tubercular, the palsied, and the tonsilitic believe that when they die their hearts become richer, their minds stronger, their bones more full of marrow. He believes that."

The diminutive farce reaches its climax when Hercules appears. He has just visualized Wieland to himself as a tiny whipper-snapper like him who now stands before him.

Hercules: Are you the man who always has Hercules on his lips?

Wieland (stepping back): I have nothing to do with you, Colossus!

Hercules: How's that?   Pray remain!

Wieland: I thought that Hercules was a stately man of middle size.

Hercules: I, of middle size?

Wieland: If you are Hercules, you are not the person I meant.

Hercules: That is my name and I am proud of it.   I know full well that when a ninny cannot find a shield-holder among bears, griffins, and swine, he uses a Hercules.

The objection, as is seen, is the same that was made to Wieland's conception of Mercury: The mystic figure has become a mere allegory, a mere name.   This reoccurs, unfortunately, in the comparisons from Goethe's old age.   There is, for example, the ugly passage in the autobiography: "The boy Cupid stubbornly holds fast to the mantle of hope when this is on the point of getting away."

Hercules: I see my divinity has never appeared to you in that kind of a dream.

Wieland: I confess that this is the first dream of that kind I have ever had.

Hercules: Then retire unto yourself, and ask the gods for your notes on Homer where we are too great for you. I believe it, too great.

Wieland: In truth you are enormous.   I never imagined you like this.

Hercules: How can I help his narrow-chested imagination?   Who is, pray, his Hercules of whom he boasts so much?   And what does he want?   For virtue?   What is the motto?   Have you seen virtue, Wieland?   I have knocked about a good deal in the world and I never met such a thing.

Wieland: Virtue, for which my Hercules does everything, dares everything, you don't know it?

Hercules: Virtue!   I heard the word for the first time in my life down here from a few foolish fellows who could not explain it to me.

Wieland: I cannot explain it any more than they can. But let us waste no words on this subject! I wish you had read my poems and then you would see that I myself pay precious little attention to virtue. It is an elusive thing.

Hercules: It is a monster like all fancy that cannot hold out against the course of the world. Your virtue reminds me of a Centaur. So long as it trots around before your imagination it is glorious, it is powerful! And when the sculptor portrays it to you, how superhuman is its form! Open it up, and you will find four lungs, two hearts, two stomachs. It dies in the hour of birth like any other deformed creature, or is never begotten except in your brains.

This anatomy does not sound especially natural in Hercules's mouth. The weapons against Wieland in this case are not taken from the same arsenal from which those came with which the Greek method of feeling and poetic fancy had supplied Goethe. In the face of anatomy and natural science the Lernean dragon, for whose heads two grew out for each one that Hercules in vain cut off, will likewise not stand the test. And just as little will the Christian angels stand the test, to whose long wings there is no corresponding vertebral muscle, though Goethe himself uses them so strongly at the close of *Faust,* Part II. But the rest of the dialogue is extremely witty, wholly antique in its basic conception of virtue as valor, and in keeping with the eighteenth century in its bold freethinking.

Wieland: But virtue must be something, it must be somewhere.

Hercules: In the name of my father's eternal beard! Who ever doubted that? And methinks it dwelt with us in half-gods and heroes. Do you think that we lived like cattle? We had the bravest sort of fellows among us.

Wieland: What do you call brave fellows?

Hercules: One who gives to others what he has. And

the richest is the bravest. If one had a superabundance of
muscle, he gave the other a sound thrashing. And remember, a real man never wastes his time on his inferiors; he
concerns himself only with his equals, or his superiors. If
one had a superabundance of semen, he gave the women as
many children as they wanted; I remember having made
fifty little fellows myself once in one night. And had
Heaven given a third more than it had given thousands, he
opened his doors and bade thousands welcome and asked
them to enjoy his goods with him.

Wieland: The most of all this is counted a vice in our
days.

Hercules: Vice? That is a fine word too! That is why
everything is only half with you, just because you reckon
virtue and vice as the two extremes, between which you
waver, instead of looking upon your middle position as the
positive and the best, as your peasants and servants and
maids still do.

Wieland: If you were to be found in the possession of
such sentiments in our century you would be stoned. Didn't
they persecute me violently for my slight attacks on virtue
and religion?

Hercules: What is there to be attacked? I have fought
with horses, cannibals, and dragons, but never with clouds,
it made no difference what form they had. He who is wise
leaves it to the wind that blows them together to blow them
apart in time.

Wieland: You are a monster, a blasphemer.

Hercules: Can't you grasp that? Your Hercules stands
like a smooth-faced fool between virtue and vice. If the
two women met me, you see, so—one under one arm the
other under the other, and then, march! And both would
be obliged to be off and away.

This Hercules does not put to shame Euripides's
idea of the demi-god of strength, who, living beyond
human conceptions of virtue and vice, can drink and
carouse in the house so long as he does not know
that the queen is lying therein dead; but when he
learns that the queen has descended to Hades and

that Admet has not said anything to him about it simply in order not to break the sacred duties of hospitality, he proceeds, in his overflowing power, to the lower world and fetches the lost one, who died out of tenderness for her husband, up again to the light of day.

VI

There are three small satiric-dramatic works from this period (1772-73) all written in the same spirit and in the same form, the Hans Sachs doggerel, a form Goethe constantly employed in his youth and even used in the beginning of the definitive edition of *Faust*.

The first is the jocund and jovial *Jahrmarktsfest zu Plundersweilern,* the model of Oehlenschläger's far more protracted and far more carefully elaborated *St. Hans Aften Spil.* It consists of fresh and vigorous outbursts in pithy verses, in which the cheerfulness of youthful mood drowns out all literary allusions. In accordance with his lamentable custom, and in a very confusing way, Goethe revised this little farce again and again. In the original plan the market-comedy on Ahasver, Haman, Mordecai and their colleagues, played at the market booths, is intended as a joke on the Rationalists, who called the Bible a pretty poor sort of book, and on the maundering pietists after the fashion of Lavater. In the second version from the year 1789, the market-comedy on the characters above noted is entirely worked over, written in German Alexandrines, and aimed at the French tragedy in general and Racine's *Esther* in particular, without having gained in sprightliness and humor. When Oehlenschläger, in 1802, imitated also the comedy within the comedy, he carefully retained the loose doggerel of Goethe's first sketch. There are several places in which the barkers follow their Goethean model quite closely. For example:

GOETHE	OEHLENSCHLÄGER *
Liebe Kindlein,	Smagfulde Pantomimer!
Kauft ein	Peer Dover og Kirsten
Hier ein Hündlein	Kimer!
Hier ein Schwein,	Valdhorn og Violiner!
Trommel und Schlägel,	Bajatser og Harlekiner!
Ein Reitpferd, ein Wägel,	Kager og Appelsiner!
Kugeln und Kegel	Insekter og Prospekter!
Kistchen und Pfeiffer,	Komedier og Tragedier!
Kutschen und Läuffer,	Nye Hegler og Karter!
Husar und Schweitzer,	Tobaksdaaser og Bonaparter!
Nur ein Paar Kreutzer	Fuglebure og Voksfigurer!
Ist alles dein,	Af Drikkevare
Kindlein, kauft ein!	En utallig Skare!
	Skynder Jer bare!

Oehlenschläger's picture of Dyrehaven is a united whole; it can be read at any time with pleasure. Goethe's work was never so seriously intended, having been dashed off simply in order to ventilate youthful presumption. But like all of these trifles from his early youth, it delights, not only at a first reading but at a second as well, because of the wealth and fullness of expression, which presages at once of genius and bears the stamp of the lion's claw. Here, as is always the case in the works from this

* Tasteful pantomimes! Peter Dover and Christina Chimer!
Bugles and violins, buffoons and harlequins!
Oranges and cakes, insects and outlooks!
Comedies and tragedies, hatchles and heckles!
Snuff-boxes and Bonapartes, bird-cages and wax figures!
All kinds of drinks! Right this way, Ladies and Gentlemen!

period, there is a good natured emphasis of the sensuous in opposition to pious cant. And now and then we meet with a vulgar expression which in the latest edition, the censor, inspired by a sense of extreme delicacy, has felt constrained to erase.

VII

Closely related to this is the little farce, *Pater Brey;* also the more elaborated scenes entitled *Satyros.*

The sentimental and hypocritical wencher ridiculed in *Pater Brey,* a certain Leuchsenring, is now wholly forgotten, though the model in this case is a matter of complete indifference. The method employed for his expulsion is also quite infantile. The girl's lover who returns home, disguises himself for a moment as a white haired old man and learns from the young girl that she does not care a straw about anyone but the absent one, and thus ousts, in a good humored way, the importunate consoler of women.

Like Mordecai in the *Jahrmarktsfest,* Pater Brey is a variant of Molière's *Tartuffe.* He is even seen through by the green grocer, and he is scorned by the returning captain who hoaxes him away (while he comes to an understanding with his lady friend) by telling him that in the neighborhood there lives a little flock who lead a very sodomitic life: they talk through their nose, go about with stout, inflated stomachs, and sniff at every Christian. Since it is the Pater's especial business and art to convert people who live like wild men, he hastens off in order to improve also these. They show him the way to

the pigsty; he returns embittered and abashed only
to be driven away for good and all.

The larger drama, *Satyros,* is, like *Pater Brey,*
directed against a false prophet.   The leading character is a satyr who, in order to get support and
help for an ulcer on the leg, goes to an anchorite
in the forest.   But this particular anchorite, as distinguished from others, resembles the very embodi-
ment of joy over nature's eternal power to pro-
create; and he expresses this joy in life in verses that
teem with the presumptive young Goethe's power of
expression:

> Das quillt all von Erzeugungskraft,
> Wie sich's hat aus dem Schlaf gerafft;
> Vögel und Frosch und Thier' und Mücken
> Begehn sich zu allen Augenblicken,
> Hinten und vorn, auf Bauch und Rücken,
> Dass man auf jeder Blüth und Blatt
> Ein Eh-und Wochenbettlein hat.

However much kindness and care the hermit
shows the sick satyr, he is dissatisfied with everything; he is not contented with milk and bread; he
wants wine and fruit which the hermit does not have.
In the latter's absence he complains that his couch is
hard and his food imperfect; he tears down the
crucifix that hangs over his bed and appropriates
anything in the house for which he has use:

> Mir geht in der Welt nichts über mich,
> Denn Gott ist Gott, und ich bin ich.

He yearns for young girls and soon wins the
beautiful Psyche.   When Hermes the Priest appears, he holds forth to him and his parish on the
gospel of nature.   Clothes are superfluous and

should be dispensed with; men should not live in houses but in caves; they should not cultivate a sad morality but should live as in the days of the Golden Age.

The references to Rousseau are perfectly plain; conspicuous indeed is the boldness with which young Wolfgang, who a short while ago had approached Rousseau through Herder, now ridicules him—only a little later to follow once more in his tracks, in *Werther*.

But more conspicuous is the fact that,—as is suspected from the satyr's fretful disposition and as has been proved by German scholars from Wilhelm Scherer on—none other than Herder himself is the model which hovered before the young poet's mind. This is revealed by his early inclination to react against teachers and philanthropists. It was only recently, as we have seen, that he, in his relation to Herder, had compared himself to the boy Georg, who tries to wear the captain's armor but cannot move about in it. A day never passed without his wishing that he could live with Herder: "That will come to pass! Just wait a while! The boy in the cuirass wanted to ride too soon and you ride too fast." Herder on his part had discarded completely the rôle of protector. In one of his letters we read: "I hear from Goethe only now and then; but however it may all turn out, he is a fellow of life and soul. Whatever he may be he will be it with all his heart and with clenched fists."

There had, of course, been diminutive collisions, but they quickly subsided because of the youth's frank and open method of reacting to injustice. When Wolfgang, the year after his association with

Herder in Strassburg, met the latter's fiancée, and simply by sending the beautiful *Fels-Weihgesang an Psyche* to her, aroused Herder's jealousy, the young man wrote a splendid and sincere letter—it was in July, 1772—in which he said:

I want to tell you that I was angry at your reply to the *Felsweihe,* and called you an intolerant priest. For the expressions "false priest" and "an impudent hand wielded the name" were without justification. If I was wrong in striking a dolorous note to your girl should you on that account go forth with fire and sword prepared to destroy?

Thus far nothing had been able to shake Goethe's exalted opinion of Herder's significance. Now, however, we see that, momentarily at least, Herder appeals to him as an exacting and, so far as women are concerned, inconsiderate person. It is not enough that the Satyr beguiled the youthful Psyche —note that the name is the same Goethe had given Caroline Flachsland in the dedication of the aforesaid poem—he also spread his coils for Eudora, the wife of the unsuspecting priest Hermes. But she sees through him and unmasks him, just as Orontes's wife unmasks Tartuffe. From the sanctuary of a temple, to which the Satyr has withdrawn and from which he has forbidden, on pain of death, anyone to follow him, there comes a loud, piercing shriek, and we learn that he is attempting violence on Eudora. In the god the animal suddenly appears. The Satyr is forced to extract himself from the dilemma by arrogantly boasting of his divine origin. Like his father Zeus, he confers an honor on that man from whose wife he fans the flies. He is disgraced, like Pater Brey, but, built on a larger scale, he departs in haughtiness and with threats.

CHAPTER IX

Reinhold Lenz—Maximilian Klinger

While Goethe was thus settling up accounts with individual contemporaries, older and younger, among whom were former patrons and future confederates, a number of young people joined his ranks, the more prominent of whom were for a time regarded as his equals. Reinhold Lenz looked upon himself, and was looked upon by others, as Goethe's peer. Maximilian Klinger wrote a wretched drama entitled *Sturm und Drang,* and thereby gave the name to an entire literary movement.

Reinhold Lenz, the son of a church official, was born at Sesswigen in Lapland in 1750. He had left Dorpat in 1768 and gone to the University of Berlin. He visited Ramler and Nicolai. In the spring of 1771 he came to Strassburg as the tutor of two brothers, barons from Courland, who were to study in Strassburg. No one could have been much less adapted to this kind of work than he. Incapable of controling himself, he was a poor guide to others.

Lenz had a neat little physique, a handsome head, was blond and blue-eyed, was noted for the vapid strain that was in him, and for his half embarrassed, half reserved nature which could on occasion pass to effrontery. He was rich in moods, whims, and bizarre ideas. He was one of those people who

175

take up with a spiritual movement in order to make
it dogmatic and to exaggerate the significance of its
tenets; one of those who convert the living gestures
of an age into grimaces. He voiced the enthusiasm
of the Strassburg circle for Shakespeare as he had
found it expressed there. He affected, when especially cheerful, the tone of the Shakespearean clown.
He wrote his work *Anmerkungen übers Theater*
after *Götz von Berlichingen* had appeared, but was
careful to note on the title page that he had read
his monograph to a coterie of Strassburg friends
two years before the publication of Goethe's drama.
Goethe doubted the contention strongly and with
chronological justice. Since he had followed Goethe
in everything else it is safe to assume that he followed him here. Lenz no longer attacked Lessing's
Frenchman as misunderstanding Aristotle; he attacked Aristotle himself and the rules in the *Poetics,*
declaring that the unities of time, place and action
were superfluous, praised Shakespeare and his character comedy in excessive language, and fixed the
essence of poetry as the imitation of nature. What
he really had in mind was the art of reality, or
realism.

In actuality it was his acquaintance with Goethe
that completely turned the young poet's head and
revamped his mind, blithe and bland as this was.
He was as far from having an individual point of
view with regard to art as with regard to life; he
had only an ambition along this line. He was possessed of Goethe and wished first and foremost to
be more than his friend; he wished to be his spiritual
brother.

He exaggerates every enthusiasm that Goethe

cherishes or has cherished. Of Rousseau he says, for example, in his notes: "Rousseau, even the *divine* Rousseau," and "Héloise, the *best* book that was ever printed in French letters (*mit französischen Lettern*)." He soon developed a sort of talent; his works, the labor of a few years, were full of whims supposed to stand for humor and disfigured by mannerisms, which were supposed to stand for style. This lasts from 1773 to 1776, years in which his loftiest thoughts concerning his supposed genius alternate with disdain for his own ability; strong imagination plays at shifts with his self-contempt.

The decisive trait, however, is his obsession for Goethe. Lenz associates with all the men and women with whom Goethe had associated in the various towns, with Salzmann, Lavater, Herder, Merck, Sophie v. la Roche, later with Wieland whom he, like Goethe, had criticized (Lenz in *Mopsus und Menalkas*). All the so-called *Stürmer und Dränger,* Klinger, Wagner, Kaiser, Maler Müller, became his friends. Half a year after Goethe's departure, he betakes himself, true to his ape-like mission, to Sesenheim and falls in love with Friederike Brion, writes poem after poem to her and, so far as he is able, in Goethe's style. He succeeded in his imitation of Goethe so well that two of the poems, *Ach, bist du fort?* and *Wo bist du itzt, mein unvergesslich Mädchen,* were ascribed to Goethe and included in editons of Goethe's works, even in the three volume collection entitled *Der junge Goethe* by the *Goethe-Kenner,* Hirzel. This is all the more striking since the last poem, which was superscribed by Friederike *Als ich in Saarbrücken,* was written while *she,* but neither Goethe nor the author of the poem, was in Saarbrücken.

Lenz's attention to Friederike seems to have been very urgent but ineffective. When Goethe in 1779 returned to Sesenheim on a short visit, he learned from Friederike that Lenz began to call constantly so soon as he had left, and that he was most inquisitive about reports concerning Goethe or letters from him, until Friederike eventually became distrustful and tried to get rid of him. When he assured her that he loved her passionately and in the face of her reserve threatened to commit suicide, it became necessary to send him away on the ground that he was half mad. But she came to the conclusion that his real purpose was to gather material with which he could debase Goethe in public esteem. She revealed her suspicion to Goethe.

Lenz had already (1776) followed Goethe to Weimar, had ingratiated himself at Kochberg into the favor of Frau von Stein who, at the very same time that she was keeping Goethe at a distance with modest dignity, accepted Lenz with calm coquetry as her teacher in English—until he finally committed some bit of asininity (Goethe calls it an *Eselei*) which resulted in his removal. Perhaps he had approached Frau von Stein by following this line of reasoning: If she had loved Goethe, she could also love him. At any rate he read verses aloud in Weimar in which he scorned the relation to Frau von Stein of Goethe as well as that of the Dowager Duchess. He wrote a defense which was regarded as a libel. Goethe had to ask for his expulsion.

It is always the same obsession that leads Lenz on. He is Goethe's shadow, his double; he carries

out his rôle as an actor; he allies himself with him
as a fellow-combatant and vies with him as a rival.
At first Goethe overestimated him; he believed in
his talent. In 1773 he writes to Betty Jacobi concerning him: "A chap whom I love as my own soul"
(*ein Junge, den ich liebe wie meine Seele*). When
Wieland rejected Lenz's attack, Goethe writes,
1774, to Sophie v. la. Roche: "Lenz is a dangerous
enemy for him; he has more genius than Wieland."
Goethe acquiesced in Lenz's sending him a manuscript "On our marriage," in which he now seemed
to subordinate himself to Goethe, now to place himself at his side, half jestingly, half seriously, but in
such a way that the two had to be regarded as
indissolubly united. This naïve claim stood out
prominently before the public in Lenz's *Pandaemo-
nium Germanicum,* in which Goethe and Lenz (in
their own names) are the leading characters who,
with similar dress and mutual aid, will ascend a
symbolic Parnassus. Here also, Wieland, Klopstock, Herder and Shakespeare appear in person.
In Lenz's *Der Waldbruder* there are likewise two
friends and rivals, Herz and Rothe, that is, Lenz
and Goethe, who are placed opposite each other.

When Lenz published his drama anonymously,
it was ascribed to Goethe by the majority and compared to *Götz.* Both Klopstock and Voss believed
in all seriousness that *Der Hofmeister* was by
Goethe. Herder even writes (November 14, 1774)
to Hamann: "Goethe now has Lenz as a rival in
his career."

In the fourteenth book of *Dichtung und Wahrheit,* Goethe has given a profound psychological
study of Lenz's character as he knew it. He com-

plains of him without anger or bitterness, though he takes it quite seriously that he published *Götter, Helden und Wieland* without his knowledge and against his wish, and intrigued in general against his former comrade. But he excuses this intrigue on the ground that it was unintentional, roguery for roguery's sake, and shows that Lenz always lived in a chimera, that his hatred as well as his charity was imaginary, that he never benefited those he loved and that he never harmed those he hated. His days were made up of a heap of nothings; he could waste so many hours because of his excellent memory which retained everything and made it bear fruit. He lived, besides, in Strassburg mostly with officers of the garrison and, fantast that he was, he gradually came to believe that he was a connoisseur of all things pertaining to military affairs. He even sent in a *Promemoria* with some good advice to the French minister of war.

As Goethe's double, he lodged with the poet's parents while on his visit to Thuringia. He followed Goethe to Emmendingen where Schlosser lived after his marriage with Cornelia. He became a most intimate friend of the family. He loved Cornelia, in his fantastic way, about as he had loved Friederike and Frau von Stein. In 1777, he experienced Cornelia's death. It was while in Schlosser's home that his grief manifested itself in madness and raging so that, after the usage of the time, he was put in chains as an insane person. Quite incapable of doing mental work of any description, he was given an asylum in the home of a shoemaker in Emmendingen where Conrad, the son of the family, became his dearest companion. He himself learned the shoemaker's trade. Having regained his health, he went first to St. Petersburg and then to Moscow, where he died in 1780.

The individual who approaches Lenz's works with confident expectation is doomed to a grievous disillusionment. His inane hatred of the unity of place gave rise to a change after every third or fourth speech with the result that hopeless confusion ensues. Of the spirit of rebellion, apart from the realm of the æsthetic, there is hardly a shimmer. In the drama there is a thick vein of plebeian moralizing.

Ludwig Tieck, in order to taunt the aged Goethe, endeavored to persuade the reader in the introduction to Lenz's works, 1828, that Lenz, with his vigorous depiction of reality, was following a wiser course than Goethe with his trend toward the ideal, the antique, the faraway, the foreign. He quotes Goethe's remark: "Ah, when I erred and went astray, I had a host of comrades," and then asks: Was he, then, in his youth really on the wrong road? And further on he raises the question why this demigod left his fatherland so soon? Perhaps "because all of his flowery dreams did not mature," as we read in Goethe's *Prometheus*.

Grant that the elder Goethe's preference for the remote and the antique was by no means invariably correct, it remains, despite this concession, quite impossible to play off a Lenz against Goethe. Lenz's dramas are prose and nothing more. His once famous drama entitled *Der Hofmeister* is supposed to serve as a warning against tutorial positions. We are shown how such an occupation incapacitates for life, promotes laziness and luxury, and through its obligatory servility causes the bitterest of humiliation. The tutor in this case has to adapt himself to the major's rude caprices and the haughty and arrogant commands of the major's wife. The boy whom he is supposed to educate cannot be persuaded to study. The young daughter, who is thoroughly in love with an absent lover, allows herself to be seduced by him, becomes with child, and is straightway driven from the home. The tutor flees.

He and the daughter both become completely unhappy but are liberated in the end. The tutor castrates himself by way of punishment for his misdeed but becomes almost immediately acquainted with a young and beautiful woman who loves him at first sight and would gladly marry him despite his wretched condition. The aristocratic young girl's fiancé then marries her regardless of her checkered past and the child she has borne.

The characters shift and waver from act to act. At first the tutor is lazy and servile but grimly enterprising in the presence of the young lady. He is merely pitiable and whining; he is contrite to the point of self-castration; he is so eager for the renewed life incident to the innocent love of which he is the object. The moral of the drama is distinctly puerile; it warns against bringing tutors into the family: One never knows what it may lead to.

The same is true of Lenz's other drama entitled *Die Soldaten* and once the equal of *Der Hofmeister* in popularity. It also has a plebeian moral warning: Never admit officers, who go about from garrison to garrison, to the women of the family. The virtue of women lies almost unnaturally close to the heart

of the young poet, famed for his multifarious infatuations.

When the tutor Läuffer protests against the fact
that the Church preserves the teaching of the Devil
and the story of Lucifer's rebellion, a second person
is expressing Lenz's opinion concerning the aims of
Enlightenment as set forth in the slogan: "In our
enlightened day, no one any longer believes in a
Hell." The reply is also in accord with Lenz's own
heart: "Consequently the entire rational world will
go to Hell." Obscurantism did not frighten the
absolving youth from that period of Enlightenment.
The tutor discourses as follows:

Take it for granted that our teaching in regard to faith
is superstition! In case you eradicate superstition, real faith
disappears too, and there remains nothing but a barren
waste in the realm of the spirit. Take superstition from
the rabble, and they will assault you. Take the Devil from
the peasant, and he will become a devil in opposition to his
lords.

The fundamental idea of *Die Soldaten* is con-
tained in a speech of the Countess to the young
Marie, who says: "He loves me, but . . ."
The Countess replies:

An officer's love, Marie, is the love of a man who is accustomed to all manner of dissipation, who ceases to be a
good soldier the moment he becomes a steadfast lover. And
since he has sworn to his king not to be anything but a loyal
soldier, you have to abide by the consequences.

In these dramas the moral of the young revolu-
tionist is not dissimilar to that which Kotzebue, a
few decades later, preached in his plays. Now and
again, Lenz as a poet of rebellion recedes to his

starting point, that is, to Rousseau. We note this change in his *Der neue Menoza*—an unqualifiedly unimportant drama, though it was at that time highly regarded and widely discussed.

It contains an attack on European culture. The exotic prince says:

> I shall leave you in peace and go home to the end that I may enjoy my inheritance in all innocence, rule over my country, and build a wall around it so that everyone who comes from Europe must first be quarantined before he multiplies his pestilences among my subjects.

Herr von Biederling replies:

> You have failed to familiarize yourself with our horticulture. . . . You would have to remain with us for ten or twenty years before you learned how we are superior to all the nations of the earth.

The Prince:

> Superior—in fraud and rascality. . . . All that you gather together remains lying on the upper surface of your reason, and degenerates into wile. Feeling you know not; you are not even familiar with the word. What you call feeling is merely varnished lasciviousness; what you term virtue is merely the paint with which you touch up brutality.

Lenz has all the essential earmarks of megolomania: lack of character, lack of bearing, envy, and importunate intimacy when in the presence of the really great. With him and Goethe it is always a case of *Du* and *Ich,* You and I, we two.

II

Maximilian Klinger, incessantly linked with Lenz, was of a different mould—superior as a man, quite inferior as a poet.

Friedrich Maximilian von Klinger (1752-1831), like Goethe, was a son of Frankfort. His father, unlike Goethe's, was an indigent policeman, and after his death his mother supported the family as best she could by running a little grocery store. The son had to fight his way through life unaided and unassured. The oppressions of his youth bred in him a hatred for all oppression and inspired him with a fighting disposition; the young *Stürmer und Dränger* who owed their name to him, regarded him as the chieftain of the spiritual revolution; by Heinse he was even called "the lion, king of beasts"; by Wieland the vampire (*Der Blutsäufer*).

He was tall, slender, well built, with regular facial features, fond, however, of giving himself a superingenious appearance. He had good manners and good faculties, docility, a strong memory, and uncommon ability as a linguist. Plebeian prudes said of him that he drank, ate raw meat, and was consumed by sexual dissipation. The really leading features of his disposition were firmness, steadfastness, and a proud feeling of independence. America, as the continent of the great republic, was the land of his longing. If Rousseau had been a significant element in the development of Herder, Goethe, and Lenz, for a personality like Klinger's Rousseau must be everything. Lenz wished to see two statues erected side by side, those of Shakespeare and Rousseau. Klinger would have been satisfied with one, that of Rousseau. *Emile* was his fundamental book, his Bible. He himself felt that he was a child of nature; everything was good as it came from nature's hand, everything was spoiled by the hand of man was his unadorned confession of faith just as it was

that of the citizen of Geneva. Even as an old man
he wrote of Rousseau: "The young man who has no
guide should choose this one. He will certainly
lead him through life's labyrinth and equip him
with power to endure the struggle with fate and
with mortals."

Whether he owed it to himself or to the Frenchman of Switzerland, there was certainly no lack of
this power in him. He became a general at the
Russian court, curator of a university, the favorite
of the Zar, and as an older man reknitted the bond
of cordial friendship with Goethe, with whom in
his younger days he had constantly associated.

If Lenz as a poet was full of provincial morality,
there is at least the spirit of social rebellion in
Klinger. And if Lenz's style is full of mannerisms,
Klinger's is full of exclamations.

As the unique product of the movement, one reads
Sturm und Drang with astonishment. The speeches
of the young men in the play sound like those of
insane persons, consisting as they do of disjointed,
hardly explicable, sentences. Confusion is so ram-
pant that the *dramatis personnae* do not know, at
the beginning of the play, that they are in America.
Having arrived in the country and being under
shelter, the leading character, who is significantly
called *Wild* though he has another civilian name,
says to his followers:

In order to help you at one blow out of your dreams, let
me tell you that I led you from Russia to Spain in the belief
that the King of Spain would begin war against the Grand
Mongolians. But since the Spanish people are lazy the
King is too. So I again prepared to travel and here you
are now in the midst of war in America. Ah, let me enjoy

to the full the fact that I am standing on American soil where everything is new and replete with meaning.

To this the hero's associate, *La Feu,* says:

War and murder! O my bones! O my guardian angels! —Pray give me a fairy adventure! O woe is me!

Here a third leading party, called *Blasius,* breaks in in the same delirious tone:

Would that the lightning would strike you dead, you insane Wild! What have you done this time? Is my Donna Isabella still alive? Heh! Can't you talk? My Donna!

When one recalls what a sensation this play created, and what significance lay in its title for later years, one would suppose that, just as the style anticipates Schiller's *Räuber,* the action would likewise have something of the spirit of social revolution in it. But as a matter of fact the play revolves around a story of grievance and vengeance in the life of private individuals.

Lord Berkley of Scotland, sixty years old and a wreck, has suffered a grievous injustice in his native land and is now living in North America. He is in his dotage. He has lost his reason out of grief over his former friend and present enemy, Lord Bushy, who has stormed his castle, set it on fire, driven him and his good wife and his little Jenny half naked from their home. Lord Berkley sits now day in and day out building houses of cards that tumble down as fast as he builds them and remind him of his devastated castle. He is nursed in this condition by his daughter, the above-mentioned Jenny who, no one knows why, is called Car-

oline. In his delusion the old man always addresses
her as *Miss,* without affixing her baptismal name (as
though the author could not write English). He
constantly says: No, Miss!, Heh, Miss!

Miss Caroline cannot share her father's immeasurable hatred of the Bushy family for she loves
Lord Bushy's son; him she can never forget: Was
his name not Carl, did he not have blue eyes and
brown hair, was he not larger than any of the boys
of his age, was he not beautiful with his red cheeks,
and was he not her steadfast cavalier?

But Carl Bushy is not unworthy of her. It is
namely he who, under the name of Wild, has led his
comrades to America on the ground that he is spending his life in the search after phantoms. He sees
the picture of his beloved Caroline in the distance
and seeks her in continent after continent.

Wild is gruff and stern to his comrades, though
they cannot resist him, perhaps because he is so big
and powerful, perhaps because they are even less
rational than he. Read for example this bit of
dialogue:

Blasius: I loathe you, Wild! I wish that you would
leave me alone for a while.
Wild: Does it occur to me to pursue you?
Blasius: I cannot endure you. Your strength is contrary
to my nature, as is also the fact that you are constantly chas-
ing after phantoms—I hate you!
Wild: As you like! At times you love me.
Blasius: (Embracing him) Who can resist you!—Boy,
boy! I have a worse disposition than you. I am inwardly
torn asunder and incapable of reuniting the threads. I want
to be melancholy. No, I don't want to be anything. You
saw my noble horse pull a small cart in Madrid. I grieved
in the depths of my soul and Isabella dried away my tears.
Glory of this world! I can no longer pluck your flowers.

Yes, he who has lost his senses, who has lost thee, eternal love, thou who holdest all things in us together!

That sounds as though it had been written by a schoolboy in the first class, or in the next to the first class. The author is not only no artist; he also lacks that sanity and balance indispensable to the creation of a character that does not act contrary to all principles of reason. One of the young men pays violent court to a ridiculous old woman, for he loves to find himself in an illusion; man must always dream, never think, in order to be happy. Another of them is silent and reserved in the presence of a beautiful young girl who loves him and cheers him up in vain until she at last makes demands of him as if she were a minx.

Naturally the lovers find each other and one of the numerous recognition scenes takes place. He: "Here I find what I have looked for in vain the whole world over. You are an angel, my lady, a magnificent, soulful creature. I came here in order to allow myself to be shot in the next battle and— and I will let myself be shot dead."—Recognition.— She: "Good Carl, you are still the same wild, brave boy."—He: "And so I find you here, Miss Berkley, and I shall keep you here, and what Wild keeps—I could choke your father in order to possess you."— The father comes and contents himself with saying bitterly: Adieu, Miss!—The old man seems to rec-ognize the features of his enemy in the young man, and yet he is almost obliged to do violence to himself in order to keep from falling on his neck. In reality he is quickly reconciled. Less prompt at reconcilia-tion is his son, a sea captain, who chafes for revenge

against the Bushy family for having placed the old
Bushy in a boat and let him drift at sea. A happy
fate drives him to land however, and he follows
up Wild, the young Bushy, with his cannibal-like
hatred. They shoot at each other but each comes off
with his life. The old Lord Bushy at last appears
in order to make his peace with his mortal enemy.
This is achieved through the ridiculous explanation
which he has kept until the very last, that all of this
family hatred is based on a pure misunderstanding:
"Berkley, one does not lie at the hour of death and
I have never lied. Here where truth and untruth
are separated, I tell you that I am wholly innocent
of the desolation of your home. The one who
caused the misfortune has long since lain in the
valley of death." And he embraces Berkley.

It is not enough that the style is intolerable; it
is also parodic. When Wild climbs a tree in order
to reach Caroline's room, the fair one exclaims:
"Hold fast, my beloved! Branches have been
known to break." He replies: "I am hanging on
your eyes." When the Captain has challenged Wild,
old Berkley asks him whether he will not be seated
at the table. He replies: "At any rate, only as a
cannibal, Mylord! I yearn for the Captain's flesh."

Klinger wrote in addition to this drama an entire
series of other dramas, among which *Otto* is the
best known in Germany because it is the first drama
of knighthood after Goethe's *Götz* which, as is
known, provoked a veritable welter of dramatic
literature on knighthood. Aside from having been
influenced by Goethe, however, *Otto* also owed a
great deal to those poets who aided in the creation
of a new dramatic norm. *Otto* contains three par-

allel actions, the first of which is modeled after the motif of Lessing's *Emilia Galotti;* the second follows the Gloucester motif in Shakespeare's *King Lear;* the third imitates the basic motif in *Othello.* Where Goethe rests on Shakespeare, his associates and imitators rest both on him and Shakespeare.

If one should seek in *Sturm und Drang,* this inchoate and notorious trash that has just been reviewed, for leading ideas or fundamental thoughts, one would be forced to say that they consist in an emphasis of human individuality. This is what the writers of the period regarded as the original and meritorious element as contrasted with social forms and class distinctions. The human is the finest, and the most easily vulnerable. It is on this account that we hear so much in the productions about affronting and offending and disgracing *mankind,* about rescuing *mankind's* honor. Goethe writes scornfully in *Götter, Helden und Wieland:* "You people all belong to the great family known as mankind's dignity—an idea abstracted from God knows where." Lenz writes of Shakespeare: "Wretched indeed is he whose bosom is not made to swell and who is not brought to feel the vast compass of the word *Mensch* on reading works of this sort."

Man's enemies are convention and custom, both of which are attacked in every scene. But they are attacked no more vigorously than are honor and prejudice, the servants and messengers of propriety. The *heart* on the contrary is the highest tribunal; it is even more: It is omnipotent. It is a question of listening to the voice of the heart. To understand the heart is wisdom; to follow it is virtue.

Before the days of Goethe that idea was neither

intelligible nor accessible in any form other than
the moral.   One worked out the good or the bad
moral that was to be deduced from a book; the
moral was the thing.   This explains why *Werther*
was regarded either as a recommendation of or a
recipe for suicide.   That it was possible to build up
a free and original work of art on inner experience
had never occurred to anyone.   But for Goethe
poetry was merely a confession of inner experiences:
"The thing that makes a poet is a full heart, full of
just one feeling."   The heart is the creative power;
this explains the commitment from Prometheus:
"Hast thou alone not done everything, thou holy,
glowing heart!"   This explains too the fact that
in *Werther* we have the programme of the book,
so to speak, in the very first lines: "Best friend, what
is the heart of man!"   And later on: "Our heart
alone creates its happiness."

CHAPTER X

WETZLAR AND GOETHE—*Werthers Leiden*— *Werthers* RENOWN

IF we look back over the leading male characters in the works of Goethe's youth, it is quite difficult to escape a distinctly unfavorable impression—that of the unmanliness of these young men. In all of them, in Werther, and even more so in Clavigo and Fernando, not to speak of Weislingen, there is a pronounced element of weakness. We detect this indeed in Faust himself. In the case of Werther, this impression is strongest at the close of the book, a close that casts a cloud over the beginning. Modern ethics, the temperaments and sensibilities of the present, are repelled: A young man takes his life out of despair at being separated from a woman who seems quite satisfied in and with her union with another man, and who in any event can endure life without him.

Modern critics have taken to jeering Goethe because he did not commit suicide on finding himself in Werther's situation. No derision could be more absurd. Why in the name of all that is reasonable should Goethe have taken his life? People affect to feel nowadays that it was a sort of belated duty he owed himself. They refuse to believe that any great seriousness is to be attached to the suicidal thoughts by which he portrays himself as having been plagued at that time. They insist that he never really thought of sending the well-polished dagger, which he kept suspended at his bedside during those days, through his heart. What are we to understand here by "seriousness?" If the term connotes only and entirely the dwelling on such ideas of suicide as eventually lead to death, then he was not "serious." But Goethe wrote very explicitly to Zelter in 1812 (he was then sixty-three years old) : "I am fully conscious of the decisions, resolutions and exertions that it cost me to escape from the waters of death." He told the whole truth when he said he wrote the novel in order to liberate himself from these feelings. Moreover, he never pretended that he felt precisely as did Werther.

Following out his father's wish, he came in the spring of 1772 to Wetzlar to practice law. The lamentable condition in which the Court at Wetzlar, then the highest tribunal in Germany, found itself, the antiquated system under which it then worked, may be seen from the fact that no fewer than 16,000 cases were then on the calendar, not a one of which was removed unless a great bribe or still greater favoritism aided in effecting a settlement. Goethe seems to have done not the slightest bit of juridical work. No trace of his stay in Wetzlar has ever been found other than the fact that he entered his name in the register on his arrival. He read Pindar and Homer. Even if he had been a more zealous jurist than he was, he would have found something to do only with difficulty. Five years previous to his coming, Emperor Joseph II had sent twenty-four chosen men as an investigating committee to Wetzlar in order to correct the existing conditions. They investigated for four years and sent three judges, who belonged to the peerage, to jail on the ground of bribery, but in the fifth year they themselves were so affected by the situation that a sharp rupture arose among them and a complete cessation of all work at the court ensued.

The town itself was ugly and murky; but beyond the gates spring had come in all its full-blown splendor. "Every tree, every hedge is a nosegay, and one would gladly be a beetle in order to hover about in this sea of fragrance." Just outside the little town was a well where Goethe sat for an hour each day and looked on as the girls came from the village to fetch their water—"the most innocent and necessary task that in olden times was attended to by the daughters of the king." He liked to lie down by one of the little brooks that flowed into the Lahn, hidden in the tall grass, with his back against a tree and his Homer in his hand, as he was lying the first time Kestner saw him. He walked to the nearest village, Gartenheim (Wahlheim in *Werther*) and there he found a quiet place by the church between two big old linden trees, which he liked best of all. Thither he had his table and chair and milk brought from the inn, and there he joked with the village children and made drawings. All the children surrounded him. they all liked him, especially three small boys no one of whom was over four years of age. They each received a creutzer daily so that the mother could buy a bit of fresh wheat bread for the soup.

At the inn *Zum Kronprinzen* where he took his midday meal he found a lively company of young

jurists the most of whom, like himself, took their
work anything but seriously. They offset the tediousness of the law by playing all manner of jokes.
Among other diversions, they formed a sort of
round table and instituted an order of knighthood.
But knights they hardly were.

To this circle there belonged two secretaries of
the legation, though they were very infrequent visitors. One of them came from Brunswick, the other
from Bremen. The one was Wilhelm Jerusalem,
an insular, irritable, pessimistic young man who
could not endure Goethe and who never came into
really close contact with him. The other was Johann
Christian Kestner, Goethe's senior by eight years,
a Hanoverian by birth and an excellent individual.
He was clam, clear-headed, and a little dry, but remarkably conscientious as a jurist despite his warm
feelings and many-sided interests. Both were destined to have the greatest significance for Goethe's
most popular work from his younger days. Jerusalem served as a model for Werther as a suicide;
Kestner was fused with the grim old husband of the
charming Maxe Brentano and caricatured as Albert.

Five years previously, in 1768, Kestner had become engaged to Charlotte Buff, then fifteen years
old. She was the daughter of the ranking official
of the German Order at the city. She was blond
and blue-eyed, healthy as healthy could be, and possessed of a charming personality. She was always
happy, quite efficient and thoroughly dependable.
Of sixteen children that the official had had, eleven
were still living. The mother was dead. The oldest
daughter was less capable than Charlotte, the second
oldest, upon whom devolved the task of taking the

place of a mother to the other ten and assuming general responsibility for the large household. Though only nineteen years of age, she attended to her duties with remarkable ease. For reading and study she had no time.

Goethe became acquainted with her at the little ball given on Pentecost evening by the young men from the Imperial Court at Volpert's house a short distance from Wetzlar. The rapture he straightway felt at the sight of her is known the wide world over. Scarcely since the glorification of Beatrice by Dante and Laura by Petrarch has the passion of any other poet been so famous.

Kestner's method of enduring the handsome and captivating young Goethe as a rival was admirable; Lotte's conduct was no less worthy and beautiful. An actual collision was avoided, or almost so. All three were united by ties of cordial friendship. But in the month of August the clouds began to gather. Goethe's passion could hardly be controlled any longer, he was jealous of Kestner and Kestner was jealous of him. A kiss which he stole from Lotte, and of which she complained to her fiancé, brought on strained feelings. In the middle of August Goethe conferred, while in Giessen, with Merck, who saw Lotte, then on a visit in Giessen, and who could estimate her real worth, though he chided Goethe and advised him to break off all connection with her. On September 11, Goethe departed in complete silence without even saying farewell.

Scarcely ten days later he had a friendly meeting with Kestner in Frankfort. They threw themselves into each other's arms. On October 30 Jerusalem shot himself in Wetzlar because of an unhappy love

affair with a young woman, the wife of a secretary
of one of the embassies. From November 6 to November 10 Goethe was again in Wetzlar gathering
all the information he possibly could on the death
which Kestner had reported to him immediately,
but concerning which he was obliged to send him a
detailed account in writing.

In January, 1774, the newly-married Brentanos
came to Frankfort. The husband was fully sixty
years old and had five children by a former marriage. His wife was a charming young woman
with a liberal education. And there she sat now,
tied down, surrounded by the stench of oil and
cheese, in the dingy store of her husband in Frankfort. Goethe came and accompanied her on the
piano with the cello. Brentano was no friend of
musical duets. "Frightful moments" ensued.

Not until February, 1774, a year and a half after
his departure from Wetzlar, fifteen months after
Jerusalem's death, but immediately after the outbreak of Brentano's jealousy, Goethe began to
write *Werther*, and in four weeks the book was
finished. The entire first part he had, in all probability, practically finished in the meantime by the
use of his letters from Wetzlar to Merck and to his
sister Cornelia. But if we consider the time that
Goethe allows to pass between the experience and
the composition we will understand why it is written with the peace of mind that is so noticeable
in the first part, abounding as it does in healthy and
vigorous vitality. And by comparing the tone of
the letters to the Kestners with those of the more
passionate parts of the novel we will easily see
where Goethe follows reality and where he does

not. Despite the inevitable melancholy, the tone of the letters is frank and free, youthful and bold, whereas *Werther* is distempered and elegiac, especially toward the close.

Just before the writing of *Werther* was begun in January, 1774, we have an effusive letter from Goethe on the merriment of the skating party. The ice cracked and creaked, the people fell and looked outlandish, and so on:

Yesterday we ate roast venison and jelly tart and drank a great deal of wine and dined with houris until one o'clock in the morning. . . . From the new Mayor, Herr Reuss, where I in a costume of scarlet and gold announced the New Year—Whither?—To the Rhine, coachman! I up the steps, where the bell rope was still hanging in the corner. —Shall I ring?—Then comes little Käthe.—Do you still know me?—The door is opened, I take her affectionately by the head and precipitate a misfortune with her coiffure.—I present myself.

That is all poles removed from the close of *Werther*.

Shortly after having made Goethe's acquaintance, Kestner gives, in a letter to a friend, the following remarkable characterization of the poet and lover, then only twenty-three years old, and necessarily repellent to the older and more sedate man in many ways:

He has many talents; he is a true genius and a man of character. He has an extraordinarily vivid imagination, which explains the fact that he generally expresses himself in pictures and similes. He himself is accustomed to say that he always speaks figuratively; when he gets older he hopes to think and to express his thoughts just as they are. He is impetuous in all his feelings though he has himself remarkably well in control. His way of thinking is noble.

He is free from prejudice and acts on the impulse without bothering himself as to whether it pleases others, as to
whether it is the fashion, or as to whether good breeding
permits it.   He hates all coercion.   He loves children and
can busy himself a great deal with them.   He is odd and
has in his conduct, in his external appearance, a number of
features that might make him disagreeable.   With women
and children and many others he stands nevertheless in excellent repute.   For women he has an extraordinary regard.
In principiis he is not yet quite fixed and is still striving after
a definite system. . . . He is not what you would call orthodox, though not out of pride or capriciousness or affectation—he discusses the leading questions along this line only
with a very few, he is reluctant about disturbing others
in their calm ideas. . . . He hates skepticism and strives
after truth. . . . . He does not go to church, nor to the
confession, and he rarely prays; since,—as he says, I do
not wish to be a liar to boot. . . . For the Christian religion
he has a very high regard, though not in the form in which
our theologians present it. . . . He strives as we have said
after truth, lays however more weight on the feeling of
truth than on proofs of it.   He has already accomplished
a great deal and has a considerable store of information,
has read much, but has not as yet thought or reasoned a
great deal.   His chief study is the liberal arts and sciences,
or more correctly speaking, he studies all sciences except the
professional ones. . . . He is in a word a quite remarkable
man.

If we compare with this portrayal the conversation between Gretchen and Faust in the catechization
scene we will see how exactly the portrayal fits:

Gretchen: Nun sag, wie hast du's mit der Religion?   Du
bist ein herzlich guter Mann.
(With women he stands in excellent repute.)
Faust: Lass das, mein Kind!
(He discusses the leading questions of religion only with
a very few.)
Du fühlst, ich bin dir gut.

(For women he has very great respect.)
Für meine Lieben liess, ich Leib und Blut.
(His way of thinking is noble.)
Will niemand sein Gefühl und seine Kirche rauben.
(He is reluctant about disturbing others in their calm ideas.)
Gretchen: Das ist nicht recht, man muss dran glauben!
Faust: Muss man?
(He is free of prejudice. He acts on the impulse. He hates coercion.)
Gretchen: Du ehrst auch nicht die heil'gen Sacramente.
Faust: Ich ehre sie.
(For the Christian religion he has a high regard.)
Gretchen: Doch ohne Verlangen.
Zur Messe, zur Beichte bist du lange nicht gegangen.
(He goes neither to church nor to confession.)
Glaubst du an Gott?
Faust: Wer darf sagen
Ich glaub' an Gott?
(He hates skepticism, strives after truth, etc.)
Gefühl ist alles.
(But he lays more weight on the feeling of truth than on the proofs of it.)
Name ist Schall und Rauch.
(He expresses himself mostly in pictures and similes.)
Gretchen: Ungefähr sagt das der Pfarrer auch, nur mit ein bischen anderen Worten.
Faust: Jeder in seiner Sprache.
Warum nicht ich in der meinen?
(He is not orthodox, esteems religion, but not in the form in which our theologians present it.)

We have already remarked that Werther in the first part, where Goethe alone is still the model, is entirely too wholesome and strong to be thought of as a suicide. His nature sense is especially healthy. Such a feeling for nature had hitherto never been detected in a German novel. Werther does not describe nature, nor does he exploit such

designations as Luna and Zephyr (as Goethe did
in his oldest poems). Everything is steeped in feeling. He feels life pulsating in nature, and he feels
its echo in his own breast:

> When the lovely valley round about me exhales its vapor,
> and the sun rests at midday on the upper surface of the im-
> penetrable darkness of my forest and only individual rays
> steal down into its sanctuary, when I lie then in the high
> grass by the babbling brook and nearer down to the earth a
> thousand different grasses of smaller kind become visible,
> when I feel the swarming of the little world between the
> blades, and countless and unfathomable little figures of the
> insects and gnats closer to my heart, and feel the presence
> of the Almighty who created us in His image, the fluttering
> of the All-Loving through space who bears us up and holds
> us in light eternal, my friend, when my eye becomes wrapped
> in dusk and the world about me and the heaven in my soul
> rest like the figure of a beloved—then I am seized with
> longing and this thought comes to me: Oh, if you could
> only express, if you could only breathe into the paper, all
> this that lives so warm and full in your soul so that it would
> be the mirror of your soul, just as your soul is the mirror
> of the infinite God! My Friend! But I court ruin in the
> desire; I succumb quite to the power of the glory of all I
> have seen.

This is the extent of his intimacy with nature; he
has confidence in her; she becomes confidential and
precious to him; he strives to reproduce nature.

That the feeling is Goethe's own is proved by the
fact that it returns, expressed in the same way, only
with less theological coloring, in Faust's monologue,
Erhabener Geist, Du gabst mir, gabst mir Alles.
The Spirit gave him Nature in all its glory as his
kingdom, the power to feel it, to enjoy it, and the
gift to look deep down into it as he would look into
the heart of a friend. He feels like Adam: Thou

leadest the files of the living by me, and teachest
me to recognize my brothers in the peaceful bush,
in the air, and in the water.

Werther who, as an artist, wishes to reproduce
nature and is grieved when he cannot find the right
word, wishes to feel divine, superhuman; he wishes
to have nature arise from within his own heart; he
would feel the instinctive joy in life that other creatures have, particularly that of the birds in their
flight:

> How often have I longed to fly far away to the shores of
> the unmeasured sea on the wings of a crane which had
> flown above me, so that I might drink the swelling, seething
> joy of life from the foaming beaker of the infinite! How
> I have longed to feel even for a moment that there was in
> the pent-up enclosure of my bosom one drop of the happi-
> ness of that being which creates all things in itself and
> through itself.

The same wish, expressed in almost the same
words, occurs in *Faust*. Faust sees the bird flying
high over his head and wishes that he himself had
wings. Even the crane re-occurs:

> Wenn über schroffen Fichtenhöhen
> Der Adler ausgebreitet schwebt,
> Und über Flächen, über Seen
> Der Kranich nach der Heimath strebt.

It is likewise during the walk on Easter evening that
Faust, seeing the light of the setting sun in the windows, which causes them to shine as if filled with
fire, longs for wings so that he might follow the
sun in its course:

> O dass kein Flügel mich vom Boden hebt
> Ihr nach und immer nach zu streben!

He would live in eternal light and clarity, with the
night behind him and the day before him, and drink
from the never-failing fountain of life, just as
Werther would have done:

> Doch scheint die Göttin endlich wegzusinken;
> Allein der neue Trieb erwacht,
> Ich eile fort, ihr ew'ges Licht zu trinken
> Vor mir den Tag and hinter mir die Nacht . . .
> Ach zu des Geistes Flügeln wird so bald
> Kein körperlicher Flügel sich gesellen.
>
> Doch ist es jedem eingeboren,
> Dass sein Gefühl hinaus und vorwärts dringt,
> Wenn über uns im Raum verloren
> Ihr schmetternd Lied die Lerche singt.

These verses from *Faust* belong to the edition from
the year 1806, and could hardly have been written
much earlier, since Goethe used for the next scene
in which Faust appears a book by Pfister on mediaeval sorcery. We know as a fact that he borrowed this book from the Weimar library in 1801.
We see, accordingly, that in Werther's love for nature and in his visionary attitude toward it there is
an element of Goethe's own vigorous and wholesome
character, an element that was preserved in his
works a full generation after this period.

Goethe has made Werther's impressions of nature conform to his own momentary feelings; and
he has done this with uncommon delicacy. Suffering from an unhappy love affair, he sees (August
18) in nature only the powers of destruction; in
heaven and earth he sees only "an eternally swal-
lowing up and eternally ruminating monster." But
he is healthy for all that.

Deep down in his soul Werther is not an un-

manly youth; and he is above all not a whimperer.
The fact is, Goethe had to have a tragic end, for
the strong passion which had thus far prevailed
would lose its poetic interest if the conclusion were
primarily idyllic. This being the case he took up
with a new model at the very last, and introduced
a few confusing facts from the world of reality, such
as Werther's reading Lessing's *Emilia Galotti,* one
of the clearest, most rational dramas in existence.
In a letter to Herder Goethe himself criticises it
as being "only thought."

He accommodated everything to this tragic close:
He had the bright summer mood of the first part
supplanted by the melancholy of autumn in the second; he dropped Homer and Homer's wholesome
views of nature and took up Ossian. Homer is a
distinct force in the first part. When Werther
cooks his own green peas in the public kitchen at
Wahlheim, his mind reverts at once to Penelope's
haughty wooers who roasted their own oxen. Now
the hazy, restless Ossianic pictures, which corresponded to the increasing morbidity, uncertainty, and
lyrical passion, gradually gain control of the theme,
until Ossian's songs—which Goethe had translated
for Friederike, and which are interpolated just before the final decision—prepare the way for death
and downfall.

The degree in which he estimated Ossian at this
period of his life is revealed by the beautiful passage in which Werther expresses his indignation
at the individual who asks him whether he likes
Lotte. Like her? One might as well ask him
whether he likes Ossian.

II

There is no one definite taste in *Werthers Leiden*. The natural and fascinating alternate with the super-sentimental and exaggerated; ingenious similes and perspicacious soul studies vie with an extravagance which could not help but seem antiquated even during Goethe's own life; indeed it made this very impression on him himself. It is fortunate that in a later edition he contented himself, on the whole, with some addenda that greatly enrich, and did not undertake another of his confusing revisions.

One quite infelicitous revision is this one of July 16: "How I adore myself since she loves me!" It corresponds to the equally unfortunate phrases that introduce the book in the editor's assurance to the readers: "You cannot help but give his mind and his character your *admiration* and your love." This contains one redundant word.

The hymn to Klopstock of June 16 is also antiquated. Lotte has mentioned his name. Werther reverts, in thought, to Klopstock, and then exclaims: "Noble man! Would that you could have seen your idolization in this look and would that I were never again to hear your desecrated name!" The meaning is: "I hope that I shall never again hear your name desecrated." It was only a few more years until Goethe, immediately after his arrival in Weimar, was to have Klopstock placed over him as a moralist, and to see himself obliged to reject him and his ideals. And from that day on he was forced to tolerate the enmity of the author of *Der Messias*. But who in our day can study Klopstock's vulgar and con-

ceited face, who can read his works without being
bewildered at the attention he received while living? It all betrays, as nothing else, the fact that
the German people were standing at that time on
a very low artistic and spiritual level. I do not
believe that I underestimate Klopstock's services
to the German language, and the part he played in
the national awakening of the German people. Nor
do I undervalue a few of his odes in which—*Der
Eislauf,* for example—there is real nature sense,
though nature *tone* they know not. But that his
main work, *Der Messias,* could so inspire—what a
testimony to the low degree of development in Germany long after the middle of the eighteenth century, after the Encyclopaedists, after Voltaire! For
non-Germans, and certainly for many Germans, it is
now impossible to read, to say nothing of enjoying,
Der Messias. It would be preferable to read Indian religious poetry from the gray days of old.
It is just as full of unction and just as empty. And
the incredible verses that are supposed to be hexameters! The fourth of *Der Messias* limps as
follows:

Leidend getödtet und verherrlichet, wieder erhöht hat

It would be interesting to know where Klopstock
fancied the accents should fall. Or take this verse:

Weihe sie, Geist Schöpfer, vor dem ich hier still anbete.

The legion of false accents corresponds to the false-
ness and fatuousness of the ideas. In such Goethe
took delight in the days of his poetic adolescence.
    There is still another of the heroes of Goethe's

youth—whom we are soon to see abandoned, even
persecuted as a fraud—that received honorable
mention in *Werther*: Lavater. The clergyman's
wife, as is announced in the memorandum of September 15, 1772, who has the nut trees cut down,
is characterized by the fact that she shrugged her
shoulders at Lavater's fanatic hobbies—just as
Goethe himself did not many years later.

In other places Werther represents, to be sure,
a point of view which the author of the book was
soon to discard, though a point of view that was
justified for a quite different reason: the proclaim-
ing of artistic naturalism as a matter of principle.
By making an exact copy of nature, Werther has
produced a sketch which is entirely successful, and
which seems to interest him. This strengthens him
in his determination to hold fast to nature alone in
the future; for it is infinitely rich; it alone creates
the great artists. Nature is here contrasted with
the rules and not, as later in Goethe's life, with the
ideals. Quite in the spirit of *Sturm und Drang* he
writes: "One can say about as much to the advantage of the rules as one can say to the advantage of
established bourgeois society." It does not yet occur
to Goethe that it is not so much fidelity to rules that
contradicts an imitation of nature. We read, to be
sure, later on in his own works:

> Nachahmung der Natur
> —der schönen—
> Ich ging auch wohl auf dieser Spur;
> Gewöhnen
> Möcht' ich wohl nach und nach den Sinn,
> mich zu vergnügen.
> Allein sobald ich mündig bin—
> Es sind's die Griechen.

The poet who, in course of time, was to relegate all strong feelings to their proper limit, so much so that in the eyes of many he appeared secretive, dry and unimaginative, takes not the slightest offense at the manifestation of any type of emotional outburst in Werther. When Lotte dotes on her little sister, who is terrified by Werther's kiss and fears lest she may grow a beard because of it, Werther almost has to do violence to himself in order to keep from falling down and adoring her. Lotte takes the child to the well and washes the kiss off. Werther exclaims with undisciplined sentimentality:

I never attended a christening with greater reverence. When Lotte returned, I would have liked to throw myself down before her as I would before a Prophet of old who had atoned for the sins of an entire people.

Had Goethe not had the poor taste to prefer, at this period of his life, the Swiss Rousseau to native French writers, he would have avoided such an outbreak.

Flaws of this kind, however, are rare; they vanish in the enraptured portrayal of Werther's infatuation. How dainty is the description of his uncertainty as to whether Lotte was trying to see him when she leaned her head out of the carriage as they drove away! And equally charming is the confession that he would gladly have kissed the boy who brought him a note from her simply because this boy had recently seen her. Beautiful and apt is also the comparison (July 26) in which he says he is drawn to her as the ships are drawn to the magnetic mountain in the fairy tale. The nails fly to the

peaks and the poor wretches are shipwrecked amid
falling boards and floating planks.

By means of a number of delicate touches that
are eventually blended into a unified whole, the
psychology of Werther is delineated with force and
grace.   Lotte upbraids him, for example, for his
"all too passionate participation in everything."
We have also a significant touch when (August 12)
Albert's nature is described as being the antipodes
of Werther's.   The occasion of this remark—in a
fine and careful preparation for the close of the
novel—is Albert's well-founded objection to Werther's playing with his pistols, even when they are
not supposed to be loaded, and Albert's commitments on the foolish element in suicide.   It is in
this connection that Werther makes use of the superbly phrased sentence that shows us the real Albert: *"Nun weisst du, dass ich den Menschen sehr
lieb habe bis auf seine Zwar."*   It is to be assumed
as a matter of fact, says Werther, that there are
exceptions to all generalities.   But so would-be wise
is Albert, that when he feels that he has made an
over-hasty remark, or has said something that is
too general or only half true, he delimits it and
verifies it beyond recognition.   A long conversation
is spun out during which Werther first defends the
actions undertaken in passion, and then, when suicide
is touched upon, contends that there are certain degrees of torture which can no longer be endured and
which consequently justify self-annihilation.

The figure of Lotte is introduced in a naïve and
natural, and in the most original, way for the heroine of a love story.   When Werther sees her for the
first time she is surrounded by six children between

two and eleven years old. Though beautifully
dressed for the ball, in a white gown with pink scarf,
she is holding a huge piece of rye bread in her hand
and cutting for each of her small brothers and sisters a slice dietetically adapted to the age and appe-
tite of the recipient in question.

Though extremely young, she is maternal and
domestic; the children love her and obey her. The
two oldest boys, having received permission to run
along behind the carriage for a short distance, kiss
her hand tenderly and cordially on leaving her.

Immediately after this we see her whirling about
in the waltz with address and charm. She is beautiful, good, modest, wholesome, and without affectation.

The second part of the novel has a wholly different character from the first. The first part is
plastic and living, the second is psychopathic. We
hear precious little about Charlotte. It is well known
that Goethe no longer uses himself as a model; he
has substituted the other. It is the situation and
the incidents in the life of young Jerusalem that
are here portrayed. Werther is now interested
more or less in another woman, who, according to
the intolerable custom of that time, is referred to as
Fräulein von B.

The new motive to Werther's former self-aban-
donment, the prejudice namely against which he as
a private citizen has to fight and the humiliation to
which he is exposed, are now introduced. The arrogance of the nobility is attacked and ridiculed, but
from an essentially conservative turn of mind: Class
differences are necessary; Werther does not forget
what advantages they have brought to him himself.

And now, after having been ejected from the Count's house on that afternoon because he, as an ordinary citizen, is not tolerated in the society of the nobility, the idea of suicide arises in his mind for the first time. "Ah, hundreds of times have I seized a knife in order to give air to my agonized heart. It is said of thorough-bred horses that, after they have been heated up and driven about in a fearful manner, they bite open a vein in order thereby to get air."

On the twenty-fourth of March Werther asks for his release as attaché of the legation. His mother had hoped to see him as a *Geheimrat* and *Hofmann* —a position which Goethe in actuality secured not much later.

A prince, who is without knowledge of men and talks only of what he has heard and read, takes an interest in Werther. This man places a higher value on Werther's reason and ability than on his heart, which—in accord with the spirit of that age— is his "sole pride." The melancholy youth thinks of going to war; he gives up the idea however when a general under whom he wished to serve shows him that this wish is more a matter of caprice than passion. In the beginning of July he changes his place of abode; he wants to visit a neighborhood apparently in order to study some mines, in actuality to be nearer to Lotte.

On the twenty-sixth of October he is again, and all of a sudden, near her. When he returned we are not told. In marked contrast to the circumstantiality with which everything is related, we have here not a word on the meeting at the end of a year. But Werther feels quite at home in her town; he seems to be welcome; indeed he cannot be imagined anywhere else. And the question arises in his mind, or rather in his soul: Suppose I went away, would they miss me, and if so, how long? By the fifth of November he has already lost his spirit; he has lost what he exaltedly calls "the sacred, inspiring power with which he created worlds about him."

The nearer we approach the end the more emphasis is laid on Werther's peculiarity as a being of nature and his estrangement from Christianity: "Has not the Son of God Himself said that they should be around Him whom the Father has given Him? But if I am not given to Him?" Werther wishes to be dissolved in nature. He would gladly renounce his human character in order, with the storm, to tear the skies asunder and move the waters.

The unhappy love affair and the social slight are taken up together. Werther's jealousy grows. Albert feels dissatisfied with the youth's advances to his wife. He is out of humor. The relation between the consorts is growing darker and darker. Werther feels moreover that his honor has been irreparably wounded through the social jilt he suffered. At the same time Charlotte is forced to ask him not to come to the house again for three days.

Suicidal instincts arise in his lacerated soul. He dreams of murdering her husband, her, himself. As to his criminal intentions the reader is skeptical. It is not set forth in a sufficiently convincing way. Then come, as a mood-awakener, the Ossianic poems. As an insertion they are too long. These are followed by the last meeting. For the first time in his life Werther feels that Charlotte loves him.

In the final letter, written in the spirit of that age, we read of *milleniums* (as in *Götz, Clavigo, Faust*) : "Lotte, milleniums can never efface these impressions." And finally the beautiful note : "Nature, thy son, thy friend, thy lover draws near—near to the infinite end!"

III

Rousseau's *La nouvelle Héloise* had appeared in 1761. This is the book without which Goethe could not have written his *Leiden des jungen Werthers* thirteen years later. Rousseau's hero, Saint-Preux, changed his clothes, donned the famous costume, the blue coat and yellow vest which Werther wears, and which Goethe himself had worn in Wetzlar. *La nouvelle Héloise* had enraptured France, indeed the whole of Europe. The story of Werther's passionate and unhappy love affair likewise received its significance from the fact that it did more than portray the casual passion and incidental misfortune of a single individual : It treated the theme in such a way that the passions, yearnings, and torments of an entire age found their expression therein.

The age saw itself visualized in this book. *Werther* depicted the right and the wrong of the full heart in its relation to workaday rules, its striving after infinity, its impulse to freedom, that freedom which reacts to the dividing lines of human society as it would to the bleak walls of a prison. In the course of a few months, the author of *Werther* became the most famous personality in German literature. Young men sympathized, first

in Germany and later in many other countries, with
Werther: they dressed and yearned and felt just as
did he. Young women wanted to be loved just as
Lotte had been loved.

As early as 1777, the book had been imitated by
Pastor Miller in his *Sigwart, eine Klostergeschichte,*
a creation on which there was showered an inor-
dinate measure of the praise that is born of fashion.
Götz von Berlichingen had been a victory in Ger-
many; *Werther* encompassed the earth. Three
French translations appeared in 1776-77. The
English translations began to appear in 1779. And
as late as twenty-five years after its publication,
Werther inspired Ugo Foscolo in Italy to write his
Jacopo Ortis. Fully thirty years later it moved
Charles Nodier in France to write his novel entitled
Le Peintre de Strasbourg. And as early as 1779,
scarcely five years after its original publication,
Werther was so famous that a certain Herr von
Leonardia of Glückstadt found, in the Captain's
cabin of a merchant ship, several Chinese paintings which portrayed Werther's sufferings. This
explains Goethe's statement in the Venetian epi-
gramme,

> Doch, was fördert es mich, dass sogar auch der Chinese
> Malet mit ängstlicher Hand Werthern und Lotten auf
> Glas!

Still less satisfaction could the author of *Werther*
derive from the fact that in a little country like Denmark it completely captivated Rahbek,[9] was imitated

[9] Knud Lyhne Rahbek, born at Copenhagen in 1760, died there in
1830. Even as a student he showed marked enthusiasm for the
theatre, and supported it through the various magazines he established. He was one of the most productive and popular writers

by Ingemann [10] in his *Varners Vandringer,* and by
Sibbern[11] in his *Gabrielis.* One thing is certain: the
fame of the book became universal. Napoleon took
it with him on his campaign to Egypt in 1798, read
it seven times, and studied it so carefully that he
could discuss a point in its composition during his
conversation with the author in 1808. Chodowiecki
and Crusius illustrated the work. Indeed even at
public markets in Germany Werther was shown
painted on cloth or canvas.

By way of petty retaliation, however, the book
aroused the embitterment of the older generation
and of the authorities. In Leipzig the sale of
Werther was forbidden on penalty of a fine of one
hundred dollars. Senior Pastor Götze, noted or

of his day, casting off lyrics apparently without difficulty—and
sometimes without inspiration—at the same time that he dedicated
his energy to the popularization of Danish literature. His wife,
Kamma Rahbek, born Heger, was Adam Oehlenschläger's sister-
in-law. Her most noted work was the founding of "Bakkehuset,"
near Copenhagen, where she opened and presided over a literary
salon such as Denmark had not known up to that time, and has
not known since. For the Rahbeks then to take up with *Werther*
meant that it would be known to literary Denmark as a whole.
Brandes himself has written a captivating monograph on Kamma
Rahbek.   —TRANSLATOR.

[10] Bernhard Severin Ingemann (1789-1862) was the Walter
Scott of Denmark. His "Varner" was written in 1813 when he
was still enveloped in the hysterical romanticism that was a part
of his youthful nature and part of his country at that time. He
wrote a series of novels portraying the life and history of Denmark
in the thirteenth and fourteenth centuries. The Danes are familiar
with him as the author of a cycle of patriotic poems entitled
"Holger Danske."   —TRANSLATOR.

[11] Frederik Christian Sibbern (1785-1872) wrote his "Letters of
Gabrielis" in 1826. It reached the fifth edition in 1893. He trav-
eled extensively in Germany, where he came under the influence
of Schelling. Though he never built up a philosophic system of
his own he did much to direct the thought of his time. His most
important work is "The Spiritual Nature and Being of Man"
(1819-1828).   —TRANSLATOR.

notorious because of his feud with Lessing, wrote in 1775 his *Kurzgefasste aber notwendige Erinnerungen* against *Werther* and, what is still more remarkable, Götze and Lessing agreed for once in a matter of literary judgment. Lessing found *Werther* flaccid and immoral since its method of reasoning was not Grecian. He wished in the place of the suicide a cynical ending, just as cynical as possible, an ending that would prove that Werther was capable of being cured of his unhappy and excessive infatuation.

In Denmark Bishop Balle[12] brought it about that the work was placed on the index by the theological faculty as a book which makes religion ridiculous and vice attractive. In Milan the resident bishop bought up an entire edition of the Italian translation and had it destroyed. Viennese critics hoped that little by little people would reject Goethe inspiration and revert to common sense. Nicolai, who wrote the wretched parody entitled *Die Freuden des jungen Werther,* had the chagrin, as he himself relates in his *Beschreibung einer Reise durch Deutschland und die Schweiz,* 1781, of seeing in Vienna, not simply a grand tragic ballet, in three acts, called *Der junge Werther,* but of attending fireworks, *Wird man es glauben: ein Feuerwerk?* known as *Werthers Zusammenkunft mit Lotte in Elysium.* This ingenious creation was divided into two parts, front fireworks and decorations. The

[12] Bishop Nicolaj Edinger Balle (1744-1816) took a middle ground between orthodoxy and rationalism. In 1791 he published a catechism that was long considered an authority. From 1793 on he held a series of "Bible evenings" in one of the Copenhagen churches. His motto was: "The Bible is its own defense."

—TRANSLATOR.

former was in five sections, depicting Werther's happy days, his union with Lotte despite the separation, and his meeting with Lotte at her final resting place. The decorations portrayed Werther and Lotte during their sojourn in the Elysian fields. There was then no lack of those elements that make for popularity and from which universal favor is wont to proceed.

CHAPTER XI

GOETHE AND BEAUMARCHAIS; *Clavigo*

THE leading character in *Clavigo,* Goethe's next more pretentious work, is far more unmanly even than Werther. The genesis of this play is as follows: In the social circle to which Goethe belonged after his return from Wetzlar, a game known as playing-at-getting-married had come into vogue. By the casting of lots, the young ladies and gentlemen were paired off and the individual couples were to consider themselves, for eight days in succession, as summer married people. This simply meant, it seems, that during this period the young gentleman in question was to regard himself as the cavalier of the young lady in question. It came to pass in the spring of 1774 that Goethe was united three times in succession to the beautiful, sixteen-year-old Anna Sibylla Münch—the girl of all young girls in Frankfort to whom his mother would have most liked to see him married. There is no doubt but that a good deal of the marriage game took place between Goethe and the young girls of the circle. Here are two sisters, Susanne Magdalene Münch and Anna Sibylla, between whom he seems to have divided his heart about equally. Then there are the three Gerock sisters, and we have Kestner's description of an accidental meeting between Goethe and the one sister Antoinette. Her face beamed at the sight;

she greeted him on the promenade with an impetuous embrace and a kiss—that is fourteen days after the disconsolate departure in the letter to Lotte, preserved word for word in *Werther*.

Goethe says that after his return from Strassburg he was constantly loved in Frankfort by a fine, amiable woman. Not until after her death did he learn of this mysterious and divine love in a way that could not help but move him. Was it Antoinette Gerock—and is she one model for Mignon?

At the weekly meetings Goethe had read aloud from Beaumarchais, especially from his defense entitled: *Quatrième Mémoire à consulter, etc. Contre M. Goetzmann, accusé de subornation et de faux; Madame Goetzmann et le Sieur Bertrand, accusés; les Sieurs Marin, gazetiers; Darnaud Baculard, Conseiller d'ambassade, et consorts.*

I do not believe that a club of young men and young women, all of them very young, would in our day choose for reading aloud such an original and such an interesting polemical pamphlet in a foreign language, the plea in a lawsuit from a man who was not yet famous, who was as yet the author of neither *The Barber of Seville* nor *Figaro*. Originality in the choice of reading matter has become rare indeed. But by way of explaining the originality in this case we must concede that Goethe belonged to this circle.

When the reading was finished, Anna Sibylla said to him: "If I were now your sweetheart and not your wife, I would encourage you to transform this *mémoire* into a drama."

The result was remarkable; this monograph had already had an enriching effect on Goethe's mind;

before the week was over the drama was finished.
The achievement was of itself not great; many a
dramatic author has worked just as rapidly, and the
work is, to be sure, not of first rank. But it is dramatic to a high degree, more dramatic than anything
else Goethe ever wrote. This was owing to the
breath of Beaumarchais there is in it. Beaumarchais's plea contains incidentally (on the occasion
of an anonymous, calumniating letter) an account
of his journey to Spain in 1764; it tells how the
audacious, self-confident, mentally superior adventurer, supplied with the very best of recommenda-
tions, undertook a journey beyond the Pyrenees in
order to have justice done to his sister and against
the Spanish writer who had brought her into public
disgrace by his conduct toward her. In Beaumarchais's account his sister has of course all the right
on her side; he himself is a knight without fear and
without reproach. Clavigo, an absolutely low-
minded individual whose business it is to deceive
him, changes his place of abode time and again in
order to deceive him, and finally effects an order of
arrest against him, but is caught up by Spanish
justice and discharged from his office and his untenable position.

Goethe takes up Beaumarchais's sketch step by
step and places it in the light in which he places
himself, though he gives a different explanation of
Clavigo's action and has him, at last, cause the young
girl's death while he penitently retires under the influence of a worldly wise but cold-hearted friend.
Goethe has incarnated himself absolutely in Clavigo's conduct toward Marie Beaumarchais. It is
his own conduct toward Friederike Brion.

The point of departure from which Goethe proceeds in *Clavigo* is the second act. With the exception of the first page and a half, Goethe has taken
the entire act, word for word, from Beaumarchais.
He has not merely copied the speeches, but also the
stage directions (such as "he becomes more attentive," "changes his expression," "loses every single
cheerful expression," "moves about on his chair in
the greatest confusion") are taken literally from
Beaumarchais's account.

It is in this crucial act that Beaumarchais, during
his unexpected visit to the famous author and keeper
of the imperial records, forces him, in the presence
of his entire body of servants, to draw up a written
statement, one that is intended for publication, in
which he confesses that he has debased, without the
shadow of right or reason, an irreproachable girl
and begs her forgiveness.

On the stage this scene is tremendously effective;
but as everyone who has seen it knows, it is excessively painful. This is particularly true of the fact
that Clavigo allows himself to be coerced into calling in his servants and signing a statement, in their
presence, which seals his own degradation and
stamps his conduct as dishonorable. The spectator
rebels at the very thought; that is no real man who
will conduct himself in such a fashion. Moreover,
one is repelled by the lack of refinement on the part
of Goethe which persuaded him to select as a hero
an individual who finds himself in this predicament.
In the pride of the first moment, Goethe wrote to
F. H. Jacobi:

That Beaumarchais's *memoires de cet avanturier françois*
delighted me, and awakened the romantic strength of youth

in me, that his character and his deed were amalgamated
with points of my own character and with deeds of my own,
and thus Clavigo became my own—all this is my good fortune, and I challenge the most critical knife to separate the
passages that have been merely translated from the whole
without mutilating it, without inflicting on the structure, and
not merely on the story, a mortal wound.

He is of course quite right in insisting that the
act could not be cut out or separated; but he should
not have challenged the most critical knife, for it
is, when in good condition, a very sharp instrument.
He who wielded it could, for example, draw attention to the fact that Goethe, by crudely appropriating the entire act without modification, has placed
Clavigo, to whom he does not deny his respect, in
a far worse light than Beaumarchais does, who profoundly despises him.

The explanation offered by Goethe is precisely the
same as that offered by Beaumarchais. He has
simply omitted the date, May 19, 1764, from the
explanation. But let us not overlook the fact that
in Beaumarchais, the servants understand not one
word of all that is said in the room.

It is the same in the original as in Goethe's work:
"You have disgraced in cold blood an honorable girl,
because you thought that she was here in a strange
country without assistance and without avengers.
That is the action of a scoundrel and a wretch. And
therefore you must now declare, by your own hand
and voluntarily, that you are a detestable person,
and you must make this statement in the presence
of your servants who do not understand us, because
we speak French (*qui ne nous entendront pas parce
que nous parlons Français*)." These words Goethe

omitted, and he had to omit them, because his characters spoke German, and in the drama it was impossible for him to make a distinction between the scenes in which this German stood for French and those in which it stood for Spanish. But he forgot that he thereby gave Clavigo a stigma which he was not later in position to eradicate.

Goethe has also in another way, by copying his text so uncritically, debased his hero where he wished to elevate him. In the drama as a whole the union between Clavigo and Marie is conceived after the fashion of the Germanic peoples. Marriage should only confirm a union between hearts. In Beaumarchais marriage is conceived after the fashion of the Romance peoples, as a secular and practical institution. Clavigo as a Spaniard has regarded it in this latter light. It is not therefore ridiculous from his point of view when he says to Beaumarchais who has scolded him: "Vanity has led me astray. I feared that I would ruin my chances of a distinguished future by this marriage. Had I known that she had such a brother, she would not have been in my eyes an insignificant, foreign woman. I would have hoped for the greatest advantages from this marriage." By a more careful elaboration Goethe could have given Clavigo's character greater dignity and thereby greater interest.

Carlos, the other leading character in the drama, is purely fictitious. In him we see, as it were, the first attempt at Mephistopheles, in whom, as is known, there is a blending of multifarious elements. Mephistopheles is the shrewd servant, his master's confidant and matchmaker; there is in him something of the harlequin and something of the clown;

but there is also in his supercilious intellect, which
scorns all emotion and leads everything back to sensual reality, something of the so-called satanic.

In Carlos we have as yet only this devil's sharp
and heartless intellect united with a passionate interest for his friend whom he admires and whom
he wishes to liberate through his mockery. Now
and then there is a sort of crayon sketch of a motif
that reappears in *Faust*. When Carlos, for example, portrays Clavigo, where a number of young
women appeal to him, either personally or in writing in order through him to make the acquaintance
of Clavigo, Carlos says:

"How many a young duenna came into my hands
on this occasion!"

This is an anticipation of the scene in which
Mephistopheles has the duenna on his neck while
Faust busies himself with the young virgin.

Merck, the model, had a Mephistopheles figure.
He was tall and gaunt, had a pointed nose and a
tiger-like look in light blue eyes. At this time he
was army paymaster (*Kriegszahlmeister*) in Darmstadt. As has been indicated above, he had a keen
intellect, poetic talent, good taste, was equally at
home in literature, art, and natural sciences, had
done a great deal of work along all of these lines,
had written scientific treatises on the animals of the
prehistoric world, satires, fables, novelettes, and
critical reviews. He impressed his contemporaries,
however, especially by his person. In this age of
hazy, unclear feelings, he had a critical judgment
that saw through all weaknesses and defects; and
he was chemically free of good nature. This latter characteristic arose in part from the fact that

he became more and more embittered and distempered as time went on, first because his marriage turned out unhappily, and secondly because of some unsuccessful business enterprises that brought him to the brink of ruin. A few years later, Goethe persuaded his Duke to come to his financial assistance by going on his bond for four thousand guilders. Merck however fell a prey to melancholy and fancied that his numerous speculations were going to bankrupt him, though his business affairs were after all not in such poor condition. He shot himself in 1791.

For Goethe Merck always cherished the most cordial affection. One time, after having been separated from him for quite a while, he chanced to see Necker's medallion of Goethe. He at once broke out in tears of joy, and had a duplicate made so that he could use this head as a seal.

One should read attentively the conversations between Carlos and Clavigo in the first and fourth acts of the drama, where he persuades his friend to break with the little girl who is holding him back and dragging him down:

Carlos (Act I): And get married! Get married just at the time that life is really beginning to amount to something! Settle down to a domestic existence, bind one's self before half of the journey has been completed, before half of the conquests have been made! . . . Be calm! She is not the first girl to have been deserted, and to have found consolation. If I were to advise you, there is the young widow across the way. . . .

Carlos (Act IV): I have borne your fate in my heart as though it were my own. You are my only friend; all other men are intolerable to me, and you are beginning to become so.

Clavigo: I beg you to calm yourself.

Carlos: Burn down one's house on which he has worked for ten years, and then send him a father confessor to preach him a sermon on Christian patience!

Clavigo: I confess to you that I was frightened on seeing Marie again! How disfigured, how pale, how consumed! And that is my fault, my treachery!

Carlos: Nonsense! Whims! She was consumptive even while your affair with her was still in full bloom. But you lovers simply have no eyes, no noses. (The realism of the expressions is pronounced enough!) Clavigo, it is a disgrace! Thus to forget everything, everything, a sick woman who will bequeath her pestilence to your offspring, so that your children and grandchildren, on reaching a certain age, will politely go out like so many beggars' lamps.

If Carlos is gruff and audacious, Clavigo in his remorse and contrition is too pitiable to be of interest. To Beaumarchais he calls himself "a wretch who is not worthy to behold the light of day." And to his friend he gives this explanation of his conduct: "Carlos, I am a very small person." This is, unfortunately, the painful truth. It is shown most clearly when he accepts Carlos's low-minded suggestion of having Beaumarchais arrested and criminally indicted for having come to Madrid in secret, for having introduced himself under a false name, for having thrown him off his guard by kind words, and for having forced a statement from him, only later to go out and spread the same statement broadcast.

If we compare, moreover, the decisive conversation between Carlos and Clavigo with the similar scene in Octave Feuillet's *Dalila* between Carnioli and Roswein, we will see that the situations are precisely alike. The shrewd friend and lover of art wants to prevent the artist from entering into a marriage which he may later regret. The various speeches in Feuillet's work teem with humorous touches: Don't you know, you triple idiot, that marriage is one of these wild and merciless laws of nature as a result of which the individual is consumed in his attempt to preserve the human race! I forbid you to put yourself under this dishonorable extinguisher.—You will stop like a locomotive that has jumped the track and whose own steam, try as it may, cannot budge it from the place.—You will have your wings clipped; you will turn sick in the limbs which you no longer have . . . and this for the sake of such a little girl who, like a Dutch woman, will plant tulips in your heart.

Goethe's Carlos is less figurative, stays closer to the earth, but makes a stronger impression. He is more fascinating than the leading character Clavigo, even more so than Goethe's Beaumarchais. How infinitely more shrewd and droll than Goethe's good fellow was the real Beaumarchais, especially as he became in time, surrounded by inner contrasts, a bold idealist and a bold man of business, as rich in plans as he was in wisdom. He has in him the instinct of the age, which brings it about that he inaugurates the Revolution with his *Figaro*. His *Barber of Seville*, published the same year as *Clavigo*, is significant for a reason other than the one that makes Goethe's drama significant.

Goethe has handled the names in the drama with considerable freedom. The unabbreviated name of the leading character was José Clavijo y Fajardo, and the name of the young woman to whom he was engaged was Louise (not Marie) Caron (not de Beaumarchais, since the title of nobility which her brother had bought did not extend to her).

The style is that of Goethe's youth; it is the style which Schiller inherited from him long after he himself had abandoned it. Beaumarchais says:

O how I feel the thirsting vengeance in my bosom! O how the magnificent feeling, the yearning after his blood snatches me from a mood of dull indecision! Vengeance! Annihilation! O how well I feel! How everything in me urges me to lay hold of him, to destroy him!

No rapier! No pistol! I will strangle him with these very hands, and then all the joy will be mine! The feeling that I have murdered him will be mine!

Conspicuous in this drama, as we have already noticed, is the marked influence of *Hamlet*. Here too the brother appears as the avenger of the deserted girl. In the scene of the burial—in both dramas—there is a conflict between the lover and the brother. And just as if copied from Hamlet's admonition to be careful on the ground that there was something dangerous in him, Clavigo exclaims: "Stop! Don't make me mad! The unhappy are dangerous." He is pierced by Beaumarchais's rapier, and in his dying hour permits, indeed, causes his magnanimity to flow on unimpeded.

It is right curious that Beaumarchais himself had had a drama, entitled *Eugénie,* performed at the Théâtre Français as early as 1767, in which he made use of his sister's biography, especially with regard to the motif of the brother who espouses the cause of the deceived and deserted girl. But he has treated the theme with such infinite discretion that no one would be apt to suspect that it is his own family history that is being dramatized. The action is transferred to England. The seducer is one Count of Clarendon, and the young girl is a daughter of

one Baron Hartley.   With this theme as a basis, he
constructed a play of intrigue in which the threads
are interwoven with remarkable skill.   The Count
has beguiled his unsuspecting fiancée into a marriage
that is wholly invalid, since he has his intendant disguise himself as a priest, and the members of his
household act as witnesses.

While the young woman under the guise of a lady
of degree is expecting her child, she learns that the
Count, who has just visited her and conducted himself as her devoted husband, is planning to enter on
the following day into a marriage with a rich and
distinguished young girl.   The brother had committed a breach of discipline as an officer as a result
of which he is leading a threatened existence.   He
is attacked by would-be assassins, but is immediately
rescued by the unexpected assistance of Clarendon
whom he does not even know.   Suddenly he learns
of the deception his rescuer has practiced on his
sister.   He protects him at first, in order to repay
him for what he has done, and then appears in the
rôle of an avenger.   In this way Clarendon comes
to regret his conduct, begs forgiveness, gives up the
idea of his financially advantageous marriage and
pleads for the hand of the young woman.   There
is a goodly measure of dignity in the way in which
the reconciliation is effected.

CHAPTER XII

LAVATER AND BASEDOW—THE JACOBI BROTHERS
—FRITZ JACOBI; *Allwill, Woldemar*

DURING his stay in Frankfort from 1773 to 1775,
Goethe, already famous, made the acquaintance of
many sorts of people. He was sought after on the
one hand by younger men interested in literature
and ever ready to avail themselves without scruple
or thought for the consequences of any plans or
ideas he might reveal in the course of his conversations. One of these was H. L. Wagner to whom
he had uncautiously read the plan of his *Faust,* in
1774. In 1776, fourteen years before Goethe published the *Fragment* with the Gretchen tragedy,
Wagner usurped the idea for his *Kindesmörderin.*
Lacking moral balance as he did, he revised it three
years later and gave it a happy ending. On the
other hand, he was sought after by such a widely
known writer as Klopstock. Having learned of
Klopstock's interest in his works, he wrote (May
28, 1774) to him in filial reverence: "Should I not
address myself to that individual while still living
to whose grave I would gladly make a pilgrimage?"
As Klopstock appeared in Frankfort he was small,
well developed, with a measured but supple bearing.
He gave the impression of a diplomat who represents, not a prince, but higher powers; he was the
representative of religion, morals, and political free-

dom. He did not like to discuss literature : he dwelt by preference in detail on skating and the breaking-in of horses. He occupied at that time a place in German literature such as first Grundtvig[13] and then Björnson held in the North. In contrast, however, to the patriarch he was a man of the world. That even his external appearance seemed to appeal to young Wolfgang is relatively obvious from his lines on Klopstock in Lavater's *Physiognomische Fragmente:*

This bland and receding forehead signifies pure human reason; the space above the eyes signifies originality and finesse; the nose is that of an observer. In the mouth there is amiability, precision and, in its connection with the chin, certainty, sureness. Over the entire face hover indescribable peace, purity and temperance.

Goethe was soon to perceive how strongly Klopstock felt that he was the moral guardian of the youth of his day; and that so far as the aforesaid temperance was concerned, the virtue was a bit tenuous.

Lavater also came to Frankfort to make the acquaintance of his youthful admirer. He too was a prophet who stood on a confidential footing with

[13] Nicolai Frederik Severin Grundtvig (1783-1872) was one of the most influential writers Denmark has produced. Reared in the spirit of the eighteenth century, he began the nineteenth as a pagan. Intimately associated with Steffens and Oehlenschläger, he studied and wrote on Shakespeare, Goethe, the Eddas, Northern Mythology and—after his "conversion"—religion. He said of himself: "I am half poet, half book-worm." He was always in some sort of contest. He was a prophet, poet, preacher, politician, translator, critic and man. Björnson derived a great deal of inspiration from his teachings. The Danes, indeed all Scandinavians, remember him possibly best for his interest in and establishment of the "high-schools." The first was begun at Rödding in 1843. There are now about 80, attended annually by about 9,000 pupils.
—TRANSLATOR.

the Lord, and who was given to casting his gaze
forward into eternity.

Johann Caspar Lavater was a theologian; he was
one of those priestly persons who, supported by
vague enthusiasm and seeming animation from on
high, exercise a tremendous influence on women and
children. In him there was a mixture of inspiration and charlatanism, such as the founders of sects
are so apt to have. It was years before Goethe saw
through him; and it was his belated enlightenment
that made Goethe, in the end, such an unmerciful
critic of the man whom he had studied with an excess
of zeal.

Lavater's chief interest and obsession at that time
was physiognomics, an exceedingly unclear and pre-
carious science for which, however, it was not difficult to gain the sympathy of a young artist to whose
articles of faith this one quite naturally had to
belong, the one on which all portraiture depends:
that the external is the internal, that the physical
is the expression and mirror of the soul. Goethe
allowed himself to be enlisted as a collaborator on
Lavater's *Physiognomische Fragmente*. E. v. d.
Hellen has succeeded in separating the part written
by Goethe from the rest. It is not of great compass though it has its interest for later generations.

Goethe protests against the mockery and indifference of his contemporaries with regard to physiognomics, and though he himself must have felt how
far it came from being an exact science it was nevertheless precious to him as the key to knowledge
pertaining to the human heart. The heart was at
that time everything in the literary world. The
affairs of the heart were also the affairs of the head

for the youth of that day. The natural scientist in him took a lively interest in the form and structure of the skull. He describes the shape of one head after another. And when one sees how he dwells with equal interest on the physiognomy of animals and that of men, when one reads his description of wolves, bears, tigers, lions, cats, otters, beavers, hedgehogs and so on, which interest him almost as much as the descriptions of the heads of Cæsar, Brutus, Tiberius and so on, one understands that, when he discovers the intermaxillary bone he will also be the man to discover the hitherto unknown congruity between the human skeleton and the skeleton of animals. Several of the individuals whom he describes later came to stand in a spiritual relation to him, Rameau and Newton among others. He describes Newton with an admiration that stands out in sharp contrast to the aversion he eventually came to feel toward him.

Interesting in the next place are the lines he wrote on a portrait of Charlotte von Stein: "It would be a magnificent spectacle to see how the world is reflected in this soul. It sees the world as it is, and yet through the medium of love. And mildness is the predominant impression."

J. B. Basedow the pedagogue, a pupil of Rousseau, had come to Frankfort at the same time as Lavater. He wished to reform the education of children along the line of coarse naturalness, and, rationalist that he was, he explained away the miracles of the Bible. Accompanied by Lavater and Basedow, Wolfgang Goethe undertook, July and August, 1774, the Rhine journey which has been memorialized in the little poem entitled *Diner zu*

Koblenz, and quoted time out of mind. He mirthfully portrays himself as sitting between Lavater and Basedow at a public table in the restaurant. While he eats his salmon and chicken Lavater expounds the Revelation of St. John to a clergyman and Basedow, in conversation with a dancing master, berates infant baptism:

> Und wie nach Emmaus, weiter ging's
> Mit Geist und Feuerschritten,
> Prophete rechts, Prophete links,
> Das Weltkind in der Mitten.

On this journey he became acquainted with Wilhelm Heinse who, though convinced of the necessity of a national basis for all art, was pining for Greece and Italy and in his fancy was revelling in pagan sensuousness. His *Ardinghello,* which was supposed to represent the sensuous, strenuous individual of the Renaissance, is spiritually more akin to Lenz and Klinger than to Goethe.

It was also on this occasion that Goethe finally became reconciled with the two brothers Friedrich Heinrich and Johann Georg Jacobi. The quarrel of former days was forgotten; peace was to reign for a season.

In the home of Frau von Laroche, a favorite authoress of that time, a friend of Wieland for many years, Goethe had already become acquainted with Fritz Jacobi's excellent wife Betty. Moreover Jacobi's and Goethe's common friend, Johanna Fahlmer, to whom Goethe in his letters had shown great confidence, and who stood almost as close to F. H. Jacobi as his own wife, had done her utmost to bring the two men together, whom she valued most highly,

and who seemed the exact opposites of each other.
Goethe decided to visit Fritz Jacobi in Düsseldorf,
and though Jacobi had found peace in faith while
Goethe was and remained a seeker, a bond of friendship was sealed.

II

From a literary point of view there are several
places in Goethe's life that might be termed points
of attraction to and repulsion from the Jacobi
brothers. Goethe's review of Georg Jacobi's self-
defense on the occasion of his connection with the
deceased Klotz has already been discussed. He also
wrote in his early years, and unfortunately destroyed, the lampoon in verse entitled *Das Unglück
der Jacobis;* likewise the above mentioned poem
Flieh, Täubchen, Flieh (So ist der Held) a parody
on the erotic tone and exaggerated tenderness between two men, occasioned by the *Briefe der Herren
Gleim und Jacobi;* it embodied not a few passages from Jacobi's poems and letters to and from
him. When we read, for example, "Roth ist sein
Mund, der mich verwundt," we have to do with a
parallel to the words of the letter "Unter tausend
Küssen sag' ich Ihnen."   Then we have the little
pamphlet from the year 1779, just recently discovered, entitled *Woldemar's Kreuzerhöhung.* It is a
jest in memory of the crucifixion which Goethe in-
flicted upon Jacobi's soft and sweet *Woldemar.*

The summer of 1779 was an especially merry time
in Weimar. Anna Amalie held as usual court at
Ettersburg, and in the last of May Merck came to
pay a visit of six weeks. One day he derided Wieland for an hour at the court table. The mirth be-

came so great that in September Wieland's aria from
Alceste, Weine nicht, du meines Herzens Abgott, in
Einsiedel's parody *Orfeus und Euridice,* was accom-
panied by post-horn and demanded *da capo.* (Wie-
land complains of this in a letter to Merck himself.)
Another Ettersburg farce was the crucifixion of
Woldemar. The friendship formed during the
Rhine journey in July, 1774, had now begun to cool.
Goethe felt that he was the target in *Allwills
Briefe.* This novel was likewise one of the books
satirically catalogued in Goethe's *Triumph der
Empfindsamkeit. Woldemar* had originally been
published in Wieland's *Teutscher Merkur,* 1777,
under the caption, *Freundschaft und Liebe. Eine
wahre Geschichte.* It provoked Goethe's derision
at the time, for it was likewise included in *Triumph
der Empfindsamkeit.* A revised edition was published in book form in 1779, under the peculiar title:
*Woldemar: Eine Seltenheit aus der Naturge-
schichte.* Goethe, having recently completed the
first sketch of his *Iphigenie,* had now become an im-
placable antagonist of the sentimental heart-effu-
sions such as had drawn nourishment from his own
Werther. He was disgusted with this hubbub of
debauchery in sentimentality and coquetish self-
idolization. And he wrote a short burlesque in
which the devil at last fetches Woldemar, delivers
a philippic on this execrable book, and nails its
two lids to a tree about as one might nail a bat's
wings to a barn door. The parody in itself is a
bagatelle on a little sheet, a student's prank, if you
please. Deviations from the original wording
amount in all to about fifty: We have *Die bren-
nende Begierde nach Menschenfleisch* instead of

Menschenherz. We read also, *Der Weisheit toll und voll,* for simply *voll.* Woldemar says: *Ich wollte, das ich mein Herz fassen könnte, wie ein Weib ihre Brust, um Dich nöthigen, es zu trinken.* In Goethe's work the devil says: *Ich wollte, dass ich sein Herz fassen könnte, wie ein Weib die Zizzen einer Ziege, um Dich nöthigen, es zu trinken.*

There is, moreover, the poem entitled *Gross ist die Diana der Epheser,* 1811, intended as a protest against F. H. Jacobi's *Von den göttlichen Dingen und ihrer Offenbarungen.* And finally, we have F. H. Jacobi's monograph, *Ueber die Lehre des Spinoza in den Briefen an den Herrn Moses Mendelssohn,* 1789. The latter is motivated by Lessing's agreement with Goethe's *Prometheus,* and thereby with Spinoza's philosophy. In conclusion it must be said that the second, revised edition of *Woldemar*—despite the treatment accorded the first edition—is dedicated to Goethe in words the first of which deserve quotation, showing as they do with how little harmony friends, who fancy that they become greater through the bonds of friendship, are at times contented:

I dedicate to you a work which, without you, would not have been begun and never finished. It belongs to you; I give it over to you; to you as to no one else. You feel these words, old friend, and you give me your hand on it— likewise as you would give it to no one else. Twenty years have passed since our friendship was begun. At that time someone asked you in my presence whether we had not been friends from very childhood! You replied that this love was so new that if it were wine it could not be enjoyed. It has now become a noble wine.

Anything even remotely resembling a fruitful impression Goethe never received from the two brothers. Yet there is a vague possibility that he took the idea of Faust's interrupted attempt at suicide from J. G. Jacobi's *Elysium,* 1774. Faust hears the singing of the Easter psalm and desists from taking his own life. In Jacobi's work the hero is just in the act of putting a beaker of water from Lethe to his lips when he is interrupted by a song.

Nor did the Jacobi brothers ever acquire a profound understanding of Goethe's real nature. Although F. H. Jacobi tried, in his *Allwills Briefsammlung,* 1776, to delineate a being like young Goethe, he succeeded in portraying nothing more than a gifted young man who is dangerous in the presence of ladies, an enemy of the law and its letter, of rules and their yeomen, a young man who follows his own natural inclinations, and who wants to allow all of his talents to attain unto their full and complete development. As to the rest, he is garrulous and of viewy diacticism. This young Goethe never was; nor could he ever acquire that type of characteristic.

III

Fritz Jacobi, born in 1743, was thirty-one years old when he became acquainted with Goethe, then twenty-five years of age. As a very young man he had come to Frankfort to study business. After spending some time in various cities, he returned to Düsseldorf to take charge of his father's affairs, ill adapted though he was to a practical life as a merchant. He received an appointment at the Electoral Court Chamber (Düsseldorf lay at that time in the Electoral Palatinate) and when Goethe came, he found Jacobi enjoying a position of unusual dignity, and living during the summer months at his country place out at Pempelfort. Goethe, whose sister Cornelia was acquainted with Jacobi's wife and sister, had been corresponding with the latter previous to his visit to Jacobi in 1774. For a time he was altogether happy in the home of the young man with the overflowing impulse to friendship. They laid bare their hearts to each other in endless conversations; they did mutual homage to the trend toward sentimentality then so pronounced; they felt like brothers who were separated "with the feeling of having been eternally united." Goethe writes to him:

You have felt that it was a source of ecstatic joy to me to be the object of your affection. Oh it is glorious to believe that each of us receives more from the other than he gives! Oh love, oh love! The poverty of wealth—and what a feeling pulses through me at the thought of embracing in another what I myself lack, and of presenting the other with what I have!

Talented youth is frequently just about as uncritical as this. It was impossible for Goethe to realize at that time that Jacobi's confidence was merely the conceit of a half-gifted youth; that his impulse to friendship rested on emptiness; that his entire stock in trade consisted of an unctuous flow of words; and that he harbored within his heart an irresistible urge to imitation.

He straightway sought to reproduce Goethe's personality, and to imitate his style. The amusing feature of this latter endeavor lay in the fact that Goethe's style of that era was not his own: it was borrowed. Under the initial and marked influence of the prophet of Zürich, who had so completely

captivated his mother, Goethe had involuntarily
imitated his method of expression: he wrote with
the same brand of open-hearted exclamations; he
assumed the function of the oracle just as Lavater
himself had done. The connection of Lavater's
sentences was ingeniously slipshod by reason of its
absolute naturalness. His language, the language
of the righteous man of nature, at its best in the
Swiss dialect, was apt to be full of shifts in the train
of reasoning: it was either bold in its frankness
or suggestive in its mysterious silence. We have
precisely the same situation in the style of Goethe's
letters from this period. Jacobi dilutes this style
first with fresh and then with consecrated water.

Goethe had read some of his *Werther* to Jacobi
before it had been published. Before it had been
published, Jacobi had finished his wretched imitation, entitled *Allwills Briefsammlung*. Allwill was
supposed to portray Goethe, an evil spirit who had
fallen into a middle-class home. From the first the
book was meant as a glorification—it appeared serially in Wieland's *Teutscher Merkur*—but before
the end was reached Goethe had effected his crucifixion of *Woldemar*, had left Jacobi's letter of grievance unanswered, and now Jacobi's changed feelings
vented themselves in a diminution of Allwill's human goodness. The book ends by having a young
girl, to whom the hero has made advances, read him
the text in an unconscionably long communication.

In the letter on Allwill's childhood Jacobi has
made a crude attempt to characterize the contradictions in Goethe's make-up. He portrays the boy's
refractoriness and bravery: "Several times he took
the guilt and punishment for his comrades on him-

self; not so much out of friendship or sympathy, rather because he was disgusted at their entreaties and cries during the execution." The blandness of the young man's conduct is emphasized in the following way: "With all this there was not a shadow of impudence; on the contrary, he was so inexacting and modest toward everyone of whom he had a good opinion, so grateful and gentle, that most people thought he was either a fool or a flatterer." The young Lucie, for whom Goethe's Frankfort friend, Antoinette Gerock, is supposed to have been the model, expresses the same contradiction in Goethe's nature in her way:

> Anyone who knows you intimately must often be surprised that you have not become either an angel of virtue or a devil of vice. The inconsistencies of your character correspond to no known formula: undisciplined sensualism, and stoic, effeminate tenderness; the utmost flippancy, and the coldest heart, the firmest loyalty; the sense of a tiger and the heart of a lamb; omnipresent and nowhere; everything and nothing.

It is this same girl who at last recapitulates the spirit of the book by saying to Allwill-Goethe, in italics: "The doctrine of intemperance, the principles of debauchery carried to the utmost limit, such are the terms for what you, with the levying of much sense, sophistry, and poetic embellishment, wish to substitute for seasoned wisdom."

As for *Woldemar*, it likewise has to do with Goethe in that Jacobi, in the preface to the second edition, insists that in the course of years he had entirely forgotten the novel and its characters (that he did not even own a copy of the book) when Goethe's *Tasso* appeared and recalled to him his own Woldemar.

He must have had the ability to fancy himself
mirrored everywhere; for the similarity is slight;
the original Woldemar is merely a self-portrait.
Fritz Jacobi lived happily with his excellent wife
Betty, born von Clermont, (perhaps the model of
Therese in *Wilhelm Meister*), and at the same time
in a relation of acute intimacy with Goethe's friend
of years standing, Johanna Fahlmer. It was indubitably one of those double relations that Goethe
had in mind when he wrote his *Stella,* 1774. Its
real nature was an enigma to him. Jacobi made a
novel out of it. The heroine of his book, Henriette
by name, equipped with infinite charm and virtue,
has been recommended to Woldemar by many men
of many kinds as a suitable and desirable wife.
Woldemar sees in her nothing more than a sister.
She brings it about, however, that Woldemar marries her friend, the fascinating Alwine. She becomes and remains the third party in their alliance,
though in perfect innocence and without awakening
a shred of jealousy. If he is absent from home, she
absents herself likewise and at the same time. For
her to live without Woldemar's company is unthinkable; nor can he endure existence without her. The
tittle-tattle of gossipy people eventually force them
to separate.

In actuality the relation was such that Jacobi's
stern old father, who in the novel has become Henriette's father, was highly enraged at his son because
of some disparaging remarks he had made in a letter. Added to this is his embitterment over one of
Fritz's errors of youth; he has had a child by a
servant girl. The story leaked out, undermined
his reputation, and perhaps caused the separation

from Johanna Fahlmer. There is a possibility, indeed even a probability, that at one time or another passion flamed up between them, for they did not associate with each other as entirely non-sexual beings.

But the novel *Woldemar* is non-sexual, insipid and vacuous. For a modern individual who is not German it is unreadable. We are forced every now and then to skip over about ten pages. The sentimentality is so intolerably thick that working one's way through it is like ploughing through a mountain of porridge. The brotherly love between Woldemar and Biederthal is so effusive in letters, kisses and embraces that it is distinctly hysterical. And like unto this is all the other love in this novel, the virtuous as well as the violent. Between man and man it is as ardent as it ordinarily is between mortals of different sex. Between man and woman it is so transcendent that the suspicion as to whether they could cherish warmer feelings for each other and be other than the angels in Heaven is done into a case of immense vulgarity or repellent stupidity.

Of preaching there is no end. The popular prejudices of the age are proclaimed just as they are in the works of Goethe's youth. But this is done in such a circumstantial way that twelve pages are covered with what could have been said in one sentence. We are informed with boundless diffusiveness that we should not allow our time to be taken up with idle, senseless, social affairs. Each one should go his own way, attend to his own business, and not try to be in perfect harmony with people of different dispositions and different minds. Here is one intelligible sentence: "Was it not foolish of a so-

prano voice to undertake a duet with a trumpet?"
All the rest can be omitted. But the author is too
self-complacent to impose upon himself such limitations.

Simplicity and veracity are desired. Objections
are taken to unnecessary luxury which Diogenes and
Rousseau would endorse. Rousseau's gospel of nature in general is preached, though with the limitations of individualism. Woldemar has always been
a preacher of abstinence. He improved on the statement concerning the camel and the eye of the needle
so as to make it read: It is easier for an elephant
to go through the eye of a needle than for a rich
man to enter into the Kingdom of Heaven. The
camel was not enough for him. Later on he made
concessions. But he continues his violent attacks on
all comfort: This it is that embitters one's life.
The man for example, who wants a saddle horse
and who finally has this wish gratified, derives pleasure from his horse for a few days and then nothing
but worry. He has to ride the horse in order to give
him exercise when he has no desire at all to ride.
Peace does not return to his soul until he has sold
the beast. There is much more of the same kind.

These are his doctrines: Use your money as you
like, have beautiful rooms and beautiful clothes, but
guard against boastfulness and arrogance, do not
try to appear what you are not, have what you have
first for yourself and let others enjoy it with you!
Your own senses, reason, will—truth, harmony—
only this! And he tells in detail the story of a country fellow who so ardently longed for a pair of
leather breeches that the life of his very soul was
spent in thinking of them. It is a question of not

filling up your soul with such useless and barren thoughts.

Woldemar has theories on everything possible. He hates, for example, the nature gardens in the English style, so much admired at that time, for a garden is art, and nature neither can nor should be imitated. The cultivators of free nature should not have the right to enjoy a peach or an apricot, not even cherries, plums, and pears. Their aliment should consist of roots and wild chestnuts. In other words, Woldemar, like the author, is so opinionated that there is nothing concerning which he does not have an opinion; and he has no opinion which cannot be turned into a dogma.

Woldemar is a disciple of the Scottish popular philosophers, of Reid and especially of Ferguson. He loves virtue; and he loves it for its own sake; he abominates any sort of hedonism. To him the epitome of false philosophy is Helvetius, for Helvetius tried to deduce morality from egotism. Woldemar has tried to cultivate the animal at the bottom of his own nature, and to develop it to the highest point of perfection of which his being is capable. But in this way the last spark of real virtue vanished and man can no more live without virtue than he can live without food and drink. He was again obliged to create a virtue from the depths of his being. There follow treatises without number on virtue. No wonder that Jacobi became a believer in revelation. In his works we never detect the slightest trace of clearness, tangibility, corporality; nothing but eternal nonsense on the old spectre virtue.

Let us see how he appealed to the Dano-German

Baggesen,[14] who met him in Pyrmont during his first journey abroad in the year of the Revolution, 1789. For Baggesen, Jacobi is "an erect, remarkably well built, handsome man, and of an indescribably agreeable disposition." The Danish poet glorifies him in a passage which begins as follows:

His great and good mind shines forth unmistakably in every feature of his face, just as, to judge from all I have heard, it shines forth in every feature of his benevolent life. In his instructive and friendly society, as in his writings, thought and feeling are married to each other. He is one of the most excellent men, one whom I love and esteem most of the men on this earth. And from the moment when I first became acquainted with his heart, my resignation and admiration do not count seven stars of the first magnitude that shine with equal splendor in my idea of the human heaven. . . . His company was for me so extremely pleasant that I gave myself up to it only sparingly out of fear lest I might lose too much when obliged to leave him.

Lucky Baggesen! But poor Goethe! And to think that this Jacobi's quasi-friendly, quasi-equal relation was to be prolonged through forty years of Goethe's life!

[14] It is not surprising that Baggesen took this attitude toward Jacobi. He said of himself in 1797: "I am by nature, art, and fate a weak, fantastic, disorderly, peculiar, and passionate mortal."
—TRANSLATOR.

CHAPTER XIII

GOETHE'S BETROTHAL—LILI SCHÖNEMANN

WOLFGANG had again fallen violently in love.
Early in the year 1775 he had been introduced,
while in Frankfort, into the home of the banker
Schönemann's widow, *née* d'Orville, a well-to-do
and distinguished lady who lived in grand style.
He was at once captivated by the charming daughter
of the family, Anna Elisabeth Schönemann, then seventeen years of age. She was a beauty and a queen
of the ball. Her hair was golden and her eyes were
blue. She was confident and superior despite her
youth. She was witty, given to mocking, inclined
to be coquetish, and charming withal. Young as
she was, it is hardly thinkable that she fully appreciated the inner preëminence of Goethe, then, too,
anything but aged. But she sang his songs to piano
accompaniment; she rode out by his side like an
Amazon in full panoply. She introduced him into
her cultured though superficial world. She drew him
in short into the charmed circle of her personality
so completely and strongly that by April, 1775,
Wolfgang and Lili, as she was called and as she is
referred to in Goethe's poems, became engaged.

The betrothal was not greeted with unmixed joy
on the part of those most immediately concerned.

248

It did not suit Goethe's mother, who would have preferred to see her son married to a more quiet and domestic maiden of the city. The attitude of his sister Cornelia was distinctly hostile. Lili's mother and her guardian were opposed to the union, partly because they were familiar with the young man's earlier infatuations, partly because she was Reformed and he was Lutheran. Lili herself was ready to flee with Wolfgang to any part of the earth. She was even willing to follow him to America in case he found this move advisable.

Those were not mere external hindrances, however, on which the engagement stranded. It was the general unsuitability that became painfully evident to the young lover so soon as the first benumbing intoxication of love was a matter of history. Lili was a woman of dignity and worth, not simply a girl of attractive appearance. This has been proved completely by the courage she manifested under and during the difficult circumstances that surrounded her later in life. But she was only seventeen years old; and she gave her worshipper, all too inclined by nature to spells of jealousy, such abundant opportunity to experience the tortures of love that their betrothal seems to have been an affair of mutual anguish, interrupted at times by kisses and caresses—as so many betrothals have proved to be. But he loved her, very much indeed. A number of beautiful and genuine poems testify to posterity on this point.

We have for example the poem entitled *Neue Liebe, Neues Leben* which, with all of its effusiveness, reveals nevertheless an impulse to escape, longings begone, crossed though the impulse is with the irresistible desire to be near her. It begins:

> Herz, mein Herz, was soll das geben?
> Was bedränget dich so sehr?
> Welch ein fremdes, neues Leben!
> Ich erkenne dich nicht mehr.
> Weg ist alles, was du liebtest,
> Weg, warum du dich betrübtest,
> Weg dein Fleiss und deine Ruh—
> Ach wie kamst du nur dazu?
>
> Fesselt dich die Jugendblüthe?
> Diese liebliche Gestalt?
> Dieser Blick voll Treu und Güte
> Mit unendlicher Gewalt?
> Will ich rasch mich ihr entziehen,
> Mich ermahnen, ihr entfliehen,
> Führet mich im Augenblick
> Ach mein Weg zu ihr zurück.

There is also the lyric entitled *An Belinden,* the last two stanzas of which show clearly what plagued him and what pulled him:

> Bin ich's noch, den du bei so viel Lichtern
> An dem Spieltisch hältst?
> Oft so unerträglichen Gesichtern
> Gegenüber stellst?
>
> Reizender ist mir des Frühlings Blüthe
> Nun nicht auf der Flur;
> Wo du Engel bist, ist Lieb', und Güte,
> Wo du bist, Natur.

But the best description of the affair is not contained in the numerous letters to Auguste von Stolberg and Johanna Fahlmer, those letters in which he now in melancholy fashion calls himself "a

Shrovetide Goethe," and now places orders for jew-
elry for Lili, the most elegant that money can buy.
The best description is contained in the humorous
poem entitled *Lilis Park*. It describes a whole
menagerie that she gathers around her as around a
fairy. Like a queen she moves about among the
various sorts of animals and feeds them. The animals compete for the position of greatest propin-
quity with regard to her; they rush over and between each other. Even Jupiter's eagle and Juno's
peacock and Venus's dove come so soon as they hear
her pip. But among this fauna there is found also
an unlicked, untrained bear that Lili has brought
into this otherwise tame company and has tamed
along with the others. And this bear is happily-
unhappy when in her company:

> Zu ihren Füssen liegt das Thier.
> Sie sieht es an: "Ein Ungeheuer! doch drollig!
> Für einen Bären zu mild,
> Für einen Pudel zu wild,
> So zottig, täpsig, knollig!"
> Sie streicht ihm mit den Füssen übern Rücken;
> Er denkt im Paradiese zu sein.
> Wie ihm alle sieben Sinne jücken!
> Und sie sieht ganz gelassen drein.
> Ich küss' ihre Schuhe, kau' an den Sohlen,
> So sittig als ein Bär nur mag.
> Ganz sachte heb' ich mich und schmiege mich verstohlen
> Leis an ihr Knie. Am günst'gen Tag
> Lässt sie's geschehn und kraut mir um die Ohren
> Und patscht mich mit mutwillig derbem Schlag,
> Ich knurr' in Wonne neu geboren.

II

We have seen what made the cursorily treated
theme in *Clavigo* attractive to Goethe: the situation
of the leading character. With this he was all too
well acquainted; he himself was in it constantly, he
was constantly troubled because he could not do
as he naturally would have liked to do; he could
not, he dared not, seize and possess precisely what
he loved. Were he to do so he would be bound
for the rest of his life. This frightened him. Were
he to withdraw he would come to regard himself
as guilty, albeit the guilt would be somewhat doubtful. And of what use was it for him to pretend a
love which he no longer felt? And how could he
help that?

It is his own exalted art in *Dichtung und Wahrheit* that has turned against him and furnished material for an indictment. He has made Friederike
so enrapturing that it seemed inhuman to desert
such a being. The apparently treacherous element
in his conduct was possibly only self-preservation,
even to a certain degree, however peculiar it may
sound, self-renunciation for the sake of art.

The break with Lili must be regarded in a similar light. However indispensable she seemed to
Goethe, he nevertheless felt that he must, some how
or other, relieve himself of this situation. In many
ways Lili would have been more worthy of him and
would have suited him better than Christiane. But
he was apparently unable to endure having his peer
at his side in daily life.

Twenty years after the affair had been broken

off, and seventeen years after Lili had been married to Baron von Türkheim, she had a talk with the wife of General Beaulieu concerning Goethe. Having learned that this lady stood in close connection with Weimar, she hoped to hear some of the details of Goethe's life and fate from her.

"I consider him," she said, "as the creator of my moral existence. My passion for him was stronger than duty and virtue. I owe my own spiritual existence wholly and solely to his noble mind. I consider myself as his creation, and I shall hang on his picture with religious veneration to my very last breath." Seeing that there was only a remote possibility that she would ever come in contact with him again, she asked the lady in question to extend this greeting to her "unforgetable friend."

Goethe's "victim" cherished then no rancor against him. Quite the contrary: she continued to be grateful to him. It was however during his affair with her, in the now happy now unhappy moments, when his mind was enraptured by her beauty at the same time that he was yearning for his freedom, when she made him jealous out of thoughtlessness and yet loved him with intensity—it was then that he wrote the two operettas, *Erwin und Elmire* and *Claudine von Villabella*, together with the drama *Stella,* as evidences of their mutual infatuation.

CHAPTER XIV

Erwin und Elmire—Claudine von Villabella—
*Stella—*THE IMPRESSION GOETHE MADE

IT has become a rather fixed custom to speak of
Erwin und Elmire as a pastoral play in the same
style as *Die Laune des Verliebten.* But there is not
a shade of parallel here, even though the one be regarded as a sort of complementary piece to the
other, for in the former the girl plagues her lover
by her coldness, whereas in the latter the situation
is the reverse. *Die Laune des Verliebten* is rococo
through and through; *Erwin und Elmire,* in its first
form, has both *Götz* and *Werther,* and consequently
all Gallic form, behind it. The play opens with a
lively scene in which Olympia, elaborated with Goethe's rare mother as a model, represents, in sharp
contrast to her daughter Elmire's inactive melancholy, the defects of modern, fashionable education
as compared with the excellent features of the old,
straightforward discipline of years ago. The scene
corresponds to the one in *Götz* where both the hero
and his wife complain of the bookish training which
in reality cripples innate ability.

Elmire even dreams of the convent as a place of
refuge (just as Elisabeth in *Götz* thinks of the monastery as an asylum for Karl). But the entire situation in this case is of no particular consequence.
Through pretended indifference, Elmire has robbed

254

Erwin of his equilibrium. He has decided to disappear from sight. His friend Bernardo tells Elmire that he has ridden out and in the loneliness of
the forest has found a noble hermit, a god-like man,
who is created to give consolation to her grieved
heart. It is naturally Erwin, who has taken his
refuge in loneliness, cultivates his garden between
the mountains, and masked, with white beard and a
long cloak, learns of Elmire's despair, and at last
throws off his mask and is united with her. The
action is as juvenile as possible, but the numerous
interspersed songs, which the Duchess Amalie set
to music in 1776, are beautiful, fresh, warm, youthful, entirely worthy of Goethe.

The little operetta, originally dedicated to Lili,
is occasioned by the pangs he suffered in his relation
to her, and had thereby its natural ground of existence, and could be compared in this form with a light
frame of youth around some excellent and beautiful
songs. Some of them are to be sure so much more
natural than the frame that a false light is thrown
upon them. Take for instance the fact that, in the
poem *Ein Veilchen auf der Wiese stand,* which Erwin is supposed to have sung constantly, it is the
men folks who compare themselves with the little
violet which the young shepherdess thoughtlessly
treads under her feet. Men who compare themselves with flowers are a trifle distasteful.

The *Erwin und Elmire,* however, of the first prose
sketch was much to be preferred to the piece that
was included in Goethe's collective works as a finished operetta. The German poet certainly did not
follow Victor Hugo's rule of correcting his faults
in a succeeding work, a procedure that is most nat-

ural and commendable. The scientist is compelled
to revise, for science progresses during the years
that his work lies still. But a poet is generally punished if he allows a later idea, or a later bit of information, or a new artistic conviction, to be incorporated in an attempt of his younger days. As is
known, Goethe had a decided inclination to do this
very thing. He could never let a work that had
once been finished get out of his hands; he laid it
on the anvil again and again, and with his deep-
seated tendency to procrastination continued to
ruminate on old plans.

He took, along with so many other things, *Erwin
und Elmire* with him to Italy, subjected it to infinite
revision, transformed it into a conventional operetta
in accord with the Italian taste of that time, and
destroyed, weakened, or denatured all that had been
naïve and innocent in the original. It is strange that
he found no more productive occupation in Italy at
that mature point in his life. It is strange that he
felt no irresistible desire to create something new.
Out of the initial sketch of this work he made a
theatrical affair, written in irreproachable iambics,
with many moralizing sentences, intended for experienced singers, male and female, but heavily laden
with academic solemnity where there had once been
a wealth of youthful gaiety. The original method
of expression, with its varied locutions and phrases
direct from Frankfort, gave way to an iambic trot
that followed the rules. There is not a single
glimpse of humor in this opera text—an enlivenment
that is bitterly missed.

II

The operetta in prose, *Claudine von Villabella,*
like the first plan of *Erwin und Elmire,* belongs to
the year 1775. The play has only negligible significance; it is fanciful and easily written, but far less
puerile than its immediate predecessor. Derived
from a Spanish source, there is naturally some action
and much sabre-rattling. It reminds in truth, more
or less, of the sword and mantle dramas of the
seventeenth century. In its first fresh form, however, it bears the impress of the age to a quite
marked degree; it also reveals the youthful Goethe's
naturalistic style. The idyllic world in which the
action takes place, and in which there is a noble
father, his noble daughter, that father's noble friend,
and the daughter's noble, visionary adorer takes on
life and activity because this noble adorer has an
irresistibly captivating brother who as a vagabond,
brawler and professional seducer causes the entire
family trouble. Since he moreover falls in love with
Claudine and, during an attempt to reach her, happens, in the total darkness in which he finds himself,
to inflict a wound on his virtuous brother, there is
material for conflict, despair, gallows-humor, and a
placable ending.

The style, like that of *Götz von Berlichingen,* can
on occasion become quite vulgar. We read for example: "What! Should he any longer allow his
brother to be led astray in this dissolute life, roaming about the country in company with gamblers and
scalawags, deceiving more girls than another man
knows of, and raising a quarrel more frequently
than a drunkard urinates!"

The drama glorifies folk songs and folk melodies.
The vagrants resemble genuine romantic robbers in
that they are masters when it is a question of singing a song to the accompaniment of the guitar. Gonzalo, the old gentleman, is a friend of folk melodies.
He says, in substance: In his day the country chap
had a good time of it; he always had a song to sing
which came from the lips and went to the heart.
And when Gonzalo does honor to nature poetry it is
because he sets great store on the natural state, *à la*
Rousseau: "Where can you find nature just as it is
with my rustic brother?   He eats, drinks, works,
sleeps and loves in a perfectly straightforward
fashion and never once troubles himself a devilish
bit about the sort of hocuspocus that is employed to
mask all this in the cities and at the courts."

Gonzalo loses himself in rapture over old songs,
love melodies, stories of murder and ghosts; nowadays one would ridicule the individual who sets a
high price on such commodities.   Crugantino informs him that, quite to the contrary, all ballads and
romances and tavern songs are now zealously sought
after and translated into many languages: "Our
æsthetes compete for them."   (It is plain that the
reference is to Herder's efforts and to Goethe's folk
song collections from Alsace.)   In this connection
Gonzalo breaks out in the spirit of *Sturm und
Drang:* "That was indeed a good idea and somewhat incredible that they are gradually returning to
nature.   They used to comb the combed and curl
the curled and run their hands through their curls
and in the meantime imagine—it is hard to tell
what."

Close to this protest from this child of nature

against flourishes we have—no less in the spirit of
the age—an outburst of a rather offensive and gran-
diloquent bit of sentimentality. Crugantino, uncere-
monious coxcomb, impetuous Don Juan and robber
captain that he is, has forgotten his cithern during a
surprise. He apostrophises himself in the following
terms:

If you had only not left your cithern in the lurch! That
was a low trick for which you deserve to be boxed on the
ears by a vile wretch. Your cithern! I could become insane! What should people say of a fellow who comes out
of a fight alive and leaves his friend to the mercy of his foes?
O fie on such a fellow, fie, fie! Your cithern, of more price-
less value than ten friends! Your companion, your playmate, your sweetheart, who incidentally has outlived all your
sweethearts!

When, at the close, Crugantino defends himself,
he expresses the programme of the youth of his age.
He has been requested to conduct himself better.
He raises a question:

What does that mean, "conduct one's self better?" Do
you know the needs of a young heart such as mine? Of a
mad young head like mine? Where is there a place in the
world for one such as me? Your middle-class society is
intolerable to me. If I am to work, I must be a serf; if I
am to enjoy myself, I must be a serf. Should not one who
has a decent regard for himself rather go out in the wide,
wide world?

This is an anticipation of Schiller's Karl Moor, who
years later expressed even more solemnly the same,
or a similar, heart-throb as the shibboleth of his
soul.

The really valuable part of this drama consists

in the few interpolated songs. Though they are not
to be numbered among Goethe's very best, they
nevertheless bear the Goethean stamp. There is first
of all the song of the vagabond:

> Mit Mädeln sich vertragen,
> Mit Männern rumgeschlagen,
> Und mehr Kredit als Geld,
> So kommt man durch die Welt.

Then there is the little song entitled *Liebliches Kind,*
and first and last the magnificent ballad, one of
Goethe's most beautiful, effectively broken off in the
middle of the closing line: *Es war ein Buhle frech
genug.* It is doubly forceful since, as it originally
appears here, it is repeatedly interrupted by dialogue
and action.

The revision of the drama, which Goethe undertook twelve or thirteen years later in Italy, is quite
considerable. As is the case with the other works
revised in Italy, it is not simply the fact that iambic
pentameters take the place of prose; it is not simply
the fact that the lyric parts have been transformed
into duets, trios, quartets and choruses with the tir-
ing and tiresome repetition of the texts of the song.
The action itself is completely changed. The wild
brother to Don Pedro is no longer in love with Claudine but with her cousin, a change which weakens the
unity and suspense of the drama. Everything was
simpler and clearer in the first form.

All that can be put down here on the credit side
of the account is exclusively a matter of individual
lyric entries. They are of high rank. There is first
of all the profound and beautiful poem which, in
just a few words, reproduces the history of the soul

of many a young man in that the conflict between ambition and love is poetized:

> Es erhebt sich eine Stimme,
> Hoch and höher schallen Chöre;
> Ja, es ist der Ruf der Ehre!

Likewise Claudine's brief song:

> Liebe schwärmt auf allen Wegen.
> Treue wohnt für sich allein;
> Liebe kommt Euch rasch entgegen
> Aufgesucht will Treue sein.

In this little verse, as every connoisseur feels, romantic poetry is anticipated. There is no doubt whatever but that this touch is repeated in such a poem as this one by Tieck:

> Liebe denkt in süssen Tönen,
> Denn Gedanken stehn zu fern,
> Nur in Tönen mag sie gern
> Alles, was sie will, verschönen.

The song *Mit Mädeln sich vertragen, mit Männern rumgeschlagen* has gained by the revision; it has become fuller in content and less elementary in tone. We notice, in fine, in the entire short lyric woof the hand and style of the master. How picturesque and Goethean is the line

> Von meinem *breiten* Lager bin ich vertrieben.

Nevertheless the impression as a whole remains that Goethe, then thirty-nine years of age, would have used his precious time in Italy to infinitely better advantage had he seen fit to create something new and forget these bagatelles of his younger days.

III

It was also during his infatuation with Lili Schönemann that Goethe felt at times like the supposedly fascinating but unquestionably pitiable hero of *Stella*. The title came, as may readily be imagined, from Swift's double relation to Esther Johnson, whom he called Stella, and the other young woman who loved him, known as Vanessa. The latter wrote to Stella to find out whether the report was true concerning her clandestine marriage with Swift. In a fit of rage, Swift rushed at Vanessa and broke with her so tempestuously and violently that she became ill and died soon after of fever. Stella pined away.

From this situation we have the name. Public opinion has been irreconcilably against Stella. In Danish literature we have Wessel's[15] coarse parody. A man who loves two women, and two women who peacefully love the same man—that seemed ridiculous. And it is ridiculous according to our bringing-up and our prejudice. But there was more than one affair of that sort in those times. We have but to think of Bürger's double marriage to two sisters, which caused such a sensation in Göttingen and thereby in Germany. There was also Friedrich Ja-

[15] Johan Herman Wessel (1742-1785) was a Norwegian who wasted his life in idleness in Copenhagen. He preferred the Bohemian shiftlessness of the "Norwegian Club" to the writing of poetry—for which he had undisputed talent. Aside from a number of humorous tales in verse, such as "The Smith and the Baker," he is best known for his parodistic tragedy entitled "Love without Stockings." All the devices known to French comedy are employed, and there is abundant cause for laughter at the bizarre conceits—and good lines. Wessel threw his life away.
—TRANSLATOR.

cobi's double relation to Johanna Fahlmer, Goethe's friend, the "little aunt," as he calls her—after Cornelia's death she became Schlosser's second wife—to whom he wrote so many intimate letters, and to his own wife, Betty, an admirable woman, who had effected a reconciliation between the poet and her husband.

Goethe himself, however, was the most immediate model for his Fernando. Again and again in his life he touches upon double moods that obviously allude to motifs of the drama. He comments, by way of illustration, on the splendid feeling that arises when a new passion begins to stir within us before an old one has completely vanished: "In a similar fashion one beholds at sunset the moon rising on the opposite side of the heavens, and one cannot but rejoice in the double ray of light from the sky."

He himself stood at that time in an easy relation to the two Münch sisters; but it was Friederike more than anyone else who, in union with Johanna Fahlmer, furnished him with the model for Cäcilie; and it was the delightful young Lili who gave him the fundamental traits of Stella's character. In her there is all the power of longing, and the intense joy that comes from meeting. It is Lili, and she alone, who even twenty years later refers to herself as Goethe's creation, that is speaking when Stella says:

How often has my whole being trembled and rung when he, in unrestrained grief, emptied the sorrows of the world into my heart! I begged him for Heaven's sake to spare himself! To spare me! In vain! He fanned the flames that surged through him into my own marrow. And thus the girl became, from the crown of her head to the sole of her feet, all feeling and all heart. And where is there a place under the blue sky to-day in which this creature may breathe and find nourishment?

He has given her the joys and sorrows of a whole world, and she is aflame to the very marrow of her bones. God bless you, she says to him after he has returned. God forgive you for being so bad and so good. God forgive you—God, who has made you so—so fickle and so true. She is lovesick, cares not at all about marriage, and does not learn until later that it is impossible.

Goethe has made a weak attempt to give the impression of a strong character in Fernando by showing the passion he arouses even in the case of his administrator. Thank God, the administrator says, that you were not a gipsy chieftain. At a mere suggestion from you I would have burned and pillaged. It is also the administrator who explains to us why Fernando has deserted the good, amiable Cäcilie: his nature will not tolerate being tied down:

I was a fool, you said to me, to permit myself to be bound. This status chokes my powers; it robs my soul of its courage; it hems me in on all sides. And there is so much to me! Think of the extent to which I might develop myself! I must out and away into the wide world!

It is in passages such as this that one feels the mighty model back of this miserable hero. Goethe will have Cäcilie restore to Fernando his original freedom, and she is to do it out of magnanimity and from the purest of motives. Fernando, however, feels bound to her just as he is bound to Stella. His relation to Cäcilie is in truth of longer standing and greater delicacy. After a moment of idyllic happi-

ness, the Medusa-head of indignation arises and
stays aloft, until the heart of a woman who feels
with strength and vigor speaks the redeeming
words: Here is nothing to be palliated, but also
nothing that cannot be expiated.

Cäcilie tells the story of the German Graf von
Gleichen who returns from the Crusade with the
beautiful Oriental woman who has liberated him
from slavery. His wife embraced the Saracen and
said: "Take everything I can give you! Take the
half of what belongs to you entirely. Take him
entirely! Leave him altogether to me!" She threw
herself on his neck, and then at his feet, and said:
"We are thine!" The close of the drama is noticeably analogous to that of the legend in that Stella
says: "I am thine!" Cäcilie concludes with the remarks: "We are thine!"

The intended effect of the play stranded on the
wretchedness of Fernando's character: he is really
too undependable, too pitiable. He takes leave of
Stella without even saying farewell and runs after
Cäcilie, having in the meanwhile learned where she
is staying. But he had not been able to live with
her! Hardly has he found Stella, to whom he promises unbroken happiness in the future, until he makes
the same promise to Cäcilie, and prepares to abandon Stella, clandestinely and again without saying
farewell. His plan is betrayed by the wrath of a
waitress at his scurvy conduct. He is pitiable, and
as a symbol of all his pitiableness stands his declaration to Cäcilie that when he could find no trace of
her, he used his time—instead at least of returning
to Stella—in fighting against the noble Corsicans
(the revolt of Paoli), whose struggle for liberty he

admired. One of Goldschmidt's[16] characters later conducted himself in a similar fashion. The reference is to his *Arvingen*. Fernando says:

I could find no trace of you. Tired of myself and of life, I entered foreign military service, put on this uniform, and helped in the suppression of the noble Corsican's liberty.

It was quite impossible, naturally, for Goethe to let *Stella* rest in peace—two parodies on it had already appeared by 1776. In 1805, he completely remodelled the ending: In later editions, Stella takes poison and Fernando shoots himself.

IV

How are we to explain the fact that all of these heroes correspond so imperfectly to what Goethe really meant by them? The explanation is not far to seek: it lies in Goethe's shyness; in his reserve; in his modesty, a modesty that saved him from displays of ostentation. He was himself the model in all his weakness. But he could not bring himself to ascribe to the characters also his own insusceptibility, his own greatness. Of these virtues we learn nothing from him; for information concerning them we are obliged to appeal to his contemporaries.

[16] Meier Aron Goldschmidt (1819-1887) was Denmark's first journalist in a modern sense. A Jew himself, he did much to call the attention of Denmark to the Jews within her boundaries. After a fairly successful attempt at journalism, he established his *Corsaren* (The Corsair) in 1840 and made it a powerful and dreaded organ until it was discontinued in 1846. He fought for the ideas and ideals of a republic, attacked absolutism from every conceivable angle—and wrote some of the best short stories that have ever been written in the Danish language. As he grew older he became more conservative. His *Arvingen* (The Heir), a novel, appeared in 1865.
—TRANSLATOR.

In the thoughtless, tactless, overweening superciliousness of youth, he had offended nearly all of
them.   And yet!   He had written his satirical review of Lavater's *Aussicht in die Ewigkeit* for the
Frankfurter Gelehrte Anzeigen of November, 1772.
There he said:

> Those who thirst after eternity always prepare for them-
> selves that particular sort of sustenance, up in Paradise, that
> tickled their palates here, whether we have to do with the
> Heaven of the Orientals, or the Beer Hall or Valhalla of the
> Northern peoples.   Lavater opens up a view for thinkers
> and scholars only.   What he says is well meant, but it does
> not come from the soul.

A year later, November 9, 1773, Lavater writes
to Herder concerning Goethe:

> It seems that we shall come closer together.   I rejoice
> with trembling.   Among all the writers I know there is no
> greater genius.   And yet, I had a kind of foreboding that
> that firm, smooth, straightforward, fraternal simplicity, that
> quiet though gorgeous humanity, would not be found in
> him in perfect proportion with his ability to think and feel.

On December 30 of the same year, however, he
writes:

> Goethe calls me brother; how shall I call him, the Unique?
> He is the incomparable, the fearfully exalted among men.
> But, dear brother, what objection have you to Christ?

Criticism of all kind is, however, soon eliminated.
Lavater writes to his friend Zimmermann:

> You would idolize Goethe.   He is the most fearful and
> amiable of men.   He would make a glorious, vigorous crea-
> ture for a prince.   He could be king.

Heinse, the author of *Ardinghello,* writes at the same time:

Goethe called on us. From top to toe, genius, power, strength, a heart full of feeling, a mind full of fire and equipped with the wings of the eagle. Resistance is impossible; he carries everything along with him.

Goethe had given open expression to his aversion with regard to the effeminate tendency of the Jacobis. As late as May 28, 1773, he sent his satire on Fr. Heinrich Jacobi to Klopstock, "the wildest I have ever written," he said, "I am sure it will never be published." Jacobi cherished a cordial grudge against Goethe, and warned Wieland against "this audacious person whose whims are incalculable." From the moment they first met, however, in July, 1773, Jacobi's hatred was metamorphosed into a species of adoring admiration. He writes to Wieland:

The more I think about it the more I appreciate the impossibility that resides in the attempt on the part of anyone who has never seen, never heard Goethe to write anything comprehensible on this extraordinary creation of God. Goethe is one possessed, one who is quite infrequently permitted to act arbitrarily. You hardly need to spend an hour with him without finding it extremely ridiculous for him to think or act other than he does.

Wieland sends the following jocular reply:

Dear brother, I beg you on bended knee to read *Don Quixote* until you have completely cured yourself of this gigantic style.

Two years later, however, the turn came to him who had been so ferociously scorned, even annihi-

lated, by Goethe in *Götter, Helden und Wieland.*
On November 10, 1775, Wieland wrote to Jacobi:

What shall I say to you about Goethe?   How completely
he won my heart at first sight!   How infatuated I became
in him when one day I chanced to sit by his side at the table!
This splendid young man!   All that I can say to you on
this subject is that since this morning my soul has been as
full of Goethe as a dew-drop is full of the morning sun. . . .
Ah, if he were to remain with us!   Between Goethe and
myself it has come to the point where the World, Sin, Death,
and Hell are no longer of avail.

To Merck he writes:

Is there another instance on record where one poet has
loved another poet with such inspired affection?   For me
life is no longer possible without this marvelous chap whom
I love as my own son.   And like a genuine father, I rejoice
to see him outgrowing me in such a delightful manner.

In January, 1776, he writes:

I have now lived nine weeks with Goethe, and have been
living since the union of our souls . . . completely in him.
Viewed from any point, from every angle, he is the greatest,
best, most glorious, human creature God has ever created.
. . . There was a certain hour to-day when I had an opportunity to see him in his full glory. . . . Beside myself, I
knelt before him, pressed his soul to my heart, and worshipped God.

During his stay in the home of Frau von Keller,
on January 1, 1776, Wieland expresses his Goethe
rapture in dithyrambic verse.   Here are a dozen or
so specimen lines:

Mit einem schwarzen Augenpaar,
Zaubernden Augen voll Götterblicken,
Gleich mächtig zu tödten und zu entzücken,
So trat er unter uns, herrlich und hehr,
Ein ächter Geisterkönig, daher!

Und Niemand fragte: Wer ist denn Der!
Wir fühlten beim ersten Blick: s'war Er!
Wir fühlten's mit allen unsern Sinnen
Durch alle unseren Adern rinnen,
So hat sich nie in Gottes Welt
Ein Menschensohn uns dargestellt.

Der all Güte und alle Gewalt
Der Menschheit so in sich vereinigt!
So feines Gold, ganz reiner Gehalt
Von fremden Schlacken so ganz gereinigt!
Der unzerdrückt von ihrer Last
So mächtig alle Natur erfasst,
So tief in jedes Wesen sich gräbt
Und doch so innig im ganzen lebt.
Das lass' ich mir einen Zaubrer sein.
Wie werden mit ihm die Tage zu Stunden,
Die Stunden wie augenblicks verschwunden,
Und wieder Augenblicke so reich,
An innerm Werthe Tagen gleich!

True enough, it is Goethe's countrymen who are
speaking here, and Germans from the age of European sentimentality at that; but it is merely a case
of outshone rivals, who are not generally inclined
to songs of praise. And let it not be forgotten, they
are men whom Goethe, in the pride of his youth,
had deeply offended.

There remains sufficient testimony to give us a
vivid idea of the impression of power and genius
which the young Goethe made on the most illustrious
of his contemporaries, and on women no less than
on men. But we know too how he, unfortunately,
with all too great conscientiousness belittled himself
as the leading character in the works of his youth,
with the result that it is almost only his weakness
that we see.

CHAPTER XV

Der ewige Jude—Hanswursts Hochzeit

AMONG the numerous plans which the young Wolfgang made in his twenty-fifth year was also the superb description in verse of the peregrinations of the wandering Jew through all ages and all lands, hoping thereby to produce a concise picture of the spiritual and ecclesiastical history of the human race. He discussed the plan and gave completed specimens of it to Lavater in June 1774, on the journey from Wiesbaden to Schwalbach, and again a few weeks later at the dinner table in Ems. Lavater speaks of the work as though it were already a finished whole. In the meantime, however, Goethe abandoned the plan completely. He never finished more than ten pages. Again we have doggerel, vivacious, warm and warlike, but far too little to give us an idea of the intended work. We can only see that it would have been a virile attack on orthodoxy and the clergy without regard to confessional differences.

The tone of *Der ewige Jude* is disrespectful. The shoemaker of Jerusalem is portrayed quite as though he were a contemporary. He had a sanctimonious mind, was half Essenian and half Methodist. Indeed he is even called a Moravian. He and his kind demand daily signs and wonders, shake their heads

at the daughters of Zion, and make greater requests
of the clergy than the latter fulfill.

The clergy were then exactly as they were in the
eighteenth century, or just as it is apt to be with anyone on taking up office.   However zealous they may
have been at first, busy as ants and wise as serpents,
so soon as they don their frocks they take it easy
and grow fat.   The philosophers of that time were
also about as they were eighteen hundred years later.
They assumed a supercilious attitude toward what
other people took seriously, though they did not
make any marked advance:

> Ihr *non plus ultra* jeder Zeit
> War Gott zu lästern und den Dreck zu preisen.

The fragment contains otherwise not a single line
on the Jew's offense against Jesus, nor does it contain any on his wanderings over the earth.   We
know only from *Dichtung und Wahrheit* that it was
Goethe's intention, among other things, to have the
Jew pay a visit to Spinoza; and it was a happy idea
to have these two characters meet face to face.
Unfortunately, it remained nothing but an idea.

We have the portrayal in verse of a situation in
Heaven between the Father and the son.   The
Father calls out two or three times in vain to His
son, who finally comes stumbling across the stars:
he has been on one of them helping a woman in
child-birth.   The Father commands him rather to
return to earth and see how things are going on
there.   The son swings down to earth, and on his
arrival is immediately reminded of the wretched
manner in which he was treated during his first
sojourn there.

The verses which depict the emotion of Jesus the
second time he breathes the air of the earth are
beautiful indeed and replete with genuine feeling.
The son is brought to realize how even the purest of
happiness has in it at least the presentiment of sorrow. He greets the earth as he saw it the last time
from the heights of Golgotha:

Sei Erde tausendmal gegrüsst!
Gesegnet alle meine Brüder;
Zum ersten Mal mein Herz ergiesst
Sich nach drei tausend Jahren wieder
Und wonnevolle Zähre fliesst
Vom nimmer trüben Auge nieder.
O mein Geschlecht, wie sehn ich mich nach dir!

He tarries for a moment on the mountain where
friend Satan tempted him; he looks about and discovers to his painful surprise that it is this same
gentleman, the Prince of Darkness, who has conquered and is ruling over the earth. Everywhere
scurvy covetousness stretches forth her greedy claws;
everywhere the prince shuts himself in with his
slaves in his marble castle and squanders nourishment enough for thousands; everywhere the golden
sign of Jesus's sufferings of the past glistens as it
depends from the breasts of those who wear it officially, idle and pudgy now that they have become.

By the Prince, Goethe manifestly thought of
Louis XV, who was contemporaneous. The country
first described is Catholic; but when Jesus goes from
this to a Protestant people he finds that precisely
similar conditions obtain. On leaving the land of
the crucifixes he comes to a land where it is impossible to feel or see that there is any God at all; he
visits a Protestant clergyman who has a fat wife;

the twain are in bed; they have many children; and
they have many tithes.

> Er war nunmehr der Länder satt,
> Wo man so viele Kreuze hat
> Und man für lauter Kreuz und **Christ**
> Ihn eben und sein Kreuz vergisst.
> Er trat in ein benachbart Land
> Wo er sich nur als Kirchfahn fand,
> Man aber sonst nicht merkte sehr
> Als ob ein Gott im Lande wär.

Accompanied by the pastor, Christ betakes himself to the city where a convention of clergymen was
to be held on that particular day. Asked at the city
gate to give his name and rank, he replies with
marked humility and modesty, "I am the Son of
Man." The scribe fails to grasp this statement
until a brandy corporal remarks by way of elucida-
tion: "His father's name must have been *Man*."
Jesus asks to be conducted to the senior pastor. He
and his companion are received, however, by no
more pretentious person than the cook who, drop-
ping a head of cabbage from her apron, says that the
pastor has already gone to the conference. It was
Goethe's plan to depict an entire group of degenerate, worldly-minded clergymen who make up the
assembly, but the poem breaks off at this point.

It is highly illuminating to compare this work on
the descent of Jesus to earth, written in the year
1774, the product of the free-thinking young man,
with the account of Christ's descent into Hell, written in the year 1765, the product of the orthodox
boy.

II

Another fragment from the year 1774, unimportant in itself though written in a fiery mood, is *Hanswursts Hochzeit.* Though farther from being complete than the above work, it testifies to the poet's most defiant and disdainful mood. It was sketched in all probability while Goethe was engaged to Lili, and while he was meditating on his own wedding.

A young man, of whom it is said that he is known the world over, and referred to as a genius from Salzburg to Petersburg, appears in fool's dress: it is Goethe himself in the guise of Hanswurst. He is told not to be so gruff, as geniuses generally are. The fragment portrays the tortures and oppressions the poet had to endure from his latterly acquired fame over the publication of *Werther.*

As a starting point, Goethe had taken an old melodrama from the seventeenth century, *Harlekins Hochzeitsschmaus,* though he retained nothing more than the title and a few characters. Goethe's Hanswurst wallows in the coarsest of linguistic expressions: he uses words which in the German of our day cannot be printed. Kilian Brustfleck—another Harlekin—the guardian of Hanswurst, challenges the latter, now that he is a bridegroom, to become dignified and never to use a wanton word. He can take his redress in silence by living just as stark mad a life as he pleases. Famous as he is, there will be wedding guests in profusion. The entire address-book of the Germanic world will be represented. Hanswurst replies in language that cannot be quoted, saying that these guests will do nothing more than

eat at the wedding feast, whereas his immediate
yearnings are of a different nature: He would much
prefer to take his Ursel along with him up to the
hayloft.

This is virtually all that has been worked out.
But Goethe amused himself by giving a list of the
names of the expected wedding guests, a list in which
he displays a genuine Rabelasian fancy. It is sufficient to name just a few of them: Ursel Blandine,
Braut; Ursel mit dem kalten Loch, *Tante;* Hans
Arsch von Rippach; Hans Arschchen von Rippach,
empfindsam; Schindluder; Thomas Stinkloch, *nichts
Gerings;* Blackscheisser, *Poet.* There is a catalogue
of no fewer than one hundred and fifty such proper
names. It was probably Goethe's purpose, when he
used them, to stigmatize some of his contemporaries
against whom he bore an unrelenting grudge.

There is a rejected outline of the twenty-second
chapter of Heine's *Atta Troll* which is constructed
on an idea similar to this. It is the chapter in which
King Solomon proposes riddles to the Queen of
Sheba. Among others there is this one: Who is the
greatest scoundrel among all German scoundrels?
The Queen mentions one name after another:

> Hundert Namen hat seitdem
> Schon die Königin eingesendet;
> Immer schrieb zurück der König:
> Kind, das ist noch nicht der grösste.

Heine's idea however, as is so frequently the case
with his poetic conceits, was carried out, though
later replaced by another poem. Goethe's plan was
left lying as a fragment of five or six pages, never
again to be taken up.

CHAPTER XVI

Knebel's Visit: Weimar—The Stolbergs; Journey to Switzerland

On December 11, 1774, Goethe received a visitor whose message was to have a decisive influence on the course of his life from that moment on: Karl Ludwig von Knebel called. He was an amiable Prussian officer, the senior of his host by five years. He had entered upon a position in Weimar as a tutor to the young Prince Konstantin. He it was who introduced Goethe to Karl August, heir presumptive to the throne of Sachse-Weimar, then on a journey through the country which included Frankfort as a stopping place.

The state to which the Prince was to fall heir was a very small one; Thuringia was in general the homestead of petty principalities. In Ruhla in the Thuringian Forest, a brook in the middle of the village separated the land of Gotha from that of Weimar. A student, in case he were a trifle jubilant, could start a quarrel with the police of five different sovereigns while taking a single walk. Even forty years later, in 1815, there were 700,000 people in Thuringia under the sway of no fewer than five Saxon dynasties, three from the House of Reuss, and two from the House of Schwarzburg. On no less than three different occasions had this country been a nursery of German intellectual and

spiritual life: In its day, the Wartburg was the home
of the Minnesingers; it later became Luther's place
of refuge; and a still more glorious fate was in store
for Weimar.

Weimar, nowadays the city of great memories—
venerable as a museum, small in compass, beautiful
and smiling, gliding in and out through avenues and
gardens in which the ducal park, intersected by the
Ilm, constitutes a sort of central point, was, at the
beginning of the year 1774, very much smaller and
very much poorer, just a little town surrounded by
wall and moat.

Over the tiny state there ruled a young, vivacious,
capable widow, some thirty years old, Anna Amalie,
as regent for her son not yet of age. She was a
Princess of Brunswick, a niece of Frederick the
Great. She was married at the age of seventeen to
the Duke of Weimar. She became a widow at the
age of nineteen, then *enceinte* with her second son.
While she herself ruled to the best of her knowledge, she took all possible pains with the education
of her oldest son. When only five years of age he
received as his tutor a certain Count Görtz, who,
however, in the opinion of his mother, tried to win
the favor of the heir to the throne by being far too
lenient toward the fiery, intractable boy. (This is
the Görtz alluded to in *Stella,* scene one, where they
speak of old political crones who start gossip.)

Anna Amalie was one of the few German Princesses who at that time did not hold the German
language in contempt. At her court both German
and French were spoken, and as her son grew up
she asked the advice of Wieland, her guest from
time to time, as to the boy's capabilities. Wieland

had just written his *Goldener Spiegel* in which he
spoke the truth to German Princes in a jesting way.
Since his letter of response strongly praised the
Prince's intellect, studiousness, love of truth, and
aversion to flattery, it came natural to the Duchess
to persuade Wieland to take over the position of
teacher of philosophy for her two sons.

There was an especial need that Karl August's
disposition be changed; he was cold, unapproachable, gruff. The tutor was to ennoble and mollify
his charge's nature. He was to make him more
accessible to other people —including his mother.

The gentle and timid Wieland had, however, done
nothing but join forces with the courtier Görtz, so
that the Duchess soon came to the conclusion that
the count and the poet together, as indeed all the
others at the court, were flattering her son, and,
with an eye single to the future, were correcting
him too rarely and too mildly. Even the secretary
of the treasury, who was constantly reminding her
of the lack of money, had an abundance for Karl
August, not yet of age. On this account the relation
between the mother and the son became tense and
bitter.

The energetic and imperious lady would not let
her boy have his own way, lest he come to grief
because of lack of early discipline. The son in turn
was highly offended because his mother slighted
him. Was she not accustomed to calling him Prince
just as she called his younger brother whom she
preferred? Should she not call him Duke, even
as a minor? The Duchess became in time so unhappy over the general dissatisfaction that prevailed
at the court that she actually thought of resigning

the regency one year before the appointed time.
Her Prime Minister dissuaded her from so doing.

Moreover, at the beginning of the year 1774, a
great misfortune befell Weimar: the sole building
of really palatial proportions, the castle and the
theatre connected with it, was burned to the ground.
This gave rise to new discord between the mother
and her determined son. Amalie, believing that the
decision should come from her, decided to take up
her official residence in three private houses that lay
side by side. But the heir to the throne, seeing that
the decision would still be in effect during the first
years of his own reign, chose, as the ducal residence,
a larger and more imposing villa, then in process of
erection. He carried out his determination, though
the house in question, having been built rapidly and
carelessly, proved to be a distinctly unsanitary and
disagreeable place of abode.

In September, 1774, the Duchess introduced Karl
August, then seventeen years old, into the council
of state; in other words, he was treated as a mature
individual. But she still denied him the title of Duke
and he, in turn, was now too proud to demand it.

Since she thought of forming a small court for
him, she asked him to tell her which of the gentlemen of the royal household he preferred. No
sooner, however, had he named some of his own
favorites when he was informed that he could choose
only from the gentlemen of the bedchamber. He
named then, among others, the master of horse,
Baron Gottlob von Stein, destined eventually to become famous on account of his wife.

The Duchess had formerly expressed quite vigorous opposition to every journey that had been pro-

posed for her son; she was even unwilling to have
him stay at a university. Now, however, she permitted Karl August to travel, though with the sole
and distinct purpose of selecting for himself a
fiancée. They ran through the lists of marriageable
princesses and the mother's choice fell on Princess
Luise of Hessen-Darmstadt. His desire to marry
was in reality no stronger than Frederick the Great's
had been when his father forced him into marriage
with a princess whom he neither loved nor knew
nor cared to know. And yet, Karl August acquiesced in his mother's wishes. The journey could
be made; Karl August and Konstantin, with their
tutors, could set out for France. They were to stop
on the way in Karlsruhe where the Princess was
then visiting, her acquaintance was to be made and,
if possible, the engagement was to be announced.

In December, 1774, the Princes began their journey, accompanied by their tutors, the above-mentioned Count Görtz and the poet Knebel, the latter
of whom was to achieve substantial fame as the
translator of Alfieri and Propertius, and especially
of Lucretius's didactic poem entitled *De rerum natura*. They were also accompanied by the master-
of-horse, Baron von Stein, and the court physician.
They arrived at Frankfort on December 10; they
could remain there but a few days. There was living at that time a young man in Frankfort whom
they were exceedingly anxious to see: He was supposed to be a genius—in the language of the age,
a Heaven-stormer—had written a dramatized history entitled *Götz* which Karl August had found
excellent, also a novel entitled *Werthers Leiden*,
which was regarded as magnificent though it had

made no impression on the heir presumptive to the throne—sentimentality was not his affair. The author had, to be sure, derided the Prince's popular teacher, Wieland, but only in a farce; moreover, the one criticised had himself admitted, with the refinement and discretion of a great talent, that the aforesaid farce was a little masterpiece of persiflage and sophistic wit. Not even that bit of facetious writing could hurt him in the eyes of the young Prince. The handsome, stately Knebel, then thirty years old and an admirer of talent wherever he saw it, took it upon himself to call on this uncommon personality. He entered the beautiful old house Am Hirschgraben wherein he found a man twenty-five years old, erect and splendid to behold, apart from his brilliant eyes. Knebel was at once all fire and flame. On being told that the Princes, who were staying at the Römischer Kaiser, were to leave the following day, he went along back with Knebel to the hotel.

Thus Karl August and Goethe stood face to face for the first time in their lives. The Prince, seventeen years of age, made a pronounced impression on the Poet: What the former said was clear and vigorous; though short and slender, he was by no means without dignity; he was quick-witted; he expressed himself in plain and simple terms; there was nothing forced or affected about him. Goethe saw that that was a prince in whom he could take hope.

But the Poet made a far stronger impression on the Prince: His mercurial liveliness, his conversation in which he gushed forth conceit after conceit and revealed an abundant store of ideas, capitvated Karl August completely. Goethe was obliged to remain

until evening. Nor was this all: the Prince invited
him to visit him again in Mayence. Knebel remained in Frankfort with Goethe so as to accompany him.

Their association was renewed in Mayence. For
Knebel Goethe was even now "the very best of all
men." This remark impressed the Prince, having
as he did a high regard for Knebel. They discussed
Goethe's farce on Wieland. With remarkable self-
depreciation, the young poet called the little masterpiece "a jocular prank." The best impression of
all was made by the fact that in a postscript to a
letter from Knebel to Wieland he himself characterized his attack as a mere joke.

In Karlsruhe the Prince's engagement took place.
He and Goethe met again, the latter having gone
there on a short visit.

II

The two young Stolbergs, both of them poets in
a small way—Count Christian was the older, Count
Friedrich Leopold was the less gifted—had just
finished their studies at the university and, after the
fashion of the time, had started out on what was
then popularly known as a *Geniereise*. Auguste von
Stolberg, later the wife of the Danish Minister
A. P. Bernstorff,[17] had for a long while been carry-

[17] Count Andreas Peter Bernstorff (1735-1797), hardly less renowned than his uncle, Johan Hartvig Bernstorff, was twice married, his two wives being the sisters of the Counts Christian and
Friedrich zu Stolberg. Entering the service of his state as early
as 1759, he remained in it until his death, except for brief periods
of "dismissal," as, for example, at the time of the Struensee affair.
He played a decisive rôle in the incidents preceding the Napoleonic
Wars, and is regarded by many careful students as one of Denmark's greatest benefactors.   —TRANSLATOR.

ing on an intimate correspondence with Goethe,
though he never came to know her personally.
Under these circumstances it was quite natural that
the brothers should visit the poet in Frankfort.
They suggested to him that he accompany them on
their journey to Switzerland. The party was further augmented by Count Kurt von Haugwitz, with
whom Goethe was soon on an intimate footing. Von
Haugwitz later entered the diplomatic service and,
as Minister of Prussia, failed to shed lustre on the
affairs of his country during the years of Napoleon's
unusual activity, 1805 and 1806. The Stolbergs
were two of the eggs Klopstock had hatched. At
this stage of their careers they were rather unset-
tled nature poets and visionaries with regard to
liberty and freedom: It was not always easy to surmise that they were counts of the blood from their
external deportment.

In the same year, Fritz Stolberg wrote in his *Ode
an die Freiheit:*

> Nur Freiheitsschwert ist Schwert für das Vaterland!
> Wer Freiheitsschwert hebt, flammt durch das
>   Schlachtgewühl
> Wie Blitz des Nachtsturms! Stürzt Paläste!
> Stürze Tyrann dem Verderber Gottes!
>
> O Namen, Namen festlich wie Siegesgesang!
> Tell! Hermann! Klopstock! Brutus! Timoleon!

As we see, Klopstock is placed between Arminius
and Brutus among the heroes of liberty. The
brothers belonged to the *Göttinger Hain* and, like
their sister, became attached to Denmark. Both of
them also became in time zealous reactionaries.
Friedrich Stolberg's conversion to Catholicism cre-

ated at that time a great sensation and caused his
break with Voss, who wrote on this occasion his
polemical pamphlet entitled *Wie ward Fritz Stolberg ein Unfreier?*

At this first meeting both brothers were tremendously enthusiastic about Goethe; the journey was
begun in Werther costume. The young men were
kindly received in Darmstadt by Merck and in Karlsruhe they met, aside from Karl August, the future
Duchess Luise von Weimar, of whom Goethe wrote:
"Luise is an angel." He gathered up some flowers
that fell from her bosom and kept them in his letter
case. In Strassburg the cordial relation with Lenz
was renewed. Goethe could not help but think, with
sorrow of course, of Friederike, whom he did not
wish to grieve with a visit so soon after his first
affair. In Emmendingen he visited his sister, then,
as he knew, physically broken down and very low-
spirited. But Wolfgang's stay had a good effect
upon her; she felt quite happy for a few days in his
presence.

The young travellers saw the Rhine Falls at
Schaffhausen. Goethe received his first strong impression of Swiss scenery which, however, aside
from *Jery und Bätely*, he never glorified, though he
kept it all so well in his mind that he was in a position later in life to entrust the reproduction of it,
with all the material for *Wilhelm Tell,* to his friend
Schiller.

In the month of June Goethe rode into Zürich
where he stayed with Lavater and made the acquaintance of a number of prominent Swiss citizens,
including old Bodmer, who had once invited the
sacred poet of *Der Messias* to spend some time with

him, and who soon felt quite surprised at the way
Klopstock flirted with all the pretty girls.   Klopstock and his host separated in coolness.   Bodmer
was then seventy-seven years old and saw in Goethe
only a hot-head.   Among his observations on him,
two are especially worthy of note: Goethe called
Brutus and Cassius scoundrels (*Niederträchtige*)
because they stabbed Cæsar from the rear; and it is
said that Goethe is planning to write a tragedy on
Dr. Faustus, a theme out of which this mad-cap
could make a better farce than a tragedy.

Goethe indulged in some mountain climbing, including St. Gothard.   From Altdorf he dispatched
a short, cordial note and a longer and no less cordial
poem to Charlotte Kestner.   A few days later he
wrote to Lili the little poem beginning:

> Wenn ich, liebe Lili, dich nicht liebte,
> Welch Wonne gäb' mir mir dieser Blick!

At the same time he jotted down in his diary the
jubilant and unsentimental exclamation:

> Ohne Wein und ohne Weiber
> Hol' der Teufel unsre Leiber.

Directly underneath this he entered the evidence of
his devotion to nature:

> Ich saug an meiner Nabelschnur
> Nun Nahrung aus der Welt,
> Und herrlich rings ist die Natur,
> Die mich am Busen hält.

At the close of July he was back in Frankfort.
He had not yet broken with Lili.   He went riding
with her, attacked though he was by another fit of

jealousy and not unaware of the dissatisfaction felt by the older generation at the thought of a union between the two. The break was imminent and he himself was at once moved and depressed. The work he had planned on *Egmont* simply would not progress.

Karl August had repeatedly asked him to come to Weimar on a visit. Goethe kept the invitation open by sending him, through Knebel, some of his works. Then, on September 3, 1775, Karl August took the reins of government in his own hands. On October 12, he came to Frankfort with his young consort. The invitation to Weimar was renewed in more definite form: Goethe, accompanied by Chamberlain von Kalb, who was then in Karlsruhe, was to betake himself to the Thuringian capital.

CHAPTER XVII

Urfaust

BUT before things had reached this stage, young Wolfgang had written still another work, this time a dramatic fragment. He seems to have got the idea at the close of 1773. He elaborated the first and larger half between October 1774, and the beginning of 1775; the second and smaller half in the late summer and autumn of 1775. Then he laid the manuscript aside just as it was until 1788, when, during his second sojourn in Rome, he took it up again and tried to work himself into the spirit and tone of those younger days. He did not publish it until 1700; it came out as a "Fragment."

What he finished however in the autumn of 1775 —he was then twenty-six years old—was, it matters not how slipshod his treatment of the theme may have been, the best bit of poetry that had been written on this earth within the past one hundred and seventy years. Goethe himself never surpassed it. Beginning with *Faust* 1775, he stands on such a height as a poet that his name is inscribed by the side of the greatest of all mortals. These eighty-nine pages contain a riotous sum of feeling, wit, fancy, and reason, an abundance of genuine euphony and such inimitable art in the portrayal of the three fundamentally human and yet symbolic characters, and in some of the subordinate characters as well,

288

that all criticism about petty points disappears before an inevitable admiration that is akin to reverence. This is written for all time; it will never be
forgotten so long as the German language is understood.

If one attempts to explain just why these pages
are, as it were, asbestos, why they can be destroyed
neither by fire nor by water nor by time, one sees
that the explanation lies first and foremost in the
fact that Goethe has gone deep down into the purely
elementary and quite original element in the life
of feeling and passion of a childlike young woman.
He has sung of that which is indissoluble in its
eternal simplicity, unshakable, as strong as granite.
In direct contrast to this he has placed the investi-
gative spirit of the man who yearns for definitive
knowledge regarding the constituency of the cosmos, the forces of nature, all the rich and mysterious meaning of life, and his intense though transitory longing for the young woman who entices,
moves, and melts him without being able to hold
him. The meeting and association between these
two is emphasized, placed in strong relief, by the
scenes between Marthe and Mephistopheles.
Marthe, humorously conceived, is the older and
more experienced neighbor, who is as if made to be
a procuress, though she herself seeks the men with
pleasurable intent. Mephistopheles is neither the
Devil of the Mediæval Mysteries and Moralities,
nor the evil incarnate of the theologians, nor the
fallen angel in his rebellion against the God of the
Bible, nor the Satan of Milton, nor the Lucifer of
Byron. He is the cynic who is never ridiculous and
revolutionary, a thorough judge of man, a witty

head without kindliness, a stranger to compassion, a
figure whose very being consists in seeing through
men and the plans of men, an agent of cold mockery
and supercilious caprice.

The Faust theme is a very old one. It was first
recorded (1587) by the bookdealer, Johann Spies
of Frankfort, and dramatized in London by Chris-
topher Marlowe (1589), the re-creator of English
tragedy. Marlowe's is an ingenious and juvenile
work. After having been carefully staged, it was
performed for the first time since the days of Elizabeth in London in the summer of 1896. The impression the performance made was more nearly
that of a Mediæval Mystery than of a Renaissance
drama. Marlowe was the first to put the spirit of
rebellion in Faust, originally merely a shade and a
conjurer. What Marlowe's Faust longs for is
power, earthly omnipotence; Goethe's Faust strives
after wisdom, earthly omniscience. The energy of
the entire Renaissance, combined with that of Marlowe himself, is to be found in the English Faust;
thirst for knowledge such as characterized the age
of Humanism, combined with that of Goethe himself, animates the German Faust. His point of departure is his grief and anxiety at the inadequacy
of his knowledge; he is depressed at the thought of
his fragmentary insight into the nature, the ideas
of the cosmos.

In Germany Marlowe's drama was first arranged
for the folk-stage and then adapted to the puppet-
theatre. In a letter from Mendelssohn, dated November 19, 1775, we learn that Lessing intended
to write a middle-class *Faust*. In reality Lessing
had two *Faust* plans in mind: one that followed

tradition and exploited spirits and devils; another in which the seducer of the leading character was to have a purely human nature. The single scene, "Faust with the seven spirits," of a *Doktor Faust,* which Lessing published in the seventeenth *Litera-turbrief,* February 16, 1759, corresponds to the old Christian view which saw something uncommonly devilish in the specially rapid gratification of the senses.

From Marlowe the tradition was handed down to Goethe, *via* the puppet-theatre, that Faust should begin with a monologue in which he lashed the faculties of the universities. Even in the *Urfaust,* 1775, this monologue has its full power and boldness. Only the introductory lines, which were a trifle unfelicitous, were speedily revised into the admirably vivacious ones that we of to-day all know by rote. Otherwise the monologue as a means of dramatic exposition was taken over by Goethe from Hans Sach's diminutive dramas, to which Goethe here reverts, as he did so frequently in the works of his youth. From Hans Sachs he had borrowed the tetrametric doggerel which in his hands continued to be naïve, but also pithy and profound. The day of the ambling German Alexandrine had gone so far as he was concerned; English blank verse—unrhymed iambic pentameters—which Lessing had introduced in his *Nathan* (1779), had not yet been mastered by him, or it did not appeal to him; free dramatic prose with its loquacious naturalism, which he had preferred in *Götz* and which his confederates, Lenz and Klinger, employed without ceasing, he retained, following the example of Shakespeare, in only a few isolated scenes.

Doggerel, however, which is genuinely German, which reminds of the national past, which he is in a position to make all the more pliable, which he interrupts now and then with a song or with rhymed iambic pentameters (even in the midst of strophic forms), with Alexandrines, with free, rhymeless, short rhythms, with speeches that are lyric poetry in themselves and that have an anapæstic swing, ingeniously and melodiously rhymed lyric poetry, doggerel which is free in its movement, bold in its bearing, jocose and mocking, though it can swell to pathos or glide over into Pindaric sublimity, into Ossianic solemnity, into song that grips the heart, doggerel— this is the favorite instrument of his soul throughout the entire epoch, and in no place has he, playing with it and on it, risen to such heights of greatness and virtuosity as in *Faust*.

He did not need to seek outside of himself in order to find the innate instinct which enables its enviable possessor to recognize and encompass existence in its unity and totality; for such a gift was Faust's own, just as it was the mark of his own inner and outer life; it was his initial incitement.

The idea of a spirit world and its power, in which he has Faust seek refuge and consolation, he had found in the works of the then noted Swedish spiritualist, Emanuel Swedenborg,[18] who had published

[18] Emanuel Swedenborg (1688-1772), though known principally for his theosophy and New Thought, had a wealth of experience in other fields. At the siege of Frederikshall in 1718 he invented a machine for the transportation of boats overland from Stromstadt to Iddefjord. In 1716 he was appointed assessor of the Swedish college of mines. But in 1743 he began to have visions and gave up all other work in order to expound the Bible as the immediate mouthpiece of God. He held Revelation XXI-2 to be the prediction of the establishment of a new dispensation. He himself never contemplated the founding of a separate church. He thought that

his mystic *Arcana coelestia* in London between the years 1749 and 1763. It is proof indeed of Goethe's immeasurable desire for knowledge that he felt inclined to, and had the ability to, plow through this mass of madness. It is proof too of his mental maturity and superiority that, though only twenty-five years old, he could use Swedenborg's teachings on spiritualism in a purely artistic way and to a purely æsthetic end without ever once becoming caught in them. A hundred and thirty years later Strindberg,[19] then sixty years of age and over, became hopelessly enmeshed in this same web of supernaturalism.

As a ghost-seer, Swedenborg was not merely *en rapport* with the spirits of men long since dead, Vergil for example; he was also informed as to the spirits of the various planets which, each for itself, comprised the individual spirits, one and all, that belonged to the sphere in question. In harmony with this teaching, much more valuable as a constituent part of poetry than of science, Goethe created the Earth Spirit, which reveals itself to Faust with terrifying visage.

Young Goethe felt that he was doubly hindered in his attempts to understand: He was not merely an individual mortal; he did not see things as they are but as they are reflected in him; he comprehended

his doctrines would in time permeate all other existing churches. The Swedenborgians were first organized in London, in 1778, under the name of "Society of the New Church Signified by the New Jerusalem." —TRANSLATOR.

[19] There is reason to believe that Johan August Strindberg (1849-1912) became entangled in the meshes of mysticism, spiritism, and cognate themes before he was sixty years old. Neither his "New Kingdom" (1882) nor his "Keys of Heaven" (1892) nor his "Damascus" (1898) nor his "Advent" (1899) can be said to bristle with clarity. —TRANSLATOR.

only the spirit that he resembled; the significance of
the Earth Spirit lay beyond him.   Moreover, as a
mortal man, he did not enter into the actual thoughts
of life; for he had only the word, and that was
inadequate.   Wagner was satisfied when he had a
method of speech that he could follow.   Mephistopheles advises the apprentice to be contented with
magnificent words.   In his very first monologue,
however, Faust gives expression to his contempt for
the science that is rooted exclusively in words and
is not able to see, to perceive, to grasp.   He wishes
to appropriate unto himself All-Nature, not in lifeless words, but in living vision:

> Schau alle Wirkungskraft und Samen,
> Und thu nicht mehr in Worten kramen.

When he dedicates himself to magic, his action is
symbolic of the fact that he, dissatisfied with the
scientifically fragmentary, wishes to become master
of ingenious powers of perception.   Goethe, as is
now known, preserved until his very death a prejudice against empirical science that progresses by
means of experiments.   Because he himself saw at
times into nature with the eye of clarified genius, he
refused to admit that a Newton, with his calcula-
tions, could make any appreciable advance.   Gradually, however, Goethe came to realize, as an investigator, the significance of self-conquest that merely
means going forward, step by step, rejoicing in such
progress as may be made, and seeing the whole in
the slightest of all.   At this early stage of his evolution, however, he is dissatisfied with anything less
than a fundamental grasp of the cosmos.

As soon as Faust gazes at Nostradamus's, that

is, at Swedenborg's, mysterious book, he has one of
those outbreaks on the whole and unity of nature
in which the youthful poet's fantastic wisdom expresses itself in words that will never be forgotten:

> Wie Alles sich zum Ganzen webt,
> Eins in dem Andern wirkt und lebt!
> Wie Himmelskräfte auf und nieder steigen
> Und sich die golden Eimer reichen!
> Mit segenduftenden Schwingen
> Vom Himmel durch die Erde dringen
> Harmonisch all' das All durchklingen!

Let no one be surprised at the rhyme, *steigen-
reichen.* It owes its origin to Goethe's Frankfort
way of pronouncing a "g." Thus he rhymes, also in
Faust, Ach *neige-*Du schmerzens*reiche,* and *Tage-
Sprache,* as in the famous lines:

> Es sagen's aller Orten
> Alle Herzen unter dem himmlischen Tage,
> Jedes in seiner Sprache.

In his younger days, Goethe always wrote "g" for
"ch" in the diminutive *chen: Gretgen, Mädgen,
bissgen.*

It annoys us to see him eradicate all the traces
of naïveté that give tone to the oldest *Faust* once
he thinks of going to press. We have but to think
of Gretchen's little monologue,

> Wie konnt' ich sonst so tapfer schmälen
> Wenn thät ein Mägdlein fehlen!

The vulgar *nit* has become *nicht,* and *nimmer* has
been changed to *immer,* in the following verses:

> Wie schien mir's schwarz und schwärzts noch gar,
> Mir's nimmer doch nit schwarz gnug war—

It is irritating too when we see the earlier lines of
her monologue,

> Ich schloss doch ganz gewiss den Schrein,
> Was Guckguck mag dadrinne sein?

being metamorphosed into the following more solemn and more nearly High German

> Es ist doch wunderbar! Was mag wohl drinne sein?

As a young student in Leipzig, Goethe had seen
Auerbach's cellar with the paintings that portray
the expeditions and adventures of Faust and Mephistopheles. In Frankfort, where he had wavered
between a pietistic belief in God under the influence
of Fräulein von Klettenberg, and the infidelity of
Enlightenment under the influence of Voltaire, he
had steeped himself in alchemy and cabala; he had
even tried his fortune with magic. But his stay in
Strassburg was decisive. It was there that the suffering Herder gave him certain characteristics for
his Faust. No one that he knew had investigated
as had Herder; no one was such a genius; no one
was so full of self-esteem; and Herder, with his
never failing satire and repudiatory sarcasm, also
gave him certain fundamental features of Mephistopheles, features that were later to be rounded out
and determined through and by the impressions
made on him by Merck. Friederike gave him the
outstanding features of Gretchen, whose name he
took from the little peasant girl whom he had loved
in Frankfort when he was but fifteen years of age.
Unreservedly matchless is the art with which
Goethe has portrayed the maidenly figure of Mar-
garethe. First we have her famous refusal of Faust's

company, then Faust's almost reverentia. mood in
her sleeping room, the picturesque monologue, *Will-
kommen süsser Dämmerschein,* which, by reason of
the purity that characterizes her surroundings, prepares us for the purity and artlessness in the life of
her soul. Attempts have been made to discover the
models which inspired Goethe in the creation of this
mood, in which he reconstructs from the frugal fur-
nishings the nature of the possessor, just as in "A
Thousand and One Nights" the wise men recon-
struct the nature of those who have passed by a certain road from the footprints left behind. There
is a poem by Georg Jacobi *An Belindens Bette;*
there are two passages in Rousseau's *La Nouvelle
Héloise;* there is the scene in Shakespeare's *Cym-
beline* where Jachimo enters the sleeping room of
Imogene. But the scene in Goethe's *Faust* preserves
its absolute originality and supplies the reader's
fancy with the elements essential to the formation
of a picture of Gretchen, which receives its first distinct outlines in the speech that moves us because of
its very plainness, and in which this poor little girl
of the humblest class depicts her life as it was and
as it is. Her horizon is her mother's house and
the garden of her neighbor, the woman across the
way. One would not believe that such matter could
be transformed into lofty poetry. Their household
is quite small. They have no servants. Gretchen
herself has to cook, sweep, knit, sew and run er-
rands. There is no man in the family. Her mother
is a widow, her brother is a soldier. There was once
a little sister who is now dead and for whom Gretchen had to be the mother. The child was born
just after the father's death, and her birth nearly

killed her mother. There the mother lay, recovered
very slowly, and could not possibly nurse the child.
Gretchen had all the work and care that arose from
attending her entirely alone. The little thing looked
upon her as her mother. She liked to lie sprawling
in her lap. Gretchen kept her cradle standing by
her bed. But she did not mind the trouble that
arose from nursing her little sister, so dear was she
to her. And then she died and Gretchen was left
alone.

Everyone who has read the skillfully intertwined
dialogue, in which the two couples are shifted in
Marthe's garden so as to entertain each other, as in
an antiphonal song, cannot help but sense the artis-
try with which the poet has the interest in Faust
take root and grow in the young girl's heart, at the
same time that Mephistopheles, conduct himself as
he may, has a terrifying effect upon her. Ingenious
too, because of its artlessness and simplicity, is the
childlike trait revealed in Gretchen when she plucks
the daisy and goes through her inimitable investigation: He loves me; he loves me not, until finally, in
exceeding joy, she holds the last petal in her hand
and says: He loves me.

Here, as in the catechization scene—a genuine
pearl in itself—it is the interplay of the most elementary in the love of woman, as in the religion
of woman, with the highest and most refined art that
makes the elementary fully effective. Max Morris,
one of the most deserving Goethe students of recent
times, a scholar who enjoys an enviable ability to
trace motifs and themes to their initial sources, has
gone through everything that Goethe can have read,
or must have read, during each stage of his life

when he was working on *Faust,* and he worked on it, as everyone knows, for over sixty years. As to the catechization scene, Morris has drawn attention to some expressions in Rousseau's *Profession de foi du Vicaire Savoyard,* in which the latter declines the attempt to penetrate the nature of God. Morris has also referred to a passage in Lavater's *Physiognomische Fragmente,* which Goethe once corrected, and in which there are some observations regarding God that seem to anticipate Faust's confession in a quite remarkable way. But let anyone study for a moment Lavater's lax, loquacious, German prose:

Oder nenn's, beschreib's, wie du willst . . . Nenn's Innigkeit, Herzlichkeit, nenn's Glaube, Liebe, Hoffnung . . . Religion, inneren Sinn, Gefühl für das Unsichtbare, Höhere, Uebermenschliche, Ueberirdische. . . . Religion. . . . lässt sich nicht lernen oder lehren . . . Die Göttlichkeit aller Dinge muss gefühlt werden.

Then think of these immortal verses, verses written for all time, beginning, *Mishör mich nicht, du holdes Angesicht!* They close as follows:

Erfüll davon dein Herz, so gross es ist,
Und wenn du ganz in dem Gefühle selig bist,
Nenn das dann wie du willst,
Nenn's Glück! Herz! Liebe! Gott!
Ich habe keinen Namen
Dafür. Gefühl ist alles,
Name ist Schall und Rauch,
Umnebelnd Himmelsglut.

A glance at Gretchen's heartfelt prayer, uttered before the devotional picture of the *Mater dolorosa* in a niche in the wall, shows that her religious inclination, however childlike it may be, is no less

deep than Faust's and hardly less independent of
formulas. This prayer is all of one casting; it is
all one gripping expression of spiritual distress; it
is so simple in its structure and so replete with power
and elementary innocence that it seems merely like
the cry of a human heart. What can be more simple
than this young girl's complaints? What can be
more commonplace than her description of the way
she waters the flowers in the window with her tears,
those flowers which she plucked in the early morning and now offers to the Madonna? And yet there
are, as careful investigators have shown, in these
few dozen lines echoes from the Prophet Jeremiah,
from the church hymn *Stabat Mater* written by a
Mediaeval monk, Jacopone da Todi, from the pictures of Mary with the sword in her heart that belonged to the days of the Renaissance, and from
Ossian's *Selma's Songs*. Once again we have the
simplest and most elementary feeling expressed in
a marvelous way after, and partly because of, having assimilated the art and poetry of many ages.

The estimable features in Faust's nature are emphasized by contrasting him with Wagner who, even
in the old folk-book, is his famulus. But Goethe
has personified that particular sort of scholarship
which was the especial object of his hatred and contempt. In just a few strokes, Wagner is portrayed
for time and eternity as the well behaved and inoffensive pedant. In the first place, he is sketched with
a view to the prevailing tendencies of that time; for
Wagner's weaknesses are those of Gottsched and
the older generation against whom Herder, and the
young men who followed him, took the field. Wagner admires a beautiful rhetoric; he sets great store

on the art of public speaking, just as Gottsched did.
In opposition to him, Faust emphasizes the value
of that eloquence which is the expression of sincerity. *Wenn Ihr's nicht fühlt, Ihr werdet's nicht er-
jagen*. Wagner studies history; he delights in steeping himself in old parchments. He labors under
the naïve optimism of that time, which indeed flourishes to this very day, and receives, as a net result
of its bizarre conceptions, the satisfaction that
comes from feeling that great progress is being
made: *Und wie wir's dann zuletzt so herrlich weit
gebracht!* Wagner does not doubt but that by
studying history he will come to know the heart and
mind of man. Faust interjects his views on this
subject. It is an answer written in lapidary style,
and for all eternity, to the effect that the knowledge
one derives while following the course of erudition
gives the advocate an insight into a lumber-room
and a trash-basket; and that knowledge of the real
secrets of human life, far from rewarding, punish
severely, and are punished:

> Die wenigen, die was davon erkannt,
> Die thörig genug ihr volles Herz nicht wahrten,
> Dem Pöbel ihr Gefühl, ihr Schauen offenbarten,
> Hat man von je gekreuzigt und verbrannt.

Wagner, who immediately after the disappearance of the Earth Spirit, enters in sleeping-gown
and night-cap, reminds of Wieland who likewise appears, in the farce, in his night-cap with the shades
and spirits of the lower world.

The war, which the young poet in the first dialogue between Faust and Wagner wages against the
academic science of his time, is continued in another

form in the conversation between Mephistopheles
and the student.   Quite significant for Goethe's
fondness for hoaxes and disguises is the fact that
Mephistopheles appears as Faust, and plays the
disguised rôle of Faust, at the very first meeting.

In this oldest draft prepared for the stage
(1774), the scene is full of the poet's personal reminiscences of the University of Leipzig; they were
later deleted on the ground that they were too local,
and consequently too unimportant.   We have remarks on the uncleanliness of students' rooms, on
the inn where the beautiful girl waits on the table,
on the monotonous food in the boarding houses
which reminded so little of home, on rancid butter.
and on the everlasting mutton and veal.

In the student's scene of the *Urfaust,* we miss the
judgment passed on the faculty of theology; nor
does it contain the immortal expression regarding
the faculty of law: *Es erben sich Gesetz und
Rechte, wie eine ew'ge Krankheit fort.*   But the
two inimitable characterizations of the faculties of
medicine and philosophy are found even here.   The
remarks on the art of the medical fraternity are admirable because of Mephistopheles's audacious, cynical wit, which quite precipitously breaks through
the paternal tone he has assumed thus far.   It is,
however, the serious and fearfully scornful criticism
that is leveled at formal logic which arouses our
keenest interest.   For young Goethe, without either
knowing it or wishing it, describes, through the im-
plication embedded in the contrast, the method by
which his own intellect grasps, his own mind creates: Not analytically, but synthetically—precisely
as did Bonaparte's twenty years later.

Deep indeed is his hatred of formal logic—a hatred with which Hegel was soon to agree and outdo—as expressed in the lines:

> Dann lehrt man Euch manchen Tag
> Dass, was Ihr sonst auf einen Schlag
> Getrieben, wie Essen und Trinken frei,
> Eins! Zwei! Drei! dazu nöthig sei.

Even more significant is the imaginative depiction of ingenious reason's all-controlling talent:

> Zwar ist's mit der Gadankenfabrik
> Wie mit einem Webermeisterstück,
> Wie ein Tritt tausend Fäden regt,
> Die Schifflein herüber, hinüber schiessen,
> Die Fäden ungesehen fliessen,
> Ein Schlag tausend Verbindungen schlägt.

It should be quite impossible for anyone who has ever read these lines just once, and who has understood them, ever to forget them. They were written by a youth of twenty-five summers. The sagacity lodged in them is uncommon; but the lack of years on the part of their author is more than uncommon.

Young as the poet is, it never occurs to him that his Faust should need rejuvenation. For his Faust is as young and as eager for life as his creator. The Goethe of twenty-five summers could not fancy such a thing as an impulse or a yearning to be made young again. But as the reading world of today becomes acquainted with *Faust,* it is wont to picture the leading character as a venerable scholar who is eventually transformed by sorcery. The scene in the Witches' Kitchen, however, in which Faust reverts to youth, Goethe wrote in 1788, while he was in Italy, obviously impressed at the time by his own rejuvenation, both as a man and an artist, the rejuvenation to which the Goethe of thirty-nine winters happily fell heir while living under the beneficent influence of a southern sun. This kind of rejuvenation must of course be regarded as symbolic of the innate ability genius has to undergo this process; to do just this thing. "Such prominent men," said Goethe to Eckermann on March 11, 1828, "are what we would call 'ingenious natures!' . . . They experience a second puberty. This explains the fact that in the case of specially endowed men we observe certain unusually fresh, vigorous, fertile periods in their old age. They seem to undergo a sort of temporary rejuvenation." But the rejuvenation, as we see, lay nevertheless quite apart from the original plan of the work.

In the completed drama there is, unfortunately, a bewildering mixture of the old and the new. We are reminded, for example, of the remarkable scene entitled *Wald und Höhle* which opens with Faust's gratitude to the Earth Spirit for having given him everything for which he had asked. The monologue gives expression to calm and restrained power, peace of soul, serenity of mind, great joy in life, and exalted study of nature. The reader is consequently surprised when, at the close of the scene, Faust, in despair, calls himself a fugitive, a man without a home, a monster without rest or peace of soul—precisely as Werther refers to himself as a wanderer over the earth. These are the words, this is the mood, of the man who has just thanked the Earth Spirit for having given him the whole of this earth as his kingdom, and invested him with absolute power to understand it and enjoy it.

The close of the scene belongs to the *Urfaust* (1774), written when Goethe, in the demoniac unrest of youth, after his break with Friederike, after his flight from Charlotte, after the dissolution of his relation to Lili, quite unable to find peace either of mind or body, pained by the loss he felt, pained even more by the loss he caused, equally dissatisfied in his yearning after world-embracing knowledge and his craving for divine creative power— when Goethe felt that he was a man without a home, a fury-lashed mortal. The beginning of the scene was written fully fourteen years later, in the charming garden of the Villa Borghese where Goethe for the first time in his life felt completely happy, and when it seemed to him that the spirits had given him all that mortal man could wish to have with impunity.

It was to be sure not very long ago that we first became acquainted with the *Faust* which Goethe wrote about the year 1775. It was unearthed by Erich Schmidt in 1887. He found, in Weimar, in a quarto volume, which contained quite a number of other things, the copy that had been made by that stout-hearted and intelligent lady at the court, Fräulein von Göchhausen.

This *Faust* has a tremendous advantage over the other so far as the conclusion is concerned. It was written in a uniform style and needs for its completion nothing but the scene of Valentine's death. If it had this, it would constitute a fully explicable and rounded-out whole in which everything is at once necessary from the point of view of logic, and

capital in quality.   There is nothing whatsoever
in it that causes the least racking of the brain.   It
could be understood by readers in almost any stage
of development—and could be placed in the hands
of anyone for a few pennies. What was later added,
partly as introduction, partly as interpolation, is
mostly of very high rank, sublime or profound or
impertinent, but in style, and frequently in spirit,
neither in the same tone nor along the same line as
the original nucleus of the great poem.

Heretofore, Goethe had imitated Shakespeare.
With the *Urfaust* he stands out all of a sudden as
Shakespeare's equal.   The figures he created in this
instance are in no way inferior to the greatest of
all ages.   Homer, to be sure, gave us Achilles and
Ulysses, Penelope and Nausikaa; Cervantes gave us
Don Quixote and Sancho Pansa, Shakespeare Fal-
staff and Hamlet, Molière Tartuff and the Misanthrope, Holberg Erasmus Montanus and Peer
Degn.   In *Faust* Goethe has created characters
which in clarity and symbolic worth are quite the
equal of any of these.   With Faust, Wagner, Mephistopheles, and Gretchen he stood, when twenty-
six years of age, on a spiritual level with the most
renowned poets Europe had ever known.

CHAPTER XVIII

ARRIVAL AND RECEPTION IN WEIMAR—
KARL AUGUST

AFTER Karl August's engagement to Princess
Luise had been solemnized in Karlsruhe, the two
Princes and their tutor continued their journey to
Paris by way of Strassburg. Though Karl August
was subject at all times to the closest custody, he
entered into such an intimate relationship with Jean-
nette Brossard that he assured her an annuity of
five hundred francs for the rest of her life.

Having assumed the leadership of the government in the fall of 1775, the Duke returned to Karlsruhe in order to marry his fiancée. At the two meetings with Goethe—one on the journey thither, one
on the return—the intended visit to Weimar was
discussed in great detail. Goethe was to be called
for in a carriage; but the carriage did not arrive.
Councillor von Kalb, who had waited for it week
after week in Karlsruhe, returned to Frankfort by
way of Mannheim.

On his arrival there, however, Goethe was not
to be found: he had already waited in vain far too
long. In the middle of October he wrote to Knebel:

Your young ducal pair requested that I should accompany
them to Weimar. I made my arrangements, packed my
trunk, put on my travelling suit, said good-bye, and then sat
and waited. Why—I do not know. Kalb, to whom I was
referred, failed to come. But I would have gone on any

way alone had it not been too dangerous in the present condition of the roads and the weather.

At last Goethe allowed himself to be persuaded by his father, who as an old republican cherished a profound dislike to princes and the servants of princes, that the Duke of Weimar had been playing a joke on him and had now forgotten him. He then decamped and started on his way to Italy, a journey he had so long wished to undertake. In Heidelberg his patroness, Demoiselle Delf, had made plans to have him appointed at the Electoral Court in Mannheim. But here he was overtaken by the estafette. The carriage had come.

On November 7, 1775, Goethe entered Weimar. No one knew that it was Helios that had come. But they all feared the favorite.

It was impossible to take him from his hotel in a court carriage as was the custom on the arrival of guests of ducal blood. As a plain citizen he was excluded from this honor. Nor could he as a plain citizen eat his first meals at the ducal table. This etiquette was changed, however, as quickly as possible.

Goethe was to be sure not ennobled by the Emperor until April, 1782. But as early as June 11, 1776, he received by ducal appointment a seat and a vote in the *Conseil* with the title of *Geheimer Legationsrat* and a salary of 1200 thalers a year. Moreover, he was presented with the park house, which became his favorite place of abode and which everyone who goes to Weimar visits again and again. But it was seven months after Goethe's arrival before he secured this fixed position.

He owned nothing. At the moment he gave up

his law practice in Frankfort he became dependent upon the good will of his father. As late as March 1776 he begs Johanna Fahlmer from Weimar to speak a good word for him with his father so that he can get a suit of clothes and a little money. He is helped out of his worst need when the Duke makes him a present of a hundred ducats. But he must have more; he must have clothes; and among other things he must have shirts and pretty good ones too. His mother would gladly have sent anything she had to her pet (*Hätschelhans,* which she always calls him, a name which the Duchess Anna Amalie adopts in the letters to his mother), but his father steadfastly refuses to send any money to Weimar, fearing that he could not in that way induce the son to come back to Frankfort.

The venerable and high-principled but narrow-minded Baron J. F. von Fritsch, Anna Amalie's confidential agent, was grievously disconcerted by the unescapable presence of this favorite, chosen from the ordinary class of mortal men. The young Duke had already been acting as though he were going to institute radical changes in the established form of government, and now he has called in as a friend and older adviser a young man who is nominally a lawyer but actually a poet who has written, among other odd things, a smart novel that treats of hopeless infatuation for a woman already legitimately attached, and which dilates at great length on suicide, just as though both of these were entirely permissible.

The Duchess Luise shed many a tear, in silence of course, over the new-comer. It was most assuredly interesting to hear him read from his manu-

scripts; but Luise had an emotional heart, while Karl
August, who had married her as a matter of duty,
who did not love her, who loved but little and but
few round about him, went dashing away on the
chase on every possible occasion and passionately
resigned himself to his chief and favorite amusement, rapid riding interspersed with hurdling. And
now, to pile Pelion on Ossa, he has taken unto himself a friend who is a wild genius, who does not belong to her social class, and who is hopelessly disrespectful to the customs of society in general.
There was no doubt in her mind but that this individual would take genuine pleasure in beguiling her
young husband into new sorts of wildness, new types
of folly, new moments of infidelity.

Little did she know that, quite to the contrary,
Goethe felt from the very first that he was her cavalier. He immediately endeavored to instill measure
and moderation into her young lord, and to be unreservedly kind toward and considerate of her. He
was captivated by the young Princess at the very
first sight; and his natural refinement of feeling, his
wholesome disposition, to say nothing of his ingenious cleverness, could not help but bring about
a good understanding wherever this was humanly
possible.

Goethe soon incurred the ill will of the ecclesiastical fraternity. For the past five years the position
of Senior Court Preacher and General Superintendent (the fearful title bequeathed by the Reformation for plain Bishop) had been vacant. Since the
Duke was tired of the gloomy, shallow Weimar
clergy, who had nevertheless been urged for the
position, he requested Goethe to recommend a suit-

able man for the place. Goethe's thoughts at once turned to Herder, his old friend and teacher, now eking out an unenviable existence as a minister in Bückeburg. He wished to repay Herder for the good he had received from him and was quite willing to disregard his irritable temperament. He even felt that real joy could arise from having this irritable person as a daily associate. The clergy of Weimar rose as one man in opposition to the appointment. A violent counter agitation was launched. Goethe was eventually compelled to inform the consistory that the appointment of Herder was in accord with the Duke's express desire. The consent of the consistory was in this way forced, but was invalid until the Town Council had officially nominated Herder. On May 2, 1776, the Duke requested the senior of the consistory to send him the decree of appointment so that he might sign it. And still there was delay. The matter was dragged out until June. The Town Council, acting not entirely on its own initiative, held the appointment up as long as possible.

Hardly had the report been spread that Goethe was in Weimar and that he was having an influence on the reigning Duke when his former friends, madcaps from the days of *Sturm und Drang,* felt something like an electric shock. The friend, the comrade, they said, had been preferred. He must do something for them; he must lead them into green pastures. It was not long until he had first this one and then that one at his home in Weimar as uninvited guests.

Lenz was among the first to arrive. His coming was a genuine misfortune for Goethe. He was so impecunious when he came that the Duke had to pay his hotel bill. He insinuated himself, as we have seen, wherever he went, could not and would not hold his tongue, started a scandal and had to be removed. Herder, who had finally been appointed, brought him the order of expulsion and sufficient money to pay his way out of town. Goethe had asked for the order and Chamberlain Einsiedel had drawn it up. And this was one of Goethe's friends!

Even before Lenz had gone Klinger came on from Giessen, three months before he was to take his examination in law, and asked for an appointment on Goethe's recommendation. He "wished to leave his conscience in silence and give himself up entirely to the ebb and flow of fate and the enjoyment of sensual pleasures." He stopped at the hotel where Lenz was living, "Der Elefant." There the three poets found each other, Wieland and Lenz and Klinger. In Goethe's garden Klinger struck up an acquaintance with Prince Konstantin and clung to him. He writes: "At his home I can eat when I want to." He drank so much with the young man that the Prince became ill. In need of money, Klinger had his belongings in Giessen sold. But when he embarked on a mad love affair with a girl in Weimar the same time that he had another in Gotha, he left.

While Lenz was still there the composer Philip Christoph Kayser wanted to come on from Zürich! Goethe had to write and ask him to please stay where he was: "I have you in my heart at all times. Send me something frequently. Please stay in Zürich! If you can be quiet I will help you."

Klinger returns and with him a charlatan by the

name of Christoph Kauffmann, one of Lavater's apostles of *Kraft*. Kauffmann had invented the name of *Sturm und Drang* for Klinger's drama, which originally was called, significantly enough, *Wirrwarr*. Twenty-six years old in 1775, he had come to Zürich from Strassburg where he had been an apothecary's apprentice. He had a long flowing mane of hair and a long beard, his entire breast was bare, he wore green russet trousers and green or red russet waistcoats. He wandered on foot with a great knotty stick in his hand and a cap of liberty on his head, fully convinced of his ability to reform and transform the universe. He called himself God's lime-hound, for he was certain that his way was God's way. He was a free mason and wished to establish educational institutions. He introduced himself at the Weimar Court in the costume above described, enraptured Caroline Herder, calumniated everybody in Weimar, so that scenes arose that necessitated his removal from the town. And this was one of Goethe's friends!

The climax of misfortune was capped when, in the beginning of the year 1776, the Duke, despite Goethe's constant appeals, somewhat indisposed as he was, undertook a forced ride from Gotha to Erfurt and back without stopping. Goethe was so vexed that he refused to dine with Karl August on his return and became so ill from sheer vexation that he was obliged to abandon a journey he had planned to Leipzig. His fears with regard to the Duke's health were entirely justified. Karl August was attacked with rheumatic pains that continued for more than a month and threatened to become chronic.

At this juncture Goethe's opponents in Weimar rose as one man against him. The poet from Frankfort was leading the Duke astray. Rescue was possible only in case he could be induced to go somewhere else. But to the dismay of the faithful, the report was spread that his stay was no longer intended as a mere visit; Karl August was planning to have him remain permanently and become his guide, councillor and friend. Nor was this all; the intruder from another town is to be given a place in the cabinet; he is to be made Minister, perhaps even Prime Minister. The plebeian adventurer is to rule them all.

Fritsch declares that he cannot sit in a council of which Dr. Goethe is a member. As God and all the world know, Dr. Goethe is incapable of doing responsible work. His appointment would be taken amiss by everyone. In case Dr. Goethe, as Fritsch liked to believe, really feels a sincere attachment for the Duke, he himself will renounce the honor that is being planned for him. He, Prime Minister that he is, must in any event send in his resignation. It was Anna Amalie's intervention that saved the day.

At this point Klopstock, Germany's super-moralist, took an active interest in the situation. On the basis of floating rumors and strong calumniations, he preferred all manner of charges against Goethe. The giddy seducer is ruining a young Prince "who was destined to the performance of virtuous deeds that will bring good fortune to his people." He claimed that Fritz Stolberg would decline the position in the council to which he had been appointed in case the people continued to live at the Court as

they had been living, in case Goethe made Karl August "drink until he was sick." Nor would the Duke
live much longer. And he really persuaded Stolberg
to decline the appointment which he had even sought
so soon as his arrival was fixed. Klopstock held
Goethe responsible for the sorrows of Duchess
Luise. He let the Stolbergs know that people in
Weimar were drinking cognac from beer glasses,
and that the Duke and Goethe had common mis-
tresses. Goethe could, if he wished, show the
Duke his letter. He even spread this about in all
sorts of copies. He felt that he was a consecrated
being. In the eyes of the older generation he was
the sovereign lord of literature. As the poet of
the *Messiah* he was placed as far above Homer
as one placed Christianity above Paganism; his odes
were regarded as superior to anything that German
literature had produced. An attack from him was
a blow that went home.

Goethe replied to Klopstock with cold courtesy,
and defiant repudiation. Klopstock wrote: "Now
I despise Goethe."

From this first experience it was made difficult
for the poet to come into a natural and worthy relation to the Prince. It is not hard to see, however,
what drew the two young men together.

So far as the Duke was concerned, it was the
longing of a young man for independence. He had
always had his mother watching over him, a mother
jealous of her power, who had even stretched this
power farther than was justifiable. He had always
had a tutor at his heels. Hardly had he grown up
when they gave him a wife that he had absolutely
never desired. Now he felt: At last I shall breathe

freely, I shall live! And just at this time he meets
this young celebrity whose slogan is nature against
custom, whose very joy of life is freedom, whose
Georg dies "defending his freedom like a lion,"
whose Götz dies exclaiming "Freedom, freedom!"
Even as a young, plain citizen's son he is filled with
the power and joy of life. What a friend, what a
teacher for a young man who had so recently been
a boy! He knows life, has already loved, suffered,
and written books of which Germany is talking,
books which the young admire, which the old condemn, or in which they, despite their dissatisfaction
with the content, honor the genius. For Karl August he is the road to a rich and free life.

For Goethe the attraction was no less strong.
For him the meeting with Karl August was a way
out, a liberation.

He had become anchored. He had been a lawyer in his paternal city, had a large practice for a
young man, a practice in which his father went
through all the documents for him and with him.
But he approached this business with secret despair.
He did not wish to become a lawyer. And Frankfort was a little world in itself, difficult to enter, and
next to impossible, for him, to leave. The wall
that surrounded the city surrounded him too. Dis-
tances were at that time enormous. From Frankfort-on-the-Main to Berlin was then a longer journey than it is now from Copenhagen to New York.
His fate seemed determined. If he went his way
as a lawyer he would become a husband, an official,
a local celebrity in the old Imperial City. But after
his engagement to Lili Schönemann had been publicly entered upon, after the preparations for the

wedding had been made and the engagement had nevertheless been broken, his life in Frankfort had become impossible. He would meet Lili's relatives everywhere; and the disapproval of what had taken place would be equally ubiquitous. He had to get out of this enclosure, away from this future, away from this dependence upon everything and everybody.

Then it was that the heir presumptive at Weimar reached forth his hand. Goethe seized it and held it fast, and with this handshake he received fifty-six years of care-free life. As to what and who he really was, this twenty-six-year-old *Geheimer Legationsrat* was not himself especially clear. He was an individual who was not particular about understanding himself. The old rule ran: Know thyself! He felt no urgent desire to know himself, for he felt profoundly that the unknown was the sum total of his being, the source of his strength. What one really was, that one learned soon enough and fully enough from others. He strove at the same time for clarity as a judge of men, as an investigator, and then as a scientist and a statesman on a small scale. He was alternately a youth who let himself drift along with the current, and a man with rich experience back of him; he was a plant-like, a growing, developing nature. And he was a mind—a mind that controls, and controls itself.

He stood at the cross-roads of life: let it break or bear! *Bricht's auch, bricht's nicht mit mir!* The poem entitled *Seefahrt* was written during the days in which he had entered upon his new destination, September 11, 1776. He portrays in it the ship as it lies in the harbor waiting for a favorable wind,

then the journey itself during which a violent storm
breaks out, and closes with the following verses:

> Doch er stehet männlich an dem Steuer;
> Mit dem Schiffe spielen Wind und Wellen,
> Wind und Wellen nicht mit seinem Herzen;
> Herrschend blickt er auf die grimme Tiefe
> Und vertrauet, scheiternd oder landend,
> Seinen Göttern.

In reality, he had brought his ship into the harbor;
into a safe little harbor where he was secure against
storm and against stranding.

II

A state in miniature; it was about the size of that
of an English lord; a small prince but a real man;
a little town and a little court; about twenty associates. Such was the inventory of his fortune. But
he was offered a field of activity and possibilities
for development. This was Goethe's opportunity.
Neither he nor his contemporaries had a clear idea
of the smallness of the state or the insignificance
of the material situation: Anna Amalie's income for
the year 1776 was 30, 783 talers and 16 groschen;
her expenditures were 28,982 talers and 21 groschen.
It makes but little difference for our purpose
whether the state and the court were large or small;
the important thing is that the poet had been pro-
moted; he had been made finer; he had been lifted
up into a higher circle than the one to which he originally belonged. People did not ask themselves, he

did not ask himself, whether this transplanting gave
favorable soil for the protection and growth of his
powers of poetic production. He himself saw in
the change a renovation of his condition, an appeal
to his many slumbering talents and capabilities.

It does no good whatsoever to reason about fate
in this case. It was to be this way simply because
it was this way. But we see that Goethe's poetic
vein practically dries up during his first ten years
(1775-1785) in Weimar. He produces just about
nothing: a few literary satires of slight value,
*Triumph der Empfindsamkeit, Neuestes aus Plun-
dersweilern,* an adaptation of Aristophanes's *Vögel*
(1777, 1780), small topical dramas such as *Lila*
(1776), or *Die Fischerin* (1778), and the drama
Elpenor (1781-83), which remained a fragment,
the little drama *Die Geschwister* (1776)—all
works that have psychological and historical interest, but all of which could have remained unwritten
and Goethe's renown would not have been one whit
inferior on that account. The valuable works which
he planned during this period, received, without exception, their final form much later. There is
Egmont, begun in truth back in Frankfort in 1775
and not finished until 1787. There is *Iphigenie,*
written in prose in 1779, but completely recast in
1786. And there is *Tasso,* likewise written first in
prose, in 1780, and then transformed into the drama
that we know, with its monumental verses, in the
year 1789.

It cannot be denied that if we except individual
lyric poems, few in number but of the highest rank,
Goethe's first decade in Weimar was a desert so far
as poetry is concerned.

The winter and spring months were completely taken up with various sorts of amusements, vigorous skating among other things, a pleasure novel to Weimar's narrow-minded society and therefore highly scandalized. Then there were various banquets, hunting parties, balls and festivities, all manner of lighter and more enduring love affairs. Aristocratic society in the decade immediately preceding the French Revolution did not take marital morality any too seriously in little Weimar any more than in other centres of culture. Morals were in general freer than they became in the nineteenth century. Some of the New Year verses which Goethe himself wrote at the change of years give us an idea of the ethical situation. There are, for example, these lines in a poem to Frau von Lichtenberg:

> Mit gutem Appetit geniessen,
> Vom Morgen bis zum Abend küssen
> Und fest sich an den Schnurrbart schliessen,
> Kann lange Nächte leicht versüssen.

We do not know to whom Goethe's flickering heart first became attached on his arrival in Weimar. When, in 1778, he succeeded in bringing to the city of his adoption that rare beauty and renowned artist, Korona Schröter, who became Duchess Anna Amalies' Court and Chamber Singer, he felt strongly attached to her and was with her daily. She was the first to sing *Erlkönig*, the first to play Iphigenie. In 1786 she published in Weimar a pamphlet of twenty-five songs that she had set to music.

Goethe glorifies her with marked warmth in the

lines he dedicated to her in that diverting poem entitled *Auf Miedings Tod* (1782):

> Ihr Freunde, Platz! Weicht einen kleinen Schritt!
> Seht, wer da kommt und festlich näher tritt!
> Sie ist es selbst, die Gute fehlt uns nie;
> Wir sind erhört; die Musen senden sie.
> Ihr kennt sie wohl; sie ist's, die stets gefällt;
> Als eine Blume zeigt sie sich der Welt:
> Zum Muster wuchs das schöne Bild empor,
> Vollendet nun, sie ist's und stellt es vor.
> Es gönnten ihr die Musen jede Gunst,
> Und bie Natur erschuf in ihr die Kunst,
> So häuft sie willig jeden Reiz auf sich,
> Und selbst dein Name ziert, *Korona,* Dich.

The young Duke was even more inconstant than
Goethe. The lady, however, Caroline Jagemann,
actress by profession, who later became the Duke's
maîtresse en titre, and who, as such, was ennobled
and made the possessor of an estate under the name
of Frau von Heygendorf, was not born at the time
of our poet's arrival in Weimar. Inconstant or not,
Goethe himself soon overcame his madness for pleasure and began the work that at once consumed his
time and concentrated his attention.

He had never felt that he was only a poet. Indeed throughout his entire life he had such a pronounced penchant for the plastic arts that it was only
natural for him to spend years, all told, in developing himself along these lines. Though he never
became more than a dilettant he found it at all times
impossible to rest until he had seen what he could
accomplish in a given line.

From his father he had inherited, first of all, the
passion for making collections; it was a passion that

never forsook him just as he in turn never abandoned it. He imparted it in truth to the Duke who,
following his example, made a serious study of the
natural sciences and planned scientific and art collections. Goethe became, as the years went on, a
naturalist of note.

There was also a decidedly practical turn to his
mind. Having entered the Cabinet, he became a
Minister with all his heart and soul. Every detail
of the administration attracted him. He interested
himself in all phases of administrative affairs with
the result that he soon had the leading public interests under his immediate and personal control. He
was made chairman of the committee on public highway, on public buildings, on the conservation of forests, and on the working of the mines. As a member
of the war commission he found himself obliged to
waste much invaluable time. During Frederick the
Great's entanglement with the campaigns of Austria,
a Prussian general set out (1779) to draft troops
from the Weimarian provinces. His act was one of
usurpation. Goethe prevented trouble by taking
personal charge of the levying of the recruits. Quite
contrary to his wish, Karl August entered into the
Princes' alliance against Austria. Weimar's military contingent, however, was negligible: The cavalry never consisted of more than a few hundred
dragoons with uniforms and spurs—but without
horses.

The government of this diminutive country—only
a few hundred square miles in area—was naturally
patriarchal. It was consequently, as Goethe's youth-
fulness prompted him to see things, his duty to be
present at every fire in the neighborhood. He led

the hook and ladder company; he presided at the meetings. And what lay nearer his heart and consumed for a long while his best strength, was the theatre of which he was director for more than a quarter of a century.

The new arrival was well received by Wieland who, because of his great and amiable talents, his good humor, his unenvious disposition, and his store of shrewdness with regard to actual life, had the fundamental prerequisites for what the English call "good company." In Herder, whom he himself had brought to Weimar, he had an intimate friend and an artistic adviser right by his side until Herder's jealousy of Goethe's friendship with Schiller and an ever increasing tendency to moralizing, destroyed the critical judgment of the Senior Court Preacher. Knebel has already been discussed. Among the courtiers there were Siegmund v. Seckendorff and Friedrich von Einsiedel, both amiable men. Among the officials there were K. A. Musäus already famous as the collector and publisher of the *Volksmärchen der Deutschen,* and F. J. Bertuch, promoter of finance and industry, all interesting personalities. There was, too, the Court Lady, the slightly deformed Luise von Göchhausen with a good head always full of merry conceits.

Despite his ability to appraise Goethe as a man, the Duke had very little appreciation for his poetry. His taste was French. One sees that his enthusiasm for *Egmont* when the drama was sent him was tepid. He would have preferred a tragedy of the orthodox French type. But as a personality he had a beneficent effect upon Goethe and Goethe upon him. The

cleverest and most beautiful testimony of their mutually happy relation is the poem *Ilemnau,* written
for Karl August's birthday, September 3, 1783. It
portrays a bivouac on the chase. The neighborhood
around Ilemnau had been the object of Goethe's
especial care. The population was pitiably impoverished. The mines in Ilemnau had been lying idle
for a long while. Goethe had had everything improved; the mines were reopened in 1784 and again
worked, though without results.

We have a description of the nocturnal gipsy
camp which the young court people constitute. The
Duke is sleeping in a hut; everybody speaks in a
whisper so as not to disturb the young lord's rest.
With distinctly valorous frankness Goethe mentions
here the mistakes of the Duke and the anxiety that
is caused by his lack of restraint. He broods over
his own lot and part in the Duke's follies. I myself,
he says, brought pure fire from the altar of liberty;
but the flame that I started was not pure. Unwisely
I sang of courage and liberty, and again of honesty
and liberty that knows no restraint (*Götz* and *Werther*). Now I sit here and feel guilty and yet happy,
innocent and yet punished.

At the close of the poem he expresses his joy at
the wholesome potentialities in Karl August's soul:

Doch rede sacht! Denn unter diesem Dach
Ruht all mein Wohl und all mein Ungemach:
Ein edles Herz, vom Wege der Natur
Durch enges Schicksal abgeleitet,
Das, ahnungsvoll, nur auf der rechten Spur
Bald mit sich selbst und bald mit Zauberschatten streitet,
Und, was ihm das Geschick durch die Geburt geschenkt,
Mit Müh und Schweiss erst zu erringen denkt.

Goethe does not conceal the fact that they are still a long distance from the goal:

> Gewiss, ihm geben auch die Jahre
> Die rechte Richtung seiner Kraft.
> Noch ist, bei tiefer Neigung für das Wahre,
> Ihm Irrthum eine Leidenschaft.

But the longer he broods over Karl August the safer he feels with regard to the future. The Duke is developing more and more happily and, in deep appreciation of his position, has restrained his liberty. He who wishes to rule and guide others must impose upon himself a great many privations:

> Der kann sich manchen Wunsch gewähren,
> Der kalt sich selbst und seinem Willen lebt;
> Allein, wer Andre wohl zu leiten strebt,
> Muss fähig sein, viel zu entbehren.

The self-control which Goethe thus brought close to the heart of the youthful ruler and disciple he eventually made into a law for himself. The attempt to canalize his passions constitutes an essential part of his own self-development. His case was not entirely unique: To a certain extent all men pass through a stage of development as a result of which they are gradually but surely changed, even completely transformed. But the majority of men merely become less pliant and pliable and in the end dry up, or they are at least rigorously toned down. Goethe's external metamorphosis is well known: The young man who had worn his heart on his sleeve, who had given the name of brother to every acquaintance of the same age or a little older, who had been on terms of *Du auf Du* with every

comrade, accessible to all, frank and open, effusively
communicative to people whom he had never seen
and never did see—Auguste von Stolberg, among
others—became now as cold as he had been warm,
as inflexible as he had been volatile, as secretive as
he had formerly been loquacious.

This took place after the friends of his younger
days began to pour into Weimar in order to use him;
long after it had become clear to him that he was at
present regarded merely as an object to be exploited,
and was to be regarded in this light the rest of his
natural days.   The relation to an intractable but
well-bred young Prince who made his future secure,
who placed him at the head of a diminutive government, who permitted him to do good and to disseminate human happiness wherever there was a field
for such effort, could not help but have an influence
on the poet's violent impulse to freedom, an impulse that he had brought with him from the days
of less restraint.   And like a genuine German, Wolfgang Goethe had deep down in his heart a desire to
serve.

In *Tasso* the Princess advises the Poet to entrust
himself to her brother.   Tasso's reply was undoubtedly an expression of the feeling that became Goethe's own a short while after his arrival in Weimar.
Tasso says:

> He is my Prince! But do not fancy that the wild impulse
> to freedom puffs up the soul within me.   Man is not born
> to be free; and for the man of noble parts there is no fairer
> fate than to obey a Prince whom one honors.

CHAPTER XIX

CHARLOTTE VON STEIN—*Die Geschwister*—FRAU VON STEIN'S BREAK WITH GOETHE—CHARLOTTE VON STEIN'S *Dido*

GOETHE met Charlotte von Stein, *née* Schardt, in November, 1775. He was then twenty-six years old. She, born on Christmas Day 1742, was almost thirty-three. Since May, 1764, she had been married to the inoffensive, though far from prominent, Master of Horse at the Court of Weimar. She had given birth to seven children, only three of whom were still living. She had the characteristics of a distinguished aristocratic lady: Naturalness and easiness, eagerness to learn, sympathies without enthusiasm, frankness and tact, and according to the claim of those who knew her, an exceedingly attractive physiognomy without being really beautiful, the fundamental trait of which was a sort of gentle seriousness. It is now impossible to pass judgment on her appearance since the four pictures of her that are preserved in Weimar, her self-portrait, the two paintings by Imhof and Meyer, and a miniature portrait in enamel by an unknown artist, are as unlike as they would be if they represented four different women. As a lady of the world and a lady of the court, she had the charm that comes from being perfectly at ease under any and all circumstances. She was naturally very superior in dignity and bearing to the young genius from Frankfort. Just after his break with his fiancée, Goethe was racked and restless. He was causing unhappiness wherever he went, wherever he went he was filling hearts with trouble. He felt as though he were being pursued, he was often in the mood to which he had given expression when he put the words on Faust's lips: *Bin ich der Flüchtling nicht, der Unbehauste!* In her presence there was peace. She straightened everything out, toned everything down, became his soother, his angel, his guardian spirit, a sort of loftier sister. He wished that his sister might have a brother as he had a sister in Charlotte. Infatuated as he soon became, he transformed her in his poems to the sort of being he needed. She became the priestess of his soul and in his thoughts, possibly also in reality, he cast himself down at her feet just as the persecuted of old were wont to throw themselves at the foot of the altar and pray for love and peace.

Thus she becomes Iphigenie in Tauris, the Priestess. He is Orestes, the brother persecuted by the furies. In one of Goethe's most beautiful poems to her there are the lines:

> Denn Du warst in abgelebten Zeiten
> Meine Schwester oder meine Frau.

Her charming presence, when he finds her or refinds her—for in remote times she was his—calms and appeases his soul; it reconciles him to fate; and it reconciles him with himself.

In the course of years he again personified himself, in another way in this material. He himself became Iphigenie. All the circumstances that later

bore down upon him in Weimar, such as loss of time
in the levying of recruits and the assessment of taxes,
the neglect of his calling, the fact that he was not
writing poetry, Karl August's lack of appreciation
of his nature, and last of all his longing to get away
from the gray sky of Weimar to Italy's mild climate,
where he was about to go when the carriage over-
took him that brought him to Thuringia—all of this
becomes the oppression that weighs down upon the
Priestess. Iphigenie's longing for Hellas and her
yearning to escape from the Kingdom of the Scythians, becomes Goethe's longing to escape from the
cold, raw air of North Germany and betake himself to the sun of sunny Italy. The King who loves
and admires and binds Iphigenie, this impetuous and
powerful King who is always on the point of becoming distinctly rude, ruler of the Barbarians that he is,
but who is good at heart and in whom the finer feelings can be evoked—that is Karl August in his relation to Goethe.

The first sketch of the drama is finished in Italy.
Goethe feels an aversion to its lack of style; he revises it again and again. In its fourth form the
work approaches a matchless tenderness in tone and
feeling. It has received the stamp of human nature
in its most refined nobility; it has become the most
inspired of the larger productions that Goethe has
created, a living monument, a tree of melancholy
planted on some of the tenderest feelings and strongest, stillest moods in his life.

It is possible that his portrayal was indebted to
Frau von Stein for these enduring merits. The individual of today who studies her nature as it is revealed to us in her letters and poetic attempts knows

full well how little she actually corresponded to the Frau von Stein that Goethe pictured to himself.

But even such a contemporary as Karl August was entirely aware of this discrepancy. As an old man (May 27, 1828), while rehearsing with Chancellor F. von Müller a thousand memories from those earlier days, remarked: Goethe always idealized his women one way or another; he loved his own conceits in them; he did not really feel any pronounced passion. His most lasting flame, Frau von Stein, was a rather good woman but by no means a great light.

Of those particular women who have been immortalized by reason of their relation to Goethe, no one of them had so much significance for him as did Charlotte von Stein. He spent fourteen years of his life in the utmost intimacy with her; and of these the first twelve were spent under her actual dominion. We find him during these years—from his arrival in Weimar to his departure for Italy—dissipating, as her admirer, disciple, friend, lover and poet, his robust and vigorous creative ability, though he does develop a certain finesse and strength in finesse, an exaltedness and sureness which he fondly imagined he owed to her, but which she herself possessed absolutely not at all.

What he did owe to her was the impression of this exaltedness and sureness. Being a blue blood herself, she was in a position to communicate to him, patrician bourgeois, bourgeois patrician that he was, a quite superior knowledge of the world as well as an aristocratic tone and bearing that can be acquired only with extreme difficulty. As her pupil, Goethe took his obligations at the provincial Weimar

Court so seriously that he squandered his real powers in writing festival plays and poetic divertissements for the entertainment of the court circle. His
real poetry during this first period lies in the misty
dew-drops sprinkled throughout his letters to Frau
von Stein, or it is condensed into stars in the form
of poems, some of which are sent her, though occasionally he does not even mention his most excellent poems, conceived and elaborated on the very
day, or the day before, he wrote to her. He did
send her the first poem, the one he entitled *Wandrers
Nachtlied,* from February 12, 1776, but he did not
send her the other, much happier, perhaps the most
purely poetic poem he ever wrote (Septembr 7,
1783), though we know that he wrote to her on
September 9, 11, 13, and 14:

> Ueber allen Gipfeln
> Its Ruh,
> In allen Wipfeln
> Spürest Du
> Kaum einen Hauch;
> Die Vögelein schweigen im Walde.
> Warte nur, balde
> Ruhest Du auch.

That is without doubt one of the most perfect
poems that has ever been written at any time on this
earth. The only poems that can be compared with
it, though they are not equal to it, are Shelley's *One
word is too often profaned,* or *The flower that
smiles today,* or Verlaine's *La lune blanche luit dans
les bois,* or *Les sanglots longs des violons de l'automne,* the most inspired verses that have been written in the century following Goethe.

In his letters we find, however, such delightful

poems as *Mit einer Hyazinthe* (April 25, 1778) which begins as follows:

> Aus dem Zauberthal dort nieden,
> Das der Regen still umtrübt,
> Aus dem Taumel der Gewässer
> Sendet Blume, Gruss und Frieden,
> Der Dich immer treu und besser
> Als Du glauben magst, geliebt.

It is here that we have the roguish and yearning poem *An Johannes Secundus*—on chapped lips—in its original and compact form, not distorted as it is in his works; and here is found, last but not least, the poem that is decisive for the portrayal of Goethe's love: *Warum gabst du uns die tiefen Blicke.* It contains one stanza that is conclusive by way of glorifying Charlotte von Stein:

> Kanntest jeden Zug in meinem Wesen,
> Spähtest, wie die reinste Nerve klingt,
> Konntest mich mit Einem Blicke lesen,
> Den so schwer ein sterblich Aug' durchdringt.
> Tropftest Mässigung dem heissen Blute,
> Richtetest den wilden, irren Lauf,
> Und in Deinen Engelsarmen ruhte
> Die zerstörte Brust sich wieder auf.

We are prepared in advance to believe the best concerning her. We are familiar with her true worth. We see what she has been to Goethe for a long time —his need, his confidante, his ideal, his consolation —for he felt spiritually lonesome in those days. We know how ill he could afford to go without seeing her for a single day. He always insisted upon giving her an account of his thoughts, of his material occupations. He sent her all the interesting letters he received and such little gifts as books, peaches, asparagus from his garden, hares he had shot, and so on. He took as much interest in her son Fritz as he would have taken in his own child. Indeed for a number of years he stood in the relation of a father to the boy.

From the very beginning she is Goethe's sole beloved, and she in turn loves him without selfishness or jealousy. He writes, March 6, 1776: "Thou one and only woman whom I love here in this vicinity, and the only one who could wish me good fortune were I to love another more deeply than you— how happy I would be, or how unhappy."

But he soon suffers bitterly from the imperfection of the situation. She seems, so far as we can determine, to have kept him at a distance for a number of years. He soon gained her heart. On the reverse side of her letter of October 7, 1776, she wrote this little stanza with the false accent at the close:

Ob's unrecht ist was ich empfinde—
Und ob ich büssen muss die mir so liebe Sünde
Will mein Gewissen mir nicht sagen;
Vernicht es Himmel, du! wenn's mich je könnt anklagen.

In September, 1776, he writes:

Why shall I torture you, dearest creature! Why deceive myself and plague you! We cannot be anything to each other, and we are too much to each other. . . . Just because I see things only as they are they drive me insane. Good night, Angel, and Good Morning. . . . In the future I shall see you as one sees the stars—think that over!

He did not keep this distance long. In December, 1778, she took him to task for his self-satis-faction:

> Wie einst Titania im Traum—und Zauberland
> Claus Zetteln in dem Schoose fand,
> Sollst du erwachend bald für alle deine Sünden
> Titanien in deinen Armen finden.

Of jealousy on the part of Gottlob von Stein there was not a trace. Goethe made love to all the ladies of the court and no one took his love very seriously. He went about it, moreover, in such an open way; he sent his daily letters and notes un-sealed, without envelope, open, to Charlotte von Stein through his messenger. He evidently feared neither the eye nor the tongue of anyone despite the fact that as early as January 1776 he began to ad-dress her in his letters with *Du*.

If Frau von Stein nevertheless allowed her adorer to pine in vain for so long it can be explained from a combination of reasons: Her sense of duty, her fear of the curious eyes and of the tittle-tattle in the little town where no one passed in at one of her doors or out of the other without being watched. She also possessed the coquetry of woman that tries to bind more firmly by refusing. Whoever has studied the life of Charlotte von Kalb, of that lady, who, for a long while and for good reasons, was re-garded first as the sweetheart of Schiller and then of Jean Paul, will recall that she, with to be sure a mixture of rashness and despondency that were constituent parts of the life of her soul, became the talk of the town, though she never resigned to any-one but her husband. And her husband she did not love; he was good for nothing. She bore him, how-

ever, one child after another at the same time that
she was nourishing a warm passion for Schiller.
There were then such women at the close of the
eighteenth century among even those who seemed to
be "Titanesses."

It is not until the year 1781, after six years of
acquaintance and friendship, that Goethe feels completely happy in his association with Charlotte von
Stein.   Then it is that their relation to each other is
one of perfect harmony.   He has, he writes, never
been fonder of her and has never come so near being worthy of her love.   He claimed that she had
expelled extraneous matter from his heart with the
thoroughness, and in the spirit, that one might
cleanse a robbers' stronghold.   She teaches his
heart, which is always in debt, to be economic,
though she gives him a richer substitute than he had
before.   On the twelfth of March he writes:

My soul has grown fast to yours. I am not going to
make a great ado about it, but you know that I am inseparable from you, and that neither height nor depth can keep
me from you.   I wish there were some sort of vow or sacrament that would make me yours, visibly and legally.   How
precious that would be to me! And my period of probation
was long enough to think it all over.

The expression, "period of probation" is significant.   When Hermann Grimm, in his book on Goethe, attempts to explain the supersensual nature of
the case, by declaring that otherwise we must presup-
pose falsehood, fraud, self-deception, even impudence, on the part of Charlotte, and coldness, rudeness and impudence again on the part of Goethe,
that is, on the part of the Charlotte and the Goethe
whom he has depicted, he does nothing more, by his

ratiocination, than to lay bare the real value of his
psychology.

Charlotte's mind "helps him to create." Her
warmth "produces a beautiful climate about him."
In April he is so happy that he feels tempted to follow the example of Polycrates and cast his ring into
the sea. On his thirty-second birthday, August
28, 1781, he writes: "I am always yours, and with
you; I am more of a serf than can be imagined."
Indeed he can compare her influence upon him only
with the influence Shakespeare has had on him:

> Lida! Glück der nächsten Nähe,
> William! Stern der höchsten Höhe,
> Euch verdank' ich was ich bin.

His adoration flattered her; it nourished the
woman's vanity in her to feel that the man who was
considered a genius, who was sought out and studied
by so many, both men and women, should be so
taken up with her. This worship on his part gave
her an entirely new position in Weimar, just as it
later gave her a position in history. It even won
her to a certain degree, though a really profound
impression upon her heart it hardly made; nor did
it awaken a resignation for him, a dedication to him,
such as he experienced with regard to her. Women
who are intensely adored are not accustomed to return the adoration with especial warmth. They accept the homage that is done them with a sort of
submission, or as a tribute that is due them. They
are but little inclined to incur extra expenses that
may be charged to the love account; they regard
these extras as right, proper and necessary.

To give Wolfgang Goethe world-bearing, finesse

of being and morals—that was the chief function
of Frau von Stein.   Among other requirements, he
was supposed to express himself in French after
the fashion of a genuine courtier.   For some time
during the year 1784 he had to write to her in
French.   This was in accord with her wish.   In accord with his own nature he was all the while maturing into an ideal development such as the world
had never seen before.

II

What her relation to him in daily life was we do
not know.   She destroyed the letters she had written to him, he having returned them.   What she
meant to him, on the other hand, from the time he
first came under her spell and for a long while after
is made quite plain from Goethe's own works.

The first of these written testimonies is *Die
Geschwister* (October, 1776).   It was performed
already in November of the same year in Weimar
with Goethe himself as Wilhelm and the young
and charming Amalie Kotzebue as Marianne.   The
drama is a disguised picture of the poet's love for
Frau von Stein, so frequently called the *sister*.   In
the drama she plays the double rôle of the deceased
mother and a living daughter.   Though it testifies
to the strength of the feeling Goethe had for Charlotte von Stein, it is otherwise a work that challenges
to sharp criticism.   It is a dull play.   It marks an
almost incredible fall from the heights on which he
stood in *Faust*.

Even the presupposition of the drama, the underlying situation on which it is based, is at once un-

sympathetic and unnatural. Wilhelm, a young merchant, has lost an adored sweetheart who, by way
of superfluous clarity, bore the name of Charlotte.
She was a widow when he became acquainted with
her, their life together had been bliss itself, she was
great and pure, the earth was not worthy of her.
He could not offer her his hand, however, for he had
just squandered his paternal inheritance and had
to devote his entire time to making his own living.
He has again succeeded in getting on his feet, but
now it is too late.

Suffering as he does from a tactless communicativeness, he reads his friend Fabrice a letter from
Charlotte, which is, as we know, a genuine letter to
Goethe from Charlotte von Stein. It is the only
one we have, and reads: "The world has once more
become dear to me. I had detached myself from
it, but I now love it again because of you. My heart
reproaches me; I feel that I am preparing trouble
for you and for myself. During the past six months
I have been ready to die, and now I am no longer
ready."

Wilhelm also wishes to read his friend the splendid letter she wrote him shortly before her end as
a farewell message. But the friend has already
heard this letter and has enough of it. Wilhelm
has in his house Charlotte's daughter, Marianne,
whom his sweetheart consigned to him as a little
baby. He offers no objection at all to having her
regarded as his sister. She herself believes she is
his sister and, we do not know why, he has not told
his friend Fabrice, who is in love with her and woos
her in her present status. But this wooing makes
it quite impossible to maintain the useless secret any

longer. Wilhelm loves Marianne, who is his deceased sweetheart in rejuvenated form. Marianne loves Wilhelm and is unable to bear the thought of being separated from him. She accordingly rejects Fabrice and the lovers fall into each others' arms.

There is in the drama, as in Ibsen's *Little Eyolf,* the motif of incest. Wilhelm's relation to Marianne is certainly uncomfortable after, and in the light of, his relation to Charlotte. Marianne's infatuation in Wilhelm is equally, or likewise, uncomfortable so long as she looks upon him as her brother.

The least happy feature of this little drama is its style: it is replete with emotion and unctuous sentimentality. At the very beginning Wilhelm receives a letter containing some money he has earned. He apostrophises Heaven in the following fashion:

Dear God! How I thank Thee for having got me out of this trouble and for securing my safety! For Thy blessings upon me in little things after I have wasted Thy gifts in great things—can I express my gratitude! But Thou doest nothing for me, as I do nothing for myself. If that dear, charming creature did not exist, I would be sitting here adding up accounts.

Much worse, however, is Wilhelm's monologue the first time Marianne leaves the stage: it is a relapse into the nauseating style of sentimentality:

Angel, dear angel! How can I keep from falling on her neck and revealing everything to her! Dost thou look upon us, O holy woman, thou who didst entrust this treasure to me? Yes, those in Heaven know of us; they know us. Charlotte, thou couldst not have rewarded my love for you more magnificently than thou didst by entrusting thy daughter in the hour of death to me! Thou gavest me all that I needed and bound me to life. I loved her as thy child, and now — still there is an illusion. I believe that I see thee again; I believe that fate has given thee to me rejuvenated; that I can now live united with thee again, as I could not, dared not do in that first happy dream! Happy, happy! All Thy blessing, O Father in Heaven!

Fortunately we have another and more important testimony to the influence of Charlotte von Stein in *Iphigenie auf Tauris*. If *Iphigenie* has been the most admired of Goethe's dramas, it is because he has saturated the material with the spirit of humanity in which his century approaches its climax. Iphigenie is a beneficent character. From her there radiates a rich and refined humanity; her beauty has so won the heart of the bold Thoas that he longs for her hand; the nobility of her soul has mollified the harshness of the Scythians. We do not have here, as in the drama of like title by Euripides, a goddess in the clouds; Goethe's Iphigenie is a nobler type of mortal; she is almost a goddess; she is reserved; she is womanly; she has a sense of right and justice, however, that induces her to risk all—her own welfare and the liberation of those who are dear to her. She cannot lie; she cannot practice deception; fraud is foreign to her soul; she must tell the King the truth; and she must secure his consent to the journey.

There has been a tendency to find a touch of Christian ethics in Goethe's Iphigenie. Entirely aside from the fact that the poet's attitude toward Christianity just at the time that he gave the character its final form was one of hostility, there is nothing in her bearing that is inconsistent with the antique. There is no less difference between the Iphigenie of Euripides who begs for her life and prefers a wretched existence to a glorious death and the later character who, composed and courageous, meets death for the common good, than there is between the Iphigenie of Goethe who at first undertakes to liberate the prisoners by a wily invention and the Iphigenie who voluntarily reveals the truth to the King because she cannot lie. Indeed even in Sophocles we find a hero that can be favorably compared from this point of view with her: Neoptolemus in *Philoctetes*. As a disciple of Odysseus he undertakes to deceive the hero and carry off the sufferer's bow to Troy, but by reason of his noble nature, and the rare Achilles blood in his veins, he suddenly suffers a complete transformation, tells Philoctetes the truth, and refuses to forsake him.

Goethe's Iphigenie is antique in the simplicity of its structure and the personality of the characters. But written as it was at the close of the eighteenth century it is also profoundly personal by virtue of the humanity that irradiates it—a humanity that sprang in part from Charlotte von Stein.

III

In order to depict the woman's nature briefly, I anticipate the course of events. We fully understand Charlotte von Stein's surprise and grief when Goethe, in 1786, without telling her of his intentions, left Karlsbad and started to Italy. A few poems that she wrote in September, 1786, give expression to a state of mind that is not far removed from despair. In one of these poems we read:

> O wie bin ich nun allein,
> Ewig werd' ich einsam sein.

One stanza runs:

> Ach, ich möchte fort und fort
> Eilen, und weiss keinen Ort,
> Weiss mein Herz an nichts zu binden
> Weiss kein Gutes mehr zu finden.
> Alles, alles floh mit dir!
> Ich allein verarmt in mir.

That the feeling of sorrow on the part of the Princess in *Tasso* is so similar can hardly be accidental:

> Es reisst sich los, was erst sich uns ergab.
> Wir lasser los, was wir begierig fassten.

There have been critics who affected to feel that the real purpose of Goethe's journey to Italy was to break with Frau von Stein; they have imagined that after ten years he had become tired of her. This is an unqualifiedly erroneous supposition. The letters Goethe wrote to Charlotte von Stein while in Italy were not published until 1886. They prove as clearly as possible his undimmed affection for her, his unchanged desire to communicate to her all his thoughts and all his feelings.

The truth is, he had now reached the point where he *could* dispense with her. Indeed, he who had once declared that Weimar was the one and only place where he could live, and who had formerly been able to breathe only in her presence, had come to the state of mind and soul where he *wished* to dispense with her; or he at least longed for another place of abode so strongly that the loss of her did not outweigh the pleasure he could derive from this new life in a new environment. He had been basking in the sunshine of the South; he had steeped himself so completely in the various phases of classical heathendom—nature, antique, renaissance, the plastic, the picturesque, the architectural—with which he felt himself spiritually akin, that when he returned home he found himself a different and a more resolute individual.

He had torn himself away from Italian soil with profound regret. Such consolation as he could visualize he sought in the fancied friends that would greet him on his return. He had, moreover, the feeling that he was bringing his friends back home a great offering. But when he arrived in Weimar his mind was at once infinitely cast down; he felt an irresistible melancholy; he saw the inhabitants of Weimar with new eyes; he saw nothing more than a narrow-mindedness that was half patrician, half plebeian. Even the climate of north Germany had become annoying to him. The German sky was contrary to his nature; the abominable weather was a vexation to his soul. "When the barometer is low and the landscape colorless, where is one to live?" Thus he writes to Herder. With the unfavorable impression regarding the climate and the general drabness of nature is fused the feeling of a chilly reception. "From Italy, rich in forms, I was thrust back into formless Germany, and obliged to exchange a bright sky for a sombre one. Instead of consoling me and drawing me to them, my friends brought me to the brink of despair. My rapture over objects that were far away, my torture, my complaints over what I had left and lost, seemed to offend them: I was wholly bereft of sympathy; no one understood my language."

Misunderstanding greeted him on all sides. The edition of his collective works, which his publisher

had begun, was coldly received: The public had
turned its fickle interest to other authors. In the
last letter the Duke wrote Goethe in Italy, the former disapproved, as we have already seen, of
Egmont. Herder, who had once admired *Götz,*
began to take offense at Goethe's liberal attitude
toward accepted morals. The *Römische Elegien*
he dreaded. His later judgments on *Der Gott und
die Bajadere* and *Die Braut von Korinth* startle by
reason of their narrow-mindedness. The friend, the
soul-sister, Charlotte von Stein, loved, adored, glorified, idolized by him for nearly thirteen years as a
woman has rarely been loved, adored and so on—
what real appreciation did Goethe enjoy from her?

He found nothing but ill humor, reproaches, and
disdainful offense because he had absented himself
for over a year and a half. She had the feeling that
a change had taken place within him while he had
been gone; that he no longer yearned to be near
her. She withdrew from him, stiff, formal and
frigid. Moreover, she at once began to lay bare
the moralizing side of her nature: She was annoyed
by the fact that the little wench (*die Dirne*), Clärchen, should be elevated to the position of the
Prophetess of Liberty regarding the future.

It was a source of immeasurable disappointment
to Charlotte von Stein that Goethe, long after his
return home, dreamed and talked only of the South.
It was human for her to regard his praises of this
South as a sort of offense to her. But it was not
tactful on her part to become bitter and distempered.
This opened Goethe's eyes to a number of things,
but especially to the fact that the individual whom
he had been worshipping at a distance as the incar-

nation of grace and charm was in reality a semi-
aged woman. He himself was now thirty-nine years
old, she was going on forty-six. He had lived in
Italy, as did also his friends, an unrestrained artist's
life with young and blooming lasses; since Charlotte
von Stein now coolly drew back and away from him,
the sensual attraction that she formerly exercised
seems to have become extinct.

Three weeks after his return from Italy, Goethe
became acquainted with a plain, healthy young girl,
Christiane Vulpius, who had brought him a petition
from her brother. She was an amiable child without either demands or jealousy; she captivated him
at once. In the middle of July 1788 she became
his sweetheart, in November 1789 she moved into
his house; in October 1806 she became his wife.

During the last days of July 1788, Frau von Stein,
seriously dissatisfied with Goethe's conduct though
utterly unaware of his relation to Christiane, temporarily moved to her country place at Kochberg.
She felt that the bond between her and him had
been torn asunder; she never spoke of him without
coldness and bitterness. But matters became far
worse when, in the beginning of the new year, she
learned of Goethe's tender connection with Fräulein
Vulpius. From now on her position with regard
to Goethe is for her "like a sickness." Passionate
embitterment against Goethe and unbounded contempt for Christiane are the feelings that fill her
soul. She leaves him a letter on her departure for
Ems in 1789 in which she seems to have demanded
the dissolution of his relation to Christiane as the
indispensable prerequisite for future friendship.

His answer of July 1 is calm and benevolent, but

declinatory. He begins with the remark that in a case like this it is difficult, and yet not difficult, to be sincere. He reproaches her for the inhospitable reception she accorded him on his return from Italy and for her numerous unkind remarks: That he could just as well have remained away since he no longer took any interest in people, and so on. "And all of this before there was the slightest reference to the situation that seems to offend you so! And what is this situation anyhow? Who gets the worst of it? Who lays claim to the feelings that I give the poor creature, or the hours that I spend with her?"

One of two things is true: Charlotte's relation to Goethe, which she broke off, was an affair of friendship only. And in this case her embitterment at his stay in Italy and his union with Christiane is preposterous. Or the relation was more than mere friendship. What hypocrisy there lies in her damning judgments of Christiane! Goethe tells Charlotte without passion and without anger, but explicitly, that he simply cannot submit to the scornful, fiendish way she treats him, and at the close he writes a passage which certainly must be taken literally (since Goethe loathed coffee), but which could only excite the wrathful lady even more:

Unfortunately you have for a long time rejected my advice concerning coffee; you have adopted a diet that is exceedingly injurious to your health. Aside from the fact that it is very difficult to overcome many impressions purely spiritually, you even strengthen the hypochondriacally torturing power of anxious ideas by an external means the harmful qualities of which you have already had abundant opportunity to observe and which you, out of love for me, desisted from using for a time to the distinct advantage of your health.

From now on and for the next ten years there is no word of abuse that Charlotte von Stein fails to use in her commitments on Goethe. She treats him as a low, degraded person, a half ridiculous figure. For her he is only the stout *Geheimrat* with the double chin, whose chambermaid is his mistress. She sides unreservedly with the fine folks of Weimar for whom Goethe was now the extinct volcano, the fallen star. But she is more passionate in her outbreaks. Again and again she is terrified to see him becoming so stout and beefy; she is shocked to see that his productions all stand on a low moral plane. She even sympathizes with Kotzebue in his malignant attacks on him. And when they meet socially she never hesitates for a minute to make the most offensive kind of remarks straight to his face.

Indifference, contempt, pity, these are the feelings she parades before the world with regard to him. To her son she writes: "Please write to Goethe; it will not be the first time we have letters from the living to the dead." Or, "concerning our former friend, I have again heard something disadvantageous; if I could only efface him from my memory!" She always speaks as though she had been "deceived by a friend." And when Christiane, in November 1793, gave birth to a daughter (who died immediately) she writes: "He is dreadfully proud of his daughter; he is as friendly as an earwig and makes French puns." Of his *Römische Elegien* we read: "For that sort of poetry I simply have no appreciation." Of his *Hermann und Dorothea* we read: "It is rather nice; it is only a pity that in the passages on the housewife who cooks on the pure hearth, Virgin Vulpius constantly destroys the

illusion." When *Wilhelm Meister* is finished she
writes of it to her son:

There are some pretty ideas in it, especially on the political relations of life, and the book begins with a feeling of
which I no longer believed Goethe, as a perfect child of
this earth, was capable. It must owe its origin to old times.
Incidentally, however, all the women in the book conduct
themselves in an undignified way; and if he does occasionally detect some good feelings in human nature, he at once
smears them up with filth so as not to be obliged to concede
that human nature has something divine in it. It is always
as if the Devil were pointing the way, lest we might make
a mistake with regard to his feelings and look upon them
as being better than they actually were.

IV

All of this is rather ugly and unrefined, though
it surpasses in no way what we would normally expect from a woman whose importance can easily
be exaggerated, and whose self-esteem was mortally
wounded. But this is not all. Quite terrifying to
any who preserves a shred of faith in humankind
and who can still be astonished at an act of stupidity on the part of a woman who seeks revenge because she is no longer loved, is the attempt at a
poetic portrayal of Goethe's personality such as
Charlotte von Stein undertakes at this stage of her
career.

History teaches us that for a prominent man
nothing is more hazardous than the nourishing of
an acquaintance with a woman who writes. If he
does not love her it is wrong: she will not fail to
use her pen by way of taking vengeance on the luke-
warm gentleman. If he loves her for a while and

then no more it is worse: the rejected lady will
take an even more violent vengeance with the help
of her faithful stationery.   Nor does it alter matters
if, as in the case before us, he found her at the beginning among those who do not write.   Wrath
over the fact that she has been unable to captivate
him forces the pen into her hand and makes a literary woman out of a non-literary one: there is at
least one book she can write—the book on him who
was so faithless.   Lady Caroline Lamb's embitterment against Byron at the beginning of the nineteenth century made her an authoress.   In her novel
entitled *Glenvaron* she stamped Byron as the devil
of dissimulation and iniquity.

It is of course easier for those who have already
appeared before the world as authoresses to have
recourse to the written word.   When Alfred de
Musset was once dead, George Sand gave in her
Elle et Lui a quite forbidding and altogether unreliable picture of him and his relation to her.   When
Chopin was dying she portrayed him in *Lucretia
Floriani* as a weak child, irrational and irritable to
the point of madness.

And think of the portraits of himself Franz Liszt
was obliged to see in narrative literature!   For
women he was the most dangerous man of his age.
His friend of years standing, Countess d'Agoult,
gave in her *Nelida* a caricature of Liszt that awakens disgust—disgust for the woman who wrote it.
She even goes so far as to deny him all creative ability.   And the anonymous authoress of the story
Histoire d'une Cosaque raged a good many years
later about the heartlessness of the celebrated artist,
which heartlessness consisted in the fact that he,

despite numerous invitations, could never be moved to show his lady admirer just a little bit of love in return.

Later on Gustave Flaubert furnished a magnificent example of how love for a muse is punished, or speaking with perhaps more accuracy, how a great poet can come to do penance for not having rejected the muse's passion at the right time. Flaubert's letters to Madame Colet show, despite the frank benevolence of which they give testimony, that throughout the years in which they knew each other she was the offensive, he the defensive party. She is embittered at the rareness of his visits and positively jealous of the persistent and apparently unfruitful work that is keeping him from her. And when their relation to each other has been dissolved she takes vengeance with unmitigated energy. She describes him first in *Histoire d'un soldat,* and then in her book *Lui,* as hard-hearted, avaricious, selfish, quite unpoetic, and talentless as an author. She even sends letters to his house in which she accuses him, who never came in contact with the Tuileries, of cringing before tyrants.

Neither Byron nor Musset, neither Liszt nor Flaubert was, however, a personality of Goethe's magnitude. And yet no one of them was treated worse or more inconsiderately than Goethe was treated by Charlotte von Stein. After the break she wrote her tragedy entitled *Dido.* In it she portrays herself as Elissa and Goethe as the poet Ogon. It is interesting to see the crimes and vulgarities that she has ascribed to this sinful wretch in whose mouth are placed modes of expression, and some of the speeches, that Goethe actually made to her.

In the first place he is the most stupid of braggarts. Nature, he says, has been able to realize its ideals in only a few beings; to them belong he and his equals: "The rest are creeping things trodden under foot, unnoticed."

He is portrayed as the most vulgar of cynics. He admits that he formerly strove after virtue and purity in all seriousness; this was due to his innate yearning to belong to the select. But he did not succeed in this; it was not becoming to him, either. And with her favorite ridicule of Goethe's figure, which was a trifle stout though by no means massive, the authoress has him continue:

I became so lean; but now just look at my cheeks, my well rounded stomach, the calves of my legs. I will voluntarily confide a secret to you: exalted emotions come from a shriveled stomach.

He is vain to the point of sheer foolishness:

I confess that I like to hear myself praised. It makes no difference whether the praise be born of generosity, flattery, or stupidity. I do not like to look behind the curtain.

He is faithless as a matter of principle: "We make promises to ourselves; and we can also break them." He is a hypocrite; his hypocrisy he considers a convenient virtue.

Elissa, who honors poetry and poets, and who once upon a time built an altar to Ogon, has at last come to see the difference between the talent and the man. She says to him:

Once I was mistaken in you; but I see you all too well; despite the beautiful curls of your hair and your elegant shoes, there are still the buck's horns and hoofs and the other appurtenances of the satyr, and for that sort of beings promises are never sacred.

He replies with Goethe's letter from June 1, 1789:

These false ideas come from a certain unhealthy drink from the use of which I have always tried to dissuade you. Drink only the juice of the grape, the noble wine, and you will soon learn to reconcile yourself to the attractive picture you make of me.

She rejects him with the remark: "I refuse to lay my safety in your hands, for your morals are dependent upon your kitchen." He refutes her once more with expressions from that letter, "It is difficult to tell the truth without giving offense," and excuses himself with the expression Goethe so frequently used, "Man must from time to time slough off his skin."

When he is alone, he unmasks himself in a monologue as a totally depraved actor:

The gestures of the actor which, by the way, I am in the habit of practicing in the presence of women, always had the best effect when I fell before their feet in a picturesque position and attracted their attention through an expression of mute passion; in this way I never missed my objective.

The sum total of his character is that he is an arch-traitor. He deserts his benefactress, the Queen (Duchess Luise), after he had tried in vain to seduce her—this motif is especially venomous—only to take up with her ill-mannered and unrefined antagonist and rival Jarbes at the moment that the latter came with armed power. Though there is some disagreement as to who is meant by certain other characters in the drama no one has ever doubted but that the poet Ogon is aimed at and meant for Goethe. It was also this very circumstance which, at the last moment, caused Charlotte von Stein to decline the offers that had been made her to have *Dido* published and performed on the German stage.

The drama as a whole is a bungling bit of work; it is so utterly without wit, style, and spirit that by the widest stretch of charity it cannot be called literature. It is on this account all the more instructive to note the enthusiasm with which Schiller in January 1797, when his friendship with Goethe was the most cordial, writes to Frau von Stein concerning the "beautiful, serene, blithe spirit" of the drama. He has such an outburst as this: "In my whole life I have read little, perhaps nothing, which showed me the soul from which this came in such a clear, true, and modest light as does this drama; I am on this account more moved than I can tell you." No one strove more zealously than he to have the drama printed; it was too as a result of his encouragement that Charlotte sent it to the theatre in Breslau.

In the year 1796 occurred the first, wellnigh voluntary, step toward a reconciliation between Goethe and Frau von Stein. It came about as follows: Schiller's little son Karl accompanied Goethe's six-year-old August to Frau von Stein's house. She took a liking to the child at once. Goethe made a conciliatory move almost immediately. It was just at the time of this incident that Frau von Stein put the finishing touches to her *Dido,* and dispatched the finished product to Schiller.

During the following years the erstwhile lovers

met each other infrequently. In October, 1798, Charlotte writes: "I see Goethe but rarely, and if I do not see him for some time, I am terrified at the way he is constantly taking on avoirdupois." Goethe's severe illness in January, 1801, softened her feelings just a little, but not so much as to prevent her from writing in the following vein on April 23: "Day before yesterday I was sitting with Frau v. Trebra in the old rose-hedge. Goethe passed by with his chambermaid at his side. I was ashamed of him to the bottom of my heart, and held my parasol before my face as though I had not noticed him."

Nevertheless Goethe strove, as though he did not wish to give up his aging friend, patiently and incessantly after reconciliation. In 1804, when he was fifty-five and she sixty-one, he announced his visit one day. The result was not wholly happy. Frau von Stein had subscribed to *Der Freimüthige*, a journal published by Kotzebue in connection with Merkel, the chief aim of which was to batter down all respect for Goethe. In its hostility to him it was iniquitous, narrow-minded, moralizing, and art-renouncing. The mere fact that Frau von Stein subscribed to it is proof of the low level of her development and the intensity of her malevolence.

While Goethe was paying her a call that lasted for two hours, a number of the magazine was brought in. She writes in this connection to her son:

I feel that he is disagreeably inclined toward me and there is such a wide divergence between our ways of thinking that I unintentionally give him pain at every moment. Unfortunately *Der Freimüthige* was brought in during his visit. He began to discuss the stupidity of the reading public that would busy itself with such a sheet. Part of that was of course meant for me. He simply did not wish to see the journal; I had to lay something over it.

The woman who had inspired *Iphigenie* ended, spiritually, as the authoress of *Dido* and a subscriber to Kotzebue's journal.

CHAPTER XX

Lila; Harzreise im Winter—Triumph der Empfindsamkeit

JUST at this period, when Goethe himself was not
preparing anything for publication, he was disagreeably surprised to see his *Sämmtliche Schriften* put
on sale by an impudent Berlin bookseller by the name
of Himburg. The enterprise was effected in secret
and contrary to Goethe's express desire. Three separate editions appeared, each one augmented, in the
years 1775, 1777 and 1779, under the title *D. Göth-
ens Schriften*. The "D" was supposed to stand for
"Doctor." Not even the name was correctly spelled.
There was much in these editions of which Goethe
was not the author, and all of them teemed with
inaccuracies. Copyright of original texts was then
unknown; nor was there any law protecting the
author in the matter of translations. It was in all
probability the fact that an outsider had obtained
possession of Goethe's writings that later inspired
him to edit the first edition of his works (in eight
volumes). This edition appeared in the year 1790.
It was also this event that induced him to revise the
dramas and operettas from his younger days, a task
that occupied so much of his best time during his
journey to Switzerland.

One of these operettas was *Lila,* a peculiar and,
for a modern reader, unsatisfactory creation. It

was a topical drama, written in December, 1776, with the distinct idea of appeasing and consoling the young Duchess Luise in her not entirely happy domestic life. Goethe is supposed to have obtained the idea from Frau von Stein who, in turn, had taken it from an old and now forgotten French drama entitled *L'Hypocondriaque*. The French drama belonged to the first half of the seventeenth century. In the drama (as in the first form that *Lila* received, the form that no longer exists) an infatuated man loses his mind because of a false report of the death of his sweetheart. She hastens to the disconsolate soul and all unite in trying to cure him of his delusions. They show him several persons who are regarded as being dead and who are brought back to life by music. The sick man at last believes that he has been wakened from the dead and embraces his sweetheart. Though Goethe's intention was to effect a cure of the Duchess's diseased mind, he arranged it, so as not to be too distinct and not to hurt anyone's feelings, in such a way that, in the first draft of the drama, it was not Lila but her husband whose mind was diseased. The piece was revised with the retention of this content first in February, 1778, and again, "beyond recognition" as the poet himself says, in February, 1788, where the rôles are exchanged and where it has received the only form in which we now know it.

Baron von Sternthal has been wounded in battle. His wife, Frau Lila, to whom this news is brought in a letter becomes very unhappy, looks for a new letter with each mail, and suspects her relatives of intercepting the post. Finally there comes a false report of the Baron's death. Lila takes a violent fever, becomes afraid of people, goes about in deep distress, looks upon her dearest friends as phantoms or shades, and even flees from her husband on his return home as though he were a spectre.

Under the treatment of a mountebank, her condition becomes worse until a capable physician makes it clear that in order to cure a case of insanity like this it is necessary to enter into all of the delusions of the patient. When Lila believes that she is surrounded by fairies and cobolds, her sisters and friends simply have to disguise themselves as such fanciful beings. The physician disguises himself as a magician, the young ladies of the house as fairies, a friend appears as a man-eating monster, and in this way—contrary to all rational modern treatment of insanity—the unfortunate Lila is cured of her ailment, recognizes her husband, and throws herself into his arms a happy woman.

There are a few wonderful verses in this drama: they are spoken by the physician who disguises himself as a magician. They express the idea of the drama much better than the drama itself. They run as follows:

Feiger Gedanken   Allen Gewalten
Bängliches Schwanken, Zum Trutz sich erhalten,
Weibisches Zagen,   Nimmer sich beugen,
Aengstliches Klagen   Kräftig sich zeigen
Wendet kein Elend   Rufet die Arme
Macht dich nicht frei.   Der Götter herbei.

These twelve lines are worth a hundred times more than all the rest.

A play such as this is of value only to literary historians. Its chivalric purpose—that of consoling a disdained duchess—does not make the operetta a

source of entertainment to us; nor can anyone who
is not entirely lost in uncritical reverence for Goethe
read it with even a slight touch of profit. Its theme
is in itself interesting rather than valuable. It is
quite characteristic of the poet that he should cherish a belief in his ability to cure a sick soul through
the ingress of environment upon the deluded conceits of the soul in distress and thus purge it of its
fanciful agony. Goethe himself was of the distinct
conviction that he possessed talent as a physician of
the soul. He had, more than once in his own life,
overcome his psychic sufferings by steeping himself
in nature and by engaging in actual tasks of one kind
and another. He fancied, on this account, that
others could be helped by the same method, that is,
by instruction. Just at the time that *Lila* was written, he tried personally such a cure. The poem entitled *Harzreise im Winter,* which needs a measure
of commentary in order to be understood, contains
an obscure passage which reads as follows:

> Ach, wer heilet die Schmerzen
> Dess', dem Balsam zu Gift ward,
> Der sich Menschenhass
> Aus der Fülle der Liebe trank?
> Erst verachtet, nun ein Verächter,
> Zehrt er heimlich auf
> Seinen eignen Werth
> In ungenügender Selbstsucht.

Among the numerous letters Goethe received
from unknown individuals there had been long, repeated, urgent, and importunate ones from an exceedingly unhappy and scribacious youth who sought
consolation from the author of *Werther* on the
ground that he could best sympathize with his tor-

tured existence. The author of *Werther*, however,
felt somewhat oppressed, but more repulsed, and let
the letters lie unanswered. Curiosity at last won the
day, and when Goethe was in the Harz (1777) he
rode, quite alone, at the close of November, in
stormy weather, to Wernigerode where the writer
of the letters, a certain Herr Plessing, was then living. True to his fondness for mystification and
incognito, the poet introduced himself as a landscape
painter from Gotha. He spoke of Weimar, where
he insisted he was well known, explained Goethe's
silence on the ground that he was overburdened with
work, had Herr Plessing himself read his letters to
him, and then made the following statement: In
Goethe's circle it has come to be regarded as an
assured fact that one could liberate one's self from
melancholy self-torture by a cordial participation in
real affairs and events that lie beyond one's immediate interests. Herr Plessing, however, scorned this
method of procedure as being quite ineffectual in
the case of his peculiar type of melancholy—which,
incidentally, cured itself a few years later.

In real life Goethe was then not conspicuously successful as a physician of the soul. On the stage he
could more easily attempt a cure by means that a
physician for the mentally diseased would reject once
for all.

II

The motif of the literary-parodic farce entitled
Der Triumph der Empfindsamkeit is not unlike that
employed in *Lila*. Written in 1777, it too revolves
around the distress of a married man the mind of
whose aristocratic wife has become deranged by

external circumstances. Though it has but slight poetic value, this little drama in six acts is psychologically interesting. It was presumably from the reading of Carlo Gozzi's *L'amore delle tre melarancie,* which was performed for the first time in 1761 in Venice, and which opens the poet's *Fiabe teatrali,* that Goethe derived the initial idea. In Gozzi's comedy—first translated into Danish by Meisling, and then felicitously adapted by Sophus Schandorph,[20] in 1894, under the title of *Three Oranges*—a prince has fallen a prey to hypochondria and bombastic, pietistic affectation of which he can be cured only by laughter. In Goethe's *Triumph der Empfindsamkeit* the literary satire is turned against sentimentality with which he himself up to this time had proved to be so infected. The drama is written with good humor; this much can be conceded. And as to its forms, it anticipates the jests of Tieck and the other German Romanticists even as to dramatic technique. We read for example: "The fifth act is now at an end; let us play the sixth." Though inspired with a measure of self-irony to the extent that it ridicules Goethe's own former stage of development, it is nevertheless far too allegoric to contain any real portrayal of human beings. We have here, in truth, what we have in the

[20] When Brandes started on his career, in the '70s, he consciously or unconsciously created a school. The more prominent members of this coterie of "realists," who set up Zola as their model, were J. P. Jacobsen, Erik Skram, Karl Gjellerup, Herman Bang, Peter Nansen, Henrik Pontoppidan and Sophus Schandorph. Schandorph fitted into Brandes's plan—the portrayal of life as it actually is—possibly better than any other member of the group. He was given to rather strong expressions somewhat after the style of Rabelais. His knowledge of the Romance languages and literatures was wellnigh perfect. He died in 1901, after having written a very great deal. —TRANSLATOR.

majority of instances in which Goethe attempts to
be humorous, comic: The attempt comes from a
poet who is so pleased with his own conceit that it
has never occurred to him how remote his production really is from having actual comic power. It is
no mere accident that Germany has never produced
a great comic writer. The German *Gemüt* is heavy
and sentimental; the witty authors in the German
language are almost invariably of foreign extrac-
tion. When Goethe tries to be satiric he becomes
as a rule symbolic, or allegoric as in *Walpurgisnacht*
in *Faust*. In this particular satire there is not the
slightest portrayal of human beings; everything is
grotesquely symbolic.

Andrason, "a humorous king," is annoyed because his queen, Mandandane, is so completely captivated by a supersentimental Prince Oronaro that
she has lost her interest in everything human, walks
only in the moonlight, sleeps by waterfalls, and carries on prolonged conversations with nightingales.
When the King asks the oracle for advice he receives
the reply, assuredly not edifying, and expressed in
hexameters, that when a tangible spectre loses its
ghostliness in contact with beautiful hands, and when
a linen sack is emptied of its entrails, the patch-work
bride will be united with her lover and perfect equanimity will return to the house of him who sought
advice.

The Prince arrives; he is sheer languishing. His
servants mention his lofty position: "You talk of
my rank, unfortunate man? What is my rank
against this *heart?*"—In the way of luggage he carries along with him a great mass of boxes and cases
and chests in which there is to be found all the things

that make a sentimental heart rejoice. In one there
is a gushing fountain, in another the song of birds,
in another a heap of moonshine, altogether an artificial nature. And just as the nature which he cultivates is artificial, just so is his love meant, not for
the real Queen Mandandane, but for the picture he
has made of her, that is to say, for a huge doll of
human size which resembles her to the minutest
detail; it even wears the same sort of costume. He
worships the doll, not her herself. When the ladies
of the court get hold of the doll, it turns out that
in its hollow interior there is a sack of linen in which,
mixed with chaff, lie the enchanted books that have
made the Prince and the Queen so daft: *La nouvelle Héloïse, Die Leiden des jungen Werthers,* the
above-mentioned imitation of *Werther* entitled *Sieg-
wart,* all books which, according to the command of
the sensible King, are to be thrown into the fire, since
no mortal man should waste his time reading them.
In this way we are enlightened as to what the oracle
meant by his hazy wisdom.

The King apparently offers the Prince his wife;
but the latter feels like a perfect stranger in her presence. She seems to have changed, a mere oaf of
the one he loves and worships. They then bring him
his doll and he is delighted. The King and the
Queen soon find each other.

The sole profit to be derived from reading the
book is the knowledge thereby obtained that Goethe
at this period in his life felt disgusted with sentimentality in literature as well as in life, just about
as Henrik Ibsen, when he created his Gregers Werle
in the *Wild Duck* was disgusted with the "ideal demand" that he himself had made in the rooms of the

cottager where an "ideal demand" could not be realized, and where it simply evoked confusion.

The drama contains a goodly number of jokes on the raging enthusiasm of that time to see and perform monodramas. At the first performance Goethe had interwoven a little monodrama, *Proserpina,* which he had written the year before (with Rousseau's *Pygmalion* as a model). In reality Proserpina has nothing whatsoever to do with *Triumph der Empfindsamkeit,* though a few of the speeches in *Triumph* prepare us for its advent. Without belonging to Goethe's happiest reproductions of Greek myths, *Proserpina* is a short work of far greater value than the heavy farce into which it was woven. In a gripping monologue Proserpina (who, as is almost always the case with the Greek gods and goddesses in Goethe's works, has a *Latin* name and is not called Persephone) expresses her grief at being torn away from the light of the sun and relegated to the mute and silent desert of the lower world. The young girls who were once her playmates seek her in vain in the flowery dale where they were so happy together. Hopeless is their grief, hopeless her own so-called happiness, her pitiable rank as a queen in the land of shades. She is afraid of all the inevitable misery she sees about her; she would gladly give the languishing Tantalus a drink of water, would gladly put a spoke in the wheel that hurls Ixion round about, and is envious of the poor Danaïdes: Not one drop of water can they put to their mouth, there is not one drop of water in their pail. But the source of greatest grief to her is the fact that she is indissolubly bound to the disagreeable and brusque Pluto, whom she cannot bring herself to call husband, and whom nevertheless she dare not call otherwise.

She trembles at the thought of her mother, who perhaps has been looking for her on the playground to ask her whether she did not wish a new dress and new pair of golden slippers, and who is in despair over her disappearance. With frenzied cordiality she appeals to her father Zeus, who, when she was little, often lifted her up in his hands so that she believed she would swing on up into heaven. This same father cannot possibly be preparing to relegate her to Hades for ever and a day.

Now this is all very well. But it has a decidedly cooling effect on the mind of the reader to learn that Proserpina's return to earth is dependent, according to the quite irrational decree of Fate, upon her ability to find something succulent in the lower world. Nor is literary reason particularly uplifted on learning that since Proserpina, as the Fates inform her, having eaten of a pomegranate, an incision equal in fatality to that made into the even more renowned apple, is condemned to Tartarus forever and a day. Her despair is complete; our satisfaction is not.

CHAPTER XXI

SATIRES ON KLOPSTOCK AND THE STOLBERGS—
SECOND SWISS JOURNEY: *Jery und Bätely*—
OPEN AIR THEATRE; OPERA TEXTS

Two humorous bits of poetry, both satires on
German literature, belong to the year 1780. The
first was Goethe's adaptation of the introduction
to Aristophanes's sprightly and facetious comedy
entitled *The Birds*. The significant feature of this
work, significant for Goethe and for the state of
affairs in the Germany of his time, lies in the fact
that the political satire of the Greeks has been made
purely literary, while the boundless and communicative sincerity of Aristophanes has been rendered
so decorous by Goethe that his *Die Vögel* could be
performed at a court festivity in Ettersburg near
Weimar. Goethe himself played the role of Treufreund, and Korona Schröter recited the epilogue
in which Goethe refers to Aristophanes as "the undisciplined favorite of the Graces." It is an expression that has remained through all these years, oft
quoted and never questioned.

Here, as in *Das Neueste von Plundersweilern*,
which was recited at the Christmas table, of the
Duchess Amalie in 1780, it is Klopstock first of all,
and his group, that constitute the target. Though

Klopstock was only fifty-six years old in 1780, he is depicted as a choleric patriarch, and scourged as the owl, that dreaded and terrible critic who would dissect all the young of the birds in order to show that they should have sharper wings, stronger beaks, and better built legs. He conducts himself precisely as do that sort of inflated and spiteful critics against whom Goethe directed his two poems *Der Rezensent* and *Dilettant und Kritiker*. The whole day long he reflects and ponders over what the other birds did yesterday. When the two irresponsible chaps, Hoffegut and Treufreund, who act as though they were birds and the friends of birds, stand before him, he asks them first whether they are writers. Since they are thought of as being German they reply "Just as all of our countrymen." They encourage him to have a law passed so that they may be better paid and protected against piracy, so that they may receive the consent of their ancestors to approach their unmarried daughters, so that they may receive the consent of married men to associate with their wives, so that they may not have to pay for what they receive, and so on. Profoundly agitated because of their shamelessness, the owl replies that there is just one course to be taken with them: They must be led forthwith either to the house of correction or to the insane asylum—a reply which possibly contains a reminder of Klopstock's moralising letter to Goethe shortly after his arrival in Weimar.

An inseparable companion and menial admirer of the owl is the parrot who stands for the then twenty-eight-year old Professor Karl Friedrich Cramer at the University of Kiel; he had already written whole works by way of glorifying Klopstock, the first in two volumes, the second (*Klopstock. Er und über ihn*) in five full volumes, both of which gave evidence of such an exaggerated and tasteless enthusiasm that they simply staggered Goethe. This is the same Cramer who later formed such an intimate friendship with Jens Baggesen, translated his works into German, and was his original companion on his great journey through Germany portrayed in *Labyrinthen*.[21] Here he appears as a fatuous repeater of the owl, hopelessly destitute of critical judgment: The owl, he says, passes judgment on everything, and that suits me quite well; I do not need to pass any judgments myself. Taken all in all, this satire is stingless. The wittiest part of the drama owes its origin to Aristophanes.

Das Neueste von Plundersweilern has, in common with *Der Triumph der Empfindsamkeit*, rabid mockery of the mournful in *Werther;* in common with *Die Vögel,* it has the ridiculing of Klopstock and his idolization. Klopstock is sketched as follows:

> Der Mann den Ihr am Bilde seht
> Scheint halb ein Barde und halb Prophet.

Cramer is scorned even more sharply than in the Aristophanic comedy:

> Ein Zögling kniet ihm an dem Rücken,
> Der denkt, die Welt erst zu beglücken,
> Zeigt des Propheten Strümpf' and Schuh,
> Betheuert, er habe auch Hosen dazu,

---

[21] Baggesen's *Labyrinthen* (1792-1793) is a description of his travels through Germany, Switzerland and France. It is one of the most sprightly and intellectual books that has ever been written in Danish. It has been compared favorably with Heine's *Reisebilder*. Baggesen himself has been depicted as a Dr. Faust who forsook his cloistered studies and went out into the world to enjoy any pleasures that might come to him by living a full and unhampered life. —TRANSLATOR.

Und, was sich Niemand denken kann,
Einen Steiss habe der grosse Mann.
Vor diesem himmlischen Bericht
Fällt die ganze Schule aufs Angesicht.

In this school two of Goethe's erstwhile friends,
the Stolberg brothers, are not forgotten. The
Counts are unmercifully raked across the coals:

Mit Siegesgesang und Harfenschlag
Verklimpern sie den ganzen Tag;
Sie kränzen freudig sich wechselweise,
Einer lebt in des Andern Preise.
Daneben man Keul' und Waffen schaut.
Sie sitzen auf der Löwenhaut;
Doch guckt als wie ein Eselsohr
Ein Murmelkasten darunter vor.
Daraus denn bald ein Jedermann
Ihre hohe Abkunft errathen kann.

All of this is sprightly, masterful, witty, but it is,
nevertheless, wasted work for posterity. It is topical poetry, intended to amuse a small, intelligent
court circle that had been initiated into the literary
conditions of that time. It does not appeal to the
German people, to say nothing of the non-Germanic
peoples, of a century and a half later.

II

On his second journey to Switzerland, made with
Karl August from September, 1779, to January,
1780, Goethe greeted his mother in Frankfort,
found his father in ill health, visited Sesenheim in
order to see Friederike, now composed, natural and

dignified, and saw Lili in Strassburg who was now
Frau von Türkheim and a mother. It relieved him
to see that Friederike cherished no rancor against
him, and that Lili seemed happy to have forgotten
him. In Switzerland he made a number of acquaintances, among others that of an excellent woman
from Zürich, Frau Barbara Schulthess, who won his
friendship and to whom we owe the preservation of
the first sketch of *Wilhelm Meister*. She had made
a copy of the manuscript sent her between 1783 and
1785. The copy was not discovered until January,
1910.

The letters from Goethe's two journeys to Switzerland (1775 and 1779), the first series included in
the edition of his *Gesammelte Werke* from the year
1808, the second not published until the *Nachgelas-
sene Schriften* came out in 1833 (in Eckermann's
redaction), were combined in the following editions
despite the fact that there is a sharp contrast between them. The first are written in the style of
Werther and are sketched in connection with *Werther*. The latter are to a high degree jejune and
occasionally dry. The first abound in the emotional
life of feeling, in the thoughts of youth and the
longings of youth; the others are the calm notes of
an observer, edited by a second person.

Let us note in the first Swiss journey that ardent
demand for freedom, the denial of the fact that
these Swiss, who wall themselves in in their towns
and live according to custom and philistinism, can
be called free simply because their remote ancestors
fought for freedom. Let us note the (as in *Werther*
and *Faust*) longing, so passionately expressed, to
be able to fly freely through the air. Verily, Goe-

the more than anyone else deserved to live to see
the invention of air-ships. He would have taken
great delight in them and would have hastened to
learn all about the use of them. Let us note also
the admiration of nature which goes so far that
Goethe in the presence of beautiful fruit prefers
ocular to palatal enjoyment, that he has not the
heart to pluck a beautiful berry, to bite into a peach
or a fig. And let us note finally, not simply the
juvenile joy that arose from gaining the good will
of a young girl in a social circle, but also the youthful and wholesome sensuousness, of the eye no less
than of the feelings, that is expressed in the unforgetable depiction at the close of the letter telling
of the first time that the nude figure of a charming
young woman was revealed to the young man. The
portrayal is so excellent that one could leave it unread for more than a generation and then recall it
line for line. In felicitously chosen words he describes this situation, extremely simple and at first
blush apparently wonderful as it is: "She began
to disrobe. What a wonderful feeling as one piece
of clothing after another fell away and even nature,
freed of all extraneous covering, seemed strange
and made an almost terrifying impression."

The letters from the second Swiss journey are
purely factual, though the view of nature expressed
in them is not on this account less sympathetic.
Right in the very first letter he strikes up a new,
superior tone. We have a description of a journey
through a mountain-pass:

The journey through this narrow pass gave me a great,
calm feeling. The elevated gives the soul beautiful rest; it

fills the soul and causes it to feel as great as it possibly can.
How glorious such a pure feeling is when it rises to the
edge without running over! My eye and my soul could
encompass the objects, and since I myself was pure and
the feeling could never offend or become false, the things
about me made a proper and legitimate impression. If we
compare such a feeling with that under which we laboriously
struggle with petty things and energetically strive to imbue
these petty things with all that can possibly be imparted to
them, and embellish them according to our ability in order
to give our mind enjoyment, and batten it on its own creation, then we see for the first time that we are concerning
ourselves with a paltry makeshift.

The passage is significant, for Goethe has consciously taken leave of the sentimental view of nature from his earlier days, the view that he ascribes
to Werther when he has him find nature now effusively good, now merely destructive, entirely dependent upon his own joyful or depressed mood. Goethe has now, in peaceful contemplation, transformed
his soul into a mirror, a pure mirror of and for nature that stands out unassailable by the changing
moods of mortal man.

In the letters from the second Swiss journey, in
contrast to those of the first, Goethe maintains a
marked silence concerning human beings (as though
they are too small to be of interest in this exalted
natural scenery) and loses himself in a description
of nature which offers one's fancy insufficient nourishment. It is rather remarkable that Goethe, with
all of his admiration for Lessing's *Laokoon,* was
never able to master the incontestable and accurate
in Lessing's theory, namely, that only that description which can be dissolved in action adapts itself
to the art of words, while the description of those

things that lie in space, side by side (as the neighborhood near Noir Mont) constitutes an appropriate theme for the art of painting. The reading of Goethe's mountain landscapes requires effort without offering satisfaction.

A far greater pleasure is to be derived from reading the poem entitled *Gesang der Geister über den Wassern,* conceived while looking at Staubbach and written in Thun. The poem portrays the incessant mutability in nature and the soul of man as the law of life:

> Des Menschen Seele
> Gleicht dem Wasser:
> Vom Himmel kommt es,
> Zum Himmel steigt es,
> Und wieder nieder
> Zur Erde muss es,
> Ewig wechselnd.

Still another fruit of this second Swiss journey is the little melodrama, *Jery und Bätely,* from December, 1779. Again we have to do with a bagatelle, intended for performance at the court in Weimar, preferably so soon as possible, that is to say, before there had been any marked abatement of public interest in the private experience of the Duke in Switzerland. To that end Goethe tried to induce Christoph Kayser in Zürich to set it to music in a trice. It was set to music by him, and also by Reichardt, A. B. Marx, Wendel, Birey, F. L. Seidel, and J. Rietz. In other words, it was uncommonly popular in its day without on that account being able to hold the interest of posterity to any marked degree. Truth to tell, the sole part of the work that is un-

forgetable is the little poem which, in its day, made
an impression upon Sören Kierkegarrd:[22]

> Gehe!
> Verschmähe
> Die Treue!
> Die Reue
> Kommt nach.

The art form in this work approaches quite close
to what the French once upon a time, and J. L.
Heiberg, later, called *vaudeville*.[23]   In the middle
of the dialogue the speakers break off in order to
sing a little song.   Aside from an occasional touch
of the Alps, there is precious little of the atmosphere
of Switzerland in this idyl.

Bätely, a sprightly and beautiful girl, who lives
with her old father in a hut out on the field, has been
amusing herself by rejecting all wooers; she is cold
and pert toward her faithful adorer Jery, though
he has the very best of intentions and a house and
a home and goods and money; he is even willing to

[22] Kierkegaard's interest in this poem may be personal.   In 1840
he became engaged to a young woman in Copenhagen, but a year
later he broke the engagement in response to the admonition of a
"tender conscience."   It was a serious affair in the light of that
day.   Kierkegaard assumed full responsibility for this odious act,
using it, later on, as the theme of his *Stadier*, in which he appears
as his own accuser and the vigorous defender of the deserted girl.
Repentance followed in the wake of his apparently unmotivated
"going away."   —TRANSLATOR.

[23] Johan Ludvig Heiberg (1791-1860) went to Paris in 1819 and
remained three years.   While there he became acquainted with
the latest Parisian novelty—the vaudeville.   On his return he tried
his hand at this genre—and succeeded.   His "King Salomon and
George the Hat Maker" was performed at Copenhagen November 28, 1825.   It was a new type of comedy and one that has since
flourished in the North as elsewhere.   In 1826 he published a
treatise on "Vaudeville as a Literary Type and its Significance."
Heiberg was also a serious student of Hegel.   His essay on "Human
Freedom" (1826) introduced Hegelianism into Denmark.
                                                    —TRANSLATOR.

take her father into his home. The old man begs
the rash and pretty girl to remember that he may
die some day, that she herself is getting older and
older, and that in case she jilts her excellent lover
she may later see herself forced to take the first
wooer that comes along. This is all in vain. The
jolly young maiden is weary of Jery's importunity
and infatuated antics. At this point the friend of
her youth, one Thomas, appears on the scene with
a herd of oxen; he listens to Jery's tale of woe and
promises to straighten out the situation. He deports
himself with a sort of simulated brutality, is going
to steal a kiss from her, is going to beat the door
down if this be denied him, he lets his entire herd
of oxen graze on the family's meadow from which
he drives their own cows. Jery reappears as Bätely's cavalier, while all the neighbors whom she has
turned down and thereby offended leave her in the
lurch. When the more puissant Thomas throws the
brave Jery in a wrestling match and then retires,
Bätely is converted; she sets Jery's sprained wrist,
nurses him, takes care of him and eventually lays,
with enthusiastic gratitude, her hand in the hand
that was raised in her defense.

That is bright, innocuous theatrical art; but one
does not need to be a Goethe in order to hit upon
such an idea.

It is quite probable that it was the court life with
its need of diversion, and its propensity for half
dilettant, half artistic performances, that inspired
Goethe to write at this particular period in his life
an entire series of melodramas. In them he not only
anticipated all the novel theatrical devices of which
the German Romanticists were naïvely proud, but

also the modern rejuvenation of that especial hobby of the ancient stage which we now know as the open-air theatre. The little operetta entitled *Die Fisch-erin* (1782) was originally written to be played in the park at Tiefurt, with shifting illumination over the Ilm by day, and by torchlight. Nor did it make an unfavorable impression when the attempt was repeated in this century. Korona Schröter composed the music for the play, and took the leading part.

The drama is especially valuable because of its lyric woof; the action is as unimportant as it is unpretentious. A young fisher maid is restless and peevish because her father and her faithful lover always stay away so long while engaged in their self-imposed activity. They are never so sure to miss the set hour for dinner as when they have not caught a single fish, and have gossipped with everyone who rode a horse down to the water, and at whose house they laid-to. She wishes to avenge herself on them for their remissness: She leads them to believe that she has fallen into the water during their absence, and found a watery grave. They arrive with an unusually rich haul, and are grief-stricken when they cannot find her. As soon as she has punished them sufficiently with fright and mental anguish, she returns and is greeted by them with intense joy; also by the neighbors who have hastened up with burning deal-shavings in order to look for her. Here, as in *Jery und Bätely,* the young girl is wheedled into a marriage every thought of which she had previously avoided out of virginal shyness. *Die Fischerin* opens with *Der Erlkönig,* and in order to give Korona Schröter, who sang the leading rôle, an opportunity to display her artistic endowment. Goethe has interpolated a number of folk songs from Herder's collection, an English song, a diverting one from the Lithuanian, a pleasing one from the German, all at once popular and merry.

Scherz, List und Rache, 1764, is an opera text in verse the greater part of which is in rhyme. Viewed exclusively from the point of view of euphony of verse, it must be ranked very high. What are Richard Wagner's texts, which after all give evidence of unquestioned poetic instinct, when compared technically with these? These verses are pliant, light, sprightly, and in some instances the arias rise to heights of unqualified excellence.

The theme, however, is of too little importance for Goethe to have wasted his time on it. An avaricious doctor has fraudulently obtained an inheritance of a few hundred ducats which Scapin and Scapine had hoped, and not without reason, to secure. The doctor is a classical type of the miser who counts his gold pieces when alone. The young couple are classical cut-throats who hatch out a scheme by which they hope to coax the money from the old man. Scapine acts as if the doctor had given her poison instead of a potion; she pretends that she is dead. Thereupon the doctor gives Scapin fifty ducats to dispose of the body in silence. During the night Scapine returns, frightens the doctor as a spectre, and befools him out of the rest of his money.

This is quite thin and hardly edifying. But there is real humor and great glamour in such verses as these:

> Gern in stillen Melancholien
> Wandl' ich an dem Wasserfall,
> Und in süssen Melodien
> Locket mich die Nachtigall.

Doch hör ich auf Schalmeien
Den Schäfer nur blasen,
Gleich möcht ich mit zum Reihen
Und tanzen und rasen,
Und toller und toller
Wird's immer mit mir.

Seh ich eine Nase,
Möcht ich sie zupfen,
Seh ich Perücken,
Möcht ich sie rupfen,
Seh ich einen Rücken,
Möcht ich sie patschen,
Seh ich eine Wange,
Möcht ich sie klatschen.

A third play of this kind entitled *Die ungleichen Hausgenossen*, 1789, is merely a series of disjected and incoherent fragments. It is likewise in prose with interpolated songs and revolves in great part around the contrast between a whining poet and a bold hunter both of whom are inanely jealous of a young Frenchman with whom Rosette is in love. In the protracted final song, written in seven-eight strophes, which Goethe has included among his poems under the cumbersome title of *Antwort bei einem gesellschaftlichen Fragespiel*, there is one single stanza that is excellent. The profit to be derived from reading this unsuccessful sketch is slight indeed if we omit these lines on Goethe's ever widening experience with women:

Geh den Weibern zart entgegen,
Du gewinnst sie, auf mein Wort!
Und wer rasch ist und verwegen,
Kommt vielleicht noch besser fort.
Doch wem wenig dran gelegen
Scheinet, ob er reizt und rührt,
Der beleidigt, der verführt.

CHAPTER XXII

Elpenor; THE PROSE OUTLINE OF *Iphigenie* —
THE FIRST SKETCH OF *Egmont*—THE FIRST
SKETCH OF *Torquato Tasso*

AT the close of the seventies Goethe began to feel
a strong attraction for the antique. One evidence
of this, aside from *Iphigenie,* is the extraordinary
and valuable fragment entitled *Elpenor,* of which
only the first two acts, and these not in Goethe's own
version, are extant. It was written in rhythmical
prose similar to that employed in the first three versions of *Iphigenie.* The manuscript from the year
1806 was to be revised for the complete edition of
Goethe's works, though he could not prevail upon
himself to undertake the task; he entrusted the rendering of it into verse form to Riemer. It is a
pleasure to state that Riemer did his work well; his
verses adhere most rigidly to Goethe's sketch in
prose. They are, to be sure, quite free, but euphoni-
ous and especially pleasing where the blank verse
glides over into trimeters otherwise so rarely used
by Goethe.

As years passed by, Goethe regarded his attempt
to create a tragedy in the Greek spirit with disfavor.
He was an unjust critic of his own ability. What
he finished is of imposing beauty.

Strangely enough, it seems to have been on the
basis of a Chinese story that he planned his Hellenic
drama. The plot revolves around ambition, mur-

der, and blood-vengeance which, when it came to be written down, appealed to him as being too harsh. But what has been done is merely the depiction of a princely youth for whom fate seems to have a lofty career in store. The portrayal of the youth, like that of his tutoress and excellent foster-mother, is entirely worthy of the author.

In some mysterious way, Queen Antiope has lost her consort in battle, while the hands of unknown murderers have robbed her of her son during a journey which the two were making together. The young prince, then a mere boy, was heir presumptive to the throne. She regards with ill favor her consort's brother, Lykus. But when she chances to see Lykus's son, Elpenor, of the same age as her own child, she begs for permission to take charge of the education of the charming child. Elpenor is to be regarded as her own son until his father and male educators lay claim to him. This is the situation at the beginning of the drama. It is the scene of separation between Antiope and her adopted son. In just a few strokes, but with an art that is at once rich and rare, innate loftiness, bravery, martial temperament, and princely spirit are depicted in Elpenor's mind. He longs after the fashion of a young Achilles for arms; like a young Alexander for an unridden horse that is his. He is at the same time aroused when he hears of violence and injustice; he wishes to restore, to reorganize, to help. Antiope gives him the details of her son's death, and places the half-grown boy, whose soul as yet knows neither hatred nor revenge, under a solemn oath: He must swear to become her avenger.

It is at this point that the tragic perspective opens.

It is manifestly Elpenor's own father who has the crime on his conscience. The Queen seems thus to initiate the unsuspecting boy into the thought of patricide; and in case he will do that, he must be willing to commit suicide. The possibility is also open that the two youthful heirs to the throne were exchanged during their childhood, so that Elpenor is really Antiope's son. The reader can imagine that, by imposing the obligations of the oath and thereby of suicide upon him, she robs herself of her dearly beloved child, the child she has had in her presence without knowing it. For a birthmark, by which the deceased was identified, is found on Elpenor's neck. And this Antiope explained on the ground of consanguinity. We do not know how Goethe intended to carry out the action; we can only vouch for the extreme value of the fragment which he himself so entirely misjudged.

There is a close connection between *Elpenor* and the prose form of *Iphigenie auf Tauris*. Goethe's oldest manuscript of the latter was lost when the library in Strassburg, where it was preserved, was destroyed by fire during the bombardment of the city by the Germans in 1870. Fortunately, however, Gustav von Loeper, who has otherwise rendered such invaluable service as a student of Goethe, had made a copy of it as early as 1858. There is another copy in the old Royal Library in Berlin; it is the one Goethe presented to Knebel. And there is still a third, for which we are indebted to Lavater, in the old Ducal Library in Dessau.

We have already discussed the relation of *Iphigenie* to Charlotte von Stein. At once emblematic and symbolic of the fact that such Grecian antiquity

as Goethe knew had come to him by way of Rome,
is the nomenclature he has employed. We have here
a creation in which everything concerns pure Hellenism, and yet there is not a shade of Greek in the
names of the gods. Zeus is called Jupiter; in the
genitive *Jovis*. Even Artemis, whose image and
sanctuary constitute the focus of the play, is called
Diana. It is, so to speak, a sign and a reminder that
the Greek art for which Goethe—and Winckelmann
too—had such profound admiration, was of Roman
origin.

One basic characteristic of the theme, which
makes it less effective, strangely enough never disturbed Goethe. The axis of the play is the contrast
between Grecian civilization and Scythian barbar-
ism. It is especially the moral perfection to which
the Hellenes had approached that is contrasted with
the Scythians' contempt for human life, and their
inherited desire for human sacrifices by way of recon-
ciling the goddess. Now, Iphigenie and Orestes,
who stand as the distinguishing figures of the Hellenic spirit, belong to the race of Tantalus—a house
of criminals in which, up to the very last moment,
all the terrors and horrors of murderous crimes are
at home. The descendants of Tantalus are at any
rate worse, and farther removed from the moral
ideal, than the Scythians have ever been. Tantalus,
whom the gods took into their confidence, revealed
their secrets to men, and was punished by being cast
down into the lower world. The son, Pelops, came
into possession of his beautiful wife through treachery and murder. Her sons, Thyestes and Atreus,
murdered out of envy their father's first-born son.
The father, who looked upon Hippodamia as being

guilty of the crime, forced her to commit suicide. Harmony between Thyestes and Atreus was of but short duration. Thyestes seduced the wife of Atreus; Atreus drove Thyestes out of the country. Thyestes, who had reared one of Atreus's sons as his own child, goaded him on to the attempted murder of his own father, whom the youth looked upon as being his paternal uncle. King Atreus had this son, whom he looked upon as being his nephew, first tortured and then murdered. Thereupon he acted as though he were reconciled, and enticed Thyestes with his two sons into the empire, had the boys seized, their flesh roasted, and served up to the father on his own table. When Thyestes, the meal being over, asked for the boys, Atreus hurled the head and feet of the murdered children down before him. On his return from Troy, Agamemnon, the son of Atreus, was murdered by his wife and her paramour. By way of punishment, Orestes, the son, has murdered his mother and Aegisthus, her lover, previous to his having come to Tauris where he meets his sister and after having been so incessantly pursued by the furies. Would it be possible to imagine anything worse than all this happening in the most barbarous family of the Scythians?

When Goethe steeped his material in the ideas of his own age, and tried to interpret divine curse or blessing on a race as a display of heredity in the biological sense of the word, he came into conflict with the antique idea in a very peculiar way; for from the antique point of view, a curse and its eradication was something quite external. In the prose play Iphigenie says:

A single family produces neither the demi-god nor the

monster. An entire series of noble men, or debased, presents the world with the joy or the horror.

How does it come that she, model of magnanimity, humanity, refinement of soul, and love of truth, came directly from a family given to every conceivable type of treachery and atrocity for five succeeding generations?

When we read the *Prosa-Iphigenie* we see how difficult it was for Goethe, after giving up doggerel, to find a new form. It apparently never occurred to him to adopt the metre of the Greek tragedy, the beautiful and solemn trimeter. He preferred prose and groped along as best he could; for this is not the prose in which he wrote the *Götz* of his younger days. Nothing is now farther removed from his mind than blunt boldness; his style has become a compromise between easy conversation and set verse, about as recitative in the opera is a compromise between speech and song. Though the drama gained much, stylistically, from the revision made in Italy, a number of features are necessarily clearer and more distinct in the prose form. We might quote by way of illustration, the trenchant though singular speech of Pylades:

Die Götter rächen an den Söhnen nichte der Väter Misse-that; ein jeder, er sei gut oder bös, hat seinen Lohn. Segen ist erblich, nicht Fluch.

In verse that reads as follows:

Die Götter rächen
Der Väter Missethat nicht an dem Sohn,
Ein Jeglicher, gut oder böse, nimmt
Sich seinen Lohn mit seiner That hinweg. .
Es erbt der Eltern Segen, nicht ihr Fluch.

The word *Es* seems to me notably unclear.

In analogy with the healing of the mental disease in *Lila,* Goethe has portrayed the healing of a diseased mind also in *Iphigenie.* After the meeting with Iphigenie, Orestes is cured of his mental sufferings. The cure is not especially convincing, nor is it effected as a result of, or on the basis of, deeper psychology. It was apparently the impulse to cure Orestes simply through association with Iphigenie as an exalted compliment to Frau von Stein that induced the poet to omit a more exact motivation.

In Euripedes's admirable drama of like title, which constitutes the basis of Goethe's drama, Orestes's insanity is kept behind the scenes. It is merely discussed at the beginning of the drama by the herdsman:

> Just at this
> One of the strangers started from his seat,
> And stood, and upward, downward, with a beat
> His head went, and he groaned, and all his arm
> Trembled. Then, as a hunter gives alarm,
> He shrieked, stark mad and raving: Pylades,
> Dost see her there?—And there—Oh, no one sees!—
> A she-dragon of Hell, and all her head
> Agape with fangèd asps, to bite me dead.
> She hath no face, but somewhere from her cloak
> Bloweth a wind of fire and bloody smoke
> The wings' beat fans it: in her arms, Ah see!
> My mother, dead grey stone, to cast on me.*

In Goethe's Iphigenie, Orestes's insanity breaks out at the same point, in the recognition scene between him and his sister. In Euripides, it is Iphigenie who reveals her identity by asking the stranger to carry a message from her to Orestes, who, by re-

* Translation by Gilbert Murray.

calling incidents from their common childhood, overcomes her doubt as to his identity. In Goethe it is Orestes who, unable to tell the noble Priestess of Artemis an untruth, reveals his name to her. And when she thereupon tells him who she is and wishes to touch him, he loses his senses and exclaims: "Touch not my locks! As from Kreusa's bridal gown, there goes out from me an inextinguishable fire. Leave me! Like Hercules, I will die, untouched by others, a disgraceful death." He continues to rave until he falls into a swoon. When he awakens, he persists in believing that he is in the lower world, surrounded by his criminal and distressed ancestors, until at last the nearness of his sister, from Goethe's point of view her pure humanity, cures him in downright magical fashion. This can be effected only after his escape from horrors that were formerly his in order that, entirely after the manner of Atreus's race, the sister as sacrificing Priestess may offer up her brother.

Just as everything in Goethe, in contrast to the antique conception, is spiritualized, so is likewise the relation between Iphigenie and the goddess whom she serves. Beautiful indeed is Iphigenie's appeal, in Goethe, to the divine sister and brother, to Artemis and Apollo:

Oh, brother and sister! Ye who bring to mortals the bright light in the boundless Heaven, by day and by night, but never shine upon the departed, have mercy upon us— brother and sister! Thou knowest, Diana, that thou lovest thy charming brother above all that Heaven and Earth encompass, and that thou always turnest thy virgin face to his eternal light! O let not my only brother, my brother found so late, rage in the darkness of insanity! And if thy will in concealing me here has at last been fulfilled, and if thou willst give blessed salvation to him through me and to me through him, then release him from the curse of the Furies so that the precious time that is given us may not be lost in fruitless effort!

Orestes replies: "Let me for the first time since my childhood feel pure joy in thy arms!" And he returns to delight in life.

Where Pylades in Euripides is the brother-in-law of Orestes by having married Electra, in Goethe he is unattached. A splendid type of sympathy arises between him and Iphigenie; it is a case of mutual attraction. We notice this especially in the fourth scene of the fourth act which, in the definitive drama, is so completely revised that the lines here quoted, and the feelings they betray, have disappeared:

When I hear thee, oh thou lovely one, my soul turns to thy consoling, courageous words as the sun-flower turns to the sun. The comforting speech of a friend is a charming gift unknown to the individual who lives alone. In his heart, thought and decision ripen slowly, whereas the fortunate presence of the beloved develop both quickly.

From the few passages that have been cited, one will feel how completely German literature lacked, at this stage of its development, a fixed and determined norm for the diction of serious drama. Everything is solemn and styleless, while in the drama upon which it is based, more than two thousand years older than Goethe's work, both dialogue and chorus are so established and steady that even in a translation, provided it be smooth, they prove unassailable by time.

As an offset to all of this, however, Goethe's

drama, even in the imperfections of the first sketch, shows an admirable concatenation of events; there is strict unity of action; it moves along with unimpeded majesty. There is not one superfluous scene. Nor is the action external; it rests entirely upon the strength of the emotions and their evolution. Despite the antique garb, the spirit of the drama is modern through and through. Where, in Racine's *Iphigénie,* a real human sacrifice such as that of Eriphile is inconsistent with the polished language and refined feeling of the hero, in Goethe's tragedy there is no grating discord. Such a tragedy an antique Hellene himself would have written—provided he had been able to assimilate the civilization of the past two thousand years.

Goethe's heroine is beyond the prejudice of antiquity. A Greek man or a Greek woman of ancient times would never suppose that he or she incurred, by reason of superior position, obligations of any sort toward a barbarian, even though he were king. A barbarian would have impressed them as little as would a slave. It would have been impossible for them to appreciate Iphigénie's uncertainty in the obligatory choice that confronts her: I must either deceive the king, or expose the life of my brother to grave danger. Vacillation of even a moment's duration would have been wholy foreign to a Greek woman of olden times. But Goethe imbued Iphigenie with a sense of gratitude toward the barbarian who had been her benefactor. It is not simply the thought of telling a lie that is repulsive, dishonorable, impossible from her point of view; ingratitude is equally so. In this particular she stands on the very pinnacle of humanity at its best.

II

In the fall of 1775, Goethe is in Frankfort spending part of his time in a serious effort to overcome his father's doubts as to the advisability of accepting an invitation to Weimar, an invitation that appealed to him strongly because of the desire for life and activity that was in him. He chances in the meanwhile upon a book, written in Latin, by Strada, a Jesuit. The book treats of the war of the Netherlands. Egmont's character and figure at once stand out before his imagination in most attractive light. He reads of the conversation that is supposed to have taken place between Egmont and Orange. The contrast between the two captivates him. Orange has begged Egmont to flee with him and from the impending danger. He reads too of the parting scene between Orange and Egmont, the former leaving with tears in his eyes, convinced that he has looked upon his noble friend for the last time. For Goethe, this becomes the contrast between the serious, sober, thoughtful man of reason, and the genial, carefree soul replete with life and power, believing in the stars and rejecting judicial circumspection. Egmont's spirit is akin to his; he is indeed blood of his blood.

Goethe closes *Dichtung und Wahrheit* with the story of how his landlady in Heidelberg, the worthy Demoiselle Delf, vigorously opposed his decision to break off his intended journey to Italy and follow the call to Weimar until, with the carriage waiting at the door, he passionately cried out to her in the words of Egmont:

As if whipped along by invisible spirits, the sun-horses of

time rush on with the light chariot of our fate, and there is nothing for us to do except to hold fast to the reins with firm courage, and guide the wheels now to the right now to the left, steering clear of a stone here and avoiding a precipice there. The end of the journey—who can tell? The starting point? It is difficult at times to remember even that.

In case this account coincides at least in part with reality, the scene between Egmont and his secretary was written as early as October 31, 1775, and probability indeed favors this conclusion. The passage reminds quite strongly of what we have said above (p. 96) concerning the poem from Goethe's youth entitled *Wanderers Sturmlied*. It is clear, as is seen from a letter Goethe wrote to Frau von Stein, February 11, 1776, that the scene between Machiavelli and Margarete von Parma was written at that time.

We are in a position then to make a rough estimate as to the parts of *Egmont* that were written early in Goethe's life: These two scenes, the folk songs that open the drama, in which there is still a slight touch of *Götz*, and last but not least the inimitable songs that bear the genius of the very best creations from Goethe's younger days.

In these oldest scenes we detect quite distinctly the use of the historical feature in the portrayal of the period, all of which Goethe owes to his reading. A number of characteristic and doleful evidences of the fanaticism of the Reformation, both Protestant and Catholic, are cited. We notice quite frequently that the poet adheres rigidly to his sources.

In the folk songs skilful preparation is made for the appearance of the hero. The soldier who serves under him emphasizes with enthusiasm his skill as a marksman; the workmen comment on his generosity; the invalid notes with pleasure his victory at St. Quentin; and again the soldier refers to his valor as victor at Gravelingen. This method of introducing the hero Schiller later employed in his masterful *Wallensteins Lager,* written under the influence of Goethe. On January 5, 1798, Schiller writes to him: "I find that I have here surpassed myself; this is the fruit of our intercourse; for only the frequent, constant communion with a nature so thoroughly opposed to mine . . . could place me in a position to push out my boundaries in this way."

The dialogue between Egmont and his Secretary shows us all sides of the hero's fascinating personality and is written with this end in view, hence in all probability first.

Read attentively this splendid dialogue! Egmont has let his Secretary wait two mortal hours. It was his intention to go straight home from the Regentess. He seems to have spent these two hours with Clärchen, and the Secretary loses all patience since he, as Egmont perfectly well understands, is expected by the Regentess' court lady, Donna Elvira. The Secretary lays the matters before his Lord that need an answer, and these answers characterize Egmont; they reveal him in every decision from a new but harmonious angle.

In the first place he shows that he is human in his understanding of his subordinates. He does not wish to hear of the outrages committed in Ghent. It pains him—as it does Goethe—to hear of doleful occurences that have taken place and simply cannot be helped.

The pictures of the Virgin have been torn down;

shall the delinquents be hanged as iconoclasts were
in former days?—No, he is tired of all this hanging.
Let them be flogged.—Women too?—No, let them
off with a warning.—He is indulgent toward the religious lunacy.—There is a soldier who wishes to
get married. The Captain hopes that the privilege
will be refused him, for far too many women are
already following the regiment, so that its bivouac
resembles a gipsy camp.—The soldier should be the
last to whom this is permitted.—Some soldiers have
outraged an honorable girl.—They shall be punished severely, and so on.—He is stern when he becomes aroused. Otherwise the answers show him to
be mostly tolerant, sympathetic, respectful, carefree,
eager to enjoy the moment, a hater of scribbling, an
enemy of formal Spanish etiquette, a foe of court
restraint, a man who in danger moves about with the
safety of a somnambulist, and feels threatened only
when frightened by a call. For him life has appreciable value only when each morning awakens to
a new joy, and he falls asleep in the evening with
new hope.

In the scene which, in all probability, was written
immediately after this one, the scene containing the
dialogue between the Regentess and her secretary
Machiavelli, another personage enters who puts the
last and final touch to the description of Egmont's
personality. The Regentess fears the secretive, reserved, impenetrable, self-sufficient Oranien. The
Secretary remarks: "In contrast to him, Egmont
goes about as freely as though the world belonged
to him." The Regentess complains, however, of
Egmont's at times offensive bearing: He conducts
himself as though he were the lord of the country

and could drive out the Spaniards at any moment in which this might appeal to him as a desirable episode. The Secretary says: "I beg of you, do not construe as dangerous his candor, his buoyant temperament which treats all important things lightly." In these scenes we have the entire character sketch in outline.

One will hardly go wrong if one ascribes the two songs which Clärchen sings to the year 1776. They are matchless by virtue of their profound charm and infinite simplicity; they have been surpassed by no other poet. The first characterizes the boldness, intrepidity, and martial enthusiasm in a young girl who loves Egmont. It stands in sharp contrast to the effeminate blandness, the juvenile piety, the fear of the judgment of the neighbor across the street, which Goethe's Gretchen displays. Clärchen's song begins:

> Die Trommel gerühret,
> Das Pfeifchen gespielt!
> Mein Liebster gewaffnet
> Dem Haufen befiehlt,
> Die Lanze hoch führet,
> Die Leute regieret,
> Wie klopft mir das Herze!
> Wie wallt mir das Blut!
> O hätt' ich ein Wämslein
> Und Hosen und Hut!

The other little song has remained with proverbial unforgetableness in man's consciousness as the imperishable, almost definitive, expression of woman's love:

> Freudvoll und leidvoll,
> Gedankenvoll sein;
> Hangen und bangen
> In schwebender Pein,

Himmelhoch jauchzend,
Zum Tode betrübt,
Glücklich allein
Ist die Seele, die liebt.

After this the manuscript lay untouched for three years. In December, 1778, two scenes were added: Alba's dialogue with the son, and Alba's monologue. A third was written in June, 1779. Before his departure for Switzerland in September of the same year, Goethe sent what he had written to Frau von Stein and asked her to keep it. He wanted to take up the work again in December, 1781, but could not finish the difficult fourth act. From March to May, 1782, he worked on the tragedy again and with real pleasure; but then he laid it aside once more, and over five years elapsed before he again took up the manuscript. He felt repelled by what he calls the unbuttoned and student-like tone. It was not until during his second sojourn in Rome from June to September, 1787, that Goethe put his hands to the work for the finishing touches and got it out of his hands.

III

Still another of Goethe's great dramas, *Torquato Tasso,* was planned during the first years of his stay in Weimar. Like *Iphigenie auf Tauris,* it was originally written in rhythmical prose and in a totally different spirit from that which animates the finished work. The completed acts in prose from those early days have, unfortunately, either been destroyed or lost. *Tasso* was begun in November, 1780; in May, 1781, two acts were done. The drama, as it stood in July, 1789, shows to a marked degree Goethe's spiritual distance from the pulsing, throbbing life in the center of Europe at that time.

On May 6, 1827, Eckermann asked Goethe what idea he had endeavored to visualize in *Tasso?* Goethe replied:

Idea? I do not know. I had Tasso's life, I had my own life, and by blending these two remarkable figures with their individual characteristics there arose the picture of Tasso over against whom I placed Antonio as a contrast in prose. The other affairs pertaining to the court and life and love were the same in Weimar as in Ferrara, and I can truly say of my portrayal: It is bone of my bone and flesh of my flesh.

It is not difficult to take objections to certain phases of this statement; and it all needs some explanatory comment.

Goethe has either been inaccurately reported, or his own memory played him false. Manso's life of Tasso, 1634, with which he had long been familiar, and in which he steeped himself when he began to study the theme, contained nothing concerning Antonio. His figure did not indeed engage his attention until 1788, when he chanced upon Abbé Pierantonio Serassi's life of Tasso. Goethe was then in Italy; Serassi's life had appeared in 1785.

Ludwig Geiger, one of the most excellent students of Goethe's life now living, has said somewhere and rightly that Goethe originally had no idea whatever of placing the poet and the statesmen side by side as opposing, complementary contrasts; that he had planned to depict the victory of genius over custom and conscience. Tasso was to triumph over petty aspirations. The poet was to be celebrated who strode forward on his victorious career, hand in

hand with his ruler.   The spiritual prince of letters
was to be the companion in effort of the prince of
affairs, the one obeying his mind, the other govern-
ing a state.

The longer, however, Goethe lived at a court
the less he became inclined to give man as man equal
standing with a prince, and the more settled he became in his conviction that his drama (as was the
case with actual history), should lead to a tragic
end.   It was difficult for him at first to see such an
unpardonable fault as that with which we are presented in the finished *Tasso* in a duel between two
courtiers, still less minded was he at first to see anything particularly offensive or irrational in the fact
that a great poet who loves, and who is loved by
a princess, should stretch out his arms to her as
though she were his equal.   Goethe soon saw all
of this in a new light.   And this explains why the
drama failed to advance beyond the second act.

Johan Ludvig Heiberg,[24] a cordial and intelligent
admirer of Goethe, says somewhere:

How does it come that Goethe's *Tasso* is so great?   Because the Poet and the Statesman stand opposite each other
as real powers, and the one circumscribes the other.   Why
is Ingemann's [25] continuation of it so poor?   Because he

[24] Heiberg was a leader among the Danish writers of his day.
In 1827 he established the *Flyvende Post,* a journal in which a
number of poets—Hans Christian Andersen, Carl Bernhard, Carl
Bagger and others—made their *début.*   His criticisms of Oehlenschläger have never been entirely superseded.   His "Elverhöj,"
played to this day, has been the inspiration of several Danish
dramatists.   He was director of the Copenhagen Theatre from
1849 till 1856.   —Translator.

[25] It is difficult to conceive of one of Goethe's works more unlike Ingemann's own than "Torquato Tasso."   He could have reproduced the spirit of "Götz von Berlichingen" or "Hermann and
Dorothea" with poetic accuracy, but a classical theme was poles
removed from his temperament.   —Translator.

made the Poet the one and all and transformed the Statesman into a mere court cringer *à la Kotzebue*.

Heiberg praises the ability to stand above one's own
work, to arrange and supervise the manifoldness of
its inspirations so that each is kept within its right
and proper limit—he praises all of these qualities,
contending that they are the essential characteristics
of the true dramatist and the real drama, and states
with emphasis that the real dramatist begets at once
circumspection, irony, grace, and illusion. In its first
form, *Tasso* would evidently not have awakened
Heiberg's admiration.

An almost naïve confession as to how the poet in
this case has sought and seen only himself in this
theme is concealed in the expression that "everything was in Weimar as in Ferrara." Goethe's
optimism and the conciliatory feature of his nature
lie back of this observation. From the beginning
he had decided to disguise his dear, humane German
men and women as Italian men and women from
the period of the Renaissance. This could be done
however only through the exercise of an arbitrariness that took no thought for the consequences.

Goethe was certainly thinking of Weimar and
not of Ferrara when he remarks concerning the
diminutive capital that "Ferrara has become great
because of its princes." The same thought was in
his creative mind when the Princess replies that it
has become great "even more because of the good
men who have come here by accident and established
mutual friendships." But there is a world of difference between Goethe's model Maecenas and the
real Alfonso II. He had the blood of the Borgias

in his veins; he patronized Tasso, as he had formerly done Ariosto, solely because of his ambition. He was narrow-minded and economical to the point of avarice. His infantry and artillery, new types of cross-bows, new cannon of various calibre, engaged his attention much more than epics and sonnets. His case reminds of that of the Electors and Kings of the House of Hohenzollern. He tried to reënforce his power through the medium of diplomatic intrigues; he suffered severe disillusionment by reason of the undpendability of faithless assistants. One of the most contemptible of these was the very Antonio Montecatino, who in Goethe's drama is the chief support of the state.

Ferrara and Weimar! Ferrara, where one made a wide detour in turning the corner so as not to have the dagger of an enemy thrust into one's heart, and Weimar, where it was forbidden by law to smoke on the streets. Nothing could resemble the Court in Weimar less than the Court of the family Este. A fearful legacy of murder, incest, dissipation, and family hatred hovered over Alfonso and his brothers and sisters: they loathed and persecuted each other. Eleanora, in Goethe's drama more nearly angelic than human, resembled in actual life a fury rather than a woman. She was wily, crafty, resolute, frigid, disputatious. If Tasso loved her and sang her praises, he could well have spared his pains. Her health, her litigation, particularly the case she instituted against her own brother, and her political intrigues occupied her attention so completely that she had no time left for love. And during one of the various conflicts that Tasso had at court with his rivals, she openly espoused the cause of his enemies. The two sisters, Eleanora and Lucretia, the two brothers, Alfonso and Ludovico, their ministers, court attendants, confidants, and court ladies constituted a circle which was as unfavorable as possible to the cultivation of refined feelings and exalted thoughts. To this group came Tasso with his host of illusions. At his arrival they were celebrating the entrance of the new Duchess, Barbara. He was completely blinded, altogether enraptured by the splendor that was unfolded before his eyes. He was not satisfied with being a mere spectator at this court drama; he wished to play a leading rôle himself; and by reason of his irritable vanity he felt humiliated at every moment. With a naïveté that reminds Danes of Hans Christian Andersen,[26] he himself confessed the chief yearnings of his life: "My highest wish has always been not to be obliged to work, to be flattered by my friends, carefully waited on by servants, petted by those around me, glorified by poets, and pointed at by the populace." This was the ideal condition which he had hoped to find in Ferrara where he so soon felt bitterly disappointed.

Tasso seems to have inherited a tendency to insanity from his mother, and from his early youth to

---

[26] Hans Christian Andersen (1805-1875) has done as much to make Denmark known in the world at large as any other individual who spoke and wrote the Danish language. His fairy tales have been translated into virtually all the civilized languages. But he was a child his whole life long. Known and honored throughout the entire world for his fantastic tales, in which is buried a wealth of homely but profound wisdom, the appearance of a review that was not kindly written could make him lose complete control of his temper, his will-power, and certainly his peace of mind. He wrote to entertain people and lived on adulation. Few men have been more naïve or wiser in the things that touch upon human nature.   —TRANSLATOR.

have led a restless and tortured existence. His
father was obliged to flee from the Inquisition and
take him along. From his thirtieth year on he lived
in constant dread of the Inquisition, suffered from
sensory delusions, heard sounds as though there
were a clock in his ear, heard voices and saw cats
and spectres. In Antonio Montecatino he believed,
he who suffered from the delusions of persecution,
that he saw the courtier among his persecutors.
When, in 1577, he fell upon a servant with a dagger,
because he imagined that this servant was a spy in
the employ of the Inquisition, the Duke gave him a
few days house arrest. But in 1579 he had Tasso
placed in a ward for the insane in the St. Anna Hos-
pital where he remained for seven years. After his
release the poet wandered about in a restless condition, lived for the most part in monasteries, suffered
severe deprivation, and died in Rome in 1595, fifty
years old.

Goethe's Tasso really gives the impression of a
man whose mind is diseased, though it is not the
poet's intention that he be regarded as insane. He
pictured his hero to himself as irritable, whimsical,
fantastic, subject to moods, as Goethe himself was
when he did not succeed in controlling himself, and
as he would have become had he not, through constant self-training, got control of himself. Naturally
Goethe did not think of himself alone but in all probability of Rousseau, irascible, suspicious, and constantly suffering from the mania of persecution as
Rousseau was, and certainly also of Lenz, who had
been heartily welcomed at the court in Weimar, just
as Tasso at Ferrara, and who had, like Tasso, made
himself impossible.

It is entirely probable that from the time of the very first sketch, the idea had hovered before Goethe's mind of causing the presence of the Princess to have a pacifying, soothing, allaying effect on Tasso, just as the presence of Iphigenie had on Orestes, that is to say, as Charlotte von Stein had on him himself. The following verses are almost an exact rewriting of what he had said again and again concerning himself in his letters to her. Tasso reveals to the Princess his feelings as he made his way through the quiet corridors of the castle, moved by passions, and finally entered for the first time the room where she, followed by her maids, appeared on the threshold:

> Welch ein Moment war dieser! O vergieb mir!
> Wie den Bezauberten von Rausch und Wahn
> Der Gottheit Nähe leicht und willing heilt,
> So war auch ich von aller Phantasie,
> Von jeder Sucht, von jedem falschen Triebe
> Mit *einem* Blick in Deinen Blick geheilt.

If we compare, however, Goethe's Tasso with the historical Tasso, and his Ferrara with the real Ferrara, we receive the same impression from *Tasso* that we receive from *Iphigenie,* as contrasted with *Götz* and the original *Egmont.* The time has come when the conception he was about to form of his own personality, his art, his life as a whole, removed him from all externality. He had begun to purify, to cleanse, to lave away the reality he had so loved and praised in *Götz* and *Werther.*

CHAPTER XXIII

Wilhelm Meisters Theatralische Sendung

SCARCELY three years had elapsed since the completion of *Die Leiden des jungen Werthers* when Goethe laid the plans of another novel, much longer than the first and originally entitled *Wilhelm Meisters theatralische Sendung.* In February, 1777, he dictated the beginning; in January, 1778, he finished the first book. But his life was so distracted and the elaboration of the novel proceeded so slowly that he did not finish the second book until five and a half years after having written the first lines. He wrote on the third hurriedly until November, 1782, and on the fourth more slowly until November, 1783. He worked on the fifth and sixth books until 1786. All of this was merely the sketch of the first four books of what many years later received the title of *Wilhelm Meisters Lehrjahre.* At the request of Herder and the Dowager Duchess Amalie, he took the work in hand again in 1791. The first two books were finished in June, 1794. And then, in 1796, more than nineteen years after the beginning had been written, *Wilhelm Meisters Lehrjahre* finally appeared.

It had become a common belief that the oldest form of the novel was lost. But in January, 1910, there was discovered in Zürich the above mentioned copy of Goethe's original plan of the first six books. They found a place in the complete work, not as they had been originally written, but changed, emended, revised and completely rearranged. The original sketch—the *Sendung,* came out in two large volumes in 1911.

By virtue of its plain, inoffensively diffuse method of portrayal, the *Sendung* contains information of an invaluable sort, not simply by way of a better appreciation of *Wilhelm Meisters Lehrjahre,* but for the entire life of Goethe as a young man and poet. He is twenty-nine years old when he begins to write the story; he continues to work at it, with interruptions of course, until he is thirty-seven. Then he laid it aside. In seven or eight years he returns to it. He subjects it to a thorough revision and completes it.

Outside of Germany the novel in its completed form has never enjoyed unreserved popularity. In the memory of the majority, it stands nowadays as massive, bulky, prolix, slow in developing, and clumsily composed. To read it requires some of the great patience that was necessary to write it. It is in very truth a spring of riches, a river that wends its way over sands of gold, but a river that meanders, winding in and out with numerous curves and bends. Just, however, because the book did not come into existence at one single stroke, or at one casting, but in such a fashion that the section originally intended as the beginning is interpolated later in modified and abbreviated form, and owing to the fact that the original plan is widened, deepened and added to—for these reasons and others that become self-evident on reading it, marked perspicuity and easy survey do not constitute its most pronounced features, though they are more evident in the first copy, this treasure that was lost and has been found.

In it the hero is not so far removed from Goethe himself. The poet has, to be sure, done everything that lay in his power to keep Wilhelm separate and distinct from his own personality. He has made the father the excellent and rational element in the marriage of the parents while he has made the mother, in as strong contrast to his own mother as possible, an intolerable woman who, after having borne her husband five children, is caught up by a passion for an insipid man, which makes her seem even more absurd and provokes all manner of strife and discord in the home.

Wilhelm's talents, on the other hand, are nearer to Goethe's own. The discriminating irony with which his unsuspecting simplicity in the novel is depicted, is not perceptible in the *Sendung*. He frequently makes himself felt through his manifest ingeniousness. He shows such rare ability as an actor, that he never abandons the stage, as he did in the novel, because of his retrograding talent. Moreover, his calling as a poet stands out undeniable and real. Here indeed we have a marked similarity to Goethe himself.

Even in the *Sendung* he dreams of establishing a national German theatre, not simply as an actor, but primarily as a dramatist. Again and again Goethe returns to Wilhelm's attempt as a dramatic author. One feels that it is in this sphere that his gifts are surest. By reason of his dramaturgic knowledge and ability, he is able at his very first appearance on the stage to take a rôle that he himself had written and to make a profound impression in it as an actor and interpreter.

Significant indeed is the explanation of what attracts Wilhelm more and more to the theatre in proportion as his feelings gain in warmth and his imagination in flight. He is confined in a city; he is caught in the current of narrow-minded urban society; he is depressed from living in a house which has no outlook on nature, and which affords him liberty neither of mind nor of heart. When he takes a walk in the open air he is unable to assimilate the impressions that become intermerged with his being.

Here it is that expressions are used which could never apply to Goethe himself, such as the statement that Wilhelm is constantly paying nature a visit, and that nature in turn treats him as her guest. Where could he go with his premonitory feelings of love, friendship and valor! The theatre becomes for him a place of refuge, a place where, under roof, he oversees with comfort all the glories of nature; where he has the entire world in a nutshell. He avers that all unnatural feelings of nature are conjured up in this one focus, the stage.

Wilhelm, like his creator, began by writing pastoral plays; and like his creator he writes them in Alexandrines. When he shows these works to his friends, they ask him whether anyone has helped him to write them. By way of reply, Wilhelm uses an expression which sounds quite autobiographic: From his very youth he has always been able to speak or write in any metre that he had heard or read. He praises the genius and calling of the poet.

The poet has received all these things, for which men strive, from nature; nature enables him to enjoy his surroundings, and feel at ease with them. The poet feels the sorrowful and the joyful in the fate of all men; and he does so without consuming melancholy or blatant delight. The poet is a teacher; he is a prophet; he is a friend of the gods and a friend of men. This innate passion for the art of poetry can be checked just as little as any other natural impulse can be checked without thereby undoing the man in question. From his very childhood Wilhelm has experienced this irresistible urge.

In the novel Wilhelm Meister is nowhere so clearly depicted as a poet, nor could he be, because he was not supposed to end his days as a spiritual creator. A whim that was possibly more than a whim of the aged poet has him close his career, in the *Wanderjahre,* as a physician.

Coördinate with his laudation of poetry as an art is his glorification of the work of the actor. With the same impulse to speak ill of her own class that has caused many an actor to refer to his profession as sheer buffoonery, Melina has said that the standing of the actor is wretched. Wilhelm replies by remarking that the same might be said of many other callings, that of the politician or the soldier or the clergyman, by way of concrete illustrations. He exclaims with something of Goethe's own strong feeling for life: There have been people who were so thoroughly bereft of humanity that they declared life as a whole to be an abominable affair. But Werner, as in the novel, stands up for his vocation. His eloquent defense against Wilhelm's contemptuous remarks concerning the standing of the merchant corresponds to Antonio's attitude toward Tasso.

Wilhelm's youthful infatuation for the actress Marianne is sketched from the very moment of the first indication of love until the union between them stands out in full flower. Wilhelm's tortures are portrayed much more forcibly than in the novel, those tortures that arose when he learned of Marianne's relations to another man. In the novel he passes an unheard-of judgment on her, though he suffers the pangs of Hell, pangs which the more mature author, however, regards with the superior air of a being too great for such emotions. In a very significant, though naïve way, Goethe disapproves, in the *Sendung,* not simply as an artist of the fact that Wilhelm resigns to his anguish by living in obscurity, cut off from the outside world; he also reproaches him for beginning to drink coffee when in this condition: "This publicly distributed poison, harmful both to body and purse, was exceedingly dangerous to him." One is reminded at once of his notorious reply to Frau von Stein when she passionately complained of his relation to Christiane Vulpius, in which he said it was clear from her letter that she had again begun to drink coffee.

Aside from coffee, Goethe also cherished a cordial detestation for tobacco. This leads him to remark that Wilhelm, in his embittered condition, "at last found happiness in his pipe." In Goethe's estimation he could not have fallen deeper. Nor is it apparent that he realizes the amusing incongruity between the despair born of infidelity on the part of a sweetheart and the joy he had from a can of tobacco. In this connection Goethe wrote an oft-quoted epigramme:

Vieles kann ich ertragen. Die meisten beschwerlichen
      Dinge
   Duld' ich mit ruhigem Muth, wie es ein Gott mir
      gebeut.
Wenige sind mir jedoch wie Gift und Schlange zuwider;
   Viere: Rauch das des Tobaks, Wanzen und Knoblauch
      und Kreuz.

All of the marvelous songs of Mignon and the Harper, the verses in which the completed work attains in reality its highest excellence, are found in the *Sendung*. There is only one difference: The songs in the novel are occasionally changed, and when changed it is always for the better. In the first form of Mignon's famous *Kennst du das Land* each stanza ends with the words: *O mein Gebieter*. In the novel there are three variants: *O mein Geliebter, O mein Beschützer,* and *O Vater*.

A lampoon which gives occasion to a superfluous scene is later omitted, while Philine's bewitching song is not written at all. Otherwise the two most remarkable characters of the work, Mignon and Philine, are as complete and perfect in the *Sendung* as in the novel. In other words, Goethe's ability to create characters was so well developed at that time that improvement was impossible. The later additions have to do largely with practical wisdom, wealth of thoughts and comprehensiveness of survey. So far as poetry itself is concerned, the completed novel is of no higher value than the masterful sketch from the days of his youth.

Philine especially is as real and corporeal a figure as there is in the book. She is frivolous and forward, bold and blithe; she is almost invariably referred to with aversion and not rarely with disgust by those about her. Yet she preserves in the eye of the reader a never failing grace. She is a great *canaille* but a greater work of art; and she disappears almost entirely in those books of *Wilhelm Meister* that were added during the revision.

There are passages in the *Sendung* that are much more effective than they are in the finished novel, because in the latter they are placed so far apart from each other that they are no longer felt as contrasts, and the effect is lost. This is the case with the two definitive comments on the advantages and disadvantages of the born aristocrats, of the grandees of this world.

The passage "thrice happy are they to be called who are aristocratic by birth," which in the novel is spoken by Wilhelm, is far more telling in the *Sendung* where the praise of prominent people is the poet's own. The passage closes with the following words that are omitted entirely in the novel: All hail to the grandees of this earth! All hail to those who come in contact with the great, drink of their fountain, and participate in the advantages they enjoy. And again all hail to the genius of our friend who made the first step toward elevating him to this advanced state! There is unmistakable evidence in this of Goethe's satisfaction at being transplanted to Weimar. It sounds like unaffected homage to the distinguished society to which he was there introduced.

Quite close, however, to this, and without question meant as a contrast to it, is the passage in the *Sendung* in which Goethe shows how easy it is for

the distinguished to win the humble; they need to
pay them just a little attention, or to bestow upon
them just a few gifts the bestowal of which does
not mean a real sacrifice. The poor, however, if
they wish to win someone, are obliged to give their
whole soul. With no little bitterness attention is
drawn to the fact that the distinguished lack respect
for art, and that they are indifferent to the best in
art; they have in short precious little aesthetic or artistic appreciation. The expressions along this line
are spoken by the actor, but it is certain that they,
like the other ones already mentioned, sprang from
Goethe's personal experience at the court of
Weimar.

The deletion of the jocose passages bearing on
contemporary events is instructive. One such is particularly so, for it obviously refers to Schiller's
Räuber. Since the book was finished during his
friendship with Schiller, and at his urgent appeal,
the statement naturally had to be omitted. It follows the description of the bivouac of the travelling troupe, and reads as follows:

We cannot conceal the fact from the readers that this
was the original scene, copies and imitations of which have
been seen on the German stage *ad nauseam*. The idea of
amiable vagabonds, noble robbers, magnanimous gipsies, and
all sorts of idealized rabble in general has its real origin in
the rest camp of this troupe which we have depicted with a
goodly measure of reluctance. For it cannot help but be
sorely vexing to find an opportunity to familiarize the public with the original only after the copies have long since
robbed the theme of its novelty and attraction

There are several passages, however, in which
the self-sufficiency and conviction of his own genius,

both admirably concealed in the novel, are given
well-nigh lyric expression in the *Sendung*. In the
former, Wilhelm frequently makes a somewhat sad
or characterless figure. After the Harper's song
on loneliness, Wilhelm has a passage in the *Sendung*
that was destined to be omitted: "The feeling of
of the nobility of his being, of the lofty goal in his
destination—to develop the sense for the good and
great among men—became once more living and
alive in him." We are told that he longed for nothing more ardently than to be able to contribute his
part "to the betterment and reformation of the
world." It seems as if Goethe had wished to refute
his earlier, and noticeably sombre, statement in
Faust:

> Bilde mir nicht ein, ich könnte was lehren
> Die Menschen zu bessern, und zu bekehren.

In a later passage—that has been taken out—
there is the statement that for the secretary of the
Count the grip with which Wilhelm took hold and
brought everything to right was something quite
new: The secretary was full of admiration for the
vivacity and dependability of feeling with which our
young poet knew how to differentiate between what
was action and effect, and what was merely narration and instruction.

Stress is laid then on *our young poet's* purely
theatrical genius, which in the case of the real
Goethe was less assured.

The passage in which Aurelie expresses her admiration for Wilhelm's talents is also found in the
Sendung. And even in it Aurelie remarks that he
recognizes things without having seen them in na-

ture; that he knows everything from within; that
he comes at almost nothing from without, or by
external means. A little later she makes use of this
significant expression; it has been modified in the
novel: "It is a fetching characteristic of *a young
poet and artist,* for you are both, though you make
no such claim for yourself. This unconsciousness
and innocence is, so to speak, the covering that envelopes and nourishes a flower bud. To be forced
from this state prematurely is a fatal misfortune."

Stress is laid on Wilhelm's unmistakable calling
as a poet, and his talents as an artist, while in the
novel he abandons all thought of the theatre when
Jarno, in his supercilious way, denies him every
spark of undisputed ability.

In the *Sendung* we find Aurelie's original disapproval of the German people. She avails herself
of a pungent expression with regard to all those
who are captivated by her: It seems to her as though
the entire nation were endeavoring to compromise
itself (she makes an erroneous use of the term "to
prostitute itself") in her eyes. In another passage,
jesting derision is heaped upon German thoroughness and tediousness. They are discussing a play
that the company is to perform: "It was a drama
in five acts, one of those that never ends, a species
of which the Germans are said to have several examples. Or maybe these are reproaches that come
from frivolous souls who admire only the foreign."

The passage has been deleted from the novel
which, condensed though it is in certain ways, cannot be entirely acquitted of the charge of diffuseness, and is to this extent genuinely German, not
merely in the best sense of the word but also in its

less acceptable connotation. Goethe nevertheless stands out even in the *Sendung,* in the original plan of the novel, as a seer, abundantly rich in the wisdom of life, and as the creator of an inimitable galaxy of living characters, now mysterious, now sensually inveigling, now clear, now complex, now passionately morbid, but all without exception forming and fashioning the leading character who is in the process of uninterrupted development down to the very last moment.

CHAPTER XXIV

PHILOSOPHICAL LYRICS—STUDIES IN NATURE:
DISCOVERIES IN ANATOMY AND GEOLOGY

DURING these same years Goethe wrote some lyric poems which show him at the height of his creative power, enrapturing as they are by reason of an imaginative force that makes itself felt though they do not seem to have been elaborated with especial care from a purely technical point of view. They are written in free rhythm and are wholly without rhyme or a fixed metre. The first of them is, to be sure, addressed to fancy; but it is not in itself noticeably distinguished because of its fancy. It reveals on the contrary a rigid and classic choice of words. This explains why these poems have retained their position in the memory of man without the affiliated aid of art.

The first one, *Meine Göttin* (1780), is a hymn to imagination and is the least important of the three. In the beginning it is a trifle conventional in the manner in which it equips fancy: to it are ascribed attributes such as the stalk of the lily, the flowing hair, the austere look. But it rises so much the higher the more simple and seemingly fanciless the expression becomes:

All the other poor generations of this thickly populated, living earth roam and live in obscure enjoyment and indistinct grief of a momentary, limited life, bent down under

414

necessity's yoke. To us, however, the god has given his most adroit, his fondled daughter. Rejoice! Grant her the dignity that would be accorded the mother of the home! See to it that the old mother-in-law, Wisdom, is not given opportunity to harm the little soul! But I know her sister, the older, more demure, my quiet friend! Would that she might not desert me before the light of my life has been extinguished, this noble doer, consoler, Hope!

The poem entitled *Grenzen der Menschheit,* written in the same vein, is simpler and more profound. Like the other poems from this same period, it has a basic tone of mortal humility. Without warning against arrogance, the poet tells in plain words of the narrow confines within which man is enclosed. If he endeavors to have his head bump into the stars, he loses his sure foothold on earth; if he stands secure on solid earth, he will rise no higher than the oak or the vine. The water of life purls by the feet of the gods in an unbroken stream; but the wave lifts us up and swallows us. Our life is encircled by a ring of diminutive diameter.

As we see, this is the poetry of thought and reflection. The same attributes must be ascribed to the third and most excellent of these poems entitled *Das Göttliche* (1782). It is the poem that begins with the simple but unforgetable words that testify to the greatness of the poet's soul:

> Edel sei der Mensch,
> Hilfreich und gut!
> Denn das allein
> Unterscheidet ihn
> Von allen Wesen
> Die wir kennen.

The poem develops, further on, the thought that nature is without feeling: The sun shines on the just and the unjust; wind and current carry the one as the other along with them. And fortune is just as arbitrary as nature: It lays hold without discrimination and at random. The law of life is unmerciful. Or, as the poem expresses it with a euphony that flatters the ear:

> Nach ewigen, ehrnen
> Grossen Gesetzen
> Müssen wir alle
> Unseres Daseins
> Kreise vollenden.

Man alone is able to differentiate, choose, judge, and give permanence to the moment. It is therefore man's duty to be helpful and good. It is entirely probable that a greater effect has never been produced by fewer words and simpler means.

Quite the opposite is true of the main poem in this vein and from the same period—that pretentious, carefully versified poem in rhymed octavos entitled *Die Geheimnisse* (1784-85). It was left lying as a brief fragment of a conscientiously planned whole. In and of itself, the meaning of the work is simple enough however poetically unsympathetic the allegorical species of poetry to which it belongs may be. The twelve knights, whom the young clergyman meets while on a tour through the mountains to a splendid convent, were supposed to represent twelve different religions, each of which has had, in its day, its period of flowering and climax. The twelve have now gathered about a single man toward whom they all feel drawn since each of them feels akin to him. Under the name of *Humanus*, Goethe glorified Herder in the loftiest

tones: He had been estranged from the same Herder when the latter, impressed by some discord, or
reflecting on the lack of natural harmony there was
between him and his friend, began to go his own
way. Then it was that Goethe appreciated the
significance of Herder all the more. In 1780, Goethe had become a member of the Anna Amalie
Lodge of Free Masons; in 1783 he was taken into
the Order of the Illuminati.

It seems as if he had laid down in this poem
the religious philosophy of Masonry, just as he did
later in the other poems, and in the mysterious activity developed by the man in the tower in *Wilhelm
Meister*. The cross surrounded by the roses in *Die
Geheimnisse* seems to allude to the teachings of the
Rosicrucians. The predilection, not so much for
mysticism—to which Goethe continued to remain a
stranger and to which in time he became almost
hostile—as for rummaging around among mysterious things, a tendency that eventually grew pronounced in him, is quite noticeable here. The teaching proclaimed is that of self-restraint, self-control,
self-conquest. It is surprising that Goethe felt that
such a ponderous apparatus was necessary for so
familiar a doctrine.

As an introduction to this unfinished poem, Goethe originally wrote, in the same metre, the poem
which at present, under the title of *Zueignung,*
serves as introduction to his complete works. It
contains a picture of exquisite charm. There is a
description of a journey to the edge of a mountain
on a dewy morning. The mist rises from the river;
the sun seems to be about to break through when,
the clouds having been dispelled, the divine form of

a woman is revealed to the wanderer. "Do you not know me?" she asks with an enrapturing voice, "I who have emptied the purest balm into your wounds, and to whom your heart has become more and more firmly attached?" "Yes," he replies, "you gave me rest; you cooled my feverish brow; you gave me the choicest of all earth's gifts. But I shall not repeat your name. For many do that, and each calls you his. When I was a wanderer I had my companions; since I know you I am alone." She stretches forth her hand after the narrow bands of clouds, and in her hand the dew becomes the purest garment: He receives the veil of *poetry* from the hand of *truth*:

> Dem Glücklichen kann es an nichts gebrechen,
> Der dies Geschenk mit stiller Seele nimmt:
> Aus Morgenduft gewebt und Sonnenklarheit,
> Der Dichtung Schleier aus der Hand der Wahrheit.

II

From his early youth Goethe had always kept in close touch with the natural sciences. In Leipzig he had attended lectures on medicine and physics; in Strassburg he had taken the course given by Spielmann on chemistry. And when, a few years later, chemistry began to make such rapid strides, he again took it up: Shortly after his arrival in Weimar we see him studying chemistry. In Jena he had Döbereiner introduce him to the art of determining and calculating chemical compounds according to weight and measurement (*Stöchiometrie*). He also participated in the experiments of Göttling and Buchholtz.

Under the guidance of Loder he studies anatomy and begins as early as 1781 to explain the human skeleton to the pupils in the drawing school at Weimar. Anatomy is one of his favorite disciplines, partly for its own sake, partly because it enables him to understand the human body as the most important object of plastic art. He studies chemistry because, during his mineralogical interests, he has felt hemmed and checked on account of his lack of knowledge of the chemical constituency of bodies, so that he has to lay mineralogy aside until he has caught up. For many years in succession he wanders through Thuringia, studies the Harz and other mountains geologically, mineralogizes and botanizes everywhere, in the middle of the eighties even at Karlsbad. As S. Kalischer has rightly said, "For him no mountain is too high, no well too deep, no passage way in the mines that anyone else has used too low, no cave too labyrinthine." Wherever he goes he studies the botanical gardens, the natural museums and collections. He makes independent observations on every optical phenomenon and draws his own illustrations. He makes collections of stones, plants, bone preparations, all sorts of petrifactions, and he himself takes passionate interest in establishing scientific laboratories in Jena.

At every point he begins anew to make observations and increase his experience. In the forests he looks up the foresters, the herb-gatherers, the essence-cookers in order to enter into the mysteries of botany. He associates with the owners of herbariums; he makes observations in his own garden; he reads everything he can get pertaining to botany in the library at Weimar as well as elsewhere.

He approaches his theories of the natural sciences
in a practical way during his administration of the
crown forests at Weimar, while in control of the
university collections at Jena, and while studying
statuary. It has already been said above that his
studies in mining in Ilmenau did not lead to practical results. The statement is correct, and yet they
did accomplish one thing: they initiated him into
the science of geology in which field his discoveries
(as is also the case in ostelogy and botany) constitute an enduring contribution to the study of natural
science in general.

The scientists of Goethe's time hurt themselves
tremendously by the treatment they accorded him
in their own field. Posterity has made reparations
for his name, though insufficient. Nothing testifies
so eloquently to Goethe's genius and to the significance of his artistic activity, to the reality of the
characters he produced and the thoughts he thought
within various spiritual fields, as his discoveries in
the realm of natural science. This is true not
simply because they prove the vast compass of his
mind, somewhat after the fashion of Pascal. Pascal's greatness as a physicist gives us confidence in
his seriousness and ingeniousness as a philosopher
of religion. We see his soul grieving under the
tortures of existence and clinging to the consola-
tions of a fanciful world. No, the testimony is
eloquent, first and foremost because these discoveries give a standard of the depth to which Goethe
sounded nature's mysteries in man and beyond
man. For, directly contrary to Schiller's philosophy, Goethe conceived of man as in no way contrasted with nature, but always included in it.

Though he never rejoiced over any of his poetic works that chanced to meet with marked success, Goethe cannot help but rejoice over his scientific discoveries—though he is prepared in advance to see them scorned without reason and besmirched without cause. Thus it is that an individual of to-day feels rapture over his astonishingly prophetic eye as a naturalist. Viewing Goethe from this angle, we feel a respect and reverence that are nearly deeper than those evoked by studying his purely poetic creations.

Goethe never enjoyed an especially strong constructive imagination; his *Wilhelm Meister* and *Faust* are both imperfectly composed. And yet he had, in a way, a most surprising eye for composition. Think of his genius along this line in the field of plastic art! For the individual who has read his article on Leonardo's *The Last Supper,* the picture from that time on invariably falls into the various groups of three persons each that Goethe pointed out. With regard to nature, this ingenious eye is shown in the discovery of the great laws of composition. And with him composition is related to uninterrupted evolution. The idea of evolution, on which all scientific studies of the nineteenth century are based, had no champion equal to Goethe in the preceding decades.

His poetically designed treatise entitled *Die Natur,* of the year 1780, a series of animated and more or less enraptured aphorisms, is a composite expression of the worship and adoration of nature, motivated if not directly inspired by Spinoza's *Deus sive natura.* The poet attempts to elucidate nature's mysterious being by citing a number of the

contrasts and contradictions involved in a conception of it. There is an express renunciation of the
personality of nature as we know it, and yet the
author has enough of the poet in him to speak as
though familiar with nature's characteristics and
methods of procedure. Swinburne expressed himself in precisely the same fashion ninety years later
in his poem entitled *Hertha*. That nature is to be
presumed as the One and All, compels us to ascribe
to it mutually contrasting and excluding propensi-
ties and purposes. Its very interminability makes
it difficult for us to pass judgment upon it. In
Goethe's utterances there is nothing but reverence
for nature, a reconciliation with its coldness, and
a love for it that is defiant at the mention of the
lack of a common measure, and that makes it
possible for us to evaluate its being, and man's being as well. Here are a few specimens of these
apothegms :

Nature! We are entwined and surrounded by it, incapable of getting out of it, incapable of penetrating it more
deeply. It takes us into the circle of its dance, unbidden
and unwarned. It drives us along with it until we are
tired, exhausted, and fall from its embrace.

It plays a drama; whether it itself sees this, we do not
know. And still it plays this drama for us who are standing in the corner.

Its children are innumerable. Toward no one is it
everywhere covetous. But it has its favorites, on whom it
squanders, to whom it makes great sacrifices. It attaches
its protection to greatness.

It envelopes man in the mists of obscurity, and spurs him
to light eternal. It makes him dependent upon the earth, leth-
argic and heavy, and constantly shakes him out of his torpor.

Man obeys its laws even when he opposes them; man works
with it even when he works *against* it.

It has no language, no speech, but it creates tongues and hearts by the help of which it feels and speaks. . . .

Its crown is love. Only through love can one approach it. It creates a gulf between all beings, and everything will consume itself. It has isolated all things in order to bring all things together. With a few drafts from love's beaker, it completely indemnifies one for all trouble. . . .

Past and future it does not know. For it the present is eternity. It is gracious. I praise it, with all its works. It is wise and quiet. No explanation can be wrenched from its body; no gift can be extorted from it that it will not bestow voluntarily. It is cunning, but with good intentions; and it is best not to notice its cunning.

A great deal of this is reminiscent of Spinoza, some of it is soon to be expressed by Hegel, and the last part of it anticipates Schopenhauer. The entire work is a didactic poem in prose and is to be regarded merely as an overture to the strictly scientific investigations and philosophic observations that follow.

Goethe's botanical studies, which led to the discovery of the metamorphosis of plants, have to do with the origin of forms. He finds one single fundamental law working throughout numerous transformations. His whole being, which was borne along on faith in unity in the manifold, on the spiritual bond that unites the apparently heterogeneous, always led him to find unity where others had divided into rubrics. It was by virtue of his ability to draw comprehensive conclusions from scattered though thorough observations that he was the first in geology to give voice to the theory of an ice age, or as he calls it an age of lasting cold, in the prehistoric world.

As a geologist he was the first to understand the

significance of the remains of fossil plants and animals by way of determining the age of the strata
of the earth.   Quite remarkable in this regard is
a letter from him to Merck, October 27, 1782, in
which he first explains to his friend that the remains of bones in the upper strata of sand belong
to the most recent age, an age, however, which from
our present method of reckoning is incalculably old.
He says that at that time the elephant and the
rhinoceros were indigenous to North Germany, and
that their remains have been washed down by mountain streams into the valleys where they are found
at present.   He also prophesies—and correctly so
—that the time will come when one will no longer
confound various petrifactions with each other; one
will arrange them with care according to their relation to the various ages of the earth.

Goethe's sole and remote predecessor in this matter is the Dane, Niels Steensen,[27] who, in 1669,
made a distinction between mountains in which organic remains are found and those in which they
are not found.   This distinction, however, is of
relatively little importance in comparison with Goethe's, and Goethe was not familiar with it at the
time.   He proceeded here, as always, from what he
had actually observed with his own eyes.   At the
close of his sojourn in Strassburg, he climbed, while
on a tour through Lorraine, the Bast Mountain,

[27] Brandes wrote these lines in 1915. Four years later he
changed them—for the benefit of the German edition—to read as
follows: "Goethe's predecessors in this field were Leonardo da
Vinci, Bernard Palissy and Niels Steensen. Leonardo did no more
than explain the presence of conchyliaceaus matter on high mountains. Palissy was as an artist only a mineralogist. Steensen's
investigations, like the studies of Leonardo and the investigations
of Palissy, remained unknown to Goethe."   —TRANSLATOR.

which consists entirely of mussels, and called to
mind—with contempt—Voltaire's mediaeval explanation of this accumulation as a "freak of nature." He understood that he was standing on an
old, dried-up sea-bed.

As an assistant in his geological studies, he employed a young student by the name of Voigt, who
drew up a mineralogical map of Weimar and Jena.
With it he felt secure; he could give an account of
the structure of each mountain and plain. He even
had Charpentier's mineralogical chart developed so
that it extended from the Harz to the Fichtelge-
birge, from the Riesengebirge to the Basalt Mountains of the Rhön. And what is more, he expressed
in a letter to Merck his great desire to have a mineralogical map made of the whole of Europe. Such
a map would have been of the greatest advantage.
Goethe was the first to think of it.

It was granite that held the chief attraction for
Goethe as a student of mineralogy. In a letter to
Frau von Stein he speaks of being "enraptured by
the granites." He dreams and writes about this
Urstein, just as he does with regard to the *Urpflanze.* Early in 1784 he dictates his treatise entitled *Ueber den Granit,* one of the choicest bits
of German prose ever written: The enormous
masses of granite inspired the Egyptian kings with
the idea of gigantic works. Pointed columns in
honor of the sun, Sphinxes, and Memnon statues
testify to their inspiration to this very day. Italian
naturalists fancied that the obelisks were erected
by a floating mass which, congealed, became granite.
But the stone was soon restored to its place of
honor. One came to see that granite was the high-

est and the deepest, the foundation of the earth. What captivates Goethe is the manifoldness in the greatest simplicity. For the general situation and the relation of the parts to each other, also the colors, all shift and change with each different mountain; indeed the masses of each individual mountain are often quite different from step to step, while as a whole it is all the same.

Whoever appreciates the attractions that nature's mysteries have for man will not be surprised to learn that I have abandoned the circle of observations I was formerly wont to cultivate and have turned to these with passionate attachment. I do not fear the reproach that it must be the spirit of contradiction which has led me away from observations and portrayals of the human heart, the *youngest,* most manifold, most movable, most changeable part of creation, *just as it is the easiest to shake,* to observations of nature's *oldest, firmest, deepest, most unshakable son.* For one will surely agree with me that all natural things stand in close connection, and that the seeking mind does not like to be excluded from anything obtainable. Grant me then—I who have suffered and still suffer many things and much from changes in human disposition, from its rapid and incessant mutability, not only in my own case, but in that of others as well—grant me the exalted rest which great, low-voiced nature's mute and lonely presence affords.

This contrasting of the human heart with granite, with a certain predilection for the latter, corresponds quite accurately to the epigramme written by way of self-defense a few years later:

Mit Botanik giebst Du Dich ab, mit Optik? Was thust Du?
  Ist es nicht schönrer Gewinn, rühren ein zärtliches Herz?
Ach, die zärtlichen Herzen! Ein Pfuscher vermag sie zu
  rühren;
  Sei es mein einziges Glück, Dich zu berühren, Natur!

Conspicuous in this little treatise on granite is a sentence which reveals Goethe's feeling for the analogy between this sort of stone, which for him is "the first and firmest beginning of our existence," and what has recently, with reference to the *Urfaust,* been called "the purely elementary, the most profoundly original element in the life of feeling, that which is indissoluble in its eternal simplicty, unshakable and firm as granite." (Page 289) Goethe writes: "So lonely, I say to myself as I look down upon this perfectly barren mountain ridge and glimpse in the distance at its foot a tiny bit of verdant moss, so lonely does man become if he but open his soul to the oldest, the first, the most basic feeling of eternal truth."

There was neither thought nor desire on Goethe's part, however, of allowing his enthusisam to lead him into conceiving of nature as something firm and fixed, finished and final. From the very first and incessantly he conceives of everything on earth as genesis, formation, transformation, development. He often says that in order to arrive at a living conception of nature we, of and by ourselves, must see to it that we become and continue as movable and formable and pliable as nature itself.

It was entirely clear to him that changes in nature take an incalculable amount of time. In this, as in other points, he anticipates Darwinism. In the contest between the Vulcanists and the Neptunists, a contest that was rife during his day, he always espoused the cause of the Neptunists, it being impossible for him to see how whole mountain ranges could be thrown up over night from a molten and flowing interior. He was, on the contrary,

saturated with and possessed of the idea that
changes in nature come about most slowly, most de-
liberately.   Thirty-four years ago I wrote concerning him: "He extends one hand to Thales, the other
to Darwin."   He himself referred to Thales and
compared himself with Thales.

In the second part of *Faust* he has Anaxagoras,
a man of eighty years, ask:

> Hast Du, O Thales, je in *einer* Nacht
> Solch einen Berg aus Schlamm hervorgebracht?

And he has Thales answer:

> Nie war Natur und ihr lebend'ges Fliessen
> Auf Tag und Nacht und Stunden angewiesen;
> Sie bildet regelnd jegliche Gestalt,
> Und selbst im Grossen ist es nicht Gewalt.

We have already seen how addicted the young
Goethe was to the use of *Jahrtausend* as a strong
expression supposed to portray the strength of the
heart's feelings and the senses' yearnings.   A few
years later *Jahrtausend* has taken on a wholly different, a profounder and a more nearly real significance as the expression for the time that nature
requires to effect its transformations.

He patiently tolerates the fact that even Herder,
whose *Aelteste Urkunde des Menschengeschlechts*
and *Ideen zur Philosophie der Geschichte,* had developed even him as a naturalist, now mocked at
Goethe for going around about with his hammer
pecking on mute and silent stones.   He is filled
with the mission of natural science; predilection for
the untrue must be exterminated, and this natural
science does.   He writes (December 15, 1784) to
Knebel: "It teaches and proves that the greatest,

the most mysterious and most magical moves along
in a perfectly regular, simple, open fashion; it must
in time heal poor unthinking, unknowing men of
their thirst for the vaguely supernatural." It is
the miracle that he has in mind.

Just as he now, in mineralogy and geology, riv-
eted his attention on the dead, the skeleton in the
earth of various lands, just so does he study the human skeleton, and that with great zeal. This leads
him to the discovery of the intermaxillary bone in
the human skull, the existence of which up to this
time had been denied by such leading osteologists
as Blumenbach, Sömmering, and the Dutch Camper.
A fundamental difference between man and other
mammiferous animals was hereby abrogated once
for all. One had made a distinct approach to the
idea of a common development of all creatures.

On March 27, 1784, he writes from Jena to Charlotte von Stein this felicitous and touching note, the
second for that day:

A few lines to my Lotte by way of saying good morning,
for unfortunately I shall not be able to say good evening.
I have been granted a delightful satisfaction. I have made
an anatomical discovery that is at once beautiful and important. You shall also have your share in it. But do not
say a word about it. A letter is bringing the news also to
Herder under the seal of silence. I am so happy that my
heart is moved within me.

Farewell! Oh how I love you! How strongly I feel
this in my happy and my dejected moments! Do not answer
my note; but let me find a few words from you in my home.
Farewell, my Lotte! Everything is going so beautifully
with me because you love me.

In the letter to Herder we read:

I have found neither silver nor gold, but I have found

something that gives me unspeakable joy; the *os intermaxillare* in the human skull. With Loder I compared the skull of man with that of an animal, caught the clue, and behold, there it is. . . . It is the keystone to man. It is not lacking; it too is there.

The bone fastened to the upper jaw and on which the incisors rest had been conceded to the ape by some anatomists who denied its existence in the skull of man; and it was precisely this lack that was made to constitute the essential difference between man and the monkey. Goethe could not bring himself to believe in the heterogeneity in the construction of the skeletons of beings that were otherwise so homogeneous. Nor was he satisfied with the mere corroboration of his find. He began a methodical comparison of the form and position of the intermaxillary bone in the skulls of all animals that he could get hold of, even in that of a young Indian elephant that he had had sent to him from Cassel. His monograph entitled *Versuch aus der vergleichenden Knochenlehre, dass der Zwischenknochen der oberen Kinnlade dem Menschen mit den übrigen Thieren gemein sei,* is of uncommon significance in that it is the very first treatise that was ever written on comparative anatomy.

The manuscript with the drawings was sent to Merck, who sent it on to Sömmering in Cassel, who in turn sent it on to Camper in Holland where it did not arrive, however, until after the expiration of nine months. The manuscript and the tables remained in Holland after Camper's death. They were not returned to Germany—to the Goethe archives—until 1894. Neither of the two scholars would have anything to do with Goethe's proofs.

This was the first great scientific disappointment the discoverer was to suffer. This it was, too, that kept him from publishing his work for so long.

In the meantime he continued his studies; he took up the anatomy of the vertebrae of the neck, from their coalescence into a single bone in the case of the whale to their expansion in the long neck of the giraffe. He planned tables for the comparison of them for each individual vertebrate animal concerned. And just as he in his study of the plant went so far that he could trace the composite forms of the flower and fruit back to a single leaf, just so did he finally hit upon the idea that the skull which surrounds the brain, as well as the vertebral column which surrounds the spinal cord, consists of vertebrae which have undergone a transformation. He thought that he could detect three such vertebrae in the reverse side of the skull: the occiput bone, and the front and back sphenoid. And then it came to pass in 1790, during his second sojourn in Italy, as he was walking along the strand of the Lido beyond Venice he found a sheep's skull so happily broken, for his purpose, that he discovered at once three vertebrae in the skull: the palatal bone, the upper jaw-bone and the intermaxillary bone. By merely seeing it with his own eyes he understood the action of the organs of seeing, hearing and smelling which, transformed, had given these their final shape. This established forever the belief in his mind that was henceforth to constitute at once his strength and his weakness as a naturalist: "That nature conceals no mystery which it does not in this place or that reveal to the naked eye of the attentive observer."

CHAPTER XXV

Prometheus: SPINOZA AND LESSING

IN the year 1785 Goethe did not feel so well
physically as he had in his younger days. Then it
was that he undertook his first journey to Karlsbad
which he was to visit so regularly later on in life.
On the one hand he was benefited by the water;
on the other he found himself surrounded there by
a circle of new and vivacious guests. The first time,
and also the second, he met there, moreover, the
dearest of his friends from the Weimar circle, the
Duchess Luise, Herder, and Frau von Stein. As
early as 1785 he had thought of fleeing from daily
life and taking a journey to Italy. But it was not
until his second stay in Karlsbad, in 1786, that he
quietly and without revealing his plans to anyone,
betook himself southward from the Bohemian
watering place and, true to his fondness for mystification, travelled incognito under the name of
Möller.

During the period from 1783 to 1786, Goethe
again takes up the intensive study of Spinoza, to
whom he had formerly said what Dante had said
to Vergil: *Tu se' lo mio maestro e'l mio autore.*
Spinoza's influence upon him he confessed at all
times. The cause of his renewed interest in the
great philosopher was Fritz Jacobi's book *Ueber*

die Lehre des Spinoza which, to be sure, did not
appear until 1785, though Goethe had become familiar with it two years previous to its publication.

This study could not help but have a pronounced
influence on Goethe. Its point of departure was a
remark made by Lessing concerning Goethe's poem
entitled *Prometheus*. Lessing had been dead but
a few years. Otherwise inimical to much that Goethe had to say and do, Lessing had declared himself
to be quite in agreement with the thought Goethe
had set forth in *Prometheus*. Jacobi's book is a
queer bit of ratiocination, diffuse in technique, and
like everything else that came from Jacobi's hand,
it was written in a self-complacent and undisciplined
manner. The copy in my own library belonged to
Adam Oehlenschläger; he had written his name in
it, though he had never cut the leaves. That Oehlenschläger bought it shows, nevertheless, that genuine
worth and real importance were attached to it even
in later years. The sensation it evoked rested, however, in no way on its intrinsic value: it was due
to the fact that, quite to the dismay of Lessing's
good friend, Mendelssohn, it revealed Lessing's religious views. Mendelssohn had believed all along
that Lessing was loyal to a personal God; now it
became clear to him that the author of *Nathan der
Weise* was a Spinozist.

In July, 1780, Jacobi had come to Wolfenbüttel
to make the personal acquaintance of Lessing. On
the first day they spoke of important matters and
various persons, moral and immoral, theists and
atheists, and Christians. The second day the critic
and poet entered Jacobi's room as the latter was
engaged in writing some letters. In order to hold

Lessing while thus occupied, Jacobi gave him something to read. Lessing returned it with the questions: "Have you nothing else?" "Yes," replied Jacobi, "here is a poem. You have yourself caused vexation on many an occasion, now you may become vexed in turn." Having read *Prometheus*, Lessing said: "I have not become vexed. I have long been familiar with this." Jacobi remarked: "Do you know the poem?" Lessing said he had never seen it before, but that he found it quite good.

The conversation continued. Jacobi said that he found it good too in its way, otherwise he would never have given it to Lessing:

Lessing: I do not quite mean that: the point of view of the poem is also my point of view. The orthodox conceptions of the godhead no longer exist for me; I cannot endure them: ἓν καὶ πᾶν (One and All)! I know of nothing else. That is what the poem aims at, and I must confess that I like it very much. *Jacobi:* Then you agree with Spinoza? *Lessing:* Were I to name myself after someone, I know of no other name.

It is no wonder that this conversation again directed Goethe's attention to the great philosopher who had died more than a hundred years previously (1677), this great philosopher who earlier than any other modern thinker had taught and proved what was Goethe's own conviction: That the truths which science reveals surpass by far the visions and dreams that science annihilates. However scholastic his philosophy was in form, in its content it displayed a hatred of scholasticism and overcame it, just as Goethe in time overcame the pedantic erudition of his day. Spinoza had found the conception of deity inadequate and imperfect, not merely on

the part of the masses but on that of the thinkers
as well.   He had come to see that it is impossible
to give the infinite a finite place; that the godhead
must be one and all or nothing; and that the divine,
if anything at all, must penetrate all.   His God did
not create nature, but was nature's being.

Naturally Spinoza did not have the conception
of life that he would have had had he known modern chemistry and physiology.   For him the universe was merely a matter of extension and thought;
he never rose to the living and fruitful infinite which
history and natural science show us ruling in boundless space.   Conceptions such as evolution and progress were foreign to him.   The world, as he conceived it, seemed crystalized.   But he saw more
keenly than anyone the idea that also captivated
Goethe's mind—the eternal identity that lies at
the basis of passing wave motions.   And he converted Goethe's dislike of the supernatural into a
hard and fixed conviction.

For Spinoza the supernatural is meaningless: An
object outside of nature would be outside of the
existent.   The prophets of olden times had been
men whose knowing and perceiving was of the same
type as our own.   The quality of being the Son of
God had not been the exclusive privilege of one
individual.   God's Son was the eternal and divine
wisdom which revealed itself everywhere, and especially in the mind of man.   Without this wisdom,
approach to the state of eternal happiness was unthinkable.   Spinoza added:

Concerning the codicils of certain churches in this connection, I must expressly remark that I do not understand
what they say.   They seem to me to speak the same lan-

guage that he uses who would insist that the circle has taken
on the nature of the square.

Spinoza, whose motto was not to be surprised,
not to be angry, not to mock nor hate nor despise
but to understand, fortified Goethe in his basic passion—his impulse to understand.

Even the historical character could not help but
arouse his living admiration. This serene and peaceful thinker had done what Goethe in his later years
had desired and praised without ceasing: He had
renounced; and his renunciation had been markedly
different from Goethe's own. The King of France
had offered him an annuity; he declined it. The
Elector of the Palatinate had offered him a professorship at Heidelberg with the remark that he
would be quite free, but with the appended comment
that the Prince was convinced that Spinoza would
not abuse his great office, with its atmosphere of
freedom, to attack the religion of the State. Spinoza
replied:

> I do not quite understand within precisely what limits I
> must use this freedom to philosophize, which one is so liberal
> as to concede me, on the condition that I do not attack the
> religion of the State.

He declined the offer; he continued to live the most
retired sort of life, earning the few pennies he
needed from day to day by grinding lenses. Like
Goethe, he had loved joy:

> It is a superstition to look upon sadness as being some-
> thing good, and to label everything wicked that causes joy.
> The Deity would have to be a jealous, envious being if it
> could find satisfaction in my personal impotence and suffer-
> ings. No, the greater joy we feel, the more nearly we attain

unto perfection, and the greater part we have in the exact nature of the Deity.

This and nothing more had been Goethe's gospel for a decade. As early as December, 1774, he had sent Merck the verses beginning, "My old gospel I bring to you once more," and in which he had extolled a joyous nature with all the exuberance of youth:

> Wer nicht richtet, sondern fleissig ist
> Wie ich bin and wie du bist,
> Den belohnet auch die Arbeit mit genuss,
> Nichts wird auf der Welt ihm Ueberdruss . . .
> Sieh, so ist Natur ein Buch lebendig,
> Unverstanden, doch nicht unverständlich,
> Denn dein Herz hat viel und gross Begehr
> Was wohl in der Welt für Freude wär,
> Allen Sonnenschein und alle Bäume,
> Alles Meergestad und alle Träume
> In dein Herz zu sammeln mit einander. . . .

Goethe remained true at heart to Spinoza until his very death, however weak and unworthy his bearing became in later years, when it was a question of standing out for academic and religious freedom. Did he not turn away from Fichte when the philosopher was accused of atheism? Did he not become highly incensed, in 1823, over the fact that mixed marriages were being allowed in Weimar between Christians and men of the tribe of Spinoza?

CHAPTER XXVI

First Edition of his Collective Writings— Journey to Italy: Antique and Renaissance

THE longing for Italy to which he had given imperishable expression in Mignon's classical *Kennst du das Land,* in the original draft of *Wilhelm Meister,* had reached the point where it could no longer be subdued. Many difficulties, however, had to be overcome. He had to obtain leave of absence from his Duke, for whom it might be difficult to find a substitute, but who would gain in independence during his absence. He had to tear himself away from Charlotte von Stein and thereby cause her anguish of heart. And he had to devise some means by which he could secure the necessary money to defray his travelling expenses; for the 1200 thalers that constituted his regular salary were quite inadequate. He had, to be sure, come into some revenue from the estate of his father, but he had allowed his mother to retain the largest part of the interest on the capital. He was consequently obliged to see whether he could not derive a measure of income from his writings. According to the plan that had been agreed upon, his collective works would make eight volumes, and his publisher, G. J. Göschen of Leipzig, declared his willingness to pay a stipendium for the entire edition amounting to 2000 thalers. This was in truth no colossal sum; but with it in hand the journey could be undertaken. Goethe tried in vain to receive more. Göschen asked whether such a sum was an easy matter: "Are two thousand thalers a mere bagatelle?"

As matters finally eventuated, it was shown that it would have been quite impossible for Göschen to have advanced a larger royalty: he did not cover expenses as it was. The first volume came out in 1787, the last in 1790. The writings were published by subscription: There were 602 subscribers in the whole of Germany. Of the first four volumes, there were sold in addition 536 copies, 487 of the fifth, 417 of the eighth. Single editions had not been more successful. Of *Werthers Leiden* 262 copies were sold, 20 of *Götz*, 17 of *Clavigo*, 312 of *Iphigenie*, 377 of *Egmont*, 326 of *Die Mitschuldigen*, and 198 of *Die Vögel*. It is not known precisely how many copies of *Faust, Ein Fragment* were disposed of. This was the end of the sales. All in all, Göschen had lost 1720 thalers by his undertaking.

This is to be laughed at and to be wept over. But Spinoza has warned us against both laughing and weeping; and he has exhorted us to comprehend. He who is at all familiar with contemporary judgment and contemporary opinion comprehends this without difficulty.

II

Salve magna parens frugum, Saturnis tellus,
magna virum: tibi res antiquae laudis et artis
ingredior, sanctos ausus recludere fontes.
Vergilius: Georgicon II, 73.

Everything that was unnorthern in Goethe, such as love of the sun and clarity and large lines, passion for the plastic and the cultivation of beauty, everything in his nature, as it had been developed, that was akin to Antique, such as his appreciation of the dignified, his detestation of grimaces, his love for simplicity, calm, greatness—all of this drew him on irresistibly to Italy. He knew the country as one knows a person that one admires and loves from mere correspondence, without personal acquaintance. And it came about that the actual sight surpassed all expectation and influenced him so strongly that the traveller soon felt that he was on the point of undergoing a complete change, a rejuvenation; he felt charmed and strengthened.

There was in him the inner sun that yearned for the cloud-free sun in the sky. As he himself (after Plotinus) said:

Wär' nicht das Auge sonnenhaft,
Die Sonne könnt' es nie erblicken.

There was in him also the classical sense for measure and moderation, for balance and sanity which, by way of illustration, had made it easily possible for him entirely to avoid exaggeration in Mignon's song, had made it possible for him to

glorify the Italy he had never seen without using a
single superlative:

> Ein sanfter Wind vom blauen Himmel weht
> Die Myrthe *still* und *hoch* der Lorbeer steht.

It was the natural scenery and the venerable art
of Italy that attracted him.   For the history of the
country he had far less appreciation.   It was not
as history, but as clear and ordered beauty that the
Antique delighted him.

We recall young Wolfgang's perfervid enthusiasm for Gothic as the national German type of
architecture with which Italy had nothing to compare.   Now he has turned his back on Gothic. He
has wheeled his preference about somewhat as one
would turn a fiery charger. Gothic has become contrary to his nature, just as every outcrop of religiosity repelled him.   The Greek temple rises before
his eyes as the home of beauty and the incarnation
of all that is sacred.   And his love of antique art
is not inferior to his reverence for the antique
temple.

The embryo of this transformation must be
sought in Goethe's studies in nature.   He had followed his sound idea of a fundamental type.
Through his discoveries in osteology he had seen
his belief in the unity between the vertebrate animal
and man corroborated.   In what he was pleased to
term the *Urpflanze* he searched for the plant type
which convinced him of unity in all species of diver-
sity.   In every field of nature that he investigated
he had found unbreakable, undeviating laws. Could
he not find similar laws in art? Is it possible that
art alone is exposed to pure arbitrariness? He felt

that in the antique he would meet the same idea of
the typical that he had met in nature: a rigid ex-
clusion of the unqualifiedly accidental.   The human
figure, in the classical drama for example, could be
traced back to single, simple forms such as Iphigenie, Antigone, Philoctetes, Neoptolomus, the sacrificed woman, the virgin who follows the law of the
heart, the proud man offended, the erring though
noble youth.   It would be possible to condense their
spiritual essence into something typical; they were
all placed in simple situations that redeemed their
entire power.

He began to look with disfavor on his earlier
impetuous and irregular productions.   He finds his
poetic form at present in law-abiding verse, in the
consistent iambic pentameter.   He begins to revise
his prose dramas; to rewrite them in this form.   He
seeks with undaunted and unabated constancy antique themes, characters such as Achilles, Nausikaa,
Palaeophron, Epimenides.   He reverts with ever
increasing frequency to ancient classical verse forms.
Even such thoroughly national material as *Hermann
und Dorothea,* or the Mediaeval beast epic *Reineke
Fuchs,* he is planning to treat, in the future, in Greek
hexameters.

Gothic has now become so contrary to his nature that in his *Italienische Reise,* composed of his
letters and diaries for the years 1786-88, and com-
piled during the years 1816-17 and 1829, he has
not a word to say regarding the Gothic churches;
he is silent concerning the picturesque palaces in
Verona with their Mediaeval stamp.   Nor does he
have a word to say concerning the Venetian Gothic

of the palaces along the Grand Canal. And what
has always seemed to me astonishing, if not preposterous, is the fact that he could not prevail upon
himself to visit the conventual church in Assisi
which, with its crypt and Giotto's frescoes, is perhaps
the most marvelous church in all Italy. Yet he loses
himself in observations on, even explorations of, the
church of Maria della Minerva, the facade of which
is the remains of an ancient temple of Minerva,
a temple with no artistic value and one which the
modern visitor who has read Goethe's enthusiastic
description views with wonderment. Even Paul
Sabatier, honorary citizen of Assisi and author of
the life of St. Francis of Assisi, who knows the city
as no one else knows it, and who once showed the
author of these lines through it, could see nothing
remarkable or in any way worthy about it. It was,
to be sure, the original remains of a temple of olden
times that Goethe saw.

By 1786 he had come to feel about as Emperor
Julian the Apostate felt fourteen hundred years
earlier. Any Christian monument had become to
him a horror. On this account he writes with the
chill of declination:

The monstrous substructures of the church piled over
each other in Babylonian fashion where St. Francis lies I
passed by in apathy.

There is no doubt but that his aversion to Christianity dates far back in his life. The sole discordant note between him and Herder after their
association in Strassburg arises in this connection.
Goethe, in the spirit of youth, replies to Herder

upon the latter's having sent him two monographs of religious content by saying that he is out of sympathy with that kind of topics, for the whole teaching of Christ appeals to him as such a sham (*Scheinding*) that his wrath, not his interest, is aroused. To Charlotte von Stein he writes (April 6, 1782) : "Here is a sheet of Lavater's *Pilate*. I have no comment to make. I am so tired of the story of this good Jesus that I could not endure hearing it from anyone, except perhaps from Him Himself." But this aversion had, earlier in his life, been united with an interest in various forms of Christianity, with pietism (Fräulein von Klettenberg) as well as with mysticism (Emanuel Swedenborg). This interest returns in Goethe's old age. *Faust* closes in a Catholic fashion, and Goethe as an older man allows himself to be led on by the Boisserée brothers into collecting convent and church paintings from earlier times. But now, standing as he is at the bright meridian of his life, he is a Pagan through and through. If he praises anything it is because it reminds him of the Antique; if he finds fault with anything it is because he sees in it a deviation from the basic principles of the Antique or from the spirit of Greek heathendom.

But what pleasure he had taken in the Dutch paintings in the days of his early youth! He studied them, as we saw above, so zealously in Dresden that he hardly had time to pay even a short visit to the section on Antique art. But the Antique arose slowly to an all-controling place in his mind. Oeser's admiration for Winckelmann and Winckelmann's own doctrines again emerge in his mind.

In contrast to the battle-cry of *Natur und Frei-*

heit from the *Götz* period, Winckelmann had set up the shibboleth of *Edle Einfalt und stille Grösse* which he has found in the works of the Greeks and which he, like Thorvaldsen [28] later, knew or felt almost entirely through what was found of late Roman art.

The degree to which Goethe had been obsessed by Winckelmann is shown by his original attitude toward the Italian Renaissance on his arrival in Italy. He travels through Florence, the inexhaustible treasure house of Renaissance art, with a stop of only three hours; he has no desire to see the city. He longs for Rome, that is to say, he longs for the Antique. And no less significant is his attitude toward Michael Angelo. When he first became acquainted with him in November, 1786, he is so overwhelmed by the master's virility that not even nature makes a good impression on him. In July, 1787, he even ranks Michael Angelo higher than Raphael. But his name soon disappears from Goethe's letters and after the initial storm of emotions awakened by Michael Angelo has subsided he reverts to the immutable calm of that art from which he had deduced his doctrines concerning the law-abiding principles of all art. This he finds solely in the Antique and in Raphael as descending from the Antique.

During his second sojourn in Rome he has no desire to revisit Michael Angelo; he praises anew,

[28] Berthel Thorvaldsen (1770-1844) went to Italy in 1796. He arrived in Rome March 8, 1797, just as Canova was at the height of his popularity. He modelled a Jason which received the unstinted praise of Canova, and from that time on his success was assured—and his type of art determined. He remained in Italy for twenty-three years. —TRANSLATOR.

and that in the loftiest tones, the Apollo of Belvedere, that slightly affected Roman lord whose
beauty, as he sees it, "transcends all conception."
Michael Angelo's art of passion no longer corresponds to his ideal; this he finds in the colossal heads
of the Jupiter of Otricoli and the Juno of Ludovisi,
castings of both of which he was careful to buy for
his private collections.

It is well to note that it is only a section of Hellenism that he understands. It is not the irreconcilably tragic, nor the Dionysian, nor the wild joy
in combat, which in the next century came to light in
the form of Pergamenian art, that faintly reminds
him of Michael Angelo. It is a diluted, a feebler
harmony that he grasps. Consequently he could
find this harmony in such tame artists as Raphael
Mengs—and Angelica Kaufmann, for whom he has
both love and appreciation.

Since the Renaissance was, among other things,
a revivification of the Antique in art, literature,
politics and especially in religion with broadsides
aimed at the Church and Christendom, Goethe's
predilection for certain phases of it is directly due
to his visionary enthusiasm for the Antique. In the
art of painting, Raphael, with his easy and simple
harmonies, continues to be Goethe's hero. He had
studied him when a young man. His St. Caecilie
in Bologna, the first painting by Raphael that he saw
during his stay on Italian soil, has for him the characteristic of genuine art in that it calms the storm
and allays the passions.

Goethe has a violent aversion for all pictures of
martyrs; he rejoices in Raphael's portrayal of the
human out and out. Concerning the art on the

Christian martyrs he says: "One is forever in the hall of anatomy, at the scaffold, near the potter's field. We have the sufferings of the hero without end; we lack and miss action; we look in vain for present interest; there is always something that is fantastically expected. We deal with malefactors or saints, criminals or fools." He detests these men in armor who kneel with folded hands awaiting a blissful resurrection.

He sees in Raphael the man who loved life for life's sake, and preferred the joy of life to all art and renown. Goethe, who never did go in for grave-visiting and to whom the study of any sort of relics was foreign, makes a pilgrimage to Raphael's tomb and admires the perfect form of his skull, just as he later did in the case of Schiller. As late as 1816 he prefers Raphael's paintings to all other art; he even places him—significant enough because of the kind of proof—above the two greatest masters of the Renaissance, Leonardo da Vinci and Michael Angelo. He even holds up against Michael Angelo such a trifle as the fact that he wasted time and talents in the marble-quarry. Without feeling the pronounced similarity between the versatile da Vinci and himself, he cites against him the fact that he toiled far too much with the technical. The equilibrium in Raphael's mind, this talent that flows from the source as from the freshest fount, is absolutely in accord with Goethe's own heart.

It is quite significant—though it has been frequently noted—that while other poets choose their themes from periods that lie far apart, Goethe treats themes only from the Antique and the Renaissance.

Schiller, for example, has his dramas take place in
the years 1300, 1400, 1500, 1600 (*Tell, Jungfrau
von Orleans, Die Braut von Messina, Wallenstein*).
Goethe takes his material at times from his own
age, to be sure, (*Clavigo* and the dramas on the
Revolution), but his Götz, Egmont, Tasso, even
the legendary figure of Faust, all belong to the sixteenth century.

The degree to which the paintings of the Renaissance were burned in on Goethe's mind is shown,
among other works, in *Faust*, Part II. Correggio's
blissful painting, *Leda and her Playmates*, is described twice. The first time is when Homunculus
awakens to life:

> Schön umgeben—klar Gewässer
> Im dichten Haine; Frau'n, die sich entkleiden,
> Die Allerliebsten—das wird immer besser.
> Doch Eine lässt sich glänzend unterscheiden
> Aus höchstem Helden, wohl aus Götterstamme,
> Sie setzt den Fuss in das durchsicht'ge Helle.

The second is when Faust stands by the river
Peneios:

> Von allen Seiten hundert Quellen
> Vereinen sich im reinlich hellen
> Zum Bade flach vertieften Raum.
> Gesunde, junge Frauenglieder
> Vom feuchten Spiegel doppelt wieder,
> Ergötztem Auge zugebracht,
> Gesellig dann und fröhlich badend,
> Erdreistet schwimmend, furchtsam watend,
> Geschrei zuletzt und Wasserschlacht.

Leda and the Swan in Correggio's portrayal has
apparently gained control of Goethe's fancy.

Even the closing tableau in *Faust*, Part II, is an

exact reproduction of three paintings from Giotto's
school from the fourteenth century on the wall of
the Campo Santo in Pisa. The song of the Holy
Anchorites

> Woge nach Woge spritzt,
> Höhle, die tiefste, schützt,
> Löwen, die schleichen stumm
> Freundlich um dich herum.

is nothing but a poetic translation of a painting
from the pre-Renaissance which Goethe saw on his
journey.

Of the Italian thinkers of the Renaissance, Goethe was strongly influenced by Giordano Bruno,
whose enthusiasm for the All-Unity of God and
the Universe he had defended as early as 1771
against Pierre Bayle's attack. These verses are
almost a translation from Bruno:

> Was wär' ein Gott, der nur von aussen stiesse,
> Im Kreis das All am Finger laufen liesse!
> Ihm ziemt's, die Welt im Innern zu bewegen.

Of the poets of the Italian Renaissance, Goethe
placed, as his *Tasso* shows, a high estimate on
Ariosto. Dante, with his gloomy pathos, was far
removed from him, and Petrarch, with his purely
spiritual love for Laura, was contrary to his very
nature.

If the Italian Renaissance stands far closer to
his heart than the German or Dutch Renaissance,
it must be said that the latter contained much that
he admires and some things that he loves. Though
indifferent to Holbein and Cranach, he never failed
to rank Albrecht Dürer very high. He who trans-

lated the blatant and boastful but doughty Benvenuto Cellini was perfectly capable of estimating Dürer's inner loyalty to reality and his true-hearted fullness of feeling.

Among the Northern poets of the Renaissance he loved the neo-Latin poet of the *Küsse,* Johannes Secundus of the Netherlands. This is shown in the above mentioned poem entitled *Liebesbedürfnis,* especially as it reads in the letter to Frau von Stein:

> Lieber, heiliger, grosser Küsser,
> Der Du mir's in lechzend athmender
> Glückseligkeit fast vorgethan hast,
> Wem soll ich's klagen, klag ich dir's nicht!

To whom should he complain, if not to Johannes, of what he suffers because of his chapped lips in being prevented from putting them to the mouth of his sweetheart?

In his polemic relation to the Church, Goethe felt related to the bellicose Latin Humanists, Reuchlin, Erasmus, Hutten, and Sickingen. Especially in his later years, when Pastor Pustkuchen published his *Wanderjahre* in opposition to Goethe's, did he make an appeal to them:

> Reuchlin! Wer will sich ihm vergleichen,
> Zu seiner Zeit ein Wunderzeichen!

He closes by saying:

> Denn gegen die obscuren Kutten
> Die mir zu schaden sich verquälen,
> Auch mir kann es an Ulrich Hutten
> Und Franz von Sickingen nicht fehlen.

His whole life long Goethe felt akin in spirit to the Renaissance. When he abandons the cultivation

of reason from the age of Enlightenment, he does
it, not as smaller minds, with the re-introduction of
the belief in revelation, but with many-sided reason
and artistic fancy in unbreakable union.   He stands
before us as the Renaissance raised to the second
power, a regeneration of Renaissance in individual
form.

CHAPTER XXVII.

NEW POETIC STYLE; *Iphigenie* IN VERSE—COM-
PLETION OF *Egmont*—WORK ON *Faust*—
Iphigenie in Delphi; Nausikaa

THROUGH his incognito Goethe wished to make
it possible to have all of his time for himself while
in Italy: He wished to waste the precious hours
neither in accepting honors, nor in paying calls on
other people. His incognito was preserved, however, except at the very first, with anything but severity. What strikes an individual of the twentieth
century is the fact that he so arranged his life while
in Italy that it meant only a local absence from Germany. In reality, his surroundings were German;
his companions were Germans. There was no
thought of association with the Italian people, to
say nothing of Italian society and intelligence. He
lived in the company of such mediocre German
painters as Bury, Lips, Hackert, and Angelica Kaufmann. During his entire sojourn in Rome he lived
in the home of the painter Tischbein, a man whom
he had previously known only through correspondence. Tischbein acted fraternally toward him. He
painted that stilted picture of Goethe, resting in
the Campagna, clad in white with a broad rimmed
hat, surrounded by fragments from the period of
classical antiquity—a base relief, the capital of a
column, and so on.

His guide in Rome was a resident German student of art, Hofrat Reiffenstein. He undertook the journey to Sicily in the company of the German painter Kniep. He associated intimately with Karl Philipp Moritz, author of the well-known novel entitled *Anton Reiser*. He was frequently in the company of that German-Swiss citizen and inept artist, Heinrich Meyer. He shared and adopted Meyer's not wholly irrational views on art. During his second stay in Rome he associated with the painter Schütz and the above-mentioned friend of his youth, Christoph Kayser, who had set some of his songs and operettas to music, and who now composed the score to *Scherz, List und Rache*. Even the Duchess Giovane, with whom he became acquainted, was a German princess.

Had he not, during his second sojourn in Rome, entered into a cordial relation with a beautiful Milanese Maddalena Ricci, who, however, soon became engaged to an Italian, he would have lived exclusively in intimate association with Germans. His Italian circle of acquaintances would have consisted solely of young and flippant individuals, except for a few relatively important personages such as the Neapolitan jurist, Gaetano Filangieri and his queer sister, an opulent Principessa, who did not set a very high price on social deportment, though she did on him. By way of exception Goethe interests himself in the original of the charlatan Cagliostro and consequently looks up the family Balsamo in Palermo.

Along with his work connected with familiarizing himself with the art treasures, he acquires and appropriates mementos and paintings; and along with his constant acquirement of Italian natural scenery through sketches of landscapes and figures, he is daily occupied with the re-reading and revision of his collective works for the Göschen edition, of which only four volumes were ready for publication when he left for Italy.

One of the domains in which young Wolfgang's conception of liberty had undergone a complete transformation was that of poetic style. It was in the name of freedom that the literary revolution against Greco-French classicism had taken place. But there was soon awakened in Goethe an aversion toward the old Germanic gruffness and formlessness in *Götz,* an aversion to the loose and lax form of *Werther.* By way of liberation from his stylelessness and formlessness, he had resorted to Hellenic material, to old Greek style. In the later sonnet, *Natur und Kunst,* he gave his new conviction an imperishable expression. He shows that nature and art seem to avoid each other, but if we cultivate art seriously, nature can glow freely in our hearts.

> So ist's mit aller Bildung auch beschaffen:
> Vergebens werden ungebundne Geister
> Nach der Vollendung reiner Höhe streben.

> Wer Grosses will, muss sich zusammenraffen;
> In der Beschränkung zeigt sich erst der Meister,
> Und das Gesetz nur kann uns Freiheit geben.

First of all he took up *Iphigenie,* and by the turn of the year 1786-87 he had rewritten the drama in beautiful iambics, pentametric as in Lessing's *Nathan,* though just as melodius as Lessing's are clear. The form here is so perfect, the measure is so simple and full, that many of these verses which express merely some humble, unimportant idea have become expressions that have been repeated time out of mind. There is Thoas's verse:

> Du sprichst ein grosses Wort gelassen aus.

Other verses express a simple picture which has never been forgotten:

> Doch es schmiedete
> Der Gott um ihre Stirn ein ehern Band.

Or take these two argumentative verses:

> *Thoas:* Es spricht kein Gott, es spricht Dein eigen Herz.
> *Iphigenie:* Sie reden nur durch unser Herz zu uns.

The scene between Orestes and Iphigenie, which opens the third act, is pure music. Read this appeal to the gods that flows from Iphigenie's lips:

> Habt Ihr nur darum mich so manches Jahr
> Von Menschen abgesondert, mich so nah
> Bei Euch gehalten, mir die kindliche
> Beschäftigung, des heil'gen Feuers Gluth
> Zu nähren, aufgetragen, meine Seele
> Der Flamme gleich in ew'ger, frommer Klarheit
> Zu Euren Wohnungen hinaufgezogen,
> Dass ich nur meines Hauses Gräuel später
> Und tiefer fühlen sollte?

The care with which Goethe has striven to keep the style antique is clearly shown by a slight change in this scene. In the older text, Iphigenie uses the expression *Gnade* as coming from Jupiter—she means Zeus. Here the word is changed into *Erfül-*

lung, a conception that is pre-Christian and corresponds to hope:

> So steigst du denn, Erfüllung, schönste Tochter
> Des grössten Vaters endlich zu mir nieder!

There is in this text, in which every sentence,
indeed every word, was weighed, balanced and refined for so many years, a concentration, an inimitable fullness, and an enrapturing rhythm, despite
the fact that the verses are unrhymed. In this way,
and in truth for this reason, the simplest picture is
indelibly stamped on our mind. Take the case of
Orestes when he speaks of the furies.

> Doch hör ich aus der Ferne hier und da
> Ihr grässliches Gelächter. Wölfe harren
> So um den Baum, auf den ein Reisender
> Sich rettete.

The lyric element breaks through, not merely in
the various passages in which the metre has been
changed so as to take on the form appropriate to
an anthem or a song, but also where it is unmodi-
fied in order to give expression to purity of soul,
spiritual elevation and unqualified refinement of
feeling. A case in point is when Thoas asks Iphigenie whether she believes that the unpolished
Scythians are capable of responding to the voice of
humanity. She replies in these light and easy lines:

> Es hört sie jeder
> Geboren unter jedem Himmel, dem
> Des Lebens Quelle durch den Busen rein
> Und ungehindert fliesst.

These verses contain the lofty and beautiful moral
of the drama. Of it, Hyppolite Taine, one of the

most excellent critics of art that ever lived, said:
"I place no modern work above *Iphigenie auf Tauris*
by Goethe."

In his *Philosophy of Art* Taine says that the
drama is beautiful even in prose and infinitely more
so in verse. The introduction of rhythm and metre
has given the work the matchless accent, sublime
clarity, and broad tragic tone at the sound of which
the mind rises above the flat tasks of everyday life
and sees before its eye the heroes of olden times.
We behold the race of primitive souls long since
forgotten, and among them the majestic maiden,
the guardian of the law and benefactress of man, in
whom all goodness and all nobility in human nature
are concentrated to the glorification of our race
and the uplifting of our fallen courage.

II

Goethe had now outgrown not simply the loose,
indefinite form but also the bombastic, overflowing
sentimentality that flourished in *Die Geschwister* as
well as in *Werther*. He feels more and more the
necessity of cutting himself off from, and reacting
against, men's familiar importunity. He was a born
aristocrat and had simply, as a result of a misunderstanding of his own frank genius, allowed himself to be misled into making acquaintances with
anybody and everybody.

The latest hero of freedom to emerge in his mind
was, as we have seen, the Netherland nobleman,
Egmont, Prince of Gaure. How distinguished in
comparison with Götz, how aristocratically amiable,
how entirely care-free in his self-complacency! His

noble, fruitful nature with its easy blood, which feels itself elevated above that of other people as above the morals of other people, becomes the Fate by which he allows himself to be led and driven. He is almost passive, and yet a brave man. He is a lover of liberty, though one does not see him fighting for it with the violent blows of a mailed fist.

He is an enchanter, beloved of all. But he is most wholesomely appreciated by a plain, pert little girl, who loves him more than all the others combined. His conception of liberty is different from that of Götz; it is less narrow. His relation to Clärchen is of a part with his idea of liberty.

The drama as a drama is without suspense and without conflict. Not all of the leading characters are entirely worthy of Goethe. Alba is far too loquacious. A little reminiscence of Shakespeare's *Julius Caesar* will show who inspired the vigorous and lively folk scenes. The characters are firmly and clearly drawn. Clärchen is one of the most charming personages known to the records of dramatic poetry. It will be as impossible to forget her as it will be impossible to forget Leonardo da Vinci's Mona Lisa, Raphael's Sistine Madonna, Shakespeare's Imogene. The choicest part of her delineation is contained in what is not said. Schiller was right when he wrote the excellent epigramme:

Jeden andern Meister erkennt man an dem, was er ausspricht;
Was er weise verschweigt, zeigt mir den Meister des Stils.

Shakespeare himself scarcely has a series of remarks and replies, which from the point of view of finesse and eloquence, can measure up to the pauses in the following. Egmont has depicted the Regentess, Margarete von Parma:

> *Clärchen:* A majestic woman! I was almost afraid to go near her.
> *Egmont:* You are not usually timid. Probably it was not fear; probably it was only virgin modesty.
> *Clärchen:* (Casts her eyes to the ground, seizes his hand, and leans against him.)
> *Egmont:* I understand you! You dear girl! You may raise your eyes again!

If Clärchen is not maid, then she is woman in all that the latter term implies.

The words *Freudvoll und leidvoll,* already referred to, have been, as it were, inscribed on the tablets of love. Egmont deserves Clärchen's love. The Egmont whom Goethe begins to create in Italy, and into whose heart he again works himself, is not the historical character. He did not owe his King enormous sums, nor was he bound to him by such means; nor is he the father of a family with eleven children, such as Schiller, in his opinionated critique, would have preferred to see portrayed. The taking off of this Egmont would have been a feast of tears to the masses; they would have revelled in sentimental weeping when they saw him snatched from his good wife and eleven little ones! Concerning this irritating review, Goethe wrote to the Duke in a tone of dry accuracy:

> The reviewer has perhaps analyzed the moral part of the work quite well; so far as the poetry of the drama comes into question, however, he might have left something for others to do.

Egmont has not become the father of a family. Nor is he in any sense of the word an effeminate,

effervescing lover like Werther, or Fernando, or
even Clavigo. He is a man. He is more loved than
loving. His little friend is the unreserved object of
his tenderness, but deep down in his soul she occupies him no more than Gretchen occupies Faust.
Faust is so little taken up with Gretchen that she
succumbs because he does not follow her fate. Even
when he sees the vision on the Brocken, the young
woman with the red line about her neck, she and her
misfortune never occur to him. Egmont remains,
despite all warnings and prayers, in Brussels when
Alba enters with his army. It was reasonable to
expect that he would do this because he could not
live without Clärchen; he did not wish to be separated from her. Goethe must have seen this motif
and rejected it. She plays absolutely no rôle in his
final determination.

And yet Goethe was fully, deeply conscious of her
worth. Without paying any attention to the doubts
that arose on all sides, he transformed her after
her death into the Goddess of Liberty. She appears
in this capacity to Egmont, consoles him in his last
dream and extends to him the laurel wreath. Consequently he can say on awakening: I die for the
liberty for which I have lived and fought and for
which I now offer my life. So serious was Goethe's
love of political liberty, and so forceful his expression of it immediately preceding the French Revolution. After this there follows a long period of
eclipse until this love of liberty finds expression for
the last time in the above quoted words which are
placed on the lips of the dying Faust.

III

In the *Italienische Reise,* March 1, 1788, Goethe tells of his deliberations anent the last three volumes of his collective works. He has just laid out the plan of his *Faust,* and he places complete confidence in the success of this operation. He admits that the writing of the drama is, naturally, a quite different affair from what it was fifteen years ago, though he feels certain that he has again found the thread:

And so far as the tone of the whole work is concerned, I am at peace. I have already worked out a new scene, and if I smoke the paper I believe that it will be impossible for anyone to distinguish it from the old ones. Since I, by reason of my long rest and isolation, have been restored to my former level of existence, I am indeed struck by the similarity to my old self, and by the slight impression that years and events have made on my soul.

Goethe deceived himself very much indeed. The scenes which he added, in Italy, to the manuscript, to the oldest plan that he had taken along, resemble the former ones neither in spirit nor in tone.

In the first place, there is the *Hexenküche* scene, in which the drinking of the magic potion effects Faust's rejuvenation, a plan that was originally never once thought of. Even the metre is no longer the rhymed doggerel but rhymed iambic pentameters. The scene is peculiarly introduced with Mephistopheles's rationalistic explanation of the possibility of rejuvenation. There is a certain strife between all the ghosts and all the phantastic beings that commingle in the witches' kitchen, the speaking monkeys of both genders, and Mephistopheles's later reply

to Faust's question as to whether nature combined
with art can not devise a better means of relieving
him of thirty years than the foolish advice, but-
tressed on magic, of an old woman. He replies:
Of course, you need, if you so desire, neither physician nor sorcery nor money. Take a hoe and a
shovel, dig in the earth, manure it and cultivate it
and live on plain food, that is the best way to re-
juvenate yourself. And when Faust can not be prevailed upon to go in for this sort of simple life,
then and not till then, Mephistopheles resorts to
the witch.

When the witch accordingly arrives and no longer
recognizes her lord and master, modernized Satan
that he is, hornless, hoofless and tailless, and when
Mephistopheles in his embitterment causes her a
fearful fright, Goethe uses an expression which
shows plainly that the scene was written in the
South, under circumstances and in surroundings that
caused all inconsistencies in nature to appear as a
bit of mere superstition known only to the land of
fog. By way of expressing his liberation from all
the antiquated apparatus, Mephistopheles says:

Das *nordische* Phantom ist nun nicht mehr zu schauen.

In order to motivate the attraction that Faust is
soon to feel for a young girl, Goethe lets him see
in a magic mirror an ideal picture of a woman, perhaps a form of Helena such as appears in *Faust* II.
Even in the old saga, which constitutes the basis, as
also in Marlowe's *Faust,* this ideal woman is united
with Faust. What, however, is more probable, is
that she is a reminiscence of the irreproachably beautiful woman whom Goethe saw disrobed, and whom

he described in the *Schweizerreise,* for the words
that he uses here recall what took place there:

Ist's möglich, ist das Weib so schön!

And strangely enough—as though Goethe had
forgotten in those days the significance that Gretchen
soon acquired for Faust, and how strongly his yearning for her is awakened—in the scene *Wald und
Höhle,* the second important scene that he wrote
in Italy, Faust speaks in his monolgue, not of the
little girl from the middle class, the leading character of the entire tragedy, but of the magic picture
in the mirror as of that to which his longing now
tends.   He is vexed because Mephistopheles
arouses his senses and exclaims:

Er facht in meiner Brust ein wildes Feuer
Nach *jenem schönen Bild* geschäftig an.

By "that beautiful picture" he evidently means not
the living Gretchen, but the ideal picture in the
magic mirror, the one that has just been portrayed
though it never again appears in the entire work.
Attention has already been drawn to the lack of
agreement between the leading part of the scene
and the close that we have in the old manuscript.

And finally there is a scene of some few pages
that was written in Italy and inserted before the
scenes between Mephisto and the student.   It is only
a fragment, the close of the rich and magnificent
double scene between Faust and Mephisto in the latter's various forms as a poodle, as a wandering
scholar, and as an aristocratic squire in a bright

red, gold embroidered costume. This fragment begins, strangely enough, with the words:

Und was der ganzen Menschheit zugetheilt ist.

In the completed *Faust,* Part I, which was published twenty years later, in 1808, there are four lines that run as follows:

Mein Busen, der vom Wissensdrang geheilt ist,
Soll keinen Schmerzen künftig sich verschliessen,
Und was der ganzen Menschheit zugetheilt ist,
Will ich in meinem innern Selbst geniessen.

The last two lines existed at least twenty years before the first two with which they rhyme.

The result is that just as carefully as the line of separation has been erased, just so little is it possible to say that the same idea is being discussed before and after the line of separation. When Goethe was sixty years old, he was confronted with the task of finding a beginning to the proposition with the lines that rhymed with *Zugetheilt ist* and with *geniessen;* and this he has certainly succeeded in doing.

Apparently the two propositions correspond quite well to each other; the first two lines treat of care, the last two of joy. But if we look more carefully we see that it does not work out exactly right.

My bosom which is completely cured of longing after knowledge, shall in the future not be closed to grief. This is the gist of the appended beginning.

But the close, which Goethe wrote on Italian soil, said a great deal more: "And everything that falls to the lot of humanity as a whole I will enjoy within my inner self." This includes both the good and the bad, both joy and sorrow. Were it simply this slight formal contradiction that arose it would not be so bad. But a new, a more serious difficulty appeared when the addition was made. The new Faust is disgusted with all his knowledge, has lost his impulse to final knowledge in the possibility of which he no longer believes, and yearns only after the satisfaction of his sensual passions:

> Des Denkens Faden ist zerrissen,
> Mir ekelt lange vor allem Wissen.
> Lass in den Tiefen der Sinnlichkeit
> Uns glühende Leidenschaften stillen!

The original Faust, with whom Goethe sympathized even in Italy, yearned on the contrary to comprehend the very soul of the universe, and so to develop his power of thinking and manner of feeling that he could think through all the thoughts of men, and feel their feelings after them:

> Mit meinem Geist das Höchst' und Tiefste greifen
> Ihr Wohl und Weh auf meinen Busen häufen,
> Und so mein eigen Selbst zu ihrem Selbst erweitern,
> Und, wie sie selbst, am End' auch ich zerscheitern.

He is much more intellectual than the later Faust. Mephistopheles has to use all the knowledge at his command, he has to exploit his full store of eloquence, when he attempts to show Faust the impossibility of obtaining what he is striving after, to wean him away from reason and science, and to fill him with insatiable desire for worthless mundane joys.

The brief monologue itself in which he does this is a masterpiece of felicitously turned phrases all of which go to show the prohibitive difficulties the individual man has in approaching the infinite. However many of the treasures of the human mind Faust has succeeded in appropriating, he feels no new power welling forth from his inner being; he finally accepts, with a display of despondence, Mephistopheles's warning against the futility of speculation.

It is nevertheless exceedingly hard to separate, with perfect accuracy, those parts of the beginning of *Faust* that were written at that time from those that were added or expanded preparatory to publishing the finished work in 1808.

Parts of what was published last of all were in high probability written many years before. It does not seem to me to be likely that Faust's desire to translate the text of the Bible into his *geliebtes Deutsch* belongs to the time after the writing of the twenty-ninth and seventy-seventh Venetian epigrammes. Their caustic and repeated sallies apropos of the difficulties arising from a poetic treatment of the German language—which is referred to unreservedly as *der schlechteste Stoff*—are not in favor of such an assumption.

On looking through the old, yellow, moldy manuscript Goethe was persuaded that emendations were in order: He toned down the expressions that appealed to him as being too gruff and gross. Gretchen's marvelous monologue at the spinning wheel —*Meine Ruh ist hin*—underwent a slight change that may be considered in the light of an improvement only from the point of view of prosody. For the words

> Mein *Schoos*, Gott! drängt
> Sich nach ihm hin

we have the more abstract and quite academic

Mein *Busen* drängt
Sich nach ihm hin.

It is perhaps on reading Faust's great monologue that we become most clearly conscious of the fact that Goethe has experienced a development the net result of which is a happy approach to greater artistic perfection. The style in which the monologue is written is exalted, melodious, virile. The iambics have a beauty, and are treated with a skill, that was unknown to Goethe until he had revised his *Iphigenie,* and rewritten it, in verse. There is nothing like it in the *Urfaust.* Delightful is the effect produced by having the animals on the land, the birds in the air, and the fish in the sea referred to as the brothers of men—somewhat as St. Francis of Assisi addressed them! Delightful also is the portrayal of nature during a storm which overturns the spruces, so that one hears the roaring and cracking of the falling trees. And finally, there is a delineation, in a serene and lofty style, of the moonlight, and the silvery figures of olden times which arise, in this soft illuminaton, before the mind of the dreaming soul!

There is no slight difference between the simple, naïve tone in the earlier erotic scene of the work, and the height of lyric eloquence to which it has now risen.

It was quite out of the question to portray anything more simple or familiar than the young girl who plucks the petals from the daisy and says: He loves me; He loves me not! But no one had availed himself of that theme previous to the days

of Goethe. It was the egg of Columbus; and its
effect was incalculable. By this addition the field
of art was extended.

IV

It is no wonder that Goethe, down in the garden
of the Villa Borghese, conceived of the Devil as a
northern spectre, taken up as he was in Italy with
figures from the world of Grecian legends. On his
journey to Bologna, he saw a painting of St. Agathe
which appealed to him as being so wholesome, so
reassuring, so maidenly, that his own Iphigenie occurs to him. Curiously enough, he conceived the
idea that he would like to read his poem to this
St. Agathe, and have his own heroine say nothing
whatsoever that would in any way offend her. Just
at the time, however, that he voluntarily decided to
continue his work on the Priestess among the Tau-
rians, his fancy took a leap to one side: He abandoned the theme for the time being, and set forth to
dream out a continuation of the action. The new
drama was to be called *Iphigenie in Delphi*; its contents were to be as follows:

Filled with the hope that Orestes will succeed in
bringing the Taurian image of Artemis back to
Delphi, Electra consecrates in the temple the axe
that has worked such fatal havoc in her home. A
Greek arrives and informs her that he has accompanied Orestes and Pylades to Crimea, and seen
the two friends led off to death. She breaks out in
a violent passion; her madness seeks revenge. In
the meantime Iphigenie, Orestes, and Pylades have
come to Delphi. The Greek announces Iphigenie as

the Priestess who committed the murder. Thereupon she seizes the axe, she whose wild excitement is contrasted with Iphigenie's sacred calm, and would strike her sister to the earth, when a happy circumstance prevents this new horror from befalling the Atridean race.

Goethe had found the theme in the textbook ascribed to the Roman grammarian Hyginus, one of Emperor Augustus's serfs. According to Hyginus, Electra goes to Delphi in order to question the oracle concerning her brother's death after having received the false report of the sacrificial act in Tauris. When the message makes it appear that Iphigenie who has just arrived, is the murderess, she snatches a brand from the altar in order to put out her sister's eyes. Orestes interferes and the recognition scene takes place. There is, incidentally, a Greek tragedy on the same theme, probably by Sophocles. (In the year 1856, Friedrich Halm took up the subject once more and wrote a tragedy on it that was performed at the Burgtheater.)

Goethe never completed more than this loose sketch; not a line of the drama itself was ever written. There are, however, some valuable scenes of another antique drama the plan of which was laid in Palermo, and of still a third in Taormina. The latter was to be constructed on a totally different basis. It took shape in his mind while he was in Sicily where he was surrounded by reminiscences of the *Odyssey*. Of this he was, as it were, possessed for a while. It is a great pity that he never collected himself at any future time sufficiently to work it out. It was *Nausikaa*.

We can see what hindered him first and foremost

from completing this drama. For two weeks in succession he had thought incessantly of a theme from the *Odyssey*, which he wished at first to treat under another name, probably that of *Arete*. But one day he chanced to stroll into the public park at Palermo in order to ponder over and muse on his theme a little more. There it befell his genius, never capable of wooing a single theme for any length of time, that another subject opened up before him. He was profoundly impressed by the fact that many plants which he had been accustomed to see growing either in pots or behind the shelter of a hot-house were here growing freely and rapidly under the open sky. His old and naïve idea of the *Urpflanze*, not as an abstraction and simplification, but as an individual species, took hold of him. He resigned himself to search in the hope that here in this fragrant garden with all its manifold plant-life, he might find the *Urpflanze* itself. Botany won the day over poetry. As he himself says: The garden of Alcinous on the island of the Phaeacians disappeared and the world garden opened its gates before his eyes.

He nevertheless finished enough of his *Nausikaa* in Palermo and Taormina to give us an idea of the interest that would have attached to the completed plan. Nausikaa is the most beautiful maiden character in the *Odyssey*, shrewd, domestic, considerate, a true but primitive princess who does not consider herself above carrying her own father's and brother's linen to the laundry. She is conversant with life; she knows how to avoid malicious gossip; she can give the stranger a bit of advice that liberates. A tender, womanly interest in the stranger is indicated in the *Odyssey*, but in accordance with the ancient conception of a seemly and aristocratic young maiden's bearing, it never for a moment transgresses the bounds of mere indication. She yearns for a bridegroom who is precisely like this man. Her father likewise, so long as the stranger has not disclosed his incognito, though he has shown himself in his true splendor, and has given abundant proof of his varied accomplishments. Up to this point, the father would gladly recognize him as a son-in-law. But as soon as Odysseus has mentioned his name, and as soon as it is made known that his wife is awaiting his arrival in her native city, this project is naturally abandoned. At his departure Nausikaa does not appear at all; she is not even referred to.

Goethe had an opportunity here to introduce a life of feeling from the modern point of view. For he had decided to have Odysseus (whom he persistently calls by his Latin name Ulysses, in accord with his inveterate custom), claim, by way of caution, that he was another individual, one of Odysseus's confederates, an unmarried man. Herein lies the first similarity between the severely tried and much travelled hero, and the famous wanderer disguised as merchant Möller. When Goethe depicted in Nausikaa a noble, much sought after maiden who had rejected various suitors, but whose soul is touched by the fate of this rare shipwrecked individual, there was a chance to show how her being underwent a transformation, and how her scruples about leading the stranger into the city of the Phaeacians was a premonition of her budding affection.

Nausikaa is grieved when the stranger wins the

favor of her brother, and obtains even the father's
permission to return home, though the oracle has
expressly forbidden such action. Nausikaa asks:
What? The best, the most excellent man I ever
met, the only one I can love, is to be taken away
from me? Odysseus comes (just as in the *Odyssey*)
to thank her for the kindness she has shown him.
He is for her a breath from the great fresh sea
with all its distant strands. She herself feels, on the
island, as though she were a prisoner. Odysseus
describes his home with its severe winter climate in
contrast to her father's rich and luxurious garden
(the climate of Weimar in contrast to that of Italy).
The sight of Alcinous's garden (described by
Homer), magnificent in every way, has the same
effect on Odysseus that the scenery of Italy had on
Goethe:

> Ein weisser Glanz ruht über Land und Meer,
> Und duftend schwebt der Aether ohne Wolken.

Nausikaa allows us to catch a glimpse of her real
emotions. Goethe puts some words in her mouth
which in the *Odyssey* her father uses concerning
Odysseus:

> Du bist nicht von den Trüglichen,
> Wie viele Fremde kommen, die sich rühmen,
> Und glatte Worte sprechen, wo der Hörer
> Nichts Falsches ahnet und zuletzt, betrogen,
> Sie unvermuthet wieder scheiden sieht.
> Du bist ein Mann, ein zuverläss'ger Mann;
> Sinn und Zusammenhang hat deine Rede. Schön
> Wie eines Dichters Lied tönt sie dem Ohr
> Und füllt das Herz and reisst es mit sich fort.

Nausikaa struggles in hope and doubt: does the
stranger love her, or does he not? She decides to

beseech her father and the other princes not to let
him go. In the hall of Alcinous deliberations are
being held bearing on the case: Shall the guest be
permitted to return home? Nausikaa's brother arrives, and enthusiastically espouses the cause of the
stranger.

Out of the one martial game in the *Odyssey,*
Goethe has made many in all of which Odysseus
proves to be in possession of the greatest skill. Just
as in Homer, loose talk has aroused him and he
has defeated all rivals. He is a hero. No one is
his equal. The assembly is finally turned in his
favor.

And then Nausikaa appears and confesses her
love. It is decided to fulfill the stranger's plea with
regard to Odysseus, but to persuade the stranger to
remain, whereupon he is obliged to make himself
known: "I am Odysseus." Since it is generally
known that Penelope is awaiting him in Ithaca,
and since the hour of separation is drawing near,
Nausikaa does not permit herself to be seen. She
feels a sense of shame. She wishes to die. Aversion
and contempt are in store for her from her people.
All the young men who wooed her so long in vain
will take vengeance on her (just as in the little
Swiss drama all wished to take vengeance on Bätely). Nausikaa tells Odysseus that he must not
judge her falsely. All of this is his own work, the
result of the untruthfulness in which he wrapped
himself. He wishes to correct what has happened,
offers Nausikaa Telemachus as a bridegroom,
wishes to return and bring his son. The two young
people are then supposed to find each other. The
father, Alcinous, is willing to accept the proposal.

But Nausikaa has already thrown herself into the sea and died.

In the discussion of this plan, Goethe traces every clue and motive back to himself. There was, he says, nothing in this work which I could not have depicted from my own life. I myself was on a journey, I was running the risk of bringing on affections which, though their end was not tragic, were capable of becoming quite harmful. I myself was in the same situation, so far from home as to be able to become interested in painting with living colors distant occurrences, travelling adventures and incidents. I myself was exposed to the danger of being regarded by the young as a demi-god and by the mature as a braggart. I was in danger of receiving many an undeserved bit of praise and of meeting with many an unanticipated hindrance. He emphasizes the fact that his personal situation made the material so attractive to him that he dreamt over it the greater part of his stay in Sicily. In accordance with his custom, however, he hesitated about writing it down until the mood had, so to speak, evaporated.

It is most reasonable to assume that when Goethe sketched the figure of Nausikaa, he had, among other models, his new acquaintance, the above mentioned Principessa, the sister of Filangieri in mind. She was a Princess like Nausikaa. At the very first meeting she invited him to visit her. It so happened that she occupied a palace so magnificently fitted out, so splendid, and so full of bespangled flunkies that Goethe said he felt, on entering it, "like the Sultan in Wieland's fairy tale." She begs him at once to sit down beside her; she asks him to accompany her to Sorrento, where she has a large estate and where the mountain air and the divine view will cure him of all philosophy, smoothe out the wrinkles in his brow, and "put him to shame before he leaves for having preferred stony and desolate Sicily to her." Concerning her brother the jurist, she always uses, in Goethe's presence, the humorous expression: The brave man! He takes an awful lot of trouble. I have already said to him quite frequently: "If you people make new laws you simply cause us new inconvenience in that we have to devise new ways of transgressing these laws. We have long since learned how to evade the old ones."

Naturally the similarity between the model and the figure in the poetic work extends no farther than the general situation; it does not reach as far as the character itself which is fundamentally different, almost the direct opposite. Nausikaa is the Greek, the Southern Gretchen. Like her she is a combination of naïveté and exaltedness. The maidenly, reserved bearing is overcome in her case too. Without considering the consequences, she gives in to the longings that fill her. In the presence of Odysseus she praises his speech; it as beautiful as the song of the poet. Gretchen says about the same: *Und seiner Rede Zauberfluss.*

We have a similar situation in Goethe's novelette entitled *Der Mann von fünfzig Jahren,* where the elderly man is loved by his grand-daughter, though she was really intended for his son.

The Major remarks in the novelette: "I would never have believed her capable of anything so unnatural." To this the young woman's mother replies that that is not unnatural in the case of a

young girl. In the same vein we have, among the
fragments in *Nausikaa,* these words:

> Und immer ist der Mann ein junger Mann,
> Der einem jungen Weibe wohlgefällt.

**In despair over being unable to compete with
Homer, Goethe alcoved the plan for ever and a day.**

CHAPTER XXVIII

STUDIES IN BOTANY; METAMORPHOSIS OF PLANTS
REVISION OF *Tasso*—RETURN TO WEIMAR:
PROFOUND DISCONTENT

IT was during the study of Italian plant forms, a new field for Goethe, that he had a number of original and valuable experiences pertaining to the dependence of growth upon light, air, and soil. And while searching for the *Urpflanze* (in the public gardens of Padua and Palermo), he arrived at those general ideas concerning the structure of plant forms that were soon to be embodied in his brochure on the metamorphosis of plants.

Initially he was so ill-informed that he firmly believed he would find the *Urpflanze* among other plants, just as though nature worked out her models until they stood in among other specimens in the same way that a model from Paris stands in the shop window along with others cut after this particular Parisian design. But four weeks pass by; he feels, in the presence of nature, that he is a creative spirit; he knows that the *Urpflanze* is his product and not the product of nature.

In Naples he writes: "The *Urpflanze* is the most truly remarkable creation in the world, and nature itself will come in time to begrudge me this creation." Observation has taught him that the plant brings forth the most varied and variegated sorts of forms simply by modifying one single organ—the leaf.

From this point of view, the formation of the leaf is a propagation which differs from the propagation that takes place in the simultaneous formation of fruit and flower only in the matter of frequent repetition. And by concluding further that a plant, even a tree, which we visualise as an individual entity, consists after all of separate parts that resemble each other and the whole, he approaches the secret of organic individuality. He was in truth prevented from penetrating it fully by the mere fact that the microscope did not clear up the life of the cell until after his day. He perceives, however, not simply so far as the plant is concerned, that the seemingly indivisible separate beings consist of a "collection of several details," as he expresses it, but that the same applies to animals and men as well.

When Goethe began his botanical studies, botanists everywhere stood under the direct influence of Linné; they were exclusively engaged in systemology. Linné had stamped microscopists and physiologists as mere dilettantists; he had also caused the defection from the investigations bearing on the anatomy and physiology of plants which had been carried on even in the seventeenth century. Linné's system was artificial to the extent that it divided the plant world according to external characteristics, such as the number and position of the stamens. With him and his disciples it was a question of recognizing and separating as many species as possible from each other.

All of Goethe's original investigations in the neighborhood of Weimar, concerning the growth of trees and mosses, or concerning plants in his own garden, had been undertaken from Linné's point of view. Goethe took Linné's writings along with him on his excursions, and classified whatever he found according to the Linnéan system, just as the botanists did in adjacent Jena. When he went to Karlsbad, he even took along with him a gardener's son from Jena, who was especially interested in giving plants their correct Latin names. He felt that the young man's assistance might be of substantial value to him.

Though Linné's system, as we have said, was artificial, he himself emphasized the necessity of a natural system, according to which plants would be grouped after their real and peculiar characteristics. French botanists, and among the Germans Batsch and Büttner in Jena, were planning to draw up such a system. Jean Jacques Rousseau, who had influenced young Wolfgang as a poet, also gave Goethe the botanist not a few suggestions. Linné and his successors taught, moreover, that the species have never changed since their creation. Goethe on the contrary saw that in certain families, such as the gentians, each individual specimen had the same external characteristics, while there were others, roses for example, in which the individual specimens differed so much from each other, partly even in the case of the decisive marks, that it was impossible to decide to which species the individual specimen must belong. In other words, he found all sorts of transitional forms in the species that were fixed according to Linné, so that his belief in the existence of

unalterably determined and unchangeable species
was shaken.

So much the more because he had studied plants
not in herbariums but on his walks out in the open;
and he had observed with his own eyes the effect
of external influences on the forms of plants. The
same species looked quite different, depending upon
whether it grew in the field or in the valley, in the
sun or in the shade, whether it was exposed to cold
or protected, whether it was richly watered, or
whether it received but little water.

In Italy his botanical belief was corroborated
and his botanical heresy was strenghtened. Even in
Padua he discovered that under the warmer suns
and the milder winter the flora as a whole took on a
quite different stamp from what it had in the North.
And even in Padua he observed (while studying a
fan palm in the botanical garden of the city) a complete series of transitions between the simple leaf
form and the compound fan leaf. He saw that the
parts of plants developed differently under different
sorts of influences, and that a comparison between
the various plant species could be undertaken with
the idea of arriving at a comprehensive point of
view in the plant world.

Though he used the miscroscope but little, he did
not adhere to the finished plant. In Rome he saw
how various plants sprouted and kept up their
growth until they acquired the finished form. The
above mentioned Reiffenstein succeeded, moreover,
in persuading him to make the attempt to see to
what extent parts of plants that had been cut off
would take root. He also studied and made drawings of abnormally developed plants, bred and ob-

served the plant forms that arose through the inter-
ference of man or from external causes, such as the
bite of an insect.

It was then not as the result of momentary
inspiration but of prolonged persistence that he approached his theory concerning the transformation
of plants; and it was with the greatest difficulty that
he had it published. Göschen refused to print the
little monograph which in later editions takes up 32
pages. The essay was published in 1790 by Ettinger
in Gotha under the German-sounding title: *J. W.
v. Goethe, Herzoglich Sachsen-Weimarischen Ge-
heimrats Versuch, die Metamorphose der Pflanzen
zu erklären.*

With Goethe it was a question of establishing, by
reference to numerous transitional forms, the fundamental thesis that all the different parts of the plant,
except the stem, are transformed leaves: On the
tiny insignificant cotyledons, after the form is pulled
apart, there follow the undeveloped leaf blades, and
then by renewed contraction the calyx, and then
by separation the corolla, and then by renewed contraction the stamens and pistils, and finally as a
result of the latest development the fruit. Goethe
raises the question in this connection as to what
causes the lateral development and contraction of
the form. His own theory is that during the growth
of the plant and the in-filtering of the sap into the
parts that lie higher, these saps gradually become
more finely filtered and thereby changed. Modern
science has not agreed with him, in so far as the
change of material does not come about so simply
as he in his day could suppose. But it has agreed
with him in the essentials in so far as he understood

that the change of form of plants in general must be dependent upon the change of material.

The little work, to this very day the basis of scientific botany, evoked a smile on the part of his contemporaries and seemed to them to be a queer delusion. Is it possible that a poet is botching around in science! This essay of just a few pages, concerning which Auguste Saint-Hilaire said that it belongs to those few books that do not simply make their author immortal but that they themselves are immortal, was received with the sympathetic lament that such a great talent could have so completely got off its right and proper course. Professional men shook their heads, while scholars in Goethe's immediate vicinity denied him the recognition they otherwise distributed with open hands. As early as 1791, Schiller was made a member of the Academy of Science in Erfurt; Goethe was not accorded this modest distinction until 1811, or twenty years later.

I

It was Goethe's original intention to take *Torquato Tasso*, which, according to the preliminary outline of the contents of Goethe's collective works in the first edition (1786), was to have only two acts, along with him to Italy and revise it while there. But he did not succeed in doing this, though he worked at it with marked perseverance. While occupation with *Tasso* stretches out over more than nine years of his life (March, 1780—July, 1789), the revision alone engaged his attention during the last three of these years.

What the Duke says to Tasso, then, concerning

his work on *La Gerusalemme Liberata* applies remarkably well to Goethe himself:

> Er kann nicht enden, kann nicht fertig werden,
> Er ändert stets, rückt langsam weiter vor,
> Steht wieder still.

In 1786, Goethe resumes work on the subject, in
February, 1787, he thinks of laying it aside for a
while so that he can devote his time to *Iphigenie in
Delphi,* works on it nevertheless in February and
March, and then puts it to one side in Rome in order
to have time to complete *Egmont.* He writes even
in February, 1788, that *Tasso* must be revised, for
as it is written it is of no account. In March he has
his plan complete. It never occurs to him for a
moment to go to Ferrara, which he had seen for
only one day, October 16, 1786, and found nauseating.   In the beautiful gardens of Florence, during
the months of April and May, he elaborated those
parts of the drama which then attracted him most,
was again seized with misgivings, found the first
two acts a failure, saw that they must be revised,
returned home with the work unfinished, and wrote
in February, 1789, to the Duke that *Tasso* was
growing like an orange tree, very slowly. But by
April he had advanced so far that he could "read"
the drama to the Duchess Luise only by narrating
the three scenes that were still lacking. He finished
it finally at the same time that the Bastille was being
stormed in Paris.

If there be one event with which the drama has no
connection other than that of contemporaneity, it is
the French Revolution. This is a drama which, in
contrast to *Egmont,* has no folk scenes, and whose

air, however fresh and clean it may be, can be characterized as court air.

But in saying this there is no intention whatsoever of making a disparaging remark concerning the drama, which is caviar for the multitude, but a wonderful work of art, not exactly as a stage drama but as a bit of poetry. There is very little stage life in it, especially because it is so difficult to find actors who can measure up to the demands made by the leading figures. But it abounds in knowledge of men and wisdom in general. This world knows of but few dramas that contain such a large number of speeches that have become winged words, standing phrases, quoted again and again, in season and out of season, rightly and wrongly. Here are a few examples:

> Es bildet ein Talent sich in der Stille,
> Sich ein Charakter in dem Strom der Welt.

It is possible to question the truth of the remark, since many a talent needs to be unfolded through many-sided influence; but it is impossible to doubt that the remark seemed to the age in which it was made, and to posterity as well, quite striking as a proverb.

The sentence

> Doch haben all Götter sich versammelt,
> Geschenke seiner Wiege darzubringen,
> Die Gratien sind leider ausgeblieben

is supposed to stamp in Tasso's mouth Antonio, and has during the past century, in round numbers, been applied to many an individual other than Antonio.

The same is true of the sentence that characterizes Leonore:

> Und wenn sie auch
> Die Absicht hat, den Freunden wohlzuthun,
> So fühlt man Absicht, und man ist verstimmt.

There have been countless applications of Leonore's remarks on Antonio and Tasso as the seeming antipodes of each other, as men who appear mutually hostile though they should be mutually complementary. There have been countless instances where two men, Goethe and Schiller for example, have been kept apart for years and years by misunderstandings and apparently contrary dispositions until at last we learn that they are simply opposite poles of the same fundamental being:

> Zwei Männer sind's, ich hab' es lang' gefühlt,
> Die darum Feinde sind, weil die Natur
> Nicht *einen* Mann aus ihnen beiden formte.

The difficulty in completely understanding men, men whose inmost nature we imagine we have thoroughly penetrated, because we have seen them and observed them for years, is expressed in this caustic remark by Tasso:

> Die Menschen kennen sich einander nicht.
> Nur die Galeerensklaven kennen sich,
> Die eng an *eine* Bank geschmiedet keuchen.

Tasso's remarks concerning the poet have been repeated time out of mind:

> Und wenn der Mensch in seiner Qual verstummt,
> Gab mir ein Gott zu sagen, was ich leide.

Students of Shakespeare will recall that he almost invariably speaks with contempt of authors and poets. Those in *Caesar* and *Timon* play a pitiable rôle. It was Shakespeare who originated the depreciatory conception of the writing individual as contrasted with the man of deeds; he has the scholar and poet fare ill in comparison with the hero. From Shakespeare this idea was handed down to Goethe and his brothers in Apollo from the time of *Sturm und Drang*.

Where, a generation later, the Romanticists in Germany as in France and in the North, outdid themselves in self-idolization, saw the poet in their creations become now a knight with a golden harp, now nothing less than the shepherd and chieftain of the people (Victor Hugo), in the mind and works of the young Goethe the poet becomes a half ridiculous, half contemptible figure.

When Götz von Berlichingen complains that "this lazy leisure simply does not suit me," Elizabeth says to him: "Then finish your autobiography which you have begun!" Götz replies: "Ah! Writing is busy *idleness*. While I am writing about what I have already done, I am vexed at the loss of time in which I might have done more."—In the same spirit Liebetraut says in *Götz* concerning him who invented the game of chess that he "was too *active* to become a scholar." In Klinger's *Otto* we have the same low grading of those who write history as contrasted with those who make history. He says in this connection: "Writers of history must have very little to do, since they merely write up what the others actually accomplish." In *Julius von Tarent,* by Schiller's predecessor Leisewitz, we read: "Whoever can be a hero knows but little about history. There is the *idler* Julius; he is familiar with so many brilliant historical examples. Had he been a man of real ability he would himself have become a hero." And in his *Räuber* (1781) Schiller says after him, through Karl Moor: "O fie, fie on this emasculated century which can only ruminate on the events of the past . . . I am disgusted with this ink-wasting century when I read in my Plutarch of great men."

But of the various writing people, it is especially the poets who are looked down upon. On this account Admet says in *Götter, Helden und Wieland*: "Euripides is also a poet and I have never in my life held poets to be more than they actually are. But he is a brave fellow and my countryman." The poet is then the symbol of weakness. One whines "like a sick poet" (*Götz*). The poet is a poor devil who deserves sympathy. Thus we read in Schiller's *Räuber*: "Poor poets, who do not have a pair of shoes to put on because they have sent their only pair to be mended" — apparently a reminiscence from the life of Corneille.

In Goethe's prologue to *Neueröffnetes moralisch-politisches Puppenspiel* (1774), he derides with unmistakable bitterness the mutual envy and jealousy of the poets:

> Dringt Einer sich dem Andern vor,
> Deutet Einer dem Andern ein Eselsohr.

> Herum, herauf, hinan, hinein—
> Das muss ein Schwarm Autoren sein.

At this period of his life the poet is always outdistanced and outshone by the hero. In Schiller's

Fiesco (1783), a painting is brought to the leading character. He throws it to one side with the words:

You boast with the heat of the poet, with the impotent puppet plays of the fancy that know not heart and that are strangers to such deeds as warm the fancy into other deeds. You throw tyrants on the canvas while you yourself are a miserable slave.

In contrast to this, the conception of the artist in *Torquato Tasso* is altogether sympathetic and profoundly appreciative. Goethe has established the bond that exists between his hero and his poet in a quite exquisite manner:

So bindet der Magnet durch seine Kraft
Das Eisen mit dem Eisen fest zusammen,
Wie gleiches Streben Held und Dichter bindet.
Homer vergass sich selbst; sein ganzes Leben
War der Betrachtung zweier Männer heilig,
Und Alexander in Elysium
Eilt den Achill und den Homer zu suchen.

There is no doubt but that the poet in the prose sketch of *Torquato Tasso* was a leading character the significance of whose calling was emphasized in all probability just as strongly as it is in the finished drama. But where the vocation is there measured on a one-arm lever, in the finished classical drama in verse it is measured on a lever of two arms. The worth of the poet and the man of affairs, or more accurately speaking the statesman, are set off against each other. It is not until this has been done that one feels that the author of the drama was able to rise superior to his own life-work, not in the spirit of immature depreciation, such as we witnessed fifteen or sixteen years earlier in his life, but by way of dispassionately showing the poet where his real sphere of activity lies, and what rôle he plays among other mortals whose existence is also justified.

At this time Goethe himself was no longer merely the poet of former days. For quite a while he too had been struggling with practical questions. As a poet he had simply met with cordial opposition from the vindicators of state routine, vindicators whom he was obliged to disarm, not by defiance nor by referring to the favor he enjoyed at the hand of his Prince, but by self-control and persistent industry.

Tasso's nature has two fundamental traits: he is sensitive and he is impulsive.

Thin-skinned in his feelings as he is, he acts without previous deliberation and follows an impulse which knows no inner restraint.

As to how *sensitive* he is, we see before our own eyes from the rapture he experiences on receiving the wreath from fair hands as a reward for the completion of his great poem. He does not see how he is to live from that hour on. He asks the Princess to remove the wreath from his head; it is scorching his hair, it is burning the thoughts from his brain like a sun-stroke, it is setting his blood in a fever. This is the height of exaltation from which he falls at the arrival of Antonio with his glacial coldness and the manifestation of unreserved displeasure.

As to how *impulsive* he is, we see for the first time when, under the impression of the cordial words spoken to him by the Princess as to how his great poem has *won* the reader, intoxicated with joy, he hopes to see his love for her requited. He picks a quarrel with the cool Antonio whom he fills with antipathy through the offer of friendship and the request of friendship in return. And we receive an even deeper impression of this feeling when, immediately after, suffering from Antonio's reserve and the doubt of his merits, which the latter in his envy and aversion allows us to catch sight of, he refers, not merely to his ability and the reward for his ability, but even goes so far as to allow himself to be dragged into a state of actual hostility. He draws his sword on Antonio in the ducal palace, and this despite the fact that, according to an old and universal law, such conduct is considered a crime and sure to be met with severe punishment.

The Prince, who understands him and pities him, contents himself with inflicting upon him a harmless arrest in his own rooms; but to Tasso's sensitive nature this is an injustice that shrieks to heaven. When an honest attempt is made on all sides to adjust and straighten out what has happened, his impulsive temperament once more robs him of his power in the drama: he takes the demure and cultured Princess into his arms and presses her to his bosom. Also, he is so imprudent and uncautious as to commit this unconventional act in the presence of two or three witnesses, to whom the deed is not exactly criminal but which, the circumstances being as they are, decided Tasso's fate and isolated the unfortunate mortal forever.

The other traits which show Tasso's sickly nature we experience only through the remarks of Antonio; they do not stand out especially clear in the picture. An Elizabethan dramatist would have made us eye witnesses to all of these oddities which Goethe took from the two Italian biographies that he used: Tasso cannot be temperate in food and drink, he fills his stomach with sweet and spiced things, never puts water in his wine, and disobeys the injunctions of his physician in general. Since Goethe does not wish to have us regard Tasso as mentally diseased, and since he himself scarcely believed that he was of unsound mind, he explains his wild dreams as being the result of his irregular life. Tasso suffered from an obsession that he was surrounded by enviers, enemies, and persecutors. He complains to the Duke of broken locks, intercepted letters, attempts on his life, and so on, but when the cases are investigated nothing can be found.

In reality, Tasso, like Rousseau and Strindberg, suffered from a distinct mania that he was being persecuted. But this does not exclude the fact that in life he often had, and in the drama he has justifiable reason, for suspicion. Leonore von Sanvitale, who tries to get him away from Ferrara in order to enjoy his society herself, is, despite her tenderness, by no means always honorable toward him. She gives him an entirely false picture of the feelings of the Princess, conceals from him the love that the Princess really cherishes for him, and does her share to deprive him of the equilibrium he sorely needs.

The manner in which the various persons who come in close contact with Tasso endeavor, for good reasons but in vain, to persuade him to abandon and forget his morbid introspection is unusually beautiful in itself; and it is elaborated with the finesse of a born artist.

The Duke makes it clear to him that Fate digs many an abyss around about us; but the deepest abyss of all is found in our own heart. He adds in a spirit of paternal kindness

Ich bitte dich, entreisse dich dir selbst.

To this Tasso replies with a fascinating, ingenious and yet evasive simile; one that quite transcends what the Duke himself has in mind. He claims that without brooding, and without the writing of poetry he cannot live. He contends that it is consequently just as idle to forbid his participation in these things as it is to forbid the silkworm from spinning, though it spins the precious web from out of its own self, and in this way spins itself to death, only to lie at last enshrouded in its own yarn as if in its coffin.

Antonio replies in words that are admirably chosen, and as profound as they are true:

> Es ist wohl angenehm, sich mit sich selbst
> Beschäftigen, wenn es nur so nützlich wäre.
> Inwendig lernt kein Mensch sein Innerstes
> Erkennen; denn er misst nach eignem Mass
> Sich bald zu klein, und leider oft zu gross.
> Der Mensch erkennt sich nur im Menschen, nur
> Das Leben lehret Jedem, was er sei.

Nor are Antonio's observations any less to the point when he says that there are times when Tasso sinks within himself as if all things had found lodgment in his own heart and the external world had completely vanished. But then suddenly, just as if a mine had been discharged, he endeavors to seize control of all he had so recently cast off and away; he endeavors to obtain in a moment things that can be secured only after years of preparation. Goethe has Leonore use an expression concerning him which he himself will use in time concerning Reinhold Lenz: He harms no one but himself.

Antonio, who perchance confuses the reader and spectator somewhat on his first appearance in so far as his conduct seems to be determined wholly and

entirely by envy and jealousy, grows in our estimation as the drama proceeds until at last he stands
face to face with Tasso as a picture of mature manhood over against uncontrolled youth, as the picture
of an individual sincere in his intentions, reasonable
in his guidance, and resolute where he was formerly
vacillating.

As is usual in Goethe's works, the heroine is fully
as attractive as the hero. Where Faust and Egmont
allow themselves to be loved, Tasso, like Werther,
is deeply and inconstantly in love. Where Gretchen
and Clärchen love without measure and without
regard, Goethe has depicted in the Princess a noble
and dignified woman who loves fervently and fully
but whose love recognizes limits and whose breeding
demands, not simply that morals and customs be
respected, but that rank and standing be taken into
consideration. Where Leonore von Sanvitale, with
all her kindness for Tasso, clings to him nevertheless
in womanly vanity, takes pleasure in seeing her own
being reflected in his mind, reads herself into his
poems and out of them, delights in the renown
that accrues to a woman who stands in such intimate
relations to a distinguished personality, and wishes
to see him honored so that she herself may be the
more honored, Leonore von Este loves him uncon-
ditionally though, as has been said, not boundlessly.

She has an edifying effect upon him. She teaches
him what is permissible and what can be presumed.
She makes clear to him the significance of dignified
womanhood. Like the assassins of the Middle Ages,
he falls back upon nature's call to mortal man:
Erlaubt ist, was gefällt. She, distrustful of the natural state of man, and having no delusions about a

Golden Age, adopts as her slogan: *Erlaubt ist, was sich ziemt.* She is conceived of in lofty fashion. She is a disciple of Plato. She gives expression to generalities that are tenable. Sincerely endeavoring to keep her adorer within certain safe limits and at the same time retain her own self-assertion and self-possession, she posits this thesis:

> Willst du genau erfahren, was sich ziemt,
> So frage nur bei edlen Frauen an

There is no escaping the fact that to the modern mind she seems to be writing poetry for albums. In her being is a basic portion of resignation. She no more believes in happiness than in the Golden Age. "Happy! Who is happy?" she asks. During the years of her approaching maturity she had been in ill health; she had been obliged to form that philosophy of life which sees good in pain and something beneficial in distress. She is reserved: It is impossible for her even to approach her own brother in Tasso's behalf; impossible for her to ask Antonio to spare Tasso; to become reconciled to him and with him. She is wont to carry out her desires in perfect stillness, personally, without appealing or applying to anyone else. She wishes to use her maternal inheritance in caring for Tasso, he himself being such an impractical economist.

It is consequently all the more effective and pleasing when this reticent, demure, resigned and temperate young woman, on being confronted with Tasso's actual departure, falls into semi-despair, confesses her love for him, shudders at the feeling of imminent loneliness, and portrays the hope she

has of seeing him in the morning, the joy of the day
when she can associate with him, and that quiet,
glowing feeling which gave to each day a full and
rich meaning:

> Die Hoffnung, ihn zu sehen, füllt nicht mehr
> Den kaum erwachten Geist mit froher Sehnsucht;
> Mein erster Blick hinab in unsre Gärten
> Sucht ihn vergebens in dem Thau der Schatten.
> Wie schön befriedigt fühlte sich der Wunsch
> Mit ihm zu sein an jedem heitern Abend!
> Wie mehrte sich im Umgang das Verlangen,
> Sich mehr zu kennen, mehr sich zu verstehen!
> Und täglich stimmte das Gemüth sich schöner
> Zu immer reinern Harmonien auf.

This sore of love, which the more plethoric and
quite demure Leonore compares to the quiet light of
the moon, is, for all that, true love such as can easily
be developed in women who, though not intensely
sensual, are nevertheless emotional and reflective.
Max Müller once upon a time published a little
book, entitled *Deutsche Liebe*, on the mutual love
between a young man and a sickly young German
Princess (a situation similar to the one experienced
by his father, the well known German poet, Wilhelm
Müller). This portrayal corresponds essentially to
the strong but resigned feelings on the part of the
Princess in Goethe's drama, who, it is perfectly
plain, is only apparently an Italian Princess from the
Inquisition at its worst, and who, it is also plain, is
thoroughly German and represents the short-lived
period of humanity.

She is just as human as she is German; and the
same can be said of the other characters of the
drama. The one feature of the work that is not

human, but one of civilization's artificialities, is the
conflict; and here lies the rickety spot in this otherwise rare bit of dramatic poetry. That a young poet
should challenge his opponent to a duel, and that in
a place which for conventional reasons is considered
inviolate, and that the gifted artist longs to embrace
a Princess whom he loves and by whom he is loved
—these are purely artificial sins; they are merely an
attempt to bombard artificial boundaries, which, just
at the time of the completion of *Torquato Tasso,*
were being turned upside down and inside out, in
the main country of Europe as then constituted, by
another type of catapulting violence that was poles
removed from the violence that had characterized
Goethe's juvenile *Sturm und Drang.*

II

Goethe had originally planned to return home
from Italy by way of Frankfort in order to greet his
mother. Nothing came of this. On March 18, 1788,
he writes quite cold heartedly from Rome to Karl
August, stating that he intends to return to Weimar
by way of Lindau, Augsburg and Nuremberg: "I
have already deprived my mother of the hope of
seeing me on my return journey and have tried to
console her by referring her to another occasion."

The last time he had seen her, after a lapse of
four years, was for just a short while in 1779; he
was then on a journey to Switzerland. His stay in
Frankfort made such a slight impression upon him
that he never even mentioned it in the description of
his travels. Nine years had now passed by during

which he had never laid eyes on his noble mother.
She had lost her daughter and was living entirely
in and for her son. Even after his father's death in
1782, Wolfgang felt neither impluse nor desire to
pay her a visit. She was living all alone in the empty
house and not until now did she have an opportunity
to get something out of her own life. From 1784 to
1788 she was quite taken up with the actor Unzel-
mann. On his leaving Frankfort she was moved,
even distressed. She never went to Weimar where
she would have been accepted and welcomed according to her just deserts. She kept up a correspondence
with Anna Amalie for four years. When Goethe
was in Cassel in 1783, he could not be prevailed
upon to take the short journey to Frankfort, though
his companion, the young Fritz von Stein, asked him
to do so. (This young man lived two years later
for some time with Frau Aja.) From Eisenach
Goethe writes to Charlotte von Stein, 1784: "They
tell me I could reach Frankfort in thirty-one hours,
but I have not the most fleeting thought of going
there. You have so drawn my nature to yours that
there is no other nerve left in me for the simplest
duties of the heart." A little later on he says: "I
have neglected my Fatherland and my mother for
your sake." *Vaterland* for *Vaterstadt* is Frankfort
dialect to the very close of the eighteenth century.

Not until 1792, as a companion of the Duke during his participation in the campaign in France, did
Goethe casually see his mother whom he, after the
fashion of man, had set aside for this cold and hot
coquette who completely dominated his existence
for so long. And of his paternal city as such he
thought only with coldness and indifference. As a

resident of Weimar he not only declined, in 1792, Frankfort's polite offer to appoint him *Ratsherr* in the place of his deceased uncle on his mother's side; he also offended the town of his birth by renouncing at last his rights of citizenship in order to avoid a city tax incurred by becoming a citizen of Frank-fort.

In two different places, Goethe has given con-sonous expression to the mood that came over him when, after an absence of over a year and a half in Italy, he returned home to Weimar: *Zur Mor-phologie. Glückliches Ereignis* (1817), and *Biog-raphische Einzelheiten. Erste Bekanntschaft mit Schiller.*

He had returned to Germany thoroughly satur-ated with the natural scenery of southern Italy and the monuments of Rome, wholly filled with the new artistic canons that had transformed his very nature. He strove without reserve after pure, clarified beau-ty, after rigid, simple form. In Germany he found not merely the young generation, but all those who could lay claim to literary interests, standing where he had stood about fifteen years ago. In this situa-tion there was, to be sure, nothing remarkable. The reading public cannot keep pace with those men who, in a given country, open up new artistic ways and determine the tastes that shall prevail. But it sur-prised him and discouraged him. He had hoped for success with his *Iphigenie* and his *Egmont;* for he had once had success with his *Götz* and his *Werther.* They made no impression; they aroused no favor-able comment; they evoked disappointment; and the author's disappointment was the keenest.

He writes: "After my return from Italy, where

I had sought to perfect myself along the line of a more pronounced definiteness and purity with regard to the varied phases of art, unconcerned as to what had taken place in the mean time in Germany, I found the works of the younger poets, and those of the older as well, standing in high repute. Among these, unfortunately, were the very ones that were especially obnoxious to me. I mention only Heinse's *Ardinghello* and Schiller's *Räuber*. The former was always distasteful to me, because it tries to ennoble and embellish sensuality and dubious ways of thinking with regard to plastic art; the latter because a forceful but immature talent had poured out in it the very ethical and theatrical paradoxes of which I had endeavored to purge myself; and he had emptied them on to the Fatherland in torrents unabated.

"The tumult which this awakened, the applause that was so generally accorded these bizarre lucubrations, by refined ladies of the Court as well as by blatant students, startled me: I had a feeling that my exertions had been wasted. The themes for the development of which I had trained myself seemed to have been set aside; my methods of education had apparently been rejected . . . Fancy my condition! I had been trying to find and nourish the purest views, and here I was, squeezed in between Ardinghello and Franz Moor."

He continues with a portrayal of the aversion he felt toward Schiller's revelling in liberty and self-determination, after the fashion of Kant, and because of Schiller's ingratitude toward great Mother Nature, who had never treated him novercally. He was always and ever contrasting liberty with nature:

"Instead of considering nature as independent, as creating from the deepest to the highest, according to law, he took it merely from a few simple, human, empirical ideas of naturalness." Such a remark as the following from Schiller's treatise entitled *Ueber Anmuth und Würde* made a quite depressing effect on Goethe: "Out of animal figures and forms, it is only nature that speaks, liberty never." As though there were a liberty outside of nature! As if it were possible to precede nature by an *only!*

This is the status of Goethe at this juncture of his career. All had turned away from him because he worshipped truth and beauty without regard to public taste and public usages. The great German public regarded him in the light of an apostate from the cause of his youth. But so much the more unalterable did he continue to remain in his adoration of nature, and his artistic ideals; so much the more vigorously did he determine to follow his course without making a shadow of a concession to the Germans. Up to this point he had not concerned himself to any marked degree with his readers; now he began to despise them.

From now on we note that tendency in him to which he gave expression, as late as 1816, in a letter to Merck. He said:

Die lieben Deutschen kenn' ich schon; erst schweigen sie; dann mäkeln sie; dann beseitigen sie; dann bestehlen und verschweigen sie.

It had at last become clear to him that he was never to enjoy universal popularity; it did not lie in his nature.

The Duke alone was cordial toward him, and appreciative of him. In accordance with the poet's wish, he exempted him from now on from all work, as a minister, that was really foreign to his true vocation. Goethe retained only the supervision of the institutions of art and science, with especial reference to the theatre in Weimar and the University in Jena.

He returned from Italy on June 18, 1788. Less than a month later, on July 12, a young working girl from Bertuch's flower factory, Christiane Sophie Vulpius, handed him, in his garden, the above mentioned petition. She pleased him then and there; he pleased her then and there. It was a case of love at first sight; it was markedly different from that of the Princess in *Tasso*. It was evoked by the arrow of Cupid rather than by that of Amor. It was no high-born love; but it was serious, enduring, natural, and innocent. Nothing could afford more reliable proof of the tenuous superficiality of the refinement and culture of the best society in Weimar at that time than the outcry that was raised when this union became known. The really modest women, from the Duchess down, were scandalized; the less modest paraded a virile contempt; the men were either excited or amused. Poor Christiane! She belonged (and there are very few women who can say the same thing) her whole life long to just one man. But she was reviled like a minx. Goethe himself encountered the solemn disapproval that is meted out to a man whose conduct is unbecoming.

Karl August and Herder were the only men in Weimar who were not offended: It simply did not lie in the Duke's nature to moralize on an erotic irregularity; and Herder, though a preacher, had not lost the liberality of his youth. Goethe's mother was the only woman who viewed the case as a perfectly normal and harmless affair. She would naturally have preferred to see her son married to a pretty, domestic young woman from Frankfort, but she was far too human to be angry at her son because he had gone contrary to a social rule, or to condemn his new friend.

She writes to Christiane as soon as her relation to Goethe became established, and after having sent her some little presents. The birth of August won her affection completely. With the innate lawlessness, incidentally, of a woman, she persisted in spelling his name "Augst." In the letters to her son she calls Christiane now "Dein Liebgen," now "Deine Freundin," and now "Dein Bettschatz." Here is the beginning of her first letter to Christiane:

That the things I sent you have caused you joy is very agreeable to me—keep them as a little token from the mother of the one you love and esteem, and who is really worthy of love and esteem.

She signs this letter, "Ihre Freundin Goethe." In another letter, to her son, written in January, 1795, she enthusiastically thanks him for his *Wilhelm Meister,* the reminiscences of which from his childhood, the puppet theatre and the rest, have given her especially keen delight, "so that she felt thirty years younger." She closes the letter in this blunt, straightforward way:

One thing more! The continuation of Wilhelm will not be put off so long—for I have not yet had it bound—don't let a person wait so long for the rest of it—for I am curious about it. Good-bye! Kiss little Augst for me—also your bedfellow.

Your faithful Mother,

GOETHE.

END OF VOLUME ONE

WOLFGANG GOETHE

Volume II

CHAPTER I

CHRISTIANE VULPIUS—*Römische Elegien*

AFTER Goethe's return home he lived in a world of Roman reminiscences. He was "the aristocratic Roman," as Herder half jestingly, half satirically called him. He fused Roman memories with fresh Weimarian impressions of his happy life with Christiane Vulpius in his collection of poems entitled *Römische Elegien*. This was the first pretentious work he wrote after his return and in order to mislead the curious he gave his beloved the Roman name of Faustina which, scarcely by accident, sounds like the feminine form of Faust. In the original sketch her name was Christina.

There was nothing of the Roman woman in Christiane herself. Her uninterrupted friendship for Goethe lasted twenty-eight years. Born June 1, 1765, she was twenty-three years old in 1788. Her father had been an official copyist in Weimar, but during his later years he fell an incurable prey to drink and eventually died of intemperance. Her brother was a capable official and energetic reviser of dramas. He had made a name for himself by his robber novel entitled *Rinaldo Rinaldini,* a work which enjoyed an enormous popularity, greater in-

7

deed than any single work of his illustrious brother-in-law.

Goethe's ardent yearning for Christiane was the point of departure of the union. It gradually developed into affectionate resignation such as a more distinguished man can cherish for an unpretentious and dependable woman friend who does not possess the excellence of training enjoyed by her protector. Goethe gave her a care-free existence. She appreciated him even though she did not understand him. By her living with him she was subjected to humiliations from those about her. She never failed to maintain a feeling of distinct and unwavering gratitude toward him. She had felt that she was too good to be cast aside after Goethe's first desire had been satisfied, and Goethe found her too good to be treated in this way. In the little poem entitled *Gefunden* he tells how, while taking a walk one day, he found a little flower out in the forest:

> Im Schattan sah ich
> Ein Blümchen stehn,
> Wie Sterne leuchtend,
> Wie Äuglein schön.

His first impulse was to pluck it; it asked: Was I created only to be plucked and then left to wither and decay?

> Ich grub's mit allen
> Den Würzlein aus,
> Zum Garten trug ich's
> Am hübschen Haus.

He replanted the flower and it grew and put forth branches and flowers.

The poems *Morgenklage* and *Der Besuch* are

on love. They tell how she absented herself from a tryst where she was expected with longing and yearning and how, at a certain visit, he took her by surprise as she lay sleeping and did not have the heart to disturb her. Goethe's charming portrayal of Christiane, half lying and half sitting, asleep in the corner of the divan, with her head against the pillow, resembles strongly an illustration of the poem.

Christiane was in no sense of the word distinguished though she was not on that account vulgar. She possessed to a rather remarkable degree the attractions of youth and beauty. She had what the French call *la beauté du diable*. She appeared better full face than profile. She was, as the *Römische Elegien* inform us, a brunette whose dark hair fell luxuriously down over her forehead while short locks curled about her pretty neck and loose unbraided hair stood up from her crown. She was a child of the people and liked that type of amusement which attracts a young girl of her social class. She was especially fond of dancing, a passion she never lost until well on in years. She did not bother herself about reading and was a poor correspondent. She amused herself by talking, attending social affairs and the theatre and associating with actors and actresses. The daughter of a factory worker, she followed her father's example. Though she never led a really dissolute life, she liked a glass of good wine; indeed she had no objection to two or three of them.

She made her protector's home charming and attractive, though she was a poor economist, especially in her later years when, racked with physical

pain, she paid so little attention to the details of
housekeeping that Goethe became financially embarrassed.   She never regarded herself as his equal;
she always addressed her Lord and Husband officially as *Sie* or *Herr Geheimrath*.   Even after the
marriage had been legalized she submitted to all
the slights to which the society of Weimar took
pleasure in subjecting her.   It was not until 1811,
when her son August had grown up and had received a title that, zealous of his rights as a legitimate citizen, she became pugnacious, even grossly
critical; she forbade Bettina admission to her home,
even though she came accompanied by her husband.
In fine, she made it known that she was a genuine
Geheimrätin.

One sees the various women in Goethe's life in
various positions and situations: Friederike when
she runs across the meadow under the open sky,
Charlotte Buff cutting bread and butter for her little
brothers and sisters, Lili at the ball, Charlotte von
Stein at her country place or at court, Christiane in
bed as a young woman, as an older woman in the
kitchen or on walks out to Belvedere.

As the years passed by, she became quite stout.
The women of Weimar, especially Charlotte von
Schiller, called her *die dicke Ehehälfte*.   But when
younger, she exercised, by reason of her solid and
exhuberant figure, her sprightly and loving eyes,
a sort of sensual bewitchery over Wolfgang Goethe,
then almost forty years old.   The mere thought of
embracing her filled him with extreme delight.
Neither daily life in the company of each other, nor
months of separation, nor five periods of pregnancy
(1789, 1791, 1793, 1795, 1802) were able to cool

his ardor or effect his estrangement, even though he never conceived his domestic fidelity as being unconditional. Of the five children, three sons and two daughters, only the first born survived. The others were born dead or lived only a few weeks. The sensual attraction is in time transformed into conventional marital affection: the sweetheart becomes the housekeeper, the housekeeper becomes the wife.

We have a letter from Schiller, the authenticity of which is not absolutely assured since the original has not been preserved. Its reliability, however, in substance in the part quoted is beyond question. At the close of the century, Schiller wrote to Count Schimmelmann concerning Goethe's relation to Christiane. Schiller's views on this subject coincide entirely with those of his wife, who was of noble birth. After having praised and defended Goethe from every conceivable angle—as an intellectual force, as a poet, as a scientist, and as a man— Schiller says:

I wish I could also fully justify Goethe with regard to his domestic relations just as I could confidently do with regard to his literary and civilian relations. Unfortunately, however, he has come, owing to some false conceptions of domestic happiness and because of a solicitous fear of the marriage vow, into a situation which oppresses him and makes him unhappy in his own home, and from which, alas, he is too weak and gentle-hearted to disentangle himself. This is the sole blot on his escutcheon; it harms no one but himself, however, and even it comes from a quite noble trait of character.

Goethe adopted the same Fabian policy here that he had employed in his literary activity. He postponed getting married so long that when he did finally make up his mind, the people of Weimar looked upon Christiane as having been irreparably compromised. It was only with extreme difficulty that she was admitted to the society of Weimar; she was never received at court. If he wished to marry her he should have done so when he took her into his home. As it was, he endured the drawbacks incident to having a woman around without a single one of the advantages that a formal union with her would have procured for him, and especially for her. Had the marriage been solemnized earlier, his son, August, would have escaped the stigma of being of illegitimate birth, a stigma that was for a considerable time a decided hindrance on his journey through life.

II

The *Römische Elegien* constitute a most charming cycle of poems. An exact knowledge of the German language is, to be sure, indispensable to unqualified enjoyment of them. When, some time ago, the *Elegien* were praised by Taine, a Frenchman who chanced to be present asked what they really were. The great critic gave this off-hand reply: *Des pastiches d'après Properce.* That they are just this Goethe himself never denied. By way of defending them and the Venetian epigrammes, he writes the introduction to *Hermann and Dorothea:*

Also das wäre Verbrechen, dass einst Properz mich begeistert,
    Dass Martial sich zu mir auch, der Verwegne, gesellt,
Dass ich die Alten nicht hinter mir liess, die Schule zu hüten.
    Dass kein Name mich täuscht, dass mich kein Dogma beschränkt.

But for all this the elegies are abundantly original. They begin by giving a few somewhat buoyant pictures of Rome, its gripping monuments, proud palaces and venerable walls, with a reference to the genius of the city. All of this glory and all of this magnificence are without meaning to the poet until he has found the one who to him personifies the city and gives it voice. He soon finds her; and then he finds joy. She gives him a place of refuge where he is in peace from politics and news, from ladies and gentlemen of the smart world. She herself is not a lady; she is not ashamed of receiving help from this doughty stranger. She yields without hesitation. But despite her hasty sacrifice, for which she had a precedent in the gods and goddesses of olden times—Venus with Anchises, Luna with Endymion, Rhea Sylvia with Mars—she has both her chastity and her pride. She loves the man to whom she has yielded. She is a widow with a little boy; she must be cautious; she must try to avoid the malicious gossip of the town. Consequently the lovers conceal their mutual understanding as well as they can. *Opportunity* is one of the goddesses they now worship.

With the freedom of the Roman poets, but with a different and more artistic spirit than, for example, Ovid, Goethe depicts the caresses that the poet gives and receives. No Roman of ancient days ever surpassed such verses as these:

Dann versteh' ich den Marmor erst recht; ich denk' und
    vergleiche,
  Sehe mit fühlendem Aug, fühle mit sehender Hand.

The close of the elegy is jocose and unforgetable:

Wird doch nicht immer geküsst, es wird vernünftig
  gesprochen.
  Ueberfällt sie der Schlaf, lieg' ich und denke mir viel.
Oftmals hab' ich auch schon in ihren Armen gedichtet
  Und des Hexameters Maas leise mit fingernder Hand
Ihr auf dem Rücken gezählt. Sie athmet in lieblichem
  Schlummer,
  Und es durchglüht ihr Hauch mir bis ins Tiefste die
  Brust.

Once again he glorifies Rome and the climate of
Italy. In the seventh elegy we find almost precisely
the same words that were quoted above (page 343)
touching on Goethe's return home. These verses
were written at the same time as the letter to Herder, though they contain a picture of the grey sky
of the North, its fog and darkness, its formlessness
and poverty of color. It is a distant, uncomfortable
memory which serves as a foil to the brilliance of
the present. In the fifteenth **elegy** he prefers a complete tribe of southern fleas to the mists in the
mopish North.

Concerning Faustina he makes the remark—it
corresponds to what was said above regarding Christiane's grace—that during her childhood and adolescence she was regarded as neither pleasing nor
beautiful. It is even so with the flower of the grape-
vine—a simile that is quite felicitous—in that it
lacks forms and color, but it brings forth grapes
that ripen and mature both men and gods.

A strong and vigorous, though sensuous, feeling
of happiness is expressed through a profound sympathy for the illustrious dead, from Alexander and
Caesar down to modern times: they are only shades,

and are never warmed in the embrace of woman. There is an exquisite depiction of his quiet, happy, domestic life with his sweetheart while the noise and confusion from the outside Roman world penetrate to the pair and suggest to the poet themes for amusement and passionate devotion. He hears the cheerful voices of the harvesters as they come home on the Flaminian Way. When they approach the Porta del Popolo he complains that Rome no longer celebrates Ceres as the goddess of grain, and seizes upon this opportunity to tell of the nocturnal mysteries which were transplanted from Eleusis to Rome, the secrets of which were, in reality, the incidents of a love-affair between Ceres and a demigod. There is a good deal of mythology in all of the poems; in all of the myths there is a good deal of eroticism. But there is neither an excess of erudition nor a superfluous tone of boldness and vulgar sensuality in them. Grace is never forgotten:

Euch, o Grazien, legt die wenigen Blätter ein Dichter
Auf den reinen Altar, Knospen der Rose dazu.

If there is no reference to any other Roman god, Amor at least receives abundant attention; and whenever Goethe delineates the sweetheart, he avails himself of the touch by which he characterises —a bit monotonously—Christiane: the locks about her precious head as she lies in bed, her head resting on his arm:

Find' ich die Fülle der Locken an meinem Busen, das Köpfchen
Ruhet und drucket den Arm, der sich dem Halse bequemt.

There is constant and dolorous reference, not simply in the elegies which were excluded from the familiar

collection, the ones now generally published with the
poem entitled *Das Tagebuch,* but also in the elegies
of which Goethe approved, to sexual diseases—
which were happily unknown to ancient times. The
abhorrence with which they are mentioned is unmistakable. The fear of infection is characterised
as the most venomous foe of pleasure. His own
beloved is lauded in unequivocal words. Convinced as he is of her fidelity, he fears no danger
from this source.

We may assume that Goethe was incited to write
these poems by his correspondence with Karl August. In February, 1788, he received a letter from
the Duke containing, among other observations, the
report that a case of sickness from which the latter
had suffered had been different and more nefarious
than Goethe had supposed. Moreover, and peculiarly enough, it contained a challenge to Goethe to
go in for a life of vigorous erotic enjoyment. Goethe
replied (Rome, February 16) :

I was good-natured enough, on the reading of your letter
which the courier brought me, to think of hemorrhoids, and
now I see that the neighborhood has suffered. Let us hope
that all the evil will be eliminated from the body once for
all by this annoying inoculation. I shall not fail to defy the
evil spirits through the application of the mysterious *sigillo.*
. . . You write so convincingly that one would have to
have a *cervello tosto* not to be enticed into the alluring garden
of flowers. It seems that your good thoughts of January
22 have dispatched their influence direct to Rome, for I
could tell you of a number of exquisite walks I have latterly
taken. This much is certain, and you, as a *doctor longe
experimentissimus,* are perfectly correct in your assertion that
a moderate indulgence such as that of which you spoke tones
up the mind and brings the body into a state of precious
equilibrium. As I have experienced more than once in my

life, just as I have also felt the irritation, when I have deviated from the broad way and was about to set out on the narrow path of abstinence and certainty.

The passage in the letter is significant by way of characterising the freedom of speech that obtained at that time between the Prince and the Poet and by way of showing the unqualified confidence that each had in the other. The introduction to the eighteenth elegy reminds one of the letter:

Eines ist mir verdriesslich vor allen Dingen, ein Andres
  Bleibt mir abscheulich, empört jegliche Faser in mir,
Nur der blosse Gedanke. Ich will es Euch, Freunde,
    gestehen;
  Gar verdriesslich ist mir einsam das Lager zu Nacht;
Aber ganz abscheulich ist's, auf dem Wege der Liebe
  Schlangen zu fürchten, und Gift unter den Rosen der Lust.

But however much the elegies may have been experienced, partly in Rome, partly in Weimar, they nevertheless remind not infrequently of Roman pictures; and they are just as reminiscent of Ovid as of Propertius. There seems to me to be no doubt at all but that Goethe, in his fifteenth elegy with its portrayal of a scene in an *Osteria,* has imitated Ovid's fourth elegy in the first book of his *Amores*.

The word *Osteria* is, to be sure, quite modern, though the scene that is depicted is Old Roman. Ovid tells how the beloved, accompanied by her husband, after having taken her place at the table, is requested to write fond words in the wine that has been spilled. Tibullus does nearly the same in his fourth elegy on Delia. She too is asked to write words of cunning in the wine. Goethe has his heroine, accompanied by her uncle, take her place at the table, where the top is moist from wine that has been spilled. And then she writes a Roman numeral *Four* by way of indicating the hour of rendezvous for the following day.

Some of these short poems are merely little jokes and intended as such. There is one in which the lover remains away because he believes he sees the stern uncle in the garden before the house. What he sees is the scare-crow. In another he tells of his detestation of the barking of dogs in general, but his delight at hearing a certain definite dog, the dog of his neighbor, bark, for he is thereby apprised of the coming of his sweetheart. In others, the nineteenth for example, which depicts the danger that threatens from *Fama,* the goddess of rumor, Goethe, in order to set forth the hostility that naturally obtains between *Fama* and *Amor,* has so interwoven and interfiltered two old, well-known myths that we wish with all our heart that he would drop mythology once for all and adhere to actual life. Even in the works of Pindar and Ovid the introduction of an excessive amount of mythology makes the enjoyment of their poetry a difficult task. And when a modern poet incessantly harks back to the myths and legends of long ago, the effect produced may be tiresome, lifeless and ineffectual.

Nevertheless, the last little poem dedicated to *Verschwiegenheit,* is a charming bit of lyric poetry. It is the companion poem to the one that cautioned against *Fama.* In this case, as indeed generally, the poet's own words come into play: *Dichter lieben nicht zu schweigen—wollen sich der Menge zeigen.* So it comes about that he who would not confide in his lady friend lest she might disapprove of his manner of living, nor in his gentleman friend lest he might become his rival, and who is too advanced in years and experience to feel that it is judicious to proclaim his secrets to the forests and the fields, entrusts them to the form of the distich and embodies them in ancient verse, just as he might deposit a precious treasure in a jewel box:

Dir, Hexameter, Dir, Pantameter, sei es vertraut,
Wie sie des Tags mich erfreut, wie sie des Nachts mich beglückt.

All in all, it must be said that, just as Goethe in his *Iphigenie auf Tauris* succeeded in imitating Euripedes and vivifying his theme with that particular spirit of humanity which predominated at the close of the eighteenth century, he succeeded equally well, in his *Römische Elegien*, in imitating and bringing down to modern times the three Latin poets whom he jestingly calls the Triumvire of Rome—Tibullus, Catullus, and Propertius. And he created, incidentally, a worthy and more nearly modern counterpiece to their erotic lyricism. There are just a few pages of the *Römische Elegien*, only twenty elegies in all, whereas Ovid's *Amores* alone consists of a half hundred poems of cognate species. Goethe's poems constitute a complete and well rounded whole. They are saturated with the sensual feeling of happiness and a warm, perhaps a little easy-going and massive, sensuality, which, in contrast to that of the poems of olden times, is distinctly heathen. It actually enjoys its indifference toward ascetic prescriptions, an attitude of which the writers of antiquity knew nothing.

It is practically unnecessary to tell of the indignation felt by the fine ladies of the day at the *Frech-heiten* in the *Römische Elegien*. Nor need we report on the manner in which the virile guardians of Zion went out after these poems with tongs of fire, with fire and tongs.

CHAPTER II

SECOND SOJOURN IN VENICE: *Venezianische Epigramme*

It so happened that Goethe had an opportunity, earlier than he had anticipated, of seeing Italy for the second time, or more accurately, one city in Italy, Venice. The Duchess Anna Amalie, accompanied by a number of people, Herder among others, had been living for some while in Italy, and Goethe had expressed a desire to call on her. It was accordingly arranged that he should meet her in Venice and accompany her home. At the latter part of March, 1790, after a journey of eighteen days from Jena, he arrived in Italy. The Duchess having been delayed in Naples, he staid at first alone in the City of the Doges until the beginning of May, and then with the Duchess and her entourage until some time in June.

The fruit of this sojourn was the *Venezianische Epigramme,* interesting in themselves, but doubly interesting as the counterpart to the *Römische Elegien.* Though written in the same metre, they are in direct contrast to the spirit of the elegies, which are peaceful, enrapture by everything ultra-montane, the product of contentment; the epigrammes are quarrelsome, dissatisfied with the piggishness and bigotry of Italy, sharp and caustic against the foreign as well as the domestic.

Much of this is owing to the fact that Goethe started on his journey a few months after the birth of his son, August. His home was then unusually attractive. He missed Christiane bitterly, by day as well as by night. He did not realize how indispensable she had become to him until this separation, the first since their union. Under these circumstances, the Italy he had idolized just a few years before now lost its attraction; and captious as he was, he saw only its shady side. He suffered from dishonesty, selfishness and extortion on the part of the foreigner, and especially on the part of the Hierarchy, which, only a few days ago, had played an insignificant rôle in his joy over the South. In the Rome of which he had written his elegies, Christiane had been the central point; in the Venice in which he was now engulfed, there was no Christiane:

Schön ist das Land, doch ach! Faustinen find' ich nicht
    wieder.
Das ist Italien nicht mehr, das ich mit Schmerzen verliess.

In these epigrammes we catch fleeting glimpses of the cynicism which the last letter to the Duke betrays. It is a wholesome cynicism; in its intolerance of hypocrisy and bigotry it calls things by their right names. They show the poet unsusceptible to the world of beauty in Venice, and so dejected in spirit that poetic creation is difficult. It is also noteworthy that in these epigrammes, and here only, Goethe is occupied, while producing, with the production itself. He speaks again and again, in a way that does not exactly entertain the reader, of the book into which the verses are introduced and raises the question as to whether a given epigramme is excellent or inferior, impudent or humble. We are not accustomed, in the case of Goethe, to be led through the kitchen; we are rather used to being conducted at once to the elaborately furnished dining room where the bounteous meal stands ready.

The disagreement with and aversion toward Christianity, which we observed in the *Italienische Reise,* has reached its climax in the *Venezianische Epigramme.* He attacks Christianity under the rubric of *Schwärmerei*—transcendental enthusiasm. Some of these observations are as harmless as this one:

Mache der Schwärmer sich Schüler wie Sand am Meere
—der Sand ist Sand; die Perle sei mein, Du, o vernünftiger
Freund!

Others reveal a feeling of violent hostility. We quote but one:

Jeglichen Schwärmer schlagt mir ans Kreuz im dreissigsten
　　Jahre!
Kennt er nur einmal die Welt, wird der Betrogne der
　　Schelm.

Imagine, by way of comparison, what the mockers of religion produced during the days of the Renaissance! Aretino himself was certainly not naïve; but his sarcastic little poems are naïve and innocent when measured by Goethe's standard. Take, for example, this epigramme (quoted from memory):

Qui giace Aretin', poeta Tosco.
Chi parlo' mal' d'ognun', fuor' di Christo,
Scusandosi cosi: Non lo cognosco.

A more direct address is given to many of these epigrammes that attack priests, bigots and palmers

(Nos. 6, 9, 11, 15, 17, 19, 21, 49, 57, aside from those excluded from the collection). They give evidence of a blending of human sympathy with stupidity, of delusion unmasked by a man of the world, of contempt for the ignorance and loquaciousness of the masses. They also pour vitriol on that old inclination on the part of the masses to accept every untruth that glitters as gold.

The pronounced and inescapable appreciation of the defects of the German language as a medium of poetic expression to which these epigrammes give ample testimony, is of unusual significance. That German, as compared with the other languages of the leading countries of Europe in Goethe's day, was uncultivated there can be no doubt. It was Goethe himself who elevated German to the position of a world language. In his poetry he placed it almost at once on a level with Italian, French, and English. With regard to prose, German was even further behind the other languages. Goethe's own prose was not infrequently prolix and heavy. He himself, however, does not list these defects of his mother-tongue that were disagreeable to him. It is more than likely that he had reference, not so much to the lack of historic development from which German suffered, as to its ponderous syntax, its throwing the verb back to the very close of a relative proposition, with the result that the reader is obliged to go through several lines before he can tell whether the person that constitutes the subject of the discussion has been murdered or embraced.

In our own day, German scholars and interpreters have endeavored to explain away the meaning of the twenty-ninth epigramme; they have tried to make it appear that the material therein referred to was not the German language at all. Such a deduction is the outcome of the patriotism that blinds and deludes. For the epigramme reads as follows:

Vieles hab' ich versucht, gezeichnet, in Kupfer gestochen,
  Oel gemalt, in Thon hab' ich auch Manches gedruckt,
Unbeständig jedoch, und nichts gelernt noch geleistet:
  Nur ein einzig Talent bracht' ich der Meisterschaft nah:
Deutsch zu schreiben. Und so verderb' ich unglücklicher Dichter
  In dem schlechtesten Stoff leider nun Leben und Kunst.

Compare this with the following, and its meaning is clear:

Was mit mir das Schicksal gewollt? Es wäre verwegen,
  Das zu fragen; denn meist will es mit Vielen nicht viel.
Einen Dichter zu bilden, die Absicht wär ihm gelungen,
  Hätte die Sprache sich nicht unüberwindlich gezeigt.

Aside from this collection of epigrammes there is still another from the same period and inspired by the same mood. In it there is no lament over the German language in and of itself. But the poet gives expression to his regret that German is so little known abroad. He defends himself in a humorous way against the charge that he writes on inappropriate topics. He contends that not one man outside of Germany understands a word of what he is saying:

"Wagst Du Deutsch zu schreiben unziemliche Sachen?"
  Mein Guter,
Deutsch dem kleinen Bezirk leider ist Griechisch der Welt.

In our day such a remark made with regard to a writer in one of the Northern languages would

seem natural, though it seems quite unnatural when
applied to German, spoken in Europe alone by at
least eighty million people and by perhaps twenty
million outside of Germany. At that time the situation was totally different. Goethe himself was
the first German to be translated on a large scale,
rarely of course in verse and least frequently of
all in verse that can be read with enlightening
pleasure.

A number of these Venetian poems revolve
around the poet's visits to *Osteria* or booths where
acrobats and jugglers made merry with their arts.
With genuine rapture he returns again and again
to the portrayal of a little girl by the name of Bettina who stood on her head, walked on her hands,
was tossed up into the air from the hands of her
father, threw a *salto mortale,* and so on. A number of epigrammes are also dedicated to some
charming and attractive little girls, who sought out
acquaintances on St. Marks Place or the Piazettas
and enticed strangers to follow them. They are
compared to the lizards of the South that run
quickly up and down the walls and then suddenly disappear in the cracks and crevices. The satisfaction
with which the description is carried out contains a
definite challenge, of the same kind that Byron and
Heine, after Goethe, delighted in making, to bourgeois dignity and self-righteousness. Goethe has
here, by way of exception, apparently started with
the intention of vexing. In one of his epigrammes
he has directed the question, in order to make his
meaning quite distinct, to himself as to whether he
saw nothing but jugglers and sinners, men and

women, and as to whether he was not admitted to good society. He replies:

Gute Gesellchaft hab' ich gesehn; man nennt sie die gute,
Wenn sie zum kleinsten Gedicht keine Gelegenheit gibt.

In the very midst of all this material that challenges there is one epigramme that has a peaceful, beneficent effect: it is the one in which Goethe expresses his cordial gratitude to Karl August. It is totally devoid of exaggeration, keeps down to this earth, and lists with approval the profane and secular things for which he feels indebted to his Duke. What good has it done his renown, what benefit has he derived from the fact, that he has been imitated in Germany and read in France? No emperor has inquired after him! No king has concerned himself about him! No other prince has cared for his needs:

Klein ist unter den Fürsten Germaniens freilich der meine;
    Kurz und schmal ist sein Land, mässig nur, was er vermag.
Aber so wende nach innen, so wende nach aussen die Kräfte
    Jeder! Da wär's ein Fest, Deutscher mit Deutschen zu
        sein.
Doch was priesest Du Ihn, den Thaten und Werke verkünden?
    Und bestochen erschien deine Verehrung vielleicht;
Denn mir hat er gegeben, was Grosse selten gewähren,
    Neigung, Musse, Vertraun, Felder und Garten und Haus.
Niemand braucht' ich zu danken als Ihm, und manches
        bedurft' ich,
    Der ich mich auf den Erwerb schlecht als ein Dichter
        verstand.

Beside this unique poem of praise for Weimar's Duke there runs an entire series of epigrammes that revert to praise of Christiane, with the repeated

assurance that in her he has obtained happiness—
the happiness for which he longed—and he has obtained it completely.   All in all one cannot say that
Goethe was pretentious or exacting; that he was
quite easily satisfied is more nearly the whole truth.

CHAPTER III

The French Revolution: Goethe's Attitude Toward It—*Der Grosskophta*: The Affair of the Necklace

GOETHE had begun his career with the youthful, revolutionary and rebellious aversion to the nobility and the princes that is natural to a son of the people. But so far as he personally was concerned, he lifted himself up above the petty caste in which he was born; he became superior to the middle-class society of the Germany of his day. He had found in time an outlet, a field of activity, and possibilities for development at the court of a prince who, though subordinate, was nevertheless sovereign. Goethe had come to see how the good and fruitful can be accomplished when and if the doughtiest and cleverest has his hand on the helm.

Moreover, his life had taught him how much importance—and how little—can be attached to the judgment of the masses.

He had grown to be forty years old and, as La Rochefoucauld has said, he who has lived for forty years without having come to detest men has never loved them. Goethe had loved men. And though he can in no sense of the word be called a misanthrope, he had been made painfully familiar with the ignorance, the envy, the prejudice of the human

29

horde.   He had come to see that, as a rule, the
opinion of the majority is either a display of stupidity, or a manifestation of rudeness.   He had come
to cherish the settled conviction that what the masses
want can never be anything else than food and drink
and general well-being.   He could not appreciate
the righteous demand on the part of the poor that
they be allowed to earn their daily bread without
becoming slaves in the attempt.   The word liberty
had to a large degree lost its charm for him.   The
time was now far distant when he and his young
comrades on the *Frankfurter Gelehrte Anzeigen*
characterised themselves as those to whom the name
of political liberty had such a sweet sound (*so süss
schallt*).

Like all ambitious and ingenious spirits, Goethe
had from the very first felt an unrestrained longing
for liberty.   This explains why the action in *Götz*
is being constantly interrupted with toasts to liberty.   But his life had taught him how differently
different people understand liberty.   He had seen
that it can be longed for personally or socially or
artistically or politically.   Refractoriness, free thinking, defiance of social customs, opposition to art,
radicalism—all of these bore a direct relation to the
general concept of liberty.   There was the individual
who longed for freedom from the religious and
political point of view, but opposed the same principle in art.   There was the other who longed for it
in art, but rejected it in politics and religion.   Liberty indeed was somewhat like a chemical element
that may or may not enter into composition with
other elements, such as nationalism and democracy.
It was made the opposite of coercion, but not the

opposite of a voluntary subjection to such coercion as that of moral discipline, or that of metrics, or social forms, or reasonable law: *Und das Gesetz nur kann uns Freiheit geben.*

At the beginning, he too had regarded liberty as being one with personal unruliness. But he had been called to educate the Duke of Weimar, and thereby himself.

Then came the French Revolution. The storming of the Bastille, as a symbolic action, caused general rejoicing in the minds of all liberty-loving men throughout Europe; and it did actually inaugurate the great deeds that followed. When closely examined, however, it was a pitiable and contemptible affair. The Bastille had long since ceased to be the prison of despotism. Its few remaining inmates were confessed criminals. The one hundred and twenty disabled soldiers that guarded it were brave and noble veterans. Its commandant was a humane man and an officer of superior honor. They who rushed in when the guards kindly opened the doors were blood-thirsty ruffians. If the practical signal for the Revolution was an ill omen, the theory that was proclaimed was no better. Sièyes posited this presumptuous statement regarding the third estate: "It is nothing; but it is to be everything." Goethe obviously had a vivid idea as to what was to be expected from and of the citizenry.

At the same time he received the impression that the age was venal; that it had its price for every buyer; that it was at the disposal af anyone whose audacity and arrogance would speculate on its bigotry; that those who would could lead it around by the nose. By the populace, however, he was poles

removed from understanding the lowest stratum
of society. The clergy had prepared men's minds
to believe anything, quite regardless as to whether
it was credible or not, and to manifest the most
humble respect for the cultivators and spokesmen of
all that was most glaringly at odds with sound judgment and reasoned intentions.

Goethe follows the life of Cagliostro and looks
into the family history of the Balsamos in Palermo
as well, for he learns that the son, Giuseppe Balsamo, who disappeared after having perpetrated
a number of mad pranks, and the notorious Count
Cagliostro are identical. He studies the history of
the Balsamos and investigates even their correspondence with the same thoroughness that he is
wont to employ in studying a plant family in botany.
He observes with alert interest the triumphs over
credulity celebrated by the boldest adventurers and
humbug-makers known to modern times. He investigates the way in which deceived, semi-deceived and
deceivers study these people and flout sound common
sense. It captivates him to follow Balsamo's metamorphosis from the obscure beginning up to and
through succeeding stages of Marchese Pellegrini
and Count Cagliostro. He indulges at the same
time his inveterate proneness to mystification when
he secures an introduction to the Balsamos by claim-
ing, without hesitation, to be an Englishman, dele-
gated to bring a letter from Cagliostro, then living
in London.

After the affair of the necklace, the immediate
precursor of the Revolution in France, had aroused
the suspicion of the masses, shaken the throne and
exposed the criminal gullibility of the society that

centrea about the French court, Goethe wove his impressions of the lawsuit together with the impressions of Cagliostro, and wrote his drama entitled *Der Grosskophta*. It is admittedly a weak, unsatisfactory product, though by no means either thin or void.

Consequently, he did not take an especially vigorous delight in liberty when the Revolution broke out. He understood it as little as did Taine or Nietzsche after him. For him it was merely an eruption of envy and avarice. He did not perceive the earthquake; the great historical pulse in it all passed by him unnoticed, unregarded.

Long before the Revolution actually began, the citizenry of France knew precisely what it wished to substitute for the then prevailing feudal monarchy. It wished to abolish absolute power and the rapacious lordship of the nobility. It was republican in its way of feeling; but it wanted the propertied classes to rule. If it hated the Catholic Church it was not because of an inborn hostility to religion but because the Church made common cause with the rulers in fleecing the people. Long before the Revolution broke out the peasant class also knew precisely what it wanted. It wanted the land that it cultivated in chronic hunger, martyred to the point of despair from the taxes it had to pay to the State, the impost it was forced to contribute to the landed proprietors, the tithes it had to raise for the clergy, and the villeinage imposed by all three in union one with another. The ever-increasing distress into which the people sank gave rise to a spirit of rebellion and brought to the fore the very necessity of a well-known law of nature.

It was far too petty then, when, in the first unsuccessful piece Goethe wrote against the spirit of
the Revolution, *Der Bürgergeneral,* he has the story
revolve around the fact that one man wants to have
access to the pantry of another, to steal his loppered
cream and put his sugar on it. In this way "the sweet
and sour cream of Liberty and Equality" are supposed to be mixed in the right proportions. Here,
as in the imperfect and incomplete but interesting
drama entitled *Die Aufgeregten,* the rebels demand
absolutely nothing that is justified.

We have pointed out above that Goethe took all
his themes from his own time, or from the Antique
and the Renaissance. Especially do his themes belong to the period from 1789 to 1799, from his
fortieth to his fiftieth years. *Der Grosskophta, Die
Aufgeregten, Das Mädchen von Oberkirch, Der
Bürgergeneral,* and *Unterhaltungen deutscher Ausgewanderter* are all based either on the theories or
the effects of the Revolution. *Die natürliche Tochter* depicts the civic order of things such as existed
previous to the Revolution, events that took place
when Goethe was about twenty-four years old. In
this group belongs also *Hermann und Dorothea* in
which the Revolution forms the background and sets
the action in motion. Among his most valuable
works on the Revolution, and written at the time of
it, must be mentioned also his excellent monograph,
Die Campagne in Frankreich (1792).

Goethe's correspondence shows that he sympa-
thised with the people in their sufferings. Their
lot in the days preceding the Revolution was not
easy. On April 3, 1782, he wrote: "The curse
of being obliged to waste the very marrow of the

country makes the maturing of pleasure an impossibility." On June 20, 1784, he wrote: "The poor people have to carry the bundle and little difference does it make whether it is too heavy on the one side or the other." In the *Venezianische Epigramme* we find this vitriolic comment on the conservatives in Germany:

Jene Menschen sind toll, so sagt Ihr von heftigen Sprechern,
Die wir in Frankreich laut hören auf Strassen und Markt:
Mir auch scheinen sie toll; doch redet ein Toller in Freiheit
Weise Sprüche, wenn ach! Weisheit in Sklaven verstummt.

Heartily displeased as he was at the imitations of the French Revolution on German soil, he was also worried over the reaction that Jacobinism in France was evoking in Germany.

Though the Minister of the little Duchy of Sachse-Weimar was intensely interested in the affairs of the commonalty and tried in many ways to improve them, he never really had a clear idea as to the burden of injustice under which the poor were laboring in a kingdom like the France of that day. He was consequently in error as to the justice with which the elementary powers in France arose in rebellion.

As a whole, the elementary, the basic, in history did not appeal to Goethe. He appreciated only the humanly great as it confronted him in *personal form*. Just as he derived his conception of the Renaissance from such real personalities as Raphael, Cellini, Reuchlin and his own heroes, Götz and Egmont, just so did he appreciate the Revolution only when he stood face to face with its executor, Napoleon Bonaparte. The great strength in the powers of the Revolution left him untouched. For him the Revolution was the inorganic, the disorderly, the break in that chain of evolution of which he came very near being the first discoverer. When the Revolution started in 1789, he was more engrossed with the ideas of evolution than at any other period of his life. Order was for him what we call composition, but composition in development. In the vegetable kingdom he had seen the root develop into a stem, the stem transformed into a leaf, and the leaf re-formed into a flower. In the animal kingdom he had seen the vertebrae transformed into the bones of the skull. In no case had there been a sudden leap; it was all merely a matter of transition. In geology he had followed the slow, millenial changes and had passionately combatted the doctrine of a sudden, volcanic overturning.

As such a sudden, volcanic overturning the Revolution filled him with horror.

II

The first of Goethe's works immediately connected with the French Revolution is *Der Grosskophta,* 1791. It is especially important because of its direct bearing on contemporary events. After the fashion of *Clavigo,* it deals not only with individuals who were still living but with events that had taken place quite recently; some of them had become closed issues only five years before. It is the famous story of the necklace that Goethe has dramatized.

The Cardinal of Rohan appears under the name of *Der Domherr.* Jeanne de St. Remy de Valois,

Countess of Lamotte, is known as *Die Marquise.*
She was the adventuress who took advantage of the
Cardinal's zeal in order to ingratiate herself into
the favor of Marie Antoinette, and who inveigled
him into buying the necklace at a cost of over a
million and a half. Her tool, Nicole le Guay, called
d'Olivia, who was disguised as the Queen and represented her at the nocturnal meeting in the palace
garden of Versailles, is known as *Die Nichte.* And
the leading character is introduced simply as *Der
Graf,* though the Count of Cagliostro himself had
nothing to do with the affair. He was imprisoned
because of his intimate association with Rohan. His
name is mentioned but once, as "Rostro." The remaining characters, as is the case with *Die natürliche Tochter,* are nameless. Goethe's unhappy
fondness for abstractions, connected with his preference for types, is responsible for the fact that
the *dramatis personae* are given rank, such as the
Colonel, the Knight, the Dean, the Count, and nothing more; it does not follow, however, that they
display the individuality which the rank implies. As
to the style, it leaves much to be desired. As to the
drama itself, it is well constructed, dramatic, and
certainly theatrical, unsympathetic though it may be
as a work of art.

The drama portrays a colossal swindler who calls
to his aid belief in spirits and conviction of the rea-
sonableness of miracles in order to impress those
about him and thereby gain power, though it is not
clear from the drama what he does or wishes to
do with this power. Without having any direct
connection with him, though supported by him, we
have the operation of an unscrupulous pair: There

is the Marquis who seduces his niece that has been
trained to appear partly as an innocent girl in a
Masonic ceremony, partly as the Princess in some
relation to the Dean; and there is the Marquise,
the shrewd, keen-sensed malefactress who pulls the
wires.   Since the young niece is not at all inclined
to serve as the tool for repeated frauds, she tells
the Knight, in whom she has confidence and for
whom she feels affection, of her wretched position,
prays to him for help, and betrays the entire intrigue
to the ruling Prince.   The drama closes with the
imprisonment of the culprits.

The conduct of the Knight is not very chivalric.
Since the entire action concerns so unexciting and
flat an affair as the pilfering of a necklace by a pair
of cut-throats and their deception in dealing with
an admitted dunderhead, and since there is not one
glimpse of humor or comedy in the drama, it must
be set down as a failure.

But this does not prevent it from being a substantial contribution to the psychology of unctuous
prophets and their gullible adherers.   Among Goethe's contemporary friends, Lavater believed firmly
in Cagliostro; in this way the phenomenon came
personally near to Goethe himself.   When he wrote
his drama the Cardinal of Rohan was only fifty-
seven, Cagliostro only forty-eight.   He explained
to his followers that he was in actuality eighty, but
by using an elixir which he sold in bottles, he looked
as though he were forty.

Since the poet originally planned to treat the
theme as a text for an opera, he wrote a few verses
under the rubric of *Kophtische Lieder*.   They contain in condensed form the action of the entire

drama. Let us look at the first lines of one of these poems:

> Thöricht, auf Bess'rung der Thoren zu harren!
> Kinder der Klugheit, o habet die Narren
> Eben zum Narren auch, wie sich's gehört!

Or examine the following lines from the second of these songs:

> Auf des Glückes grosser Wage
> Steht die Zunge selten ein.
> Du musst steigen oder sinken,
> Du musst herrschen und gewinnen
> Oder dienen und verlieren,
> Leiden oder triumphiren,
> Amboss oder Hammer sein.

Compare the great skill of such verses with the affectation and sentimentality that characterise the monologue in prose from the *Grosskophta*. The Dean speaks:

A profound stillness prophesies to me my immediate good fortune. I hear not a sound in these gardens which otherwise, owing to the kindness of the Prince, are open to all pleasure seekers, and on pleasant evenings are frequently visited by a lonely, unhappy lover, and even more frequently by a joy-crowned, loving couple. I thank thee, divine light, that thou seest fit to envelope thyself to-day in a quiet veil! Thou delightest me, O brisk wind, thou threatening, murky rain-clouds, that thou wardest off the frivolous folk who generally swarm back and forth through these paths, fill the arbors with laughter, and rob others of their sweetest joy without securing any genuine joy for themselves. O ye beautiful trees, how ye seem to have grown in the last few summers!

It would appear that there lay in German prose a hidden temptation for Goethe to go over to the

Kanzleistil of emotion. Here, as in *Die Geschwister,*
he evokes and justifies the question: Was the fault
inherent in the language, or was it his own? The
language, we dare not forget, was undeveloped in
his day. We have already seen that, in the *Venezianische Epigramme,* he laid the blame on the language; on the German language.

CHAPTER IV

THE FRENCH REVOLUTION: *Der Bürgergeneral;*
Das Mädchen von Oberkirch

THE following little drama, *Der Bürgergeneral,*
is the product of Goethe's activity as director of
the Weimar Theatre. A number of unpretentious
French dramas, in German versions, had been performed in Weimar and Scapin, who had received
in German the ill-sounding name of "Schnaps," was
played with marked success by a certain Herr Beck
who had come to Weimar in 1793. Goethe created
the Scapin-figure of this drama for him, and chris-
tened it "Schnaps." There is, incidentally, this peculiarity about awkward German farces: In order
to evoke laughter from the plain people, they pooh-
pooh probability, whereas laughter is excited in the
farces of other civilized nations through inconsistencies that are really born of an unimpeachable
inner logic.

In a country town that belongs to a liberal, refined, young nobleman, there lives an exceedingly
happy newly married couple, Görge and Röse.
Schnaps comes to Röse's father, Märten, and informs him that the renowned Jacobins in Paris have
heard of his cleverness, and in order to win him
over to the cause of freedom and equality have just
appointed him Citizen's General. As proof of all

41

this, he has in his possession a tri-colored cocarde
and a regimental coat, which, in reality, he had
stolen from a French soldier who had been taken
prisoner. The real purpose of his visit, which
Görge had welcomed in no way, is to get a square
meal free of charge. He breaks open the cupboard
in the house and finds a large plate of loppered milk.
While the coming revolution is being proclaimed in
the village, he regales himself with milk, cream,
sugar, and rye-bread. But just as he is consuming
his repast, Görge appears on the scene and gives
him a sound trouncing. The cries and screams call
the attention of the district judge to the unusual
proceedings. That functionary hastens up to the
scene of activity and, finding the cocarde and the
uniform in the house, is on the point of arresting
its occupants. But the sensible nobleman appears
in time and adjusts such embarrassments as have
arisen.

That does not in truth seem to have much connection with the French Revolution; and yet it does:
The entire drama is interspersed with references
to it. Schnaps demands that Märten shall be free
and equal; he imagines he already sees the people
dancing around the tree of liberty. When Märten
tells the nobleman that Schnaps first acted kindly
toward him only later to break open the cupboard
and take whatever he wanted, the nobleman replies:
"Just like his comrades! In the provinces, where
his type have carried on their work of devastation,
and where gullible idiots at first rejoiced over what
was taking place, they began with compliments and
promises and ended with violence, theft, and ban-
ishment of the high-minded people."

It has a rather depressing effect to feel that Goethe saw nothing in the Jacobins but criminals, and that in order to give a poignant portrayal of their character he could think of nothing better than the appropriation by force of a bottle of loppered milk. Moreover, it is distinctly aggravating to think that he wasted his time writing this insipid nonentity and left the serious and in some ways significant drama of the Revolution from the same year, *Die Aufgeregten,* lie as a fragment. The middle and conclusion of it are only hurriedly sketched. It is a lasting pity that he did not finish it instead of *Der Bürgergeneral.*

Die Aufgeregten is well planned, gives an excellent impression of the echo made by the Revolution in a rustic village, and contains some interesting characters, one of whom especially stands out clear and distinct among Goethe's heroines.

An estate is being managed by an intelligent Countess on behalf of her young son. For no less than forty years the peasantry have litigated against the estate, which demands soccage and the up-keep of certain roads. The peasants consider themselves exempt on the ground that an agreement had been entered into which limited the rights of the Countess and protected them. But the document has in some unexplained way disappeared. If the Countess had only herself to take into consideration, she would have dropped the case long ago for the sake of humanity. But since she is merely the administratrix of her son she feels duty bound to have the case brought up before the court at Wetzlar.

In the meantime the ideas of the Revolution have reached the neighborhood, and the peasantry is

aroused by a certain "Tinker Politician." He is the
grandson of Holberg's [1] politicaster and makes
himself out as such. He is called Breme von Bremenfeld, is a barber and a surgeon, holds himself in
high esteem both professionally and politically, and
unites Hermann von Breme's conviction of his unusual ability as a political leader with Gert West-
phaler's smooth loquaciousness. He is really superior to the latter in that he has a measure of talent
as an orator. Goethe has amused himself by having
him use expressions in one of his speeches which remind of Antony's oration in Shakespeare's *Julius
Caesar*.

We are introduced to an entire galaxy of personages. There are a couple of young girls of the burgher class, one of whom, Breme's daughter, is in
love with a young baron who pays her importunate
court; there are a number of peasants; there is the
tutor of the Countess's young son who is excellently
portrayed, in just a few strokes, as a Jacobin fanatic; there is an intelligent and deserving councillor
who is the spokesman of Goethe's own ideas and
who, somewhat like Goethe, inspires respect because
of his bearing; and there is the Countess's young
daughter Friederike who, though only half grown,
is a sportswoman full of family pride, veracious,
determined, a hater of nonsense and effusive bu-

---

[1] Holberg wrote "Den Politiske Kandestöber" in 1722, one of
the most fruitful years in the history of Northern literature. The
comedy has thirty characters as contrasted with the fifteen in *Die
Aufgeregten*, a title that Goethe gave his play only after much
deliberation and hesitation. He had at first decided to call it
"Breme von Bremenfeld." Had he done so, its relation to Holberg's comedy would have been more evident. Holberg's influence
on Goethe is even more pronounced than Brandes' comments
would lead one to believe. —TRANSLATOR.

reaucracy. On hearing that the cringing officer is suspected of having made off with the lost document, but that countless difficulties are in the way of a definite settlement of the affair, she levels her gun at his head and would have shot him down without any more ado had he not been frightened into making a clean confession and telling where the document could be found.

There is in her something that we rarely find in Goethe's characters—inveterate energy and indiscriminate resoluteness. The action itself is diverting; the spirit of the play is humane; the jocular conception of the German revolutionists is quite free from rancor. It is moreover interesting to see a Holbergean character taken over and varied by Goethe. It is only a pity that in one single scene this character is lifted out of the comic style where it belongs by poetic right: This is where Breme uses the most fearful expressions in abusing his daughter because she refuses to be his blind tool against the Baron, whom he wishes to capture and lock up. Such a move is a novel and unmotivated testimony to the fact that the comedy was not Goethe's strong point.

It is also unfortunate that the excellently planned drama of the Revoltion, *Das Mädchen von Oberkirch,* the manuscript to the introductory scenes of which was not found until 1895, remained a fragment. The little that was worked out gives an exalted idea of the rest of which only an indistinct glimpse can be derived from the outline as found among Goethe's papers. The action takes place in Strassburg during one of the first years of the Revolution, and is introduced by a conversation between two people of noble birth. The Countess, whose estates have been plundered, sits knitting in her apartment in the city, when her nephew, the Baron, enters and tells her of her sons and daughters who have emigrated but who have escaped only with their lives. The sons are in the army [in Coblenz, then], the daughters have found a quiet place of refuge; they embroider and sew in order to make their living.

After a great deal of hesitation and self-evoked argument the Baron comes out with a statement telling just why he has appeared: He intends to get married and to marry out of his class. The Countess is shocked; but she becomes rebellious when she learns that the object of his choice is her own lady in waiting or companion, Marie. The Baron shows that his conduct is not simply the outcome of warm feeling; it is the result of good politics as well. Under the present threatening conditions he will do best to marry a woman from the people. Moreover, Marie is the Countess's foster-daughter rather than her servant. The conversation is interrupted by Pastor Manner, a young preacher, whose assistance the Baron needs as an offset to the aunt. Marie has really all sorts of virtues: She is pretty without being arrogant, amiable without being coquetish, obliging without being self-humiliating. But when it becomes evident that Manner is also seriously in love with Marie, the latter emphasizes the political uselessness, even the unreasonableness, of the intended union, to which the Baron, as we in time learn, has as yet not acquired the consent of his beloved. The powers that be (in Manner's words: the rabble) will pay no attention to such a marriage. The Baron would, to be sure, not free himself from suspicion by this course, but he would make Marie also seem a fit subject for distrust.

The outline of the play contains only a few local names and designations, hardly thirty words in all, exclusive of the verbs. I believe I catch a glimpse of just this much from this fact: It is Manner and not the Baron to whom Marie feels drawn. As one of the common people, she is favored by the *sans-sculottists*. Moreover, it is her beauty that brings it about that she figures in the Cathedral as the goddess of reason, in which capacity she is worshipped and adored. But the rôle is contrary to her nature; she protests against the ideas whose interpreter she has been forced to become. She is thrown into prison and the two men who love her take common counsel as to how she can be rescued. This is a guess and is not meant to be anything more; but it seems to me that the words of the outline support it.

To the group of plays from the Revolution there belongs finally the larger and more significant work entitled *Die natürliche Tochter*. But since it was not planned until 1799, and not completed and produced until 1803, discussion of it must be postponed. It shows evidence of a complete change in the poet's dramatic style.

CHAPTER V

Die Campagne in Frankreich, 1792: GOETHE ON
THE BATTLE FIELD—*Reineke Fuchs*

IF we wish to see Goethe at his freshest and happiest as a student of the Revolution, we have to read his *Campagne in Frankreich,* 1792. Though the book was not published until 1820, it consists exclusively of his diary which he kept on the field during the action. It is a notable piece of work because of the ease and calm with which it is written.

In July, 1790, shortly after his second return from Italy, he had accompanied Karl August to Silesia where the latter took part in the manouvres while Goethe himself spent most of his time studying Kant and Osteology. When the Duke, in 1782, participated in the campaign of the Allied Powers against revolutionary France, Goethe (after one visit in Frankfort and another in Mayence) followed Karl August to the front, and met him at the close of August in Longwy. The campaign was an absolute failure; it was abandoned when the French were victorious at Valmy. The retreat of the Allied Powers was an affair of sheer dissolution. Goethe realized, in person and at first hand, how completely he had underestimated even the outward strength the French Revolution could develop. The impression, however, did not lessen his aversion.

48

The feature of it all that especially gratifies the reader of his diary is his perfect equanimity coupled with his insatiable desire for knowledge. Nothing escapes him. No optical phenomenon such as the refraction of a colored shard in a fen—which evokes a treatise on the science of color. No rare osteological phenomenon, nor any mineralogical one either, fails to receive due and disciplined attention from him. During the battle at Valmy he studies the beautiful species of stone found in the neighborhood. During the siege of Mayence he searches in the charnel house among the decayed bones: "The best ones had already fallen into the hands of the surgeons."

He narrates and portrays with vividness. One sees one's self the young girls who received the Allied forces in Verdun, and about whom Victor Hugo has sung. Goethe seems not to have learned the terrible fate that was subsequently in store for them. He depicts the bayonet squad as it rushes headlong down a steep declivity, like a waterfall; and he does so with a clarity which no other author, whose specialty was the depiction of the visible (Théophile Gautier for example), has ever surpassed.

Goethe did not experience cannon fever. He gloried in the fact that every danger tended only to make his mind more bold, even rash. Amid the thunder of the cannon he calmly rides up to Fort La Lune. He studies his condition and is satisfied with his pulse while under fire. Still he notices that something unusual is taking place within him: "It is as if one were in a very hot spot and were so completely permeated by the heat that one feels one's self in complete harmony with the surrounding element."

On September 19, 1792, we have a remarkable
utterance from him. He tells how in the morning
everyone thought only of bayonetting and gobbling
up all the Frenchmen, and how he himself felt absolute confidence in an army such as that commanded
by the Duke of Brunswick. After the unsuccessful
attack, however, each man fought for himself; dependence upon one's neighbor was out of the question. Finally someone called out to Goethe asking
him what he had to say since it had become a custom
for him to be the enlivening element in the party.
He replied: "From today and from this place
there begins a new epoch in the history of the world,
and you can say that you were present."

The incident has been regarded with suspicion.
Some have felt that it was a later fabrication, a parallel observation having been found in the diary
of a German officer, a diary, incidentally, which
Goethe borrowed while elaborating his own monograph. But he must have used the expression; for
he tells in his book on the siege of Mayence that
the officers who heard this prophecy afterwards
believed that it had been literally fulfilled, for the
French abolished at that time the old Catholic calendar. His remark, as he himself emphasizes, naturally has a quite different meaning. Even before
the battle of Valmy Goethe felt that a new era was
dawning.

At no time does he appear to better advantage.
He portrays his various experiences, his weariness
and hunger, his longing for a bed and something to
eat, his blind confidence in the fate that seizes him
while in the midst of all manner of infectious diseases, his joy on receiving his trunk and with it his

manuscript on the science of colors. He makes
some quite discriminating remarks on the difference
in the character of the Prussian and the Austrian
non-commissioned officer, expresses his thoughts
concerning a monument from the age of the An-
tonies which he sees now for the second time, and
discusses his relation to the philosophy of Hemster-
huis. This latter inspires him to set forth straightway his own definition of the beautiful. It runs in
this vein: "The sight of the law-abiding animate in
its greatest activity and perfection which goads us
on to re-production and brings us to feel that we are
animate and in the greatest of activity ourselves."
The definition has been declared to be ingenious;
if so, it may also be described as droll.

Die Belagerung von Mainz gives a profound
impression of Goethe's innate humanitarianism and
personal courage. When Mayence is taken and—
together with the French garrison—the Germans,
who, as republicans, had aided the French, file out,
the common people became of course enraged at
these German republicans. Just in front of Goethe's
house there is seated on horseback a tall, handsome
man; at his side is his sweetheart in man's attire
and likewise very beautiful. He is an architect suspected of pillaging and incendiarism. The rabble
rush upon them in the attempt to injure them.

Thereupon Goethe, who has been watching from
his window, springs down into the street and tells
them to halt in such a commanding tone that they
immediately desist from further attacks. Goethe
succeeds in saving the life of the man that had been
threatened.

To a friend who cannot forbear saying that, with

actual danger to himself, he has saved the life of
a stranger, perhaps of a criminal, Goethe makes
the remark that has been quoted time out of mind:
"There is simply something in my nature that makes
me rather commit an injustice than submit to disorder."

The expression is constantly being twisted so as
to mean just the opposite of what Goethe indubitably had in mind. Thus, not long since, the celebrated German General Keim used it against the
Goethe League as evidence that Goethe would have
found the judicial murder of the Spaniard Fran-
cisco Ferrer wholly justifiable. Quite the contrary;
he pleads here for the utmost clemency; and he
understands by any injustice that he may be obliged
to commit the tempering of justice with mercy, or
the allowing of mercy to pass for justice.

The remark shows how far removed he was from
bloodthirstiness toward the revolutionists, who were
in truth directly contrary to his innermost being.

After the conquest of Mayence, Goethe turned
back, visited his brother-in-law, Schlosser, in Heidelberg and his mother in Frankfort. Frau Aja was
now living in pecuniary embarrassment because of
the war tax which the French army under Dumou-
riez had levied on the city. She was forced to sell
her wine cellar, her books and her paintings. Goethe was not yet financially able to save her from this
loss and privation.

II

After his return to Weimar Goethe took in hand
a bit of work which was of a quite different nature

from anything that had formerly engaged his attention: He began a revision of a folk poem, the old beast epic on the cunning of the fox, in hexameters, just as it had been treated when the oldest parts of it were written in Latin in the tenth, eleventh, and twelfth centuries (*Ecbasis, Isengrimus, Reinardus Vulpus*). The French redactions of the thirteenth century had greatly expanded the material; the Dutch *Reinaert* was made the foundation for all later versions in German. In 1752 Gottsched had published the prose translation which Goethe undertook to versify under the title: *Heinrichs von Alkmar Reincke der Fuchs.*

The exercise in writing hexameters which the *Römische Elegien* and the *Venezianische Epigramme* had given Goethe, together with the inclination that he had gradually developed to see preëminence in ancient art forms, beguiled him into the oddity of choosing the hexameter as the cloak for the naïveté and satire of the Middle Ages. Form and substance do not in this case coincide, they do not harmonize. The hexameter is ill adapted to the German language and has on that account been practically abandoned in our day.

It was dissatisfaction with the age and perhaps embitterment over the complaint against Louis XVI which caused Goethe to have recourse to the old beast saga: "Had I hitherto," he writes in the *Campagne in Frankreich,* "been obliged to surfeit myself to the point of loathing with street, market, and mob scenes, it was really inspiring to look into this mirror for courts and regents. For though the human race is even here quite naturally portrayed in its unfeigned brutishness, everything happens, if not in an exemplary, at least in a jocund way, and good humor is nowhere impaired."

It is a diligent piece of work Goethe has done; so far as the very art of language is concerned it is quite and entirely worthy of him. Oehlenschläger, however, who translated it into Danish in 1806, used exorbitant language when he said: "In my estimation, *Reineke Fuchs,* in Goethe's version, is the most beautiful imitation we have of the Homeric poems."

Though the work was revised by Goethe's aesthetic friends—Knebel, Wieland, Herder—before being sent to the publisher, a few linguistic and metrical rough spots have remained. A verse such as

Fehlet Euch alles im Hause, so gebt eine Maus her—mit
    dieser
Bin ich am besten versorgt.

cannot be acquitted of the charge of an awkward dactyl: *Maus her mit.* In a verse such as the following,

Selbst verschont ich des Königs nicht, und mancherlei Tücken
    Uebt ich kühnlich an ihm

the meaning has been reduced to haziness for the sake of the meter; for it is obvious that the unblemished prose of it would be: *Sogar des Königs verschont ich nicht.*

There are passages in which Goethe did not exercise sufficient care in comparing the old texts, with the result that negligible but amusing errors have crept in, for the familiar reason that one of his predecessors made them only to be imitated by another and later. In *Reinaert,* for example, we read *een paer Kerspetten;* in *Reineke* we read, as the result of an error in imitation, *gude Kersebern.* *Kerspetten* are waffles; *Kersebern* are cherries. Goethe therefore refers in his work to this queer menu:

So ging inch mit ihm und bracht' ihm behende Kirschen und Butter.

We understand full well Goethe's delight in appropriating and reproducing all the old popular experience and wisdom of the animal fables, so much of which applied to his own time, indeed to all times. It makes delightful reading. We are highly amused, by way of illustration, when the fox devotes his eloquence to picking at the Pope's legates, abbots, prelates and nuns, and when the badger replies: "Uncle, I find it quite remarkable that you confess the sins of the others: No one would make a better monk than you."

And how imperishable is that story of the peasant and the serpent! The former found the latter caught in a trap—and freed his potential foe after he had taken a quite solemn oath never again to harm him. A short while elapsed, and the serpent, beginning to feel the inconvenient pangs of hunger, would strangle the man and devour him. The man complained; the serpent indulged in a political affirmation:

"Das ist mein Dank? Das hab ich verdient?" So rief er.
    "Und hast Du
Nicht geschworen den theursten Eid?"—Da sagte die
    Schlange:
"Leider nöthiget mich der Hunger; ich kann mir nicht
    helfen;
Noth erkennt kein Gebot, und so besteht es zu Rechte."

That is the political morality of the twentieth century, just as it was of the twelfth century.

Throughout the entire work, large in volume and poetic in content, Goethe has interpolated but two brief passages in which he has given expression to his personal convictions: The one is quite in the spirit of the poem of the Middle Ages, which never lacked a reason to see the clergy in a culpable light; in the other, Goethe voices his aversion to all revolutionists. These few lines have been attacked with imbecile violence as grating against the fundamental tone of the old beast epic; and they have been defended with a zeal that is in no way less exaggerated. They are found in the eighth song, lines 152-160, and lines 171-177. The passage on the clergy runs as follows:

Freilich sollten die geistlichen Herrn sich besser betragen,
Manches könnten sie thun, wofern sie es heimlich voll-
        brächten;
Aber sie schonen uns nicht, uns andere Laien, und treiben
Alles, was Ihnen beliebt, vor unsern Augen, als wären
Wir mit Blindheit geschlagen; allein wir sehen zu deutlich.
Ihre Gelübde gefallen den guten Herren so wenig,
Als sie dem sündigen Freunde der weltlichen Werke behagen.

Apart from the solemnity of the style, there is really nothing to prevent this from having stood in the old folk poem. Goethe's lines on the men of the Revolution sound undeniably more modern:

Doch das Schlimmste find' ich den Dünkel des irrigen
        Wahnes
Der die Menschen ergreift, es könne Jeder im Taumel
Seines heftigen Wollens die Welt beherrschen und richten
Hielte doch Jeder sein Weib und sine Kinder in Ordnung,
Wüsste sein trotzig Gesinde zu bändigen, könnte sich stille

Wenne die Thoren verschwenden, in müssigem Leben er-
  freuen!
Aber wie sollte die Welt sich verbessern? Es lässt sich ein
  Jeder
Alles zu und will mit Gewalt die Andern bezwingen
Und so sinken wir tiefer und immer tiefer in's Arge.

These two short passages contain literally everything there is of Goethe himself in *Reineke Fuchs*.
It cannot be denied that they express not merely a
pronounced indifference to politics, but an excessive
insusceptibility to the revolution that was then taking place in the minds of the people. They express
also a certain underbred satisfaction with existing
circumstances. This is seen most clearly in the conservatism to which the latter quotation gives voice.

CHAPTER VI

SCHILLER AND BAGGESEN; SCHILLER AND DEN-
MARK — SCHILLER'S YOUTH; SCHILLER AND
VOLTAIRE; SCHILLER AND CAMPISTRON —
SCHILLER AS HISTORIAN AND PHILOSOPHER
—BEGINNING OF THE FRIENDSHIP BETWEEN
GOETHE AND SCHILLER

IN 1790, Jens Baggesen visited Friedrich Schiller in Jena. In June, 1791, he received, through a note from Countess Schimmelmann, wife of the Minister of State, the unfounded news concerning Schiller's death, fourteen years before it occurred. Though Baggesen, smitten as he was with all the mawkish sentimentality of the age, exaggerated the expression of his grief (in his language it was despair for which he asks Providence to forgive him), the effect of the rumor made a profound impression, not merely on Baggesen himself, but on all the men and women who at that time stood highest in cultured Denmark.

Count Schimmelmann and his wife, also the Danish minister at The Hague, Schubart and his wife, who had previously planned to go on an excursion from Copenhagen to Hellebaek, now united to celebrate Schiller's memory at this beautiful spot, at that time isolated and charming because of its very wildness. Baggesen and Sophie von Haller, together with the above mentioned company, betook themselves to the home of Count Schimmelmann at Sölyst, where the Emilie fount now flows. Baggesen,[2] without the slightest foreboding of the unpleasant news, had latterly been so completely taken up with Schiller that when he opened his trunk he found that the books which he had sent on ahead for recreation in bad weather consisted almost exclusively of the works of Friedrich Schiller.

They had planned to sing Schiller's *Ode to Joy* under the most agreeable circumstances. Now they had to listen in abject sadness to a recital of it by Baggesen. He began: *Freude, schöner Götterfunken, Tochter aus Elysium.* The clarinets, flutes and horns joined in. They sang the chorus, the ecstatic hymn of human love, the expression of a stronger faith in a loving Province in fact than Schiller maintained in daily practice:

> Seyd unschlungen, Millionen!
> Diesen Kuss der ganzen Welt.
> Brüder! Ueberm Sternenzelt
> Muss ein lieber Vater wohmen.

Baggesen had written several verses in German in honor of Schiller and promised on oath to live true to his spirit. Then four young couples of youths and maidens, clad in white and crowned with blossoms, entered and danced as shepherds and shepherdesses.

[2] Baggesen was captivated, soul and body, by the *Sturm und Drang* movement in Germany. He adored Voss and worshipped Klopstock. He considered himself a disciple of Wieland and married Albrecht von Haller's granddaughter. His friendship for Reinhold lasted until his death. But before Schiller he bowed in reverent admiration. If his grief at the news of Schiller's alleged death seems extraordinary it was in keeping with his life. It was difficult for him to seem or be unaffected. —Translator.

The following day Baggesen read aloud scenes from *Don Carlos,* passages from the unfinished history on the defection of the Netherlands, and poems such as the *Götter Griechenlands* and the *Künstler.* In Hellebaek, the very name of which reminded of Hellas, they felt hellenically disposed:

> Unser todter Freund soll leben,
> Alle Freunde, stimmet ein!
> Und sein Geist soll uns umschweben
> Hier in Hellas' Himmelhain.

Owing to the condition of his lungs, Schiller had in reality been near death's door. And just as the unsubstantiated report of his demise reached Copenhagen, the true enlightenment came bearing on the wretched economic plight in which the poet was slowly but surely pining away. Then it was that the two Danish friends with German training, two men who had been brought into an alliance by the familiar *Weltbürgergeist,* Duke Frederick Christian of Augustenborg and Count Ernst Schimmelmann, agreed to assure Schiller an annual pension of 1000 talers (3600 marks) for the coming three years. With this aid the poet could resume his work. It would otherwise most probably have been closed with *Don Carlos.* (It is difficult to refrain from the thought that had Schiller died at the age of eighty-five instead of forty-five, and had he reaped the modern harvest in the way of royalties from his dramas, Mr. Rockefeller's income would hardly have surpassed his.)

At the close of 1791 he wrote to Körner:

I at last have time to read and collect and work for eternity. Before the three years shall have elapsed, I can find a position in Denmark, or the Mayence plan shall have materialized, and then I shall be fixed or the rest of my life.

He cherished unbroken gratitude toward his two benefactors, though he never saw them. His desire to visit Copenhagen was prevented only by ill health.

At the expiration of the three years, in June, 1794, Schiller met a fate that was better than an appointment in Denmark would have been: He made the intimate acquaintance of Goethe.

When twenty years old, Fritz Schiller, as a poor, distressed, and defiant student at the Karlsschule in Stuttgart, had caught a glimpse of Goethe who, as a handsome, stately young *Geheimrat,* dressed in court costume, and accompanied by Karl August, had paid the school a brief visit. Nine years had in the mean time passed by, years of poverty and passion, endured under the pressure of petty military despotism, in rebellious moods, in erotic joy and anguish, in an eternal struggle for mere existence, carried along by an ambition that was only partly satisfied.

Schiller had come to Weimar in 1787; Goethe was then in Italy. During the Christmas of 1784, he had made the acquaintance of Karl August in Darmstadt, and had given public readings from his own works before the local court. He read the first act of his *Don Carlos* to the Duke himself, privately. His reward for this was the bestowal of the title of *Herzoglicher Weimarischer Rat.* When Goethe returned from Italy, Schiller was out in the country, at Volkstädt, near Weimar.

He had become attached to the Lengefeld family, was patronized by the mother, and attracted by the

two daughters, Caroline von Beulwitz, and Charlotte, who afterwards became his wife. Schiller was
eager to make Goethe's acquaintance; he felt certain he would see him at the home of Frau von Stein
at Kochberg. It lay but a short distance from Volkstädt. He was quite unaware that Goethe returned
from Italy with the conviction that Schiller's influence was a power inimical to his own efforts. Nor
did he realize that Goethe was no longer an habitue
of Kochberg, and that he was destined never again
to become such. Schiller was hurt; he was offended;
he could not understand why Goethe failed to take
the slightest notice of his presence: It was such a
short distance from Weimar to Wolkstädt. He
might, however, have known that his criticism of
Egmont was ill inclined to open the way to Goethe's
traditionally locked heart.

In September, 1788, however, the wanderer
chanced to go on a visit to Frau von Lengefeld in
Rudolstadt, and there met Schiller. In addition to
the three Lengefeld women, Frau Herder, Frau von
Stein, and Frau von Stein's mother were also present. Goethe was courteous; but he did not have
anything to do with Schiller personally.

Schiller wrote to Körner concerning the first meeting with this man whom he had admired for so long:

The first sight of him lessened to a marked degree the
exalted opinion I had formed with regard to his striking
and beautiful figure. He is of medium height, unbending,
and walks erect. His face is unfeeling, though his eyes are
expressive, vivacious. You like to look at him. Though he
is serious, there is something benevolent and good in his mien.
He is a brunett, and seems to be much older than he really
is according to my count. His voice is exceedingly agreable,
his power of narration is marked by fluency, intellectuality,

and vivacity. You like to listen to him, and when he is in a good humor, which was more or less the case on this occasion, he speaks willingly and in an interesting way. Our acquaintance was quickly made, and without the least coercion. The company, to be sure, was so large, and the others were so eager to engage him in conversation, that I had no opportunity to be with him for any length of time, nor to speak with him on any but general topics. He speaks gladly and passionately of Italy. What he told me concerning Italy gave me a most striking and vivid picture of the land and the people.

What is not said, though it is implied, is the fact that Schiller was bitterly disappointed. He had hoped for some remark from Goethe which would show that he recognized his worth as a poet; Goethe discoursed on Italy. In the autumn, Schiller moved to Weimar. Goethe avoided him with such infinite care that Schiller never had a single chance to see him. But there he was, without a position, with marked ability, and as it would seem, with very poor prospects. Goethe recommended him for a vacant professorship at the University of Jena. The chair of history at Jena had been made vacant through the call of its former incumbent to Göttingen. That was a neat way by which Goethe could remove Schiller from Weimar. In December, 1788, Schiller accepted the call, incident to which he paid his respects to Goethe, hoping that he might finally approach the grand master on this occasion. Goethe's minister acknowledged the call; he confined his conversation exclusively to the professorship at Jena and was most profuse and voluble in the expression of his desire to see Schiller succeed in his new post. There was no fixed stipend attached to the position when Schiller entered upon the duties of his office in May, 1789. In January, 1790, the Duke granted him an annuity of two hundred thalers. In February of the same year Schiller married Charlotte von Lengefeld. In January, 1791, he had a violent tubercular attack. On the road to recovery, he suffered a relapse that brought him face to face with death. Then it was that help came from Denmark.

II

Schiller's letters to Körner from February and March, 1789, betray the dissatisfaction, even desperation, which Goethe's kindly negative deportment had evoked in the poet who was his junior by ten years.

He writes:

To be near Goethe often would make me decidedly unhappy. He never has moments during which he pours out his heart even to his most intimate friends; he is not to be got hold of; I believe he is an inordinate egotist. . . . He is benevolent, but only as a god, without giving of himself —which appeals to me as being consistent and carefully deliberated behavior intended to make effective the keenest enjoyment of egotism. Men should not allow any such creature to rise up among them. Because of all this I dislike him, though I love his mind with all my heart and think very high of him. . . .

He has awakened in me a queer blending of hatred and love; a feeling not dissimilar to that which Brutus and Cassius must have cherished toward Caesar. . . .

I prefer to let you know me precisely as I am. This person, this Goethe, is forever in my way, and he reminds me all too often that fate has treated me unkindly. How gently his genius has borne him up above fate! How I have had to fight up to this very moment!

That Schiller's fate had been unspeakably hard in comparison with Goethe's admits of no doubt. But in order to appreciate the instinctive aversion which he felt toward Goethe, we must first become clear as to how Schiller conducted himself, spiritually, at this particular period of his life; nor must we overlook the huge gulf that lay between his mental point of view and that of Goethe.

With his first play, *Die Räuber,* unbaked though it was, Schiller as a born dramatist had produced the most effective drama of the German stage. As the author of this drama, published in 1781, and the next two plays of the next three years, *Fiesco* and *Kabale und Liebe,* Schiller belonged, heart and mind, to the period of Storm and Stress. All three plays are in prose; in all of them the rhetoric and bombast were in keeping with the style of the period; in all of them there was abundant strength.

In *Die Räuber* there was a breath of world history. This drama by a young man who, up to this time, had lived to see nothing but the detestable and petty tyranny in the military academy at Stuttgart, preludes the revolution that was soon to shake Europe. Franz Moor was the old form of State's "tyrant"; Brother Karl was the man with the sympathetic heart, discovered and depicted by Rousseau. The two brothers together personified the social forces of the eighteenth century in clash and conflict with each other during the French revolution. Otherwise nearly everything in the play was unreal. If we except the robbers, whom Schiller copied from his own comrades, the remaining characters belong either to the realm of shades (as Amalia and the old Moor), or to the theatrical stock in trade (as

Daniel and Hermann). Karl Moor was the prize work of a youthful imagination; Franz Moor was a combination of Edmund the wicked brother of *Lear,* Iago, and Richard III.

The part of the drama which deals with the rivalry between two brothers, the one good, the other bad, was a common theme of the period. We have but to recall Klinger's *Die Zwillinge* and Leisewitz's *Julius von Tarent* (1776). The latter was Schiller's most immediate prototype. Julius corresponds to Karl Moor, Guido to Franz, Blanca to Amalia. The horrors are heaped up even more strongly, in that Guido murders Julius, while the Prince, their father, who corresponds to the old Moor, puts his own wicked son to death.

But the spirit of revolt itself and the dramatic tempest motif were Schiller's own; and it was he who created Karl Moor as the champion of humanity. He rejects and abandons a degenerate society and throws down the gauntlet to its laws.

In *Fiesco* Schiller had shown himself less dependent upon models; he had indeed made marked technical progress. His tragedy had an admirable vigor. In the leading character he had created an interesting and more consistent personality than his previous hero. With the exception of Muley Hassan, the other male characters are of little account, while the women are just as unreal as Amalia.

In *Kabale und Liebe* Schiller had attacked primarily the caste system. Begun in captivity and continued through adversities and humiliations, the drama was written in the most unhappy period of the poet's life. It was a *bürgerliche Tragödie* similar to other bourgeois tragedies of the age; the most immediate prototype in this case was Gemmingen's *Der deutsche Mausvater;* but as a love tragedy it surpassed them all. At the close, however, the characters in the play disintegrate under Schiller's inept hands. He caused the righteous young lover to poison his sweetheart because of a silly suspicion. Nevertheless, he has given us a picture of his own age, just as it was, gloomy and sinister, but so strong and in certain respects so true, that the play even to this day belongs to the fixed repertoire of the German theatre.

With his early productions, Schiller had been on the way to establishing a national theatre. His persons came near to being individuals. His prose was continually growing better. With his next work, *Don Carlos,* he started out on an entirely different road upon which he continued until his death. His talent was Europeanized; he gave up Shakespeare as a model and put himself in the power of the French—with constant protest against them. In this he simply followed Lessing's example, who, with praise for Shakespeare and words of contempt for the tragedy-writer Voltaire, had produced his masterpiece, *Nathan der Weise,* as a pupil of Voltaire and in Voltaire's spirit. When Schiller gave up prose and began to write verse, he seemed to have forgotten what he had previously learned, and went in for glittering rhetoric. At the same time he supplanted his individuals with types.

The first prose sketch of *Don Carlos* written in Bauerbach, has not made much progress over *Kabale und Liebe.* As this was a *Familiengemälde* in a private home, just so is *Don Carlos* a *Familiengemälde* in a royal household. The leading character in this case, the young prince, has been a Ferdinand on a higher social plane, with higher potentialities, and was to be a hero after Schiller's young heart. In like manner, Princess Eboli, in the original sketch, was to have been Lady Milford in duplicate, only raised to a higher degree. On April 14, 1783, Schiller wrote to Reinwald from Bauerbach: "If I dare use the expression, Carlos gets his soul from Shakespeare's Hamlet, his blood and nerves from Leisewitz's Julius, and his pulse from me."

In the finished drama, however, Don Carlos, in consequence of a change in plan and because of the introduction of Marquis Posa into the plot, is only a shadow of his friend, only a shadow of the man who was originally to have been his intimate and confidant. Posa dominates the entire play. Carlos is toned down into an ideal youth in love with his blameless stepmother. The drama is drawn out to immeasurable length. The plot and action, worked over and revised through fully five years, became confusion worse confounded.

It was Dalberg, the intendant of the theatre in Mannheim, who, as early as the spring of 1782, drew Schiller's attention to the theme. It was Dalberg who, in 1783, had Schiller appointed to the post of theatre poet in Mannheim. But in Mannheim French taste prevailed; French literature was read and there, more than anywhere else, tribute was paid to Wieland. Dalberg, who valued French drama and underestimated Shakespeare, demanded the revision of *Fiesco* so that it would be in accord with the prevailing taste, and in harmony with the ideals of Wieland. This demand had such an in-

fluence upon Schiller that his spiritual development
from the point of view of the drama became thoroughly French. All French tragedies were written
in verse; the theme of *Don Carlos* was precisely the
sort the French liked. It was akin to Racine's *Mithridate* and *Phèdre*. Schiller cherished a profound
respect for Racine. And when illness hindered him
in his original intention, he translated *Phèdre* into
German verse. He wrote to Dalberg on August
24, 1784: "Secretly I also entertain a more than
feeble hope of sometime performing an important
work for the German stage by transplanting the
classical plays of Corneille, Racine, Crébillon, and
Voltaire to our own territory."

Voltaire's influence upon the German drama of
the eighteenth century had been overwhelming. He
was more easily understood than his less realistic
predecessors. The philosophic optimism with which
the Germans had become familiar through the
philosophy of Leibniz and Wolff had prepared the
people's minds for him. They liked the dramatic
conflict in his works; it resulted in spiritual progress
and moral improvement, even though the hero lost
his life thereby. In his works, the leading persons
from the time of Louis XIII and Louis XIV were
modernized by an ingrafting of such sentimentality
as Rousseau and Diderot had glorified and had
taught the Germans to admire. His dramas were
Tendenzdramen; they made propaganda for the
cause of freedom in religion and politics, shrieked
abhorrence at fanaticism, at the Inquisition, at superstition, and at fire and brimstone in the service
of the oppressed in faith. No hero can have
thoughts more akin to Voltaire than Schiller's **Mar-**

quis Posa. All these youths *à la* Schiller in the later tragedies, who are noted in German textbooks as distinctly Germanic, the very ones whose idealism, like that of Max Piccolomini, is supposed to be national, are none other than heroes of the *Sturm und Drang* period who have felt the cosmopolizing influence of Voltaire.

Weisse, Cronegk, Brawe blazed the path that Schiller followed. When Schiller revised *Don Carlos,* he stood at the parting of the ways. Should he follow Shakespeare and Goethe, or Voltaire and Lessing? His philosophic-poetic *naturel* made the choice for him. He simply could not set up the human and the concrete as a point of departure after the fashion of Shakespeare and Goethe, and then have this transformed into poetry. Owing to his deep-seated preference for abstract ideas, he proceeded from thought and poetry to the human. His creative works consisted in giving thoughts a framework and then clothing the framework. He always proceeded from an idea, just as Voltaire and Lessing had done.

His Posa is certainly at the same time the most Voltairesque and the most Schilleresque of his creations. He incarnated himself with all his ideal yearnings in the Spanish *Marquis.* In his mind's eye, nevertheless, he had a distinctly French model for his *Don Carlos* in Campistron's *Andronic.*

The Greek emperor Colojanus Palaeologus has robbed his son Andronicus of his beloved, Irene of Trapezunt, and married her himself, just as Philipp II has robbed his son, Don Carlos, of his beloved, Elizabeth of Valois, and taken her in marriage.

Depuis près de deux mois qu'on épousant **Irène**
L'Empereur s'est lié d'une nouvelle chaîne
Qu'enlevant la Princesse à son fils malheureux
D'une fois tant jurée il a rompu les noeuds.

The son, like Don Carlos, is beloved everywhere throughout the empire, but nowhere more than by the rebellious Bulgarians, with whose messenger he fraternizes and whose wish it is to have him for their leader, just as the rebellious Netherlanders appeal to Don Carlos to be their ruler.

Il s'est de tout l'Empire attiré l'amitié,
Vous voyez qu'il soutient les rebelles Bulgares
Chaque jour l'envoyé de ces peuples barbares
L'entretient.

The Prince, just as Don Carlos, merely wishes to come to the help of the oppressed:

Léonce, vous verrez, avec combien de zèle
Des peuples opprimés je défends la querelle. . . .
Qu'on me laisse partir, que jaille en Bulgaire!

When he encounters the rejection of his desire to go to the maltreated and rebellious province, he, like Don Carlos, will travel in secret. The emperor condemns him to death. He can choose his way of meeting death, so he has his veins opened in the bath. The innocent Empress takes poison.

What is so noteworthy here is the fact that this old French play from the close of the seventeenth century is, despite its Byzantine name, founded upon the self-same source which inspired Schiller, namely, Abbé de Saint Réal's *Dom Carlos, Histoire Espagnole.* Campistron himself made this statement in an older preface which is not prefixed to the

drama, and which I did not discover until the above
was written.

It was the impossibility of placing the characters
of the Spanish court on the stage in Paris which
forced the poet to disguise it as Byzantine. This
explains why Schiller resorted to the old drama, and
accounts for the fact that the most original character in his *Don Carlos,* Marquis Posa, in his most
original situation, in the scene with Philipp II, has
already been portrayed in the French text. Let
us compare Léonce's appeal to the Emperor with
Posa's celebrated appeal to Philipp, in the tenth
scene of the third act:

> Fais si bien, juste ciel, que ma plainte le touche!
> Tout un Peuple, Seigneur, vous parle par ma bouche;
> Un Peuple qui toujors à vos ordres soumis,
> Fut le plus fort rempart contre vos Ennemis. . . .
> Cet heureux temps n'est plus; ces guerriers intrépides
> Sont en proye aux fureurs de gouverneurs avides;
> Sous des fers odieux leur coeur est abbatu,
> La rigueur de leur sort accable leur vertu;
> Tout se plaint, tout gémit dans nos tristes Provinces;
> Les chefs et les soldats, et le peuple et les princes.
> Chaque jour sans scrupule on viole nos droits,
> Et l'on compte pour rien la Justice et les Lois.
> En vain nos ennemis à nos peuples soutiennent,
> Que c'est de votre part que leurs ordres nous viennent.
> Non, vous n'approuvez point leurs sanglants attentats.
> Je dirai plus, Seigneur, vous ne les savez pas.
> Ah! si pour un moment vous pouviez voir vous même
> Pour quels coups on se sert de votre nom suprême;
> Que ce saint nom ne sert qu'à nous tyranniser,
> Qu'à mieux lier le joug qu'on nous veut imposer;
> Alors de vos sujets moins Empereur que Père
> Vous ne songeriez plus qu'à finir leur misère.

In a letter to Körner, February 12, 1788, Schiller
tells of an argument which he had with Wieland.

When the conversation centered upon French taste, Schiller offered to make each individual scene of any French writer of tragedy, whosoever he be, truer and at the same time better. (This recalls Lessing's boast in the *Hamburgische Dramaturgie*) : "Name me one play of the great Corneille, which I dare not undertake to improve. He (Wieland) brought up my *Carlos* in order to refute me, *since just in this particular instance I perpetrated the very fault which I had censured in the French.*" As may be seen, Wieland had a critical eye for the affiliation of Schiller's tragedies with the French. More than this, Fritz Jacobi cracked the only joke in his life on *Don Carlos*. He called the drama "a cold palace, where there is the smell of an overheated stove."

If Schiller's creative powers as a poet were hereafter for some time at a standstill, it was owing to the fact that he turned to the study and writing of history. He had always been philosophically inclined. Hardly since the days of Lucretius had any poet been philosophic to such a high degree. Poems such as *Die Götter Griechenlands,* 1788, *Die Künstler,* 1789, and *Das Ideal und das Leben,* 1795, reveal a philosophic gift of high order that has espoused poetry and begotten a beautiful art of narration.

But even now we can see from what has been said concerning Schiller how sharply Merck's expression to Goethe fitted him: "You try to give the real a poetic form. *The others* try to make the so-called poetic real"—which furnished Merck with an unfavorable testimonial.

III

As a historian and philosopher no less than as a poet Schiller belonged mind, heart and soul to the eighteenth century; and what is more, he continued to hold out against the influence of intellects, which in the eighteenth century prepared the way for the nineteenth.

From 1786 to 1791 he had buried himself with inspired zeal in the study of history; and because of this very fact he attained at the close of his life as a poet that reality which stands so decidedly at odds with his original Rousseau-like point of view and imparts to his later works a merit that is rare.

But his conception of history and historiography was poles removed from Herder's. In the first place, he did not write the history of peoples but of leading characters; in the second—and more important—his fundamental view was teleological: It sought and found the end and aim. His serious interest in history had been aroused by Kant's *Idee zu einer allgemeinen Geschichte in Weltbürgerlicher Absicht* and his *Bestimmung des Begriffs einer Menschenrace,* both of which interpreted the past in advance of experience. Schiller felt (rationalistically and withal poetically) that the task of the historian was to impart to that which has been handed down a higher harmony. Never losing hold of the optimism which began in the age of enlightenment, he believed that history contains a sort of divine judgment: *Die Weltgeschichte ist das Weltgericht;* and he reshaped history in accordance with this basic point of view. Like Voltaire, he wrote history with a philosophic end in view and with artistic vividness. The History of Charles XII by Voltaire was and remained his model for historical depiction. He put his own ideas and those of his age into the struggles of the past. This method was not so successful in converting the Thirty Years War, with its religious fanaticism, into a struggle for freedom of thought; it adapted itself better to the rebellion of the Netherlands, despite the fact that at bottom this revolution lay fully as distant from the contemporary struggle on the part of the German intellectual aristocracy against Lutheran orthodoxy.

Schiller began his study of Kant's philosophy with the *Kritik der Urtheilskraft,* published in 1790, hence with that particular part of Kant's *Kritik* which must have interested him most, the *Aestetik.* And when he received that year a small sum of money from Denmark, he decided (as he told his friend Körner January 1, 1792) to use the three years, in which freedom from economic pressure was assured him, in entering into the teachings of the philosopher of Königsberg. Kant had insisted that the idea of beauty was purely subjective, dependent upon mere personal taste; Schiller tried to look upon beauty as real, tangible, and defined it as freedom of appearance (*Freiheit in der Erscheinung*) : Nothing is self-determined; everything stands in a position of reciprocal dependence, though the value of an entity rests upon the degree in which it approaches freedom. Since beauty has nothing to do with the thing, but with its appearance, things are beautiful in so far as they seem free. To be sure this definition was not real; for whether things seem free or not, depends naturally upon the ob-

server. The definition, however, made a profound
impression upon the age.

Noteworthy for Schiller's philosophic striving
was the fact that, over against Kant's definition of
joy resulting from beauty, namely, *disinterested
agreeableness* from which a deep gulf separated the
aesthetically pleasing from the useful, he tried, in
the spirit of former times, to emphasize the mutual
interdependence of art and morality. In the wake
of Shaftesbury, he contended that aside from the
beauty of the human form, which awakens disinterested approval, there is still such a thing as *win-
someness:* beauty in movements, and the movements
are not beautiful unless they express a feeling or an
idea, therefore something moral. Then there is
dignity, another expression for something moral,
that is to say, for the exaltation which signifies the
victory of man over his lower nature.

In conformity with his assertion concerning the
inseparability of beauty from ethics, Schiller attacked the rigid distinction which Kant, with his
categorical imperative, had made between pleasure
and duty. He deprived duty of its harshness and
also made its fulfillment a joy. There is grace in the
epigramme:

Gerne dien' ich den Freunden, doch thu' ich es leider mit
    Neigung,
Und so wurmt es mich oft, dass ich nicht tugendhaft bin.

He repudiates Kant, is so far as his desire leads
toward a full, harmonious life, and that can only be
approached by *man's aesthetic education,* that is to
say, by the discipline of the mind to the beautifying
and evaluating of the beautiful. The cultivation of

beauty liberates from low sensuousness on the one hand, and from the sovereignty of calculating reason on the other.

The art of poetry especially is the true fountain of youth:

Glaubt mir, es ist kein Märchen! die Quelle der Jugend, sie rinnet
Wirklich und immer. Ihr fragt, wo? In der dichtenden Kunst.

But the art of poetry was of a double nature, for modern poetry had to have its peculiar characteristics as over against ancient, and Schiller had to assure the justification of his poetry as over against that of Goethe: Poetry was therefore partly naïve, partly sentimental. He approached these two conceptions, not by the road of experience, but *à priori,* and here as little as anywhere else did he concern himself to the slightest degree with the conception of an historic development. (See John G. Robertson: *Schiller. After a Century*).

IV

In Jena, Batsch had founded a "naturalistic society" with splendid collections and valuable apparatus. Goethe took pleasure in attending its periodical meetings. Once in the year 1794 he met Schiller there. They left accidentally at the same time. In the course of the conversation that spun itself out between them, Schiller remarked with reference to the lecture that had been held, that such a piecemeal method of dealing with nature could not attract the layman. This was water on Goe-

the's wheel; he replied that this manner of observ-
ing nature was hardly more satisfactory for the initiated, and that there existed still another way of
portraying nature, namely as working and living,
as striving from a whole to individual parts. Schiller did not rightly understand, did not clearly see,
how such could proceed from experience.

They came to Schiller's house; the conversation
enticed Goethe in. He depicted for Schiller the
metamorphosis of plants in a general way, making
clear to his mind a sort of symbolic plant. Schiller
listened attentively, but shook his head and replied:
"That is not an experience; that is an idea." Goethe was nonplussed, became slightly offended, and
felt that they had neared the crossroads where their
paths lay apart. Schiller's insistence upon freedom
toward nature in his essay on *Anmut und Würde* entered his mind and he said: "It is at least pleasing
to me to have ideas without knowing it and to see
them with my own eyes." Schiller replied politely,
as a cultured Kantian, who stood in the presence
of an obstinate "realist" (as Goethe called himself).
But neither of them gave in. What was for the
one a matter of experience was for the other an
à priori idea.

The initial step toward a closer relationship had
however been taken. The personal attraction that
emanated from Schiller's noble and striving nature,
from his exalted mind and immensely fertile intellect, did not fail of its influence. And when his wife,
whom Goethe had admired from her childhood on
and who in turn had grown up in reverence for him,
did what lay in her power to effect an enduring understanding between the *disocuri*, between these two

great souls who had for so long remained at a safe distance from each other, then it was that the feeling of unalloyed friendship began to take root in both of them. In their spiritual views they could be compared to two hemispheres which could and should fit perfectly together each one complementing the other.

And just at this time Schiller wished to start one of those journalistic enterprises by which he tried, on several occasions, to eke out an existence. Having assured himself of the necessary coöperation of Fichte and Wilhelm von Humboldt, he next sought to win Goethe as a collaborator. This was essayed in a quite nice and profoundly reverential letter dated June 13, 1794, to which Goethe replied most graciously: "It will afford me genuine pleasure to join your society." By August 23, the relationship had developed so far that Schiller, in a letter which fills four printed pages, was in a position to open up his heart to Goethe and show him how well and thoroughly he understood him.

He traced the contrast between Goethe and himself back to a contrast between quickness of perception and discriminating understanding (intuition and analysis). A man with Goethe's mental equipment had no reason to borrow from philosophy; on the contrary, it could learn from him. Philosophy could merely dismember what is given it; but genius was the power that gives. Goethe sought for the necessary in nature but by the most difficult road in that he strove to create the individual from the whole. From an understanding of the simplest organisms he came to the point where he could understand the most highly developed organism, man, ascended from All-Nature's building materials. It was "a grand and heroic idea," which showed full well how completely his mind controlled his conceptions and confined them in one beautiful unity.

If Goethe had been born in Greece or in Italy, he would have been surrounded from birth by a world that is beautiful and an art that idealizes. As it was, he had to create a Greece from within himself. In the space of time during which the young soul is being formed, he had been surrounded by imperfect forms and by a harsh, northern climate; he had already assimilated his unamiable environment when his victorious genius detected the lack and proceeded to make amends. He had been forced to devote himself to remoulding the less desirable world that had forced itself upon his powers of imagination, and this could come about only in accord with guiding concepts. Consequently he who had been wont to move from a basic view to abstractions, was now forced to pursue the opposite road, to transform conceptions into views and thoughts into feelings, because he as a genius could create only from feeling and view.

This, wrote Schiller, was his conception of Goethe's spiritual mode of progression, and Goethe himself knew best whether he was right. But what Goethe could not know—because genius is always a secret unto itself—was the full harmony existing between his own philosophic instinct and the oldest and purest results of inquiring reason. One would think that there must be a sharp distinction between the speculative mind, which proceeds from unity, and the intuitive which proceeds from variety. But if speculation sought experiences with pure and stead-

fast mind, then intuition in turn sought the law with
free and independent mental power. They met each
other half way.

Intuition had, to be sure, to do only with individual beings, speculation only with species. But
if intuition was ingenious, it produced individuals
with typical characteristics; and if speculation was
no less ingenious, it never lost sight of the experience that comes from seeing, but produced class beings with a potentiality for life and a clear relation
to reality. Quickness of perception on the one hand
and thoroughness of investigation on the other were
perfect complements.

Thus Goethe and Schiller each had his field of
activity defined; and despite Schiller's profound
sense of modesty, he felt assured of nearness to
Goethe by virtue of his marked creative ability. It
was here, too, that he felt called upon to tell Goethe,
once for all, how that long conversation between
them had set his world of ideas in motion.

Goethe replied to his letter with genuine cordiality. In his life too that conversation had left its
tidal mark. He had once more had opportunity to
appreciate the honesty and rare earnestness in everything that Schiller did or wrote. But it is not Schiller alone who is to be benefited by the coöperation;
Goethe is also to come out of it with renewed energy and clarified vision. There is so much in him
that is dark, hazy, unfixed, hesitating.

In his reply, Schiller blessed the fate that had
finally brought them together. How wise it was to
let chance take its course! He had often wanted
to come nearer to Goethe; now they had met each
other just at the right moment. He himself was

a hybrid. His imagination interfered with his world of thought; cold reason disturbed his writing of poetry. And in addition to all of this, illness had threatened to destroy his physical strength just at the time he was beginning to make full and correct use of his mental powers.

It was in this connection that he accepted an invitation from Goethe to spend several weeks at his home in Weimar. On his return to Jena he was quite overwhelmed by the mass of ideas his great friend had awakened in him. It would take a great deal of time merely to unravel and disentangle them; but he confidently hoped that not one of them would be lost.

Such, then, was the introduction to the unbroken coöperation between two of the most prominent men of modern times. A union more beautiful, and more productive of the results that endure, can be referred to in only the rarest of instances throughout the history of the entire world.

CHAPTER VII

THE BEGINNING OF *Wilhelm Meisters Lehrjahre;*
SCHILLER'S ENTHUSIASM — WISDOM IN *Wil-
helm Meisters Lehrjahre*—CLASS DIFFERENCES
IN *Wilhelm Meisters Lehrjahre*—CHARACTER
PORTRAYAL IN *Wilhelm Meisters Lehrjahre*

SHORTLY before Goethe had made Schiller's more
intimate acquaintance he had taken in hand the
frayed manuscript of *Wilhelm Meister* with the
idea of revising it. In June, 1794, he finished the
first two books. He thereupon sent Herder a copy
of the first book and invited him to dinner in order
to hear his opinion. But he was painfully disconcerted when Herder proved to be exceedingly vexed,
even "appalled," at the beginning of the novel.
Herder wrote to a sanctimonious woman friend:
"These Mariannas and Philinas, this whole business
in truth, I detest." He hoped that the poet in the
course of the novel would brand both of these
women as worthy of contempt. But if they were
introduced in this fashion at the beginning, the hero
would thereby be besmirched throughout the rest
of his life. So spiritually cramped had Herder become that he took pleasure in nothing of which he
could not approve morally.

How refreshing it was then for Goethe to receive
the inspired gratitude of Schiller, when *he* received

the beginning of the novel, immediately upon its publication. Goethe lamented the fact that his relation to Schiller had not been established before the publication was started. Schiller devoured the introduction with rapture and found absolutely nothing in it which did not stand in perfect harmony with the work as a whole, and the entire work was considered admirable. Disheartened by Herder's lack of understanding, Goethe had sent Schiller the book with anxiety and distrust. The effusive homage of his friend set his mind at ease, just as it filled him with a desire to complete the elaborate work so soon as possible.

Indeed Schiller gave him far more than mere encouragement; he gave him ideas as well. A reciprocal fructification between these two great minds was called into being. Goethe later wrote in this connection: "For me that was a new springtime in which everything germinated joyously and sprang forth from the seed which opened and from the branches whose leaves burst forth."

The theme around which *Wilhelm Meisters Lehrjahre* revolves wholly and entirely is one with which no novel in the literature of the world had previously dealt. It was a conception unknown to earlier times and one that has become almost foreign to modern times. The theme was Education. As a rule novels treated adventure or love or the struggle for one of various aims such as the winning of a sweetheart or the liberating of a prisoner or the overcoming of an obstacle or the conquering of an enemy. This novel treated education.

Rousseau's *Emile* had turned upon training; that was something quite different from education. Even in ancient times people had believed in training. Education in the sense in which the word was formed and conceived of in Germany at the close of the eighteenth century was something radically different.

We see nowadays that there was an age, such as Goethe has created, the interests of which centred on this point, an age in which neither money nor social position nor pleasure nor power nor knowledge was the aim, but proper development of the soul in accord with its inborn ability and innate power.

We see a youth groping about through life and being formed into what he is actually capable of being and becoming, and what the name connotes, a Master.

The question arises whether fortunate environment is not the first, last and sole condition that can guide a man to a lofty goal. The answer is more or less negative. There is no doubt but that the circumstance of birth is the initial point of departure from which the goal is indicated and by which we are directed to it. But between the beginning and the end much will be wanting in case education, and *nota bene* early education, does not make a man what he can become. It is entirely possible that the individual to whom we ascribe genius would be in a far worse position than he who possessed only general qualities, for the highly gifted can be misguided much more easily, he can be thrust aside on false roads much more forcefully and completely, than he whose talents are smaller, whose gifts belong more nearly to the class that we call average.

The hero asks somewhere whether genius cannot liberate itself and heal unaided the self-inflicted wound. "By no means"—it is said—"or at most only in part." No one is to imagine that he can overcome the first impressions of youth. He who has grown up in praiseworthy freedom, in concourse with good men, and whose master has taught him what he needs first in order to understand more readily that which is to follow; he who has learned what he never needs to forget, never needs to unlearn, will come to lead a more worthy life than he who has allowed his original powers of youth to be led into delusions from which he is afterwards obliged to free himself.

He whom fate takes charge of is to be extolled as fortunate, says Wilhelm: It trains each one according to its way. Fate, we are told, is a superior but expensive tutor. I would always prefer to be beholden to a human master's reason. For wise fate has an especially clumsy organ through which it works. This organ is chance. Chance seldom executes accurately and dependably what fate has once decided upon.

In response to Schiller's plea, Goethe appended in the latter part of his book a more penetrating explanation of the symbolic expressions *apprentice* and *master*. We are told that this depends, relatively, upon education. The majority wish merely a household remedy in order to attain prosperity, a mere prescription by which to attain wealth and good fortune.

From the very beginning the hero of the novel is a seeker; he fancies that others can give him what after all can come only from himself. He is without particular character, a football of persons and circumstances. But he is at heart—as is said of

him in time—"as arrogant as Scipio, as liberal as
Alexander, infatuated, too, now and then, but not
rancorous toward his rivals." This last virtue is,
however, not an especially noteworthy one since he
rarely has rivals and the few that he does have are
fairly harmless. Goethe has imbued Wilhelm with
his own longing for harmonious development, his
own striving to make headway in the larger life of
this world and of art. And, albeit the fact is never
expressly stated in so many words, and though Wilhelm himself almost seems to be overlooked, he has
also given his hero that intriguing amiability which
wins women without fail. Marianne and Natalie,
Philine and Mignon, Aurelie, the Countess and
Therese, each succumbs in turn. It is Wilhelm's
own nature and not the extraneous and never failing power that gradually and in due time leads him
along the path that is right.

Lacking experience as he does, the hero places
an inordinate value on the experience of others and
on the results that follow therefrom. He fairly
gathers and garners up opinions and thoughts, retains in his memory the true intermingled with the
false, and follows strange lights as guiding stars.
This man's bitterness and that man's icy contempt
infect him. The most dangerous personality for
his type of independence is Jarno, who reminds us
of Merck. Jarno passes correct and accurate judgment upon individual occurrences, but he generalizes them so that they become false in the end.
Jarno acts, however, as a beneficent force. His
enemies speak incessantly of his restless head and
his sharp tongue. But why? Because the anthropo-
morphic rabble stands in mortal fear of brains. If

they only knew how frightful a monster stupidity is, they would fear it—and not brains!

Wilhelm is exposed to the delusions of the striver; and particularly to the delusion of seeking education where for him there is no education. He is exposed also to the idea of imagining that he can acquire a talent—the talent for acting—for which he has absolutely no natural aptitude. He feels that the time he has spent in trying to become an actor lies behind him as an infinite emptiness, since nothing from this period has become a part of him. His error is grievous. Everything with which he comes in contact leaves its mark upon him. Everything contributes, unnoticed, to his education as to to the education of all.

The sole danger for all of us lies in the desire to give an account of our own stewardship; in this way we become either arrogant or depressed. The safest method to pursue is always to perform the task that most immediately confronts us. The education he has in mind is freedom from prejudice. "I hate the French language with all my soul," says Aurelie. The reply is: "How can one hate a language to which one owes the greatest part of one's development, to which even now we must still owe a great deal before our existence can acquire form."

The education he has in mind is contrasted with bourgeois morality and the claims of bourgeois society. Toward the close of the novel (Book 8, Chapter 1) Wilhelm cries out: "How superfluous is all this moral strictness since nature, in her good way, moulds us for the highest we are to become. Woe to every kind of education which destroys the most effective means to true education and interests us in the final aim, instead of making us happy while on the road itself."

The education he praises is contrasted first with the orthodox and then with pious education in general. In the section on "the fair soul" there is developed, in contrast to orthodoxy, the purest religious life of the emotions, an existence which is purity not merely in itself, but which imparts purity to its surroundings, a nature whose independence is proved in the impossibility of assimilating something which does not harmonize with the noble and amiable spirit that lies at its root. But where Natalie, the niece of the woman who is entitled "the fair soul," is described, the former's earthly being is portrayed (without emphasis) as of a higher mould than the fair nature of the other, which was moulded so conscientiously that it became overrefined. We become acquainted with Therese before we become acquainted with her friend, Natalie. Therese has the cleanliness of a Dutch woman in everything physical and spiritual, in all her relations, external and internal. Jarno once denied her the three beautiful graces, Faith, Hope and Charity; for her, he said, knowledge took the place of Faith, confidence that of Hope, steadfastness that of Charity. She herself admits that she knew nothing higher than clarity and cleverness until Natalie's richer being overcame her and inspired her. When in Therese's presence we feel simply the happiness that comes from acquaintance with a being so serene.

Natalie, on the contrary, is portrayed as a creation of a more ideal sort; her harmony, due to her lofty education, is richer; her love of harmony is innate. We conceive of Therese as the good spirit of the house, as the sensible woman who, aside from other accomplishments, is well versed in counting and reckoning. Natalie's education carries along with it ingenious quickness of perception. With regard to the great fundamental question in the book, as to whether one should let nature take its course and thereby go astray, or whether one, where possible, should anticipate and ward off the danger, she has nothing to say; such a question is foreign to her mind. She thinks neither of delusions nor of dangers; she simply does not see such things. But everywhere among men, she sees a need, a want: she sees it in the case of the child who cannot even stand on its feet, and in the woe of the old man who has lost his strength. What her eye is trained by nature to detect, is the quiet craving for activity, the inclination for a talent, gifts along a hundred different lines. She sees what no one has drawn her attention to; she seems also to have been predestined to see only this. And wherever she observes a lack or a want, she is ready with a substitute, a remedy, an aid. She has, until she becomes acquainted with Wilhelm, never loved passionately though she has always loved.

Great stress is therefore put upon what her brother Lothario says at the close of the book. "It is incredible what *an educated person* (note how flat this expression has become in our day, this expression which then signified a new world) can do for himself and for others, when, unconscious of any desire to dominate, he has the disposition to become the guardian of many, leads them to do at the right time what they all would gladly do, and

directs them to the goal which the majority keep
well enough in view, though they themselves miss
the road. . . . My sister, Natalie, is a vivid example of this type of individual. The method of
procedure that nature has ascribed to this fair soul
will always remain unattainable. She surely deserved this title of honor far more than many others,
indeed, I dare say *even more than our noble aunt,
who in her time was the fairest nature known to
our circle."* Fräulein von Klettenberg was the model
for this aunt.

II

Though Wilhelm develops from within, he is both
guided and punished by fate. He does, in time,
penance for everything, including the insignificant,
and for all errors in judgment and action. Just as
there is bitter cruelty in the fate which pursues
Faust in that the dissipation of a few nights results
in the homicide of Gretchen's mother, her brother,
her child and herself, so is there cruelty in the fate
that pursues Wilhelm unwilling ever to let him go.

When eighteen years of age, he had had an affair
with an actress by the name of Marianne. He sees
a man slink away from her house; he finds an in-
criminating note in her scarf. He deserts her, innocent though she is, without questioning her, or
listening to her, or even so much as letting her know
his address. He allows her to be condemned and
bear her child alone and deserted; the truth is not
made known to him until her death when it is too
late for reparation.

Accompanied by a number of actors, he comes

to the castle of the Count; a mild infatuation ensues
between him and the Countess. A frivolous Baroness, who wishes to involve the Countess in an unpleasant affair, disguises him by dressing him up in
the Count's housecoat and placing him in the latter's
chair. The Count enters; he imagines he sees his
double at his desk; he loses control of himself; he
becomes sanctimonious, Quakerish, simple-minded.
On one single occasion, and then just as she is taking
leave of him, the fair young Countess presses Wilhelm to her bosom. The act is of momentary duration but she so bitterly regrets this unique outburst
of passion that a mad idea finds lodgement in her
brain: She has pressed a locket which she has been
in the habit of wearing against her breast; a can-
cerous sore that will completely undermine her
health has developed from it. It is a morbid fancy;
but it transforms her; it ruins her.

Goethe wished to show here how cruelly life
itself punishes and avenges and consequently how
superfluous moral preaching is. He emphasizes
this theory with special force where Wilhelm feels
called upon seriously to moralize for Lothario,
whom he does not know personally but whose behavior toward the actress Aurelie seems to him
in the highest degree reprehensible.

Aurelie has told Wilhelm the history of her life.
Once upon a time she contracted a rationalistic marriage. When her husband was at death's door, she
became acquainted with the distinguished Lothario.
In company with some Frenchmen, he had fought
with marked distinction under Lafayette in the
American colonies. He approached her with quiet
demeanor, with open kindliness, and talked so sym-

pathetically about himself, that she rejoiced to see herself for the first time rightly appreciated. She says concerning Lotario, for whom Karl August's brother, Konstantin, is the model: "He seemed accustomed to feminine favor; that attracted my attention; he was not in the slightest way flattering or obtrusive; that made me carefree." In this way Goethe prepares us for the impression Lotario is to make: "With each rôle that I played, I always felt as though I were praising him and speaking in his honor; for this is the way my heart felt, it made no difference what I said." And when they applauded her playing, there was a cry within her: "That I owe to him." When Lotario leaves her, she seeks death. Like Ophelia and Emilie Galotti, she plays her own misery and desertion; but she feels this so keenly she would just as willingly play unclad. Then she dies in despair over the loss of Lotario.

The dying woman has charged Wilhelm to give her last greeting to her faithless lover. Indignant as he is, he prepares a strong upbraiding speech in true pharisaical fashion. He arrives at Lotario's castle where he meets him surrounded by a few highly cultured men, conspicuously worldly wise and somewhat hard-hearted, one of whom, Jarno, is as full of contempt for man as Wilhelm is full of ignorance of men. More than this, an exalted little sweetheart, Lydia, is found in Lotario's presence.

Lotario has nothing to do with Wilhelm, taken up as he is with other affairs (a duel which a deserted sweetheart has foisted upon him out of rage at a third whom he has preferred. . . . Lotario's sweethearts seem innumerable). There lives also in his neighborhood the woman (Therese) who is his secretly chosen bride, but from whom, because of a tragic misunderstanding, he lives apart. He looks upon her as the daughter of a person with whom he had an alliance during a journey. In her love and adoration for him, she regards everything he does in a favorable light and concedes him everything, even all of his inclinations toward other women.

Wilhelm cannot bring himself to deliver his speech; he is overcome by the man's superiority and straightforwardness. In truth, Lothario, in the novel represents the masterful personality in full action. With him all is survey, activity on a large scale, and incessant advance. He carries every one along with him. Wherever he is, he has a world unto himself. His nearness inspires and enflames. He acts not merely upon the individual, but upon the whole, not merely on the adjacent, but on the remote as well. He is, to put it briefly, the genius of the novel.

In direct contrast to him, we have a portrayal of an old physician who influences only the most immediate circumstance, merely creating a means to activity, not imparting activity itself. Perhaps Lothario destroys in one day what it took the physician years to build up; but perhaps Lothario imparts in one day power to replenish a hundredfold what has been torn down.

Furthermore, Wilhelm cannot bring forth his accusation, for the Countess is Lothario's sister, while Lothario is too magnanimous to rebuke Wilhelm. The hero feels by no means sufficiently guiltless to cast the first stone. The models, incidentally, for the Count and Countess were Count and Countess Werthern, the latter of whom was Karl August's intimate friend and the sister of Freiherr von Stein, the restorer of Prussia.

Wilhelm is enthusiastic about Lothario. When Lydia and he are on the way to Therese, he exclaims: "Oh Fräulein, what a man he is, and what men are those who surround him!" His admiration for Therese augments his admiration for Lothario: "It is only natural that such a distinguished man should attract the souls of remarkable women. How widely the influence of real manhood and the character of worthy beings extends!"

Wilhelm finally succeeds in beginning his speech in honor of Aurelie, though in a modified form: "I intended to criticize you bitterly," and so on. But he is unable to reply to these simple words of Lothario: "Most assuredly does my behaviour deserve censure. I should not have exchanged my friendship toward her for love. Alas! She was not lovable when she loved; and that is the greatest misfortune that can befall a woman." Wilhelm then merely remarks, quite tolerantly, that we cannot always avoid the blameworthy, cannot always avoid the fact that our points of view and methods of acting are turned aside from their sane and natural course.

Goethe has once more elaborated the thesis that life itself avenges and punishes adequately. Instead of composing sermons to mortify others, it were better for the preacher to deliver his sermons into the mirror. Preaching is unnecessary; unnecessary too is the repentence and absorption in religious books, such as Lydia indulges in when she meets with adversity. Therese, who speaks for Goethe, does not see how anyone can believe in a God who appeals to us through books and stories; for does not the heart reveal everything? For her the moral is not a sickening medicine but a rational and wholesome diet. To moralize otherwise is to imitate the rustic barber who parts everybody's hair with the same comb.

Superficial, prejudiced and idiotic readers have concluded from such expressions that the moral standard of this book is not what it should be—of this book which can be called "The Wisdom of Wolfgang Goethe" with even more justice than that volume entitled "The Wisdom of Jesu Sirach." Take, for example, the inexorable severity displayed in the portrayal of Wilhelm's relation to Mignon. Of itself it is beautiful; but it is cruel. The child loves him and he the child; yet he becomes her murderer.

Owing to the frivolous talk of Philine and other young girls, the idea becomes irresistibly attractive to Mignon of spending a night with her beloved, with never a thought of anything other than a lovers' tryst. But just as she is on the point of entering Wilhelm's room, she sees with dismay that a rival has forestalled her. Philine locks the door. The child feels a hitherto unknown, even unsuspected anguish. Her heart, which had been throbbing with longing and anticipation, stops beating; it stands perfectly still; it feels like a lump of lead in her bosom. When Wilhelm is eventually betrothed to Therese, and Mignon sees how the latter hurries to meet him and embrace him, she grasps at her heart, falls with a cry to the ground, and dies. And thus Wilhelm, through no fault of his own, becomes her murderer.

There is a passage in the book which throws radiant light on the fate of characters of this sort. Wilhelm once promised the company of actors to stand by them through thick and thin. When the time, however, comes that he feels he must leave them, he suffers acute pangs of conscience at the thought of breaking his vow. He is blind to the fact that his presence is quite superfluous; he is unaware that not a one of the actors took his promise seriously.

In this connection the author points to the current belief that our circle would feel an immeasurable loss at our departure. The gap is easily filled; we discover how dispensable and easily replaced we are. "One should never promise," says Wilhelm.

The intelligent Frau Melina replies to this: "We consider it a disgrace to ourselves not to keep a given promise. But, alas! a good man promises with his mere existence, with his mere presence, far too much. The confidence he evokes, the expectations he awakens, are infinite. He is and remains the debtor without knowing it."

In this way we see that, although the crux of the novel lies in the intellectual, not in the moral, since it centers upon the problem of *Meisterschaft,* no moral question is omitted. The book revolves about education as an intellectual, and especially as an artistic process. It is in this sphere that it contains the results of penetrating experience and exhausting rumination. It is more than Old Testament-like wisdom that we read in the *Lehrbrief* (after an introduction with the quotation from Hippocrates:

Art is long, life short, judgment difficult, opportunity fugitive:

Mimicry is instinctive; but that which we should imitate is not easily recognized. The remarkable is seldom found; less seldom payed tribute to. The distant entices us; not the steps which lead to it; with the summit before our eyes, we often go astray. Only a part of art can be taught; the artist needs the whole. Who knows but the half, always goes wrong and chatters a great deal; he who possesses the whole wishes only to work and talks seldom or slowly. The halfway ones have neither secrets nor strength. *Their knowledge is like baked bread, tasteful and satisfying for one day; but flour cannot be sown, and seed is not supposed to be ground.* . . . The spirit in which we act is the highest. Conduct is conceived and reproduced only by the spirit.

It is for the sake of clearness, upon which Schiller insisted during the process of elaboration, that this distinctive life wisdom has been introduced into the novel. For the book has undoubtedly suffered from the fact that it was worked out after an entirely different plan from that according to which it was originally designed. There was a good and simple intention in the fact that the main section concerned itself with actors and histrionics, since poetry and dramaturgy were supposed to be Wilhelm's real calling. That his attempt at poetry should be mere dilettantism, his enthusiasm for the dramatic profession only a whim, his demeanor as an actor devoid of all talent, is disconcerting. Wilhelm seems thereby somewhat incapable of taking his fate into his own hands.

The fruitlessness of striving after arbitrary independence is thrown therefore into sharp relief. "What we would gladly hold, we must let go, and undeserved benefits intrude." The feeling for what one might term the rush of life's stream as over against the growing man's power to swim begets a melancholy belief in fate.

Just as Wilhelm originally wavers between the calling of business and that of art, just so does he subsequently waver. He is helpful, good, unprejudiced, but weak in character; determinable and undetermined. Wilhelm once spoke in the presence of Jarno with bitterness and despondency. Jarno's reply is unforgetable: "It is well and good that you are vexed and bitter. It would be still better, if you would become really enraged."

With this "really enraged" the character of the man is supposed to be laid bare. But the ideal that flits before our eyes is the complete mastery of life, ennobled with harmonious education. There is not one glimpse of political trend, not to mention political ambition or feeling for the state. The mind alone shall be freed. Of other freedom there is no mention. Will in this far-reaching novel of education is an unknown and unnamed power.

III

The background of the novel is the condition and color of society as it existed in the eighteenth century; as it existed in the eighteenth century preceding the Revolution and preceding Rousseau. Class distinctions ran deep; marriage duties were taken quite lightly. When Wilhelm feels attracted to the Countess he forgets that she is far above him in birth and rank. Of this lapse of memory we are informed; we are not informed, however, of the discrepancy in etiquette that arises from the fact that

the Countess is married.   Indeed the distinctions in
the various ranks of society are so keenly felt that
the aristocratic, while at dessert, discourse on "dogs,
horses, and actors."   It is characteristic of the age
that the abbots speak more immorally than the actors.   The abbot says, by way of illustration, in
the coolest sort of way: "The Baron had a little
affair with a lady which caused much more sensation
than was really necessary, for she merely wished to
make too great use of her triumph over a rival."

The general thesis of the novel is, that in Germany as it existed at that time the nobleman alone
can develop himself personally and harmoniously.
The burgher is too dependent; his personality is lost.
The nobleman can have influence; the burgher can
only work.   The nobleman alone can experience the
interesting.   Beyond the pale of higher society the
interesting can only be experienced on the stage.
The ideal of middle-class happiness, as portrayed
by Wilhelm's brother-in-law, held no attraction for
him.   Werner does not yearn for luxury; he merely
asks for rational enjoyment.   Precious stones make
no appeal to him; he wants interest-bearing capital.
He wants to earn money.   He will live economically
and well.   Though he does not wish any superfluous
wardrobe, what he has is to be of the very best.
Wilhelm, whose sole desire is to educate himself,
after the fashion of the best noblemen of that day,
exclaims: "Why should I manufacture good iron
when I myself am full of slags?   Why try to put
my house in order when I am at odds with myself?"

Since he does not enjoy the freedom inherent in
and common to the best society, he is drawn to the
freedom that goes with the dramatic profession.

Though a surrogate, it is better than nothing. As an actor he can, if only on the stage, have all manner of experiences—moods, feelings, sights, and so on. But it is not only the life of the stage that attracts him; he is taken up with the gipsy-like freedom associated with the stage and its devotees.

Goethe manifests a certain predilection for *al fresco* scenes such as the theme requires. The actors arrive at the Count's castle. The wind blows through the high gateway. In total darkness, rain and cold, they shiver and shudder; the women are frightened, the children weep. Finally they place a few bundles of fagots in a huge fireplace. It is only for show. The smoke blows out and fills the room; the fire leaps forth in crackling flames; they fear that the castle will be endangered. It is a scene such as could be introduced into Théophile Gautier's masterful *Capitaine Fracasse,* written long afterwards, which opens with a description of the *Castle of Misery* at which a band of travelling players arrives.

Or follow with Goethe the roving troupe, wandering through the forest in war time, with long hunting knives in embroidered straps and pocket-pistols in their belts! The women are slowly drawn forward in the wagon; an actor goes along at its side, whistling. Wilhelm himself wanders along, constantly accompanied by the tight-rope dancer, Mignon, and the erratic old harpist in his long cloak. The cloak is tucked in his belt; he carries the harp. They camp over night after the fashion of hunters and charcoal burners. Their strange clothing and weapons gives them the appearance of foreigners.

What is all this but the youth's longing for free-

dom from all ensnaring ties? What else but the
love for the fatherland and native-land of all artists,
that old gipsyland to be found everywhere and situated nowhere? What else but love for the saun-
tering life in contrast to the fixed life, the life beset
with pursuits and aims!

Wilhelm severs his connection with the troupe
of actors and buys himself an estate near Lothario.
His brother-in-law, Werner, informs him that people know of his life with dissolute young noblemen
and actresses—an indisputable reference to the rumors which Klopstock believed concerning Goethe's
initial relation to Karl August. Wilhelm replies
by expressing his utter indifference to public opinion.

If we compare, however, the hero as he appears
in the novel with the Wilhelm of the *Sendung* we
see that Goethe has forced him back within and
confined him to a much more delimited field, just
as he did with Torquato Tasso in the final form
of the drama. Originally Wilhelm was to found a
national German theatre; and there was the material
in him to do so. Later on Goethe subtracted all
such ability from Wilhelm and the plan naturally
failed. Tasso likewise, as originally conceived, was
to enjoy the position of friend and peer to his prince.
But in the finished work he fell from this height and
was made as unlike his poet as possible.

IV

Goethe's ability to develop characters was extraordinary. No one has produced a galaxy of
personages of more pronounced individuality than
he. Since at the bottom and basis of his own char-

acter, however, the nature-growing, nature-binding is more marked than the life of volition and practical energy, his women stand out clearer and more forcible than his men. Even his aged Faust has not one doughty deed to look back upon.

In contrast to this his women are unforgetable. This is true not merely in *Wilhelm Meister* but in the earlier works. And yet, at the very time that *Wilhelm Meister* was being finished we note a retrogression even in his ability to depict women. Mignon and Philine, both creations of the earlier *Sendung,* are shown in *situations;* they have a more vigorous influence than some living persons of our acquaintance. Therese and Natalie, on the contrary, are merely *described.* The descriptions reveal uncommon psychological finesse, but we do not see them. We merely read about them.

Just as Gretchen's character is depicted in five monologues, and Clärchen's in two short ditties, Mignon's likewise is set forth to its very depths through the instrumentality of a few songs. We have *Heiss mich nicht reden,* which expresses the mysterious element in her nature; *So lass mich scheinen, bis ich werde,* which voices her premonition of an early death; *Nur wer die Sehnsucht kennt, weiss was ich leide,* which acquainted us with her longing; and *Kennst Du das Land,* more widely known than any of the others and through which she utters her ardent longing for a life in common with her lover on Italian soil.

Few of Goethe's characters have imprinted themselves more sharply on man's mind, drawn as it is with firm and simple strokes. She is invested from the very beginning with the mixed impression of a

boy and a girl that she makes when she appears in
her silk jacket with slashed sleeves and long, black,
curly hair. She is not described; she is revealed.
She seems to be only twelve or thirteen years old.
Her brow is mysterious; her mouth is true-hearted
and frank, though a bit too compressed for a girl
of her age and inclined to twitch to one side.

Later we become acquainted with her heteroclitic
actions. She springs up and down the stairs, slides
over the banisters, or sits perched up on a wardrobe. She has a way of her own of greeting people;
Wilhelm she greeted with folded arms. Furthermore, her language is distinguishable by its mixture
of French, German and Italian, though we are not
supplied with illustrations. Mention is made of her
clothing, patched but clean, not, however, in detail,
as when Therese or Natalie is described. The monumental expression has been found.

From an artistic point of view, Philine is an even
more remarkable character. She is all life from the
top of her head to the tip of her toes, on which hang
her high-heeled slippers; they flap back and forth.
She too is depicted through everything that she does
and says; she too portrays herself in a matchless
song:

> Singet nicht in Trauertönen
> Von der Einsamkeit der Nacht,
> Nein, sie ist, o holde Schönen,
> Zur Geselligkeit gemacht.

In contrast to the clear-cut, glowing Mignon,
Philine is the epitome of charming exuberance and
lazy, likeable frivolity. Goethe alone among German poets has succeeded in making such a woman

lifelike and lovely. When Heine attempts to depict a character of this sort, he invariably becomes impudent and the character becomes a mere doll. He does not possess Goethe's Prometheus-like powers, nor his innocent Paganism.

Philine is revealed slowly and gradually. Wilhelm catches sight of a well-shaped woman. Her blond hair falls unloosened about her neck. She is seen in a window and has him ask for flowers. Stroke connects stroke—with a long intermission— until the graceful character moves before our eyes. She is cleverly sketched by the art which makes us see how many dislike her, and how many she cajoles. She is mischievous and roguish, but seldom condescends to be coquetish.

Goethe has made his Wilhelm somewhat ridiculous by the excess of virtue he unfolds when he finds her slippers in his room. But Mignon is anything but ludicrous when, after having danced as a maenad to the sound of her tambourine, she, madly jealous of Philine, bites Wilhelm in the arm. Because of her very aversion, Aurelie paints Philine with the most certain strokes of the brush, so that she seems doubly entrancing: "How contrary she is to my nature, to my inmost being, even down to the slightest details. Her brown eyes and blond hair, which my brother finds so fascinating, makes no appeal to me whatever. The scar on her forehead is so repellent to me, so indicative of something base, that I always want to draw back ten paces from her." "Her deportment is culpable," says Wilhelm, "but I must do justice to her character." "Character!" shrieks Aurelie, "do you believe that such a creature has character? Ah you men! I know every one of you. You are worthy of just such women!"

This flaming hatred and naïve jealousy depict Philine even more vividly than the longing she awakens. She is sweet frivolity in feminine form, the true Eve. A charming creature is she, enveloped in her magnificent blond hair hanging about her bright face with its kiss-thirsty mouth, unforgetable because of the beaming humor and the joyousness, lightheartedness, and changeableness of her nature. There radiates from her an atmosphere of deeply subjugating voluptuousness.

She and Mignon complement each other by contrast. Mignon, the child of a southern clime, with her dark eyes, is the direct counterpiece to Philine. Her beauty is stern and cold, her being smouldering passion, her lot in life the abuse of fate. She is bound to her protector by the magic of gratitude and a childish affection. She is the child who all at once feels that she is no longer a mere child. While Philine seeks Wilhelm at night time to give him a hearty embrace, Mignon crawls in at night to stay with him as a dog at his feet. So it is that she is suddenly seized with awakening passion, and is speedily consumed by it.

Philine seems to have sprung from Goethe's brain. But the impression of all the seventeen years in which he struggled with the novel seem concentrated in the figure of Mignon. The conception of her figure arose, in all probability, when a company of rope dancers visited Weimar in 1777. The song *Kennst Du das Land* is from 1782. The poem *An Mignon,* addressed to Maddalena Ricci, the beautiful Milanese, is of considerably later date. The poem *Euphrosyne* was inspired by the actress Christiane Neumann, Becker by marriage, who stood so close to Goethe's heart. It portrays her as a child in relation to Goethe. Written in the year 1798, it depicts Christel Becker in a situation which recalls Mignon, and with the use of a Mignon-like expression, she "seeks her teacher, her friend, her father."

Goethe upbraids Madame de Staël somewhere for considering Mignon an episodic figure; he even goes so far as to say that she it is, on the contrary, around whom everything revolves. She is the burning longing for a life in complete resignation and an overardent enthusiasm requited with love; she is the hope for deep passion in deep happiness; she is a being from a higher world, at once elf and maid of a southern clime—a child of the copse with acrobatic grace and angelic goodness. But just as Shakespeare's Othello and Beaumarchais's Figaro and Hugo's Hernani are essentially known to the public at large as characters in the operas of Verdi and Mozart and Rossini, just so does the European and American public know Mignon and Philine merely from the operatic stage as creations of Ambroise Thomas.

CHAPTER VIII

Die Bekenntnisse einer schönen Seele

A CENTRAL point of the large circle of women in the book is occupied by the figure of a sort of Protestant nun, the refined canoness, portrayed in the sixth book, which is incorporated in the novel as an episode.

Bekenntnisse einer schönen Seele is Goethe's unique attempt to portray a religious existence. With this exception, not only in the novel but elsewhere as well, Goethe eludes the religious. The society in the tower is meant as a kind of substitute for what the church was in former days, that is to say, it is to be taken symbolically: It is a higher society without traditions and without dogma though it serves as a substitute for Providence and the clergy.

This explains the introduction of an entirely new poetic cult, of a new ritual with its choir and antiphonal choir and ceremonies without ceremonial, in *Wilhelm Meisters Lehrjahre* on the occasion of the death of Mignon; likewise in *Die Wahlverwandtschaften* at the burial of Ottilie.

In the confessions of a fair soul Goethe attempts to depict also the beauty and poetry of a pious disposition. With this end in view, he took up the notes and events in the life of Fräulein von Klettenberg, reviewed and revised them to suit his purpose, though he adhered so exactly to his material that all the events related and all the personalities depicted are reproduced true to reality.

The title, "The Confessions of a Fair Soul," sounds in our ears a bit emotional and sanctimonious. But these notes have nothing to do with the sanctimonious or the emotional.

The young woman whose development into Moravian religiosity and inspired pietism we follow here has originally a rather healthy nature, clear, intelligent and refined as she is. She is more nearly bold than timid. She is at first worldly, though almost incorporeally inclined—a nature fond of reality, in which, however, the lasting conception can be developed of living in inner communion with her God. But this religious propensity is brought on by several hemorrhages, the first of which takes place as early as her eighth year.

Her unusual thirst after knowledge and her powers of conjecture date from the first awakening of her reason. If she takes medicine, she wants to know the origin of the herb from which the medicine is made. When she learns to cook it is a feast for her to cut up a chicken or a pig. Her father dilates to her on splanchnological activities as though he were lecturing to a student. Her childlike wish is to get hold of a little sheep in which there is concealed an enchanted prince. She becomes acquainted with a boy while dancing, with whom she begins to fall in love: "Now I really have the little sheep for which I wished." They write to each other and rave about each other until they are separated.

The old French language teacher warns her. In a composition written under a fictitious name she related the story of her affair with this young chap.

The teacher says: "The good Phyllis had better take care; that can easily become serious." Offended, she asked him what he means by *serious;* he gives the half-grown girl some advice that is far too straightforward and plain. Blushing deeply, she contends that Phyllis is a demure young girl.

Now she becomes acquainted with a crowd of young people, happy-go-lucky young men without any real education. These were the German court people "and this class had at that time not the slightest *Kultur.*" The majority of them led improper lives, and their conversation with her concerned itself with indecencies. This offended her and made her act coldly toward them; at times their impropriety became shameless, whereupon she answered them rudely.

The old language teacher had, moreover, solicitously explained to her that not merely a girl's virtue but her health as well was in danger from intercourse with such men. She depicts her horror for them, her anxiety when one of them comes near her: "I guarded myself from any glass or cup from which they had drunk, indeed even from the chair from which one of them had risen." In this way she soon feels isolated, spiritually as well as physically. For the understanding of the soul this is important, because it shows us how, through fear of contagion thus ingrafted on the nature of a refined woman, the joy from a sensuous life is at once disturbed at its source.

Now follows the acquaintance and friendship with an excellent young man, Narciss. When he, quite unblameworthy, because of an outburst of jealousy in a gathering, is felled by a blow and the thrust of a sword, and she binds up his wound, the feeling which she in her quiet mind had nourished for him, bursts out like a flame struck by the air.

She thinks now and then of God, but always puts him off with only a ceremonious visit and then always wears fine clothes: her virtue, her honor, her special merit. But He seems not to have noticed her in this finery. She does not take this especially to heart; she has what she needs, health and well being; her contention is that God is not concerned further with her, because she herself is not much occupied with Him. Here begins this "most delicate interchange of the subjective and the objective" which for Goethe is the clear mark of religiosity.

She refers Narciss to her father, and they become engaged. She receives all her education from him. Good came of the association, according to her conception, in that "the submission so necessary and fitting for the feminine sex began" when she as betrothed strove to adapt herself to the wishes of her lover. In the meantime, however, they become totally at odds concerning the limits of propriety. She wishes to be safe and grants no freedom; he finds this "diet" quite severe, praises her principles and seeks at the same time to undermine them. But she always keeps the warning of the language teacher before her.

In the meantime she has become a little better acquainted with God; she was thankful to Him for giving her this man who was so dear to her. She complained to Him about that which made her solicitous, and did not notice that she herself had yearned and wished for this very thing. But when the whole world, with the exception of Narciss, was dead for her, she was often lonely in society, and complete isolation was most agreeable to her, because in it were developed her powers for conversing with God concerning her feelings and thoughts. God and love did not cross each other. Her love fitted in with the whole plan of creation. In vain did Narciss give her books which derided everything invisible and supernatural, including even yearning for knowledge on the part of woman. She became conscious of self-contradiction in the last instance: "Like all men he mocked at learned women and nevertheless educated me continually."

It is a question of his gaining promotion to an office. She prays to God about this in his behalf. He is, however, not appointed, and she conceives it as her religious duty to be satisfied therewith, since this mishap also must be intended for her real good. And now the mildest emotions enter into her soul; she feels that with the aid of heaven everything can be accomplished. He has less power of resistance against this adversity than she; consequently she must console him. And the milder and the sweeter the inner experiences have been up to the present, all the more often does she seek to prolong them and find consolation where she has found it so often.

The most of us are acquainted with experiences of this sort, particularly from the days of our youth. The impulse to prayer is a natural one and is awakened moreover by our environment. In the beginning there is not a shadow of a doubt but that the prayer is addressed to an unqualifiedly receptive being. Gradually, in the case of not a few, the consideration of and for this being decreases, or it disappears entirely. In the place of real prayer there arises a state of composure, of inner calm. The soul releases itself from tormenting anxiety and solicitude, seeks an inner, central point, finds its balance little by little and enjoys the feeling that it is being supported. Its poise is so much the surer because it believes it is being borne. It does not conceive of poise otherwise. It calls to mind those tribes of people who believe that the earth **rests** upon a tortoise and an elephant.

Since the soul is in this way concentrated in devotion, in prayer, in purpose, it will not suffer itself to be disturbed by temptation or torn by disappointment and sorrows. It feels itself purified, free, happy, far cleaner and stronger than when it was cowed, merged into everything that befell it, and lay broken-hearted and discouraged. It takes delight in its purity and independence. It rejoices in its strength, for it has moments when it swells with power. All this is still purely human, so to speak.

But in the case of many people, especially women, the personality feels that it is not merely supported, but comprehended, seen, observed. It finds itself face to face with the Invisible, the Almighty, the All-Good, which wills only its good, its very highest good. And then it feels irresistibly strong, for it has God with it and behind it in its struggles, and at the same time it feels infinitely humiliated, for it receives not the slightest measure of strength from itself. But it can move mountains.

Mere tendency towards God makes the soul happy. It seeks for itself its inner life after the fashion of one who is sensitive to cold, and wishing to become warm, seeks the fire. A shadow, a hindrance of some sort may, nevertheless, intervene.

And thus it happens in this instance to the narrator. She asks herself why her soul feels at times so repressed, so retarded in its efforts to attain unto the lofty heights that stand out as her spiritual objective. She discovers that the prime difficulty lies in her distracting and dissipating occupation with unworthy things. She would much prefer to deprive herself of all social life, of dancing and playing and of whatever else made up a part of the social customs and pleasures of her day. She would like to withdraw from all such amusements and diversions entirely. But by such action she offends Narciss who stands in incessant fear of ridicule. For his sake then she endures all these things, which in her heart she regards as folly, harmful folly. But the thought of them and her attitude toward her present life give her more and more concern.

She is going on twenty-two years old. The innocent pleasures appear to her no longer innocent. Furthermore, she knows of higher joys, of joys that strengthen in adversity and give comfort in misfortune. The struggle in her soul is soon ended. Even though there be something in her which causes her to yearn for sensual pleasures, she can no longer enjoy them aright. Just as he who is fond of wine, she argues, takes no pleasure in drinking it when he stands by a full cask in the cellar where the mephitic air is on the point of stifling him. Narciss has apparently been unable to conquer her senses. There is in her not merely a decisive measure of solicitude; there is also an element of real disgust at his erotic longing.

She is sufficiently unprejudiced not to condemn in any way a worldly life in others. She is not unmindful of the fact that a given food may in and of itself be healthy, though it is harmful to her. There is, at the same time, no use to try to induce her to commit an act on the ground that it is not immoral for others. In this way, the gap between the betrothed becomes wider and wider, until they are separated. She still loves him, but she no longer feels the need of him. She breaks with him. And now that she is free, and there is no longer any secret of her unctuous dread of diversions, she feels even less than ever the need to conceal her great love for art and science. She paints; she reads; and she finds an abundance of congenial society.

Another hemorrhage and prolonged physical weakness produce a renewed intensification and pressure of piety. She feels happy at knowing that just as certain as respiration is a sign of life, just so certain is she not without God in this world. She feels as if she were near Him, as if she stood before Him. But she heartily disapproves of Lavater's appeals to the orthodox to give publicity to examples of real grantings of prayer. She feels that just as momentous as each inner experience has been at the critical moment, just so flat, unessential, ineffectual, and improbable would the narrative sound if she were to quote single details. What she dares say is that she never returned empty-handed when she sought God in trouble and in need.

But she has never for a second feared Hell; the idea of an evil spirit and of a place of martyrdom after death could nowhere find a place in her range of ideas. Nor does she know at all the thing called sin. But through communion with the invisible Friend she perceives the sweetest enjoyments of all her life power. The impulse to enjoy these good fortunes becomes so great that she gladly relinquishes everything that might interfere with it.

At this period she makes a new and significant acquaintance in her development. She becomes acquainted with Philo (the later minister and chancellor K. von Moser) a man of heart, wit, and talent, but a man who wades in feminine favor and constantly seeks new relations with women. In her eyes he is a Wieland-like "Agathon" living a life of enjoyment. They become attached to each other; he is tempted to give this nun-like creature his complete confidence. She anxiously forebodes "fearful external and internal complications" for him and becomes lost in melancholy over him.

She thereupon suddenly hears an inner voice: "You are no better than he," and is startled. Throughout an entire year she feels capable of all degrees of wickedness, murder, theft, and voluptuousness. It is the human, weakly erotic sympathy in the mature woman. She *will* not in her heart be considered better than he; she understands his temptations and faults. That voice is the voice of blood, of the instinct of love, which wakes for the last time and drives her over into faith, faith which is essentially love. For she herself says: "Such is not cured by the practice of virtue but by faith."

Now what is faith? How can it help her accept the story of a past event as true? Faith must be a condition in man's own mind; she therefore implores the Almighty: "Give me faith!"

One day she was leaning over a table hiding her

tear-stained face in her hands. What did she feel then? It was as though a gust of wind, a blast, were bringing her to the cross on which Jesus died. "It was a gust of wind," she says, "I can call it nothing else, *just like that by which our soul is borne to a faraway lover,* an approach which to all appearances is far more natural and truer than we suppose." From this moment on she knew what faith was.

In addition to inner clarity, equanimity, and fulness in her soul there now comes emotionalism. To the poise, freedom, and purity of the soul in the moral domain, to this consecrated naïveté, is added ecstasy which in her nature is nothing more than the transfer of the stifled erotic longing to the realm of religion. She feels a power to arise that is wholly new to her: "In such presentiments, words fail us." . . . Just so does a love-sick woman also speak. Her expression coincides letter for letter with that from the lips of a girl who is deeply in love, and whose love is reciprocated. "I could rise up above that which formerly menaced me, just as a bird, singing and without difficulty, flies up over the fastest stream opposite which a dog remains standing with fretful barking."

Now in place of the poise of peace, the security of ecstasy like that of a somnambulist enters her mind. When she finally attempts to give a conception of her condition, she writes: "I no longer remember a prayer. Nothing appears to me in the form of a law. It is an instinct which leads and directs me aright. I follow my conviction with liberty, and know as little of limiting destinies as of remorse." This is, as we see, the quiet and humble expression of a free person. It is what the Russian advanced *Intelligentsia* calls the immediate condition.

What especially attracted and profoundly fascinated Goethe is evidently the fact that the moral striving in this case is overcome in a way that renders ethics superfluous. It is nevertheless most interesting to observe the incessant intermingling of that which actually takes place in the soul, and the reflection of the soul's agitations, resulting as it does in the phantastic representation of a hovering, as it were, in the metaphysical world.

The same thing happens here that happens at a familiar and frequently performed physical experiment. An object that obeys all the laws of earthly existence, including the law of gravity, (a person, for example, who lies stretched out on a table) appears, because of a false conception that is itself conditioned by law, to be floating in the air as a supernatural, celestial phantasm. But if this figure be beautiful, it is just as beautiful even though it in reality be bound to the earth and its floating be a mere illusion.

Without one word by way of interpretation, without having written one sentence in his own name, without having set down one single idea that could flected in this same woman's mind, floating freely in the vast celestial expanse near her divine redeemer.

Moralists even to this very day have not entirely not have come just as well from the orthodox Moravian woman, Goethe has pictured the soul of a fair and noble woman both as it is, subservient to all conditions of earthly existence, and as it is, respent their rage on *Wilhelm Meister*. Vischer, Germany's greatest aesthetician, wrote concerning the novel a few years before his death: "One does not need to be a *Bierphilister* in order to inquire whether it is in the nature of things that an eighteen-year-old shop boy becomes a happy father. Not that a poet dare not say as much, but this situation calls for a final act in which his old man, who hears about it, at least locks him up for a week on bread and water. . . . And on Philine the poet dwells certainly with more satisfaction than logic demands."

Vischer's conception does not glitter with wit nor his mode of expression with finesse; at any rate he should not have entirely forgotten the detailed dwelling upon the confessions of the Moravian woman, these confessions which give the work so heavy a counterbalance to Philine's roguishness.

Among contemporaries it was Schiller who could best evaluate the confessions; be praises them because they avoid the "trivial terminology of devotion." This section, which accentuates so strongly the abrogation of law, accords harmoniously with the spirit of the entire work of which the confessions are but one single link. The spirit in *Wilhelm Meister* proceeds in truth from the dissolution of duty's harsh claim and the defense of freedom along the lines of beautiful naturalness. The spirit of the novel teaches that the road to freedom is through the gateway of beauty.

Hence the embitterment over the work on the part of the pious, the moral, the sanctified, the earlier friends, men and women. Hence the scandals of Klopstock, Stolberg, Claudius, Jacobi, and Schlosser. Hence the remark of Frau von Stein that there

are some "beautiful thoughts" in the book, but that
"wherever Goethe has experienced something of
the noble feelings in human nature, he attaches to
them a little dirt."   Hence Herder's exclamation at
"a certain unclean spirit in the book," his purifying
himself from complicity, his insistence that Goethe
no longer troubles himself about "the good, the
noble, the moral grace," until he comes near setting
his own humanity based on morality up against Goethe's based on beauty.   The latter wrote concerning
this in one of his letters to Schiller: "And in this
way, the old, half true, Philistine hurdy-gurdy melody buzzes without ceasing, to the tune that art shall
recognize the moral law and subordinate itself to
it.   It has always done the first and must do so . . .
If it did the second, it were lost, and it were better
to hang a mill stone about its neck and drown it than
to let it slowly give up the ghost as the outcome
of acquiescence in this utilitarian platitude."

It was not fortuitous that Goethe entitled that
insertion "the confessions of a *fair* soul."   The
beauty of the life of the soul is the central thought
of the entire work.   It is psychological.   A type of
psychic beauty such as is portrayed here in the lower
religious form is, according to Goethe's intention,
supposed to appear in a more complete, purely human form in the person of Natalie.   Lothario, consequently, at the close of the novel, when Therese
relinquishes Wilhelm to Natalie, pronounces the
above-quoted judgment on Natalie's conduct, which
is regarded as an unattainable model.   He calls
her "this beautiful soul" and adds: "Indeed she
deserves this appellation of honor more than many
others, *even more than our noble aunt herself.*"

In *Wilhelm Meister,* Book VIII, Chapter 5, we have a portrayal of Natalie's castle. Sphinxes of granite guarded the main entrance to the great hall, "the hall of the past." The doors, of Egyptian style, are somewhat narrower at the top than at the bottom, while their iron wings prepare us for a sombre, even horrible sight. One was therefore pleasantly surprised on entering the hall to see that art and life had abolished every touch of death and the grave. Not even the sarcophagi and urns round about made a disheartening or disturbing impression. Everything gleamed with marble and azure; all this splendor was effective from a purely architectural point of view. Directly opposite the entrance, on a splendid sarcophagus, was a marble statue of a stately man resting on a cushion. He held a scroll in his hands which he seemed to be studying with marked attentiveness. On it were inscribed the words: *Remember to Live!*

Remember to Live! That is the complete *Wilhelm Meister* in three words. It is Goethe's laconic *memento vivere* flung out in happy defiance and quiet sublimity against all concerned with the opposite. It is the challenge to inflated piety and the *memento mori* of Christianity.

Remember to Live! What does it mean? Not that we are to scrape together as many sensual enjoyments as possible. It means that we are to get the best out of our lives. What did the expression *to live* mean to Goethe? To him it signified the preservation of the beauty of the soul that leads to freedom. Never to feel one's self as a mere means to an end, but as one who does not need the law.

CHAPTER IX

DEFECTS IN GOETHE'S NARRATIVE ART

GOETHE'S art of narration is distinctly inferior
to his unique lyric power and his ability to depict
characters. He composes his novels after the old-
fashioned pattern. He depends far too much on
the effect of surprises, remarkable coincidences and
romantic circumstances. His epic style, antiquated
from the beginning, becomes more so as he grows
older. It is this that intimidates the half-educated
from the study of his narratives.

Even the unprejudiced reader finds it odd that
he should begin his *Wahlverwandtschaften* with a
sentence like this: "Eduard—thus we call a rich
Baron in his prime—had spent a fine April afternoon in his garden." Not even an admitted bungler
would begin a novel with such a sentence to-day.
He would do anything to avoid a parenthesis after
the first word, nor would he dream of introducing
a *we* at the very outset and thereby detract from the
unhampered manipulation of the name and general
content.

No matter how fresh and vivid the narration of
Wilhelm Meisters Lehrjahre may be at times, the
reader is repelled at other times by the method of
elaboration. We demand of the modern author
that he understand his business and be able to depict
everything that should be depicted. To use the

122

word "indescribable" or admit that "such no pen can describe," is a manifestation of weakness at odds with writing in the twentieth century. But Goethe constantly refers to his lack of ability. On the occasion of Wilhelm's first conversation with the harpist, we are regaled with the following: "We might become ever so diffuse and yet we would not be able to describe the charm of the hasty conversation if we attempted to reproduce the remarks of our friend with the adventuresome stranger."

Occasionally Goethe even promises to tell the reader something on another occasion: "The master of horse would like very much to learn the origin and life history of Friedrich; the latter then related an adventure he has already told on a number of occasions and with which we intend to make our readers acquainted at another time." Or take this instance further on in the novel: "Wilhelm wrote down many such conversations, and we will, since we dare not break off the narrative so often, present it to our readers at another opportunity; it is entirely likely that they will be interested in such dramaturgic attempts."

A fire breaks out in the course of the novel during which the harpist, who seems to have become insane, wants to murder Wilhelm's child with a knife. Mignon prevents him from so doing. Wilhelm hurries away after the non-plussed harpist, entices him into a summer house and, Goethe writes, "carried on with him a remarkable conversation, which, however, in order not to pain our readers with disconnected ideas and solicitous feelings, we prefer to suppress rather than to give at all, to say nothing of setting it forth in detail."

It is by this inartistic means that Goethe holds
back the secret in the harpist's life, disagreeable as
it is, until the very close of the novel. He has been
passionately in love with his sister Sperata without
once suspecting his blood relationship to the young
girl. Mignon is his daughter by Sperata. Begotten
in incest, she was later on abducted by the tight rope
dancers. The harpist was loath to part with his
sweetheart, even after he had learned precisely who
she was; and not once had he been willing to admit
of any break in the love between brother and sister
—until he and she were separated from each other
by force.

We and the characters in the novel learn of this
secret, with its romantic by-product and the incredible impression it leaves, when it is far too late to set
in motion a real play of feelings. It is suppressed
when it might well be suspected and related when
it is entirely superfluous.

A peculiar result of the constant intrusion of the
narrator is defective diction as soon as direct discourse becomes necessary. Goethe has manifestly
laid inadequate stress on distinguishing and individ-
ualising. While Martha in *Faust* speaks after the
fashion of an old matchmaker, Marianne's maid
and confidant, old Barbara, talks like a book. We
do not see her for ourselves; her language is abstract
and literary. How wholly different, how much better, Voltaire portrays such an old crone, even when
she appears in one of his admittedly didactic novels
of philosophic intent! "And Felix?" Wilhelm asks.
The woman of many years replies: "Your son
by this lovable girl, whose sole misfortune was that
she loved too tenderly . . . I am not going to run

off! Wait and I will fetch you a document that will cause you both joy and sorrow."

What produces the strangest effect of all in Goethe's method of narrating is the trite pretense on the part of the author that he himself was the invisible observer of the scenes he sets forth. The very close of the first chapter, with the happy meeting between the two lovers, reads as follows:

Wilhelm entered. With what vivacity she rushed to meet him! With what ecstasy he embraced the red uniform! With what delight he pressed the silken bodice to his breast! Who would dare describe, who would be so bold as to give expression to, the joy of two lovers? The old woman went away mumbling something to herself and we depart with her and leave the two blissful souls alone and undisturbed.

This is amusing and nothing more. The aged but loquacious matchmaker trips away and the invisible narrator follows suit, in *pluralis majestatis,* in order not to cause embarrassment. It is all strange, almost as much so as when Goethe remains in certain tender scenes, of which the novel has a plenty, and joins in the chatter. For example, when Wilhelm and the Countess embrace for the first and last time. Among other observations we are regaled with this one:

"Her head rested upon his shoulder and no thought was given to the locks and ribbons crushed and dishevelled by assuming this position. She put her arm around him; he embraced her tightly, pressed her again and again to his bosom. Oh, that such a moment cannot last forever! And woe to the envious fate which disturbed our friends in this brief moment!" It is evident that the narrator would grant them the complete enjoyment of culpable pleasure.

Most remarkable of all is the style in which the narrator himself declares that he is uncertain as to how the situation appeals to the imagination of the persons depicted. After having practised her ingratiatory arts upon Wilhelm long and in vain, Philine one day sits down by his side, or more accurately speaking, on his lap and caresses him in full view of all who chance to pass by. She derides him because he sits there like a stick, as inanimate as a stone. About to leave him, she says: "Please stay so that I can find my stone man on the bench when I return."

Goethe adds: "This time she did him an injustice; for however much he strove to control himself in her presence he would, *in all probability,* had he been with her in a place convenient for amusement, not have let her fondling go by unheeded." The thoroughness with which this phase of the matter is treated is pedantic, to be quite conservative.

Still queerer, however, is the clumsiness of the style in the depiction of the relation between Wilhelm and Philine the day following the clandestine visit by night to his sleeping chamber. Wilhelm does not know, because of the darkness, which woman it was who had visited him. This is an infringement on one's sense of probability.

A little later we read: "On leaving Philine whispered to Wilhelm: I must have left my slippers behind; please don't lock the door. These words throw him into profound confusion. His surmise that the guest of the previous night had been Philine is strengthened, and the reader is forced to share

this opinion, especially since we cannot discover the
reasons which made him doubtful and which must
have instilled him with another curious misgiving."
Reasons, incidentally, which have already been definitely hinted at but which Goethe has forgotten
because he wrote the book after too long an intermission.   We learn, too, at the close, that Mignon
had also intended to do this very thing.   It was
her plan to sneak into Wilhelm's room on that very
same night.   According to the original plan it seems
that she and not Philine was to pay the visit.

As a superfluous supplement to this bizarre system, as a result of which the author frequently does
not know the hero's thoughts and is not always
aware of what really takes place, must be added
the fact, for modern readers even more antiquated,
that others do know what the hero is thinking about,
and are aware of what takes place even though it
occurs in secret, in the dead of night or within the
silent mind.   There are, for example, the men in
the tower, the secret society of the omniscient, with
the abbot at its head.   The eighteenth century was,
to be sure, the age of Freemasons, Jesuits, Rosicrucians and numerous other secret societies.

It is never chance but reason that directs Wilhelm's fate.   When the society of actors is to play
Hamlet an unknown individual turns up to take the
part of the ghost.   He slinks away unseen but leaves
his veil behind on which the warning, "Flee, young
man, flee!" has been imprinted.   Wilhelm's guide
has considered it high time to wean him away from
association with actors.   We would hardly anticipate such architecture nowadays in a dime novel.

It finally comes out that Jarno knows even Wil-

helm's secret thoughts, thoughts expressed to no one.
There is, by way of illustration, the motif of the
secret benefactor suspected of being a recruiting
officer, who wants to press him into military service
against his will. Wilhelm feels poignant grief at
knowing that whatever he does he is watched and
guided. He had felt that he was unobserved and
free.

Yet what do these imperfections signify in comparison with the breadth of vision and horizon of
the novel as a whole? What are they in comparison
with its wealth of characters, each unforgetable,
and its depths of knowledge concerning and insight
into the mysterious workings of the human soul?

Though this anticipates the course of development, it is worthy of note in this connection that in
the looser composition of Wilhelm's *Wanderjahre*
the narrator makes himself much more felt. We
are left with the impression that in those days a
novel was written to be read in the long winter evenings in lonely, isolated homes, the family gathered
around the centre table and regarding the poet as
their personal friend.

In the introduction to the excellent narrative
interwoven at this point, *Der Mann von fünfzig
Jahren,* Goethe discloses to us his initial plan: He
wishes to adapt himself to the custom of the
highly honoured public by entertaining in sections.
He will bring out the present narrative serially.
But then he found an uninterrupted discourse more
suitable to his purpose.

In the novel the hero has translated several verses
of Ovid for a charming young lady. But as he is
about to give them to her he finds himself in a dis-

tressing situation. The young woman in the poem
is depicted as a spider. Should the lady who is to
be favored with the translation see an allusion to
her own personality she might find the comparison
offensive. Then we are regaled with this surprising
comment: "We do not know how our friend extricated himself from this difficulty. We must refer
the incident to others over which the muses are
kind and shrewd enough to cast a veil." That is
naïve.

In not a few points Goethe departs from his established prose form of later years. Having com-
mented on the excellence of a certain painter, he
says: "In order not to be accused with putting
good-natured readers off with vague, empty phrases
which they are not in a position to verify, I reproduce the judgment of a connoisseur concerning the
work of this artist. For several years he has been
studying the works of this painter and of others of
the same school." Then we are treated to a section of real or fictitious essays in art criticism.

All form comes to a dead stop when, in the introduction to the *Wanderjahre,* we read: "He
[Wilhelm] began to read." But instead of telling
us that what Wilhelm read, Goethe says: "But
if we find it convenient not to let the good man read
further, our friends will hardly take it amiss. . . .
Our friends have undertaken a novel and since it
has occasionally become more of a didactic poem
than is right we find it advisable not to put our
readers' patience to a still harder test. The papers
shall be printed in another place."

As time went on Goethe's prose thereby lost its
clarity and warmth. He could now and then even

go over to pure *Kanzleistil* and write *solches* and *dasselbe*, as in the following:

Ist nun das Gras von ihnen geschlagen und zu Heu getrocknet, so werfen sie *solches* von den Höhen in tiefere Thalgründe herab, wo *dasselbe* wider gesammelt . . . wird.

This is due in part to the fact that his powers of observation weakened with age; he fused pictures from memory.   It is due also to his inclination to shatter illusions, to reflect the work within the work, a conceit which the German romanticists inherited from him.

In *Die Wanderjahre* Wilhelm meets a painter who has read *Die Lehrjahre*.   He is enchanted by the dead Mignon and wishes to paint her in appropriate surroundings.   They arrive at "the great sea," by which Goethe—as he tells Eckermann—meant Lago Maggiore.   We read: "Couched under the cypresses they saw the laurels rise up, the pomegranates ripen, the orange and lemon trees in bloom, and the fruit at the same time gleam out from the dark foliage."

We feel here Mignon's song of her country; we feel, too, the joy for the strongly picturesque which in later years predominated in Goethe's works, especially in his verse, and which makes the style in the second part of *Faust* so new and surprising, at times even Rembrandtesque.

Whereas Goethe, in the poetry of his youth, was interested mostly in the psychic, his creative writing changes, as years go by, its principle of style and dwells in his old age preferably on that which is revealed to the senses and enriches them in a mysterious way.

CHAPTER X

Voss's *Luise* AND Goethe's *Hermann und Dorothea*

Johann Heinrich Voss, founder of the *Göttinger Hainbund*, friend of Klopstock and Claudius, ardent opponent of Wieland, zealous rationalist, and lover of virtue and the fatherland, had, during his impecunious days as tutor and schoolmaster, assimilated a comfortable amount of philological information. When thirty years of age (1781), he published his excellent translation of the *Odyssey*, followed by many other translations from Greek and Roman antiquity. He was the first German who controlled the hexameter, and made it melodious in the German language.

As early as 1783 he published, as a fragment, the second song of his idyllic poem *Luise;* it did not appear in its entirety until 1795, caused an extraordinary sensation, and met with great success. Voss was living at that time as rector in Eutin, a position which his friend of that period, Fritz v. Stolberg, had procured for him. Since Eutin then belonged to Denmark, Voss had, as Baggesen relates in *Labyrinthen,* "determined to learn Danish." It remained a matter of determination. This and the acquaintance with Baggesen is all the share that Denmark has in him.

Luise became significant for Goethe's production, for immediately after the completion of *Wilhelm*

Meisters Lehrjahre, in September, 1796, he began
the elaboration of *his* idyll in hexameters, *Hermann
und Dorothea,* which, despite its grandeur and value
along other lines, would never have come into existence if Voss's poem had not preceded.

Luise is a vicarage idyll which makes its appeal
because the verses are excellently built up with correct, weighty spondees and lightly moving dactyls
in a set scheme, where not one accent is false; and
which repels because of the bland way in which all
family emotions are sugarcoated with sentimentality
and saturated with emotional weeping.

There is sympathetic delight in landscapes and
a vivid sense for plant and animal life. The landscapes, incidentally, leave a distinctly Danish impression. Since the hero is a country parson, the
deism of the poet makes itself felt in ever-recurring
prayers of gratitude and incessant laudation of
God's dominant, fatherly goodness toward his many
and varied creatures, all of which has a decidedly
old-fashioned ring. On the other hand, the poet
is a militant rationalist. When the wise and good
are enumerated, Socrates is not forgotten; nor is
Voss's good friend, Mendelssohn. They are listed
side by side with the apostles and prophets—somewhat as Oehlenschläger groups together "Jesus on
High, Baldur, Socrates."[3]

We have a legend that tells how St. Peter let
a Catholic, a Calvinist, and a Lutheran sit outside
of Heaven's gates on one and the same bench, while
all within sang the praises of one and the same
God.

[3] Oehlenschläger wrote (1835) a tragedy entitled "Sokrates,"
the death scene from which was read to him a few hours before
he died.   —TRANSLATOR.

The legend begins as follows:

O Himmelswonne, wir freun uns,
Alle, die Gutes gethan nach Kraft und redlicher Einsicht,
Und die zu höherer Kraft vorleuchteten; freun uns mit
  Petrus,
Moses, Konfuz, und Homer, dem liebenden, und Zoroaster,
Und, der für Wahrheit starb, mit Sokrates, auch mit dem
  edeln
Mendelssohn! Der hätte den Göttlichen nimmer gekreuzigt.

Though the combination of names in this passage is rather striking, the one in which the greatest plastic artists are catalogued is even more so. It contains the names of Praxiteles, Phidias—and Angelica Kauffmann.

No idyllic poet of ancient times was ever so idyllic as Voss. All the persons are of immaculate character, the men as well as the women, plebeian just like the noble, servants along with the masters. Everything in this parsonage smells good, tastes good, sounds good. The unique disharmony arises when the young parson, about to drink a toast (proposed by Luise's father) to his beloved Luise of eighteen summers, takes hold of his glass so high that it does not quite clink *comme il faut.* Voss's rivals, who do not write such excellent hexameters, receive this gentle dig:

Tausendmal hab' ich ihn, Sohn, an die Erzuntugend erinnert!
Klappt nicht immer sein Glas wie ein spaltiger Töpf und
  des neuern
Dichterschwarms ungeschliffner Hexameter, welcher daher-
  plumpt
Ohne Takt und Musik, zum Aergernis? Kann er nicht
  anders?

This is the only false note struck in *Luise* and there can hardly be a difference of opinion as to its

insignificance.   Otherwise everything that takes
place is ideal; fortune means good fortune; in so
far as there is feeling it is that of joy.   The author
carries on a bit of coquetry with himself as the poet.
The first is when they sing the new song which "our
friend in Eutin" composed—he was then in Grünau
—a hymn to international brotherhood.   The second is when the wedding song is sung in honor of
Luise and her bridegroom.   It is ascribed expressly
to "our Voss in Eutin."   It is a rather vapid but
well-meant song in praise of marriage.

When Goethe published *Hermann und Dorothea*
two years later, the tendency in many circles, especially in those in which Voss's friends were in the
majority, was to place *Luise* above the new epic
poem.   Goethe's effort was referred to as a relatively weak imitation.   But neither for enlightened
contemporary opinion nor for posterity has there
been the slightest doubt concerning the relative value
of the two works.   Goethe's superiority is incalculable.

If, however, one wishes to get a clear impression
of the reawakening of Greek antiquity, as revived
by Voss, let him compare the *Der Achtzigjährige
Geburtstag,* or his *Luise,* with André Chenier's contemporary revivification of ancient poetry on French
soil.   Such a comparison will enable us to see why
Voss produced the ancient idyll in housecoat and
slippers, fitted it out with pious sentimentality and
gave it spiritual impetus, while Chenier, his junior
by eleven years, born of a Greek mother and permeated with Attic spirit, was throughout free in
mind and sober in the expression of emotions, and
chaste in style even when erotic.   Voss was chaste

even in his handling of his material; his passion is merely the Protestant passion of married life. But in his style he is unchaste. There is not a trace of attempt to govern and control the joy of beauty: it smacks and weeps; it is undisciplined and run-away.

What Goethe did was to bring an anecdote of the year 1734 down to his own time, transfer it from Salzburg to the Rhine, and incidentally make use of the turmoil of the revolution and the general flight of people *en masse* as a background in the portrayal of the fortunes of private individuals. His poem is marked throughout by the finer and grander elements in his own character just as it reveals his plastic conception of men and situations.

Hermann und Dorothea does not belong to Goethe's most interesting works; it has no great inner wealth; it is without the horn of plenty. But it is grand, classical, clear and on a lofty stylistic level. It strikes the chord upon which half a century later Johan Ludwig Runeberg [4] plays both in his compositions in hexameters and in his individual bits of poetry. It is the first real poetic work on the Fatherland that Goethe wrote since *Götz von Berlichingen*. It is artistic and yet quite simple. It

[4] Brandes has reference, it would seem, to Johan Ludvig Runeberg's (1804-1877) *Hanna* (1836), a charming idyl of Finnish life, written in hexameters. Runeberg was recognized, for a while at least, as second only to Tegnér among Swedish poets. Though born in Sweden, he spent his entire life in Finland, where, as a tutor in small Finnish villages, he became familiar with the life of the people, a familiarity which he used to good purpose in his poetry. Though influenced by the Greeks and Goethe, he was of exceptional originality. He did a great deal to link the country of his birth and the country of his adoption together. He lectured for a while at the University of Helsingfors on Roman literature. His romance in verse entitled "Grafven i Perrho" was awarded the gold medal by the Swedish Academy. He founded the Helsingfors *Morgonblad,* which dealt chiefly with æsthetic and literary questions and exerted a marked influence.　　—TRANSLATOR.

idealizes types of German men and women. Though it revolves about the affairs of a small town, it is a stranger to the outstanding faults of Voss's *Luise,* though it is probable that with regard to purity and correctness in versification Voss is superior to Goethe. The latter could occasionally allow a trochee to stand for a spondee or commit other small sins against prosodic perfection.

The great public in as well as out of Germany has had its impression of both Hermann and Dorothea spoiled by Kaulbach's illustrations which, like Cornelius's of *Faust,* either overlook or blur that particular feature which constitutes Goethe's peculiar merit: his measured dignity and spiritual temperance which abhor all that is theatrical and avoid depicted heroism. There is a wholesomeness and simplicity about *Hermann und Dorothea* that render affectation impossible. But how affectedly Faust behaves when, according to Cornelius, he offers his arm to Gretchen! What figures of Teutonic strength Hermann and Dorothea have become at the hands of Kaulbach! They have become supernaturally big and totally unnatural as types.

Goethe's own strength lies in his holding fast to the *modesty of nature,* even where he strives after the typical and representative. We have seen that his men are not always manly; but his women are always womanly. In this case the hero is equipped with an extremely sympathetic, unostentatious manliness, while the heroine makes an even more sympathetic impression, despite her hardy courage that enables her to use a sabre so effectively. But she possesses more penetrating feminine qualities, such as self-sacrificing goodness, easily awakened though earnest affection, and, like the hero, unqualified humanity.

In his ecstatic admiration for ancient literature Goethe amused himself by giving the nine short songs into which he divided his idyllic epic names after the nine books of Herodotus, one for each of the nine muses. And the muses did not fail him.

First and foremost the work has an exceptionally wide horizon. Its very first lines give the reader at once a view out over the fate that has befallen a train of fleeing refugees, out over the Rhine, which, powerful stream that it is, constitutes one of the protective boundaries of Germany designed by nature. These same lines give a view in on the daily life of the little town on the Rhine with its dignitaries, the host and hostess of *Zum goldenen Löwen,* the Pastor, and the Apothecary. In the way of thinking and mode of living of the inn-keeper and his wife we feel that we recognize young Wolfgang's parents: The father domineering and persevering in harmless snobbery; the mother clever and unprejudiced. Each is gifted with a good head and a loving heart. And Hermann has inherited the excellence of both; he is at once sturdy and affectionate. He is also patriotically inspired as no other of Goethe's young heroes; he bewails the fact that, as an only son, he was not called to the colors. He grieves over the fact that Germany is not united and makes this virile speech:

Wahrlich, wäre die kraft der deutschen Jugend beisammen,
An der Grenze verbündet, nicht nachzugeben dem Fremden,
O, sie sollten uns nicht den herrlichen Boden betreten,
Und vor unseren Augen die Früchte des Landes verzehren,
Nicht den Männern gebieten und rauben Weiber und
       Mädchen!

In clear fashion and unmistakable form Dorothea
makes her first appearance before the reader, and
before Hermann as well: She is guiding with her
long staff the oxen before the heavily laden wagon.
We see her walking with stately tread and womanly
bearing; she makes the impression of some lofty,
consoling power. She alone takes charge of the
young mother who lies stretched out on the straw
of the wagon. Dorothea appeals to us as the em-
bodiment of care and unselfish devotion, so much
so and so strongly that we understand quite well
Hermann's involuntary impulse, not merely to surrender to her the linen that the patient needs, but
to entrust her with the distribution of all the food
and drink given him by his mother for the needy
emigrants.

Not a word is used at this first meeting to describe
the girl as beautiful or impressive. Through the
deep impression, however, that she has made upon
the manly youth, and by reason of the ardent desire
he manifests to see her again, and to secure her for
his parent's home, her figure stands out in the reader's imagination as a charming creation, a captivating creature. Her history and her delineation are
put on the lips of the Judge who accompanies the
fleeing band.

Goethe has likewise entrusted to the Judge the
portrayal of the picture of the times. It is the Judge
who says what Goethe has to say regarding the expectations which had been aroused by the outbreak
of the Revolution, and which had so quickly been
brought to naught. The words are at once passionate and poetic:

Denn wer leugnet es wohl, dass hoch sich das Herz ihm
    erhoben,
Ihm die freiere Brust mit reineren Pulsen geschlagen,
Als sich der erste Glanz der neuen Sonne heranhob,
Als man hörte vom Rechte der Menschen, das Allen gemein
    sei,
Von der begeisternden Freiheit und von der löblichen
    Gleichheit. . . .
Schauten nicht alle Völker in jenen drängenden Tagen
Nach der Hauptstadt der Welt, die es schon so lange
    gewesen
    Und jetzt mehr als je den herrlichen Namen verdiente?
Waren nicht jener Männer, der ersten Verkünder der
    Botschaft,
Namen den höchsten gleich, die unter die Sterne gesetzt
    sind?
Wuchs nicht jeglichem Menschen der Muth and der Geist
    und die Sprache?

In this way the Judge shows, in resentful and striking words, how the first joy over liberty and the original faith in popular fraternity was followed by a succession of keen disappointments, one more austere than the other. And through the ingenious argument that a conquering enemy can be noble minded, as in this case it was, but that an army in retreat, in fear of death, filled with lust for murder and pliancy in the exercise of violence, is and remains purely bestial, the transition is made to the portrayal of Dorothea's heroism in her struggle on behalf of the little girls against the plundering and rapacious rabble. We still do not know how she looks; but we do know that she is high spirited.

At last, in the sixth song of the idyl, we have the description of her, set forth in the most natural and clever way. The Apothecary has been looking for the girl among the crowd of fugitives and has

guessed her identity from the old calico and the blue
pillow-slip which she has swathed about the new
born child. Hermann's mother had sent her the
clothing. He next recognizes her red stomacher
which, prettily laced, supports her rounded bosom,
the black bodice and the freshly ruffled frill which
lies gracefully about her chin. Above this he notes
the fine oval of her head and her heavy braids
wound about the silver pin. Though Dorothea is
sitting down, we easily discover the symmetry of her
tall form; and where her skirts stop we perceive
her well shaped ankles. Instinctively and from the
text we feel that her figure is commendable in every
detail.

Here as elsewhere in this genuine masterpiece
the description is revealed in narration. This is
real throughout, and never sentimental, though it
is constantly inspired by emotions; its fundamental
tone is noble. It is real poetry.

It is no wonder that *Hermann und Dorothea*
won the popular favor that was so frequently and
unjustifiably denied Goethe's other works. Here
was not the slightest detail that might give offence
of any kind. Family and fatherland were glorified,
and though every line was written with extreme dignity, nothing was tame or insipid. An unassuming,
everyday theme was treated in a grand and enno-
bling style.

CHAPTER XI

FRIENDSHIP WITH SCHILLER; COLLABORATION ON
Die Xenien—COLLABORATION ON
SCHILLER'S *Balladen*

THE ever-growing friendship with Schiller dominates this period of Goethe's life, though it is well
to remember that it was not a friendship between
equals. The two had a high regard for each other,
but they were what the Romans called *non aequo
foedre amantes*. There was the difference in age
and the difference in rank. They were perhaps
equally drawn to each other, but what Schiller offered was a most zealous incitement to poetic activity, considered by Goethe at the time as highly
encouraging. What Goethe contributed was a
wealth of ideas which suggested their own form,
greatly augmented Schiller's spiritual stock in trade
and determined for the time being his productive
tendency. While Goethe's circumstances had made
him a *grand seigneur,* who worked only when the
spirit moved him, Schiller, by natural inclination
and because of his economic indigence, was a littera-
teur who founded magazines, was supposed to supply
the copy, and pressed both himself and others to
write for them.

This means of producing, under stress and tension, was capital for the hectic, fiery Schiller but

was ill adapted to Goethe's nature, which created when it had to but otherwise lay dormant. In a letter to Wilhelm von Humboldt of 1803, Schiller writes of Goethe: "It is deplorable that he allows the familiar habit to get the upper hand. He busies himself with everything possible but is unable to concentrate himself on some one thing." That is said of Goethe!

We meet, consequently, for the first time in Goethe's works with a conspicuous lack of originality in the contributions which Schiller pressed from him for his magazine, *Die Horen.* Under the collective title of *Unterhaltungen deutscher Ausgewanderter,* Goethe submitted a series of tales that are nothing but a rehash of ghost stories, replete with spiritism and exploiting the worn themes of the creaking desk and the enchanted table. They were taken from mediocre French memoirs. It is all an adventure in rebus style with incomprehensible allegories; and in the execution there is at once irksome garrulity and intolerable diffuseness.

The best of the series, the one on the honorable *Prokurator,* is such a tale as was found amusing in the fifteenth century when *Cent nouvelles nouvelles* were in vogue. They appeal to a contemporary as abounding in questionable taste and brutal psychology. In this particular narrative we have to do with the purely outward preservation of virtue on the part of a woman, though the lady in the case would gladly dispense with it altogether. A lawyer, the procurator, goes to the city where he makes the acquaintance of a young woman whose husband, having set out on a long journey, insists that should she be unable to endure her temporary and enforced

singleness, she is to choose none but older men as
her lovers. She feels a passion for the procurator.
But he, long since past the days of early youth and
immensely demure, leads her to believe that he has
taken a vow that binds him to complete abstinence
for many months. Out of love for him, the young
woman remains chaste during the time of waiting
and the virtuous friend of the family extends the
time until the husband returns home. It is such
episodes that transpired in an age when no appreciable difference was made between a stable and
an alcove. But when published five hundred years
later for the moral, we feel repelled.

The tales are set in a frame from the time of the
Revolution. As in *Das Mädchen von Oberkirch,*
the large family of a Baroness have been obliged
to flee from the left to the right bank of the Rhine
where they associate with a *Geheimrat,* who, after
the fashion of the *Hofrat* in *Die Aufgeregten,* is
scrupulously conservative. He comes to blows, argumentative if not physical, with Carl, the nephew
of the Baroness, who is strongly in favour of the
guillotine and hopes to see it rigidly employed on
German soil. In order to preserve calm, stories
are told. The narrative which closes the series and
which Goethe called *Das Märchen* is held in high
esteem in Germany and is indeed excellently adapted
to German readers in so far as it gives unlimited
opportunity for the development of hermeneutics.
After repeated and diligent readings I must confess my absolute inability to find any meaning in
this exacting and irritating work, written, as it
seems to have been, with the same proneness to give
the reader riddles to solve that prompted Goethe

a little later to write his *Weissagungen des Bakis.*
The purpose of art, however, is not to treat the
reader as a burglar in that the cupboards are so
constructed that no fiend can open them unless he
has a half score of ingenious keys and can insert
them at the right place by means of a magic word
known only to the initiated. It seems probable to
me that *Das Märchen* is built up on symbols of Freemasonry, that the Kings—Wisdom, Strength, Light
—correspond to the lodge expressions Wisdom,
Strength, Beauty, and that the King's initiation corresponds to the liturgy of Freemasonry. I have
read from the interpreters that the work is supposed
to signify some such idea as the victory of culture
over nature as raw material. For my part it is a
matter of indifference as to what it means. It is
not a business of art to create complicated and incomprehensible allegories.

Die Horen was not long lived; it lasted only from
1795 to 1797. Subscribers became fewer and fewer.
The organ had from the very beginning found it
impossible to live up to its name, for according to
its programme it excluded precisely those two topics
that were uppermost in the minds of the people :
religion and politics. A number of its articles
were tiresome, or at least devoid of general interest.
Goethe's contributions could not make good the defects of others. His *Unterhaltungen* did not rise
far above mediocrity. His superb *Römische Elegien* frightened the common bourgeois public, informed as it soon was by the critics that these poems
were immoral. His translation of *Benvenuto Cellini's Life,* a deserving though not perfect work,
called for readers with a yearning sense for the

Italian Renaissance—which was then lacking in the demure German commoner and his wife.

Indefatigable and restless as Schiller was he had, even before *Die Horen* was discontinued, begun a new joint undertaking, the publication of a series of *Musenalmanache*. They continued to appear for six years in succession (1795-1800).

In the year 1796 the *Almanach* brought out Goethe's and Schiller's combined *Xenien* (the Greek word for gifts of the guest), very short poems in hexameters and pentameters in which the allies, according to Schiller's proposal, were to be concerned with everything and everybody that was displeasing to them in the sphere of German letters. The *Xenien* were to be the Doom's Day for contemporary German literature, for magazines, criticisms, publishers, and the public; they were to hurl a mortal blow, a felling shaft against whoever appeared to one of the two great confederates (very frequently to both) as a catch-penny writer, as a perverter of good taste, or a dilettant, or as deceptively bright, or mawkish, or dull, or vain, against anyone who had opposed them, and had made stupid or rancorous attempts upon their work, their souls' redemption.

They opened fire with an attack upon magazines which indeed were truly of no account and stupid, as magazines not seldom are. They ridiculed old-fashioned, honor-crowned poets such as Gleim, Nicolai the Berlin rationalist, hated equally by Goethe and Schiller, adherents to the French Revolution, such as the musician and journalist Reichardt, who had, nevertheless, so long been closely allied to Goethe as the composer of his songs and operettas;

the pious, nonsensical Count Fritz v. Stolberg, who had passed disparaging judgment on Antiquity as heathen. They even extended over the quite young of the rising generation, those who, like Friedrich Schlegel, had glorified Goethe at Schiller's expense. Schlegel incurred this famous Distich:

Was sie gestern gelernt, das wollen sie heute schon lehren,
　　Ach was haben die Herrn doch für ein kurzes Gedärm!

The *Xenien* were to a surprising degree joint productions. The two poets discussed them together, wrote them together. One would produce the idea, the other the form. And yet, for all that, the majority of those concerned succeeded in finding the originator. From a number of them we know definitely by the theme alone who wrote them. There is *à priori* no doubt but that the scientific ones are written by Goethe, the philosophic by Schiller. Moreover, the style of the two poets is so dissimilar that they cannot, as a rule, be mistaken. Each has in this scant form produced a handful of small masterpieces which no one who has read them can ever forget. To be sure, Goethe's are the most copious, but Schiller's are the keenest, the wittiest, and have more marked points. Take, among Schiller's epigrammes, this one on the majority of scholars:

O wie viel neue Feinde der Wahrheit! Mir blutet die Seele,
　　Seh' ich das Eulengeschlecht, das zu dem Lichte sich
　　drängt.

Or its counterpiece on science:

Einem ist sie die hohe, die himmlische Göttin, dem andern
　　Eine tüchtige Kuh, die ihm mit Butter versorgt.

Or the humorous one on learned societies and their members:

Jeder, sieht man ihn einzeln, ist leidlich klug und verständig;
  Sind sie *in corpore,* gleich wird euch ein Dummkopf
    daraus.

Or the deep and witty one on moralizing dolts:

Herzlich ist mir das Laster zuwider, und doppelt zuwider
  Ist mir's, weil es so viel Schwatzen von Tugend gemacht.
"Wie, du hassest die Tugend?"—Ich wollte, wir übten sie
    alle.
  Und so spräche, will's Gott, ferner kein Mensch mehr
    davon.

Nor is it at all difficult to cull out individual epigrammes from among those written by Goethe which rise high up above the personalities and squabbles of everyday life and contain eternal verities. Such, for example, is the one on the investigators who find a reason and aim for everything in nature, and who know full well that the cork tree was created so that bottles could have stoppers:

Welche Verehrung verdient der Weltschöpfer, der gnädig
Als er den Korkbaum schuf, gleich auch die Stöpfel erfand!

Or take this sally created for him who demanded that poetry should have a moral purpose and ethical aim:

"Bessern, bessern soll uns der Dichter." So darf denn auf
    Eurem
  Rücken des Büttels Stock nicht einen Augenblick ruhn?

Now all this is excellent. But the great mass of *Xenien* are not up to this standard. So soon as they become personal—and they do so in many, many places—so soon as they have a distinct address, attack an old newspaper that no man of today ever heard of, or an old magazine which can now be found only in half a score of dusty, muggy copies in German university libraries, or a novel that none of us has ever read or even heard mentioned, or a definite passage in a description of travels by Stolberg that is thoroughly stupid, or a clumsy phrase in the work of a schoolman like Manso, then they are absolutely unreadable and impossible. They are a feast and a festival for Dryasdust, a divine mouthful for commentators who can write a full page on each distich. But what are the rest of us to do with them?

It is difficult in this connection to hold back a heresy to the effect that this entire personal *Xenien-Kampf,* in which Germany's two greatest poets invested so much, was simply wasted trouble and stands as an instructive witness to the tenuous knowledge of men and the enormous naïveté of two prominent writers who always lived in a little provincial town. They imagined in all seriousness that they could overcome mediocrity. It never once occurred to them that mediocrity is omnipotent. They fancied that they could annihilate those they struck in public esteem; of course they only made them doubly popular. They deluded themselves into believing that they who were right by reason of special gifts would receive and enjoy justice from their contemporaries: Schiller was at that time thirty-seven years old, and Goethe was forty-seven.

The protest that was raised against them, the sympathy that was nourished for the attacked, the lampoons that rained down on the heads of those

two demi-gods, and the vats of undiluted dirt that
were emptied on these coryphaei, who believed that
they, like Apollo, could send shafts from the vault
of heaven and each foe would receive his due
amount of mundane punishment, must have taught
them that they had produced no outward effect by
their polemics. The only thing they accomplished
was exercise in the writing of excellent verses of a
certain definite kind for which they no longer had
any use.

Renan would have said concerning them that they
had too much anger and not enough contempt. Or
to be more accurate: It was Schiller, the younger,
the more pugnacious, the genuine *literateur,* who
felt in his element when he wielded blows on journal-
ists and editors; it was Schiller who carried Goethe
along with him, dragged him down from Olympus,
and induced him to beat away at the heads of daub-
ers and smearers. But the whole enterprise was
energy wasted and time lost. The wretched becomes
stronger by being attacked; it thereby comes to believe that it actually is, and is strengthened in its
dangerous belief that it really exists. As Hegel
says: Only the reasonable is real.

In a letter dated November 21, 1795, Goethe expresses to Schiller a touching assurance that it will
be easy to visualize to the reasonable public the
deranged madness of those who are narrow-minded
and stupid on general principles. By declaring war
on half-measures in all domains, Goethe felt they
could put an end to the secret feud that was being
waged against both of them through the exploita-
tion of silence, misinterpretation, and oppression.
Had there been a reasonable public there would

have been no call for these *Xenien;* and the unreasonable saw in them only blotches on the honor of
the two poets.

II

A collaboration of a far more pleasing and fruitful sort between the two friends was that which
was entirely unpolemic. They laid their themes before each other, discussed them together, and then
gave each other mutual criticism while the poem in
question was being worked out. Their collaboration
stretches out over wide fields. It begins with the
writing of a series of ballads during which each
subjects the ballad in question to the judgment of
the other. Whoever wishes to acquire an exhaustive
idea of what Goethe meant to Schiller in this special
domain should take as an illustration Schiller's work
on the beautiful ballad entitled *Die Kraniche des
Ibykus.*

Schiller first brought the theme to Goethe's attention and told him what he wished to make out of
it. On July 19, 1797, Goethe hopes that the *Kraniche* will soon, while on their annual flight, come
near him. On July 21, Schiller is going to try his
fortune with them. Not until August 17 does he
write to Goethe, after some days' work, as follows:

At last you have *Ibykus.* It is to be hoped that you will
be satisfied with it! I must confess that when I actually
began to work on the material I found more difficulties than
I had anticipated. But it seems to me that I have overcome
the majority of them. The two main points upon which
so much depended seem to me to be these: In the first
place, it was necessary to bring real coherence and connection into the narrative which, in truth, the raw fable does
not have. In the second place it was necessary to create a

certain mood so as to bring out the right effect. I simply
could not put the finishing touch to the ballad, when I completed it last evening, and it is a matter of great moment
to me that you read it before I finish it, so that I can avail
myself of your observations.

It turned out that in this form the ballad appealed
to Goethe as being far from perfect; and it is most
captivating to see with what docility and talent Schiller uses every reasonable suggestion that was given
him by his friend. "The raw fable," as Schiller
called the theme, was as follows: Some cranes
that have been witnesses to the fact that two murderers fell upon and killed a travelling poet become
the agents through which the crime was discovered,
in that they reappear over the theatre in which the
poet's drama was being performed, so that the robbers, in superstitious terror, confessed their crime.

Goethe wishes to have the beginning of the ballad thoroughly revised, and one can see that Schiller
added four entire strophes of eight verses each. And
then he wishes to have a strophe added after the
one in which the Erynnies on the stage withdrew.
Schiller acquiesced. Goethe's letter of August 22
shows that he too laid out a plan for a poem on the
same theme. But he gave it up when Schiller finished
his sketch, just about as he gave up the idea of treating the legend of *Wilhelm Tell* as an epic when he
handed over the material to Schiller for dramatic
treatment.

Goethe writes:

Die Kraniche des Ibykus is in my opinion a quite successful bit of work. The transition to the theatre is very beautiful and the chorus of Eumenides is at the right place.
Since this turn has been discovered the entire fable can no

longer be thought of without it, and in case I could find a desire to struggle with the theme, I would likewise be compelled to take up this chorus.

Now a few remarks. (1) The cranes as birds of passage should be an entire flock that fly over Ibykus as well as over the theatre; they come as a natural phenomenon, as much according to law as the sun or other regular changes in nature. In this way the miraculous element will be removed, for they do not need to be the *same* cranes; they are perchance only a part of the great flying flock, and the incidental really constitutes in my estimation the mysterious and odd in the story.

(2) After verse 14, where the erynnies withdraw, I would insert a verse by way of portraying the mood into which the contents of the chorus brings the spectators, and go over from the serious observations of the good to the indifferent diversion of the ruthless, and in this way let the moping murderer come with his exclamation stupid, raw, and high, and yet distinct only to those sitting closest by. Then there should arise a quarrel between him and those around him until the populace become aware of what is taking place, and so on. In this way, as well as in the *flight* of the cranes, everything will be done in a natural fashion and, as I see it, the effect will be increased. As it is now, the 15th verse begins in too high a voice and too significantly; we almost expect something different from what actually takes place. And if you will be a bit more careful here and there with the rhyme, the rest can easily be attended to. I wish you all manner of success with this fortunate work.

In order to obtain more light on the subject, Goethe returned to the ballad the next day. Since Schiller had been so successful with the middle part, Goethe wished to have a few strophes added to the exposition. As he saw the situation, even the wandering Ibykus should catch sight of the cranes; as a traveller he should compare himself with the wandering birds, just as a guest in a foreign land compares himself with the birds that are, as it were, visiting there, and from their flight he should see a good warning for himself and in this way, while in the hands of the murderers, appeal to the cranes as his witnesses. Hereby these birds came to occupy an exceedingly important place and the impression of their being could be fused with the impression of the avenging goddesses in the tragedy. Goethe emphasized the fact that he himself in his own sketch had found nothing more that was useful.

But this was by no means negligible. We see at once how exactly he himself thought the matter over, and how nobly he had left everything to Schiller that had ever occurred to him concerning this idea.

The veracious Schiller answers (August 30) with the confession that he, as a poor observer, knows in reality nothing about cranes except what he has read in a few literary comparisons to which they gave rise. He again avails himself of this opportunity to comment upon the fact that a rich and vivid experience greatly facilitates poetic invention. Then (September 7) he makes clear the points in which he has followed Goethe's suggestions, and those in which this has not been possible. The exposition is now not so thin, the hero of the ballad is more interesting, the cranes fill the imagination of the reader to a much higher degree, and engage his attention so completely that they are not forgotten when they are seen for the second and last time.

On the contrary, Schiller has not been able to see his way clear to have only those sitting nearest hear the exclamation of the murderer and then have the excitement pass gradually over the entire assembly.

That would weaken the general effect and dissipate attention just where the expectations were the most impatient. He has avoided the miraculous entirely, a plan that he had in mind, indeed, when he first worked out his sketch. A natural occurrence was to cause the flock of cranes to fly over the theatre. The drama itself has neither affected nor frightened the rude murderer; but it has reminded him of his crime and in this way he is seized by the sudden appearance of the cranes and involuntarily shrieks out. Since he sits high up in the amphitheatre, where the common people sit, he sees the cranes before they hover over the middle of the theatre. In this way his exclamation precedes the observation of the cranes by the spectators. Moreover, his shriek is heard to a better advantage, in Schiller's opinion, just because his seat is so elevated. The latter is a grave mistake on the part of Schiller, a mistake which he shares, however, with all who build tribunes for speakers. Those who speak or exclaim are never heard to a better advantage than when they are at the very bottom of the amphitheatre.

In the course of time Schiller sends his finished ballad to Böttiger in order to learn from him whether anything in it is contrary to and inconsistent with ancient Greek customs and usages. It seems to me that Böttiger might have remarked that the spectators in the Greek theatre never sat, as they do in Schiller's ballad, close up against each other on the *benches*, but on the steps of the theatre, and that even if there existed supports under the stage that these never could have been just about ready to break down from the weights of the spectators, who

absolutely never squeezed close in around the stage.
But Böttiger found nothing whatsoever that was
at odds with Grecian custom, and since Schiller had
done his best, he was now quite at ease.

The genesis of *Die Kraniche der Ibykus* is a
beautiful example of the artistic seriousness and consciousness with which the two poets worked together
solely and alone for art's sake. There was no
money to be made by writing a ballad, and very
little honor from the writer's contemporaries; and
least of all could the unnamed collaborator expect
any honor or profit therefrom. In this way, however, a short, irreproachable work saw the light
of day, which, like the rest of Schiller's ballads that
live in the consciousness of the German people, is
an eloquent expression of rare heroism or mysterious justice.

CHAPTER XII

GOETHE'S *Balladen*—GOETHE'S SATIRICAL POEMS

THERE is no oratory in Goethe's contemporary ballads. But in the best ones at least, there is something that is far better. In the weaker ones, such as the *Der Schatzgräber,* there is a certain amount of instruction, good suggestion and seasoned advice given impressively, in *sotto voce,* whereas Schiller always speaks in a loud, full tone. *Der Schatzgräber* gives in a subdued tone simple rules of living expressed pithily:

Tages Arbeit, Abends Gäste!
Saure Wochen, frohe Feste!

A masterpiece of technique, and written with a splendid irony which quite controls the graphic power of imagination, is *Der Zauberlehrling,* the story of the venerable wizard's pupil, the dilettant who, the master being absent, wishes to carry on his arts. But he is not able to exorcise or dispel the spirits he himself has conjured up. It is the ballad of all mimicking bunglers. Goethe found the material in Lucian's *The Liar* and has exploited it in a most fascinating manner. It is artistic and it is instructive. Instead of a mortar, which in Lucian is commanded to fetch some water, Goethe has used nothing more pretentious than an old broom, the idea being that this is an object which comes within the immediate activity of all men.

The effect of the shifting verse accent in the al-

ternate strophes is remarkable. It visualizes at
once the witchery and the unrest in the mind of the
apprentice. Content and form are one when, for
example, the boy cries out to the broom:

> Stehe, stehe!
> Denn wir haben
> Deiner Gabe vollgemessen!
> Ach, ich merk' es! Wehe! Wehe!
> Hab' ich doch das Wort vergessen.

The little cycle, *Der Edelknabe und die Müllerin,
Der Junggeselle und der Mühlbach, Der Müllerin
Verrat, Der Müllerin Reue,* is without exception
graceful, erotic, and written in French spirit. *Der
Müllerin Verrat* is Goethe's version of an old
French ditty which he several years later translated
in its entirety for *Wilhelm Meisters Wanderjahre*
(Book I, Chapter 5).

The German poet has appropriated the roguish
frivolity of the French text; in the later translation
the rendering is somewhat heavy as over against the
flippant content. Compare:

En manteau, manteau sans chemise,	Woher der Freund so frü1 und schnelle,
Non que l'ami pût en manquer;	Da kaum der Tag in Osten graut?
C'est que la sienne lui fut prise	Hat er sich in der Waldkapelle,
En lieu charmant à remarquer:	So kalt und frisch es ist, erbaut?
Surpris en cueillant une pomme	Es starret ihm der Bach entgegen;
Pomme de vingt ans au moulin,	Mag er mit Willen barfuss gehn?
On l'avait mis nu comme l'homme	Was flucht er seinen Morgensegen
En le chassant de cet Eden.	Durch die beschneiten wilden Höhn?

From the later translation:

> Gar wunderlich von warmer Stätte,
> Wo er sich bessern Spass versprach,
> Und wenn er nicht den Mantel hätte,
> Wie grässlich wäre seine Schmach!
> So hat ihn jener Schalk betrogen
> Und ihm das Bündel abgepackt;
> Der arme Freund ist ausgezogen,
> Beinah wie Adam bloss und nackt.

It is instructive as furnishing an insight into the nature of the two friends, that, at the same time that Schiller in his ballads was glorifying the haughtiest courage incident to daring deeds (*Der Taucher*), the heroic fidelity that goes through fire and water only to be crucified (*Die Bürgschaft*), chivalry which exposes itself to the talons of lions and tigers but spurns the reward therefor (*Der Handschuh*), shrewdness and heroism coupled with beautiful humility (*Der Kampf mit dem Drachen*), courageousness which effects great achievements and in resignation is content with the sight of the beloved (*Ritter Toggenburg*)—while Schiller was thus engaged, Goethe, by dint of his fondness for the feminine sex, cannot let go of the passionate, returns in these ballads here and there to the rococo tone of his youth, and in the two ballads in which he rises to greatest heights and far above Schiller, is again the eroticist, though in the loftiest and purest style.

Die Braut von Korinth and *Der Gott und die Bajadere,* the two greatest ballads in the German language, were both produced in the first half of the month of June, 1797. After having written them Goethe paid so little attention to them and laid so little stress on them that in a letter to Schil-

ler, June 10, 1797, after both had been finished,
he writes in a purely jesting tone: "Luck to you,
and let your diver be drowned as soon as possible.
It is not bad that just as I have brought my two
pairs into the fire and out of it, you have sought the
opposite element for your hero."

As the main source for the *Die Braut von Korinth,* Goethe availed himself of an anecdote from
a collection of Greek miracles, written by a Lydian
named Flegon, one of Emperor Hadrian's serfs.
This serf published among other things a description of the island of Sicily, and told of Hadrian's
life and exploits. Of his book on miracles a few
fragments are left and among other things one
(unquestionably fictitious) letter from a governor of
a province (procurator) to an official at the imperial
court:

The letter tells how Filinnion, daughter of
Demostratus and Charito, though dead, is secretly
united with Machates, the guest of her family.
The nurse takes them by surprise, sees the young
girl sitting on the young man's couch, calls as loudly
as she possibly can to the parents, and requests them
to get up and see their daughter. Charito is at first
moved; she weeps and declares that the nurse is
beside herself. But finally she goes to the guest
chamber; the couple that have been seen by the
nurse are now sleeping in the dark. She catches
sight of just a few clothes and a profile, and decides
on this account to come again the next morning
and then perhaps take her daughter by surprise.
But when she returns in the morning the young man
is alone. The mother plies him with questions and
in his bewilderment he confesses that Filinnion has

visited him and that the young girl, who longed for
him, had said to him: "I come to you wholly without the knowledge of my parents." As an evidence
he gives Charito a gold ring that he has received
from the young girl and a ribbon that she forgot to
bind about her breast when she left. He is forced
to promise the mother to show her her daughter,
in case she returns. All await her the next night.
She comes to the young man, sits down by his bed,
eats and drinks. He declines entirely to believe that
his friend is dead; he fancies that some one has
robbed the deceased of her garments and jewels and
sold them to the young girl's father. The parents
appear on the scene, recognize Filinnion and, mute
with astonishment, embrace her in this condition.
But she says to them: "O Father and Mother, how
unjustly have you deprived me of the three days
during which I had permission to be in my parents'
house with your guest! You will have occasion to
deplore your curiosity. I return to the place that
has been set aside for me. It is not without the will
of the Divine that I have come here."—And she
falls down to the earth, dead.

The writer of the letter tells that he himself has
had the grave opened, has found it empty except for
an iron ring and a gold beaker, such as Filinnion had
received from Machates on the first night. The
young girl's body lay in the chamber of her parents.
The young man took his life soon thereafter from
grief.

As becomes clear at once, the narrative furnished
Goethe with nothing but the crude material. The
idea contained in the ballad, its protest against the
morals of asceticism, against the placing of the

young girl in the convent, is not found in the narrative; and certainly there is no evidence in it of the wild pathos, the tremendous verve, in which the condition of the soul of the two leading characters is placed. And least of all does the narrative contain the wonderful art with which the strophes are composed in that, as is now more and more frequently the case in Goethe's works, there is the seriousness and calm of dignity in the first half and the fiery haste of passion in the second.

More than ten years previous to this, in 1788, Schiller wrote his *Götter Griechenlands* in which he gave expression to precisely the same mood that here seizes Goethe. In Schiller's poem we read:

> Finstrer Ernst und trauriges Entsagen
> War aus eurem heitern Dienst verbannt,
> Glücklich sollten alle Herzen schlagen,
> Denn Euch war der Glückliche verwandt.
> Damals war nichts heilig als das Schöne . . .
>
> Alle jene Blüthen sind gefallen
> Von des Nordens schauerlichem Wehn!
> Einen zu bereichern unter allen,
> Musste diese Götterwelt vergehn.

We read in Goethe's poem:

> Und der alten Götter bunt Gewimmel
> Hat sogleich das stille Haus geleert.
> Unsichtbar wird Einer nur im Himmel
> Und ein Heiland wird am Kreuz verehrt,
> Opfer fallen hier,
> Weder Lamm noch Stier,
> Aber Menschenopfer unerhört.

Grief over the destruction of the old gods is in Schiller's work as deep and genuine as in Goethe's.

But his poem is a poem of thought, singularly distant from life and reality. Though it praises the world of the senses it contains not the slightest breath of living sensuality. What an unforgetable expression has Goethe, on the contrary, given here to the fiery yearning:

Heftig fasst er sie mit starken Armen
Von der Liebe Jugendkraft durchmannt:
Hoffe doch bei mir noch zu erwarmen,
Wärst du selbst mir aus dem Grab gesandt!
Wechselhauch und Kuss!
Liebesüberfluss!
Brennst du nicht und fühlest mich entbrannt?

Liebe schliesset fester sie zusammen
Thränen mischen sich in ihre Lust;
Gierig saugt sie seines Mundes Flammen
Eins ist nur im Andern sich bewusst . . .

When, at the beginning of the nineteenth century, Wolfgang Menzel led the fashion in German literature and discovered three kinds of personal vanity and six kinds of tendencies toward voluptuousness, he saw in *Die Braut von Korinth* "the expression of that voluptuousness which yearns for the body, which, even in the terrors of the grave, seeks the enjoyment of the taste of putrifaction in love with beautiful apparitions." But even this critic found a public, as this kind of critics always does, which is as imbecile as themselves and which admires them for their "morality."

Die Braut von Korinth is a ballad of twenty-eight stanzas without, however, seeming long. It gives rather the effect, because of its lively tempo and hurried beat, of marked brevity. It is so charming that we read it again and again, so complete a painting, so fiery a lyric, so fresh and clear a sketch of life, that it belongs to the not numerous group of eternal works of art.

A companion piece to this, and of the same rank, is the legend written at the same time, entitled *Der Gott und die Bajadere*. This ballad is shorter and more condensed; it has only nine stanzas. But it too was written for eternity.

Goethe took the material from Sonnerat's *Reise nach Ostindien und China in den Jahren* 1774-1781. But to this no one attaches the slightest bit of importance. He has treated, in an amazing Goethe-like way, a theme which, by its very nature, is purely Schilleresque; he has depicted what Schiller invariably poetized as a matter of preference: Heroism which, inspired and of its own free will, elects a lamentable death. But in Goethe's work it is a woman, not a man as in Schiller's *Der Taucher* or *Die Bürgschaft*, who seeks death. Why? Because of a passionate love which is at the same time the flaming ardor of perception and unconditional submission. If there was one theme ill adapted to Schiller's powers it was a loving dancing girl; if there was anything the portrayal of which seemed intended for Schiller rather than Goethe, it was that enthusiasm which seeks self-destruction and leaps into the flames in order not to survive. But Goethe has conquered the theme; it is Raphael-like; and it is written with matchless ease.

The admirable composition of the stanza is more ingenious than that of the sonnet; it is original, too. It seems as though it were adapted to just this sub-

ject and no other. If there be skeptics, let them
be converted to faith by this:

> Bei der Bahre stürzt sie nieder,
> Ihr Geschrei durchdringt die Luft;
> Meinen Gatten will ich wieder!
> Und ich such' ihn in der Gruft.
> Soll zur Asche mir zerfallen
> Dieser Glieder Götterpracht?
> Mein! er war es, mein vor Allen!
> Ach nur eine süsse Nacht!
> Es singen die Priester: Wir tragen die Alten.
> Nach langem Ermatten und spätem Erkalten,
> Wir tragen die Jugend, noch eh' sie's gedacht.

It has always appeared to me as especially effective that the trochees of the first eight lines have
a pronounced tendency to go over into anapests.
But quite overwhelming is the masterliness whereby
the three concluding lines in these nine strophes alternately relate, dance, paint, explain, kiss, scream,
sound the organ, boom, and fly.

II

Less value attaches to the individual satirical
poems that Goethe wrote at this period: *Musen
und Grazien in der Mark*, and *Der Chinese in Rom*.
The former is a persiflage on one now hopelessly
forgotten Schmidt von Werneuchen; the latter is a
quite witty satire on Jean Paul.

The former is of special interest because it is
one of the countless proofs of the aversion Goethe
felt toward the spirit of Mark Brandenburg—the
spirit of Berlin. Goethe's relation to Prussia was
anything but cordial. Even in *Der ewige Jude* there
is an outcry against the Prussian capital:

Hier ist des Landes Mittelthron.
Gerechtigkeit und Religion
Spedieren wie der Selzerbrunn
Petschirt ihren Einfluss ringsherum.

In *Die Vögel* we have this bit of sarcasm inspired
by reflection on the Prussian eagle:

In the north there now exists the greatest reverence for
the image of the eagle. It can be seen portrayed with well-
nigh perfect ubiquity, and the peoples bow before it even when
merely carved by a bungler or painted by a dabbler. It is
black; there is a crown on its head; it opens its mouth wide;
it sticks out its red tongue; it always displays a pair of ready
claws. No one can feel wholly at ease who looks upon it.

During Goethe's sole and only sojourn in Berlin,
for a few days in May, 1778, in the company of
Karl August, he felt so ill-humored that he could
never be prevailed upon to repeat his visit. He
writes, May 19, 1788, from Berlin to Charlotte von
Stein: "This much I can say: The greater the
world is, the more offensive the farce becomes, and
I can swear that no indecency, no asininity in Jack
Pudding lampoons is so disgusting as the carrying-on
of the great, the half great, and the puny among
each other." His depression of spirits is so lasting
that as late as October 30, 1809, he writes to Zelter:
"I at least still pass my days in Weimar and Jena,
two provincial little towns which God has preserved
thus far, though the noble Prussians have tried to
devastate them in this way and that."

As a result of this aversion to the general spirit
of Berlin we must consider his feud of years standing with Nicolai, who appealed to him as the representative of Berlin. And it is only as a result of
this dislike that we can justify a poet of his rank

in writing polemics against such a poet as **F. W. A. Schmidt.**

Under the title *Musen und Grazien in der Mark* he parodied the *Kalender der Musen und Grazien,* published by the book-dealer C. Spener in Berlin, 1795. This came out as a continuation of the former *Neuer Berliner Musenalmanach,* made public by F. W. A. Schmidt and I. C. Bindemann. Through this effort Goethe brought it about that Pastor Schmidt came to be looked upon in the future as the poet of vulgarity and unjustifiably coarse naturalness—if this can be called a result. As is well known, Goethe's closing statement is often quoted to this very day:

> Wir sind bieder und natürlich,
> Und das ist genug gethan.

But was it worthy of Goethe to attack a tiny, insignificant clerical poet who had never done anyone any real harm, and whose verses moreover are not particularly inferior to those of Goethe's model and master Voss, to which he gave the vote of cordial approval a year later? In 1889, Ludwig Geiger published under the same title as Goethe's famous poem a selection of the verses by Schmidt that had been so ridiculed; it turned out that, in reality, they were no worse than poems frequently are.

Der Chinese in Rom, the satire on Jean Paul, is a half-score lines in distich form which Goethe wrote out of irritation over an expression which he considered arrogant, and which had been used by Richter in a personal letter to Knebel. The Chinese finds all the buildings in Rome heavy and squat. He had expected to find small columns of wood, carved work and gildings. Goethe adds, in a rather prosaic way, that it is possible to see in this incident the symbol of many an ultra-enthusiast who compares his aerial chimeras with the eternal coverings of solid nature and calls the healthy sick in order that he may logically ascribe health to his own diseased being.

Poor Jean Paul was not responsible for the fact that he was portrayed as a sort of anti-Pope to Goethe by the people who hated the latter even more than they loved the former. By his writings he had made friends and patrons in Weimar. Wieland regarded him highly and called him the German Yorick and the German Rabelais. The comparison with Sterne has more reason and foundation than that with the great French monk and physician.

Herder commended Jean Paul. For Knebel and Einsiedel his books were favorite reading. Charlotte von Kalb, left in the lurch by Schiller, wrote to him with glowing enthusiasm and had him visit her in Weimar (1796). Hardly had he arrived in June, when he felt an overwhelming fascination in her presence. Since Charlotte stood close to Herder, it followed as a matter of course that Jean Paul associated intimately with the latter. If only for this reason, Schiller and Goethe received the new-comer coolly. For Herder and Wieland formed at this time, in the castle of the Dowager Duchess, a sort of secondary court to that of Karl August's, where people were busied conversationally with heaping abuse upon Goethe and Schiller. Because of jealousy at the friendship between the two, Herder had become exceedingly bitter.

Quite apart, however, from this personal rela-

tion, it was wholly impossible for such a styleless
penman as Jean Paul to stand before the tribunal
of the *Dioscuri*. The mere fact that he larded his
novels with detached ideas and paradoxical figures
which he had jotted down in notebooks for future
use could not fail to have a terrifying effect upon
them. For real antipathy on the part of Goethe
though there was no ground. And the cordiality
in Jean Paul's mind was deserving of a measure of
kindliness and praise from the two noted writers.
Ludwig Börne wrote correctly concerning Jean Paul
on the occasion of his death: "In the countries one
counts only the cities; in the cities only the temples
and towers and palaces; in the houses their masters;
in the various peoples their leaders. . . . Jean Paul
went out into the narrower, more obscure ways and
sought out the town that had been neglected.
Among the peoples he counted the human beings.
In the towns he counted the roofs, and under each
roof the hearts."

But it was not merely Jean Paul's formlessness
that irritated Goethe. It was his indistinct political
liberality and his excessive faith in the rapidity of
political progress that made Goethe tired of his personality and impatient with his art.

CHAPTER XIII

GOETHE'S COMPOSITIONS IN PROSE TO CHRISTIANE:
Pausias; Amyntas; DISTICHS—GOETHE
AND HOMER: *Achilleis*

IT is quite within reason to believe that Goethe
had Christiane in mind when he wrote *Der Gott und
die Bajadere.* The rejection the dancing girl suffers in being relegated to the dead, unmarried to
her dead god, the words, "Nur die *Gattin* folgt dem
Gatten," draw the attention of the reader to her.
Goethe wrote at the same time, in the same metre
as *Der Chinese in Rom,* an entire series of short
poems, all of which owe their origin to his happy
domestic life with Christiane.

In *Der neue Pausias und sein Blumenmädchen* he
transferred the scene to ancient Hellas and prefaced
it with a quotation from Pliny in order to conceal
the otherwise patent allusion to the fact that she had
been employed in a flower factory. The quotation
from Pliny runs as follows: "Pausias of Sicyon, the
painter, had fallen in love, as a young man, with
his fellow townswoman, Glycere, who had great
inventiveness in the binding of flower wreaths. They
emulated each other; he became a master at imitation. Finally he painted his beloved, sitting, busied
with a wreath." In the form of a dialogue the first
acquaintance of the two is glorified and her unassuming skill is praised as a talent "at poetizing and
painting with flowers." The way in which they

became acquainted is remodelled; and a contest is added during which Pausias protects the girl from an importunate lout, wins in this way her gratitude and finally her herself.

The sight of an apple tree surrounded by ivy, which Goethe saw on his third journey to Switzerland in September, 1797, gave rise to the poem *Amyntas*. It reminded him of the way in which Christiane had become entwined about his life and was drawing nourishment from him, though she had become indispensable to him. Amyntas addresses this poem to his physician Nikias (the eleventh idyl of Theocritus is addressed to a physician of this name). We understand that Nikias has requested Amyntas to practice abstinence and temperance in the presence of his sweetheart, since their living together has had the harmful consequences that he no longer has the slightest bit of energy left for mental work. But he beseeches the physician not to enforce such a stern and rigid cure upon him and compares himself with the apple tree, which begged that the ivy might be retained when the people began to take it away piece by piece:

Nahrung nimmt sie von mir; was ich bedürfte, geniesst sie;
  Und so saugt die das Mark, sauget die Seele mir aus.
Nur vergebens nähr' ich mich noch; die gewaltige Wurzel
  Sendet lebendigen Safts ach nur die Hälfte hinauf. . . .
Nichts gelangt zur Krone hinauf, die äussersten Wipfel
  Dorren, es dorret der Ast über dem Bache schon hin
Ja die Verrätherin ist's! sie schmeichelt mir Leben und
    Güter,
  Schmeichelt die strebende Kraft, schmeichelt die Hoffnung
    mir ab . . .
Süss ist jede Verschwendung; o lass mich der schönsten
    geniessen!
  Wer sich der Liebe vertraut, hält er sein Leben zu Rath?

The thirty-seven distichs printed under the rubric *Sommer* in the little collection entitled *Vier Jahreszeiten* also revolve around Christiane. But the tone is fresher; and the method of presentation is less painful. In one single distich Goethe lays bare the entire secret of his relation to Christiane:

Neigung besiegen ist schwer; gesellet sich aber Gewohnheit
    Wurzelnd, allmählich zu ihr, unüberwindlich ist sie.

The majority of these poems treat such themes as joy over lines discovered in his sweetheart's hands, embraces, kisses, and passion in general. A few of them are serious in tone; two of them are especially so. The first betrays Goethe's occasional doubt as to her fidelity; but it praises at the same time the deep significance of the illusion:

Sie entzückt mich, und täuscht mich vielleicht. O Dichter
    und Sänger,
Mimen! lerntet Ihr doch meiner Geliebten was ab!

The second affords consolation for the mutability of beauty by emphasizing the beauty of what is past and gone:

Warum bin ich vergänglich, o Zeus? So fragte die Schön-
    heit.
  Macht ich doch, sagte der Gott, nur das Vergängliche
    schön.

The charming elegy entitled *Metamorphose der Pflanzen* is also addressed to Christiane. In it he attempts to explain to her in the simplest way possible his fundamental idea concerning the development and metamorphosis of the plant; he closes with a personal reference to her and her only. The change of form in the plant is conceived of as sym-

bolic of the growth and change in their love for
each other:

O gedenke denn auch, wie aus dem Keim der Bekanntschaft
 Nach und nach in uns holde Gewohnheit entspross,
Freundschaft sich mit Macht in unserm Innern enthüllte,
 Und wie Amor zuletzt Blüthen und Früchte gezeugt.

It cannot be denied that Christiane's humble
character has been accorded signal honor in Goethe's poems along with the more brilliant and refined women who aroused his passion and enjoyed
his homage.

II

During these years Goethe became more and
more interested in Hellenism. Just as ten years
later Thorvaldsen found it impossible to conceive
of art in any other form than Grecian, and persisted
in making his costumes Greek even though his
themes were modern, just so did Goethe now strive
to write and feel after the fashion and in the spirit
of the Hellenists of olden times. He was unmindful and unaware of the self-contradictory element
in this method of procedure. The Homeric poets,
as all the world must know, never tried to write
precisely as men had felt and written three thousand
years previous to their day.

The factor in Goethe's young days that drew him
to Homer was the straightforward naturalness he
at that time fancied he had found in him. Now,
after his journey to Italy and his association with
Schiller, he detected in the Homeric poems the ultimate laws for the art of poetic portrayal. Up to
this time he had lacked the courage to compete with
Homer. But when F. A. Wolf published his *Prole-*

gomena (1795), which essayed to do away with the
unity in the *Iliad* and the *Odyssey,* and to divide
them into a number of different rhapsodies, and
after Goethe's initial objection to the idea had been
overcome, he no longer found it presumptuous to
vie with the individual Homeric songs. In his elegy
Hermann und Dorothea he paid his homage to
Wolf, and referred to himself as the last of the
Homerides:

Erst die Gesundheit des Mannes, der endlich vom Namen
  Homeros
 Kühn uns befreiend uns auch ruft in die vollere Bahn!
Denn wer wagte mit Göttern den Kampf? und wer mit dem
  Einen?
 Doch Homeride zu sein, auch nur als letzter, ist schön.

At the close of December, 1797, Goethe made a
diligent study of the *Iliad,* for it seemed to him that
between it and the *Odyssey* there still remained sufficient room for an epic poem; and the temptation
to write such a poem was all but irresistible. It
should be done quite in the spirit of the *Iliad.* However unimportant Jean Paul Friedrich Richter may
be when compared with Goethe, it was after all more
natural to write *Leben, Tod und Ehestand des
Armenadvokaten Siebenkäs* (the humorous history
of a mendicant advocate from Jean Paul's own time,
who becomes a bigamist after he has pretended to
be dead in order to rid himself of his wife) than
to try to write a poem "quite in the spirit of the
Iliad."

From a number of Goethe's individual remarks
we can at least derive a general idea as to how his
epic on the death of Achilles was to take shape.
Achilles knows that his death is imminent, but he

falls in love with the Trojan Princess Polyxena, and
because of his great love for her forgets his fate.
But we no longer know whether, according to Goethe's plan, Achilles was to find love in return and
endeavor to escape the death that had been prophe-
sied for him before Troy by fleeing with Polyxena,
who would then take her life from grief over his
death, or whether Polyxena was to leave Achilles's
love unrequited and betray him to the Trojans,
whereupon he would fall a prey to the arrow of
Paris.

In vain did Schiller give Goethe the wholesome
advice not to take Homer as his model at all but to
mould the material wholly in accordance with his
own nature. Goethe strove—partly by the use of
Homeric adjectives—to come as near as possible
to the Greek poetry of olden times. Finally, after
long hesitation, he began the work. He finished
only the first canto of *Achilleis*. This was written
in March and April, 1799. He never touched the
theme again.

This first canto shows, in the introduction, how
Achilles had had an enormous burial mound erected
on the sea-coast for himself and his friend Patroc-
lus, whose body the falling flames have just consumed. Then we are led to the mansions of the
gods where Hera derides her son Hephaistos for the
industry he has used on the weapons of Achilles,
since the death of the latter is a question of only
a few days. When Thetis makes known her agony
arising from the fate that is quickly to befall her
son, Hera overwhelms the mother with scorn and
jealous hatred because of the passion she has awakened in the heart of Zeus. When the latter speaks

a few words of reconciliation, Hera begans a positive quarrel. But Pallas Athene appears on the scene, speaks to the goddess, and confesses that none of the heroes of either the past or the present have been so dear to her as Achilles. This comes as a slight surprise, since we have believed up to this point that Odysseus was her favorite. It is a matter of great grief to Pallas that Achilles is to die so young:

Ach, und dass er sich nicht, der edle Jüngling, zum Mauine
Bilden soll! Ein fürstlicher Mann ist so nöthig auf Erden.

When Achilles stands in the depth of the grave, as though at the bottom of a beaker, while the Myrmidons heap up the earth all round about, Pallas, in the form of Achilles's friend Antilochus, accosts him and begins a cordial conversation in order to encourage him to look upon his fate through eyes that know not despair. Achilles declares modestly and composedly that at some time in the future many passers-by will look upon this mound and say: "There lies buried by no means the least worthy of the Achaeans." Pallas replies with enthusiasm:

"Nein, so redet er nicht," versetzte heftig die Göttin;
"Sehet," ruft er entzückt, von fern den Gipfel erblickend,
"Dort ist das herrliche Mal des einzigen grossen Peliden
Den so früh der Erde der Moiren Willkür entrissen."

She felicitates him most heartily on the prospect of an early death:

Ja, soweit nur der Tag und die Nacht reicht, siehe verbreitet
Sich dein herrlicher Ruhm, und alle Völker verehren
Deine treffende Wahl des kurzen rühmlichen Lebens.
Köstliches hast Du erwählt. Wer jung die Erde verlassen
Wandelt auch ewig jung im Reiche Persephoneia's,
Ewig erscheint er jung den Künftigen, ewig ersehnet.

Athene returns again to her consolatory remarks, saying that the name of Achilles will sound forever from the lips of singers; his renown will become so great that that of other brave men will fade in comparison with his. It is then that Achilles praises friendship as the chief gratification of brave men; and in the expressions he uses it is—it seems to me —clear that Goethe had Schiller in mind and the joy he experienced from the hand clasp of his friend, now that the *Xenien* struggle is over. Achilles says:

Denn mir ward auf der Erd nichts Köstlichers jemals
    gegeben
Als wenn mir Ajax die Hand, der Telamonier, schüttelt,
Abends nach geendigter Schlacht und gewaltiger Mühe
Sich des Siegs erfreuend und niedergemordeter Feinde.

So far as the metrical form, the versification in general, is concerned, the entire work is quite worthy of Goethe. But how little within the range of the great German poet this ancient meter in reality lay is shown by an individual hexameter so awful as this one:

Wilder Amazonen zum Todeskampfe heranführst.

Much ado has been made of the fact that in *Hermann und Dorothea* Goethe had originally rendered the following verse quite unrhythmical by the insertion of the redundant *und*:

Ungerecht bleiben die Männer, *und* die Zeiten der Liebe
vergehen.

And time out of mind the amusing answer has been quoted which Goethe gave to the younger Voss when the latter drew his attention to the error: "Let the seven-footed beast stand!" Later, however, he deleted the impossible *und*. But this carelessness is so trifling when compared with the striking lack of sense for the harmony of verse which is brought to light when *Amazonen* has to be pronounced with two false accents: one on *ma* and one on *nen*. This is necessary in order to arrive at anything that even faintly resembles a real hexameter.

CHAPTER XIV

GOETHE'S STUDIES IN OPTICS: BROODINGS OVER THE NATURE OF COLORS; GOETHE AND NEWTON—*Die Farbenlehre:* ITS ADHERENTS AND OPPONENTS

THROUGHOUT all the years that Goethe and Schiller lived in such close spiritual communion, the former was always engaged in experiments relating to the nature of colors; he brooded over the subject well nigh without interruption. Goethe went through life with his eyes open. He was ever interested in the weather; he studied its changes, and made observations concerning them. He gave long and reasoned attention to the formation of clouds. The world of color became for him, consequently, one in which he felt at ease. It had been his wont to pass in and out of the homes of artists. He himself had sketched and painted. In Italy he had buried himself in the study of ancient and modern art. And, as he remarks in §4 of his first *Beiträge zur Optik,* Italy's natural scenery had disclosed to his eyes a "fairy-like" harmony of colors.

Even as a young student in Leipzig, he had been a witness to Winckler's optical experiments that were undertaken in sympathy with Newton's teachings.

178

In Italy he had studied the technical side of the
art of painting. He had questioned painters as to
whether they knew of any guiding principle concerning coloring. They shook their heads. At his
request Angelica Kauffmann had made experiments
in colors, had painted a picture gray in gray, and
then tinted it with a slight superficial coloring; she
had also painted a landscape in which all the blue
colors were wanting. Color phenomena in the sky
had interested him at the same time: green shadows
at purple red sunsets, the bluish tinge of distant
mountains.

When Goethe returned to Weimar, he borrowed
Büttner's excellent set of optical instruments. Büttner had just moved from Göttingen to Jena. Goethe wanted them in order to make some experiments.
But as usual he had a great many other schemes on
hand just then, and the prisms lay untouched for
some time. Büttner became impatient and asked
that they be returned. At last he sent a messenger
to Weimar to get them. Goethe cast one final look
through the prism. It became an epoch-making
moment in his life. He knew that white light should
be broken and scattered into colors when seen
through a prism. He expected consequently to see
the white wall of his room taking on colors of the
rainbow; but to his surprise it remained white; only
where some dark object made a line on the wall
was he able to detect more or less distinct colors,
and at last the cross piece in the window frame was
seen to be brightly colored, while there was no trace
of color visible in the light gray sky. Without much
reflection—presumably as a result of intuition—he
found that a boundary was necessary to produce

colors, and "an instinct" induced him to say aloud to himself that Newton's theory was false.

This among other things shows that instinct, which at the beginning of the twentieth century has again been praised so loudly and unreasonably as a scientific guide, can become, even in the case of the most excellent of men, a quite misleading power. What Goethe saw, coincided entirely with Newton's theory. Newton had never denied that colors seen through a prism are visible only when and where the light and the dark delimit each other; but he had combatted the idea that this mutual delimiting of the light and the dark produced colors; and he had ascribed to the boundary line a value only as a condition which brings it about that the picture of the color becomes visible.

Every physicist of Newton's day had learned from him that from the white wall, which Goethe saw, there proceeded rays of just as many types of light as there are degrees in the refraction. The rays that are more strongly refracted at one point are crossed by those that are less strongly refracted at another point, and from their infringing upon each other in this way white is produced. Only on the edges did the partly less refracted partly more refracted types of light become disclosed, and consequently the one edge had to appear yellow red, the other blue violet, while the middle was and remained white.

Goethe, who believed that the truth had all of a sudden been revealed to him, and that by virtue of his talent as a seer he had made a discovery in the science of optics just as he had formely made scientific discoveries in the fields of anatomy, geology,

and botany, requested Büttner to allow him to keep
the prisms. In 1790 he began to make a serious
study of optics and to carry on a number of optical
experiments. He became more and more convinced
that Newton's theories concerning light were false.
That he could not persuade any of the physicists of
his day to share his conviction deterred him in no
way. He had become accustomed to having natural
scientists completely underestimate at first every ingenious hypothesis he proposed.

It is here that we detect one of those misfortunes
which arises from the fact that professional men are
not infrequently irresponsive to and unappreciative
of new finds. It not simply strengthens the pachy-
dermic characteristics of the masses and gives food
to their prejudices; it also fills him who has been
the victim of such refractoriness with so great a
contempt for men that he does not, even when he
is on the wrong road, pay the slightest attention to
the criticism of his colleagues. It makes the same
impression on him that the shepherd boy's cry made
in the fable: He was not believed when the wolf
really came.

In his feeling for unity and belief in wholeness,
Goethe felt himself blocked by the theory of Newton
according to which white light is a composition and
colors, consequently, take their origin from light.
He was able only for a short while to adhere to
the Wolfian conception of the *Iliad* and the *Odyssey*
as consisting of individual rhapsodies; he soon returned to the belief that Homer was an individual.
Of the *Xenien* we have this one against Newton:

Spaltet immer das Licht! Wie öfters strebt Ihr zu trennen,
Was, Euch Allen zum Trutz, Eins und ein Einziges ist.

And this one:

Welch erhabner Gedanke!   Uns lehrt der unsterbliche
    Meister,
Künstlich zu theilen den Strahl, den wir nur einfach gekannt.

There is an exact connection between these *Xenien* and this epigramme against Wolf:

Scharfsinnig habt Ihr, wie Ihr seid,
    Von aller Verehrung uns befreit,
    Und wir bekannten überfrei,
    Das Ilias nur ein Flickwerk sei.

Mög unser Abfall Niemand kränken!
    Denn Jugend weiss und zu entzünden,
    Dass wir ihn lieber als Ganzes denken,
    Als ganzes freudig ihn empfinden,

Wolf, however, was no less right than Newton. Goethe's point of departure was the circumstance that for a painting light and shade are two equally justifiable forces upon the correct distribution of which rests the illusion which is to be evoked. It is also on this distribution that the general color scheme depends. Since the painter cannot possibly reproduce sunlight with all its intensity, his task consists in the reproduction of differences of light and varying degrees of clarity. Since on the light side yellow and yellow-red predominate, just as on the dark side blue and blue-red, Goethe found that to the contrast between light and shade the contrast between warm and cold colors corresponded. Yellow and blue became for him what he calls polar contrasts. It is to be presumed that he had observed in Italy a kinship between blue and black, between blue and shade. In this way he was prepared, as a result of his studies in art, to proceed with the unscientific assumption that colors arose through the interaction of light and dark, of the light and the non-light. He saw of course that every color is darker than white, and he consequently called the colors for half light half shade, and ascribed to them all something of the characteristics of shade.

Johannes Müller, one of the greatest physicists of that time, indeed of all times, a physicist who owed an incalculable debt to Goethe even with regard to his work on optics, could not help but reject Goethe's views as to the origin of colors for the very simple reason that neither shade nor dark is anything positive. "Dark," he says in his manual on human physiology, "is physiologically only a part of the eye where the retina is perceived in a condition of rest."

While in Italy Goethe had made searching studies in aërial perspective, that is to say, in the artistic reproduction of air light, in so far as this, entirely according to the degree of opacity of the air, manifests various gradations and receives things to be revealed in finely shaded tones. "Aërial perspective, (says Goethe in his *Italienische Reise*) really rests on the important thesis that all transparent media are to a certain degree murky. The atmosphere is always more or less non-transparent, especially in the South with its high barometer, dry weather, and cloudless sky, since one can there observe a very perceptible gradation of objects that are but a slight distance from each other."

In this way Goethe approached the *Urphänomen* upon which he rests his arguments in optics, just as he rested on the *Urpflanze* in morphology.

It was a question with him of finding the origin

of colors after he had rejected Newton's theory
which deduced them from light. Since he manoeu-
vred about with the concepts light and dark, white
and black, and since with the weakening of the light
and the darkening of the white, there can arise only
shades and gray, he found the especial cause that
produces colors in *the unclear media (die trüben
Mittel)*.

He had observed that when the dark was seen
through an indistinct medium that was lighted by
having light fall on it, a blue color arose which became more and more light and pale the darker the
medium became; and it became darker and more
subdued the more transparent the dark medium became until the color finally passed over into the most
beautiful violet. He had noticed that if one looked
through an indistinct medium at a clear, colorless
light, this appeared yellow and with increasing indistinctness in the medium it went over to yellow-
red or ruby-red.

This revelation of colors through media that are
not entirely transparent, Goethe calls the *Urphänomen,* which neither necessitates nor permits further explanation. This *Urphänomen* is the corner-
stone of his doctrine.

Physicists could, however, at once prove that the
Urphänomen by no means encompassed all cases
that might arise. The sun, for example, often appears silver white, when it stands high in the heavens
and is seen through a stratum of clouds or through
a bit of colored glass or dark gauze. According
to Goethe's theory it should appear yellow. Likewise the color of the sky when seen from a high
mountain appears blue. When the air, however,

so high up becomes more and more pure and less
opaque, it should, according to his theory, appear
violet. All this, which was easily and fully explained
according to Newton's theory, was inexplicable according to Goethe's.

Likewise with regard to the completing colors,
Goethe, as an artist and a lover of art, allowed himself to be led, through his experiences, into a false
theory. When the painter mixes blue and yellow, he
gets green; there is no doubt about that; but not by
a mixture of spectral colors. According to Goethe,
green originates in the spectrum only when the yellow edge approaches the blue, a situation that was
supposed to be brought about by removing the
screen a sufficient distance from the prism. But
those colors give in truth green only when they are
themselves greenish. It is impossible to compound
green from plain yellow and blue in the prism.

A fundamental question in Newton's optics was
this: Can the individual colored parts of the spectrum be separated from each other? He found the
solution of this question in the experiments in which
he applied at once prisms and lenses. But in every
case in which Newton in his experiments unites
prisms and lenses, Goethe refers to the second, sup-
plementary part of his *Farbenlehre* which, as is
known, never appeared.

Goethe had ordered Newton's works as early as
1790; he gradually tried all of his experiments.
They seemed to him, judged *à priori,* artificially
done and complicated so as to conceal the real state
of affairs. He wanted to perform for his own good
the simple, basic experiments. His *Beiträge zur
Optik* was published in 1791. *Erstes Stück* was ac-

companied with illustrations. *Zweites Stück*, with new copper plates, came out in 1792. Later he wrote his *Versuch, die Elemente der Farbenlehre zu entdecken,* without publishing it. And on this he worked year after year, heaped up and arranged an enormous mass of material, the largest he ever collected in his life, until finally, in 1810, he published his work entitled *Zur Farbenlehre,* in two large volumes, with a number of appended drawings. The first volume is in two parts, one of an argumentative, one of a polemic nature directed against Newton's optics. Of the second volume only the first and exceedingly valuable part, *Geschichte der Farbenlehre,* came out. To this we will return subsequently. From this time on there followed a complete series of supplements to the theory of colors, the most voluminous bit of writing that Goethe ever produced.

No one will regret, if only for the sake of the language, the reading of the contributions to optics from the year 1791. The description is of classic clarity, as beautiful as a beautiful poem. There is in it the love of a great poet and a great naturalist for nature, love for every rare phenomenon in nature and for its common occurrences as well, at least for those he had observed. In the very introduction, however, we scent his opposition to Newton, an opposition which amounted to a passion as the years passed by and recognition was not forthcoming.

In the *Xenien* of 1797, Goethe directs attack upon attack against Newton, just as though he were some mediocre poet or miserable magazine publisher of that time and not the scientific genius upon the results of whose investigations all modern culture, down to Einstein, is constructed.

From the score of epigrammes against him we quote a few. They betray the severity and certainty of victory on the part of the misguided Goethe.

Liegt der Irrthum nur erst wie ein Grundstein unten im Boden,
  Immer baut man derauf, nimmermehr kömmt er an Tag.

Hundertmal werd ich's Euch sagen und tausendmal: Irrthum ist Irrthum
  Ob ihn der grösste Mann, ob ihn der kleinste beging.

"Newton hat sich geirrt?"—Ja, doppelt und dreifach.— "Und wie denn?"
  Lange steht es gedruckt; aber es liest es kein Mensch.

Leidlich hat Newton gesehen und falsch geschlossen; am Ende
  Blieb er ein Brite; verstockt schloss er, bewies es so fort.

Das ist ein pfäffischer Einfall! Denn lange spaltet die Kirche
  Ihren Gott sich in Drei, wie Ihr in sieben das Licht.

As we see, Goethe in his combative zeal goes so far as to see a parallel between Newton's theory concerning the refraction of light into colors and the dogma of the Trinity which he so detested.

Like all of his contemporaries, with the exception of Kant, Goethe speaks of colors as a phenomenon of nature which is independent of the sense of light. He came very near to the conception that light and color are only our impressions, but he never drew the logical conclusion therefrom.

When he appropriated Plotinus's mystic view in the above quoted verses,

      Wär nicht das Auge sonnenhaft,
      Die Sonne könnt' es nie erblicken,

he thought that there was, so to speak, a light dwelling in the eye.   Since the various beings must be
homogeneous in order for the one to be susceptible
to the other, he avers that the eye is trained for the
light by the light within it.   What we term light
perceptions were to him a relation between something tangible within us and something tangible
without us, between something undivided within us
and something undivided without us.   Goethe, who
had made such splendid progress in other domains
through the use of his two open eyes, had a violent
aversion to the *camera obscura*.   He even accused
Newton of falsification because the latter, in his
experiments in the dark room, spoke of rays when
in truth images appeared which were changed by the
refraction of light.   He would not even concede
the significance of the Frauenhofer lines in the sun
spectrum, because they showed only when the light
was allowed to fall through a crevice.   The decom-
position of light, like the subdividing of Homer,
was to him a species of vivisection, and filled him
with the same repulsion which vivisection inspires in
every layman.

One of his apothegms in prose (No. 864) reads:

Man in and of himself, insofar as and provided he uses
his sound senses, is the greatest and most accurate physical
apparatus there can be; and it is indeed the greatest misfortune of modern physics that it has, as it were, isolated experiments from man and shows a willingness to recognize nature
only as it is manifested through artificial instruments.

He writes:

> Freunde, flieht die dunkle Kammer,
> Wo man Euch das Licht verzwickt
> Und in kümmerlichem Jammer

Sich verschroben Bildern blickt.
Abergläubische Verehrer
Gab's die Jahre her genug.
In den Köpfen Eurer Lehrer
Lasst Gespenst und Wahn und Trug!

II

In the beautiful section entitled *Konfession des Verfassers,* with which the *Farbenlehre* closes, Goethe expresses his gratitude to those individuals who by their good-will and loyalty have assisted him in his investigations. There is the Duke of Weimar to whom he is indebted in general for the conditions that have made an active and satisfying life possible, and who gave him a place in which to work, and freedom so that he might work. Duke Ernst of Gotha opened to him his physical cabinet, whereby Goethe was enabled to repeat his experiments and carry them out on a large scale. Prince August of Gotha made him a present of some simple as well as some compound prisms, imported from England. Prince Primas of Dalberg gave his experiments unbroken attention; he even supplied some of his treatises with marginal notes in his own handwriting. Among the scholars, there are anatomists and men of letters and philosophers—but not one single physicist.

With Lichtenberg, the physicist and witty satirist, he corresponded for a while, but when Goethe became urgent and tried to secure Lichtenberg's agreement and "vehemently followed up the disgusting Newtonian white," Lichtenberg broke off the correspondence and left the letters unanswered. His friend Heinrich Meyer (the Swiss painter) on the

contrary, to whom he was also indebted for instruction along other lines, collaborated with him and
helped him in a goodly number of his experiments
by making drawings in color. And at last Goethe
mentions with effusive cordiality, among the men
who have helped him spiritually, his "irreplaceable
Schiller." He writes:

Owing to the great naturalness of his genius, Schiller not
only grasped the main points with marked rapidity, the
points upon which everything depended, but he also, owing
to his reflective power, urged me to hasten on to the goal
toward which I was striving.

It leaves a melancholy impression to see the
Farbenlehre close with gratitude to a number of
princely gentlemen who placed assistance of one sort
and another at Goethe's disposal, and to a number
of men who were laymen and laymen only, such as
Meyer and Schiller, men who held up his courage
by their friendship after he, through his stubborn-
ness, had repelled all the real physicists of his age.
Meyer's participation was naturally concerned
only with the artistic, just as Schiller's had to do
with the cultural in general in Goethe's optical investigations. But it is to the sympathy of these
two men, and of these two alone, to which Goethe
clings while carrying out his work. On January 24,
1798, he writes to Schiller:

Not until I firmly determined to consult you and Meyer
and no one else did I again feel joy and courage; for the
repeated frustration of hope that others are going to help
and coöperate always sets one back somewhat.

This unquestionably explains the fact that after
Schiller's death his joy in the theory of colors for-

sook him. In a conversation with Eckermann he said:

The delusions and errors of my opponents have been too widespread during the past century for me to hope to find a companion on my lonely way at this late day! I shall remain alone! I seem like a shipwrecked individual who clings to a board that is large enough for one and no more.

In the year 1798 he writes hardly a single letter to Schiller in which he does not speak of his theory of colors. In one dated February 14, he gives Schiller for the first time his famous division of colors into three classes: the physiological, the physical, and the chemical. The physiological are determined by the condition and activity of our eye. The physical arise from the influence of the rays of light and the waves of ether, and are therefore prismatic colors. The chemical are the colors of bodies, stones, walls, clothes, and so on.

It was a great scientific achievement for those days to place physiological colors first, and to characterize them as the foundation of this teaching. That part of Goethe's *Farbenlehre* which portrays the physiological colors was, on this account, epoch-making. He became one of the founders of physiological optics, just as he had been one of the originators of philosophic botany and osteology. Hence we can say that his genius forsook him, in reality, not even in this much contested domain.

His chief merit lies in the fact that he was one of the very first to become attentive to and mindful of the phenomena of sight in their scientific sequence, and to elaborate these phenomena in a model fashion. The section on physiological colors is regarded as a classic. Physicists of our own day ascribe also

to other parts real importance, because of the accuracy with which Goethe has told of his various
experiments.

The phenomenon of colors, which had hitherto
been regarded as accidental, delusive, or morbid,
Goethe traced back to the healthy sight concerning
the characteristics of which we never received anything reliable until color phenomena had been studied, and the real relation of the eye to them had
been investigated. For Goethe, hallucinations, so-
called sense deceptions, are optical truths. He says
it is blasphemy to speak of an "optical delusion."
He contends, as we all do nowadays, that we study
the normal activity of the eye to the best advantage
in those instances in which the phenomena of the
world about us, the physical world, do not correspond to what is seen. That is precisely what Taine
said, seventy years later, in his book entitled *De
l'Intelligence.* In this treatise Taine formulated,
and quite correctly so, this profound idea: *La perception extérieure est une hallucination vraie.*

Schiller, whom Goethe had convinced of Newton's supposed delusions, saw nevertheless with distress that his friend was losing himself in hypotheses
over against which he, as a layman, stood in a shaky
and skeptical frame of mind. He wrote, consequently, on November 30, 1798, to Goethe as
follows:

This much, however, has become clear to me: A main
objective in your method will be to separate from each other,
and to keep separate, the purely factual and polemical part
from the hypothetical, so that the evidence in the case, and
the evidence bearing on Newton's *falsum* (!) will not become confused with the problematic part of the explanation.

The advice, to be sure, was good, but Goethe saw at once that he could not meet the demand; that he could not depict the actual altogether apart from the various conjectures that bore on its complete explanation. In his reply he took pains to emphasize the idea that "every lecture, indeed every method, is in itself hypothetical," that it rests, in other words, on an assumption.

He had the philosophers on his side, not simply Schelling, the philosopher of nature, but also the hostile brothers, Hegel and Schopenhauer who, at odds on everything else, were at one in their appreciation of Goethe's theory of colors. Among contemporary physicists, Seebeck and Schweigger were the only ones who, for a time at least, subscribed to Goethe's views. The renowned physiologist of the coming generation, Johannes Müller, who by 1826 had agreed, with reservations, with Goethe, came eventually to limit his sympathies to the section dealing with physiological optics. And it is this physiological part of Goethe's *Farbenlehre* which, according to the conception of modern scientists, retains its epochal significance. It had a decisive influence on Schopenhauer's monograph *Ueber das Sehen und die Farben* and it left its trace on such men as Himly, Troxler and especially Purkinje, with whom Goethe had associated personally from 1802 on.

It is, however, first and foremost the recognition from Johannes Müller on which posterity lays weight. As a student twenty-five years of age, he sent Goethe on February 5, 1826, his book entitled *Zur vergleichenden Physiologie des Gesichtssinnes des Menschen und der Thiere*. He declares that

his work would hardly ever have been finished had
he not spent several years studying Goethe's *Farbenlehre*. Along with the book he sent a letter in
which he said, among other things and in substance,
the following:

I too appear as one among many who wishes to testify to
you how I have understood the master's teachings. But
what inspires me with greater confidence is the fact that in
my case it is a question of a cause that lies close also to your
heart, the theory of colors and the metamorphosis. After
your investigations have been an inspiration to me for years,
not only as to method but also as to the character of my
efforts to penetrate the secrets of living nature, the good fortune has at last come to me to tell you publicly how the
seed that has produced magnificent fruit in all branches of
science among the older generation and that will bear no less
important fruit in the generations to come, has also had a
beneficent and fructifying influence on me. I owe everything
to your sagacious teachings. And now I entrust to your
kindly nature and forbearance this book, in the hope that you
may feel a desire to examine more carefully the gift hereby
dedicated to you from a disciple of yours, who, up to the
present, has been unknown and reserved.

Though Johannes Müller, as was quite reasonable, later took objection to Goethe's opposition to
Newton, this letter, coming as it does from the particular man who afterwards became the most prominent representative of the morphological tendency
in zoölogy, as well as the originator of experimental
physiology in Germany, is a full and fresh laurel
wreath to Goethe as a naturalist, even in the sole
domain in which he was partly mistaken.

CHAPTER XV

ESTABLISHMENT AND MANAGEMENT OF THE
THEATRE IN WEIMAR—GOETHE AND
CHRISTIANE NEUMANN: *Euphrosyne*

FROM early childhood on, the stage had had its
attraction for the author of *Götz*. The puppet
theatre described in *Wilhelm Meister* constitutes
one of the greatest curiosities in the Goethe House
at Frankfort to this very day. In 1775, when Goethe came to Weimar and brought life and enjoyment along with him, dramatic production was for
him (as it was for Voltaire) the noblest of the
major amusements.

Even before his day the Duchess Anna Amalie
had been a zealous exponent of the theatre. First
she called the Koch troupe from Leipzig; it had
cultivated the operetta. It was succeeded in 1771
by Seyler's troupe which could boast of the two sole
theatrical celebrities of pronounced fame in Germany at that time: Konrad Ekhof and Madame
Hensel. It is of these that Lessing speaks at
great length in his *Hamburgische Dramaturgie*
(1767-68). From Hamburg, where it had been
their intention to found a national theatre, they had
come to Weimar and given performances at the
castle. But the fire of 1774 left them homeless;
they moved on to Gotha where the Duke took them
into his service for a while.

On Goethe's arrival in Weimar there was neither
a fixed nor a wandering troupe; there was not even
a building in which performances could be given.
The standing of the actor and the business of acting
were on a low level. For this very reason the dilettant comedy and amateur theatre afforded great
amusement. And since there were no professionals,
society took it upon itself to play comedy. Goethe
naturally became the leader. Karl August and his
brother Konstantin, the men and women of the
court, Goethe, Knebel, Bertuch, Musäus, Korona
Schröter performed dramas with real passion, now
under the roof of a redoubt building in Weimar,
which the excellent theatrical master, Mieding, had
arranged, now out in the open, anywhere in fact
that they could find a suitable place:

> In engen Hütten und im reichen Saal,
> Auf Höhen Etterburgs, in Tiefurts Thal,
> Im leichten Zelt, auf Teppichen der Pracht
> Und unter dem Gewölb der hohen Nacht.

If Mieding, at whose death Goethe wrote one of
his most beautiful poems, (*Auf Miedings Tod*),
was an excellent machinist, Goethe was in one person the poet and the director and the regisseur and
the leading actor of this dilettant theatre. In the
capacity of actor he played the rôles of Wilhelm in
Die Geschwister and Orestes in *Iphigenie*. It was
not until the year 1783 that he withdrew from these
diversions.

In 1780 a new building was erected for the performance of masquerades and dramas. From 1784
a troupe under the direction of Joseph Bellomo gave
performances three times a week, at first mostly of

Italian operettas, and then of serious drama.   But
at the beginning of the year 1791 Bellomo and his
company went to Grätz.   The Duchess had decided
even a year before their departure to erect a court
theatre in Weimar and to place Goethe at the head
of it.   In April, 1791, Germany's one really great
actor, Friedrich Ludwig Schröder, then director of
the theatre in Hamburg, stopped for some time in
Weimar and with him Goethe discussed in detail
the art of acting and the practical management of a
theatre.

Finally in May, 1791, the far famed court theatre
in Weimar was opened with a performance of
Iffland's *Die Jäger* preceded by a prologue by Goethe.   The first lines of the prologue tell us that
the beginning is always difficult.   It then shows that
should the artists take only themselves into consideration, they might cheerfully go ahead and hope to
make their talents, great or small, felt.   But when
they remember that in a case like this it is a question
of making various powers harmonize, of working in
unison, they feel the difficulty of the undertaking:

> Von allen Enden Deutschlands kommen wir
> Erst jetzt zusammen, sind einander fremd
> Und fangen erst nach jenem schönen Ziel
> Vereint zu wandeln an, und Jeder wünscht
> Mit seinem Nebenmann es zu erreichen.
>
> Denn hier gilt nicht, dass Einer athemlos
> Den Andern heftig vorzueilen strebt,
> Um einen Kranz für sich hinwegzuhaschen.
> Wir treten vor Euch auf, und Jeder bringt
> Bescheiden seine Blume, dass nur bald
> Ein schöner Kranz der Kunst vollendet werde,
> Den wir zu Eurer Freude knüpfen möchten.

The enterprise was quite successful; but as Weimar was too small a town to be able to provide sufficient auditors for a large number of theatrical evenings, plays were given in summer in smaller towns in the vicinity, always in Lauchstädt which must be considered as a branch, most frequently, however, in Erfurt.

When the troupe returned from Lauchstädt in October, 1791, the theatre was opened with a new prologue by Goethe which is unfortunately nothing but sheer prose, clothed in iambics. Of greater value is the epilogue which closed the year December 31, 1791. Goethe had it recited by Christiane Neumann, then only thirteen years old, surrounded by a group of other children. It is patriarchal:

> Liebt Euch,
> Vertragt Euch! Einer sorge für den Andern!
> Dies schöne Glück, es raubt es kein Tyrann,
> Der beste Fürst vermag es nicht zu geben.

After an attempt for a year and a half, Goethe disbanded the troupe, retained only its most superior members, and formed a new one, into which he introduced strict discipline. He paid great attention to order and punctuality at rehearsals, demanded that all rôles be memorized thoroughly and accurately, and laid the greatest stress upon correct and distinct enunciation. He instilled first and foremost into his actors the elements of correct pronunciation, punished carelessness and indistinctness, and challenged every ancient routine.

Already seriously engrossed, he assumed in addition the burdens and torments of a theatre director. An incessant secret opposition carried along with it the uninterrupted spreading, by discontented actors, of unfavorable reports among the people concerning new plays and their anticipated misfortune on the stage. By December, 1795, Goethe already had his share of discontent and wished to resign. But Karl August begged him not to let the reins slip from his hands; he submitted, but cast about in the meantime for a first class stage manager.

He believed that he had found the right man when, in the spring of 1796, August Wilhelm Iffland, Germany's greatest actor next to Schröder, came to Weimar, his association throughout sixteen years with Dalberg in Mannheim having become looser and cooler. Iffland was given a brilliant reception. He played thirteen rôles of the most variegated sort; his acting was looked upon as being beyond reproach. He appeared in many plays that are now hopelessly forgotten, though he also took the part of Egmont, despite the fact that he was ill adapted to tragedy for a number of reasons, including lack of compass and resonance in his voice. But in bourgeois comedies and dramas, he was a master who could touch any chord in the human soul with equal dexterity. He was sincere and simple, an enemy of bombast. He adapted himself to the ensemble of effects, or more correctly speaking, he formed a whole about him.

From the Duke's side as well as from Goethe's everything was done to make Iffland a fixture; but the scheme was not a success. The National Theatre in Berlin called him to its leadership, and Weimar was in no position to compete with the capital of a kingdom.

However eagerly Goethe tried to retain Iffland,

and however thoroughly he had discussed histrionics
with Schröder five years previously, neither of these
two men corresponded in reality to his ideal of an
actor; in truth they both strove toward a different
goal, Schröder as a genius and Iffland as a virtuoso.
At heart they were the antipodes of Goethe as theatre directors, just as they as dramatic authors were
poles removed from him.

Schröder was versatile. He could improvise
after the fashion of the actors in the *Commedia
dell' arte;* and he could play rôles from all the leading literatures with the utmost precision. He was
the man who had given German actors as a class a
feeling of self-respect; previous to his time they
were regarded as vagabonds and decadents. He
was closely akin to Goethe in so far as he wished
that every play should make a complete and collective impression, that every rôle should be totally lost
in the whole. His battle-cry was nature. Rhetoric
and plastic art did not thrive under him. But as a
result of this everything received a sort of work-a-
day stamp. In his hatred of declamation he robbed
the tragedy of its swing and splendor.

For Goethe on the other hand the classical theatre was the ideal. The time had long since passed
when he called himself a naturalist. He now regarded himself as an "Idealist." In matters of
rhetoric, plastic art, and mimicry everything should
be first and foremost in good style. Goethe's actors
should never forget that they were there simply for
the sake of the spectator; it should not be their business to create an illusion but to give examples of
noble dignity. They should never for a moment
turn their back upon the public; in case there were

several of them, they should stand on the stage in a semi-circle. Since Goethe as the leader of a theatre would avoid above all things else the slurring of words, the chief stress was laid not on natural accent but on distinct pronunciation, especially upon a beautiful, almost singing style of recitation. Not nature but beauty was for him the highest law.

It does not seem, however, that Goethe, the "Idealist," felt personally that he was in any way at odds with Schröder, the "Realist," for there is no actor whom he honored more highly. He wrote in Schröder's album, 1791:

Viele sahn dich mit Wonne, dich wünschen so viele zu sehen.
  Reise glücklich! Du bringst überall Freude mit hin.

And what is more, he later wrote in Schröder's album Lessing's familiar lines:

Kunst und Natur
Sei auf der Bühne eines nur!
Wenn Kunst sich in Natur verwandelt,
Dann hat Natur mit Kunst gehandelt.

So far as Iffland is concerned, whom Goethe studied quite carefully, it is entirely probable that he is the model of the exceedingly interesting character Serlo in *Wilhelm Meister*. Of Serlo it is said, with a pun on *gebildet* and *bildlos* (just as Iffland, he came from Mannheim to Weimar):

He came to that part of Germany where, in the cultivation of the good and the beautiful there was no lack of truth, though there was frequently a lack of intellect. He could no longer accomplish anything with his masks; he had to try to influence the heart and the soul. The monotony which then prevailed on the German stage, the vapid cadence and ring of the Alexandrines, the perverted and vulgar dialogues,

the dryness and commonness of the spontaneous tone of the
moralists, he had soon caught and noticed at once what
pleased and moved.

By virtue of his excellent memory, it was possible
for him to recite not merely an individual rôle with
the precise accent of any favorite actor, he could
even learn an entire play by heart, and could perform an entire play alone, quite regardless of the
circumstances that surrounded him. His vehemence
gave the impression of strength; his flattery passed
for tenderness. He soon played better than the
models he had at first imitated, and he learned what
so few actors ever seem to learn—to exercise economy and discipline in the modulation of his voice
and the use of gestures.

Of Serlo we read in *Wilhelm Meister*:

He was cold at heart; he really loved no one. With the
remarkable clarity of his glance, he could not esteem anyone,
for he saw in reality only the external characteristics of people, and these he introduced into his mimic collection. His
self-consciousness was, moreover, deeply offended if the applause was not general. He made such a careful study of
the devices that win applause that, not only on the stage but
in real life as well, he was constantly ingratiating himself
into the favor of his associates. His mental equipment, his
talent, his manner of living worked together in a surprising
way, so that, himself unaware of what was taking place, he
developed into a really perfect actor. Indeed, with an apparently rare and quite natural coöperation of effects and
counter-effects, his diction, art of speaking, and mimic gestures arose, as the result of unceasing practice and with an
ever increasing knowledge, to a very high degree of truth,
freedom and candor.

II

Among Goethe's poetical works there is an elegy entitled *Euphrosyne*. It preserves most cordial reminiscences of the most gifted actress at the Weimar Theatre, a young woman trained in her profession by the master himself and loved by him at the same time. She died in September, 1797, eighteen years and ten months old.

Her father, Johann Christian Neumann, belonged to the company that had come to Weimar with Bellomo. He had died in 1791, shortly before the company had been dissolved. His daughter, Christiane Neumann, was born December 15, 1778, and had made her debut on the Weimar stage when she was but eight years of age. She played the part of the page in Engel's *Der Edelknabe*. She revealed such pronounced talent that the Court, captivated by her, requested Korona Schröter to supervise her education. When thirteen years old, she had recited a prologue by Schiller with such perfect skill that the Duchess Anna Amalie had her painted in this situation—that of the Goddess of Justice.

But as early as 1791 Goethe had begun to study rôles with the child and the same year she made her artistic debut in Shakespeare's *King John* as the boy Arthur, who is to be blinded with a red hot iron. Goethe himself had put the play on the boards from the very first rehearsal and, astounded by the naturalness and genuineness of Christiane's acting, had made Arthur the real center of the drama and had brought all methods of procedure on the part of the other actors in harmony with Christiane Neumann's.

In *Euphrosyne* we are told how Goethe, at a general rehearsal, was so moved on seeing the young girl lying on the stage as the wounded Arthur that he picked her up in his arms and bore her away.

In the poem it is she who, like a shade after death, speaks to him:

Freundlich fasstest du mich, den Zerschmetterten, trugst
    mich von dannen
    Und ich heuchelte lang , Dir an dem Busen, den Tod.
Endlich schlug die Augen ich auf, und sah Dich in ernste,
    Stille Betrachtung versenkt, über den Liebling geneigt.
Kindlich strebt' ich empor und küsste die Hände dir dankbar,
    Reichte zum reinen Kuss dir den gefälligen Mund,
Fragte: Warum, mein Vater, so ernst? Und hab' ich
    gefehlet
    O so zeige mir an, wie mir das Bessre gelingt!
Keine Mühe verdriesst mich bei Dir, und Alles und Jedes
    Wiederhol' ich so gern, wenn Du mich leitest und lehrst.
Aber Du fasstest mich stark und drücktest mich fester im
    Arme,
    Und es schauderte mir tief in dem Busen das Herz.
Nein, mein liebliches Kind! so riefst du, Alles und Jedes,
    Wie du es heute gezeigt, zeig' es auch morgen der Stadt!
Rühre sie alle, wie mich Du gerührst, und es fliessen zum
    Beifall
    Dir von dem trocknesten Aug' herrlich Tränen herab.

She soon became not merely the idol of Goethe, but of the Court and the general public as well. Wieland said of her that if she made equal advancement for a few years to come, Germany would have but *one* actress. Unfortunately mad havoc was played with the talent that had matured so early and with the young character developed ahead of her years. It seems that Germany at that time had no law forbidding marriage with children. In the summer of 1793, Christiane, then fourteen years old, was married to Becker, the actor at Weimar, whose unconscientious heartlessness did not deter him from having her become the mother of two children before she was sixteen. Her health suffered a fatal shock. In her fourteenth year she played the rôles of Emilia Galotti and Minna von Barnhelm. When seventeen she undertook a variety of different rôles including several from Shakespeare, the page in *Don Carlos,* and a number of boys' and girls' parts in Iffland's *Reise nach der Stadt, Die Jäger, Der Herbsttag.* These last named plays, in which the lighter style did not call for unusual physical or vocal power, were admirably adapted to her talent and condition. Goethe wrote the niece's rôle in the *Grosskophta* for her. Of her Iffland said: "She can do everything. She will never sink to the plane of the artificial transport of sentimentality, which for our young actresses is and remains the most serious fault of all."

In the summer of 1797 she died at the age of eighteen. In her death the theatre of Weimar suffered an irreparable loss. She could never be replaced, not even by Amalie Malcolmi (married to Pius Alexander Wolff) nor by Caroline Jagemann, though the former achieved substantial renown while the latter won for herself a position of absolute power.

CHAPTER XVI

GOETHE'S COLLABORATION WITH SCHILLER ON *Wallenstein*—GOETHE AND CAROLINE JAGE-MANN; HIS STRUGGLES AS THEATRE DIRECTOR—COÖPERATION OF GOETHE AND SCHILLER AT THE WEIMAR THEATRE

AFTER the death of Christiane Becker, Goethe turned to Schiller as the one individual from whom a renewal of Weimar's theatrical existence might be derived. Inspired by Goethe, Schiller resumed work on his *Wallenstein*. He had begun it in prose, but it took to wing and flight only with rhythmic treatment. The drama was destined to mark an era against the naturalistic, bombastic prose of the dramas of chivalry and the plebeian and emotional elements in the plays of Kotzebue and Iffland which then constituted the chief repertoire of the German stage.

As a poet Iffland was the antipodes of Goethe. But Goethe's admiration for Iffland, the actor, remained unweakened. In 1798, Iffland returned to Weimar to play as a guest. At his arrival Schiller lay sick in Jena. He found one single opportunity to see Iffland in Rousseau's scene entitled *Pygmalion;* Caroline Jagemann played the rôle of Galatea. When the heroine came to life at the close of the piece, Iffland was playing away without restraint in

206

monologue and pantomime. He lost himself entirely in declamation and all manner of violent outbursts; he assumed plastic attitudes and moved his hands about by way of depicting various feelings. To Schiller such acting was shocking; Goethe found that in comparison with it his own actors were mere "reporters."

Thereupon Goethe betook himself to Jena in order to discuss a number of things with Schiller, among others his *Wallenstein* and the affairs of the theatre in general. Schiller had the genius of associating with actors in a direct and friendly fashion; he treated them as his comrades. Goethe kept them at a distance; his attitude was cold. Nevertheless Eduard Genast's *Tagebücher* show that he could be paternal and benevolent if the spirit moved him. With an antique slant such as both Goethe and Schiller had, it was easy for them to come to a complete understanding with regard to the theory of the art of acting. For both of them, the typical, not the individual, was the chief aim to be sought after. The special function of the actor was not to depict the figure but to form a sort of ideal masque, and to render his part cleanly and with grace. Actors had long been accustomed to a flat, everyday prose. Now they were to learn verses by heart; and to recite them correctly and with force. And these verses Schiller was now striving to bring much nearer to daily speech than he had done in *Don Carlos*.

The real difficulty was to find an actor who could give life to Wallenstein. The greatest actor in all Germany would not be good enough. However, Schröder was celebrated for his natural treatment of verse.

Schröder's second directorship of the theatre in
Hamburg came to an end in 1797, and though he
was but fifty-three years of age, he withdrew to isolation in the country.   It seems that Schiller, as
early as the beginning of 1798, had turned to him
for advice with regard to Wallenstein.   Goethe's
good stage manager Kirms had also been in touch
with him.   The preliminaries, carried on in the main
by Weimar's factotum, Böttiger, extended to inter-
minable length; Schröder said neither yes nor no.
At Goethe's request Schiller then introduced into
the beautiful and magnificent prologue to *Wallensteins Lager* these four lines which allude to
Schröder, and which were recited at the first performance in the restored theatre.

> O! möge dieses Raumes neue Würde
> Die Würdigsten in unsre Mitte ziehn,
> Und eine Hoffnung, die wir lang gehegt,
> Sich uns in glänzender Erfüllung zeigen!

But despite the fact that Goethe himself sent the
much admired copy of this prologue together with
a friendly invitation, Schröder remained steadfast
in his original determination to turn his back on the
stage for good and all.   They were now forced to
be satisfied with lesser talents.   Wallenstein was
played by a local artist named Graff.   Though not
exactly brilliant, he at least satisfied the author and
his great friend.

II

Caroline Jagemann who, as an actress and a
singer, dominated the theatre in Weimar from 1797
to the death of Karl August in 1828, was born in

January 1777. She was the daughter of Anna Amalie's librarian. At the age of twenty, she appeared as a singer on the stage of her paternal city after having enjoyed a schooling of three years under Iffland in Mannheim. She was extremely beautiful, had an uncommon voice, pronounced ability as an actress, and became at once the all-powerful friend of Karl August,—became what he himself called "eine Gesellschafterin seiner Erholungsstunden."

By nature she was domineering, wily, enterprising, and ruthless. In her very first year as a member of the society in Weimar she demanded that Frau Weyrauch in Lauchstädt, an excellent singer, relinquish a certain rôle in her favor. The demand was met and Caroline Jagemann sang the part. The complaint from the offended artist was laid on the table and since her colleagues sided with her, great difficulties were in store for the board of directors. The Weyrauchs asked for their release but were bound for the time being by contract. The next year the same thing was repeated and the Weyrauchs left Weimar for good and all. During a rehearsal of Mozart's *Don Juan,* Caroline Jagemann demanded peremptorily that the director of the orchestra, Kranz by name, have the musicians play, not according to his own leadership, but in time and tune with her voice. At the performance Kranz carried out his own will in the matter and Fräulein Jagemann was unable to keep time. The result was so humiliating to Goethe that Kranz was temporarily removed as director of the orchestra and never again permitted to direct the operas in which Caroline Jagemann sang.

As a matter of course, she was always at odds

with the rest of the staff, including the stage manager and the director. She never lost sight of her self-appointed goal: autocratic sway on the stage. Here the creator and maintainer of the theatre, Goethe, stood in her way and for twenty years in succession she put countless intrigues into effect to have Goethe's influence broken and to have him removed. Chancellor F. v. Müller reproduces, 1808, a conversation with Goethe in which the latter said that if he had been minded to see Caroline Jagemann once a week and persuade her to be more sober, everything would have gone smoothly. But since she was utterly without logic, since she wished to be the center and nothing less, since she wished to live and have a good time, she demoralized every situation and every home into which she was admitted, though she was not a really malicious person.

At the theatre she surrounded herself with obedient slaves, one of whom was the actor Becker, another was the bass singer Stromeyer, her very intimate friend of many years who assisted her in everything.

Originally she had been most effective as a singer; but when Christiane Becker died she also took over the leading dramatic rôles. She brought to grief the principle that Goethe had so zealously defended, that of having the individual disappear in the effect as a whole. Her beauty as well as her double talent made her the favorite of the public. She was the Duke's favorite anyhow, and she knew that she would always be protected by him. When she was thirty-two, Karl August made her a member of the nobility, invested her with the name of Freifrau von Heygendorf, and enfeoffed her.

The opposition she led against Goethe gradually undermined the morale of the theatre. She never undertook, however, a decisive move against him until the close of the year 1808. Just a little before the performance of the opera *Sargino* the tenor Morhard sent in a doctor's certificate to the effect that hoarseness prevented him from singing. The prima donna became embittered and exclaimed: "If the dog can't sing, let him bark!" She referred the matter to the Duke who dutifully punished her with an arrest of one week in her private rooms and gave Goethe the brusque order to have Morhard removed without any payment of salary other than what was due him from the previous week. Moreover the director was to see to it that Morhard was beyond the boundaries of Weimar within a fortnight. All that Goethe could accomplish in this affair was to have the time extended to a month. But now he begged the Duke without ceasing to give him his release as director of the theatre. The Duke refused and tried to retain Goethe's services by giving him absolute sovereignty, Goethe having demanded this as the one condition on which he would stay. At last the entire matter was adjusted: Goethe was to have nothing whatsoever to do with the opera, and Fräulein Jagemann was always to have an under-study, so that the operas could be performed when she refused to play in Lauchstädt.

And so the storm subsided for a while. But in the next year the arrogant Stromeyer again caused trouble. On this occasion Goethe gave in at once and a number of important changes in the management of the theatre followed. They arranged an intendancy, an entire commission as a matter of fact, on which a certain Count Edling and Goethe's own son were given seats. But he himself remained of course, nominally at least, the actual leader. They were unwilling to accept his advice; but they were also unwilling to accept his resignation.

On the birthday of one of the princes, in February 1817, Kotzebue's *Schutzgeist* was announced as a gala performance contrary to Goethe's wish. He again asked for his release and was again refused. But in the spring of the same year, while he was over in Jena, they played, April 12, *Der Hund des Aubrey de Mont-Didier,* a farce in which a poodle was the hero. Goethe at once sent in his resignation and on the following day he received from Karl August a note granting his request. The expressions are humorous, since the Duke always addressed Goethe by *Du* in private correspondence:

My most dear Herr Geheimrath and Minister of State!
The observations that you have made to me convince me that the Herr Geheimrath and Staatsminister wishes to be relieved of his duties connected with the management of the Court Theatre, though I know that he will not on this account fail to support the artistic department of the theatre with advice and deeds. . . . Herr Geheimrath and Staatsminister receives herewith my profound gratitude for his excellent services of former days,—and I hope that he will use the greater freedom he will henceforth enjoy as a reason of this change to the very best advantage of the important and artistic institutions to which he has up to the present devoted himself with such marked zeal. . . .
KARL AUGUST, *Grand Duke of Saxony.*

When we recall that Frau von Heygendorf was forty years old at this time, that she had been the intimate friend of Karl August for twenty years, and the sympathetic companion of Stromeyer for eleven years, it is quite impossible to deny her the recognition that is due her.

III

During Schiller's lifetime he and Goethe worked together in a cordial and fraternal way for the welfare of the theatre at Weimar. Schiller's dramas constituted a most excellent repertoire. In addition to this he directed the rehearsals not merely of his own works but of Goethe's as well, including the latter's translations. He staged *Egmont*. He supervised the rehearsals of Voltaire's *Mahomet*. If this was not a success it was not Schiller's fault. The *Mahomet* that was played was not really a translation but a subdued revision in another metre. Numerous changes were made for the sake of greater clarity. Propagandistic issues were weakened, toned down, or omitted entirely. Additions were made with a view to the Weimar of that time. It was the same method that Goethe employed in his adaptation of Voltaire's *Tancred*.

Goethe had asked Schiller to revise *Macbeth*. Schiller acquiesced, of course. But his treatment of iambics, his long, eloquent periods, the emphasis he laid on the sonorous art of speech in general, were all directly contrary to the pithy spirit and other excellent features of Shakespearean verse. As for Shakespearean prose—Schiller and his English predecessor were the antipodes of each other. The author of *Kabale und Liebe* was a stranger to prose such as is spoken by the porter in Shakespeare. Truth to tell, Schiller, and Goethe as well, could not appreciate the effect of contrast in the works of the great Britisher. Just as Serlo in *Wilhelm Meister* persuades the hero, in a production of *Hamlet,* to omit anything that might possibly impair the unity of impression, just so did Goethe persuade Schiller, who had formerly been influenced by the Antique, to omit the vulgar but excellent monologue in prose spoken by the porter. He substituted for it a pious song which is poles removed from Shakespeare both in tone and temperament. The fact is that both Goethe and Schiller, once the ardent devotees of Shakespeare, eventually came to the point where they made a sharp distinction between the comic and the tragic in art. The French had undergone a similar reform. Both adopted Napoleon's slogan: *J'aime les genres tranchés.*

For this reason Goethe substituted, in his version of *Romeo and Juliet,* for the sprightly introductory scenes in which the men of the two hostile families challenge each other to fight, a chorus during which the servants of the Capulets decorated the palace for a masquerade. The humorous scenes among the servants in the first act were discarded, also the jests of the musicians before Juliet's burial. Even the nurse's drollness and loquaciousness and Mercutio's whims and wit were deleted; she became a mere matchmaker, he a mere jester. And the entire story of Queen Mab was omitted.

Of the two stage directors, Schiller was as a rule the gentler, Goethe the sterner, though Schiller could also become angry. During a general rehearsal of Schiller's adaptation of *Macbeth,* Goethe, Schiller, and Heinrich Meyer were looking on. The actor Vohs was quite uncertain as to his memory. Goethe called the stage director, Anton

Genast, down to him and said very bitterly: "What in the world is the matter with this Herr Vohs? He doesn't know a word of his rôle; how can he play Macbeth! Are we to stultify ourselves before the dignitaries and the general public? The performance for tomorrow shall be canceled, and you need not bother about keeping the reasons for the cancelation from Herr Vohs and the rest of the staff." But in the meantime Schiller brought Goethe to reason, praised Voh's artistic composure and genius, which were to bring him safely over all rocky places, and the performance was given.

It met with great success. The applause increased from scene to scene. At the close of the second act Schiller came on the stage and said in his Swabian dialect: *Wo ischt der Vohs?* And when Vohs came forward embarrassed, with bowed head, Schiller said: *"Nein, Vohs! ich muss Ihne sage: meischterhaft, meischterhaft! Aber nun ziehe Sie sich zum dritte Akt um."* Then he said to the stage manager: *"Sehe Sie Genascht, wir habbe Recht gehabt! Er hat zwar ganz andere Vers gesproche, als ich sie geschriebe hab, aber er ischt trefflich."*

But however amiable and good-natured Schiller was as a director, it was nevertheless easily possible for him to lose his poise when he encountered irrational opposition. At a rehearsal of Goethe's translation of Voltaire's *Tancred*, Goethe had asked Schiller to keep a diligent eye on an actor by the name of Haide who played the leading part, and who began to fan about and fight with his hands and whistle with his voice so soon as he became excited. Schiller made some objections to this method of playing; but the good Haide paid no attention, in-

deed he even stopped and tried to explain to Schiller
in detail why he played thus and so. Then it was
all over with the dignified calm of Friedrich Schiller.
He cried out in bitter anger: *"Ei was! mache Sie's,
wie ich's Ihne sage und wie's der Goethe habbe will.
Und er hat Recht; es ischt ä Graus, das ewige Vagire
mit dene Händ und das Hinaufpfeife bei der Recitation.* The actor stood as if thunderstruck. No
one had ever seen Schiller in this frame of mind.

He himself put his *Maria Stuart* on the stage and
attended the rehearsals with untiring energy and
genuine appreciation of theatrical effect. The scene
in which the queen receives the sacrament gave rise
to strong objections. Herder protested against the
profanation that arose from acting the holy communion. The scene was given but once, since even
the general public found it distasteful.

One consequence of the tendency to go back to
antiquity on the part of the two great companions
was the performance of Terence's *Die Brüder*. It
was played not simply in Roman costume but also
in accordance with the customs of Terence's day, in
masks, masks however which did not cover the entire
face, only the forehead, nose, and chin and in this
way expressed the character of the rôle. The eyes,
mouth, and cheeks were uncovered. The play
amused and drew full houses. But the other dramas
of Terence and Plautus were too far removed from
the German public. And as is known, A. W. Schlegel's adaptation of Euripides's *Ion,* one of the antique dramas that Goethe's *Iphigenie* called forth,
was a total failure. The wretched drama by his
brother Friedrich Schlegel, entitled *Alarcos,* met
with the same fate.

As an homage to Duchess Anna Amalie, Goethe himself wrote a little festival play in classical style that was performed with masks and in which he used for the first time in his life Greek trimeters, relieved every now and then by trochaic verses. It is the delightful little bagatelle with the forbidding name of *Palaeophron und Neoterpe*. It is an exceedingly clever allegory, introducing modern times as a beautiful young woman, accompanied, to be sure, by two naughty youngsters, Gelbschnabel and Naseweis, and ancient times as a dignified and sensible man, accompanied by two impatient old people, Griesgram and Haberecht. But so soon as Neoterpe and Palaeophron have given their companions a farewell, they are in a position to understand each other perfectly; they even make each other happy and give to each the wreath. Finally modern and ancient times jointly do honor to the lofty lady who long ago established the league between the two.

Two years later, Goethe wrote for the opening performance of the new theatre in Lauchstädt another prelude. This was somewhat more elaborate; it was another allegory entitled *Was wir bringen*. After a fashion which is not without charm, and in which verse and prose alternate, an old German couple and a number of symbolic figures with Greek names, *Nymphe, Phone, Pathos* (naturally ballet, opera, and drama) are united with the god Mercury who seems somewhat Latin-like in the midst of all this Greek and German. The *obligato* homage to the Princes is not lacking. In this case it is Karl August as the ruler of the country, Elector Friedrich of Saxony, the King of Poland as the benefactor who, after his consort had been restored to health

in Lauchstädt, had had the neighborhood adorned
with gardens and promenades. In order to effect
a more reasonable unity, an attempt is made in the
play to see in Märten and Mutter Martha Philemon
and Baucis themselves, of whom however the couple
never once in their lives have heard.

All of this is topical poetry written expressly for
the theatre. While director, Goethe wrote a great
deal more in the same vein. The most important
part of the piece is the sonnet, *Natur und Kunst, sie
scheinen sich zu fliehen.* It appears here for the
first time, spoken by Nymphe. The line, *Wer
Grosses will, muss sich zusammenraffen,* fitted quite
well into the work that interested Goethe from day
to day at this period of his life.

CHAPTER XVII

COMPLETION OF *Faust*, PART I

VIGOROUSLY challenged by Schiller, the author of *Faust. Ein Fragment* again went to work on his most fruitful theme in the year 1797, after having completed *Hermann und Dorothea*. He endeavored to elevate it, to saturate it with symbolism, and to give it a broad base from which it might rise without doing violence to spiritual logic. On the other hand, and quite unfortunately, he took it upon himself to weaken this very coherency that had been so slow in developing. He ruthlessly dissipated, if he did not destroy, the total effect by the insertion of whatever pleased him. It seems that there was a period in his life when he felt an ineluctable impulse to use *Faust* as a strong box into which drawers might be inserted to be filled as opportunity offered and inspiration came.

He had already written an admirable poem entitled *Die erste Walpurgisnacht*, depicting the embitterment of the old Druids at the triumphal march of Christianity. It is still another poem in which Goethe manifested his hatred of the religious negation of nature. In this cantata, arranged for several voices, we find a vigorous opposition on the part of old Germanic heathendom to the worship of the

219

new God whose priests and confessors are accused
of slaughtering heathen women and children. The
following is a characteristic stanza:

> Diese dumpfen Pfaffenchristen,
> Lasst uns keck sie überlisten!
> Mit dem Teufel, den sie fabeln,
> Wollen wir sie selbst erschrecken.
> Kommt! Mit Zacken und mit Gabeln
> Und mit Gluth und Klapperstöcken
> Lärmen wir bei nächt'ger Weile
> Durch die engen Felsenstrecken.
> Kauz und Eule
> Heul' in unser Rundgeheule.

When Goethe wrote *Walpurgisnacht* in *Faust,*
his poetic point of view was an altogether different
one. Since he had had the devil himself appear in
his poem, he could not logically protest against him
as an imaginary or fabulous being. With fresh,
vigorous, and teeming imagination he took up with
the Blocksberg superstition, and had his Faust and
Mephistopheles spend Walpurgis Night on the
Brocken with will-o-the-wisps, wizards, and witches
old and young. The picture of the landscape is
marvelous; the verses, the serious as well as the
humorous ones, have an extraordinary amount of
color-depicting and sound-producing power. Here
is a painting replete with mystery, though it is but
two lines long:

> Wie traurig steigt die unvollkommne Scheibe
> Des rothen Monds mit später Gluth heran!

Here is a jovial stanza concerning two tall granite rocks at Schierke, the names of which are "The
Snorers:"

Seh die Bäume hinter Bäumen,
Wie sie schnell vorüberrücken,
Und die Klippen, die sich bücken,
Und die langen Felsenmassen,
Wie sie schnarchen, wie sie blasen!

The hobgoblins in the spring night are delineated
with all the skill of which the poet was capable. In
the characterization of the witch-like creatures, the
portrayal is marked with coarse sensuality. Mephistopheles, and the witches as well, make constant use
of expressions which, in the various editions, have
been denoted only by dotted lines; their exact wording can be determined only by the rhyme. There
is a mixture of the generally uncomfortable and
disagreeable compounded of wild salacity, rank
smells and disgusting stenches with something of
Höllenbreughel's comic and grimaces. The impression made is tremendous when, in the midst of all
this run-away lechery, the vision of the decapitated
Gretchen suddenly appears before Faust. In the
Paralipomena, which were omitted, though they are
found after the tragedy in some editions, the obscen-
ity of the scene is much stronger.

From an artistic point of view, however, all of
this belonged to the picture of the world and the
picture of life that *Faust* was supposed to give. We
are repelled, however, when, in the midst of all this
witches' dance, Goethe's old and now otherwise
hopelessly forgotten opponent Nicolai is introduced
with vast scorn as a *Proktophantasmist,* that is, as
one who sees visions with his posterior parts. The
reference is to the fact, but little known to later
generations and quite without interest to any human
being, that Nicolai suffered from hemorrhoids and

in consequence of these, from delusions, and that he endeavored to cure himself by applying leeches to the more nearly designated section of his anatomy. Nor is this all. Four old gentlemen appear on the Brocken, a minister, a general, a parvenu, and an author, each of whom pecks and hacks away in his little stanza at the coming generation. The effect of this is null, quite so.

These however are all negligible matters; little specks. We are astounded and amazed, on the other hand, to see that Goethe, just before the strong closing scene with Gretchen in prison from the *Urfaust*—unhappily entitled *Oberons und Titanias goldene Hochzeit*—has had the heart to insert fifty strophes, *Xenien* in an abbreviated meter, each one with a blow to the left and a blow to the right against his contemporary opponents. Every vestige of the illusion is destroyed, and that on purpose. We have a reference to the deceased machinist Mieding; rationalists and artists who pay excessive attention to costumes are ridiculed. There is one Hennings, the editor of certain magazines. At the mention of his name, his two journalistic enterprises, *Der Musaget* and *Genius der Zeit*, are covered with derision. There is Lavater as a crane, with an illusion to the odd way he walked. And there is Nicolai as a persecutor of the Jesuits, snuffing about after those whom he hates.

This was done by the same Goethe who had had Schiller trim *Macbeth*, and who himself had deleted every phantastic expression or bit of exuberant jollity from *Romeo and Juliet* which did not appeal to him as being necessary to paint the moral and adorn the tale. Fortunately, his labors on the mas-

terpiece were not limited to such crimes against the
general spirit of the work. He wrote the touching
introductory poem entitled *Zueignung* in which he
tells how he feels on returning to his *magnum opus*.
His initial auditors were dead and departed:

> Sie hören nicht die folgenden Gesänge,
> Die Seelen, denen ich die ersten sang;
> Zerstoben ist das freundliche Gedränge,
> Verklungen, ach, der erste Wiederklang.
> Mein Leid ertönt der unbekannten Menge. . . .

There follows *Das Vorspiel auf dem Theater*,
consisting of a conversation carried on by the manager, the theatre poet, and the jester. The idea
he seems to have derived from Kalidasa's *Sakun-
tala*. It came out in English in 1789; Goethe had
read it and appreciated it. In the speeches of the
manager, he has assembled the sum total of experiences, bitter for the most part, to which he himself
had been subjected as director: contempt for the
public, insight into its taste for what is both bulky
and piecemeal, its utter inability to appreciate poetry, and so on and on. We have this reference to
the poet:

> Was träumtet Ihr auf Eurer Dichterhöhe?
> Was macht ein volles Haus Euch froh?
> Beseht die Gönner in der Nähe!
> Halb sind sie kalt, halb sind sie roh.

He requests the poet to adapt himself to the
public's undisciplined taste, so that he and the
theatre can go on. In the reply of the poet Goethe
has expressed his glorification of the profession of
poet, as did Shakespeare in the fifth act of *Mid-*

summer Night's Dream. The entire passage deserves study. Here is the main part of it. His
intention is certainly serious, showing how, while
time runs on without division or stopping, day after
day, the poet interrupts the succession of days, and
from one section forms a harmonious whole:

> Wenn die Natur des Fadens ew'ge Länge,
> Gleichgültig drehend, auf die Spindel zwingt,
> Wenn aller Wesen unharmon'sche Menge
> Verdriesslich durch einander klingt,
> Wer theilt die fliessend immer gleiche Reihe,
> Belebend ab, dass sie sich rhythmisch regt?
> Wer ruft das Einzelne zur allgemeinen Weihe,
> Wo es in herrlichen Akkorden schlägt? . . .
> Wer flicht die unbedeutend grünen Blätter
> Zum Ehrenkranz Verdiensten jeder Art?
> Wer sichert den Olymp, vereinet Götter?
> Des Menschen Kraft, im Dichter offenbart.

The *Vorspiel* is followed by the *Prolog im Himmel* motivated by the introduction to the *Book of
Job.* More in accordance with the Old Testament
than with the later development of the rôle of
Mephistopheles in the work in which he directs so
heinous a crime as the murder of Valentin in an
unfair duel, the devil is conceived of as a sort of
buffoon at the angels' court of the Lord, and one
of the servants of the Lord among others. The
Lord himself is inclined to tolerate him, gives him
to man in attendance as a sting, as a stimulant, who
shall prevent man from growing slack in his activity
and sinking into torpid imbecility. To the angels,
on the contrary, he delegates the spirit of progres-
siveness. While the devil is the power which stead-
ily wills evil, but involuntarily produces good, the

angels are conceived with the love of everything on earth. Their task is to secure by enduring thoughts what they would otherwise let slip by as fugitive phenomena. Goethe has put on their lips an antiphonal song, more beautiful than any psalm, in which the sublime has received an expression of exalted power. The first angel sings:

> Die Sonne tönt nach alter Weise
> In Bruder sphären Wettgesang,
> Und ihre vorgeschriebne Reise
> Vollendet sie mit Donnergang.
> Ihr Anblick giebt den Engeln Stärke,
> Wenn keiner sie ergründen mag.
> Die unbegreiflich hohen Werke
> Sind herrlich wie am ersten Tag.

At the beginning of the poem Faust's monologue on suicide is added, which, with the beautiful, sublime flow of its iambics that strongly clashes with the doggerel of the preceding dialogue, reminds of the turn of the century. There is also a wonderful Easter song of the angels, worked out on the basis of an old Christian Easter psalm, with its *terza rima* which tingles and rings like a silver bell, that moves the despairing Faust, and calls him back to life.

The elaborate scene *Vor dem Tor,* immortal in its fresh beauty, one of the most youthful and vivacious parts of *Faust,* must, though not written until now, certainly have been planned many years before. Since the burgher speaks of the Turkish War, it is probable that the speech was written during this war, so that, though omitted from the *Urfaust,* it must have originated in 1774. For that was the year in which peace was settled between Russia and Turkey at Kystsjyk-Kainards-ji. The passage runs :

> Nichts Bessres weiss ich mir an Sonn—und Feiertagen
> Als ein Gespräch von Krieg und Kriegsgeschrei,
> Wenn hinten, weit in der Türkei
> Die Völker aufeinanderschlagen.

The peasant song under the linden tree, *Der Schäfer putzte sich zum Tanz,* must likewise be of earlier origin; for in Book II, Chapter 11, of *Wilhelm Meister,* which came out in 1795, Philine asks the harpist whether he knows the melody to this song. He plays and she sings it; but Goethe adds there that he cannot tell it to his readers for they perhaps might find it dull or even improper. Fortunately he has here thrown his scruples to the winds.

It is impossible to read Faust's Easter Morning monologue without admiration and enthusiasm. It is difficult to find anything more beautiful and picturesque than the speech beginning *Vom Eise befreit sind Strom und Bäche.* The landscape in the spring with its hail storms and melting snow is depicted with a freshness and assurance that enrapture. Strikingly true in its benevolence is the application of the idea of resurrection in the case of poor creatures who, on that morning, catch for the first time in a long while the glimpse of a new sun and a breath of fresh air :

> Denn sie sind selber auferstanden ;
> Aus niedriger Häuser dumpfen Gemächern
> Aus Handwerks—und Gewerbebanden,
> Aus dem Druck von Giebeln und Dächern
> Aus der Strassen quetschender Enge
> Aus der Kirchen ehrwürdiger Nacht
> Sind sie Alle ans Licht gebracht.

The subsequent monologue between Faust and Wagner, of singular excellence, shows how much time must have elapsed since Goethe originally planned the leading figure. He has now forgotten a few individual touches that contradict each other. As is known, one of Faust's very first utterances is that he has never laid up honor for himself:

> Auch hab ich weder Gut noch Geld
> Noch Ehr und Herrlichkeit der Welt.

Here, a few pages later on, we see him honored and esteemed by the peasants as a benefactor. Every father points him out to his son. All question and rush up and hurry along in order to see him. The music and dance stop. The rows are opened. Hats are tossed in the air. But little more was needed, and they would have knelt before him as the common people do before the sacrament itself when it is carried along the streets of Catholic countries.

This does not harmonize especially well with the outbreak at the beginning: *Es möchte kein Hund so länger Leben!* The harmony is likewise tenuous between the determination on the part of Faust to go in for magic at the beginning of the work and his boundless contempt a few scenes later for his father's alchemystic attempts, the results of which were that the patients died like flies, so that his father and he himself were more of a plague to the neighborhood than the pest itself. But this is of very little importance where there is something to admire on every page; the point is that these frequent self-contradictions are disconcerting.

In the scene that immediately follows between

Faust and Mefisto as a wandering scholasticus, in
which every other speech has become a standing
phrase or apothegm, we are also conscious of the
fact that considerable time has elapsed between the
composition of the various scenes. When Mefisto
has finished speaking, he wishes to go. Faust does
not wish to let him go; he would like to hold on to
the devil now that he has got him in his power.
Mefisto begins with all his might to enchant; he
calls up spirits who, singing in chorus, so stupefy
Faust that he falls asleep. Mefisto even conjures
up a rat that can gnaw through the pentagramme
which prevents him from crossing the threshold;
finally he disappears. Faust awakens a disappointed
man. But quite soon Mefisto knocks at the door;
he is back again. It was then really not necessary
to go to all of this trouble in order to escape. The
placing of the wager follows, the contract is agreed
upon. Faust's outbreak against the conditions of
life on this earth, the life that he himself has led, is
a bit of unusual poetry; it expresses the pessimism
of mature manhood:

> Verflucht voraus die hohe Meinung,
> Womit der Geist sich selbst umfängt!
> Verflucht das Blenden der Erscheinung,
> Die sich an unsre Sinne drängt!
> Verflucht, was uns in Träumen heuchelt,
> Des Ruhms, des Namendauers Trug!
> Verflucht was als Besitz uns schmeichelt
> Als Weib und Kind, als Knecht und Pflug. . . .

It was not until 1808 that the entire first part of
Faust was accessible to the public; and there were
even then not a few who comprehended the significance of the poem. Wieland admired this "barock-

ingenious tragedy which was dissimilar to any tragedy that had ever appeared, or that ever would
appear." He made the remark, too, that Goethe
had the same meaning for the poetic world that
Napoleon had for the political world. Jean Paul
forgot the injuries he had suffered from Goethe and
greeted in *Faust* a "posthumous Shakespeare." Rahel Varnhagen, one of the very first to appreciate
the general value of Goethe, had also a full understanding of *Faust*. Schelling said of the work that
it was "the greatest poem of the Germans, com-
parable only to itself." It was moreover the Romantic School that took it upon itself to glorify and
explain *Faust,* for it appealed to its members as a
romantische Tragödie. Friedrich Schlegel, like
many a man after him, compared Goethe, as the
author of *Faust,* with Dante Alighieri.

The work has indeed acquired a significance for
our day that is akin to the significance the *Divina
Commedia* had for the Middle Ages. All the forces
that ever moved Goethe come into their own in it;
they climb up and glide down and "reach to each
other the bright gilded vessels." The yearning of
the young man, the fate of the lover, the lonesome-
ness of the genius, the rich experience of the mature
man—all of these worked together and played their
part in its composition. And round about it and
through it the imperishable has been approached.

What difference does it make if the first part of
Faust is not a homogeneous work with an individual
harmony when it is so replete with independent
harmonies that are after all united! They are all
dominated by Faust's yearning for the infinite in
wisdom, in enjoyment, and in power.

The more developed the reader the less he will be offended by the heterogeneous nature of the individual scenes; and the undeveloped reader, who is simply and once for all accustomed to a wrong understanding, has now had more than a century to discover the heterogeneousness of the poem—and he has not yet succeeded: he does not feel it. He is satisfied with the many thoughts the work calls into play in his mind; he is rejoiced over the many better feelings it calls into play in his life. And he is right.

CHAPTER XVIII

Die natürliche Tochter—BREAK BETWEEN GOETHE
AND HERDER; SCHILLER'S DEATH

IT was in the year 1800 that Goethe, while suffering from frequent indisposition, wrote the matchless Easter Walk in *Faust*. The end of the century
was imminent. The time immediately preceding
midnight of December 31, 1800, he spent in serious
conversation with Schiller. The century to which
Schiller belonged heart and soul was over; the century to which the first fifty years of Goethe's life
belonged, with its ideals of humanity and cosmopolitanism, was past and gone.

At the beginning of January he was seized with
a grave illness that affected him for a considerable
time. In the opinion of later physicians, it seems
to have been a case of violent influenza with symp-
toms of meningitis, and abscesses which, aside from
making him uncomfortable in general, closed his
eyelids. A long period of unconsciousness marked
the beginning of his discomfiture; a tumor on his
eye lasted until well on in March. Insomnia and
nervous restlessness continued until the summer,
when he sought relief in the baths of Pyrmont.

It has long been customary to contend that Goethe's sense for the secrets of art and nature dulled
his feelings for the social and political phases of
life. This is untrue. We have already seen how

231

profoundly the French Revolution interested him
and how he tried, in his way, to set its ideas and
events aright. In *Die natürliche Tochter* he puts
some of the victims and coöperators on the boards
incognito. He moved his source forward in point
of time. The *Mémoires historiques de Stéphanie-
Louise de Bourbon-Conti* had appeared in 1798.
They told of the stern fate that had befallen a
daughter born out of wedlock to the cousin of Louis
XV, Prince Louis de Conti, by Countess Mazarin.
The Prince had received permission from the King
to give his illegitimate daughter the rank of a princess; but her legitimate brother ardently strove to
prevent this by using force, falsehood, and deception.

The Princess was Goethe's contemporary, his
junior by thirteen years. When, in 1801, he undertook to poetize her affair and her fate, he moves
her up to his own time, since the King in the drama
is evidently Louis XVI, and the Princess's father,
the Duke, the King's disloyal and revolutionary
kinsman, bears some similarity to Philippe Egalité.
What we possess of this work is a single drama of
a trilogy that had been originally planned. We
have the same feeling here that we have everywhere:
Goethe's mind was insusceptible to the great revolutionary emotion.

This drama that has been so unjustly depreciated,
condemned for so long in an unreasonable way,
makes its appeal to us on purely *human* grounds.
Indeed, if we of today are to derive pleasure from
Goethe's works at all, we must look for the human
element in them; we must read them naïvely, personally, and try out what they say to *us*—wholly

regardless of what others have seen in them. How
can anyone attach importance to Huber's remark
that *Die natürlich Tochter* is "as smooth as marble
and as cold."

Goethe steeps himself in the tragic fate of an individual without being able, without wishing, to give
us an especially strong impression of the general
spirit and public life. In the domain in which Schiller moved about naturally and freely, Goethe could
scarcely breathe. But the entire age is reflected
in the tragic fate of this individual.

We learn that the King is too mild; that he
thereby makes enemies for himself; that the Duke
belongs among those whom he fears. The enthusiasm the Duke's daughter cherishes toward the King
is beautiful, just as the King himself is a high-minded
man. He is informed that the Duke, out of a whim,
has concealed his relation of father to Eugenie,
though this is an open secret. The King replies:
There is something noble in this action. It is natural that one conceal a great deal that everybody
knows:

> O lass dem Menschen diesen edlen Stolz!
> Gar Vieles kann, gar Vieles muss geschehen,
> Was man mit Worten nicht bekennen darf.

In this excited and disturbed time the young Princess Eugenie puts unalloyed faith in the people.
The King solemnly reminds her that democracy is
not the sole force deserving of sincere consideration:

> Wenn Dir die Menge, gutes, edles, Kind,
> Bedeutend scheinen mag, so tadl' ich's nicht,
> Sie *ist* bedeutend. Mehr aber noch sind's
> Die Wenigen, geschaffen, dieser Menge
> Durch Wirken, Bilden, Herrschen vorzustehn.

The most beautiful part of the drama as an individual element is this purely human factor: The
father's boundless joy when his daughter, whom he
thought a misfortune had befallen while on a daring
riding tour, stands liberated and safe before his
eyes; and the father's despair when he really loses
his daughter.

But no less profound is the *political* teaching of
the drama. We see from it how the most rebellious
act can be carried out by a well meaning man when
he tries, for example, to prevent an even greater misfortune, a murder. We see how political actions
are executed without a shimmer of regard for the
permissible, how a subordinate—somewhat as happened a century later in the Dreyfus case—calmly
practices every sort of baseness that his superior
officers demand of him. Goethe has studied and
appreciated what has been called political Jesuitism
—without the Jesuits being held responsible for the
expression; they are, as a rule, personally excellent
people.

In the drama, the lay brother, who causes a misfortune by his false testimony to the effect that the
Princess is dead, is no longer willing, when seized
with ambition, to be the mere tool of the timid, but
wishes also to have a seat from now on in the
council.

In the development of the action there are two
features of supreme importance. The first is the
marriage proposal made by the lawyer. He offers
her his hand as the best means of making it possible
for her to remain in the country; and he makes her
the offer in a dignified and attractive way in that

he emphasizes the significance of the protection that comes from having a private home:

Eugenie: Bist Du in Deinem Hause Fürst?
Gerichtsrath: Ich bin's
    Und Jeder ist's, der Gute wie der Böse. . . .
    Nicht Heldenfaust, nicht Heldenstamm, geliebte,
    Verehrte Fremde, weiss ich dir zu bieten,
    Allein des Bürgers hohen Sicherstand.
    Und bist du mein, was kann Dich mehr berühren?
    Auf ewig bist du mein, versorgt, beschützt.
    Der König fordre Dich von mir zurück—
    Als Gatte kann ich mit dem König rechten.

The second feature is the originality in Eugenie's development. At first she refuses the lawyer's proposal. Then a great change takes place within her. She forces the private cares of her life into the background under the impression of the general distress of the situation. She no longer wishes to leave her country; she will share the danger and the possible victory with her countrymen:

    Nun bist du, Boden meines Vaterlands,
    Mir erst ein Heiligthum; nun fühl ich erst
    Den dringenden Beruf, mich anzuklammern.

And she offers her hand, with refinement of soul and queenly bearing, to the rejected suitor on the condition that she retain the control of her own person:

    Nun sei's gefragt: Vermagst du hohen Muths
    Entsagung der Entsagenden zu weihen?
    Vermagst du zu versprechen, mich als Bruder
    Mit reiner Neigung zu empfangen, mir,
    Der liebevollen Schwester, Schutz und Rath
    Und stille Lebensfreude zu gewähren?

Since he would rather do anything than lose her he agrees to this arrangement. Unfortunately,

Goethe let also this plan lie. There is only a brief outline instructive in itself, of the drama that was to follow.

The peculiarity of *Die natürlich Tochter* that especially attracts the attention of the reader is the method of treatment, the change that has taken place in Goethe's dramatic style during his continued flight from the individual, and his continued tendency toward the typical. In this drama with its eleven characters, Eugenie is the only one that has a proper name. The others have only rank, position. They are evidently meant to correspond to norms, just as Goethe believed in a rule for male and female proportions in ancient statues.

Corresponding to this is the fact that the style is somewhat affected. In the conversation between Eugenie and the lawyer, or between Eugenie and the governess in the fourth act, Goethe has adopted the stichomythy of the ancient tragedy. In the second act one reads with astonishment the sonnet that Eugenie writes and declaims. It is at once stiff and gloomy, written in a senile style. But worst of all is Goethe's dread of the designations for the things of everyday life. He reminds us of the old French poet Delille with his circumlocutions, all of which is poles removed from the bluntness of style in the works of Goethe's youth. One hardly believes one's own eyes when one reads from the author of *Götz* this circumlocution of the word for *uniform:*

> Was reizt das Auge mehr als jenes Kleid,
> Das kriegerische lange Reihen zeichnet!

Significant indeed is also the fact that in the first scene of the fifth act we are *told* ot a situation which reminds us in its essential points of Clärchen when she seeks in vain to call the citizens to arms to liberate Egmont. The difference lies in the fact that Eugenie herself is to be helped and freed. But whereas in Goethe's young days the scene was depicted before our eyes so that we ourselves experience it, here it is narrated in a report just as in a French tragedy from the seventeenth century:

Hofmeisterin: Und riefst Du nicht das Volk zur Hilfe schon?
Es staunte nur Dich an und schwieg und ging.

The immediate life that pulsates and throbs has disappeared from Goethe's dramatic art, however moved by emotion and rich in thought it had continued to be.

II

The drama, stupidly and crudely parodied by G. Merkel in his *Kakogenia,* was performed in 1803 in Weimar, Lauchstädt, and Berlin. Schiller, Karl August and Fichte found it pleasing; Knebel and Friedrich Schlegel condemned it.

Herder died in the same year. Though he had had a pronounced influence on Goethe as a young man, the mature Goethe turned to other sources of human inspiration. Goethe himself has told us in his *Biographische Einzelheiten* of his last conversation with the friend of his youth. It took place at the castle in Jena where the two men stopped shortly after the performance of *Die natürliche Tochter.* Goethe had already heard of Herder's most favorable remarks concerning the play. These were all the more pleasing to the poet since they led him to believe that a renewal of their former friendly relation was possible.

One evening Herder came to see Goethe; they were living under the same roof. He discussed the drama with the unaffected air of a connoisseur, praised it in an intelligent way, and shed so much light on its real meaning that Goethe felt he had really not understood his own creation. But then, to Goethe's great surprise, he ended with such an outbreak against him that Goethe felt the offences he suffered were irreparable. "I looked at him," Goethe writes, "and replied that the long years of our association terrified me to the point of actual consternation. We separated; I never saw him again."

Goethe does not tell us what Herder said; he expresses himself quite impersonally:

How easy it is to offend or distress one by reminding him, in free and easy moments, of his own defects or the faults of his wife or his children or his home or general status as a citizen, particularly if one does this in cutting, trenchant and epigrammatic language. This was one of Herder's earlier shortcomings, one from which he never completely freed himself and which at last estranged everyone who might otherwise have been his friend. We can overlook the mistakes of youth and regard them somewhat as we regard the transitory sourness of fruit that has not entirely ripened. But let faults of this kind be continued until late in life and they bring us to despair.

And thus the relation, at one time fatherly and later fraternal, which Herder bore to Goethe came to a close with a sharp dissonance.

Among the spectators at the performance of Goethe's drama was a woman who did not understand German. This woman was Madame de Staël.

She was staying at the time in Weimar and collecting, there more than anywhere else, material for her book entitled *Ueber Deutschland*. It was a book that was destined to draw the attention of Europe to modern German literature as it was then beginning to manifest itself. In his notes Goethe has done justice to Madame de Staël, though it is obvious that she irritated him with her incessant questions and by her pronounced inclination to jump from one topic to another. She is treated in another place (in my "Main Currents") so exhaustively that further discussion of her at this point may be omitted.

During this same year, Schiller's most renowned dramas were performed on the Weimar stage. *Die Braut von Messina* and *Die Jungfrau von Orleans* were both produced in 1803, also Schiller's translation of Racine's *Phaedre*. In March, 1804, there was a performance of *Wilhelm Tell*. Schiller, who was soon to dominate the stage in Germany, already dominated that of Weimar. But his health was undermined. Death carried him off in May, 1805, then only forty-five years of age.

This loss made Goethe a lonely man. The friends who in the future were to offer him a species of substitute, the frequently mentioned Heinrich Meyer, who lived for a long time in his house, Dr. Riemer who from the very beginning became attached to him, first as the tutor to his son and then as his own private secretary, and his Berlin correspondent, the musician Zelter, were in no case his mental equals, nor did they stand in general on his level. And the loneliness increased. The Duchess Anna Amalie died in 1807, and in September, 1808, Frau Aja, his

mother, passed away. The last years of her life had
been sweetened by a long visit from Christiane and
her grand-son, "Augst," as she called him.

But let us turn back to the years 1804-1805. As
an epilogue to a dramatic performance of Schiller's
Glocke, Goethe wrote his *Epilog* which contains the
profound portrayal of the friend he had lost, and
in which the repeated refrain, *Denn er war unser,*
rings so true and so strong! In these stanzas Goethe has portrayed Schiller for all time. There is
room for but two of them:

> *Denn er war unser!* Mag das stolze Wort
> Den lauten Schmerz gewaltig übertönen!
> Er mochte sich bei uns im sichern Port
> Nach wildem Sturm zum Dauernden gewöhnen.
> Indessen schritt sein Geist gewaltig fort
> Ins Ewige des Wahren, Guten, Schönen,
> *Und hinter ihm in wesenlosem Scheine*
> *Lag was uns Alle bändigt, das Gemeine.*

> Nun glühte seine Wange roth und röther
> Von jener Jugend, die uns nie entfliegt,
> Von jenem Muth, der früher oder später
> Den Widerstand der stumpfen Welt besiegt,
> Von jenem Glauben, der sich stets erhöhter
> Bald kühn hervordrängt, bald geduldig schmiegt,
> Damit das Gute wirke, wachse, fromme,
> Damit der Tag dem Edlen endlich komme.

This *Epilog* contains the whole of Schiller, clarified, with his ideal striving, his hectic zeal, his invin-
cible youth, and his fighting spirit which brought
him victory on victory—after his death.

CHAPTER XIX

GOETHE'S *Propyläen;* THE BIOGRAPHY OF WINCK-
ELMANN—GOETHE AND DIDEROT; RAMEAU'S
Neffe—BATTLE OF JENA, 1806

GOETHE had learned from Schiller the art of
founding short-lived magazines that no one wished
to support. He established as early as 1798, in
order to spread his views concerning plastic art, the
periodical entitled *Die Propyläen.* Its aim was to
develop the artist, to interest him in thorough and
scientific study of the human body, to make clear
the relation between the artist and the public, and
especially to liberate the artist from the taste of
the public. It demanded that the highest standard
be set in the discussion and criticism of a work of
art. It was in this journal that Goethe published
a series of his treatises on the science of art, such
as *Ueber Laokoon, Der Sammler und die Seinigen,
Ueber Wahrheit und Wahrscheinlichkeit der Kunst-
werke, Ueber den Dilettantismus,* and other themes.
Schiller assisted in the elaboration of the last named
treatise. In all of them Goethe combats the idea of
merely imitating and copying nature.

Goethe and Heinrich Meyer alone constituted
the firm W. K. F. (Weimarer Kunstfreunde) which,
after *Die Propyläen* had been discontinued, kept on
committing itself on all manner of questions pertaining to art, and to propose prize tasks. It is to

241

this series of efforts that Goethe's most important
work of this kind belongs, his book on *Winckelmann,*
written in the years 1804 and 1805. This book is
a part of an elaborate work on the great art student. It contains both his letters to a friend,
Berendis, and treatises on him by Heinrich Meyer
and F. A. Wolf.

Goethe's work is grounded first of all in the
love he naturally cherished for Winckelmann; for
Goethe was the poetic representative of that very
conception of the Antique which, through Winckelmann, had become the Germanic, and which from
an artistic point of view, was soon represented—
through the influence of Zoëga—by Thorvaldsen,
while from the point of view of architecture, it was
taken up by the Bavarian King Ludwig, who surrounded his beer-drinking Munich with an Old
Greek shell. Winckelmann was of course the true
author of Neo-Classicism in Germany, and Goethe
could not help but feel deeply indebted to him. To
this was added the fact that for a long time he was
vehemently aroused by the reverential whining, the
saccharine pining, the lay-brother sanctimoniousness,
the systematic hero-worship which the German Romanticists had just then made fashionable. Wacken-
roder's *Herzensergiessungen eines kunstliebenden
Klosterbruders* and Tieck's *Franz Sternbalds Wanderungen* were both fundamentally opposed to
Goethe's method of thinking and feeling. And, it
sounds amusing at present, the Romanticists had
begun to compare Tieck favorably with Goethe. In
a little country like Denmark, to which the movements from Germany are always somewhat belated
in arriving, it was felt as late as 1860 in romantic,

that is literary, circles that it was quite correct to refer to Tieck and Goethe as poets of equal merit. The paintings of the New German school, corresponding as they did to *Sternbalds Wanderungen*, could only be an abomination to Goethe. His monograph on Winckelmann was accordingly aimed at the Romanticists. It became his pagan confession of faith.

What he wrote is in no sense of the word a biography. It does not concern itself with chronology; it characterises Winckelmann under such short rubrics as paganism, friendship, beauty, Catholicism, Greek art, and so on. Here is a sample, not written in Goethe's most lucid prose:

The delineation of the antique temper with its eye fixed on this world and the goods thereof, leads at once to the observation that such superiority can be the product only of a pagan mind. That self-confidence, working on what is near at hand, reverence for the gods as progenitors, admiration for them almost only as works of art, resignation to an all-powerful fate, and the purely earthly faith in posthumous renown—all this belongs so necessarily together, forms such an inseparable whole, is united into a human existence promised by nature itself that in the case of the heathen an imperturbable soundness dominates in the enjoyment of the highest moment as well as in sacrificing, indeed even in the painful hour of self-immolation.

After having established Winckelmann's paganism in this way, Goethe is obliged to explain, and to explain away, his conversion to Catholicism, and to show that it was utterly unlike the conversion to Roman Catholicism which Friedrich Schlegel and his wife were then on the point of undergoing, and the conversion to Catholicism which Tieck's wife and daughter did undergo in Rome.

Goethe writes:

The pagan temper radiates from all of Winckelmann's actions and writings. . . . His remoteness from every sort of Christian way of thinking, indeed his very aversion to this sort of thinking, must be kept in mind when we attempt to pass judgment on his so-called change of religion. The parties into which the Christian religion is divided were to him a matter of utter indifference, since he, according to his own nature, never belonged to any of the churches that adapt themselves to these various divisions.

We are also shown how the impecunious Winckelmann looked about long and in vain for assistance. Help could be expected only from the court in Dresden; but this court confessed the Catholic religion, so that there was no other way for him to receive favor and mercy than that which was directed by the father confessors and other clerical persons:

He felt that in order to be a Roman in Rome, in order really to grow into the life there, it was absolutely necessary to belong to the Catholic Church, to accept its faith and adapt himself to its usages. The result showed, too, that without this resolution he would not have reached his goal; and it was made easy for him because the Protestant baptism had not been able to make him a Christian, he having been born a genuine pagan.

Goethe continues with the admission that it besmirches one to change his religion, since people value enduring will above everything else, and the less important they are, the more zealously they demand that one shall hold out in that place where one has been set. But he explains that the matter has, in addition to this serious phase, another which is lighter and easier, since there are certain conditions of which we by no means approve though they have a sort of attraction for us. By way of making his point clear, he uses expressions that were especially calculated to annoy the German Romanticists. Dorothea Mendelssohn had become separated from Veit in order to marry Friedrich Schlegel; Caroline Michaelis had become separated from A. W. Schlegel in order to marry Schelling. Goethe writes:

> If I may be permitted to use a simile, I should like to say that the present situation is similar to that we have in the case of wild game which tastes far better to the fine palate when it has a slight tang than when it is fresh cooked. A divorcee and a renegade make a pleasing impression upon us. . . . But for Winckelmann there was nothing attractive about the Catholic religion; he saw in it merely a mask in which he eneveloped himself; he expressed himself in harsh terms regarding it.

It is no wonder that Friedrich Schlegel sought relief by pouring out his boundless contempt for Goethe's *Winckelmann*. It is no wonder that the most cynical and best paid man among the men belonging to the political-religious reaction, Friedrich Gentz, wrote (1805) to Adam Müller in the following words:

> The treatise on Winckelmann is godless. I would not have expected such a bitter, treacherous hatred for Christianity from Goethe, though truth to tell I have been looking for something malicious from him on this subject for quite a while. What indecorous, faun-like joy he seems to have felt on discovering that Winckelmann was a born heathen!

Posterity has judged the work otherwise: Gervinus called it "the best German biography."

II

Though Voltaire published nearly everything he wrote, some of it, to be sure, anonymously—caution dictated his action—Diderot never collected his works; he never bothered about publishing them; nor did anyone else concern himself with them, or see to it that they were given out to the public. He died in 1784, and works of the rank of *La Religieuse, Supplément au Voyage de Bourgainville, Jacque le Fataliste* never came out until 1796. *Ceci n'est pas un Conte* was published in 1798, *Paradoxe sur le Comédien, Promenade du Sceptique, Le Rêve d'Alembert* in 1830. The masterpiece of all, *Le Neveu de Rameau,* was not published until the Restoration.

This last work, however, as well as several others, existed in various manuscripts which passed from hand to hand. Schiller got hold of one of them from France and sent it to Goethe with the request that he translate it. Goethe, who was wise enough to appreciate the uncommon value of the dialogue, undertook the work with pleasure. His translation appeared in 1805, an excellent bit of work which (with the necessary toning down of individual expressions and phrases for the German public) reproduces the tone and style of the original—in so far as this can be done. For it is impossible to deny that the prose from 1762, overflowing with life and inspirited ingeniousness, stood above all the German prose that was written forty years later; nor can it be affirmed that Goethe's own prose style attained at any time the high level of that on which the prose of the original dialogue moves.

The depiction of the endowed and brilliant sluggard and cynic, Rameau's nephew, is a work of art of first rank. Through its slipshod superiority and branding contempt Diderot had used the figure as a means—just as Goethe and Schiller did, too pointedly and directly, in the *Xenien*—of mowing down, through his casual remarks, his own and his fellows' malicious and hateful opponents, a Palissot, a Fréron and others, though he praises, indirectly and with brave loyalty, all that is valuable in his French contemporaries, such as Voltaire, Buffon, d'Alembert, and Helvetius. Salutary indeed is this depraved Rameau's thorough knowledge of men and his contempt for men; salutary also is his extraordinary musical insight and finesse.

As a bit of description the scene in the Café *de la Regence* is especially admirable. He walks up and down the floor, begins to sing Italian, French, tragic, comic melodies, some thirty different pieces one after another, transforms himself, becomes mad, becomes gentle, now imperious, now grinning, imitates a young girl in distress, a priest, a king, a tyrant, gives commands or is submissive, sobs, complains, laughs without ever once departing from the tone or the tact or the character, so that all rise from the chess tables and gather around him in a merry jubilee. But he does not notice it; he is so taken up with his own business, so inspired that he resembles a madman. He sings a recitative in which a prophet paints the destruction of Jerusalem and there is not a dry eye in the house. He imitates all the instruments, a horn, a fagott, a oboe, small flutes and strings; at last he becomes a complete theatre, dancing men and dancing women, women who sing and men who sing, an orchestra all to himself. In other words, he anticipates possibly the greatest work Victor Hugo ever wrote, *Le Satyre,* in which the Faun little by little becomes Pan and, singing, reproduces the universe while all the tame and all the wild animals, all the gods and all the goddesses, listen.

In the notes Goethe praises Voltaire in the most earnest, though in the most droll fashion, by ascribing to him forty-five great characteristics. But he grasps this opportunity to tell the public and his opponents some sharp truths. He makes the point that, taken as a whole, the public is incapable of passing judgment on any talent whatsoever; to do this practice and study are necessary. And with regard to Palissot he says:

In Germany we have also instances in which evil minded people, partly in flying sheets, partly on the stage, try to harm others. But he who does not allow himself to become exasperated at the moment, can calmly await the result; in a short time it is as if nothing had happened. It is only presumption and sham merits that need to fear personal satire.

III

The battle of Jena was fought on October 14, 1806; Prussia collapsed. The beaten regiments scurried through the streets of Weimar in the wildest sort of flight. All the wagons were overloaded with fugitives. The French had taken Altenburg near Weimar, and were firing over the town at the Prussians posted in the rear. The bullets passed over the houses without doing any harm to them.

The city, by force of circumstances, became a prey for plundering. The officers and the cavalry did what lay in their power to protect the citizens and the property and to help out in other ways. But they were nearly powerless against the fifty thousand uncaged soldiers who, after having broken into the stores and emptied them, took such food and drink as they found, seized linen, money and silverware, smashed furniture, and lighted watchfires in the squares and parks. Murat and the other generals endeavored to restore order; but not a few places were burned.

By the fifteenth the suffering was extreme: There was no bread to be had in the town. The Duchess was in the castle in which most of the women of Weimar had found an asylum. Towards evening Napoleon arrived. The Duchess went out to meet him; she spoke a few words to him regarding the excessively hot weather, and the hardships they had to endure. He replied abruptly: *Ce sont les suites de la guerre.* Thereupon he asked to be shown to his rooms.

On the following day Duchess Luise was formally announced to him. He received her standing, and allowed her to remain standing. He reproached her because the Duke was an officer in the Prussian army and had led his soldiers against him. The Duchess did not permit herself to be disheartened: She asked Napoleon what would have been his judgment if one of his family, as closely related to him as the Duke was to the King of Prussia, had, at the outbreak of the war, taken leave of the army to which he had for so many years belonged, Napoleon was impressed: He informed her that for her sake he would spare the country—on the condition that the Duke withdraw from Prussian service immediately.

Goethe's house was spared from fire and plundering. A few brutal soldiers did, to be sure, rush in upon him with their swords and would perhaps have wounded him had not Christiane thrown herself between him and them and in this way protected him; and with a great deal of presence of mind, she offered them a few silver candle sticks with which they went their way. Later on the highest of French officers were billeted in the house. Among others Marshalls Augereau, Lannes, and Ney, but only for a short time. Riemer relates, as an eye-witness, that after the French soldiers had secured admission to the house Goethe quietly went up to them and asked them what they wanted and whether they had not already received everything that they could reasonably expect: They had already been quartered in his house. The dignity of his very figure seems to have instilled a certain amount of respect in them. They became all of a sudden exceedingly polite. They simply appropriated a glass of wine and asked him to clink glasses with them, which he did. And then they went away, decently and in order.

In a letter of warning which General Victor issued soldiers were forbidden to disturb "the distinguished scholar," Goethe. In a similar letter, issued by Augereau, he was called "a man who is commendable in every way." And in the letter of the French Commandant of the city the wording is even stronger: "With regard to the great Goethe, Weimar's Commandant will take all measures to protect him and his home."

A few days after the battle, and undeniably under the feeling of gratitude to Christiane for her courageous and expedient conduct, Goethe wrote the Superintendent of Weimar: "During the last days and nights an old purpose of mine has come to maturity. I wish to recognize, fully and civilly, as *mine* my little friend who has done me so much good and who has now lived through also these trying times." And in perfect quietness he was married to Christiane.

The storm that had swept over Weimar never once shook his admiration for Napoleon. He had seen him rise and win victories wherever he went. In vain had he used his powers of persuasion to prevent Karl August from becoming a general in the Prussian army. And he had looked on with perfect equanimity when, during the battle, Napoleon formed the *Rheinbund* consisting of German Princes though under French supremacy. He felt somewhat as did Hegel who, on Napoleon's entrance into Jena, wrote as follows: "It is a peculiar feeling to lay eyes on an individual man who from this time on will rule the world." Goethe himself had written in his diary of August 7, 1806, these words: "The squabble between the servant and the coachman on the box excites us more than the dissolution of the Roman Empire." He meant the downfall of the German Empire that had been established at Verdun in 843.

CHAPTER XX

GOETHE AND BETTINA; GOETHE AND MINNA
HERZLIEB—*Pandora*: A DRAMA—GOETHE AND
NAPOLEON—NAPOLEON AND WIELAND

ON April 23, 1807, Bettina Brentano, then
twenty-three years of age, entered Goethe's home.
She came from his mother, whose favorite she had
been, and whom she questioned on all the details
of Goethe's childhood and early youth. She wished
to make use of these data in the book she was then
planning to write on his life. Bettina was the grand-
daughter of Sophie von la Roche, Wieland's old
friend, the daughter of Maxe Brentano, who had
felt a passion for Goethe, and who is one of the two
models of Lotte in *Werthers Leiden*.

Immediately after her arrival in Weimar she had
gone to Wieland, whom she had never once seen
before, in order to beg him for a letter of introduction to Goethe. She received this card written in
this German:

Bettina Brentano, Sophiens Schwester, Maximilianens
Tochter, Sophie la Rochens Enkelin, wünscht Dich zu sehen,
lieber Bruder, and giebt vor, sie fürchte sich vor Dir, und
ein Zettelchen, das ich ihr mitgebe, würde ein Talisman
seyn, der ihr Muth gäbe. Wiewohl ich ziemlich gewiss
bin, dass sie nur ihren Spass mit mir treibt, so muss ich
doch thun, was sie haben will, und es soll mich wundern,
wenn Dir's nicht so wie mir geht.

She had loved and adored Goethe from her childhood, not after the fashion of Rahel in purely spiri-

tual idolization and reasoned reverence, but with an admiration which, half sensual, half mental and altogether fiery, would ingratiate itself as importunate amiability, make itself indispensable through a burr-like hanging-on, and vehemently insinuate itself into good graces through enthusiasm's highest flight up and above all mountains.

In Goethe's room she stretched out both hands toward him and became at once utterly unconscious of herself. He pressed her to his heart: "Poor child, did I frighten you?" Those were his first words. He placed her on the sofa opposite himself. And thus the two sat for some time in silence. He broke the silence: I presume that you have read in the newspaper of the great loss that we recently suffered through the death of Duchess Amalie.—No, she said; I never read the newspapers.—Is that so, I thought you were interested in everything that takes place in Weimar?—No, I am interested only in you, and I am far too impatient to go leafing around in newspapers.—You are a friendly child.—Long pause.—Then she leaped from the sofa and threw herself on his neck.

From childhood on she had had this youthful boldness. In Marburg there is shown to this day a tower up which she used to creep and crawl and then draw the ladder up after her in order to be alone. She had the suppleness of a juggler in her limbs and in addition something of the childlike *Schwärmerei* of Mignon. She was a Mignon transferred to actual life, with the same charm and much less seriousness.

In the book entitled *Goethes Briefwechsel mit einem Kinde,* which she published after his death, in 1835, she has treated her own letters freely, inserted many things and much which seemed to her might have been felt; and she gave the entire affair a more passionate coloring. She wished to make it appear that Goethe was quite taken up with her in 1807-1808. She really thought so at that time, for he was accustomed to send the poems that he had just written along with the letters. It was excusable that she should think that these sonnets were addressed to her. It was inexcusable for her to turn them into prose and then introduce the prose into her letters so as to make it appear that Goethe had simply set her thoughts and feelings to rhyme. She is punished by the comic element that arises from the fact that the most of these poems were addressed to Wilhelmine (Minna) Herzlieb.

From May to September of this year, Goethe was living in Karlsbad in intimate association with the famous Prince of Ligne, the German-born French Minister Reinhard, the geologist Werner, and Metternich's literary mouth-piece, Friedrich Gentz. In November Bettina returned to Weimar. Goethe now had enough of her and her passion. He had, though he himself was unaware of it, fallen deeply in love with a young girl as unlike her as possible, a quiet girl of the instinctive sort, beautiful with her charming figure and fascinating, small oval face, innocent and shy, the foster-daughter of the bookseller Frommann in Jena, to whom Goethe paid daily visits during that autumn. We have one single declaration by Wilhelmine concerning him:

Goethe had come over from Weimar so that he might work out his beautiful thoughts for humanity in peace and quiet. To our great joy he lived in the castle, for had we not been so near to his residence, who knows whether we would have seen him every evening. He has to look out for his health a little bit now too. Otherwise he seems well. He was always so cheerful and social that one felt indescribably happy and yet painfully moved withal in his presence.

She writes to a friend that, after listening to the golden words that flowed from his lips, she would retire to her room in the evening and then the tears would gush forth and there was but one thought that could console her:

We mortals are not all born for the same degree of excellence; each of us must strive and work according to his talents in that place where fate has placed him, and that is the end of it.

Goethe's love for her was deep. Those sonnets are of course addressed to her which play with her name, and which Bettina had the naïveté to believe were meant for her; she even insisted in so many words that she was the originator of them. And what is more, Goethe constantly dreamt of Wilhelmine while he was working on his *Pandora*. She is also the model of Ottilie in *Die Wahlverwandtschaften*. She did not marry until fourteen years later, in 1821. The marriage was soon dissolved; she became insane and died in 1865.

It was in Frommann's house that Goethe came into constant association with Zacharias Werner, one of the most disagreeable of the German Romanticists. Like all of the Romanticists he wrote sonnets. The year before, Frommann had published a translation of Petrach's sonnets that made a distinct impression on Goethe; and he now began to com-

pete with Zacharias Werner in the writing of sonnets.

The form was contrary to Goethe's nature,
though he mastered it as he did every other verse
form. He had in earlier days so frequently expressed his aversion to the restraint imposed by
the fourteen liners that, now that he was writing
sonnets, he treated this aversion in his lines. But
it is not amusing for a modern reader to read the
sonnets that treat the sonnet itself, such as numbers
11, 14, and 15, though some of them possess great
charm. There is, by way of illustration, *Freund-
liches Begegnen,* which tells how the lover, wrapped
up in a mantle, meets the young girl, attempts to
pass by her without slipping the mantle to one side,
stops, involuntarily throws the mantle off, and—
she lies in his arms.

As is usually the case, Goethe's skill is more certain when he allows his women to commit themselves
than when he relegates this function to his men. A
few of his sonnets reproduce letters by women; one
from Bettina and one from Minna Herzlieb. The
close of the sonnet in which (in my judgment) it is
Bettina who writes, has a high degree of perfection:

> Ich mag heut'gen Tag Dir nichts vertrauen,
> Wie sich im Sinnen, Wünschen, Wähnen, Wollen
> Mein treues Herz zu Dir hinüber wendet:
>
> So stand ich einst vor Dir, Dich anzuschauen,
> Und sagte nichts. Was hätt ich sagen sollen?
> Mein ganzes Wesen war in sich vollendet.

The sonnet in which the infatuated woman remarks that she would greatly prefer to post the

white, untouched paper than to write upon it herself, since *he* would then probably cover it with
words of love, contains without the slightest doubt
a play on her name: *Lieb Kind! Mein artig Herz!
Mein einzig Wesen!* It is even more certain that
the seventeenth and last sonnet, entitled *Charade,*
refers to Wilhelmine. In it there is a riddle, the
solution of which is *Herzlieb.*

II

Pandora is a mythological drama which Goethe
planned—but never finished—while he was stirred
with passion for a young girl who was removed from
him by forty years, and by his own marriage of
some time previous to the present affair. It is one
of the most unpopular works he ever wrote, at once
artificial and affected, written in ancient Greek style,
and confined to the circle of Hellenic myths. Chemically devoid of naïveté, it is done in the tone of
tiresome virtuosity, and is weighed down with complicated and solemn metrical forms. The fragment
is cryptic and allegoric, a work of art created for
philologists and professors. The language is unusually abstract, the substantives rarely have articles. And yet, there is much rhythmical resonance
in the work—such as we find in scholarly, technical,
absolute music.

Prometheus and his brother Epimetheus are the
two leading male characters. Prometheus, having
completely abandoned the idea of further fighting against Zeus, is engaged in an active life on
earth. He is the originator of fire, and for this
reason also the creator of industry. He has like-

wise done much for art, especially the art of the smith. As a maker of weapons on a large scale, he has all manner of people in his employ, and equips them for the business of war. He is the prehistoric Krupp. In contrast to him, Epimetheus is the dreamer and the brooder. His whole mind is taken up with the charming Pandora, who once was his but who was forced to leave him. His entire life is filled with longing for her return. He has by her a daughter, Elpore, an airy creature with the morning star upon her head; she disappeared with her mother, but now she reveals herself to Epimetheus, and in a beautiful song characterises herself as something that can perhaps be called the erotic hope and the dreamed of petition. In addition to her, Epimetheus has a daughter Epimeleia, who lives with her father. She is a young being whom Prometheus's son, Phileros, loves. But out of foolish jealousy he wishes to murder her; he does wound her before the eyes of her father—all of which makes a rather disagreeable impression. The whole of her culpability lies in the fact that just as she left her door ajar in order to receive Phileros, a young shepherd, who forestalled him, pushed the door open and was in the act of doing her violence. After this her lover no longer believes in her innocence—which is rather fatuous.

The best part of this drama is Epimetheus's expression of his love for the beautiful, and his loss of the charming one in whom he is infatuated:

> Wer von der Schönen zu scheiden verdammt ist,
> Fliehe mit abgewendetem Blick!
> Wie er, sie schauend, im tiefsten entflammt ist,
> Zieht sie, ach, reisst ihn ewig zurück.

Or as he says in another place:

> Der Seligkeit Fülle, die hab ich empfunden,
> Die Schönheit besass ich, sie hat mich gebunden,
> Im Frühlingsgefolge trat herrlich sie an.

The rhythm in this drama is altogether deserving
of study. Goethe has tried, with success, the effect
of meters hitherto unused by him. He has given,
in singularly felicitous fashion, expression to the
primitive bluntness of seasoned soldiers. They sing:

> Wir ziehn, wir ziehn   So geht es kühn
> Und sagen's nicht.   Zur Welt hinein,
> Wohin? Wohin?   Was wir beziehn,
> Wir fragen's nicht   Wird unser sein.
> Und Schwert und Spiess   Will Einer das,
> Wir tragen's gern.   Verwehren wir's;
> Und Jen's und Dies   Hat Einer was,
> Wir wagen's gern.   Verzehren wir's.

The drama was built on a large scale. The continuation that was planned indicates that Goethe
wished to depict by symbols of a serious nature the
entire development of human culture from prehistoric times to the domination of art and science.
He was occupied with the work from 1807 to 1809.
Then it was put aside forever.

III

Napoleon, after the battle of Jena, was moved
only by the dignified deportment of the Duchess
Luise not to vent his wrath so thoroughly upon
Weimar. Something happened also after the conclusion of peace which was objected to on the part
of Karl August and which could not help but arouse
Napoleon and show him that the people of Weimar

were unfriendly to him: donations of money to Blücher and the reception of dismissed Prussian officers into the court service of Weimar. But since the Emperor of Russia, at that time Napoleon's ally, was the brother to the hereditary Princess, the Duke could appear without causing too much unrest at the Congress of Erfurt in 1808, where four kings and thirty-four princes, in addition to the two emperors, met by appointment.

Goethe did not wish to be present but was expressly requested by the Duke to appear. He was far from seeing in Napoleon the destroyer of the fatherland. He had never known any German fatherland. He wrote on July 27, 1807: "When people complain about a whole which is supposed to have been lost and which, however, no human being in his lifetime ever saw in Germany, much less bothered about, it is impossible for me to conceal my impatience." He did not look upon foreign supremacy as a disgrace and nourished no particular animosity towards it. Quite the contrary. In place of a countless number of badly governed little principalities there had come to be a smaller number ruled in a relatively modern spirit, in harmony with the principles of the French Revolution. They made their impression upon him only now that they were embodied in a great personality. No one wanted to pick a quarrel with Germanism; none of the German princes under Napoleon, least of all Jerome in Westphalia, upon whom Napoleon had depended to win his subordinates' affection, and who had Goethe's friend, Count Carl Reinhard at his side, Jacob Grimm as librarian, and the historian Johannes von Müller as minister of instruction.

By force of good politics, Napoleon together with his marshals and envoys, brought German science and literature into real repute. Hence Goethe's disinterestedness, mortifying to the nation, toward the German's so-called struggle for liberty against Napoleon, a struggle for national independence, but which merely tended to call back into existence all the reaction of the past. Hence his words: "It will do them no good; the man is too big for them." Hence as late as July, 1812, his poem of homage to Marie Louise and Napoleon when the Empress came to Karlsbad. The hope which the poem expresses was not well founded in 1812: *Der Alles wollen kann, will auch den Frieden*. It expresses, however, joy over the birth of the King of Rome:

> Und wenn dem Helden Alles zwar gelungen,
> Den das Geschick zum Günstling auserwählt,
> Und Ihm vor allem alles aufgedrungen,
> Was die Geschichte jemals aufgezählt,
> Ja reichlicher als Dichter je gesungen—
> Ihm hat bis jetzt das Höchste noch gefehlt;
> Nun steht das Reich gesichert wie geründet,
> Nun fühlt er froh in Sohne sich gegründet.

When Napoleon, in October, 1808, learned from his Minister Maret that Goethe was in Erfurt, he made an appointment with him for the following day. He had read *Werther* seven times during his youth and had followed Goethe's career with interest and attention.

As Goethe appeared in the doorway, Napoleon raised his head from the dinner table, motioned to him to come in, cast one glance at him, and made the historic remark: *Vous êtes un homme!* That

is the best comment that has ever been made on
Goethe. While Napoleon was giving various orders
to Daru and his lieutenants who came in to make
their reports, he plied Goethe with questions about
his dramas. Daru told the Emperor that Goethe
had translated Voltaire's *Mahomet*. "That is not
a good drama," said Napoleon, and then proceeded
to show how absurd it was for Mahomet to give
such a disparaging picture of himself. He himself
wrote a derogatory critique of *Mahomet* while at
St. Helena. He then brought the conversation
around to *Werther,* and with the insight of the
tactician drew Goethe's attention to the fact that
he had not adhered to the theme of unrequited love
as the basis of suicide, but had fused this motif with
the irrelevant one of an offended sense of honor.
He then quoted another passage from *Werther*—
a passage Goethe could never be persuaded to mention—and said: "Why did you write it? It is not
natural." He then proceeded to justify his objection in detail. Goethe writes: "The observation is
quite correct." He conceded, and apologized for,
the unnaturalness of the passage in question; he
had made use of an artistic trick in order to produce
certain effects. The Emperor was satisfied, turned
again to the drama and made, according to Goethe
himself, "some very significant comment, such as we
would expect from one who had studied the tragic
stage of France with the greatest attention, and had
felt deeply the deviation of it from nature and
truth."

After closing a series of remarks, he usually said:
"*Qu'en dit Monsieur Goethe.*" He discussed likewise the Fate Tragedy that was just then coming

into vogue and made use of an expression that strikes us with surprise coming as it did from a fatalist; "What do people mean anyhow in our day by Fate? Politics, that is Fate."

He interrupted himself then and spoke with Daru and Soult on political affairs. Then he questioned Goethe as to his personal position and the Court of Weimar: "I answered him naturally. He seemed satisfied and translated my expression into *his* language so that it became clearer than I could have expressed it myself." The Emperor showed his approval again and again, when Goethe said anything, and made him laugh so heartily by his jovial comments that Goethe believed he would have to beg his pardon.

Several days later Goethe was made a member of the Legion of Honor. In a letter to Maret in which he thanks him for it, we read: *Votre Excellence voudra se faire interprête vis-à-vis de sa Majesté des sentiments que je suis incapable d'articuler, et que je voudrais pouvoir témoigner par un dévouement parfait.*

On the sixth of October Napoleon announced himself as guest at the home of the Duke of Weimar. He took his actors with him and now, on Goethe's stage, Napoleon's company—among whom were Talma and Mlle. Georges — played "The Death of Caesar" by Voltaire.

When Caesar said:

Je sais combattre, vaincre et ne sais point punir.
Allons, n' écoutons point ni soupçons ni vengeance,
Sur l'univers soumis regnons sans violence!

all eyes turned toward Napoleon.

After the performance there was a ball. Napoleon took Goethe aside and said with reference to the dramatic production: "The serious drama could very well be a school for princes as well as for the people; for in certain ways it is quite above history. . . . *You* ought to portray the death of Caesar, more magnificently than Voltaire has done, and show how happy Caesar would have made the world if the people had only granted him time in which to carry out his lofty plans."

A little later: "You must come to Paris! I make this definite request of you! You will obtain a larger view of the world there, and you will find a wealth of themes for your poetry."

The strength of the impression that Goethe made on Napoleon is best shown by the fact that when the Emperor, after his fearful defeat in Russia and his mad sled-ride through Europe, arrived at Weimar he asked, while they were exchanging horses, about Goethe and requested the French Ambassador to extend him his greetings.

But the impression that Napoleon made on Goethe was deeper: "The greatest mind the world has ever seen," exclaimed Goethe to Boisserée. His admiration went so far that he at that time in the house of the Wolzogens found it absolutely right that anything which stood in the way of such a justified genius should be removed. He defended Napoleon's conduct when he had a pretender like Enghien and a demagogue like Palm shot so as to give the public, once for all, a conspicuous example that would prevent it from constantly interfering with the plans of the genius.

Goethe was deceived by Napoleon's straightforwardness and amiability toward him. However frequently the King and Queen of Prussia might come to Weimar, they never took any notice of him. Frederick the Great, his senior by thirty-seven years, scorned, as an old man, his *Götz* and had not the slightest appreciation of his personality. Napoleon, his junior by twenty years, understood him thoroughly.

It *did* seem to him that Napoleon had crowned his career, "had put the dot over the 'i' of his life," as he expressed himself. He wrote to Cotta: "Never has another individual of higher rank conducted himself in this way toward me; with an especial degree of confidence he gave me a place in the world (alongside of himself) and did not remark in some dubious tone that my personality was agreeable to him." In other words, for the first time in Goethe's life, he had stood face to face with his equal. Neither Herder nor Schiller, nor anyone of the other many friends who associated with him, had ever been his peer. In October, 1808, the two greatest men on this earth at that time met in mutual understanding.

When Napoleon so forcefully asked Goethe to come to him, live near him, and exchange Weimar for Paris, he was in a serious frame of mind, and for one moment both indeed caught a glimpse of the phantasmagoria of the Maecenas that Frederick had tried to be for Voltaire—but did not become—and which now, though with reversed rôles, Napoleon should be for Goethe. Paris could have been the best point of departure for his influence on world literature. It did not come to pass. This one meeting alone was written in their stars. But for the first time in his life Goethe met his equal in genius.

IV

There was another of Weimar's celebrities whose acquaintance Napoleon wished to make, and to whom he showed genuine good will: It was Wieland, then seventy-five years old. The especial reason why he was pointed out is quite noteworthy by way of proving that in a highly gifted man there is at times material for a prophet.

In the March number of Wieland's magazine *Der neue teutsche Merkur,* 1798, a prose conversation is carried on between two fictitious persons, the German Wilibald and the Frenchman Heribert. The German expresses himself on the condition existing in France, then racked by party schisms, makes it clear to the Frenchman that such a republic can survive only with difficulty. The antipathy toward royal power could easily slip over into the opposite. The Frenchman expresses the hope that France's good genius will save it from such retrogression, while the aversion to new revolutions will lend approval thereto. The German maintains that the various parties are so zealously militating against the good spirit of the French nation that one can assuredly count upon the desire for peace. But he has a bit of advice to give the French, and unless he is very much mistaken, his method is the sole way of saving French society from the destruction that is becoming more imminent every day despite its material victories and conquests.

Herbert asks what this sole means of salvation is. Wilibald replies that since the French no longer wish a king, and since they can as a matter of fact not have a king so long as there are members of the House of Bourbon living, there is only one thing left for them to do, and that is to chose a dictator.

Heribert: A Dictator?

Wilibald: Or a *Lord Protector* or a *Protarchon.* The name makes precious little difference, just so it is a man in whom you can safely vest unlimited power, just as one appointed in dangerous times a Dictator in Ancient Rome. . . . He would have to be an amiable young man with great, high-minded endowments, with the most excellent talents for war and peace, with untiring activity, with as much shrewdness as courage, with the firmest character, clean morals, simple and unpretentious in his manner of living, always in control of himelf, . . . at once open and resolute, flexible and hard, mild and inexorable, everything in its time. In short, a man such as is found but once in a century, and whose genius could hold the respect of all the others and overpower them. . . . But for a number of reasons he should not be a real Frenchman; and if he after all had a foreign name, so much the better. He must have already given many proofs of the fact that he really possesses the powers I find necessary to make your Dictator a success; and of the talents mentioned, I cannot omit a single one. If he had already acquired a great name for himself in the world and enjoyed general esteem, I do not see what he would lack that would prevent him from becoming the rescuer of you yourself, indeed of the whole world. And the extraordinary feature of it all is, you do not need to go out first and search for this man, for, owing to a happy coincidence, a coincidence which could be called únique, *he has already been found.*

Heribert: I presume you mean Buonaparte.

Wilibald: Of course I do.

Heribert: For how long a time should he be appointed?

Wilibald: For as long as he holds out. I fear you will lose him all too soon. The longer the better therefore.

The results of this vaticination were most remarkable. Two years later an English magazine,

St. James Chronicle, which was always detecting the
influence of the Jacobins and of the secret society
called the Illuminati, contained (January 25, 1800),
a bitter article against Wieland as the tool of this
society. The sagacious sheet had found out that
Wieland, whom it persistently called Weiland, was
an accomplice of the Illuminati, had advised the
French what to do with regard to Bonaparte, and
the French had followed his advice. The article
reads (in translation):

However strange it may seem, a German writer has had
the temerity to give, in one of his magazines, the French
some advice concerning Bonaparte, who was then far away
in Egypt and totally forgotten by the French, and they have
followed his advice literally. . . . It is impossible not to
detect the secret motives and means of this abominable sect,
with its untiring efforts it is accustomed to employ to reach
the most culpable goal. The dialogue between Wilibald and
Heribert is nothing in the world but a suggestion from
Weiland's pen, inspired most likely by the Illuminati, who
have been endeavoring to familiarize Europe with their
plans and to make their hero acceptable to the French people. Conspicuous indeed is the corruption in that they insist that there can no longer be any thought of a king, so
long as the legally justified but unsuccessful Bourbons exist.
Notice, too, the exaggerated description of the virtues that
the dictator must necessarily have and the contention that
the description fits Bonaparte, who is after all only a successful adventurer who, in his brief and gigantic career,
has been the incarnation of all the crimes that are found in
the most gruesome of tyrants without a single one of their
good traits. All of this cannot leave the slightest doubt in
anyone's mind but that this large and loathsome gang is
working effectively and in secret.

A few words concerning the prophecy and the
embitterment it awakened in England must have
called Napoleon's attention, ten years later, to the

old German writer. He talked with him for some time at the court ball, October 6, and took delight in his spiritual good humor. The conversation revolved at first about Tacitus, from whom Napoleon insisted that he had never learned the slightest thing. He expressed vehement opposition to the admiration for him, and called him an unjust libeller of men. Tacitus hated tyrants, but he, Napoleon pronounced his name without fear. Tacitus found criminal motives for the very simplest actions, made all Emperors criminals together, so that one could admire his genius in having seen through them. He had not written a history of an empire, but had given excerpts of law-suits. His work treated of complaints, complainants, and of people who had their arteries opened. And what a style. I am not an expert Latinist; but the murkiness of his writing is undeniable if I may depend at all on the ten or twelve translations, in French and Italian, that I have read. Am I not right, Monsieur Wieland? But I am boring you. We did not come here to discuss Tacitus. Just look how well Emperor Alexander dances.

He continued to discuss the affairs of the Greek and Roman republics, and the benefits mankind had received from the Christian religion in olden times. When Wieland had an audience with Napoleon in Erfurt, the latter talked with the former in a most intimate tone, and plied him with questions concerning his domestic affairs.

CHAPTER XXI

Die Wahlverwandtschaften

IT had long been Goethe's plan to insert a series
of novelettes in the continuation of *Wilhelm Meisters Lehrjahre* which would throw light on what he
considered the most basic element in human life:
renunciation and resignation. He was now nearly
sixty years old. He compared, as he had done in
Werther, man's yearnings and longings with the
obtainable. Now, as then, he saw the innate power
of the passions beating away against the rock of
social order. Now, as then, he followed the swell
with a sympathy such as is found in those people
who know precisely what they are talking about.
But the impression as a whole was no longer one of
youthful despair; it was rather a melancholy assurance of the inevitableness of renunciation. Had
he not recently been obliged to renounce Minna
Herzlieb?

It soon became evident, however, that the novelette, as it grew in his mind, was going to be far too
elaborate for *Wilhelm Meisters Wanderjahre*: it
grew into a work that was complete in itself. It
was finished many years before the *Wanderjahre*—
to which it proved to be vastly superior.

Various experiences in Goethe's past life were
utilized as elements of the work at present taking
shape in his mind. In 1771, thirty-eight years, in

other words, before the appearance of the novel,
he had gone on a journey through Alsace and had
visited the Alsatian Ottilieberg where, according to
a legend, a beautiful and pious countess had sought
refuge from the world, and where a chapel still bore
her name.   From this we have the name of the
heroine, the motif of the chapel itself, and the
miracles of the dead body.   Moreover, Goethe's
fifty-eight years did not prevent him from being
passionately loved by two young women, Bettina
Brentano and Minna Herzlieb.   This was in 1807.
For the latter of the two he cherished an ardent
affection.   It is however impossible to see from the
sonnets addressed to her—they are playful and
rather flirtatious in tone—just how warmly Goethe
had loved in these years, and what a thorough-going
study of passions he planned and carried out.

For him the attraction that one person has for
another, mutual attraction, seemed in his present
state to be a physical necessity, a demoniac power
which works with law-abiding magic.   Since he
found this force at work even in the lower stages of
nature, such as the chemical attraction and repulsion
of bits of matter for each other, he took up with
the expression *Wahlverwandtschaft,* or "elective
affinity," which the Swedish physicist Bergman[5] had
introduced some twenty years previously.

[5] Torbern Olof Bergman (1735-1784) entered the University of
Upsala in 1752.   His father wished him to study theology; he
wished to study science.   In order to please both himself and his
father he studied both and injured his health.   While convalescing
he made some important discoveries in botany.   In 1768 he was
appointed professor of chemistry at Upsala, though it was a phase
of science of which his knowledge was not profound.   He began
to study it in a quite serious fashion and wrote a number of articles on it.   Of these the most important is his "Elective Affinities"
(1775).   —TRANSLATOR.

The local descriptions that consume so much space in the novel and constitute so important a part of it were based on the environs of the castle at Wilhelmsthal near Eisenach. It had been founded by Karl August. The splendid garden, the three fish ponds, and Ottilie's favorite spot, all so vividly portrayed in the novel, have their counterpart at the castle. He availed himself right lavishly of the opportunity to describe the natural surroundings, but not as is done to-day, in order to emphasize the influence of nature on the souls of men. His purpose was rather the reverse: He wished to visualize the contrast between man's supremacy over such nature as surrounds him from without, and man's subjection to the nature that is within him. Hence the part played by horticulture, architecture and engineering on the one hand, and the "elective affinities" on the other.

None of Goethe's more pretentious works is constructed as is this one. And none, absolutely none, has such a profound and coherent, though schematic, composition. Epic writing comes as far from being Goethe's strong point as does dramatic. Neither in *Wilhelm Meister* nor in *Faust* is there much coherency; both works lack unity. As if in the anticipation of an unusually long life, Goethe was never in a hurry to finish anything. He let his works lie, took them up again and again, inserted other works in between those that had previously been written, and completed the entire product at a late period and frequently in a distinctly careless fashion. He reminds us, in this connection, of one of the greatest minds this earth has ever known—a mind that his resembled in no other way—that of Michael

Angelo. As the result of a hardy and heroic self-criticism, Michael Angelo left the majority of his works unfinished.

Die Wahlverwandtschaften consists of two equal parts, each divided into eighteen chapters, and each containing a mass of parallel features of a symbolic or allegoric nature. They call to mind Dante's method of procedure in the *Divine Comedy*. The work has moreover a strict, almost rigorous motivation, with precise and quite conscientious attention to details. For Goethe this is an innovation; it is a spiritual novelty. There is hardly anything that he disdained in his earlier days as he did logical motivation. Take such a fundamental question as the following: Why does Faust forsake Gretchen? Goethe never answers this question. Here however we have, so to speak, an unbroken net in which each mesh fits exactly into the next following.

It would be unfair however and uncritical not to remark that the work contains an enclave. Let us call it by its right name, a digression. Goethe's inescapable inclination to retard the decision has prompted him to make the first larger half of the second part—almost a third of the entire work—of unnecessary and excessive breadth. Had this been condensed into about twenty pages, the work would still be what it is, a masterpiece, but then it would also be a highly diverting, even thrilling book for the great majority.

In accordance with the tendency of his later years, Goethe has sought the typical. This hovered before him constantly, not only in his scientific investigations but also in his poetic activity. By this we are not to understand that he took either a supercilious or an entirely neglectful attitude toward the individual. The opposite assumption would be more nearly correct. But what he wished to do here was to portray a permanent, fundamental relation, and by steeping himself in the individual instance so passionately, as though it were the only one of its kind, he came upon peculiarities that are not unique but seem to belong to certain forms common to human development. He ventures to assume the existence of natural laws.

In *Werther,* Goethe himself had, so to speak, gone through an assault of the passions. Here he looks down upon them from above somewhat as one watches the materials in a laboratory. Though this novel, the only one that Goethe ever wrote with a single guiding idea, revolves about marriage, it treats marriage primarily because the conflicts in private life were the ones that Goethe best understood. The real basic theme and subject of the novel however is more comprehensive than this statement would seem to indicate. *Die Wahlverwandtschaften* treats every single conflict that arises between the natural powers in man and existing human relations.

Goethe does not judge; he merely thinks. He never thinks in a Christian or moral way, but in unqualified harmony with a cryptic pantheism of nature.

At the beginning of the novel, the situation is as favorable as possible. We see a married couple of high rank, opulent in material goods and in the enjoyment of a wholesome life. He and she had early felt drawn to each other; but they had been separated by external forces. Both had been married before: He to a woman much older than him-

self, she to a man who was indifferent to her. They
both became free. Eduard urges Charlotte to give
her consent to marriage. She hesitates for a long
while. When she finally yields, the goal of their
life seems to have been reached.

It is now her wish that they shall live wholly for
each other. She sends her only daughter away, and
removes her niece Ottilie. They plan a life of mutual entertainment. For the moment their scheme
is to take up the scattered, confused leaves from
his diary and make something coherent and attractive out of them. They are both fond of music;
they play together. Eduard plays the flute irregularly: his art is like his life. First he plays too fast;
then too slow. Charlotte, more gifted than he,
accompanies him in such a way that the tempo of
the whole becomes just right, however much individual passages may be out of time. Then Eduard
conceives a fancy for reading aloud; but he has
this trifling oddity: He finds it quite intolerable to
have someone looking on his book while he is
reading.

Eduard wishes to have the friend of his younger
days, the Captain, visit him. Charlotte opposes the
idea; she has a presentiment that some misfortune
will arise therefrom. Eduard pleads their development; he insists that they have learned reason
through experience. He emphasizes their consciousness. Charlotte replies: "Consciousness is an inadequate weapon."

These are the characters: Charlotte, dignified and
cultured. We picture her to ourselves as being tall
but rounded out, the *grande Dame* in every sense
of the word. She is susceptible to strong impres-

sions, but abounds in self-control and good sense.
Eduard is restless, passionate, an artistic nature,
spoiled by his first marriage with a woman older
than himself, quite unaccustomed to self-denial, incapable of resignation, and with a tender spot in
his soul, a spot that always bleeds, figuratively
speaking.

Eduard entreats; he implores her to accede to
his wish regarding the Captain. She finally does
so, with no little display of reluctance. It is at this
point that Mittler is introduced. He is a character
necessitated by the basic thought of the novel. It
would always be easy to identify him with living
models. But as Goethe has arranged his rôle, he
is quite removed from the sphere of such circumstances as go to make up reality. He is a marriage
fanatic as such. First he was a priest, then a law
student. At the present stage of his life he tarries
only where there is something to be straightened
out, something to be fixed up between married
people. Everything is in excellent condition in the
case before him, so he leaves immediately.

The Captain comes. Charlotte tries quietly to
get him away by securing him a position. He proves
to be all tact and consideration, a practical man,
efficient, wise as to the things of this world, a man
of integrity. Eduard tries to make use of his
talents; he will employ him in the carrying out of
the improvements he is planning to make on the
estate. The Captain takes up with the idea, determined though he is not to offend Charlotte's wishes
concerning the arrangement of the garden.

The very first consequence of his coming however
is that Charlotte becomes more and more lonely;

for the two men are constantly together. He involuntarily keeps Eduard away from her.

The fourth leading character, Ottilie, is now introduced, at first by remarks made about her. We are prepared for her introduction by a letter from her inspired teacher at the educational institution she has been attending. In this way we become acquainted with her gentle disposition, her temperance in food and drink, and her rather frail health: She suffers frequently from pains in the left side of her head. Through a number of small, portrait-like features her personality is thrown into quite distinct relief. She writes slowly and stiffly; she writes a child's hand. She is unable to understand anything that does not follow from the immediately preceding, but give her all the intervening steps and she will grasp the most difficult situation. She wins no prizes in school; she has talents; special skill she does not have. Her charm is revealed indirectly through the cordial interest her teacher takes in her. We note that he pays attention to the very smallest features of her character and her personality, not omitting the habit she has of making a kind of warding-off gesture every now and then with her hand.

Eduard is quite devoid of any sense of order; the Captain on the contrary, who always works with a definite goal in mind, is order personified. It is under his leadership that the archives are arranged in the castle; the papers are all carefully classified. They likewise establish a first-aid society, and set up a domestic apothecary shop. This latter gives rise to extended conversations bearing on fundamental principles in physics and chemistry.

This, in substance, is what is said: We call those
natures and materials related which, when they
meet, quickly influence, indeed mutually determine
the fate of each other.   Such are nature-relation-
ships, mind-relationships.   They do not become
interesting, however, until they cause dissolutions,
separations.   The chemist is the artist of separations.   The term *elective affinity* has been formed,
for it looks as though some relations were preferred
to others.   When limestone, for example, is placed
in diluted sulphuric acid, the latter reacts on the
lime and forms gypsum.   The airy acid is disen-
gaged, separated.   "Poor acid," exclaims Charlotte.

It then becomes the privilege of the acid, we are
told, to unite with water, form mineral water and,
as a mineral spring, bring the diseased back to a
state of reconvalescence and complete health.   From
her moral point of view, Charlotte has an objection
to raise.   She insists that we do not have to do here
with choice, hardly indeed with natural necessity,
but with an occasion or an opportunity which creates
relations just as it makes thieves.   She forgets that
natural necessity creates the occasion, gives rise to
the opportunity.

The result of this conversation for the reader
is as follows: We see human life portrayed in the
lower stadia of nature.   In the depths of nature we
see these materials and beings which are really not
living, and which seem quite lifeless, entering after
all on the point of actual activity.

Ottilie's arrival necessitates a change in the distribution of the living quarters.   Eduard and the
Captain occupy one wing of the castle, Charlotte
and Ottilie the other.   Ottilie is not excessively com-

municative; Eduard finds her entertaining. Just as when she was in school, she eats and drinks too little, and yet she looks so well that she is a feast and a consolation for men's eyes. They compare her to an emerald: She is as beneficial to the eyes as it is. A characteristic feature is her complaisant obligingness which, if not hindered, rises to actual servility. If anything falls on the floor, she picks it up; she does this even for the men.

Eduard and the Captain lay new plans and introduce new improvements. A Swiss-like cleanliness is made a feature of the town. In order to prevent its being filled with the numerous roaming beggars, they institute this bizarre custom: They place small sums of money in the outmost house of the town so that these indigent wayfarers will not receive support until they come to the end of the town.

Fine little traits, such as the fact that the Captain forgets to wind his watch, prove the general absorption and distraction. Time is forgotten out of a feeling of mutual good will and rare happiness. Charlotte had had the moss hut made quite narrow; really only for two. Mention is made of this at the very opening of the story, though we are told that it can hold three, even four. And now for the first time there are four in it.

Eduard begins to admire Ottilie, to love her. He expresses a tender affection for her. He begs her, by way of illustration, to take off the medallion she wears so that there may be no danger of her pressing it against her breast and thereby causing a dangerous sickness. (We see that the portrayal of this idea interested Goethe in a quite real and living way; it is the same motif that is given a tragic turn in *Wilhelm Meister*.)   Ottilie's and Eduard's hands meet, "the two most beautiful hands that were ever clasped."   He asks her to decide where the new house he is planning to build is to be located.   The corner-stone is to be laid on Charlotte's birthday, which Eduard wishes to celebrate so that he can later pay due and becoming homage to Ottilie apropos of the same event in her life.

The two grow more and more closely together as time goes on, though their habits are so totally different.   She likes to remain in the house; he is never satisfied unless he is outdoors.   But their inner agreement is proved by their constant association with each other.   If he reads aloud, she looks over his shoulder and it does not annoy him at all.   They play selected music together and never out of time, though he plays irregularly.   The others look upon all this as upon the harmless diversion of two good children who love each other.   And the other two likewise make music in ensemble.

The corner-stone is laid.   The address which the young mason makes has a direct bearing on the teachings of the novel.   The corner-stone, he remarks, might be laid without ceremony or ado, for it rests in its position by reason of its own weight and without the mortar:

But the mortar will not be omitted; cement there must be.   For just as in the case of human beings who are bound to each other by nature, but who are bound even more firmly together when cemented by the law, just so it is with the stones whose forms fit together, but which are held even more firmly when held by this binding matter.

This is the basic problem in the book: If two

people have a natural affection for each other, are they held together even more firmly by the binding influence of the law?

The mason empties his glass with a toast to the health of those present, and then tosses it high in the air so that it may be broken to pieces on falling to the ground. But it is caught up by one of the bystanders. We are inclined to interpret the incident as a dubious omen: This glass on which is engraved the monogram of the master of the house, E-O (Eduard Otto), remains intact.

Mittler arrives and delivers an enthusiastic speech in praise of marriage. To him it is the keystone and corner-stone of all civilization; to attack it is to attack the very foundation of social order. It must be inviolable, for it brings so much happiness that the isolated unhappiness caused by it is as nothing in comparison. Why indeed speak of unhappiness at all when the real root of the trouble is impatience? That marriage is at times uncomfortable and inconvenient is also good, and constitutes an additional reason for preserving the tie. Some are married who would like to be free; and some would like to be rid of their consciences, to which and with which we are likewise married.

Mittler is driven off by the arrival of a Count and a Baroness whom he does not wish to meet; for they are his opposites, spiritually speaking. They are also the opposite of economy in the epic construction of the work. They have long been in love with each other, but they are both married. The Baroness has succeeded in obtaining a divorce. The Count's wife however has refused to give her consent to the complete annulment of her marriage.

On this account the two lovers can spend only the summers together. They come every year on the stroke of the clock, each on a different road, up to the castle or the manorial yard, where they have established a rendezvous. They have been meeting here for years; they are quite welcome because of their naturalness, their refinement of manner, their dignity, and their complete lack of affectation.

The Count contends that we are as a rule surprised when our hearts cease beating in unison. The conventional close of the comedy, marriage as the end of all things, he avers, has confused our ideas on this subject. At first we act quite involuntarily, as though the relations established on this earth were much more enduring and durable than reality shows them to be. In the end we are surprised at their evanescence and mutability. The Count suggests that marriages be entered into for a period of five years, with the privilege of renewal. Marriage should be indissoluble, if at all, in the case of a third marriage, in which state of affairs both parties could be supposed to have had a double antecedent experience. The institution, he asserts, has a loutish element in it; it destroys the most refined and tenderest of feelings; its blunt certainty is grim and demoralising. His idea is that marriage as an institution is either useless, as in the case of the mortar between the foundation stones, or distinctly nefarious, as when two substances or powers are joined together which exercise a mutually repellent influence over each other.

That same evening Charlotte is made to see that in all probability the Captain will receive an appointment that will take him away from them. To her this is a peal of thunder from a cloudless sky; she is obliged to conceal her passion and despair under the cloak of external or visible calm.

In the meantime the Baroness observes, quite to her displeasure, the mutual attraction of Eduard and Ottilie for each other. She takes the side of Charlotte, silently and by virtue of that unconscious alliance in which married women stand with regard to those who are unmarried.

The story has now reached the point where each of the two consorts is taken up with a woman who is not his spouse, and the other way about. And from this point on the course of events is cared for with the familiar refinement, and occasional boldness, of mental, spiritual and psychical motivation.

Late that evening Eduard and the Count have a long talk with each other. The newly arrived Count praises Charlotte's beauty; he finds her feet especially charming because of their smallness. He recalls with enthusiasm how she formerly shone at court. He asks Eduard to take him to the apartment of the Baroness: He has thus far had no opportunity to see her alone, and, having been separated from her for so long, he has a great deal to say to her.

Having accompanied the infatuated Count, Eduard stands for a while by Charlotte's door; he is tempted to knock. She has been weeping, and has sent her maid away. She lets him in. A mutual transposition of identities ensues: The unsatisfied yearning for an absent person conjures up before each of them the picture of another.

The following day, Eduard receives the copy of a manuscript from Ottilie; it is for him. On the

last pages he recognizes, with unfeigned amazement, his own handwriting; this she has assumed.
A declaration and first embrace follow. From this
moment on Eduard scarcely has enough self-control
to conceal his passion during an ordinary conversation.

At the same time however that the first real meeting took place between Eduard and Ottilie, the Captain and Charlotte feel irresistibly drawn to each
other. The motif is executed parallel and symmetri-
cally, just as in an old-fashioned drama. The yawl
in which they are sitting has run aground. He carries her in his arms from the boat to the land, and
they exchange the first and the—last kiss.

Different people act differently when in love.
Eduard is undisciplined; Charlotte controls herself
perfectly. She observes Ottilie, keeps close watch
on her. The situation however is growing worse
and worse; it is becoming envenomed. Eduard begins to complain to Ottilie about the other two. She
replies, rather flippantly, by disclosing to him a
derogatory remark the Captain made to Charlotte
concerning his flute-playing. This offends him; it
wounds his very heart. He now feels relieved of
all duties; considerate he need no longer be. He
is of the distinct conviction that Charlotte herself
merely wishes to get rid of him.

Everything now has a special meaning for Eduard. He detects an omen in everything that happens. Ottilie's birthday is to be celebrated. It
suddenly occurs to him that he planted the most
beautiful trees in the garden in the year of her
birth. A little research shows him that he planted
the trees on her very birthday. From this coinci-

dence he deduces a mystic connection between her
and himself. He buys a whole trunk full of beautiful and costly things for her.

One day, when Eduard is about to have the fireworks set off from the central dam in the large fish
pond, the explosives that had been collected into
one place are discharged. One of the dams, just
then crowded with spectators, breaks. A boy is on
the point of being drowned when the Captain res-
cues him and hastens away from the festivities.
Charlotte follows him. In course of time all those
present join them. Eduard then has fireworks just
for Ottilie and himself all alone.

The Captain departs that same night, and quietly.
Charlotte's resignation is complete. She is composed to the extent that she looks forward to a
future that is to be serious but not necessarily unhappy. Eduard however is transported to another
world; he is captivated by his love as by an intoxication of good fortune.

Charlotte now holds the centre of the stage. She
addresses some vehement reproaches to Eduard for
his passion but can, as was to be expected, make no
impression upon him in this way. Since neither of
the husbands is able to overcome the resistance of
the other, Eduard elects the rather passive means
of solving the difficulty by simply leaving and going
on his way. He does so however with the express
threat that he will somehow get possession of Ottilie in case Charlotte sends her away.

He settles down quietly in a lonely place. Where
Charlotte, with her naturally active temperament,
finds occupation for herself and Ottilie by interesting herself in the education of the children of the

neighborhood, Eduard has nothing to do but to brood in an idle and ineffectual way over his anguish.

The section of the novel that follows is treated with a sentimentality that is quite foreign to the modern mind. We can even assert that a sentimentality such as this is totally affected in its presentation. When Mittler, who soon becomes intolerable to the reader, looks up Eduard in order to persuade him to return to the right way, the latter portrays his fanciful life in the loneliness: "I write sweet, confidential notes in her name to myself and answer them and then keep both the letters and the replies." His one joy is in drinking from the glass with the monogram. As this has proved to be unbreakable, so are all the circumstances, all the relations, that fate determines. For it seems that everything in his previous life has been merely "a prelude, a retardation, a pastime, a killtime, until he became acquainted with her."

And so Mittler goes away from him and to Charlotte. She hopes that everything will come to a happy end, and that Eduard will return to her: "How can it be otherwise, since you find me in the condition in which I am?" Mittler exclaims: "Do I understand you correctly?" She begs him to take the message to Eduard; he declines, remarking that for such any messenger is good enough. He regards the entire affair as settled, so he must be off to other places where his presence is more needed. Goethe has experienced no doubt regarding the plausibility of his plan. He asks us to think of Mittler as spending his entire time, day in and day out, going from place to place, trying to keep married people married and together.

This is, incidentally, the turning point of the book.
Eduard's nocturnal visit to Charlotte has borne
fruit, and from now on the whole situation is fundamentally changed. Eduard is in despair; he draws
up his last will and testament, and goes to war to
fight "under a general with whom death is probable
and victory certain." It is all so unhistorical that
it is quite impossible to determine whom Goethe
had in mind.

There follow, during Eduard's campaign and the
Captain's absence, the above mentioned multitude
of subordinate events and accessory figures that delay the coming of the catastrophe. There is a
lawsuit, a discussion of memorials to the dead, building enterprises, and the introduction of the young
and amiable architect who interests himself in the
castle church. He falls in love with Ottilie. He
paints the ceiling of the chapel with the figures of
angels that resemble Ottilie. There follow the
arrival and stay of Ottilie's former teacher, and the
visit of two travelling Englishmen one of whom
relates a story bearing on the Captain's youth. And,
interwoven among the other events and episodes,
we have laid before us a series of extracts from
Ottilie's diary. These are in truth only partly in
keeping with Ottilie's mind; they serve rather as a
spiritual emporium for Goethe's own reflections,
being merely sprinkled here and there with observations that might come from Ottilie.

Here we have for the first time the comparison
that has since become so trite about the red thread
that runs through the cordage of the British navy.
Just like this noted thread does Ottilie's passion for
Eduard run through all her thoughts.

The following is a specimen of an aphorism that is really conceived after Ottilie's own heart: "Voluntary dependence is the most beautiful condition imaginable, and how would it be possible without love." Such desultory thoughts as the following however point plainly to the elder Goethe as their author:

There is no external sign of courtesy that does not have a deep moral basis. The right sort of training would be the one that would give at once the sign and the basis.

This aphorism would make a suitable motto for Herbert Spencer's *Ceremonial Government*. It discloses the mind of a venerable thinker.

The following came from the experience of a man of the world: "Fools and sages are equally harmless. Half fools and half sages are the really dangerous members of the human family."

We feel, too, the experience of a great poet and a profound observer back of such an expression as this: "Mediocrity has no greater consolation than this. Genius is not immortal." The same applies to this thought. "The greatest men are always connected with this or that weakness of their century."

The parallel figures and features that are introduced into this lengthy *entre-acte* help to emphasize the peculiarities or the position of the leading personages. The crude and secular, though externally radiant Luciane, Charlotte's daughter by her first marriage, is the exact opposite of Ottilie. Likewise the Count and the Baroness, who now appear as united and happy, are contrasted with the separated lovers. The teacher and the architect are the opposites that complement each other. The architect, with an enthusiasm for art that reminds of Goethe's own, has the appreciation of a real artist for plastic and picturesque beauty. At Christmas time he arranges living pictures; Ottilie has to represent the Madonna. Goethe writes in rapture concerning her: "In this figure she surpasses everything that any painter has ever portrayed." His enthusiasm could hardly be expressed in more visionary terms. He refers to her as "the heavenly child." His style even rises to this lyric height: "The trees should have been given life, and eyes to see, in order to rejoice in her." One feels that Ottilie is Goethe's conception of the Madonna.

Where the architect has an appreciative insight into the combined grandeur to which the physical world gives expression, the teacher, who cordially disapproves of the blending of the divine and the physical in the realm of sacred art, regards the formless as the most sublime. He has the inborn fear of an Israelite or a Mohammedan of seeing the celestial made idolatrous by being put into corporeal form. His interests are confined to a single issue: the training and development of the mind. In his own field he makes some discriminating, indeed quite surprising observations. He calls "change without distraction," for example, the right and ultimate solution of the teacher's problem. He hurls out into the world this striking paradox: "Women are created to stand alone." He explains his meaning in the following terms:

A man longs to be with a man. He certainly would have created one had he found none on the earth. A woman, however, could live for all eternity and never once think of creating another woman.

That is, if she had a husband of her own.

With his old and passionate interest for Ottilie, the teacher would like to take her back to the boarding school; for she has been torn away from regular and coherent instruction. Goethe makes the admirable observation that Ottilie, though obliged to confess this much, did not after all understand her teacher; for she no longer found anything that was incoherent when she thought of her beloved, and she did not see how there could be anything coherent without him.

As soon as she learns that Eduard was exposed to all the dangers of war, she suffered profound distress. Later on, this anxiety became duller and less acute until it amounted to nothing more than apathy. Goethe then makes the genuine observation that fear can be strained and brought up to a certain point, but not beyond this point. The law is applicable to Ottilie.

Charlotte gives birth to a boy. It has been named Otto after its father; but Otto is also the baptismal name of the Captain. Nor is it wholly a matter of accident that the feminine form of Otto is Ottilie.

Mittler appears and makes one of his vigorous speeches at the baptism. His remarks are so copious that they have a fatal effect. The decrepit old priest would have liked to sit down. As it was he was obliged to listen to Mittler while standing. The embarrassment due to this predicament entirely escapes the attention of the eloquent speaker. He finally talks the venerable priest to death. In this indirect way, Goethe pours out a measure of harmless ridicule on the head of the doughty matrimonial negociator.

In this way, birth and death are brought into

immediate juxtaposition. The taking off of the old priest seems like an ill omen for the existence of the infant. It is given over to the care of Ottilie. But, wonder of wonders, its facial expressions, its bodily features, are those of the Captain. Its eyes, large and black, are Ottilie's.

At this juncture Eduard returns from war covered with badges of distinction. He longs to go home. Out in the park he catches sight of Ottilie with the child. He makes himself known; he sees the child; he notes the similarities. The child spells the doom of his marriage: It was, he says, begotten in dual adultery. In other words, this child is Goethe's mute criticism of Eduard's and Charlotte's marriage.

Eduard and Ottilie now resign to the belief that they can belong to each other. It is the ephemeral culmination of the mood just before the tragedy. The child falls from Ottilie's boat into the water and dies. Fate exercises its gruesomeness here as in *Wilhelm Meister,* where Wilhelm's ungrounded suspicions become responsible for Marianne's desertion and lamentable death.

The news is brought to Charlotte. Thereupon she consents to the separation, for fate has willed it. But now Eduard is confronted by definite resignation with regard to him himself, on the part of Ottilie. She fancies that only by renunciation will she be able to expiate her guilt. She undergoes a complete change in the depths of her heart; she is freed from her intense desire to serve, freed also from contrition, and is to this extent at rest. But she slowly wastes away, for she eats almost nothing.

The daily life begins again between the two

couples, apparently just as in days of old. They
talk together, play their musical instruments in ensemble, and Eduard reads aloud while Ottilie looks
over his shoulder. But it is nothing more than a
faint reflection of their former life.

The attraction of Eduard and Ottilie for each
other now becomes almost magical. There is no
longer need of actual contact; it is enough simply to
be together. If anyone had kept either of them at
one end of the building, the other would voluntarily
have reached that same end. It seems as though
they are only one human being, so completely are
they occupied with the unconscious and perfect love
that arises from their common existence.

Eduard's birthday draws near. Ottilie accordingly unpacks the trunk he gave her a long while
ago so that she may adorn herself for the first, last
and only time with the gifts he lavished upon her.
Some well meant, and in themselves by no means
unreasonable, expressions of zealousness on the
part of Mittler evoke the ultimate dissolution.
He contends that nothing is more barbaric than acts
of interdiction and suppression. Positive commands
alone, he insists, are good and beautiful. He criticises vehemently the Ten Commandments. Honor
thy father and thy mother is the sole exhortation
that has sound meaning for him. The fifth commandment he finds decidedly imbecile; it sounds as
though people would take special pleasure in going
out and killing some one—as though such an act
would be agreeable to any mortal man! Instead
of forbidding children to kill people they should
have instilled in them the desire to help people, to
do them good. As to the sixth commandment he

becomes infuriated at the mere mention of it; it intrigues the curiosity of the young out on to quite dubious paths; it is coarse; it is indecent. Instead of this each one should have it brought close to his heart that the path to pursue is the one that will promote the happiness of married people, and will teach them to overcome the obstacles that stand in their way.

At this moment Ottilie enters; but she withdraws immediately and in silence when she hears the subject that is being discussed. This incident she does not survive. The encounter with the remarks that are being made about the sixth commandment, and the reminder that she has transgressed it in spirit, gives her the death-blow. She dies, having been previously consumed by hunger.

She is buried in the chapel. The miracles at the grave recall in a remarkably subtle manner the miracles at the Ottilieberg, which had been the poet's point of departure. On her deathbed Ottilie has made Eduard promise that he will not do violence to his own life. He refuses however almost consistently to eat and when, as a result of carelessness on the part of a servant, the precious glass is broken, he likewise refuses to take almost any nourishment in liquid form. He dies, and Goethe closes the sentence in which he says that this heart, so moved but a little while ago, has at last found perfect peace, with the rationalistic application of religious terminology: "And since he passed away with his thoughts directed to the Saint, we may well call him blessed."

Such is the course of events, such is the basic thought in this renowned novel, Goethe's most perfect production from his older days, the model of all later novels of a tragic character that are based on married life. It is the melancholy book of a student of nature. Its art is somewhat antiquated as viewed by the modern mind; it belongs to an age that is gone. The personages do not stand out especially sharp before us; it is rare that we hear them speak with their own voice. We have to do with the author; he explains the characters to us. We do not hear their conversations in their entirety, or with the animating force that accompanies the spoken word. We hear instead Ottilie's monologues, and of these freshness is not a consistent attribute. But the features of the novel that gave it its initial renown, and that have retained its interest to the very present, are not to be sought in the art of execution; these are to be found in the cleverness, the genius of construction, and the originality and profundity of the underlying idea.

Man is not seen here struggling with men, or seized by a passion, or developing innate talents. This book is neither a novel of adventure, nor of love, nor of crime, nor of education. Man is not seen here as the new beginning which takes up where nature leaves off; he is seen rather as a part of nature, in the grip of nature, and subjected to its laws which, totally indifferent to the individual's welfare, unite, dissolve, join, and separate.

We see a man and a woman joined together in such a way that there is apparently every reason to believe in the seriousness and permanency of the union. Those are not young, flippant persons that make up the characters of this book. It is the second marriage in the case of both parties, and both parties have been yearning for this second marriage for quite a while. The relation bursts however with a centrifugal force, though it bursts without an external break. Neither he nor she breaks the marriage in the vulgar connotation of the term. It breaks in truth for the very reason that it has been preserved. The child that is born and which, by a freak of nature, destroys both is the child of both. But this new life, born of custom, the life under which newly awakened passions flourish, opens the abyss beneath their feet.

With his wonted originality, Goethe has chosen an instance in which the child, as is so frequently the case, holds two people together who really do not harmonize at all. At the beginning of the novel, Eduard and Charlotte have no children. They do not become parents until the discord has begun; and their child which, under other circumstances, would bring the mother and father more closely together than ever and cause each the joy that attaches to parenthood, merely binds them externally. It doubles their anguish in truth instead of reënforcing their happiness. And its death does no more than make a bad situation worse.

In *Hermann und Dorothea* Goethe had depicted the happy finding of each other on the part of a young man and a young woman; their union was idyllic. In *Die Wahlverwandtschaften* he visualized the seamy side of domestic life, portrayed the passions as dark powers, and set forth marriage as an institution which constitutes for some an easy and useful cloak for their feelings, for others a straitjacket.

CHAPTER XXII

GOETHE AND SOCIAL POLITICS; GOETHE AND AMERICA

THAT social politics and social ethics lay beyond Goethe's interests, if not beyond his reach, has become an almost proverbial belief. It is a belief that is poles removed from the truth. Even in the eighteenth century he took a cordial interest in social questions, as can be seen by the immense space taken up in his consciousness by the affairs of the North American Colonies, and the emigrations from Europe to them. Lothario, in *Wilhelm Meister,* emigrates to America in order to find virgin soil for his enterprises. Jarno follows him across the Atlantic to the end that he may avail himself of the advantageous situation his predecessor has created there. It is in the *Lehrjahre* however that Lothario, like Goethe himself, expresses the belief that every man has an opportunity, also in Europe, to work and to improve things in many ways. He exclaims: "Here or nowhere is America!" That is to say, one finds his America everywhere.

But at the beginning of the nineteenth century, Goethe studies the prominent French socialists, Saint-Simon and Fourier, the Englishman Owen and also the English utilitarian philosopher Jeremy Bentham. He loses himself in plans for the refor-

mation of society.   He ascribes this duty to the
person who in the *Wanderjahre* is called the Uncle.
There had also been an Uncle in the *Lehrjahre;* he
had transformed his castle into a temple for artists.
It is the castle where Mignon's burial takes place.
But the Uncle in the *Wanderjahre* is an American
who is now living in Europe.   Though permeated
with the old civilization, he is a practical man.   His
grandfather emigrated.   He has now returned to
his estate in Germany, supervises it as a free vassal
and also as the most conscientious worker.   On his
belongings we read: *Possession and Joint Property.*
He exploits them for others; he is as economical as
a parsimonious individual can be—for others.   He
is not simply a giver, but also a promoter.   For
example, he presents industrious farmers with young
shoots from his plantations, is inexorable to slipshod and dilatory tenants who let the place run
down.   With him everything is useful.   It is indeed
from the useful that he wishes to rise and to mount
up to the beautiful.

In the oldest edition of the *Wanderjahre* Goethe
still (1821) looks upon emigration as an oddity, as
an absurdity.   But by 1827 he has changed his mind.
No one is a more radical state economist than the
old Goethe, the Goethe approaching his eightieth
year.   He does homage to America:

> Du hast es besser
> Als unser Kontinent, der alte,
> Hast keine verfallene Schlösser
> Und keine Basalte.
> Dich stört nicht im Innern
> Zu lebendiger Zeit
> Unnützes Erinnern
> Und vergeblicher Streit.

We notice the mineralogist in the remark concerning the basalt rocks, though they have since been found in various parts of America, and the mind that always looks ahead and forward in the remarks concerning useless memories. Goethe is still the same he was nearly fifty years previous to this time, when he wrote:

> Es erben sich Gesetz' und Rechte
> Wie eine ew'ge Krankheit fort,
> Sie schleppen von Geschlecht sich zu Geschlechte.

Goethe turns in this case with aversion away from the Old Europe. In his new edition he has Wilhelm exclaim: "In the Old World everything goes along in a blundering jogtrot. In the Old World the new is treated in an antiquated fashion and that which is growing according to cramped rules."

The singular Uncle has had his watchword, *Besitz und Gemeingut,* attached as an inscription round about on his various buildings, somewhat as the Oriental peoples adorn the walls of their houses with excerpts from the Koran. In this connection Goethe develops, by means of a dialogue, his ideas concerning the ownership of capital and the enjoyment of life. He is of the opinion that every man has a right to preserve and augment whatever possessions fate has given him. But the individual owner in question must always involuntarily be thinking how he is to arrange things so that others may have part and share in his goods. He himself is appreciated only in so far as others enjoy his possessions along with him. A prince is also honored because he imparts his power to others and gives other people employment. A rich man is honored because he gives of his superabundance to others. A musician or a poet is envied because his very nature is communicativeness itself.

Man should hold fast to any sort of possession that he may rightly call his own; he must make it a central point from which common property proceeds. Nothing is more absurd, nothing is more foolish, than to follow out the injunction of Holy Writ and give one's goods to the poor. It is much more praiseworthy to take good care of them, to leave the capital intact, but to let the interest, as time goes on, accrue to the benefit and joy of everyone.

The bizarre Uncle has studied the great Italian jurists Beccaria and Filangieri (Goethe's acquaintances from Naples) who jointly embody the breaking-through of the humanity of the eighteenth century as contrasted with the barbarous practice of law in previous times. Beccaria's goal was this: The greatest good to the greatest number (*la massima felicitá, divisa nel maggior numero*), which Goethe reproduces in abbreviated form in German as follows: *Den Meisten das Beste!*

The Uncle revamps this motto into the following: *Vielen das Erwünschte!* For, we read, one can neither find nor know "the most," and much more difficult is it to determine what is "best." But there are always many round about us. We become acquainted with their wishes. We can take into consideration what they should wish. And therefore this nameless Uncle plants, builds, equips incessantly and with a goal immediately in sight: No child shall want for a cherry or an apple; no mother shall be without cabbage or turnips.

Of salt and spices he has a whole storehouse. He
lets others look after tobacco and brandy; according
to his way of viewing things these are not necessities.
Significant for Goethe's love of liberty with regard
to small things is this touch: The Uncle cordially
dislikes having his meals served at the stroke of
the clock. The *à la carte* meal, ready at any hour,
is to him the acme of modern civilization.

CHAPTER XXIII

Wilhelm Meisters Wanderjahre

Wilhelm Meisters Wanderjahre, originally intended as a continuation of *Wilhelm Meisters Lehrjahre,* never became this in any sense of word. It would have been much better if Goethe had not given the leading character the name of Wilhelm, and had not made Wilhelm's son Felix and his education and training the center of the work, for he thereby nourished a delusive idea and strengthened it by re-introducing the names of a few of the persons of the older novel. But these appear completely changed. There is Jarno, for example, now wholly taken up with mining, and known to those about him as Montan.

The work on this detailed book, which is really a collection within a frame of a number of short stories that do not concern Wilhelm, stretches out over an appalling number of years. One of the stories, *Die neue Melusine,* is supposed to have been told in Sesenheim as early as 1772 and written down shortly thereafter. The embryo of other stories such as *St. Joseph der Zweite,* and *Der Mann von fünfzig Jahren,* seem to belong to the year 1797, though the latter was not really designed until 1807. The story entitled *Die pilgernde Thörin* and the first two chapters of the novel were published separately in a *Taschenbuch für Damen* in 1808 and

1809. There was published in the same place in
1815 *Das nussbraune Mädchen,* though not in its
entirety, and in the same place in 1816-1818 *Die
neue Melusine* which, as we have seen, is supposed
to have been written forty years previously. And
finally the fragment *Der Mann von fünfzig Jahren,*
which had been in process of completion for twenty-
one years—apparently not a long time. In 1820
Goethe wrote *Wo steckt der Verräther?* and at the
close of the year he has progressed so well with his
work on the novel that he can afford to have the
printing begun.

As has been pointed out, he rests the frame of
the work as a connecting idea as much as possible
on the development of the individual for the public
and society in contrast to the ideal of a purely personal training and development such as that around
which the *Lehrjahre* had revolved. The social dominates here, or according to the intention of the poet,
should dominate. It has two especial organs which
remind us more of Plato's *State* than the beginning
of the nineteenth century: *Der pädagogische Pro-
vinz,* in which the peculiarities of the individual were
to be developed as rapidly as possible, and *Der
Wanderbund* which works in opposition to emigration. In return, Wilhelm, who loves and worships
his wife Natalie, pledges himself to her to something so bizarre and epically impossible as this: He
is to spend not more than three days at a time under
the same roof and not to leave an inn without going
at least a mile away from it. This alliance, which
goes under the name of *Die Entsagenden* (the sub-
title of the novel), imposes upon its members this
no less bizarre and romantic obligation: When

they meet they are never to discuss the past or the future; they are to confine their attention to the present. By this arrangement Goethe in all probability wished to bring it about that Wilhelm and Jarno would not need to go back to reminiscences from the *Lehrjahre* when they see each other, the contents of which no longer stood out clearly in his mind.

In 1821, as the outcome of severe diligence, Goethe succeeded in forging together a sufficient amount of successful and unsuccessful material to make the appearance of the first part of the *Wanderjahre* a possibility. For the second part a provisional plan had been laid. The book was well received and the shameless forgery from the Preacher Pustkuchen, which came out at the same time under the same name, did it no great harm. But Goethe did not feel like going to work on this odd creation again; it was not until 1827, the year in which he completed the *Helena* act of the second part of *Faust,* the act parts of which he had read to Schiller as early as September, 1800, that he resumed work on the *Wanderjahre.* He remodelled the first part, which had to be revised for the sake of continuity, and was going ahead with the second and third parts when he was grievously depressed by the sudden death of Karl August in the summer of 1828; the work did not appear until 1829. It was unfavorably received.

In actuality the *Wanderjahre* falls into two parts; one is poetic and contains the novelettes; the other is didactic and contains the narrative with its Utopias. If we read these novelettes attentively, we cannot help but be struck by the personal element in a number of them. When Goethe was between fifty and six years old, his age apparently gave him a great deal of concern. He was especially interested in the question as to whether a man of that age could win the love of a young woman and retain her love against a younger rival, especially if this younger rival happened to be his own son. Just as the relation between father and son (Wilhelm and Felix) is of the greatest significance for the frame, just so is the relation between a father and a son who fall in love with the same girl touched upon frequently in the novelettes. One is tempted to believe that Goethe and his son August now and then felt an attraction for the same girl, or she for both of them. This is not at all incredible when we recall that, when August in 1817 became engaged to, and married, Ottilie von Pogwisch the young, sprightly, clever woman was much later somewhat taken up with her father-in-law, perhaps as much as with her husband.

He was presumably thinking of himself when he wrote this humorous little verse:

Aspasia, wie das Sonnenlicht,
Begünstigt zwar so manchen Wicht,
Doch mag ich gern bei ihr verweilen,
Eine Kartoffel theilt man nicht,
Doch lässt die Ananas sich theilen.

. In *Die pilgernde Thörin* (a revision of a French story entitled *La folle en pélérinage*), the gadabout and mysterious but refined and, to her lover, steadfast beauty comes to a castle where she is hospitably received by the father, who, in course of time, feels so strongly attracted to her that he offers her his hand and his heart. But right at this very moment

his own son also falls hopelessly in love with the
fascinating guest and competes for her in such vehement fashion that she finds the situation unendurable
and disappears.

The same chord is struck, gently, in *Wer ist der
Verräther?* The young Lucidor is selected by his
father, a professor, and his father's intimate friend,
an official, for the younger and livelier of the latter's
two daughters, Julie by name. Julie finds inexhaustible entertainment in the professor's house when
he instructs her in geography and topography; she
knows all the harbors and the towns with their
towers, cupolas, and minarets. She is in truth just
as much interested in the professor (he has no
name) as she is in his son.

But Lucidor, when he comes as a wooer to the
official, feels much more strongly drawn to the older,
quieter, more sedate sister Lucinde than to the
younger and jollier Julie. On account of this he
feels a certain amount of anguish which, as his stay
in the house is prolonged, goes over into despair.
His father desires, and expects, his union with the
younger sister who makes advances to Lucidor in
a straightforward and unsuspecting way. The older
sister seems bound to Antoni, the much travelled
and experienced friend of the family. When the
young man is alone in his room in the evening, he
gives vent to his torture in passionate monologues.

At last all the obstacles disappear as if by the
waving of a magic wand. The professor who arrives on the scene because the engagement is to be
announced seems to know all about his son's coolness toward Julie; nor does he blame him for his
indifference. Since Lucidor does not dare to go to

Lucinde, she herself declares to him frankly and openly that she knows of his—presumably concealed —love for her and she assures him that his love is not unrequited. He shall, she says, not be afraid of causing Julie distress, nor must he fear Antoni as a competitor, for everything has been straightened out between these two. And when he, in blank astonishment, asks how it comes that everybody in the house and out of it knows all about his secret, the explanation is given, an explanation which undeniably makes the entire novelette quite juvenile, that he has the bad habit of talking to himself and that the entire family, the acoustics of the house being matchless, have from the very start been well informed as to his disappointment in Julie and his ardent admiration for Lucinde. Moreover, they have informed his father of the true state of affairs long ago.

In *Der Mann von fünfzig Jahren* the question is raised whether a man who is fifty years old can still be regarded as young, and whether he can seriously fall in love with a really young woman. The Major—he has no name—has for sometime looked upon himself as an old man. He meets a friend who is an actor. This actor not only knows the principles of reasonable hygiene, but also the use of paints and all manner of cosmetic remedies and aids which bestow upon the user an artificial youth. He is ten years older than the Major and looks much younger. The Major applies the cosmetics and is rejuvenated after having learned to his astonishment the day before from his sister, the Baroness, that if her daughter Hilarie's heart is no longer free, it is not owing to the fact that she loves the

Major's son, for whom the father intended to compete, but the father himself, her uncle, in whose head she never seems to have found any gray hairs, on whose face she never seems to have detected any wrinkles, these, too, having been removed by artificial means.

Hilarie, deeply in love with her uncle, wants to be his forever; they become engaged. At this point the son arrives, the young lieutenant, and tells his father that he has no desire whatsoever for the hand of Hilarie, nor does he wish to be united to her; a young widow has aroused his passion and captivated him body and soul. The father is to meet her and approve of his choice. But he suspects from the son's description that the beautiful widow will pay as little attention to the young man as she pays to her other wooers.

The Major finds in her one of those amiable feminine beings who try to catch all men. With extraordinary skill she at once makes him the chief and central point of her society. To the young lieutenant she praises the father at the son's expense. To the father she never once mentions the son. But the son, who imagines that he is being loved, is in the seventh heaven.

The beautiful widow does not give the Major an opportunity to woo for his son. She herself coquettes bravely with him, finds his poems better than those of the son though he himself insists that he is a mere dilettant. When the man of fifty years is so indiscreet as to tell his sister of the strong impression that the young widow has made on him, the sister becomes peevish. Goethe remarks, and rightly so, that one must never talk to one woman with enthusiasm about another. Women regard men as buyers in a market; the men allow themselves to be deluded by the wares that are placed in the best light, whereas women, with their keen eyes, appreciate at once that these very same wares have precious little value. She finds moreover deep down in her heart that Hilarie is too young for her brother, and that the widow is not young enough for her nephew.

Weary, weather-beaten and wet-through, the young lieutenant arrives one evening at the house of the Baroness. It is to be presumed that he has been jilted by the beautiful widow. He has to be put to bed and is nursed and consoled by his cousin. When, on the next day, he appears in his father's clothes, a transformation takes place in Hilarie's soul. In her heart Flavio gets the advantage of his father.

One evening as Flavio and Hilarie are skating together they discover a third party on the ice. Hilarie wishes to avoid a stranger, but when he encircles the young girl they discover that it is the Major. Hilarie is so dismayed that she loses her balance and falls. This situation is portrayed vividly and compactly, though the rest is rendered, in places at least, in *Kanzleistil*.

We come to the explanation. The Major understands that he has been demoted from first lover to father-in-law, and since at the same time the chamberlain, who rejuvenated him with cosmetics, has taken his final leave, the Major renounces, under force of circumstances, after the fashion of all others who renounce, the idea of fighting against old age which has at last really appeared.

There is a great deal of actual experience and perhaps one or two personal confessions in this story, about the best novelette in the entire work. But it is written with constant reference to the reader, so that the real course of events is sprinkled with an old man's chatter. How much better Goethe wrote when he *wrote* than now when he *dictates!*

The next story, *Die neue Melusine,* is more briskly and coherently executed. *Melusine* is a fairy tale, though not like H. C. Andersen's fairy tales for children, nor is it easily understood and transparent as are the Danish fairy tales. Goethe's story is totally devoid of childlike simplicity, though it gives evidence of an unusual inventive power. A young man on a journey meets in an inn a beautiful young woman who shows him kindness, though no favor, and who entrusts to him a box that she owns. He is requested to take it with him for her from town to town. He must always rent an especial room for the box adjoining his own. For his trouble he receives a purse of gold with which he is expected to proceed economically. Since he however spends the money in riots and revels, his fair one comes to him one evening from the side room and supplies him anew with apparently inexhaustible riches. At times they travel together on the journey; at times he travels entirely alone with the box. The beautiful young lady becomes more affectionate toward him, their relation becomes quite intimate; the consequences are soon noticeable. The beautiful body no longer has the same bearing. One night, as the young man is travelling all alone in his carriage, he sees to his astonishment a light through a crack in the box and discovers that his sweetheart is on the inside, in miniature; she sits reading in a doll's room.

In course of time she tells him that she is really a little dwarf, that she has received permission from the king of the dwarfs to transform herself into a human being, to love a man, and from him to have the dwarf's blood, which naturally grows thinner and thinner, renewed and strengthened. However precious she has been to the young man up to this point, he no longer loves her with the same warmth and vehemence. One evening they are invited to a large party; Melusine entertains by singing and playing; her companion is not at all musical and in one of his tantrums he abuses her by calling her a *dwarf*. He regrets his rude conduct and begs her pardon. She is not exactly angry at him, but she is firmly determined to desert him. He begs and beseeches. She says that they can remain together on just one condition: He must become just as small as she. This takes place; they live for some time right happy together in a doll's palace and associate only with dwarfs, her relatives, her friends.

The good relation is broken when her parents demand that they become really married. A gold ring is placed on his finger. He hates, he loathes this gold ring, succeeds at last in having it filed off, grows up again to the height of a normal man and again finds himself in the inn where he had originally made the acquaintance of the lovely Melusine.

The teaching that may be deduced from this is rather uncertain, and rather manifold. It may mean to the woman one loves. It may mean that a man that one should never speak a mortally painful word

cannot feel happy in the long run while living with
a woman who drags him down, debases him, de-
grades him. It may mean that the most cordial
sort of relation can be broken off when it is to receive the stamp of the marriage vow. And it may
mean a number of other things.

Though not written for children, this fairy tale
could, if slightly modified, amuse them also.

A quite unimportant but frolicsome jest is the
little story entitled *Die gefährliche Wette* which revolves around nothing else than just this: A band
of young fellows are sitting at a hotel window. They
see a distinguished and stately man, well on in years,
get out of his carriage and enter the hotel. Since
he seems accustomed to being treated with profound
respect, one of the young madcaps bets the others
that he can take this fine and mighty gentleman by
the nose and move that self same nose back and forward without being molested therefor. Each of
them promises him a gold piece if he can carry out
his undertaking. The young man announces himself to the aristocratic old man as an especially deft
barber, and before the open hotel window he takes
him by the nose and shaves his upper lip.

He returns to the group; they break out in such a
howl of jubilee that everybody in the hotel learns
of the wager; and the dignified old gentleman—so
that the story may contain a moral—sends his servants to give the party of youngsters a sound thrashing. They depart in great haste, while his son, who
has discovered the ringleader, gives him in a duel
a wound that cripples him for life. The moral
solemnity of the close grates on the innocence of this
unimportant students' prank.

In *Nicht zu Weit,* ingeniously planned but poorly written as it is, the contents of an entire novel are compressed into just a few pages. It depicts a case of marital misfortune and unhappiness on the part of two people each of whom is an excellent individual. By reason of her frivolity the wife brings the husband to the point of despair, so that both are tempted to enter into a new union where new disappointments await them.

It is plain that these various and variegated stories do not stand on the usual lofty level of Goethe's art. They are interesting simply because they were written by a great personality whose heterogeneous forms of expression all belong to the picture of the man as a whole. But had these stories been written by a lesser hand, they would not fascinate.

And there is even less artistic value, though decidedly greater psychological interest, to be attached to that part of the *Wanderjahre* which is purely didactic. In the first place there is the section called *Lenardos Tagebuch,* unhappily divided into parts that lie far removed from each other. It is distinctly touching to see in this section how thoroughly Goethe studied the spinning and weaving of cotton in Switzerland, and his intensely spiritual conception of a practical trade as *eine strenge Kunst* from which all frivolity is banished in contrast to the *freie Künste* in which there is so much talentless dabbling. There is a portrayal in this story, with the foresight of one who knows, of the danger that threatened the tradesman at that time when the introduction of machinery was imminent; they are told that there are just two courses open to them: to emigrate, or to set up machines of their own. The amiable story is collected around the charming description of *Frau Susanne,* called the Beautiful-Good (apparently from the Greek *Kalé-k'agathé*) in which Goethe has finally succeeded in sketching an exceedingly fascinating woman who is just as sensible and just as mentally independent as she is captivating when she stands in the presence of the other sex.

One sees from the efficiency with which the author allows her to defend the freedom of her thoughts, placed as she is in a pietistic society, that the fine, poetic conception of the Christian legend, which is discussed in the attractive idyl entitled *St. Joseph der Zweite,* does not carry with it any noticeable concession to belief in dogma.

The way in which Goethe at this stage of his life will have religion understood and practised is best seen in the pedagogical province from the *Wanderjahre,* where all religion that is based on fear is rejected, but where the religious life is based wholly and entirely on a worthy feeling such as reverence, *Ehrfurcht.*

There is no reason why we should dwell on the romantic frame out from which the threads stretch into the various narratives. It is far too clumsily worked out and far too muddled. The leading characters are Wilhelm himself, who ends his career as a surgeon, the half supernatural character called Makarie, the sun-woman, a higher unity of Natalie and "the fair soul," Wilhelm's son, Felix, who loves and eventually marries Hersilie, the daughter of an art-loving collector. In contrast to his father, Felix loves just one woman his whole life long. And then at last a number of individual characters

from the *Lehrjahre* are re-introduced, the most of
whom are no longer recognizable.   There is Philine,
for example, now a quiet woman who spends her
time at a useful and practical occupation: she cuts
out dresses.

The entire affair revolves around such an impossible epic hinge as a jewel box into the possession of
which Felix has come at the beginning of the novel,
but to which the key is missing.   Then, in the third
book, Hersilie writes to Wilhelm telling him that
Friedrich (from the *Lehrjahre*) has found the right
key to the box.   The remarkable key is even described in the text.   It is said that this is the usual
way of things in life.   One had, for example, a very
precious wooden cross, the arms of which, unfortunately, turned out to be spurious; they had been arbitrarily attached by an artist far inferior to the artist
who had made the original cross.   But years later the
man comes, through a remarkable coincidence, into
the possession of the genuine arms.   The coincidence
is certainly untypical.   The great majority of us
never find jewel boxes, nor do we have fitting keys
sent us at the opportune moment.

The *Wanderjahre* marks a receding wave in Goethe's spiritual life.   There is much in it that is beautiful and profound, but it would have been quite
impossible for so recognized a master to write a
book of such breadth and disorder had he not been
fully acquainted with the ability of the German people to tire itself out in patient admiration, and never
to find any of the works of its favorites of excessive
murkiness or prolixity.   But on this occasion it was
shown that even that ability had its limitations beyond which it was impossible to go with impunity.

CHAPTER XXIV

Pustkuchen's *Falsche Wanderjahre*

THERE lived at this time a little Protestant preacher, as stupid as he was conceited, in the forsaken hole called Wiebelskirchen near Ottweiler. His lofty name in full was Johann Friedrich Wilhelm Pustkuchen. He was born in 1793 and was consequently no less than forty-four years younger than the Goethe whom he honored with his sincere hatred and in whom he saw a danger to, if not the actual destruction of, German literature and German spiritual life. Even before Goethe had published his *Wanderjahre*, Pustkuchen had finished his continuation of the *Lehrjahre*. He published, without betraying his exalted name, his *Wilhelm Meisters Wanderjahre* in Quedlinburg, in four volumes. It is a glorious work in which to receive enlightenment. Not that it has the slightest value. It is soft, sweet, empty and pharasaical. But it gives one an insight into the way Goethe's pious contemporaries regarded his character and activity. It is a pity that its stupidity is not so condensed as it is in Wolfgang Menzel's criticism of Germany's greatest man. And yet, it is stupidity pure and undiluted and doubly diverting because of its conventionality: It is masterful morality, perfect piety. And it is always "sweet to listen" to his sort of

315

mindless matter, as Welhaven [6] well says. Goethe, however, was not gifted with the talent of deriving pleasure from this spiritual *genre*. Among other epigrammes which the *Wanderjahre* induced him to write, there is this one. Flatter Pustkuchen it does not:

> "Was will von Quedlinburg heraus
> Ein zweiter Wandrer traben!"
> Hat doch der Wallfisch seine Laus,
> Muss ich auch meine haben.

In his *Wanderjahre,* Pustkuchen has Wilhelm come to a castle where he is hospitably received by a captain and his fair daughter. Through the former, the author expresses his settled convictions regarding literature. They are not, however, meant as mere personal opinions; they are decisions handed down by the highest court. They effect in time a conversion to more wholesome views on the part of the hitherto deluded Wilhelm.

After making clear, and strongly emphasizing, the fact that the hero has led a planless and dissipated life up to this point, the Captain inveigles

---

[6] Johann Sebastian Cammermeyer Welhaven (1807-1873) had abundant opportunity to listen to the arrows of attack as they flew by. In the firm belief that the culture and civilization of Norway should be brought in line and put on a level with the rest of Europe, he assailed Wergeland's efforts to make Norway stand out as a separate, distinct, and intensified entity. The aims of the two men were in reality more or less similar. Welhaven did all in his power to restore and reinvigorate Norway's past. He had a patriotic enthusiasm for old Norse poems and sagas. His sonnet cycle entitled *Norges Daemring* (1834) brought him lasting fame. He wrote critical studies of Ewald and Holberg. But none of this prevented him from becoming a storm-centre of attack. The poem to which Brandes refers runs as follows:

> Det var ham sôdt at lytte
> Mens Pilene flôj paa Bytte
> Til Buesnorens Klang.   —TRANSLATOR.

him into a discussion of German books. It is during this discussion that Wilhelm admits that Goethe is his favorite author.

The writer explains this as follows: Because of his distracted method of living, Wilhelm has always been a few decades behind the actual state of literature at any given time. And since he has appeared, in his capacity as an actor, in various dramas by Goethe, this poet rather than another made an impression on him for the very reason that he found in Goethe's works the formal training after which he had been striving. There never was any distinct belief or well founded enthusiasm in Goethe's books such as is to be found in those of Herder, Klopstock, and Schiller. Goethe's books make very slight demands on the reader, since they view all human relations from the point of view of social custom.

The first thing the Captain does is to attack *Die Wahlverwandtschaften*. In it love is degraded to a mere physical necessity, even to a force that works in opposition to the plan of the universe as elaborated on the basis of moral beauty. All of the characters of the book are mediocre individuals, totally devoid of inner clarity and trustworthy strength. And so on. In other words, Pustkuchen, by virtue of his inner clarity, is fully acquainted with all things, including the plan of the universe.

The Captain's sister makes the point that all of Goethe's men are devoid of real manliness. They have no regard for the sacred relations in life, nor do they have that faith which binds us all together and makes us safe. No girl could ever find a friend in any of them.

The Captain drives the point home that Goethe, in his poetry, is a materialist: He does not worship the invisible God but visible beauty. Nothing that is worshipped and admired by mankind is considered sacred in Goethe's works. He never portrays the ideals of faith, nor the most sublime thoughts, nor the eternal destiny of man, nor piety, nor truth, nor justice, nor pure love, nor steadfast courage. All this has become a chaos in which, under delusions and dirt, individual remains of the divine go idling about. And especially is it to be noted that Goethe never understood the nature of the clergy as a class, nor the poetic side of them as clergymen.

As a result of this eloquence the Captain succeeds in converting Wilhelm, until he too exclaims:

This, then, is that admired Goethe, the poet I placed above all others, and through whose art I was trying to educate myself for the very reason that I thought that all humanity was reflected in it. And it just happens that the greatest characters, the heroes of liberty and patriotism and moral strictness and faith and love and friendship, all of these are absolutely lacking in his works. For us there is then a world without heroes, a world in which shrewdness, sensuality, the passions of the weak, aristocratic education and good will are the only principles and concepts that are given recognition, and in which the purity of just one woman (he means "the fair soul") is conceived of as a sort of miracle; and the attempt is made to explain even this as the result of her physical temperament. Is *that* humanity?

And Faust, this heroic spirit who even outdid the Devil in wild power, becomes in Goethe a hero just like all his other heroes. The events go on their marrowless course just as they do in a *bourgeois* drama. What an Aeschylus or a Dante or a

Shakespeare would have made out of this German Prometheus!

The time when Goethe knew how to strike the fundamental note of the age seems to the Captain to be past. Even the Schlegel brothers have begun to have a kind of premonition of a higher type of poetry than Goethe's. More and more frequently does this once so highly praised poet come to hear that he lacks poise, measure and balance. The ease and comfort which he tries to substitute for inspiration can never possibly be looked upon by others as a life principle.

In the third book the Captain compresses his charges into these words. Goethe's chief fault lies in the fact that he misunderstands the real nature of the Germans; he is a representative only of the miserable, formless, licentious, modern times, not of the original German disposition. He never understood the meaning of loyalty. But loyalty is German. There is only one sort of life that he can portray: the faithless, honorless, hybrid life such as the Gipsies lead. This he can depict in bright colors.

The town clerk has lent the Captain's daughter some of Goethe's books: "You must not read them," her father says, "I have looked at them and locked them up in the cupboard. When the clerk comes you can give them back to him." It was the judgment of the Protestant parsonage on the destroyer of German taste and underminer of German morality. Professor Schütz in Halle published a book of 400 pages in which he compared Goethe's *Wanderjahre* with that of Pustkuchen, conceded to each of them its advantages, but the greater number of advantages to Pustkuchen's. On this occasion Goethe wrote some verses in which he treated Schütz as a kitchen police:

> *Pusten,* grobes deutsches Wort!
> Niemand, wohlerzogen,
> Wird am rein anstand'gen Ort
> Solchem Wort gewogen.

> *Pusterich,* ein Götzenbild,
> Grässlich anzuschauen,
> Pustet über kľar Gefild
> Wust, Gestank und Grauen.

> Will der Pusterich nun gar
> Pfaffenkuchen pusten,
> Teufelsjungen-Küchenschaar
> Wird den Teig behusten.

Neither moralizing nationalism nor ebullient clericalism was routed from the field by this play on an ill sounding name.

CHAPTER XXV

Goethe's *Tafellieder; Gesellige Lieder*

THE Goethe with whom we have thus far been concerned was the solitary, the poetising, the effecting, the investigating, the struggling Goethe. Then we saw him not rarely face to face with another, either loving and loved, or like unto Castor in his relation to Pollux in Heaven, in constellation with a twin star, Herder, or Schiller, or Napoleon.

But there is still another Goethe, the social. The solitary man as a worker was also a social nature to a high degree who, with his brilliant mentality in control, never sank irretrievably into bitterness and aversion. He could curse the entire human race one day and speak cordially with a visitor the next:

> Der Teufel hol' das Menschengeschlecht!
> Man möchte rasend werden!
> Da nehm' ich mir so eifrig vor:
> Will Niemand weiter sehen.

> Will all das Volk Gott und sich selbst
> Und dem Teufel überlassen!
> Und kaum seh' ich ein Menschengesicht,
> So hab' ich's wieder lieb.

In Weimar, at the Court as well as in his home, he was constantly organising social circles. One time it was a *Cour d'amour* after the fashion of the Minnesingers, another it was merely a table company. He saw to it that no false note should arise through the entrance of some disinterested individual who was not congenial to the circle. How harshly he acted toward Kotzebue, for example, I have already discussed in the fourth volume of my collected works. It was for these circles that Goethe wrote during the first two decades of the nineteenth century his *Gesellige Lieder,* songs for which there is certainly even now no equal.

Some of them, such as *Stiftungslied, Frühlingsorakel* and *Die glücklichen Gatten,* possess the naïveté of the folksong and yet are free of the heaviness that characterizes after all so many folksongs. Goethe's *Lieder* are borne aloft as it were by a joyousness and a manifestation of good spirits. Through nearly all of them there runs the susceptibility, on the part of the poet, to the joys of the table. This is in keeping with his unfailing optimism and acts as a logical protest against hangdoggedness, woebegoneness and general repudiation of human nature. Two of the *Lieder* are parodies on pious and religious songs. One renunciatory song of the time began with the line, *Ich habe geliebet, nun lieb' ich nicht mehr.* Goethe wrote, in protest, as late as April, 1803, though nigh on to sixty-four years old:

> Ich habe geliebet, nun lieb' ich *erst recht!*
> Erst war ich der Diener, nun bin ich der Knecht.
> Erst war ich der Diener von Allen;
> Nun fesselt mich diese charmante Person,
> Sie that mir auch Alles zur Liebe, zum Lohn,
> Sie kann nur allein mir gefallen.

As a witness to Goethe's enjoyment of a well-prepared dish and to his deep-set fondness for a glass of good wine, two of the following stanzas

begin, *Ich habe gespeiset, nun speis' ich erst gut!*
and *Ich habe getrunken, nun trink' ich erst gern.*
The final stanza runs:

> Drum frisch nur aufs Neue!   Bedenke Dich nicht!
> Denn wer sich die Rosen, die blühenden, bricht,
> Den kitzeln fürwahr nur die Dornen.
> So heute wie gestern, es flimmert der Stern,
> Nur halte von hängenden Köpfen Dich fern
> Und lebe Dir immer von vornen!

Goethe's preference for good wine is prolonged
throughout his entire life.   In every record of a
person who sat at his table as guest there appears
a statement as to how frequently red wine, or a
rare old Rhine wine, was offered him; and if anyone at the table mixed water with his wine, he was
accustomed to exclaim: Who taught you that horrible habit?—Ladies at whose house he visited frequently expressed their wonder as to how much he
could stand.   Many emphasized the finesse of his
senses of taste and of smell which made him an unusual connoisseur of wines.   A courtier of Weimar
by the name of Schwabe proves this for posterity
by relating an anecdote concerning a certain test of
this sort that Goethe stood one day.

Karl August had gathered a small circle about
him.   At dessert various kinds of good wines were
tried, when the Court Marshall von Spiegel asked
permission to have a wine without a name brought.
Several of the men declared that the wine was Bourgogne though they could not define it more closely.
When the Duke himself, who was a connoisseur, had
also said "Bourgogne," the affair was looked upon as
settled.   Goethe tasted it and tasted it again, shook
his head and put the glass down.—"Your Excellency

seems to be of a different opinion," said the Court Marshall. "May I ask what name you would give the wine?"—"I don't know it," answered Goethe, "I should think it is a choice wine from Jena which has been lying for some time in a Madeira cask."— "That's just what it actually is," said the Court Marshall.

The song *Vanitas Vanitatum vanitas!* is, as the last mentioned poem, also meant as a parody. There was a spiritual song, which began: *Ich hab' mein Sach Gott heimgestellt.* Goethe wrote:

> Ich hab' mein Sach auf Nichts gestellt,
> > Juchhe!
> Drum ist's so wohl mir in der Welt,
> > Juchhe!
> Und wer will mein Kamerade sein,
> Der stosse mit an, der stimme mit ein,
> Bei dieser Neige Wein.

In seven stanzas it runs through all the circles of life precisely in the same spirit and with the same refrain. The strophe on women is especially neat in its form:

> Auf Weiber stellt' ich nun mein Sach
> > Juchhe!
> Daher mir kam viel Ungemach;
> > O weh!
> Die Falsche sucht' sich ein ander Theil,
> Die Treue macht' mir Langeweil',
> Die Beste war nicht feil.

The song entitled *Dauer im Wechsel* is beautiful without being flippant. Its lightly flowing verse depicts the fleetness of life, the impossibility of rejoicing for any length of time over the florescence of the fruit tree since the west wind shakes down a flowery rain, and the impossibility of twice swimming in the same stream. Art alone gives something that is lasting:

> Danke, dass die Gunst der Musen
> Unvergängliches verheisst:
> Den Gehalt in Deinem Busen
> Und die Form in Deinem Geist.

The *Tischlied* is the expression for a charming healthfulness. It is one of many among these beautiful poems that seems produced in that state of incipient intoxication which makes an excellent head clear-sighted, imparts to a fully developed nervous system the bliss of the moment, and makes the imagination, deluded in satiation, spread forth its wings and rise up from the earth empowered to soar:

> Mich ergreift, ich weiss nicht wie,
> Himmlisches Behagen,
> Will mich's etwa gar hinauf
> Zu den Sternen tragen?

It is the true song of society. We hear the clinking of the glasses while the stream of life grows broader and the good feeling increases until it finally embraces the entire human race, and the group at the table, grown merry to excess, end by drinking its health.

Even more dithyrambic is the poem *Weltseele*, with all of its metaphysical profundity which, though not formally belonging to the table songs, must be classed with them because it was written in 1804, and because of its spirit:

> Vertheilet Euch nach allen Regionen
> Von diesem heilgen Schmaus!
> Begeistert reisst Euch durch die nächsten Zonen
> In's All und füllt es aus!

Friends are to fill the universe, hover through the expanse, encircle the limits of the sun and the planets, and influence vigorously by the act of creation which has not yet been wholly consummated. Immediately preceding this poem, and intended as an introduction to it, there is an epigrammatic stanza on the universe and its God. It is dry and sharp in its effect:

Im innern ist ein Universum auch!
Daher der Völker löblicher Gebrauch,
Dass Jeglicher das Beste, was er kennt,
Er Gott, ja seinen Gott, benennt,
Ihm Himmel und Erden übergiebt
Ihn fürchtet und womöglich liebt.

Extremely exuberant and permeated with spirit is, finally, the magnificent table song, *Generalbeichte*. It is in the form of a general confession of sins of omission for which friends, both men and women, have to reproach themselves. They have on their conscience the neglect of the good things which life has offered them, and which through ignorance they have let slip. This song corresponds to Bettina's remark in a letter: "I have forgotten the strawberries I ate in the garden: those that I left still burn in my soul."

Ja, wir haben, sei's bekannt,
Wachend oft geträumt,
Nicht geleert das frische Glas,
Wenn der Wein geschäumet,
Manche rasche Schäferstunde
Flücht'gen Kuss vom lieben Munde
Haben wir versäumet.

Some of these poems belong to the year 1804, others, the last one quoted for example, to 1807,

Gewohnt, gethan to 1813, *Kriegsglück* to 1814, and the extremely graceful *Offne Tafel*, the revision of a French table song, to October, 1813. The uproariously jolly *Ergo bibamus* was written in 1810. Goethe, then, was about sixty years old when these lyrics came from his pen. It is obvious that so soon as he expresses himself in verse he is in full possession of his youthful powers, though at this period of his life as an author his prose had already begun to lose its freshness.

Zelter was, as a rule, the original composer of these songs. A great artist he was not. But he was willing, docile and enthusiastic. He adapted himself to the poet's plans in every way and without question.

CHAPTER XXVI

Geschichte der Farbenlehre

BETWEEN April 1805 and April 1810, Goethe completed the elaborate work which he modestly called *Materialien zur Geschichte der Farbenlehre*. In very truth, this treatise is exactly what Johannes Müller called it: a spiritually historic portrayal of natural observations. Though the material is far from being well moulded, and though Goethe is frequently content with excerpts and translations from the countless scientists who, from the earliest times to his own, had interested themselves in the problem of colors, he nevertheless set the mark of his own personality on the entire production and permeated it with his own reason. It is only when he approaches Newton that we find traces of the controversialist. And even Newton, as a man, is delineated with intelligence and relative sympathy.

Permission must be granted a layman to limit the discussion to individual sections which for one reason or another are especially instructive and in which the personality of the author is conspicuously brought to light.

The section entitled *Zur Geschichte der Urzeit* is written with Goethe's established genius. He begins with the rainbow and with the impression it has made upon primitive people among the various tribes. It revealed all at once the entire color scale. To a character-forming people such as the Greeks, it became an amiable girl, Iris, a bringer of peace, and generally speaking a messenger of the gods. To other tribes it was the impersonal sign of peace. The remaining color phenomena in the air were, in ancient times, less taken into consideration; the morning glow alone was personified as Eos or as Aurora, or among the Hindoos as the goddess of the dawn.

Though not much attention was paid to the colors *above* one, people made so much the more of colors *about* one, of dyeing materials which were found everywhere. The pleasing in colors, in that which is motlied, was immediately felt, and since finery is a necessity to man almost more than the actual needs of life, the application of color to the nude body or to clothing soon came into use. Fruit juice, blood, metallic oxide, decayed plants, the mud from the fords of large rivers, everything in fact that left spots, was material for coloring. Tattooing arose with the inunction of color. A color varied in value according to its permanency. The juice from the purple mussel grew into high repute. The art of dyeing could quickly be perfected, since mixing, rummaging, and dabbling has a great attraction for primitive beings. They made new tests as they went along. For a race of people as conservative as the Egyptians, Hindoos, and Chinese, who quickly approached a high degree of perfection in coloring, their technique became religion; they proceeded from a certain pious conception. More advanced peoples longed for a momentary influence; they wished to gain approval and earn money.

The oldest peoples were acquainted only with the practical side of colors. The study of the theory

began with the Greeks. Goethe has given a lucid
résumé of the various and variegated opinions that
have been handed down from the Hellenic thinkers,
from Pythagoras and his followers, who explained
the differences in colors from the different blending
of the elements. The colors of animals were supposed to be due to the food they ate. He sets forth
the views of Empedocles, Democritus, Epicurus,
Zeno, Plato and Aristotle. It is almost pathetic to
observe the thoughtfulness and zeal with which the
philosophers of antiquity, who lacked all the apparatus for scientific study known to modern times,
tried to explain to themselves and others the mystery
of the genesis of colors. Plato believed that a flame
emanated from every body and that its parts were
perceived in the sense of sight. The eye itself was
considered in *Timaeos* as a fire which causes the
light to flow forth from the eye as from a lamp.

Aristotle regarded this as wholly erroneous: the
eye is aqueous, not igneous; else why does it not see
in the dark. The eye is not, as Democritus believed,
reflected in objects; the objects, on the contrary, are
reflected in the polished surface of the eye. Otherwise the thing in which any object is reflected, water,
for example, would see just as well as the eye. But
the eye sees nothing. Light is, so to speak, the
color of that which is transparent. The presence
of something igneous in something transparent gives
light, the absence thereof darkness. In this way the
oldest thinkers groped about and felt their way
around looking for the solution of the enigma.

Goethe runs through all the Greek names for
colors in order to derive an idea as to how many
shades the Greeks knew and what impression they

made upon them. Then he goes on to the Romans and gives, in good hexameters (most likely Knebel's), the section from Lucretius's *De rerum natura,* in which the latter explains the origin of colors. He denies that when something appears to us as white that it is white in the material itself. He holds that matter is colorless.

The individual who is blind from birth knows all materials though he has never seen a color. Each color easily changes before our eyes into another; which is adequate proof that it is not a fundamental element. If the waves of the ocean were in themselves dark, they would not whiten into foam; if the throat of the dove had a different color in itself, it would not, when looked upon in the sunshine as it turns its neck, seem now red, now emerald green, now cast a gleam like the blending of copper and gold, called in ancient times *pyropus.*

Goethe interweaves at this juncture a hypothetical history of colors in the works of the Greek painters. Though sketched, it is to be presumed, by Heinrich Meyer, Goethe himself placed his own construction upon it in the essay, that immediately succeeded, and which has to do with color and the treatment of color in times long since passed. This essay emphasizes the fact that among the Greeks science was an art; human powers and forces were in no way excluded from their scientific activities. With their abysmal presentiment, their keen and certain eye for the present, their mathematical insight, their physical preciseness, lofty instinct, clear understanding, agile imagination, amiable delight in the sensuous, nothing was wanting to them. Goethe remarks in this connection—he was rarely without his unpre-

meditated efforts in the realm of surprises—that
no race, perhaps, has ever possessed these elements
to such a degree as the German of his day. The
Germans lack, he avers, neither depth nor diligence.

Under the rubric of *Lücke,* Goethe next proceeds
to fill out the vacant space, the gap, between antiquity and such science as emerged with the coming
of Roger Bacon in the thirteenth century. His
observations, though general, are well reasoned.
He surveys the various authors from century to century; his knowledge is sound. In olden times, all
wrote in Mediæval Latin. Where Scaliger (1484-
1558) is referred to, Goethe expresses the opinion
that science would have gained much in freedom
and in gaiety had the plain, flexible Greek language
been used instead of the harsh and commanding
Latin. Paracelsus and the alchymists are treated
cursorily; Bacon of Verulam is discussed in detail
and comprehensively, but not with an excess of sympathy.

Goethe emphasizes the thoroughness and conscientiousness with which they proceeded, in the first
half of the sixteenth century, at the expense of the
impulse toward freedom with which individuals of
the second half of the century rebelled against authority. Then came Lord Bacon. He wiped away,
as with a sponge, everything which up to that time
had been written on the tablets of humanity. Galileo, Kepler, Vossius and other scientists are discussed and compared with each other in this portrayal of science in the seventeenth century.

Goethe inserts at this juncture, with amusing irregularity, a history of color in the pictorial art of
the Renaissance. He begins with Cimabue, discusses

the Florentines and Venetians, dwells on Masolino
and Massaccio, on Titian and Giorgione, characterizes briefly Leonardo, Raphael, Dürer, Holbein,
becomes enamored of Correggio, singles out Cara-
vaggio, displays a vigorous interest in Guido Reni,
passes over the French quite hurriedly, and ends by
stressing the services which Oeser, Raphael, Mengs
and Angelica Kauffmann rendered in Germany. Nor
does he omit Reynolds in England; nor David in
France, whom he holds up as the conqueror of
Boucher's "vapid, salacious mannerism." He also
expresses his opinion of Greuze's sentimentality.

Then we come to Isaac Newton, whom he compares to Tycho Brahe[7] as the one who misconceived
a basic principle and stubbornly asserted the accuracy of his mistaken ideas. He comments, of course,
on Newton's great powers. He was one of those
investigators who produce from themselves a complete world without taking the trouble to ascertain
whether it harmonises with the real world. In this
section, dedicated to Newton as a personality,
Goethe speaks still better of him. He calls him a
"systematic, sound, well-tempered man, devoid of
passion and knowing not envy." He admits that
Newton's mathematical talent lies beyond his own
horizon—which was indubitably a pity and the
source of very great and lasting harm.

[7] In a sense, Tycho Brahe (1546-1601) was the most famous
Dane that ever lived. He studied at Copenhagen, Leipzig and
Augsburg and became the most advanced astronomist of his time.
His protector, King Frederick II, fitted out an observatory for
him on the island of Hveen, now Swedish territory, in the Oere-
sund. When his patron died, in 1588, Tycho Brahe went to
Prague in response to a call from Emperor Rudolph II, where he
himself died. It was his teachings that enabled Kepler to build
up the Copernican system. Brahe himself regarded the Earth as
the centre of the cosmos.   —TRANSLATOR.

CHAPTER XXVII

Goethe and Voltaire

THE greatness of Voltaire's personality makes discussion of it at this point imperative. Goethe's opinion cannot be passed over in silence; nor can it be studied without interest.

In the superciliousness of youth, and with youth's lack of critical acumen, Goethe had held Voltaire up to ridicule. But so soon as he came to years of mental and spiritual maturity he translated a number of Voltaire's works, and in the notes to his translation of "Rameau's Nephew" he showered lavish praise upon his great predecessor in the world of letters. If this homage could not be sustained, it was due to a genuinely scientific reason.

While a fugitive in England, Voltaire had been initiated into the teachings of Newton; on his return to France he came out as Newton's enthusiastic apostle. Through the influence of "the divine Emilie" (the Marquise of Châtelet), Voltaire had kept up his studies in mathematics and physics. This had enabled him to explain Newton's theories to the French people, indeed to all Europe. In 1738 he had published at Amsterdam his book entitled *Elémens de la philosophie de Newton mis à la portée de tout le monde*. And in his letter to the Marquise he had made himself the special interpreter and mouthpiece of Newton's teachings with regard to color.

> Il déploie à mes yeux par une main savante
> De l'astre des saisons la robe étincelante.
> L'émeraude, l'azur, le pourpre, le rubis
> Sont l' immortel tissu dont brillent ses habits.
> Chacun de ses rayons dans sa substance pure
> Porte en soi les couleurs dont se peint la nature.
> Et confondus ensemble, ils éclairent nos yeux.
> Ils animent le monde, ils emplissent les cieux.

Goethe shows why Voltaire felt impelled to lay before good society in France anything and everything that was calculated to entertain, instruct, excite—and shake it. Voltaire left nothing undone. He portrayed feelings and tendencies, past and present, far and near, spiritual as well as natural phenomena. His talent and his genius were equally great, and both made themselves felt, no matter what form they assumed. He soon became the undisputed master of his race. Goethe was sincere though somewhat misguided, when he found fault with the method by which Voltaire had blindly joined the school of Newton. There is point only in the way he attacks the inadequate drawings with which Voltaire had had his work illustrated.

The occasion arises, and calls for settlement at this point, to draw a comparison between the two great minds who, by virtue of their positions as incontestable centres of literary and intellectual life in Europe, were destined to relieve each other.

Goethe and Voltaire resemble each other very little in mental construction; they are akin in that intensity and universality that gave them dominion in the spiritual world. Voltaire covers an even broader field than Goethe. Even granting that in natural science he was merely a disseminator, and not a creator, of ideas, he had after all a grounding in mathematics which Goethe lacked. As a physicist, he was without Goethe's independence and yet, in contrast to his gifted successor on the throne of literature, he abounded in that hard, sound sense which enabled him to grasp the fundamental meaning and value of Newton's investigations. Human understanding was in fact in his case developed to such a marked degree of clarity, conciseness, and brilliancy that it became the exact equivalent of genius.

In the writing of history he anticipated Goethe, and was in general his superior. His *Histoire de Charles XII* and his *Essais sur les Mœurs* were both influential works.

If Goethe did not attain during his own life to such world sway as did Voltaire, it was due solely and exclusively to the language in which each wrote. Voltaire took over a language which constituted even then the court tongue of all Europe. It was the language of diplomacy; it was the most adaptable, flexible, and elegant of all; it was a language created, as it were, for concealed thoughts and allusions, alike adapted to derision and pathos, to the obscuring or the revelation of ideas. He developed it in verse, in the species of poetry of which he was the complete master—the epigramme—and made it the organ for the most subtle wit and brilliant reasoning. This is best discerned in his *Poésies fugitives*. And in prose, in which it already excelled, he developed it in the direction of firmness, solid-

ity, force, and illuminating clarity. Voltaire never
wrote a nerveless or marrowless paragraph.

Poet in the sense that Goethe was a poet Voltaire
never succeeded in becoming. He was a dramatist
who, like Euripides of old, made the tragedy the
organ for new ideas. He was a pamphleteer who
could arouse a whirlwind of laughter and was therefore to be feared. He was the author of short,
philosophic novels that penetrated everywhere and
won the minds of men through an appeal to reason.
And he was, what Goethe never could be, a fighter.
He was the champion of tolerance, the lover of
freedom, the spokesman of justice. He made the
mighty tremble through the power that lay in his
pen.

Voltairean audacity was not in Goethe; he had his
own brand; it was spiritual in both form and substance. In comparison with Goethe's pantheism,
Voltaire's deism is local, limited and old-fashioned.
Compare both of them to Spinoza and note Voltaire's inane condemnation of the great Jewish-
Spanish-Dutch liberator as an atheist. Goethe, on
the other hand, not merely understood Spinoza; he
allowed himself to be filled with his spirit; and he
wrote in his spirit.

With the exception of the epigramme and the
satire, Goethe is far superior to Voltaire. That his
German prose is inferior is quite easy to understand.
The prose to which Goethe fell heir was not much
more than the embryo of a real medium of written
expression; it merely had in it the makings of a
real prose; it was either *burschikos-sentimental* or
it was stilted, wooden and affected, after the manner
of eighteenth century style in Germany. In the

works of Wieland and Lessing it had only to receive form in order to become French. Under the management of Goethe it became full and emotional, rich in thought, but all too often formless and rickety. As a great author, though not a great lyric writer, Voltaire had said: "Every species is good except the tiresome." German prose tended to become tiresome—even in Goethe's works.

Goethe was superior to Voltaire as a poet for one reason that lay beyond the control of either: Voltaire was all mind (in the sense of *esprit*); he was a prodigious talent, a darting, unquenchable flame. Goethe was all nature; he was an expression of All-Nature's very being. Viewed from this angle, his equal has possibly never lived on this earth. Then there is another reason for Goethe's lyric eminence: The German language, so long spurned and maltreated, became, what the French had been for ages, a world language. And happily enough, and not without significance, this is one case where the cause and the result were coeval and coöperative.

We are forced to concede one small personal superiority to Voltaire; his position in and attitude toward the society of royalty was commendable. From his very youth he had been wont to associate with lords and ladies of high degree. Fully aware of his intellectual endowments and acquirements, he considered himself their equal. That gave his position a saving grace. He moved about among them with complete ease; he never appeared subservient other than in a purely formal way demanded by the etiquette of the age. It is true that his letters to kings, empresses and other lofty personages rarely failed to flatter. But they flattered him first. And his flattery is so elegant and witty that to read it is a distinct pleasure. Think of his numerous epistles to Frederick the Great! They flatter, but back of them lie self-assertion and criticism, sharp, caustic and corrective.

Goethe, on the other hand, as the son of a middle class father and the comrade of an unimportant duke, had the German's innate respect for the social hierarchy developed to such a high degree that it gave him unequivocal pleasure to envelop himself with all the formulæ of subserviency prescribed by the court. His flattery is devoid of mental reservation or betrayal of his mental superiority. Without moving an eyelash or permitting a smile, he can tell how a certain Prince of Reuss with a number running up into the thirties had always been a gracious lord. He can write about a Russian Grand Duchess, something that Börne in his time abused him for: "Her Royal Highness, the Grand Duchess, was so benevolent as to grant me the gracious privilege of inscribing some poetic lines in her elegant and magnificent album." In 1810 the young Italian-born Empress, Maria Ludovica of Austria, came to Karlsbad. She treated Goethe decently, even kindly; he raved about her, though she was quite tenuously gifted. With German literature she had at most a distant familiarity. Ludwig Geiger has shown how, in 1809, she confused Schill (the courageous Prussian officer) with Schiller. Of the latter the extent of her criticism was confined to the safe observation: "He is known for his writings." And indeed the only remark that she is known to have made concerning Goethe himself is the following in German that puzzles and in orthography that needs repair:

Der berühmte Verfasser machte darüber eine anspielende Poesi. But Goethe was all taken up with her; she was an Empress, and she had paid him some attention.

He sang of her arrival in Karlsbad, her chalice, the position she occupied, her departure, and even her non-committal consort in the following meek and mirth-provoking stanza:

> Von seines Auges mildem Blick entbrennet
> Ein heilig Feuer, das uns nie entweicht;
> Und wie man erst des Sommers Kräfte kennet,
> Wenn sich im Herbst der Traube Fülle zeigt,
> So zeige sich, wenn er von uns getrennet
> Der Segen wirksam, den er uns gereicht,
> Und werde so, beim glücklichsten Ereignis
> Die kleine Stadt des grossen Reiches Gleichnis.

Karl August was awarded the title of Grand Duke at the Congress of Vienna in 1815, though the girth of his dominions was not noticeably increased. Goethe immediately sent in his felicitations in the following swollen words:

Ereignet sich's nun, dass Höchstdenenselben für so vielfaches, redliches, inneres Bemühen auch von aussen ein gebührendes Beiwort ertheilt wird, so benutzen wir es mit Freude, wenn die Hof-und Kanzleisprache uns nunmehr erlaubt, dasjenige als ein Anerkanntes auszusprechen, was sonst bei aller Wahrheit als Schmeichelei hätte erscheinen können. Eurer Königliche Hoheit haben bisher den kleinen Kreis bis ins Unendliche erweitert, indem Sie in einen jeden einzelnen der Ihrigen ein gemässe Thätigkeit zu erregen und zu begünstigen gewusst. Möge Höchstdenenselben eine lange Reihe von Jahren gegönnt sein, um in eimem ausgebreiterten Wirkungskreise eben diese Wohlthat fortzusetzen.

When we read this kind of verbiage we are inclined to allow Voltaire full indulgence for all the frolicsome tricks he played against his contemporaries in Germany—those tricks which German snobbishness has found so irritating to its sensitive morals. Voltaire did not spare Maupertuis right before the eyes of his harsh benefactor, Frederick the Great. Nor did he forget Frederick himself.

It is sometimes a relief not to be weighed down with a huge amount of respect for those in momentary possession of great power. This has, however, nothing to do with the deeper ego of the two great men. If we would derive a sharp and definite idea of the contrast between the nature of Voltaire and that of Goethe, it is only necessary to study Goethe's poem entitled *Gross ist die Diana der Epheser*. It had been called forth by Fritz Jacobi's book entitled *Von den göttlichen Dingen und ihrer Offerbarung*. Remember how Voltaire reacted toward writers of this kind. And think what he would have done in this case. He would have approached it with the sharpest ridicule. He would have shown up the illogical phases of it. He would have appealed to reason. He would have demonstrated all that is contrary to reason in revelation as championed by Jacobi. He would have waged war high up in the air—where Kaulbach's "Battle of the Huns" is continued.

But Goethe—he never once appeals to *raisonnement;* he goes in for nature. He merely contrasts the cultivation of nature with mental chimeras. He portrays the goldsmith in Ephesus as he steadfastly works in his shop for the honor of the Ephesian Artemis, the goddess with the many breasts, the worthy symbol of nature. Even as a child the goldsmith had knelt at her throne and begun to mould

with religious zeal the girdle under her breasts which
is adorned with so many beasts of the field—the
stag and the hind and other wild animals.   Suddenly he hears from the street that a god who dwells
in the brain back of man's stupid forehead is supposed to be far more powerful and far more worthy
of worship than the goddess who rules All-Nature.
He works along quietly.   The relevant verses run
as follows:

> Als gäb's einen Gott so im Gehirn
> Da hinter des Menschen alberner Stirn,
> Der sei viel herrlicher als das Wesen,
> An den wir *die Breite der Gottheit* lesen.
>
> Der alte Künstler horcht nur auf,
> Lässt seinen Knaben auf den Markt den Lauf,
> Feilt immer fort an Hirschen and Thieren
> Die seiner Gottheit Kniee zieren,
> Und hofft, es könnte das Glück ihm walten
> Ihr Angesicht würdig zu gestalten.

That is Goethe's position expressed in a masterful simile.   Where Voltaire, through the power of
his position and his pugnacious temperament, was
forced into incessant attack, either straight ahead
or by detour, upon the forces of the past which
limited his freedom and which he therefore wished
to destroy, Goethe moved along in calm and quiet.
He felt that the negative soon became antiquated.
Unperturbed as he always was, he influenced the
world about him in a positive way and because of
his persistence.   Over against the so-called supernatural he set up his deeply emotional cultivation
and reproduction of nature.   He made poetry out
of his harmony with and penetrating insight into
nature.   Voltaire was all mind; Goethe was all nature.

CHAPTER XXVIII

GOETHE'S LIFE: *Dichtung und Wahrheit*

IN 1808 Cotta brought out a new edition of Goethe's collective works. He was enabled to survey his complete body of letters for the first time. He had never wished to have his works published in chronological order. As he looked at the new edition it occurred to him that they had been published strictly in accord with his wishes. There was no order. Fiction and criticism stood out in wild topsy-turvydom. There were sections and headings and rubrics, everything but clear arrangement. He saw what a disconcerting effect this would have on the general public. He was seized with a desire to relate those incidents of his life which would clarify the genesis of his works and put them in their proper light.

At first he hardly thought of more than a *biographia litteraria.* But the task grew as he worked on it and thought about it. He saw that his explanation must be laid out on a broad basis if it was to be at all satisfactory; that the places where the events occur must be described; that the conditions of the time must be visualized; that personal influences, historic relations and the state, or states, of spiritual life accurately delineated. As a critic of others he had seen how most historians make the mistake of assuming too much on the part of their readers. He himself had said in his review of Johannes von Müller's biography that there was one thing an autobiographer should never forget: the younger generation for whom he writes has a very flimsy idea concerning the period immediately preceding, while posterity, for whom he none the less writes, has an even flimsier. Nothing is to be assumed; everything is to be related.

He had reproached this historian for his inept modesty. Modesty, wrote Goethe, belongs where one is personally concerned. It is clear that in good society no one should be forward; each should seem the peer of the other. But in the case of a free, written production we demand truth. When a man writes his autobiography, as did Müller, and is wholly silent as to the great influence he had had for a certain period of time, we understand neither the slights that he suffers again and again, nor his victory over the obstacles that were placed in his way.

The word *Bescheidenheit* does not suit Goethe very well, though it is better than such antinomic expressions as vanity and arrogance. His strength and his art lie in the fact that, though he always explains himself in an indirect way, he is never concerned with himself, never broods over himself, never makes a specialty of himself, but is made to stand out before us as a living figure in the portrayal of the cross-fire of impressions under which he moves forward.

He soon came to feel the difficulty of self-portrayal, especially in the portrayal of others who, for a hundred reasons, dared not be named (Lili Schöremann, for example) or concerning whom it

was impossible for him to tell the entire truth (as
in the case of Karl August and his Weimar contemporaries). He limited his portrayal therefore to
the first twenty-five years of his life, discontinuing
it at his call to Weimar. And even of these years
he published only the first three parts in succession
(1811, 1812, 1814) and let the fourth part, in
which Lili, who was still living, simply could not be
omitted, lie unpublished. It was not published until
1831.

The book is written with calm of mind; it is also
artistic. There were famous and admired autobiographies previous to Goethe's. There was in olden
times, that of St. Augustine, which is a confession,
the story of a conversion. In more modern times
there was Jean Jacques Rousseau's *Les Confessions,*
unquestionably a presupposition for Goethe's. It
is an apology; it is an unveiling; it is the autobiography of a self-righteous and self-admiring cynic.
This is the way I was; this is the way I felt; all of
these noble feelings I nourished; all of these detestable deeds I did; yes, that is how bad I was.
But I dare anyone to step forward and say: "*I* was
better." Rousseau is convinced that no man living
can truthfully make this assertion. On this account
and in advance he calls the reader a boaster and a
liar who contends that he has lived a more beautiful
or more worthy life. This impressed the populace,
and evoked applause from the dismayed.

In Danish literature we have the autobiographies
of two poets, Andersen and Oehlenschläger. Andersen called his book *Mit Livs Eventyr* (The Story
of My Life). It tells how miraculously God has
led him onward and upward from poverty and ob-

scurity to a position in which he is the peer of the most prominent, the guest of princes and kings. It first shows us how superciliously he was treated and how slighted he was of men, and then how he was recognized and admired. Goethe does not regard himself as having been under the especial protection of the guardian angel of spiritual phenomena and prodigies; and his account breaks off before he had attained to any sort of external prominence.

Oehlenschläger's autobiography is a plebeian book. It contains a loquacious account of everything possible including quite a number of valuable anecdotes. But it is a book without plan, and alack and alas, it is a book without brains.

As all the world knows, the life of the great majority of more prominent individuals is either an incessant struggle or an early surrender. Life has made them either tread-mill slaves or prisoners who cannot extricate themselves from the fine meshes of the tenacious net in which they have become hopelessly entangled either by the power of external circumstances or as a result of their own actions in days that are no more. Having reached the years of complete maturity, we see them either renouncing the attempt to attain to anything like substantial fame, or they live in a delusion, perfectly transparent to others, that they have actually approached the pinnacles of distinction. Were the better of them to sit down and write the stories of their lives we would be regaled with an account of their struggles against unfavorable circumstances that lay beyond their immediate control, or against enemies and enviers and emulators. We would see their figures in the fray.

In Goethe's autobiography, we see his life lifted up above the life of others, and all the more easily, too, since he meets with no especial animosity or opposition.• Men and things submit to him. A Frenchman has said: "There are very few human beings who control life in general and their own lives in particular." In his autobiography we see Goethe's personality borne along and aloft by a degree of self-control which even in the matter of passion never yields entirely and thereby proves its ability to control life in general as well as the lives of others.

What Goethe gives us in his *Dichtung und Wahrheit* are the points of departure for the history of the evolution of his personality. It is not a story of his struggles. Previous to his twenty-sixth year he had no opponents. He does mention, once in a while, some unimportant individual such as Nicolai, but Nicolai was never a considerable opponent. His world renown was so firmly established when he wrote the account of his life that he needed neither to refer to it nor to depend upon it. Nor does he say one single word about it. The book is merely an introduction to his growth, first as a mind and then as a poet.

Let us take two important poets who lived at the same time in Denmark: Ewald [8] and Wessel. They

[8] Johannes Ewald was a combination of Edgar Allen Poe, Theodor Körner and himself. The son a clergyman, he joined the Prussian army and then the Austrian and deserted from both. When fifteen he became engaged and when his fiancée married another man he sought relief in increased dissipation. The wonderful and miraculous were his chief attractions. Of his great genius there has never been the least doubt. His "Kong Christian stod ved höjen mast," translated by Longfellow, has become a national song of Denmark.   —TRANSLATOR.

came to grief from self-stupefaction. Or take great poets from the same time, or a little later, in Europe—Byron in England, Kleist in Germany, Alfred de Musset in France. The one voluntarily wasted his life, the other committed suicide, the third met the fate of Ewald and Wessel. Remember too the numerous individuals who stranded on the reef of self-praise from Chateaubriand to many a modern ass, and then we will feel the real significance of the unique feature of Goethe's autobiography: he merely wishes to portray his development.

Among the creative minds of more modern times there is a type of artist who has succeeded completely in producing a small but monumental work that will stand the test of ages. We have but to think of Daniel Defoe's *Robinson Crusoe*, Abbé Prévost's *Manon Lescaut*, Bernardin de Saint-Pierre's *Paul et Virginie*, Adalbert von Chamisso's *Peter Schlemihl* and H. C. Andersen's[9] *Eventyr for Börn*.

Then there is another type of artist in the case of whom everything depends upon the effect of his works. In this class belong such pious painters as Fiesole, who wish to arouse reverence, and such impious writers as Diderot, who wish to make propaganda. To this group belong all moralising and reformatory writers. They write with a purpose. They wish to educate or to develop or to encourage. Of this group the greatest example is unquestionably

[9] Brandes leaves an erroneous impression by his reference to a "little" work in the case of H. C. Andersen. His "Fairy Tales for Children" appeared in instalments. Taken collectively, they constitute a considerable body of "immortal" literature. His dramas and novels may be dead; but his tales for children are still read, and to read them all takes time.   —TRANSLATOR.

Voltaire. Throughout the entire body of his writings, historical, scientific and poetic, throughout his witty letters, his philosophic tales, his satirical verses, and his tragedies with their clandestine thrusts, there is the sole and incessant endeavor to reform, to persuade, to arouse, and to enlighten the mind of the reader. Voltaire's aim is to function as an innovator, a renovator, and a ventilator. For him the work that he writes is a means to this end.

The rarest and most refined type of artist after all is the one whose sole and fundamental aim is to develop himself. Leonardo da Vinci and Michael Angelo are conspicuous examples; but each of them was relatively unconscious in his striving, though by no means naïve. In this regard Goethe is the modern type, the prototype. He yearns least of all for full self-recognition or self-consciousness as an artist; though he is conscious of his restless self-development, he himself is the secret and the solution of his being. He had the same experience that other great artists of this type had: The passion with which they strove to approach an inner ideal made it difficult for them to leave finished works. Think of the hundreds of different tasks with which Leonardo struggled! How long he painted on his masterpiece *Mona Lisa!* How few finished paintings he left behind as monuments of this genius of his which never ceased trying! The same with Michael Angelo. How much he tried and how much he had to give up! What a number of statues he left half finished! They stand, half bound to the marble blocks, mute and yet eloquent witnesses to the fact that it is difficult for the master to give expression to his soul as it grows richer day by day, to his genius that is recharged without end. But even in his case it is not so easy to detect the restless self-development as it is in the case of Goethe.

This is owing to the fact that Goethe was the first great poet and writer whose life lies so completely spread out before us that in every essential point we can see the connection between his work and his life, or more correctly speaking between his work and his constantly shifting human nature. Even his artistic or scientific works, otherwise of less value, are interesting because of the insight they give into the life of the soul of a very great man.

From the point of view of criticism in earlier times, the history of literature connoted something about books; it had to deal with books. The author of these lines, however, has the weakness and the strength to be more interested in the man than in his book. He likes to look through the book into the man back of it. If the man himself is meritorious and deserving of respectful study, then even one of his less important works is instructive, for it reveals his personality. And it is, after all, the personality that constitutes the really great work of art.

Little Denmark has been relatively rich in renowned talents. Thorvaldsen [10] and Oehlenschlä-

---

[10] Brandes's attitude toward Thorvaldsen is that of all dependable critics of the present. Thorvaldsen was remarkably successful in his imitation of the Pagan spirit. When he attempted to imitate and reproduce the modern spirit he failed, not entirely, but partly. His statue of Lord Byron is a case in point. Originally intended for Westminster Abbey, it was set up in the library of Trinity College, Cambridge. The general public knows him probably best for his "Night" and "Morning," reliefs which he is said to have modeled in one day.   —TRANSLATOR.

ger [11] were both very great talents, though no one can truthfully call them great men. If we go through their art, and then on back to the men behind it, we meet in both cases wholesome, vivacious, richly endowed, dispassionate beings who never rise very high, who never go very deep, who never show that they have anything of the fountain-like in them; nor of the duplicate and reënforced foundation. And we return to their works, beautiful as the best of them are, and enrapturing as the effect of their individual creations may be.

When Goethe undertook to write his life, he found it ill advised and impossible to depend entirely on his memory. He had to proceed much as he proceeded when he wrote the lives of others, of Winckelmann and Hackert. He endeavored first of all to supply himself with material. An acquaintance of his in Frankfort, I. H. Schlosser (not to be confused with Goethe's brother-in-law, who died in 1799) gave him some information concerning his paternal city, and sent him books which he might need for the description of the Frankfort of his childhood. Fritz Jacobi and Knebel told him what

[11] Adam Gottlob Oehlenschläger (1779-1850) played a great rôle in the rejuvenation of Danish literature. Danish romanticism, if not modern Danish poetry, began with his *Guldhornene* ("The Golden Drinking Horns"), after which he wrote a long series of dramatic works. Influenced by Germany, he in turn had his influence on the romantic school in Germany. Aside from his poetization of Northern themes, he did much, in conjunction with Thorvaldsen, to revive the antique. His "Correggio" was written in German while he was in Rome. In his *Hrolf Krake* (1828) he has one character (Hjalte) represent Denmark, another (Bjarke) Norway, another (Vöggur) Sweden, and in this way he made a plea for an ideal Scandinavianism. His wide acquaintance with the literary men of his age in various parts of the world did much to make Denmark known abroad. Longfellow knew him quite well. —TRANSLATOR.

they remembered. He went carefully through an entire series of volumes on the affairs of the Court at Wetzlar. He was forced to regret that he had destroyed some of his own private papers. His letters to his sister he had had sent back to him. He took it upon himself to leaf through old numbers of the *Göttinger gelehrte Anzeigen,* and of Nicolai's and Wieland's critical magazines, in order to visualize to himself the judgments that had been passed upon him by his contemporaries of the preceding generation. For the portrayal of his childhood and his early youth, Bettina had supplied him with everything she had learned from the stories told her by his mother. He made use of this material in an unconcerned fashion though various parts of it bear the stamp of her embellishing fancy. And in not a few instances he depended upon his memory which played him false in little things, a fact that called forth spiteful and foolish attacks.

The depiction of people and places is without exception happy. As is usually the case with Goethe, his women are more sharply conceived and better reproduced than his men, though several of his male portraits are unsurpassable. The description of the literary condition in Germany at that time is unquestionably beyond reproach so far as the Germans are concerned, but there is no picture of the spiritual physiognomy of Europe at the moment Goethe started; Germany's spiritual life at that time was not especially interesting.

In the composition we notice with displeasure the tendency mentioned above to draw parallels between situations that had actually been experienced and corresponding ones in books. We notice also the art, perfectly natural on the part of a dramatist and here carried out at great length, of preparing us for everything that is to follow, making the basis clear of that which is to be developed, and warning us of approaching events. We notice also another dramatic agency that is employed in Goethe's dramas, namely, the bringing on of personalities who are supposed to complete, to complement, each other (as Egmont and Oranien, Tasso, and Antonio). It is perfectly plain that Herder and Goethe, Lenz and Goethe, Merck and Goethe, Lavater and Basedow, are all meant as contrasts. And finally we notice that tendency which, as we have already seen, had become more and more pronounced in Goethe's art, to see and to hold fast to the typical. He portrays those parts of his life that the reader knows from his own life. He generalizes the particular incident so that it becomes doubly interesting. The individual event becomes a symbol.

CHAPTER XXIX

KARL AUGUST AND NAPOLEON: 1813

IN May, 1812, Napoleon stopped for some time in Dresden while on his way to Russia. Karl August had a conversation with him and deferentially advised him not to undertake the Russian campaign. Through his daughter-in-law, Maria Paulovna, he was closely related to the Russian imperial family. Napoleon paid no attention to his advice; he cherished, and not without cause, deep distrust for the Duke of Weimar.

Six years previous to this conversation Napoleon had imposed a tax of 2,200,000 francs on the little duchy as a condition of peace. It was done because Karl August had participated in the war. Moreover, the Duke in company with the other Ernestine dukes, had to place a regiment, *Herzöge von Sachsen,* at his disposal. This regiment took part in various campaigns, fought in Tirol and Spain and now had to prepare to fight against Russia. Up until November the regiment lay near the Baltic where it suffered so severely from the snow fields of Lithuania that the majority of the men died, or were taken prisoners.

On December 15, 1812, Napoleon came in all quietness through Weimar on his hurried sled trip. Formally, his standing at the court was the very best. He had even, in 1808, invited himself to be

its guest when he came from Erfurt. But he had,
as a result of the fact that some malicious remarks
on the part of Karl August had been brought to his
attention, made it incumbent upon Davoust to open
all letters to and from the ducal family.

Napoleon's distrust was so deep-seated that, when
an attempt was made on his life at Schönbrunn in
the fall of 1809 (by the young Friedrich Staps), he
held fast to the belief that Karl August was the
instigator.

Nothing however was farther from Napoleon's
mind than unreservedly to reveal this distrust. For
that he was far too completely in control of himself.
He felt and knew that the prudent thing to do was
to show all manner of attention to the members of
the *Rheinbund* regardless as to whether they were
more or less hostile to him or whether their country
was great or small. He received Karl August's
second son, Bernhard, in Paris. He appreciated the
young man's bravery. After the battle of Wagram
in 1809 he personally decorated the seventeen-year-
old son with the star of the Legion of Honor, and
though his parents prevented his participation in
the Russian campaign by sending him on a compara-
tively long journey to the South, Napoleon was all
amiability toward him. The Prince remained in
Paris for four months.

But in the spring of 1813 the war broke out anew.
The King of Prussia instituted his defection and the
Prussian people rose up against foreign dominion.
Karl August's heart was with Prussia, but as one
of Napoleon's least powerful vassals, he pretended,
under duress, the greatest sort of affection for the
Emperor. The first request that the French Am-

bassador, St. Aignan (March 14, 1813) made on
the Saxon courts was that they should re-equip their
military contingent, the former having been destroyed in Lithuania. One is amazed, at the present,
at their lack of strength. The combined forces of
the Saxon courts amounted to 800 men. Weimar
had almost no officers. On March 30, 376 men
marched out from Weimar under the leadership of
a certain Major von Lyncker toward the Thuringian
Forest. Of these 200 were recruits; they remained
at Berka by the Ilm; the others were led to Ruhla
near Eisenach. On April 3 the forces of Sachse-
Gotha-Altenburg, Sachse-Meiningen, and Sachse-
Hildburghausen joined the forces from Weimar and
formed *one battallion* the companies of which were
distributed among three small towns. Only ten days
later about fifty Prussian Husars and cavalrymen
pressed forward to Ruhla. They captured the entire battalion without resistance and led them to
Blücher's headquarters where they voluntarily became incorporated in the Prussian army.

Nothing more painful could have befallen Karl
August in his relation to Napoleon, who already
distrusted him. His position became even more
difficult when the rumor (a baseless one) found
credence that a company of Cossacks who had put
some exhausted French soldiers to flight were in
actuality disguised students from Jena.

And we must add that Karl August's own vacillating rashness made his situation still worse.
When a squadron of Prussian Husars under Major
Blücher, the son of the general, entered Weimar,
the Duke invited the Major to dine with him. During the dinner the report was brought in that a very

considerable number of French soldiers were marching against Weimar. Blücher was obliged to rise
from the Duke's table in order to oppose the latter's allies. On that same evening the French General Souham entered Weimar, and now it was *his*
troops who were to be billeted on the town and
looked after generally. The Duke's confidential
agent on this, as on many other occasions during
these years, was the resolute and shrewd Privy
Councillor, later Chancellor, Friedrich von Müller.
But he had been so imprudent as to decipher a code
to two Weimar officials who, in a letter which the
French outposts intercepted and read to the Commandant of the place, had said that the French
were the pest, the Prussians were the physicians.
The French general became enraged and the entire
ducal family came within a hair of being made prisoners. The two officials just barely escaped being
shot down as traitors. As the result of a great deal
of trouble and not a little boldness, von Müller
succeeded in a personal conversation with Napoleon
in appeasing his resentment. During an audience,
however, Napoleon called the Duke his unquestioned
foe and characterized him as being "the most restless Prince in Europe" (*le prince le plus remuant
de l'Europe*) who never tired of spinning and weaving intrigues against him. The seditious speeches
which the professors in Jena delivered to their students were moreover made known to Napoleon, so
that he threatened to burn Jena that same evening.
Von Müller directed his thoughts into other chan-
nels by showing the Emperor that he was running a
great risk of forever blurring the fame that was
immortal because of his conduct at the battle of

Jena in case he now committed such a gruesome act against the town.

When Karl August came to Erfurt the next morning to pay his respects to Napoleon he was by no means received in an unfriendly way; the Emperor assured him that when he came to Weimar he would pay the Duchess a visit.   He did so the next day, April 28.   When he arrived at the castle he paid, according to an eye-witness, the young Eduard Genast, not the slightest bit of attention to Karl August, who stood at the foot of the stairs, but went straight to the rooms of the Duchess.   When she begged him to show mercy to the two officials on whom the death sentence had been pronounced, he made the prompt reply: *Je le vieux bien, et je suis charmé de pouvoir faire une chose qui Vous soit agréable, Madame!*   When he left, Karl August and his son accompanied him on horse.   During the ride the Emperor again noticed him and talked with him and his escort cordially and at great length.

But the very next day Napoleon made Karl August feel his hard hand, as is evident from the beginning of the following letter from the Duke to his near friend, King Friedrich August of Saxony:

The Emperor and King seemed to be in some doubt as to the feelings that Your Majesty cherishes toward him and expressed the wish, that Your Majesty would declare himself openly; His Majesty *commanded* me to repeat his very words to you: The King of Saxony must come out frankly and say whether he is for me or against me.   He cannot complain of my conduct toward him; I have done everything for him.   But his action at Torgau was equivocal.

The King of Saxony sent Napoleon an humble communication, and all the more promptly since he had learned of Napoleon's victory at Gross-Görschen. The French again had the largest part of Saxony in their possession, and on his arrival in Dresden Friedrich August found that also there it was French troops who formed the espalier along his route.

After his victory at Bautzen, Napoleon made severe demands, in Dresden, on Karl August. In the place of the contingent that the Prussians had captured, he was naturally supposed to form a new one. But this was a small matter in comparison with the burdens imposed upon him by the support of the Napoleonic army that was marching through Weimar and his obligation to improve the fortress at Erfurt (aside from supplying it with provisions). For three months in succession little Sachse-Weimar (with 120,000 inhabitants) had to feed 600,000 men and an unknown number of horses.

To all of this must be added the difficulties placed in Karl August's way by the Lützow *Freikorps* and the swarm of Cossacks when they attacked French troops on Weimar territory. Napoleon believed (or acted as though he believed) that the Duke was an accomplice and made him responsible for any injury his soldiers suffered within the confines of Weimar. The Duke was obliged to humble himself in order, if possible, to ward off anger. Read this congratulatory communication to the man he hated, after the battle at Bautzen:

Since my very ardent prayers (*mes voeux fervents*) for the success of Your Majesty have been heard, I praise divine mercy therefor and lay my most submissive congratultaions. Sir, at your feet. Would that Your Imperial and Royal Majesty would condescend to accept the expression of mv profound submission (*les èmanations d'une profonde sou-mission*) and of the affection I have consecrated to Your Majesty.

In the course of only three weeks (March 27—April 19) Sachse-Weimar, aside from feeding the army as usual in the four different stations at Eisenach, Weimar, Buttelstedt, and Jena, was supposed to supply Erfurt with 200,000 pounds of meat, 100,-000 rations of biscuit bread (*pain biscuité*), 100,000 rations of ordinary biscuits, 10,000 hundredweight of meal, 200,000 bushels of oats. Concerning the last item, it was as a matter of fact impossible to scrape up more than 11,000 bushels in the entire country. For the building of the fortress at Erfurt, they were supposed to supply at the same time, 15,341 logs, and 153 wagons and 1940 redoubt workers per day.

During all this misery, the idea ripened in Karl August's brain of appealing to Napoleon to promote him from Duke to Grand Duke in compensation for this socage, since a few strips of land had been added to Weimar, including Blankenhagen in the domain of Erfurt and some other Erfurt enclaves. Every morning while in Dresden Karl August put in his appearance at Napoleon's levees in order to state his wish and to make it clear to the Emperor that he would be in a better position with this higher rank to give satisfaction as the middle-point in Thuringia which the French army then needed, and so on. Napoleon merely replied: *On ne m'avait pas dit que vous désirez cela,* which was neither "yes" nor "no," and therefore equivalent to "no."

In the meantime Karl August amused himself as a genuine child of the eighteenth century splendidly in Dresden, then a sort of Paris and in which a quite diversified worldly life had been developed. From there he went to Teplitz where he took his usual cure and where he met not simply Goethe but also many members of the Austrian peerage and his son, the crown prince, as well as his daughter-in-law, Maria Paulovna. The new battalion that the French government had requested had in the meantime been raised. Berthier had given the suggestion: *L'Empereur ne connaît d'autre attachement que de se prêter à ses volontés.*

"Our contingent," writes the Weimarian Minister von Fritsch, August 3, is *au grand complet, i.e.,* 800 men have been raised; a commander, an adjutant and 8 officers have charge, and the most of the soldiers can march moderately well. Under fire, however these heroes might become more dangerous for their neighbors and officers than for the enemy." The fact is they could not shoot.

For Karl August however the all-important question was the securing of the title of Grand Duke. He had a petition drawn up in which it was said that the House of Weimar, which had once been so brilliant, had lost little by little in the course of centuries, until it had sunk below other royal houses above which it formerly towered. To Napoleon he addressed these pathetic words:

Would that it might correspond at once to His Majesty's magnanimity and political interests to restore the ancient splendor to a princely house which deserves a place alongside of the house of the Medicis in that it has made liberal use of all the means in its power to beautify art and benefit literature, while it has at the same time favored science by making itself a place of refuge for the illustrious men of the nation.

Should this idea succeed in arousing His Majesty's interest, and should His Majesty have the good grace to accord the idea a place in the extended series of great questions that are now concerning him in this period of reconstruction, His Majesty would soon be convinced that among all of his allies there is none that is more zealous, more grateful, more loyal than the house of Weimar which boasts, incidentally, of having furnished French history with some famous heroes. (The reference is probably to Bernhard von Sachse-Weimar. It could hardly refer to Moritz von Sachsen, since he did not descend from the house of Weimar.)

By reason of the special hope that this petition would be granted, a hope based on the near kinship to the Russian Court, it was a question of interesting Russian in the dynasty of Weimar; Maria Paulovna was appointed to win over the Zar, her brother, to the project. Young and sprightly though she was, she did not appeal to the ambitious ruler as being sufficiently energetic.

Karl August went to Ilmenau where he unexpectedly met Goethe, who had likewise been highly invigorated by his stay at the watering place. On the very next day, he went on a four-hour ride with his Duke.

On July 13, Karl August had written from Teplitz to Voigt: "Goethe is as if new-born." The festivities for Napoleon's day (August 15) had been held in Dresden on August 10. Goethe had come to Dresden in order to be present. The city was illuminated. He walked about in the crowded streets for several hours, and as the letters from that period show, spent the rest of his time in the art galleries. On August 11, he climbed up the two hundred and thirty steps of the tower of the Church of Our Lady in order to see the sunset. His birthday was celebrated in Ilmenau. In a letter to Christiane he described the homage that was done him, including the concert given late in the evening in the open air. This was the contribution of the town council. On the following evening there was a ball. Goethe returned to Weimar on September 2.

Karl August was, to be sure, disheartened by Napoleon's victory at Dresden, assured though he was as to the eventual outcome of the war since the allies were overcoming the French generals one by one. At the same time he invited the Commandant of Weimar, Colonel Seguy, to his Court, and accorded the French officers who chanced to be passing through the town the most cordial reception.

On October 10 the Austrian army marched into Weimar and it was even better received. Karl August wrote to the Zar and asked him for 2000 cossacks for his protection in case Napoleon should elect to march from Saxony through Weimar. But on the night following October 21 a colonel of the cossacks had Karl August called from his bed in order to tell him of the decisive victory that the battle of Leipzig had brought the Allies. At first the Duke was unwilling to believe the Colonel since he had no written evidence of the victory; he distrusted him and believed that he was really in the service of the French and had come to take him away as a hostage. Karl August was, however, soon enlightened as to the true state of affairs and French troops in the immediate vicinity of Weimar, near Ettersburg, were defeated in an engagement by Russian and Prussian cavalry.

On October 24 Emperor Alexander, his brother, Konstantin, and their escort of diplomats and generals, arrived at the castle in Weimar; and on the next day Emperor Franz of Austria came. The little castle could hardly contain all the lofty lords. Karl August began again to use all his energy to obtain the promotion he so passionately longed for. Maria Paulovna was again made an especial agent; a petition was again sent in, this time to Emperor Alexander who, however, was unwilling to make any definite promise. The troops of the Allies poured into the town in masses. The victors were hungry; there was an incalculable amount of plundering in Eisenach and other places. Goethe's assurance that his fate was highly to be praised in comparison with that of many others rested on the fact that he escaped being plundered, though he had a great deal to suffer from the many high and exacting Austrian officers. With Count Colleredo-Mansfeld at their head, they lived for three days in his house. According to his diary his house had to be *cleaned* on October 26.

The distress of the civilian population increased. Contagious diseases, especially typhoid, spread. The Duke was in extreme financial embarrassment which had to be met by a loan. He entered into an agreement with the allied forces, placed a few thousand men at the disposal of their army, took over the command of the third German army corps, and united with its leaders in forcing the French out of Belgium. From here he went to conquered Paris and took the cure on the way home at a bathing resort in Aix-la-Chapelle. In Paris he urgently requested Alexander to confer upon him the title of Grand Duke. The latter referred him, however, to the Congress in Vienna then about to take place.

The Duke went to Vienna in person and spared no pains to secure the title so ardently longed for and the slight increase in territory corresponding thereto. He succeeded.

CHAPTER XXX

GOETHE AND THE ORIENT; *West-Oestlicher Divan;* MARIANNE VON WILLEMER

ON December 1, Goethe wrote to Sara von Grotthuss: "Everything again echoes with want and misery." A few days later he complains to Knebel over the fact that "accounts come to us from all sides concerning the death of excellent people." It was typhoid infection making its way into the towns and villages that lay next to the roads along which the armies had marched.

Goethe had just then finished the three parts of *Dichtung und Wahrheit* referred to above. The passionately enthusiastic rise of Young Germany against Napoleon, brought on by defection, did not move him; it did not inspire him to song. He said time and time again:

Is it in accordance with my nature to write war songs while sitting in my room? Out near the watch fires where at night the horses of the enemy's outposts are heard neighing, I could feel a certain desire to do just that sort of thing. That, however, was not my life and my affair but the life and the affair of Theodor Körner. His war songs clothe him excellently. War songs would have been to my unwarlike nature and unwarlike mind a mask ill-fitted to my face. I have never been affected in my poetry.

He experienced, after the manner of strong minds, a deep inclination to keep himself and his

366

ideas untouched by the surf which was dashing up around him; he had to bury himself in something with which none of the people about him were occupied, but which could captivate, develop, and enrich him himself. And so, in 1813, he plunged into Oriental poetry. Even in early youth Goethe had felt attracted by it. He had read the Old Testament time and time again with as much critical acumen as he could then command, at any rate with independent conception. He understood Hebrew. As late as 1797, midway between *Hermann und Dorothea* and *Faust,* he had written a treatise, *Israel in der Wüste,* which betrays much thoughtfulness.

Through Herder he had already come into contact with Asiatic poetry, and had long known something about Hafis. But in 1813 the Orientalist Hammer, from whom Herder expected most, had published a translation of Hafis's *Divan* in two stately volumes. It was Hammer who initiated Goethe into the study of the nature of Western Asia. Though he taught himself Arabic and a little Persian, he did not in any way come in touch with the richer poetry of India. It was Hafis first and foremost who enraptured him.

He zealously rejects the mystic interpretation of Hafis's poems:

> Sie haben Dich, heiliger Hafis,
> Die mystische Zunge genannt
> Und haben, die Wortgelehrten,
> Den Werth des Worts nicht gekannt.

> Mystisch heissest du ihnen,
> Weil sie Närrisches bei Dir denken
> Und ihren unlautern Wein
> In Deinem Namen verschenken.

The translation he had in mind could not compete with the later, and excellent, one by Daumer through which Hafis became so dear to the readers of the next generation. But his penetration into the spirit of Hafis was adequate. He soon came to feel perfectly at home in the wealth of Persian poetic art, due, no doubt, to the fact that he saw historical resemblances between his own age and that of Hafis. As Hafis had poetized his joy in existence, his delight in life, at a time when Timur-i-Leng inspired peace-loving and peaceful people with fear by his campaigns of conquest, so he himself was living in an age of revolution in which a powerful conqueror had burst old political bonds and welded new ones which in turn were being rent asunder.

After the battle of Leipzig Goethe found a genuine fountain of youth for his lyric genius in the poetry of the Orient. He was the first to introduce it into German literature. These studies were, to be sure, interrupted by the necessity of glorifying contemporary events pleasing to Weimar in theatrical performances, festival plays and topical poems. This occupied his time and used up his energy at the beginning of 1814. But in July of that year he went to Wiesbaden, and Frankfort, in order to live for himself and compose for his personal enjoyment. Only a few individual poems from the lyric masterpiece of later years, the *West-Oestlicher Divan,* were written down when, in the fall of 1814, he received, through his acquaintance with Marianne Willemer, the decisive impulse to complete **his** work.

Willemer, an active and well-to-do citizen of Frankfort, had for many years stood in a friendly relation to Goethe. He had, as a young banker, in 1788, supplied Merck with a loan of four thousand gulden for the payment of which Karl August went security. This was done at Goethe's request. When Christiane Vulpius came to Frankfort in 1797, and 1806, to straighten out the affairs of Goethe's mother, Willemer was, on both occasions, one of the few who were really attentive and helpful to her. He was a forceful writer on Enlightenment and popular deistic philosophy. He wrote several weak dramas, occupied himself a great deal, as an admirer of Pestalozzi, with the problems of education, and eventually became one of Börne's collaborators on *Die Wage*. He was highly respected as a business man and as a Frankfort senator; and he took part for a time in the management of the theatre. The Prussian government granted him the title of *Geheimrat;* the Austrian government honored him with a diploma of nobility. He had been twice married and had three daughters and one son. In 1797, when but thirty-six years old, he became a widower for the second time. His oldest daughter, Rosette, was married in 1799 to the distinguished patron of art, Johann Städel.

Marianne Jung was born at Linz in Austria, 1784. In the fall of 1798 she came with her mother to the theatre at Frankfort. She became a member of the ballet when only fourteen years of age. In the rôle of a little harlequin who crept out of an egg she enchanted Clemens Brentano who memorialized her in his portrayal of the young dancer, Biondinetta, in his *Romanzen vom Rosenkranz.* Her talent for singing and acting awakened attention, her amiability won her friends. Among her ad-

mirers was Willemer who, as a member of the theatre boards, became acquainted with her and thought
of adopting her, charming child that she was.

First, however, he wanted to find out whether
she had a good heart. He disguised himself as a
peddler, took a large piece of satin with him, and
offered his wares at the house where Marianne lived
with her mother. When the women wouldn't buy,
he began to weep and related a heart-rending story
of the misfortunes that had reduced him to poverty.
Thereupon both mother and daughter began to weep
too; they bought the satin. Not long afterward,
Willemer, who had repaid the mother all the income she had received from her daughter's talent,
took the sixteen-year-old girl one evening after the
performance to his home, had her reared with his
own daughters, and gave her a thorough musical
education.

From a poem which Clemens Brentano, in 1803,
addressed to Marianne one can see that he was at
the time very much taken up with her. He taught
her to play the guitar and one day when she struck
a wrong note, he told her in his forcible and bitter
way that her position in Willemer's house was a
false one, whereupon she burst into tears. Willemer
fell into a rage over Brentano's remark and called
him a snake whom he had warmed at his bosom.
The following Christmas he had himself, among
other gifts, packed in a chest and dumped at Marianne's feet. There was as yet no mention made of
marriage.

The living of the beautiful young singer at the
home of a widower naturally afforded opportunity
for all manner of derogatory comment; but Mari-

anne was otherwise received on the best of terms in
the entire Willemer circle. She was the favorite
of the Bethmanns, appreciated by the young geogra-
pher, Carl Ritter, and associated constantly with
Bettina Brentano and the latter's sisters. When
Willemer, in 1810, started on a trip to Switzerland
and Italy he took Marianne and his daughters along
with him.

The German authors who have written on Marianne von Willemer, such as Th. Creizenach and
Hermann Hüffer, have proved in zealous German
fashion how unthinkable it is that there existed any
intimate relationship whatsoever between Marianne
and Willemer before marriage. Individual expressions by Goethe sound otherwise. After an absence
of seventeen years, Goethe came to Frankfort, July,
1814, travelled from there to Wiesbaden where he
remained a month, was the guest of the Brentano
family for the first week in September, stopped again
in Frankfort at the home of old friends for two
weeks, from where he went on September 24 to
Sulpiz Boissérée in Heidelberg. Three days after
his departure the fifty-year-old Willemer entered
into marriage with the now twenty-nine-year-old
Marianne. It is not improbable that Goethe en-
couraged him in this action; the position of Marianne had become more exposed since the daughters
had married and left home, and Goethe uses the
following strong expression about the marriage:
Rettung der jungen Frau and calls it *eine grosse
sittliche That Willemers.* His attitude toward the
newly married couple was most cordial. In October,
1814, after his return from Heidelberg, he was
often at the beautiful villa of the Willemers, *Die*

Gerbermühle, near Frankfort.   He won the hearts
of the daughters of the house by his amiability and
susceptibility to impressions.   We have indisputable
proof of this in the enthusiastic portrayal of his
personality from the pen of the oldest daughter,
Rosette Städel.

In Frankfort nothing at all was done in honor
of Goethe.   In order to punish, in a jesting way, his
former colleagues in the management of the theatre for their indifference, Willemer inserted in a
suburban newspaper a description of an elaborate
Goethe celebration in the theatre.   He spoke of a
decorated box, prologue, gala performance of *Tasso*
and crowning of Goethe on the stage with wreaths
from the busts of Vergil and Ariosto.   The description was in truth copied by numerous German papers, later recopied from them, and incorporated in
some of the older Goethe biographies.

The poet's relation to Marianne took on a new
and more cordial character in 1815.   After a prolonged sojourn in Wiesbaden he came, on August
12, to Frankfort and immediately went out to *Die
Gerbermühle* where he lived until September 8.   The
character of the intimacy between the man of sixty-
six years and the woman of thirty grew to be fine,
rich, and warm.   She had already written some
verses, including a number of poems on current topics.   Now, in the course of a few weeks, she developed into a real poetess.   Indeed the few verses
she addressed to Goethe during this brief period
are of so great value that it is not excessive praise
to refer to her as the most gifted poetess Germany
or Austria has produced.

Of evenings Goethe would read aloud from his poems, or Marianne would sing his songs as they had been set to music: *Kennst du das Land,* and *Der Gott und die Bajadere.* According to Goethe's own statement she sang the latter "as beautifully and feelingly as it can be sung," though he did not like to hear it from her lips: He fancied, as he remarked to Sulpiz Boisserée, that this legend of a dancing girl who is elevated to a lofty existence, through love to be sure and yet in a most painful way, would affect her too strongly, and remind her too much of her own lot. The assertion is adequate proof that Marianne's own life, in her younger days, on the stage and in the home, was exposed to unenviable temptations.

One evening Goethe read aloud a series of new love poems; Willemer fell asleep; his young wife, who was listening, placed a yellow, turban-like scarf over her head. In this way she entered into the spirit of the rôle of Hatem's Oriental friend. There follow a multitude of half modern, half Oriental poems of the highest rank from him to her and her to him. On the longest day of the year he had addressed the poem to her beginning *Süsses Kind, die Perlenreihen,* which was not published until 1837. The hatred of the cross to which it stands a witness induced him to postpone its publication. She wore a cross on a pearl necklace; as a Mohammedan he is passionately vexed thereby:

> Diese ganz moderne Narrheit,
> Magst du mir nach Schiras bringen!
> Soll ich wohl, in seiner Starrheit,
> Hölzchen quer auf Hölzchen singen?

He compares her with King Solomon's many wives
each of whom tried to convert him to her idol:

> Isis' Horn, Anubis' Rachen
> Boten sie dem Judenstolze—
> Mir willst du zum Gotte machen
> Solch ein Jammerbild am Holze!

But he closes with the declaration that he will not
seem more cantankerous than Solomon. Even the
Mexican idol, Vitzliputzli, would become a talisman
for him if worn on her heart.

The first poem that Goethe now directs to Marianne is the one that begins: *Nicht Gelegenheit macht
Diebe, sie ist selbst der grösste Dieb,* and which
closes with the remark that he detects mercy in her
shining eye, and in her arms rejoices over the happiness of renewed youth. It is in this poem that he
says he is impoverished. She replies with the poem
Hochbeglükt in deiner Liebe in which we have the
following: "Don't jest in that way! Don't talk
about poverty! Does not love make us rich? When
I hold you in my arms no one's happiness is greater
than mine."

The poems containing Suleika's question and Hatem's answer concerning the ring which he gave her,
but which slipped from her finger in a dream and
fell into the Euphrates, is the next poem which
Goethe produced during his sojourn at Marianne's
home and revolves in all probability around a question she really put to him, for the poem closes with
these words:

> Also träumt'ich. Morgenröthe
> Blitzt ins Auge durch den Baum.
> Sag' Poete, sag' Prophete!
> Was bedeutet dieser Traum?

The expression *sag' Prophete* is evidently intended for *sag' Goethe!* The answer reminds Suleika of how the Doge of Venice became espoused to the Adriatic, and closes with the assurance that Suleika has espoused Hatem to her river, her terrace, her grove, and that here his mind shall be consecrated to her until the very last kiss.

On the same day that Goethe left Marianne's home and came to Heidelberg, he wrote to her the beautiful, unrhymed, dithyrambic poem, *Die Schön umschriebenen,* and so on. He admits that he praises himself for the love and happiness he owes her, for this self-praise is a stench only to the jealous; to friends it is a rich perfume. She overwhelms him with happiness when she throws her passion to him as she would throw a ball so that he can catch it and throw her his ego in return. He sends her poetic pearls which her passion's powerful surf washed up on the shore for him who stood on life's desolate strand. With it she adorns her neck, her bosom!

A few days later, during Goethe's stay in Heidelberg, where Marianne and Willemer were to meet him, she composed the exquisite song of longing entitled, *Was bedeutet die Bewegung?* Goethe incorporated it in his *Divan* with just a few, negligible, and in part not even felicitous textual emendations: "What does the motion mean? Does the east wind bring me glad tidings? The fresh fluttering of its wings cools the heart's deep wounds. It plays caressingly with the dust and whirls it up into light clouds, and so on, but its gentle whisperings brings delightful greetings to me from my friend. Even before these hills grow dark I shall be sitting quietly at his feet. Let the east wind continue on its course; may it serve happy men and sorrowful; here, where the high walls glow, it finds the one so much in love:

> Ach, die wahre Herzenskunde,
> Liebeshauch, erfrischtes Leben
> Wird mir nur aus seinem Munde,
> Kann mir nur sein Atem geben.

The changes Goethe made are slight indeed. Among them there is one improvement: *Bringt der Ost mir frohe Kunde* in the place of *Bringt der Ostwind*. He has also made two other changes which only tend to lessen the value of the original: *Diene Freunden und Betrübten* in the place of *Diene Frohen und Betrübten*. And he felt called to make the following changes in Marianne's stanza:

> *Marianne*
> Und mich soll sein leises Flüstern
> Von dem Freunde lieblich grüssen;
> Eh' noch diese Hügel düstern,
> Sitz' ich still zu seinen Füssen.

> *Goethe*
> Und mir bringt sein leises Flüstern,
> Von dem Freunde tausend Grüsse;
> Eh' noch diese Hügel düstern,
> Grüssen mich wohl tausend Küsse.

Marianne's rhyme is better, just as the picture she sets forth is more beautiful. The song as a whole is an imperishable masterpiece.

The following morning and evening Goethe wrote, in Heidelberg, two of his most excellent poems to Marianne. The first is the chestnut poem, moulded with noble simplicity about a single visualization. The introductory stanzas depict the leafy chestnut tree with the prickly green fruits cradled on the swinging boughs. The last show how the brown kernels ripen in the shell until it bursts:

> Doch immer reift von innen
> Und schwillt der braune Kern.
> Er möchte Luft gewinnen
> Und säh' die Sonne gern.
>
> Die Schale platzt, und nieder
> Macht er sich freudig los;
> So fallen meine Lieder
> Gehäuft in deinen Schoos.

The diction has at once the extreme facility of the folk song and the refined verbal conciseness and simplicity of the classical song. On the very same day he wrote this poem which differs completely in style and content:

> Ist es möglich! Stern der Sterne,
> Drück ich wieder Dich ans Herz!
> Ach was ist die Nacht der Ferne
> Für ein Abgrund, für ein Schmerz!

The poem, grand in its porportions, unfolds with massive splendor from this fundamental feeling of the unnatural anguish of separation. In order to explain it, an entire theory of world creation is portrayed; we see disunion, dissolution, and distance arise in accordance with God's plan; we perceive the importance of love is everything. There is a wonderful Michel Angelo-like grandeur in this stanza:

> Als die Welt im tiesften Grunde
> Lag an Gottes ew'ger Brust,
> Ordnet er die erste Stunde
> Mit erhabner Schöpfungslust.

Und er sprach das Wort: Es werde!
Da erklang ein schmerzlich Ach!
Als das All mit Machtgebärde
In die Wirklichkeiten brach.

It sounds like an interpretation of a painting in
the Sistine Chapel on the creation of the world.

Everything was silent, everything was gray in
gray; then God created the dawn, which unfolded
from the darkness a harmonious play of colors, and
all things that at first stood apart from each other,
now sought each other in mutual attraction:

Sei's Ergreifen, sei es Raffen,
Wenn es nur sich fasst und hält!
Allah braucht nicht mehr zu schaffen,
Wir erschaffen seine Welt.

There is in these lines a genuinely creative heat, the
tremendous power of the all-embrace.

From these Heidelberg days there is furthermore
the antiphonal song between Hatem and Suleika,
beginning

Locken, haltet mich gefangen!

It is dedicated to the beautiful brown serpents entwined about her head. In this he stresses the
glowing youth of his heart despite his gray hair.
It reads:

Nur dies Herz, es ist von Dauer,
Schwillt in jugendlichstem Flor;
Unter Schnee und Nebelschauer
Rast ein Aetna Dir hervor.

That the poem is purely European and, despite
its Oriental dress, entirely personal in its conception

and content, is revealed by the fact that the word
Hatem is inserted instead of Goethe which would
rhyme perfectly in this stanza:

> Du beschämst wie Morgenröthe
> Jener Gipfel ernste Wand,
> Und noch einmal fühlet *Hatem*
> Frühlingshauch und Sonnenbrand.

The following beautiful poem in reply is by Marianne and not by Goethe:

> Nimmer will ich Dich verlieren!
> Liebe giebt der Liebe Kraft.
> Magst Du meine Jugend zieren
> Mit gewalt'ger Leidenschaft.
> Ach, wie schmeichelt's meinem Triebe,
> Wenn man meinen Dichter preist!
> Denn das Leben ist die Liebe,
> Und des Lebens Leben Geist.

It is nothing short of amazing that a young
woman who, previous to these weeks, had never
produced anything other than jesting or jeering little
poems for the amusement of her friends or relatives,
should all of a sudden rise up to Goethe's heights
in this masterful way, adapt herself to his style, and
remain on a level with him.

During those days she wandered around with
Goethe through the ruins of the Heidelberg castle
and out about the castle itself. In the dust on the
edge of the castle fountain Goethe wrote her name
with his fingers in Arabic letters. Concerning this
he says in his poem that he no longer writes symmet-
rical rhymes on paper as smooth as silk, no longer
encloses them in golden vines, no, he writes them
in the moving dust and yet the strength with which

they are written endures and forces its way down to
the very centre of the earth:

> Dem Staub, dem beweglichen, eingezeichnet,
> Ueberweht sie der Wind; aber die Kraft besteht,
> Bis zum Mittelpunkt der Erde
> Dem Boden angebannt.

It was on September 24, while taking a walk by
the castle, that Goethe thus wrote Marianne's name
in human memory. A few hours later, the Willemers returned to Frankfort. Goethe and Marianne
never saw each other again. In a poem dated September 26 he placed these deep words on her lips:

> Volk und Knecht und Ueberwinder,
> Sie gestehn zu jeder Zeit:
> Höchstes Glück der Erdenkinder
> Sei nur die Persönlichkeit.

On September 28 she wrote in her home her other
immortal masterpiece, the poem of longing and be-
reavement which she addresses to the west wind and
which, though it assuredly cannot be placed by the
side of Shelley's magnificent ode on the same subject, belongs to those verses which the Germanic
people will not cease singing for centuries. It begins with the familiar lines:

> Ach, um deine feuchten Schwingen
> West, wie sehr ich dich beneide!
> Denn du kannst ihm Kunde bringen
> Was ich durch die Trennung leide.

There is a tenderness here such as is not to be
found in any of Marianne's other poems, a pain of
regret and languishing, and a fear of causing her

beloved grief by talking of her own sufferings. The west wind cools her tear-reddened eyes:

> Doch dein mildes, sanftes Wehen
> Kühlt die wunden Augenlieder,
> Ach, für Leid müsst' ich vergehen,
> Hofft ich nicht, wir seh'n uns wieder.

In both of the stanzas quoted Goethe has changed the text a little. The last one sounds better in his emendation:

> Sag ihm, aber sag's bescheiden:
> Seine Liebe sei mein Leben;
> Freudiges Gefühl von beiden
> Wird mir seine Nähe geben.

In October Mariane sends Geothe a poem in ciphers which they had agreed to use. From this Goethe forms the beautiful and intensely passionate poem beginning

> Dir zu eröffnen
> Mein Herz verlangt mich.

The close of the poem contains woman's burning erotic love:

> Mein Leben will ich   Kraft hab ich keine
> Nur zum Geschäfte   Als ihn zu lieben
> Von seiner Liebe   So recht im Stillen.
> Von heut an machen,   Was soll das werden!
> Ich denke seiner,   Will ihn umarmen
> Mir blutet's Herz.   Und kann es nicht.

But the poetic account of the two approaches its fullest, its most imperishable expression, in the prodigious poem with which Goethe closes the *Buch Suleika,* the song in which he ascribes characteristics

to his sweetheart that remind one of the hundred
names believers give to Allah. Not even in the
warmest days of his early youth did Goethe ever
write anything more charming than this love poem:

> In tausend Formen magst Du Dich verstecken,
> Doch, Allerliebste, gleich erkenn' ich Dich;
> Du magst mit Zauberschleiern Dich bedecken,
> Allgegenwärt'ge, gleich erkenn' ich Dich.

The last two stanzas of the poem run as follows:

> Wenn am Gebirg der Morgen sich entzündet,
> Gleich, Allerheiternde, begrüss' ich Dich;
> Dann über mir der Himmel rein sich ründet,
> Allherzerweiternde, dann athm' ich Dich.

> Was ich mit äsusserm Sinn, mit innerm kenne,
> Du Allbelehrende, kenn' ich durch Dich;
> Und wenn ich Allahs Namenhundert nenne,
> Mit jedem klingt ein Name mit für Dich.

Goethe and Marianne von Willemer kept up their
correspondence throughout the rest of his life, in
other words, for seventeen uninterrupted years. In
March, 1831, Goethe decided to return all of her
letters to her. He enclosed in the package a little
poem and a note in which he begged her to leave
the package untouched "bis zu unbestimmter
Stunde," that is to say, until his death. He left
the package lying, however, for fully eleven months;
he did not send it to her until a month before his
death, on February 10, 1832. A few weeks later
he received Marianne's promise that she would conscientiously preserve the package. Then he wrote
to her, just once more and for the last time, on February 23. On March 22 he breathed his last.

The little poem that was sent with the letters reads as follows:

> Vor die Augen meiner Lieben,
> Zu der Brust, der sie entquollen
> Einst, mit heissestem Verlangen
> So erwartet, wie empfangen—
> Zu der Brust, der sie entquollen
> Diese Blätter wandern sollen;
> Immer liebevoll bereit,
> Zeugen allerschönster Zeit.

The octogenarian feels anew, even here, the tension and longing with which he always expected these letters and the joy with which he received them.

Let us compare for a moment, in our thoughts Marianne von Willemer with Bettina von Arnim, her near acquaintance. Each is thirty years old. In the life of each Goethe marks an epoch. In the presence of each he stands as the senescent man in the presence of a very young woman. Bettina feels attracted to him strongly and fantastically, just as he feels attracted to Marianne. Each became a poetess of rank. But where Bettina tries to encircle her head with a halo of glory by usurping unto herself the honor for some of Goethe's very best sonnets, Marianne gives him, without a moment's hesitation, the most beautiful poems she ever produced. He publishes them under his own name, and does her the honor of recognizing them as being the equal of his own. He was so rich and great that he was not dishonored by so doing; on the contrary, he conferred honor when he took. Not until several years after her death was the secret brought to light. But in one of her poems she uses these beau-

tiful and touching words to Goethe concerning her
verses:

> Wohl, dass sie Dir nicht fremde scheinen:
> Sie sind Suleika's, sind die deinen.

Bettina was like the resplendent bird that comes
flustering and comes blustering; Marianne's being
was the attraction that beauty and grace and a very
great talent exercise when they work together, in
harmony, and when they work quietly, peacefully.
This explains those so significant words in her poem
to the west wind: "Tell him, but tell him modestly,
that his love is my life."

CHAPTER XXXI

DUALISM IN GOETHE'S FACULTIES

THERE was in Goethe, as there is in various other minds of first rank, a double faculty: There was the one that gilds things over; and there was the one that sees things soberly, unmercifully, just as they are. His being is like a cord woven together of two threads: reality's understanding and reality's glorification. It was easy to inspire him; it was not difficult for him to be sagacious.

Nature laid him out after a harmonious plan. He took pleasure in life and delight in men. But as to his unreserved freedom from illusions, even as a young man, that drama of his entitled *Die Mitschuldigen,* written in his extreme youth, is abundant evidence. And we have even more testimony to his strength of character in this connection in his attitude toward the French Revolution. He who once upon a time said that we have but one alternative, that of being either anvil or hammer, could naturally place but little confidence in those people who wished to emancipate the entire human race.

It was his inspiration for nature, his enthusiasm for it, that gave him a feeling of security. And poet that he was, nature was not indifferent to the fate of man. Quite the contrary: nature, as he felt it, stood opposite man as a beneficent power. In his visionary treatise entitled *Die Natur,* 1780, he said: "Nature brought me into life; it will also

lead me out. I put my trust in it; let it rule over
me, for it will not despise its own work. It is not
I that talk about it. No, everything that I have
said, true or false, it itself has said; it is responsible
for all; all merit belongs to it." Nature spoke a
similar language, years later, in Swinburne's
Hertha:

> I the grain and the furrow,
> The plough-cloven clod
> And the ploughshare drawn through
> The germ and the sod,
> The deed and the doer, the seed and the sower, the dust
>   which is God.

It was this intuitive and fundamental view of
life that constituted a bulwark for Goethe against
the rising tide of bitterness. For this tide rises in
all vigilant human souls. And if one's character
be really strong, and one's eye really sure, so that
he is in a position soberly to deduce correct results
from his own personal experiences, he is mortally
apt to tie up in a joyless harbor laden with a cargo
of contempt for human kind.

Bitterness arises in Goethe also, a deterrent to
which was his life in common with Schiller whose
nature was antipodal to his own. Yet when he, in
speaking of Schiller's struggle for advancement, says
in his memorial poem to the author of *Wallenstein*,

> Damit das Gute wirke, wachse, fromme,
> Damit der Tag des Edlen endlich komme,

this so fundamentally Schiller-like characteristic was
what Egmont calles "a strange drop in his blood:"
he did not have an especially strong faith in this
future in which the noble dominates. We have seen

him, however, at this same period making a big concession to optimism, to Schiller, to his native country, and to the idyllic strain in his own nature by the dignified and wholesome poem *Hermann und Dorothea*. Thereupon he glides over into the mood of renunciation which we have already had occasion to observe.

But he takes a decisive turn in *West-Oestlicher Divan*. In this resignation has disappeared; joy in life has triumphed. The poets of Western Asia had brought this about. He conquers, not merely the general oppression of old age, but also the specific melancholy superinduced by the war. *Buch Suleika* is a copious and joyous testimony to the power and enrichment of life. There is, too, not even a faint tang of gentle softness in these love songs.

Manly seriousness characterizes the *Divan* from beginning to end. Bitterness is neither excluded from it nor restrained in it; it is merely confined to the space allotted it by the poet. It is the drop of quinine in the wine. The *Buch des Unmuths* is an instructive counterpart to the *Buch Suleika*. In it Goethe has assembled once for all his feeling of dissatisfaction and spirit of resentment. The verse fits in with that of the *Buch der Betrachtungen:*

> Was bringt zu Ehren?
> Sich wehren.

In one of the poems he portrays the apparent good will of the Germans and their actual animosity toward him. The last two verses read:

> Sie lassen mich alle grüssen
> Und hassen mich bis in Tod.

With an insight free of illusions into conditions as they really were, and with an unmistakable appreciation of the hatred they felt toward him, and the hypocrisy with which they concealed it, he set forth in the final supplement to the book his own self-esteem—that armored weapon which enabled him to face the worst with calm:

> Was? Ihr misbilligt den kraft'gen Sturm
> Des Uebermuths, verlogne Pfaffen!
> Hätt' Allah mich geschafft zum Wurm,
> So hatt' er mich als Wurm geschaffen.

It is also in this book that, under the title of *Wanderers Gemüthsruhe,* he indited the outburst, profound to the point of madness, which revealed what he had endured from the rabble of his time, and how he had raised himself up and above mere disgust at its vituperative mouthings:

> Uebers Niederträchtige
> Niemand sich beklage!
> Denn es ist das Mächtige
> Was man Dir auch sage. . . .

> Wanderer! Gegen solche Noth
> Wolltest Du Dich sträuben?
> Wirbelwind und trockner Koth,
> Lass sie drehen und stäuben.

But he never allows himself to be overcome by his scorn for mankind. In prosperity and adversity he preserves his spiritual superiority and lets his wisdom pertaining unto things of this life at last come out in these simple words:

> Wonach soll man am Ende trachten?
> Die Welt zu kennen und nicht zu verachten.

Up to the very end he continues to exercise his talents in all possible fields; he cultivates his mind as one cultivates his garden. He feels how necessary it is to have a general survey of history in order to understand the present:

> Wer nicht von dreitausend Jahren
> Sich weiss Rechenschaft zu geben,
> Bleib' im Dunkeln unerfahren,
> Mag von Tag zum Tage leben!

The great men who die young remain forever fresh in our memories as young men. Those who approach old age lose, as a rule, as time goes on, a great deal of their attraction. They often turn against many things that inspired them in their youth. They dry up inwardly or, like so many artists of second rank, they become senile virtuosos. They live surrounded by the wreaths with pale ribbons that once were bestowed upon them.

Goethe never loses a minute in thinking over his greatness or his renown. He feels as Voltaire did when he called our mind a flame which must be kept alive with all the means at our disposal. He was old even when a young man, for he had in those years that are ordinarily the years of visions, and visions only, a keen and sober sense for the reality of everything that is natural, even for that which is wholly affected, which is a mere leading astray of real nature. He never went out of his way for the base or the undeserving. Every fundamental line in the jeering physiognomy of Mephistopheles was drawn by a young man between twenty-three and twenty-five years old.

And when old in years he was still young in soul;

for he had preserved alongside of his powers of
observation the ability to be enraptured, to be inspired, to love and to worship unmoved by all his
experiences, disappointments and bereavements.
The dualism of his natural gifts gave him at once
his precociousness and his inextinguishable ability
along the line of self-rejuvenation.

CHAPTER XXXII

Epimenides Erwachen: A FESTIVAL PLAY

ON May 7, 1814, Iffland, as director of the National Theatre in Berlin, sent a request through Kirms, second in command to Goethe in theatrical affairs, to the great poet asking him as the first man of the German nation to lend his assistance to the theatre in Berlin by writing some drama which, occupying if possible only about twenty minutes, might serve as a curtain-raiser at the gala performance that was to be given when, as was to be expected, the King of Prussia accompanied by Emperor Alexander came, in about four weeks, to Berlin. It was a question of doing honor to the Russian Emperor and "the rare friendship" that bound him to Prussia's King. Emperor Franz of Austria, whose participation had been so effective, would naturally have to be remembered; there would also have to be some reference to the Crown Prince (Bernadotte) of Sweden.[12]

Goethe was staying at that time at the new sulphur bath of Berka a few miles from Weimar. He

[12] Jean Baptiste Jules Bernadotte was born at Pau, France, in 1763, and died at Stockholm in 1844. From 1794 to 1809 he was a French general. In 1799 he was French minister of war. In 1804 he became a marshal of France, served with distinction at Austerlitz in 1805, and was elected crown prince of Sweden in 1810. In 1813 he commanded the army of the north against Napoleon. From 1818 to 1844 he was King of Norway and Sweden.
—TRANSLATOR.

found the request entirely honorable; dismayed however as he was by the brevity of time, he answered
at first reservedly. But a few days later he had
already fixed upon his idea and sent in his program
for a work on a relatively large scale. It soon became evident that there was no great haste; they
could give the poet ample time. The performance
was arranged tentatively for October 19, the anniversary of the battle of Leipzig. But on September
22, Iffland died suddenly and the performance was
postponed until March 30, 1815, the anniversary of
the entry into Paris.

It was perfectly natural that Iffland should direct
his request to Germany's greatest poet. To whom
else could he have gone? Heinrich von Kleist, the
man best adapted to the solution of the task, had
taken his own life, when thirty-five years old, on
November 21, 1811. Theodor Körner, next to
Kleist, the poet most deserving of such honor, had
fallen, when scarcely twenty-two years old, in an
engagement on August 26, 1813, the same day on
which he had written his famous *Schwertlied*.

Goethe was not well suited for the task. He had
not participated in the military rise of the German
people, had not hated Napoleon, was not a Prussian,
had always been far away from Berlin, not to speak
of the theatre of Berlin. It was impossible for him
to express, without affectation, the feelings of Prussian patriotism that were to fill a work such as had
been requested. If ill-fitted on general principles
to write to order, he was especially unfit to execute
this particular order.

It is odd indeed that the very motif to which the
task directed his powers of imagination was in

actuality neither this nor that topic pertaining to
the history of Germany, or more accurately speaking, to the history of Prussia (such as Kleist had
taken in *Der Prinz von Homburg*), but to a theme
from Grecian mythology, and to a nondescript
figure at that—to Epimenides. We know nothing
of him except that he slept away, as the result of
an especial fate, an entire period of his life, and
oddly enough, found thereby, sage that he was, his
power as a seer reenforced.

If there was one occasion for which ancient
Greece was not appropriate this was it. But at this
period of his life Goethe, despite the fact that he
was just now beginning to concern himself with
Oriental poetry, was so eager to see everything
from the Greek point of view that he had to do that
even in this case. The same passion for ancient
Hellenism made itself felt much later in the North.
When Christiansborg Castle burned down in 1884,
Denmark's most famous architect, Theophilus Hansen,[13] returned a year later from Vienna, where he
was then living, to Copenhagen with a plan for the
rebuilding of the castle in which he—vastly over-
estimating my influence—tried to interest me. The
plan was for a long, low building in the style of pure
ancient Greek such as he had employed in the public
buildings he had erected in Athens. I said with a
smile: Must everything be Greek here too? He

[13] Theophilus Hansen (1813-1891) studied at the Academy of
Art in Copenhagen until 1838, when he went to Athens, where he
remained for eight years and became an instructor at the Athenian
Institute. In 1846, Ludwig Förster brought him to Vienna, where
he remained, with interruptions, until his death. He was the
architect of some of the most noted buildings in Greece and Austria. See: "Theophilos Hansen und seine Werke." By Niemann
and Feldegg: Vienna, 1893.   —TRANSLATOR.

answered quite seriously: Yes, everything *must* be
Greek.

That is precisely the way Goethe felt. He wished
above all to avoid anything that was distinctly modern, such as the Prussian uniforms of that time. On
this account he stipulated that the soldiers of his
drama should wear the costume of the ancient Order of St. John which, according to his fancy, looked
"nobler." Iffland had contended that the Prussian
people "would not recognize their honor-crowned
soldiers in this disguise." Having taken this pre-
caution, he received the permission to use the latest
Prussian cavalry uniform. In the frame of Epimenides this uniform must have created an impression similar to that made by the soldier in Berlin
who stands in the Greek guard house in Unter den
Linden wearing a Prussian *Pickelhaube*.

Goethe had arranged his prelude in such a way
that it portrayed a European rather than a national
German liberation. He could consequently utilize
Epimenides as a cipher in a sign language that would
be perfectly intelligible to Europeans. But the symbolic figure was not a requirement, nor was it clear.
Goethe had to guard against the possibility of making Epimenides, the seven-sleeper, stand for the
King of Prussia who had hesitated so long about
giving the countersign for a rebellion. It is more
reasonable to suppose that he had himself in mind
when he depicted Epimenides: He had been inactive
for so long, and now that Napoleon had been conquered, he took it upon himself to glorify the victors. He did not however wish to depict himself
as having been asleep during the critical era through
which he and his contemporaries had just passed.

He had in truth lived through it with his senses on the alert; he had been active in a marked variety of ways.

He caused a decidedly strong effect on the stage by having Epimenides, on awakening, become astonished at finding everything so different from what it had been when he fell asleep. He brought to light and service, in truth, the entire stock of experience that is at the command of one who knows the theatre from the practical side. Epimenides having fallen asleep, and the martial music having pealed forth, he directed that all lights on the stage be covered with yellowish red glass so that the theatre might be flooded with a reddish gleam of fire—the unpropitious sign of the horrors of war.

Furthermore the characters are allegories: the demon of war, the demon of oppression, the demon of cunning, all sorts of genii, and finally as leading characters, Faith, Hope, and Charity; of these *Charity* is to call forth the idea of the Emperor of Austria and his patriarchal relation to his people, *Faith,* the idea of the zealously believing Emperor Alexander, and lastly *Hope* in the garb of Minerva, but with the face of the deceased Queen Louise, is to represent Prussia. In this way Faith, Hope, and Charity become now once and for all great powers. England as *Steadfastness* receives a modest place in their vicinity.

Love refers to the Emperor of Austria with the words:

Ich suche Den mit liebevollen Blicken,
Der liebevoll bei seinem Volk verweilt,
Der treuen Seinen neubelebt Entzücken
Mit offnem, holden Vaterherzen theilt.

Faith refers to Alexander and the burning of Moscow:

> Zum Ungeheuren war ich aufgerufen,
> Mir dienten selbst Zerstörung, Blut und Tod;
> So flammte jüngst an meines Thrones Stufen
> Der Freiheit plötzlich furchtbar Morgenroth.

There is no lack of flattery for the mediocre Friedrich Wilhelm III: *Hope* contends that all three sisters live inspired by his good fortune:

> Ich will gestehn den Eigennutz, o Schwestern!
> Für jedes Opfer fordr' ich meinen Lohn,
> Ein selig Heute für ein schrecklich Gestern,
> Triumphes-Wonne statt der Duldung Hohn:
> So hab ich's ihm versprochen, ihm gegeben,
> Von diesem Glück beseelt wir alle leben.

It was only in the year 1815 that anyone in Berlin could see Faith, Hope, and Love for himself in the figures of Russia, Prussia, and Austria; and it certainly does not increase Goethe's renown that he as a poet for a set occasion had to become the official spokesman for this idea. The effect is wholly ludicrous when this legendary figure from ancient Greece discusses Frederick II of Prussia:

> *Epimenides:* Und wir sind alle neugeboren,
> Das grosse Sehnen ist gestillt,
> Bei *Friedrichs* Asche war's geschworen
> Und ist auf ewig nun erfüllt.

As a soldier's chorus Goethe applied the virile war song from his *Pandora*, parts of which have already been quoted. But since it did not fit in with the time, he wrote a new warrior's chorus with a refrain-like repetition of Blücher's nickname of Marshall *Vorwärts* and directly referring to him:

> Und so schreiten wir, die Kühnen,
> Eine halbe Welt entlang;
> Die Verwüstung, die Ruinen,
> Nichts verhindre Deinen Gang
> Hinan!—*Vorwärts*—Hinan!
> Und das grosse Werk sei gethan!

This song was naturally more effective at the time than any other element in the drama. It was meant to be popular and it was, though it did not harmonize with the style of the drama in general. How different was the homage that Goethe paid to Blücher two years later when he wrote in lapidary style the inscription on his monument in Rostock!

> In Harren und Krieg,
> In Sturz und Sieg
> Bewusst und gross!
> So riss er uns
> Von Feinden los.

It is distinctly pathetic to see Goethe in *Epimenides* so completely approving of the vulgar German conception of Napoleon as the representative and emissary of the Devil that he has his genii sing:

> Doch was dem Abgrund kühn entstiegen,
> Kann durch ein ehernes Geschick
> Den halben Weltkreis übersiegen,
> *Zum Abgrund muss es doch zurück.*
> Schon droht ein ungeheures Bangen,
> Vergebens wird er wiederstehn!
> *Und Alle, die noch an ihm hangen,*
> *Sie müssen mit zu Grunde gehn.*

Since Goethe himself belonged to those who felt attracted to Napoleon, this exulting certainty, that

all of those who are still attached to the fallen
Emperor on the island of Elba must eventually come
to grief, does not especially become him in the eyes
of posterity.

The superiority of the work lies wholly in its
lyric and linguistic phases.   There is tremendous
verbal power in the very first words of Epimenides:

> Uralten Waldes majestät'sche Kronen,
> Schroffglatter Felsenwände Spiegelflächen
> Im Schein der Abendsonne zu betrachten
> Erreget Geist und Herz zu der Natur
> Erhab'nen Gipfeln, ja zu Gott hinan.

There is in *Epimenides* a well written stanza which
gives allegoric expression to Napoleon's defeat in
Russia.   It begins as follows:

> Von Osten rollt Lavinen gleich herüber
> Der Schnee—und Eisball, wälzt sich gross und grösser.

At the close of the stanza England and Sweden
receive their coveted compliments, though Goethe's
geographic memory is a bit defective in that he has
The Belt represent Bernadotte:

> Vom *Ozean,* vom *Belt* her kommt uns Rettung,
> So wirkt das All in glücklicher Verkettung.

There are, moreover, a number of beautifully
written stanzas in which freedom is glorified.   These
words are put on the lips of *Hope* with a great deal
of sense for theatrical effect:

> Nun begegn' ich meinen Braven
> Die sich in der Nacht versammelt,
> Um zu schweigen, nicht zu schlafen,
> Und das schöne Wort der Freiheit
> Wird gelispelt und gestammelt,

Bis in ungewohnter Neuheit
Wir an unsrer Tempel Stufen
Wieder neu entzückt es rufen
      (mit Ueberzeugung, laut)
Freiheit!
    (Gemässigter)
               Freiheit!
(Von allen Seiten und Enden Echo)
               Freiheit!

It is however only painful to consider the sort of freedom which the year 1815 inaugurated for Germany (as for Europe). Freedom from French supremacy undoubtedly, but at the same time the worst condition of bondage, both spiritual and political, which the nineteenth century has ever known.

The German public was very naturally displeased with *Epimenides* as falling far short of the expectations of a festival play that was supposed to glorify the fatherland and victory, and to be what the Greeks called an *egkomion*. Neither can it be denied that, compared with Aeschylus's *Persians* and Shakespeare's *Henry V,* it was a complete fiasco. But the work was written to order; Goethe struggled in this case with a task which he could avoid only with difficulty and could not solve at all. *Epimenides* reveals the limitations of his talent, and the weaknesses of his character.

CHAPTER XXXIII

CHRISTIANE'S DEATH; AUGUST'S MARRIAGE; GOETHE AND BYRON—GOETHE AND ULRIKE VON LEVETZOW; *Marienbader Elegie*

ON June 6, 1816, Christiane died after prolonged and painful suffering. Her convulsions became so heart-rending toward the end of her illness that her servants fled in terror-stricken distress. She had been gradually sinking for an entire year, worn out by her anguish and perplexed by her household worries. These had recently become more burdensome than ever, since the woman who had been her chief support married Dr. Riemer.

Goethe's grief was intense; he locked himself up in his room where he gave way to violent sobbing. He wrote this heart-felt verse:

> Du versuchst, o Sonne, vergebens
> Durch die düstren Wolken zu scheinen,
> Der ganze Gewinn meines Lebens
> Ist, ihren Verlust zu verweinen.

The truth is, Goethe had never ceased to appreciate Christiane's real value. In her he had a reliable, faithful, modest, kind-hearted wife—just as a wife was supposed to be in the conception of an ancient Greek.

We have a proof, of its kind, even of the physical attraction that she had for him in the poem entitled *Das Tagebuch,* 1810. This poem is not included in his works; it is coarse and massive rather than salacious or indecent; it contains some thoughts that are beautiful, though it has in it one stanza that is written in remarkably poor taste in that it is a com-

posite of the vulgar and the blasphemous: It depicts a *stranded* effort on his part to embrace a
woman who is not his wife. Through the invocation
of good intentions and German thoroughness it is
possible to interpret the poem, after all, as an homage to the woman who bore him his children; and
this is the way it has been interpreted in Germany.
But Goethe paid homage to Christiane in more
charitable and becoming ways. In 1817, his son
August was married to Ottilie von Pogwisch, a
young woman of an aristocratic family. She was
quite fascinating and had unusual social ability, as
a result of which she made an amiable hostess in
Goethe's home. But she was by nature restless,
giddy, changeable, capricious, and wasteful. Her
husband had some talent for business, the special
aim of which was to make advantageous use of his
father's productions and secure for himself a liberal
inheritance. But he was always very much oppressed by his father's superiority, got along poorly
on this account with his wife, and eventually fell a
hopeless prey to the drink habit. By means of
patronage he secured, when still a young man, a title
and position; but he was quite devoid of any sort
of efficiency.

In 1816, Lord Byron rose up on Goethe's horizon.
The master read with interest Byron's *Corsaire* and
Lara. And in 1817 he began to perceive the mysterious relation in which he stood to that contemporary mind which, since the disappearance of
Napoleon from Europe, concerned him more than
any other mind of his time. A young American
had presented Goethe with a copy of Byron's *Manfred*. With astonishment and living interest Goethe

saw for the first time how his own poetry had affected a great mind of another people which, incidentally, was amply independent and as unlike his
own as possible. He saw that Byron had assimilated his *Faust* though he had changed its motives;
he was astonished at the despair that lay so far from
his own being, the murky flames of which shot out
from *Manfred* toward him. He introduced the
work and the author to the German reading public,
though he was credulous enough to take up with and
spread the romantic legend that had just then been
started concerning Byron : He was supposed to have
fallen in love with a woman from Florence; this
woman had been murdered by her husband; and
the following night the husband was found dead on
the street though suspicion for the murder could not
be fixed upon any definite individual. Byron had
left Florence and was now dragging these ghosts
around with him in his soul.

Goethe translated Manfred's despondent and
world-weary monologue, and from this time on he
remained in constant touch with Byron and wrote
articles on his *Don Juan* and *Cain*. Byron, feeling
a profound admiration, sent Goethe his *Sardanapalus* with this dedication :

To the illustrious Goethe.
A stranger
presumes to offer the homage of a literary vassal to his liege
lord
the first of living writers
Who has created the literature of his own country
and illustrated that of Europe.
The unworthy production which the author ventures to
inscribe to him is entitled
Sardanapalus.

Byron's next tragedy, *Werner,* brought another dedication to the German poet: *To the illustrious Goethe by one of his humblest admirers this tragedy is dedicated.*

In 1823, a young Englishman by the name of Sterling brought Goethe a message from Lord Byron, then about to leave in order to dedicate his last strength to the Greek Revolution. Goethe gave him the poem which reached Byron in Leghorn and in which a heartfelt emotion is expressed:

> Ein freundlich Wort kommt eines nach dem andern
> Von Süden her und bringt uns frohe Stunden;
> Es ruft uns auf, zum Edelsten zu wandern,
> Nicht ist der Geist, doch ist der Fuss gebunden.
>
> Wie soll ich Dem, den ich so lang begleitet
> Nun Etwas Traulichs in die Ferne sagen?
> Ihm, der sich selbst im Innersten bestreitet
> Stark angewohnt, das tiefste Weh zu tragen.
>
> Wohl sei ihm doch, wenn er sich selbst empfindet!
> Er wage selbst sich hoch beglückt zu nennen.
> Wenn Musenkraft die Schmerzen überwindet;
> Und wie ich ihn erkannt, mög er sich kennen!

And again six years later, after Byron's death, Goethe wrote a little poem in his honor, which begins:

> Stark von Faust, gewandt im Rath
> Liebt er die Hellenen;
> Edles Wort und schöne That
> Füllt sein Aug' mit Thränen.

The man does not exist who does not willingly and gladly grant Byron, living and dead, the honor that is due him. Moreover, he fully deserved Goethe's interest by reason of his filial relation to

him. Goethe gave him, too, a place in the second part of *Faust*. But the fact remains that Lord Byron did not understand German; that he had no knowledge of *Faust* at first hand; that he had indeed none of Goethe in general.

On the other hand, it is a melancholy fact that Shelley's name never occurs in Goethe's works; that the great lyricist lived and died unknown to him. It is not simply that Shelley, by reason of his exalted genius, was worthy of appreciation by the individual who first used the word *Weltliteratur;* he had entered into his life in a quite different way; he had entered into the spirit of *Faust* in a way that was closed to Lord Byron. In 1822, he translated the *Prolog im Himmel* with the antiphonal song of the angels. He also gave a masterful reproduction of the scenes on the Brocken in the Harz. But with all this, it seems to have been written down in the book of fate that Shelley was not to receive the recognition due him while living.

In 1819, Goethe celebrated in complete stillness his seventieth birthday while riding in a carriage from Hof to Karlsbad. He received of course many congratulations. Even Frankfurt did him honor by arranging a gala performance in his absence.

He had now come to that point in life where it was natural for his friends of equal age to disappear, while the great personages with whom he had come in touch and to whom he had stood so near were no longer living. In 1819, Fritz Jacobi and Fritz Stolberg died. Napoleon's death took place in 1821, Byron's in 1824, Charlotte von Stein's in 1827, while in 1828, Goethe, then almost eighty years old, was struck by the death he felt so deeply, that of Karl August. In 1830, the Duchess Luise and his son, August Goethe, died, the latter in Rome. It fell in short to his lot to survive those who had meant so much to him. Time and time again he was obliged to collect himself and overcome his grief by work.

II

In the year 1822 Goethe once more burst forth in erotic passion. Scarcely had his heart burned out when it caught fire again. The one phœnix had gone up in flames, another had arisen from the ashes. In 1806 Goethe had become acquainted with Frau Amalie von Levetzow, the memory of whose charm had never departed from him. In 1821 he saw her again in the company of her parents with her three daughters, Amélie, Bertha, and Ulrike. This was only for a short while, in Marienbad. But when he returned to the bath in the summers of 1822 and 1823 he was constantly with the Levetzow family. The youngest daughter Ulrike had charmed him; he felt as happy as possible in the family's company. In 1823 the attraction grew into a passion. He had not, as a twenty-one-year-old man, loved Friederike Brion more vehemently than he now as a seventy-four-year-old-man loved Ulrike von Levetzow. At the mere sound of her voice far away on the street he seized his hat and hastened out.

There was a child-like expression in her brown eyes and well formed mouth; and in accordance with the fashion of the time she wore her brown hair in short curls. I must confess, in passing, that to judge

from the portraits, both her mother and her two
sisters were more beautiful than she, however young
and sprightly she herself may have been. And yet,
it is not the degree of beauty that decides a passion.
When Amélie one day asked Goethe whether he
liked her dress he said: "Ulrike's is prettier." The
answer is typical. Ulrike still remembered that
reply in her ninety-fifth year (she died unmarried
when she was almost a hundred years old) and remarkably enough, Goethe jotted down in his note
book the fact that the dress was of checkered Scot-
ish material.

There is only one point in which Ulrike's memory,
seventy-seven years after the event had taken place,
and just like a woman, played her false: She insisted
that her relation to Goethe had never been other
than that of a granddaughter to her grandfather.
What she affirmed is true; Goethe was seventy-three
years old when she, seventeen years of age, became
acquainted with him; but his passion was as ardent
as that of a young man and it left her by no means
unmoved. It is utterly unthinkable that she lived
without being kissed and was a stranger to caresses.
The picture of her daily reception of him in the
poem entitled *Elegie* bears the full stamp of authenticity:

> Wie zum Empfang sie an den Pforten weilte
> Und mich von dannauf stufenweis beglückte,
> Selbst nach dem letzten Kuss mich noch ereilte,
> Den letztesten mir auf die Lippen drückte:
> So klar beweglich bleibt das Bild der Lieben
> Mit Flammenschrift ins treue Herz geschrieben.

It seemed to Goethe that Ulrike was necessary
for the continuation of his life. He decided to make

her his second wife; and even before he had assured himself of her consent—and that of her mother— he took steps to put his house in order for her reception. He had in the very beginning, in letters from Marienbad and Karlsbad whither he had followed the Levetzows, betrayed his secret to his daughter-in-law in covered words, though they were transparent to her. But when in the interim between his two visits to Marienbad he appeared before his son and told him his intention of entering into a new marriage, painful scenes occurred in which Ottilie's sister, Ulrike, also took part. August, who saw himself threatened in this way of the enjoyment of the inheritance to which he was soon to fall heir, turned the raw side of his nature toward his father, so much the more since he was also irritated by Ottilie, who felt extremely ill disposed at having a mother-in-law in the house who was much younger than she. August threatened to leave his father's house, a move which Goethe certainly could have endured. The son gave his tongue free play. Children not infrequently regard their parents as existing for their sake and theirs alone.

Up to this point the young girl had, however, certainly not taken her relation to Goethe seriously. She had just come home from a boarding school in Strassburg, had read Voltaire and other French authors of that time, but she had never read a word of Goethe, in whom she saw His Excellency, the famous Minister. When Goethe accordingly asked the Grand Duke to woo for him, and the latter carried out the commission, both the mother and the daughter were surprised and considered the affair almost as a joke.

Karl August assured them that Goethe was quite
in earnest. He told Ulrike that she would be the
first woman in Weimar, that he could confer upon
her all possible marks of distinction, and that she
would not need to be separated from her people.
He would give them a well furnished house in Weimar. To the mother the Grand Duke gave the
assurance that he would care for Ulrike's future.
Since she in all probability would survive Goethe,
he would settle an annuity of 10,000 thalers upon
her.

Frau von Levetzow, who had firmly made up her
mind never to persuade her daughter to get married,
asked Ulrike whether she was inclined to accept the
offer that had been made her. She said that she
would in case she were thereby fulfilling a wish of
her mother. Frau von Levetzow said that Ulrike
was far too young for her, as her mother, to wish
to see her married; but the offer was so complimentary that she would have to decide for herself.

The daughter gave a negative reply on the ground
(according to what she said seventy-seven years
later) that Goethe already had a married son in the
house whom he did not wish to dislodge. Regardless, however, as to what the ultimate reason for her
final decision was, the filial affection that she cherished for Goethe had in all probability an insufficient
amount of the element of abiding passion.

It was a hard blow to Goethe. His forced renunciation touched his heart. In February 1823 he had
been very ill; he had a convulsive cough and steady
pains about his heart (*Pericarditis*). He was often
unconscious and delirious. After his return home
from his sojourn at the watering place in November,

he became so ill that his friends despaired of his life. His cough and fever returned, he again had pains about his heart as a result of an inflammation, and in addition to all of this he lost his courage and his eagerness to work. Reconvalescence was a slow process.

As an evidence of the passionate experience of those years, the familiar poem entitled *Die Aeolsharfen,* a poetic conversation between him and Ulrike, and *Trilogie der Leidenschaft,* with especial reference to the *Marienbader Elegie,* are and remain monumental among Goethe's productions. In the *Aeolsharfen,* 1822. which gives expression to the pain at parting when neither can live without the other, and in which the grief on her part is as pronounced as it is on his, the most beautiful part of the poem is the comparison of his sweetheart with the rainbow, a wonder that is always new and always equally joyous:

> Ja, Du bist wohl der Iris zu vergleichen,
> Ein liebenswürdig Wunderzeichen,
> So schmiegsam herrlich, bunt in Harmonie
> Und immer neu und immer gleich wie sie.

The little poem entitled *Die Aussöhnung* was addressed to the distinguished Polish pianist Frau Marie Szymanowska, who had been with Goethe at Marienbad in 1823; she was accompanied by her sister Fräulein Kasimira Wolowska, whose praises he also sang. She visited him in Weimar, and Frau Szymanowska's beautiful playing had an assuaging effect upon the poet's rent soul. It was she who six years later gave Adam Mickiewicz and Odyniec letters of introduction to Goethe, and thus brought about an acquaintance between Poland's greatest poets and Germany's.

The introductory poem, entitled *An Werther,* was the last part of the trilogy to be written (1824). It contains a portrayal of the melancholy conditions of human life. It is beautiful and dignified. But the poem entitled *Elegie* is the one in which everything depends in fact on the psychological and poetic. It should be read line for line for its melancholy is deep, its life experience is rich, and the expression, though somewhat abstract, is free from flourishes; the despair is unveiled as it rarely is in Goethe's works. No attempt is made to veil the anguish.

The portrayal of how he was received into Paradise, of how blessed he felt there, and of how terrible it was to be driven out, is exquisite:

Der Kuss, der letzte, grausam süss, zerschneidend
Ein herrliches Geflecht verschlungner Minnen:
Nun eilt, nun stockt der Fuss, die Schwelle meidend,
Als trieb' ein Cherub flammend ihn von hinnen;
Das Auge starrt auf düstrem Pfad verdrossen.
Es blickt zurück, die Pforte steht verschlossen.

It seems to him now as though his sealed heart had never been opened; despondency, repentence, self-reproach, and sorrow fill it. Is the landscape in its beauty, or the vault of Heaven in its grandeur, no longer existent? He sees nothing but *her* form as an airy phantom in space. He recalls, how, in her presence, he was what men regard as pious. In beautiful verse he gives the meaning of the word:

In unsers Busens Reine wogt ein Streben
Sich einem Höhern, Reinern, Unbekannten
Aus Dankbarkeit freiwillig hinzugeben,

Enträthselnd sich den ewig Ungenannten:
Wir heissen's: fromm sein!—Solcher sel'gen Höhe
Fühl' ich mich theilhaft, wenn ich vor ihr stehe.

She is to him the one who disposes of *yesterday* as
uninteresting and of *tomorrow* as that of which we
know nothing; she implores him to view the present
with joy and determination. But he cannot. The
moment he is separated from her all is misery; his
heart is filled with trouble; his spirit knows neither
will nor decision. He has lost the cosmos; he has
lost himself. The gods have doomed him to destruction.

Thus it seemed to him in his mood of profound
depression: The gods had doomed him for the
time being to intensified loneliness, and to increased
mental activity, not in communion with men who
were approximately his equals and from whom he
could learn, but with his spiritual inferiors; with
those who, faithfully receiving, seized with avidity
and preserved the thoughts and ideas that came to
him as a result of conversation. The gods doomed
him, in other words, to conversation with Eckermann. For it was precisely at this time, in the year
1823, that Johann Peter Eckermann, an indigent
young man with a reasonable love for the art of
the spoken word, came to him, and offered him his
services. After having taken part in the wars
against Napoleon, Eckermann had studied Klopstock and Schiller, though he eventually found his
ideal in Goethe. He went on foot from Göttingen
to Weimar, was received by Goethe and retained by
him as an apprentice. Goethe had been impressed
by his manly seriousness, his feminine dependency,

and his receptivity. With him Goethe talked for years, not so much for the moment as for posterity, and he even read Eckermann's notes through—which somewhat vitiates the impression for us—and gave a part of them his personal approval.

CHAPTER XXXIV

Zahme Xenien; Invektiven—Sprüche in Prosa

IT had been a long while since Goethe had had acquaintances from whom he could learn. The last instance in which such a fate befell him was when Sulpiz Boisserée came on from Cologne and paid him a visit. He and his brother Melchoir had taken upon themselves the task of doing honor to Old German art. They had collected the mediaeval statuary and paintings which, on the abolition of monasteries and charitable institutions, were thrown on the market in great masses, or they were treated with such scorn that out of altars table-tops and window-shutters were made.

Boisserée reminded Goethe of his youthful enthusiasm for the Cathedral at Strassburg. This was his means of interesting him at present in the Cathedral at Cologne. He had persuaded Goethe to sit for hours in the thorough study of Old Dutch and German art; he had held him to it in fact until he was saturated with a Van Eyck.

He never found it entirely possible, however, to convert Goethe to his way of thinking. Goethe remarks in his apothegms that the dry and naïve, the

413

rigidly demure and scrupulously righteous, in primitive Northern art can also be found in the oldest works of the Florentines and the Venetians. The most that can be said in his favor is that he broadened Goethe's horizon.

This, however, was a long while ago, fully ten years previous to the moment under consideration. At present Goethe is the giver; a Heinrich Meyer could do no more than agree with him; an Eckermann could merely give the clue for a conversation. The value of Eckermann's work is not to be disparaged; nor are the kindred works of Chancellor von Müller, Falk, Riemer, and Soret. These works all stand as evidence of Goethe's extraordinary many-sidedness. But the communicator has on the one hand merely the value of an interviewer; and on the other hand it is injudicious to overlook the fact that every conversation noted down in this way is of necessity colored by him who wrote it, and is on this account quite unreliable.

Of infinitely greater value than the conversations with Eckermann and the others, all of which are now splendidly arranged in chronological order, and thus made easily accessible, in W. von Biedermann's large work entitled *Goethes Gespräche,* are the short apothegms in verse and prose written by Goethe himself. They constitute a rich source of knowledge pertaining to the master's ways and means of thinking during his later and more mature years.

The few in verse are partly basic thoughts concerning life and the world in general, partly polemic sallies aimed at literary foes and assailants. The first—the *Zahme Xenien*—have the greatest value.

Some of them contain incontrovertible wisdom. There is this one, by way of illustration:

> Gut verloren—Etwas verloren.
> Musst rasch Dich besinnen
> Und Neues gewinnen.
> Ehre verloren—Viel verloren!
> Musst Ruhm gewinnen,
> Da werden die Leute sich anders besinnen.
> Muth verloren—Alles verloren!
> Da wär es besser, nicht geboren.

Others defend freedom of thought as over against importunate religionists and nationalists. Goethe asserts his Pantheism in this forceful verse:

> Was soll mir Euer Hohn
> Ueber das All und Eine?
> Der Professor ist eine Person,
> Gott ist keine.

He makes the unforgetable and eternally true remark concerning knowledge, ability, and inherited emotional nature:

> Wer Wissenschaft und Kunst besitzt,
> Hat auch Religion;
> Wer jene beiden nicht besitzt,
> Der habe Religion.

Along exactly the same line we have this verse of freedom:

> Den deutschen Mannen gereicht's zum Ruhm,
> Dass sie gehasst das Christenthum
> Bis Herrn Karolus' leid'gem Degen
> Die edlen Sachsen unterlegen.

He expresses his contempt for Philistinism in the monumental lines:

> Was ist ein Philister?
> Ein hohler Darm,
> Mit Furcht und Hoffnung ausgefüllt,
> Dass Gott erbarm!

He pours out the full beaker of his scorn over the Nationalists who made propaganda for the word *Deutsch* being written *Teutsch* and for the entire debate concerning this pitiable question.

> An die T. . . . und D. . . .
> Verfluchtes Volk! Kaum bist du frei,
> So brichst Du in Dir selbst entzwei.
> War nicht der Noth, des Glücks genug?
> Deutsch oder Teutsch, Du wirst nicht klug.

From precisely the same point of view he expresses (in contrast to his own weakness in *Epimenides*) his disgust for the patriotic derision of Napoleon:

> Ich kann mich nicht bereden lassen,
> Macht mir den Teufel nur nicht klein!
> Ein Kerl, den alle Menschen hassen,
> Der muss was sein.

Of essentially psychological and symptomatic interest are the minor polemic poems against Kotzebue, Merkel, Böttiger, Spazier, Pustkuchen, and all the rest of them, whose spiritual livelihood consisted in the persecution of Goethe and whom he hated according to their just deserts and yet not enough to allow their attacks to go unnoticed. As it is they have become unforgetable through his rejoinder, while all the praise they heaped upon each other at the time would never have kept their names from oblivion.

Goethe amused himself by calculating that if he could live a hundred years longer, healthy and satisfied as he had been for the most part, Merkel (also the enemy of Tieck and the Schlegel brothers), Spazier (Baggesen's guide in *Labyrinthen*), and Kotzebue would not have any rest in all that time. but would daily write a pasquinade against him which would give no less than 36,500 not counting the intercalary days:

> Gern würd' ich dieses holde Wesen
> Zu Abend auf dem Abort lesen,
> Grobe Worte, gelind Papier
> Nach Würdigkeit bedienen hier.

The tone is furthermore this:

> An Schmierern fehlt's nicht, nicht am Lob der Schmierer
> Der rühmt sich selbst, Den preiset ein Verleger,
> Der Gleiche den; der Pöbel einen Dritten.

To be sure Goethe did not himself publish a single verse of his *Invektiven;* they were gathered together and given out after his death.

II

The same applies to the no fewer than 1055 *Sprüche in Prosa,* this treasure-house of wisdom which, with a few individual exceptions, lay untouched while Goethe was living. His grudge against the public had become so great that he was wholly out of patience with it; he no longer bore any sort of relation whatsoever to it. The hatred of his own age that had seized upon him is probably best shown by the fact that when he finally, as the result of extraordinary exertion, finished the second part of *Faust,* between the middle of the year 1827 and July 1831, he sealed the manuscript with seven seals and laid it aside in peace and quiet for posterity, fully convinced that his contemporaries would simply misunderstand it and make all sorts of maliciously stupid remarks about it.

Goethe's apothegms in prose are, though not worked out in pointed form, of no less value than Pascal's famous paradoxical *Pensées* or La Rochefoucauld's and Chamfort's sharp and witty desultory thoughts. Unlike Pascal, there is no *à priori* taking sides in Goethe's apothegms with some supernatural power. Unlike La Rochefoucauld, Goethe brings to light no great zeal to scent out and lay bare human egotism. Unlike Chamfort, he does not express his contempt for and hatred of men in caustic form.

His standpoint is that of a man who, in mental superiority, surveys all human life, becomes the servant of no particular dogma, is in the power of no mood or passion, but by virtue of his innate greatness calmly looks down upon things as they actually are from his lofty heights above.

When, once in a long while, he does concern himself with religious questions, he does so, not after the fashion of Pascal, in the anguish and passion of self-torment, but with peaceful profundity. He says: Piety is not a goal but a means of approaching the highest state of civilization through the cleanest mental serenity. Consequently those people who set up piety itself as the goal are for the most part hypocrites. He does combat the value of asceti-

cism. He simply says, laconically and with biting
ridicule: The Hindoos in the desert vow that they
will eat no fish. When he touches upon the Bible,
he says: There is a great deal of wrangling concerning the advantage and the harm that have come
from the spread of the Bible. Harm comes from
the spread of the Bible when it is used, as it has
been, dogmatically and fanatically; good comes
from its spread so long as it is used humanly and
as a source of knowledge.

With his profound experience as to what it means
to each individual to be able to work and mature in
peace, Goethe could not help but look with fear and
disquietude upon the newspaper literature which
was just then beginning to flourish. It was only
in its infancy at the time, but it was even then doing
its part by way of hindering the serene growth of
individuals and making the progress of great men
difficult. He writes:

The greatest misfortune of the age lies in the fact that it
never permits anything to mature; it consumes the present
moment in the coming one; it lives forever from hand to
mouth; it never gets anything done. We already have newspapers for the various hours of the day. Everything that
one plans, everything that one simply has on hand or in one's
mind, everything that is still far from completion, is dragged
out into publicity. No one dares be happy or sorrowful
without thereby creating a pastime for the others. Do the
fortunate really believe that the unfortunate person should
be allowed to die decently and in order as the old gladiators
used to die before the eyes of the Roman rabble?

It is not infrequent that Goethe portrays his own
character. He writes: I keep a good many things
to myself, for I would not discomfort other people.

I much prefer to let them rejoice where I am annoyed. The greatest happiness is produced by that which improves our defects and corrects our mistakes. As a rule it is a man's knowledge that determines what he shall do and what he shall leave undone. There is, therefore, nothing more terrible than to see ignorance in action. The greatest respect that an author can show the public is never to do what it expects of him, but what he, following such light as he has at that stage of his development and with regard to the development of others, looks upon as being right and useful. The active man tries to do what is right; whether right happens thereafter is not his affair. Writing history is a means of getting rid of the past. Instead of contradicting my remarks, they should act in my spirit.

Thus his apothegms run. Concerning the incessant accusation of self-praise to which he was forced to listen he writes: They say that self-praise stinks; it may be true. But as to the odor of alien and unjust censure, for that the public has no nose.

Goethe's practical wisdom induces him at times to note down small, everyday, but strikingly correct experiences such as this one: We never really become acquainted with people when they come to us; we must go to them in order to find out what they are really like. But his method of noticing the most important traits of character is quite different. In the *Xenien* he had often expressed his detestation for those people who were simply incapable of recognizing the good sides of someone else. Here he writes: Face to face with the great superiority of another person there is no other means of safety but love. He had always found the lack of ability to recognize greatness a wretched characteristic. Here he says: There is a proverb according to which no man is a hero to his valet. This comes from the fact that it takes a hero to appreciate a hero. There is no doubt at all but that the valet fully appreciates his equals.

While pondering over the reasons why great men perform such marvelous deeds, he gives expression to this apparently paradoxical idea: To live in the idea is equivalent to treating the impossible as though it were possible. In this way events arise at which the world is astonished for a thousand years.

In deep appreciation of the difficulty encountered by the man of action when he tries to take into consideration all the things that the spectator feels are justified, he utters this profound and boldly formulated thesis: The man of action is always conscienceless; it is only the observer who has a conscience. He takes consolation in the rigid coherency of his own life: That man is happiest of all who can bring the close of his life into connection with the beginning.

Remembering the great amount of time that he has wasted trying to teach and educate people who were impervious to instruction he writes: Not everyone to whom one makes fruitful remarks becomes thereby productive. It often happens that something that is old and well-known occurs to him. While he recalls how many men he trained who never thought of doing anything else but tripping him up at some later time, he writes this rich and pithy sentence: I stumbled over the roots of the tree which I myself had planted. Pausing to reflect on the number of times he has been mistaken in men, he forms this weighty judgment: One is never deceived; one merely deceives one's self.

In leisure hours, and therefore in many of his aphorisms, reminiscences of his opponents have risen up before his mind and he has been astonished to find that they did not have, so to speak, distinct physiognomies but in their triviality they resembled each other like drops of water. He expresses this politely: You all have the same nature, like the sea, to which one gives various names but which is all salt water together.

He is reminded of the jealousy of his enemies. He repeats in his own name Ottilie's aphorism: There is no greater consolation for mediocrity than this, that genius must die. He remembers how these men have toiled in order to give their calumniations the appearance of superior and nourishing wit: You have whipped the dirt to see if it would not become cream. And yet they received the names that they have from themselves: Filth glitters when the sun shines.

He found no support from the public which soon became accustomed to him and tired of him: A rainbow that stands for a quarter of an hour no longer attracts the attention. He balances up his account with his own age: The present generation is of too little value for us to do anything for *it*. We must work for the past and for the future, that is to say, we must try to recognize the merits of the past and increase the worth of the future.

But despite all his dissatisfaction he does not complain of his lot. It can to be sure befall one that he be soundly flailed by fate, but ruthless fate crushes only the straw: the grain never feels it and springs lustily about on the threshing floor.

He knows full well that the others wish to harm him, but he doubts their ability: The empirical-moral world consists mostly of bad will and envy. The really wretched take an interest only in malevolence; there are people who simply cannot go astray for they never undertake anything reasonable. But this does not lead them to anything.

In the relatively small number of reflections that Goethe has devoted to literature, he strikes at not a few of his countrymen's besetting sins. He remarks, for example, that the Germans (but not only the Germans) have the gift of making the sciences *inaccessible,* and that certain of their books seem to have been written, not that we may learn something from them, but that we may see that the author was *erudite.* He expresses his detestation for the literary vulgarity that claims to be humor: There is nothing so base but that it will appear humorous if expressed with grimaces. He jests with the activity of translators: Translators are to be regarded as zealous matchmakers who praise a half veiled beauty as being exceedingly amiable. They merely awaken an irresistible longing for the original.

He cries out with the vehemence of his youthful days against the so-called patriotic art: There is no patriotic art, there is no patriotic science. Both art and science need and belong to the whole world.

He explains why he—and for this he had been roundly abused—prefers to pass judgments on foreign rather than on German literature. This is owing to the fact that one in a foreign country (presumably) pays no attention to his judgments, and one cannot be impolite at a distance. But in the very presence of people one feels as little inclined as one does in good society to say anything offensive, and a disapproval is always regarded by an author as an offense.

He defends himself against the charge that his writings are unclear. He who wishes to reproach an author for being unclear must first look into his own mind and soul and see how things are there. Even an exceedingly distinct work is illegible in the twilight.

· He jests with his countryman's intolerable boasting about German *Gemüth,* which was denied him: The Germans should not pronounce the word *Gemüth* for thirty years; in this way a new *Gemüth* would gradually arise. As it is the word simply means being tolerant with weaknesses including one's own.

And last of all he makes this illuminating remark concerning reading and learning: We really learn only from those books which we cannot criticise; the author of a book we can criticise would have to learn from us. (From *Sprüche in Prosa,* Nos. 41, 42, 138, 332, 23, 163, 38, 46, 64, 76, 99, 104, 113, 369, 389, 391, 343, 162, 133, 106, 577, 476, 124, 392, 148, 79, 584, 183, 208, 210, 930, 71, 108, 258, 485, 601, 705, 299, 293. And apparently also from Nos. 125, 345, 72, 130, 316.)

CHAPTER XXXV

Faust, Part II; Impressionism of Style

DESPITE Goethe's quite late remark to Eckermann and others to the effect that the second part
of *Faust* was in and on his mind for at least a half
a century, he seems in his youth to have considered
what we now call the first part of the poem as a
complete whole in itself. Nothing with regard to
the theme in the original work points to the fact
that there was any thought of continuing it. It is
not until the years 1797-1801 that the plan shows
a glimmer of continuation. A few details were
worked out: the Baccalaureus scene, which however
really belongs to the first part, and which contains
the constantly recurring derision on the part of
Goethe with regard to that particular sort of originality which derives from total ignorance of what
has already been produced by others. We have
also the beginning of the *Helena* section, which is
now the third act, and which had been submitted to
Schiller.

It was not until 1806 that Goethe interpolated
the scene of the wager between Faust and Mephistopheles in the first part, which made a continuation
not merely possible but obligatory.

The essential thesis of the oldest, the real *Faust*
lies first in its threefold sally against the rhetori-
cians with their belief in the historical rules of ora-

tory, these "jingling-tingling" fools who can neither
feel nor speak in a simple, straightforward manner; secondly against the pedantic investigators and
writers of history with their belief that the past
can be called to life without poetic sense; and finally
against the censors of society with their imbecile
persecution of thinking heretics, of the few who have
been aware of some truth which they are forbidden to utter and who, consequently, have been crucified and burned from the time of Arild on. The
author of this *Faust* feels that he is the liberator
from the cold and outward rhetoric of the preceding
age and of Germany's first historic drama. He
feels also that he is the celebrator in song of that
old and great and mystic heretic—Prometheus.

In the scene in the witches' kitchen, interwoven
in Italy, 1788, there is a revelation of classic paganism in the attack against the Trinity:

> Es war die Art zu allen Zeiten,
> Durch Drei und Eins und Eins und Drei
> Irrthum statt Wahrheit zu verbreiten.

As has already been pointed out, Faust sees in
the magic mirror a lovely woman who lies couched
after the fashion of Titian's Venus in the Tribuna
of Florence. She is perhaps a Helena form. The
scene closes with these significant words by Mephisto:

> Du siehst mit diesem Trank im Leibe
> Bald Helenen in jedem Weibe.

If Goethe has given his Italian heroine in the
Römische Elegien the name of Faustina, there now
arises before his mind another heroine with a name
far more familiar to antiquity, and she it is with

whom he wishes to provide his rejuvenated Faust. In order to reach perfection, final development, the acme of culture, the Gothic Faust of legend, just like Goethe himself, had to be espoused to the Antique. Marlowe, the *Faustbuch,* and German tradition pointed him the way: Faust conjures up Helena from the lower world and makes her his beloved. From the point of view of antiquity, Helena was the personification of beauty.

Think of the significance that this detached conceit from the age of the Renaissance had for Goethe! What a symbol this Helena became for his basic view that had been in the process of development for an entire generation! When Gretchen, the little Gothic girl, was dead, her place could be worthily filled only by the very queen of beauty from ancient Hellas, by that queen who in her own person represented the ideal for whose sake Goethe now stood alone, but to which he will remain forever true. And somewhat earlier than the time at which he collects all his energy in order to work on *Faust,* he completes, during the years 1825-1826, the third act of the work and ascribes to it, as an independent whole, the significant title of *Helena,* a title he afterwards removed.

Critics, who (like Orlando's horse in Ariosto), aside from some respectable characteristics, have the unfortunate one of incompetency, have contended that Goethe was incapable of reproducing the external world. This ability, which developed more and more in his lyric poetry as years went on, made the art of his old age impressionistic, which it had never been in his youth, and induced him to develop a new and astounding originality.

His *Divan* forms the transition to his new lyric, descriptive style. Here, for example, from the *Buch Suleika* is a verse so thoroughly saturated with golden, red, and green colors that it reminds one of the coloring of Rembrandt:

Schau, im zweifelhaften Dunkel
Glühen blühend alle Zweige,
Nieder spielet Stern auf Stern,
Und smaragden durch's Gesträuche
Tausendfältiger Karfunkel.

But it is in the second part of Faust, elaborated with incessant, indefatigable work during the years 1827-1831, that is to say, from the time he is seventy-eight to the time he is eighty-two years old, that his new style comes to the fore. It transcends his former style just as the style of the old Titian transcends that of the young Titian, or as Beethoven's ninth symphony towers above all the other symphonies (Richard Hamann: *Der Impressionismus in Leben und Kunst.*)

The second part of *Faust* is in reality only lyric poetry. Its fascination lies in the verbal art with which Goethe attempts to reproduce all sensations: Auditions from the slightest whisper to the rolling thunder, visions in all shades from the variegated world of color, which he had so carefully investigated, the flaming, the sparkling, the gleaming, the dazzling, that which billows and floats in light, and that which wavers and quivers; odors in all degrees of fresh scent, perfume, refreshing fragrance, irritating effluvia down to rank stench. When for example Goethe has Mephisto depict Hell, he obviously had in mind the strong smell of sulphur; he

has Mephisto introduced with a remark to the effect
that the devils began to cough:

> Die Teufel fingen sämmtlich an zu husten,
> Von oben und von unten auszupusten;
> Die Hölle schwoll von Schwefelstank und Säure.

The sense of feeling also finds expression here
both with regard to the gliding, and to the heavy
and solid:

> Wie war die Welt mir nichtig, unerschlossen,
> Wie ist sie nun seit meiner Priesterschaft
> Erst wünschenswerth, gegründet, dauerhaft!

At times Goethe, just as the German romanticists,
intermingles various senses: The light has sound,
or the sound has odor. So overrefined have his
never obtuse senses become. Homunculus's light
not only shines but sounds:

> *Mephisto:* Lass deine Leuchte, Kleiner, tönend scheinen!
> *Homunculus:* So soll es blitzen, soll es klingen.
>   (Das Glas dröhnt und leuchtet gewaltig.)

Or still more refined: color-impression, sound-im-
pression, and odor-effect are blended:

> Von buntesten Gefiedern
> Der Himmel übersäet,
> Ein klingend Meer von Liedern
> Geruchvoll überweht.

Heaven is as it were concealed back of the variegated plumage of birds, and a resounding, strongly
odorous flow of song rushes in from over yonder.
The very first scene in the second part of *Faust*
mixes programme-like sensations: The light not
only dazzles, but creaks, rattles, booms, and is con-

ceived of as the music of the trumpets and bassoons.
Ariel sings

> Tönend wird für Geister-Ohren
> Schon der neue Tag geboren.
> Felsenthore knarren rasselnd,
> Phöbus' Räder rollen prasselnd,
> Welch Getöse bringt das Licht!
> Es trommetet, es posaunet.
> Auge blinzt und Ohr erstaunet.

Thereupon follows Faust's description of the sun-
rise and his comparison of it to the satisfaction of
hope and desire. Goethe here, as throughout this
entire period, in aversion to the worn-out small
change of the language, coins new, concise, and effective words such as *Erfüllungspforten—flügeloffen.*
He shows how passionately, despite his years, he
conceives of the fullness of life in the fulfilled desire:

> So ist es also, wenn ein sehnend Hoffen
> Dem höchsten Wunsch sich traulich zugerungen,
> Erfüllungspforten findet flügeloffen.
> Ein Flammenübermass; wir stehn betroffen.
> Des Lebens Fackel wollten wir entzünden,
> Ein Feuermeer umschlingt uns, welch ein Feuer!
> Ist's Lieb, ist's Hass, die glühend uns umwinden,
> Mit Schmerz und Freuden wechselnd ungeheuer?

The monologue ends with the description of the
waterfall and the rainbow above it, so that we feel
the moisture, the spray, the foam, and the splendor.
Lastly the philosophy of this style is given in the
significant words that this colored radiance is all
that we can grasp of life:

> So bleibe denn die Sonne mir im Rücken!—
> Der Wassersturz, das Felsenriff durchbrausend,
> Ihn schau' ich an mit wachsendem Entzücken
> Von Sturz zu Sturzen wälzt er jetzt in tausend,

Dann abertausend Strömen sich ergiessend
Hoch in die Lüfte Schaum an Schäume sausend.—
Allein wie herrlich, diesem Sturm entspriessend
Wölbt sich des bunten Bogens Wechseldauer
Bald rein gezeichnet, bald in Luft zerfliessend,
Umher verbreitend duftig kühle Schauer!
Der spiegelt ab das menschliche Bestreben.
Ihm sinne nach, und Du begreifst genauer:
Am farbigen Abglanz haben wir das Leben.

Even in the first part of *Faust* he says of the snail
that it is guided at once by sight and touch and
smell:

Siehst du die Schnecke da? Sie kommt herangekrochen;
Mit ihrem *tastenden Gesicht*
Hat sie mir schon was *abgerochen.*

Goethe succeeds in giving us, in this his last stage
of development, what the art of painting cannot
give because of its very nature,—the momentary
shifting of the vision of light and color and the quiv-
ering in motion itself:

Blinkend, wo die Zitterwellen
Ufernetzend leise schwellen.

Or take this bit of fireworks:

Irrfunkenblick an allen Enden,
Ein Leuchten, plötzlich zu verblenden.

Or this, which, as Hamann has strikingly said, reminds us of Velasquez's *The Lance:*

Die Piken blinken flimmernd in der Luft
Im Sonnenglanz durch Morgennebelduft.

Or this beautiful night, a nocturne which is more
than Whistler-like, an invocation directed to the

stars, beseeching them to shine down upon the
Nereids frolicking in the sea:

> Blicke ruhig von dem Bogen
> Deiner Nacht auf Zitterwogen,
> Mildeblitzend Glanzgewimmel;
> Und erleuchte das Getümmel,
> Das sich aus den Wogen hebt!

Note how much sympathetic observation of the
color-accustomed and color-loving eye there is in
the following words concerning the light billows
which rise and swell along the dark shore:

> Siehst auf und ab lichtgrüne, schwanke Wellen
> Mit Purpursaum zur schönsten Wohnung schwellen?

What an immeasurably great artist this octogenarian was! Consider how with changing, ever striking expression he depicts the skulking and hulking
of a fog cloud through space, as viewed from a high
mountain:

> Ein dunkler Nebel deckt sogleich den Raum.
> Er schleicht sich ein, er wogt nach Wolkenart,
> Gedehnt, geballt, verschränkt, getheilt, gepaart.

The artistic pith and power of the last expression
is matchless. There is a tone depiction of corresponding vigor. We hear the wind whistling in the
rushes along the shore, in the weeping willows, in
the aspen foliage:

> Rege dich, du Schilfgeflüster,
> Hauchet leise, Rohrgeschwister,
> Säuselt, leichte Weidensträuche,
> Lispelt, Pappelzitterzweige!

Goethe far surpasses the German romanticists in
sound effect which, incidentally, was their specialty.

He anticipates the song of the Rhine maidens by Richard Wagner in the line: *Wir säuseln, wir rieseln, wir flüstern Dir zu.* He has powerful stanzas with almost pure A-sounds:

> Waldung, die schwankt heran
> Felsen, sie lasten dran,
> Wurzeln, sie klammern an,
> Stamm, dicht an Stamm heran.

On the other hand, the song of the sirens, they who worship all the gods of the universe, contains nothing but O-sounds:

> Wir sind gewohnt
> Wo es auch thront,
> In Sonne und Mond,
> Hinzubeten; es lohnt.

It is in truth in its verbal, descriptive, and musical skill that the second part of *Faust* is so instructive, so aesthetic, so suggestive, and stands on such a high plane. And the artistic is after all the chief desideratum. The demonstration of the rational element of the poem, its plan, the clarification of obscure passages, and of what Goethe has mystified into it, consciously or in the interests of his art— all this furnishes topics for professors of literature in Germany and North America to lecture on. This is admittedly an essential phase of the business, but it is of far less interest to us.

From a purely intellectual point of view, there are a number of unsatisfactory features in the construction. The point that was to be proved was indeed the fact that the angels can save him who constantly strives—which is equivalent to saying that he is

deserving and should not be lost. But unfortunately
this is precisely what Faust has not done: He has
neither striven nor acted. He has made, with the
assistance of Mephisto, some worthless paper money
for use at the Court of the Emperor, and he has
arranged a series of Court festivals. This can
hardly be called striving. He has brought Helena
up to the world of men. This, however, though
an act, is an act in the interests of amusement rather
than in those of diligent service. And he has robbed
Philemon and Baucis of their little home. This is
an act, but an unreservedly reprehensible one. And
after this career, he is to be redeemed by the inter-
cession of a woman whom he has treated with undisciplined cruelty, and then abandoned for ever
and a day. In this which was supposed to represent
the logic of the work, real logic is quite far off, and
altogether thin if found at all.

Faust derides the idea of studying the far-away,
the world beyond, as though he were speaking in
the name of the poet himself:

> Nach drüben ist die Aussicht uns verrannt,
> Thor! wer dorthin die Augen blinzelnd richtet,
> Sich über Wolken Seinesgleichen dichtet.
> Er stehe fest und sehe hier sich um!
> Dem Tücht'gen ist die Welt nicht stumm,
> Was braucht er, in die Ewigkeit zu schweifen!

There is then immediately revealed to us the
Roman Catholic Heaven with the angelic choir, the
choir of penetential sisters, the blessed youths, the
*Mater gloriosa, Pater ecstaticus, Pater profundus,
Chorus mysticus, Pater seraphicus,* even down to
St. Francis of Assisi, whose church Goethe once dis-

dained to see. There is not much here to offer lovers of logic.

And yet, when the mystic choir voices its dark concluding stanza, we are filled with a mood as though we heard a Pagan-Christian Sibyll's words of wisdom; by virtue of the lofty art of the poet, these almost impenetrable words have remained engraved in the memory of generations:

> Alles Vergängliche
> Ist nur ein Gleichnis;
> Das Unzulängliche
> Hier wird's Ereignis;
> Das Unbeschreibliche,
> Hier ist es gethan;
> Das Ewig-Weibliche
> Zieht uns heran.

This entire world of legend was nothing but a symbol. The inadequate—inadequate as is every human work—here come most nearly being satisfactory, indeed it even marks an epoch. The indescribable—in the sense of inexhaustible—takes place here before our eyes. The eternally feminine, the maidenly, the maternal, the enigmatic, attracts us just as the lap of nature attracted Goethe's manhood, and as partly *die Mütter,* partly Helena, attracted his Faust.

CHAPTER XXXVI

Helena; THE THIRD ACT, THE FIRST PART TO BE WRITTEN—FIRST ACT—SECOND ACT— FOURTH AND FIFTH ACTS

THE third act of the second part of *Faust,* the poem originally entitled *Helena,* was the first one to be written. It constitutes more or less of a whole; it is relatively complete in itself. Study it, and it shows, without unusual difficulty or the arts of exegetic interpretation, what Goethe intended to make the kernel, the heart, of this great new work of his. That is, it makes this point clear to him who has followed and examined the historical development of Goethe's own soul. As we have already intimated, the kernel was the marriage of the legendary Gothic hero to the antique ideal, the symbolic history of that stage of development in the life of the leading character in which he, precisely like the poet that created him, conjured up and worshipped the Hellas of days gone by.

By this time, reflection had dislodged the naïveté in Goethe's works which had made him such a spiritual force in the days of his youth. The power of imagination was still luxuriously rich, the inventiveness extraordinary. Of conceits and apercus there

is no end. But we have already had occasion to
see how the ability to portray *individual figures* has
been swallowed up and lost to view by the tendency
to delineate *the typical*. In the second part of
Faust everything has become symbolism. The figures derive their value, not from their individual
and personal psychology, but by virtue of the lyric
expression in which they clothe their inner soul.
Here is depth; for here is thought ingeniously
worded. Here is beauty; for here is lyric poetry in
which an art that is rare rejuvenates the language
and widens the reproduction of nature to hitherto
unapproached boundaries. But the ability to form
figures, to create characters, has weakened. The
seer no longer says, and that with vigor, *this is;*
quite the contrary: the brooder appears on the
boards with his explanatory *this means*. These figures are not compact but transparent; one sees
through them into the meaning back of them. They
give their own meaning. They are not even pictures: they are symbols. They are not of flesh
and blood so that they can be embraced or hewn
down or pierced through. They are ghosts that
disappear before a puff of wind or magic word.
They vanish in the mists that enshroud them. The
entire work is so eldritch that the illusion is often
destroyed by the poet himself through the voluntary
introduction of a participating personage whose un-
reality is altogether obvious.

We find ourselves before Menelaos's palace in
Sparta. Helena appears, having returned home
from conquered Troy, accompanied by her maid-
servants, a chorus of captured Trojan women. The
time is far distant when Goethe had his Iphigenie

speak in modern iambic pentameters. Helena speaks
in rigid, weighty classic trimeters; the cadence of
her speech is heavy, though solemn, and beautiful.
The chorus joins in precisely as in an old Greek
tragedy.   But a figure appears which brings an
alien and ugly element into this welter of beauty
arisen from the lower world; it is a tall grim woman,
Phorkyas by name, who sets herself up as the direc-
tress of the palace during the queen's absence.   With
her raucus and domineering voice, she not simply
frightens the captured girls who accompany Helena,
but even dares to remind the queen of her past in
a way that cannot help but be quite painful to her.
Helena sublimely sets her aright, though she still
refuses to acquiesce.   She is Mephisto himself in the
garb of a woman.

When the queen steps across the threshold in order once more to take possession of the palace, and
to bring the gods their due sacrifice, Mephisto, as
Phorkyas, tells her that she herself is the victim!
Menelaos has given the command that she shall be
sacrificed with the polished ax that lies at the foot
of the altar, while her hand-maidens shall without
exception be hanged.

Helena resigns with calm dignity, though she cannot forego asking whether there is not some way
out of this situation.   Phorkyas enlightens her by
saying that there is; and from the answer we are
reminded that we are all of a sudden no longer in
the time of ancient Greece, but in that of the Middle
Ages.   There lies nearby a strongly fortified and
beautifully fitted out castle inhabited by a strange,
warlike race ruled over by a great and intelligent
chieftain.

Mephisto at once sends Helena and her followers to the inner court of the castle. After the servants and squires have marched down in a long procession to the bottom of the steps, Faust comes slowly and pompously, wearing the knightly court costume of the Middle Ages and extends to Helena his lavish homage. He leads along with him, in chains, the keeper of the tower, Lynceus, who should have announced her coming but forgot to attend to his duty. In beautiful verses Lynceus defends himself with, to be sure, a gallantry unknown to ancient times: Helena's beauty has so blinded him that he neglected to blow the horn that hung by his side; as an infatuated lover he brings her chests full of treasures, pearls, and precious stones. Some of his courtesies are a bit antiquated, as when he has the ruby turn pale in comparison with the blush on her cheek—it is difficult to conceive of Helena as being so brick-red. His use of the word egg-drop as a circumlocution for pearl is, however, beautiful; the homage implied in it at least gives the reader the impression of the queen's remarkable beauty:

> Nun schwanke zwischen Ohr und Mund
> Das Tropfenei aus Meersesgrund;
> Rubinen werden gar verscheucht,
> Das Wangenroth sie niederbleicht. . . .
> Denn Du bestiegest kaum den Thron,
> So neigen schon, so beugen schon
> Verstand und Reichthum und Gewalt
> Sich vor der einzigen Gestalt.

With the proneness to artistic double reflection such as we have already noticed in Goethe, and which the German Romanticists developed into a

formal system, the poet has Helena become astonished at the rhymes in Lynceus's speech; she asks
what this is, what it means:

> Erstaunen trifft mich, fragen möcht' ich viel.
> Doch wünscht ich Unterricht, warum die Rede
> Des Manns mir seltsam klang, seltsam und freundlich.
> Ein Ton scheint sich dem andern zu bequemen,
> Und hat ein Wort zum Ohre sich gesellt,
> Ein andres kommt, dem ersten liebzukosen.

And now the dialogue between Faust and Helena is
continued in rhyme verse.

Spiritually and physically the two come nearer
and nearer together. The chorus sings—and says—
that they are sitting right out in the presence of the
people, shoulder to shoulder, knee to knee, hand in
hand. That Goethe's ability to depict the mutual
erotic intoxication is no longer that of his youth is
seen in the dialogue between Faust and Helena:

> *Helena:* Ich fühle mich so fern und doch so nah,
> Und sage nur zu gern: Da bin ich! Da!
> *Faust:* Ich athme kaum, mir zittert, stockt das Wort,
> Es ist ein Traum, verschwunden Tag und Ort.
> *Helena:* Ich scheine mir verlebt und doch so neu,
> In Dich verwebt, dem Unbekannten treu.
> *Faust:* Durchgrüble nicht das einzigste Geschick!
> Dasein ist Pflicht, und wär's ein Augenblick.

When Menelaos and his army threaten to make
a sudden attack, Faust mobilizes his military force
and here, where Faust after the victory divides his
land among those who have been true to him, Goethe's lyric poetry once again rises as high as it has
ever risen in descriptive strength. We have for

example these lines from Faust in his conversation with his generals:

> In Stahl gehüllt, vom Strahl umwittert,
> Die Schaar, die Reich um Reich zerbrach,
> Sie treten auf, die Erde schüttert;
> Sie schreiten fort, es donnert nach.

Or consider this description of the countries' stock of cattle and their flora

> Vertheilt, vorsichtig, abgemessen, schreitet
> Gehörntes Rind hinan zum jähen Rand;
> Doch Obdach ist den Sämmtlichen bereitet,
> Zu hundert Höhlen wölbt sich Felsenwand.

The picture of the tread of the oxen in the first line is vivid and veracious. In the following stanza the oak and the maple are portrayed with equal warmth:

> Altwälder sind's! Die Eiche starret mächtig,
> Und eigensinnig zackt sich Ast and Ast;
> Der Ahorn mild, von süssem Safte trächtig,
> Steigt rein empor und spielt mit seiner Last.

We have seen how strongly the relation to Byron concerned Goethe; it was a filial relation in which the English Lord placed himself with regard to the author of *Faust*. In Goethe's estimation, and according to the idea prevalent at the time, Byron was the greatest poet of Europe after Goethe himself. If later generations have found that Byron was overesteemed in countries other than England to the extent that there were in England in his day such poets as Keats and Shelley who, from a purely artistic point of view, were superior to him, there is nevertheless not a shadow of a doubt but that he alone had historical and political influence of the first rank; and that he was the only one who created schools in three or four different countries. Byron's brave determination to bring personal and economic help to struggling Greece, even more than his beautiful death, moved Goethe profoundly. He felt a desire to glorify his young and brilliant colleague, and since he had gradually become accustomed to looking upon *Faust* as a station and depot for everything that captivated him, it lay near to him to erect a monument to Byron in *Faust* itself.

He conceived, consequently, the singular idea of having the tender association between Faust and Helena result in the birth of a son, a young genius, without wings to be sure, but springing up like a faun, or like a chamois leaping and bounding from cliff to cliff. Euphorion's ambition is similar to that of Icarus: He wishes to rise up above the earth, to move back and forth, unrestrained, free, through the air. For the time being there is no mountain peak that is too high for him.

All of this is allegory. There is sound sense in it too when Euphorion—the son of Achilles in the legend—is supposed to be the son of Faust. But it becomes unclear when Byron is also supposed to be the son of Helena. For just as it is clear that Byron descends from the Danish Normans (the name is *Björn*), from Shakespeare and Pope and Voltaire and Rousseau, just so is it clear that there is nothing in his life that leads back to *ancient* Hellas. His relation to Greece consists of his valiant effort to convert it into a *new* Hellas.

Goethe obviously saw him in a different light from that in which we see him. What we admire most in Byron the artist is the wild humors of *Don*

Juan; in Byron, the man and statesman, it is his bold spirit in unbroken rebellion against sham, hypocrisy and coercion. These are not the features that enraptured Goethe. He saw in him a young Apollo, a figure gloried by a Hero's death, with a halo of poetry, or the crown of Greece, about his head. And consequently he has—rather peculiarly—Mephisto himself pronounce these inspired words upon him:

In der Hand die goldne Leier, völlig wie ein kleiner Phöbus,
Tritt er wolgemuth zur Kante, zu dem Ueberhang; wir
    staunen,
Und die Eltern vor Entzücken werfen wechselnd sich an's
    Herz.
Denn wie leuchtet's ihm zu Häupten? Was erglänzt ist
    schwer zu sagen,
Ist es Goldschmück, ist es Flamme übermächtiger Geister-
    kraft?
Und so regt er sich geberdend, sich als Knabe schon ver-
    kündend
Künftigen Meister alles Schönen, dem die ew'gen Melodien
Durch die Glieder sich bewegen; und so werdet Ihr ihn
    hören.

As characteristic of Byron, Goethe places these lines on the lips of Euphorion:

Das leicht Errungene
Das widert mir;
Nur das Erzwungene
Ergötzt mich schier.

Lines such as these express the contrast between the vigorous instinct for nature in Goethe's being and the defiant element in that of Byron. Thus far the poetic illusion, in so far as adventurous and fantastic traits can illude, is preserved to a certain extent; it had to be. But when Euphorion, in his

first attempt at soaring high up through space, falls
to earth and is crushed, and when the chorus, which
consists of captive Trojan women from the castle
of King Priam, strikes up a dirge that can allude
to just one person, to George Noël Gordon Byron,
then we feel quite beyond the age, and quite beyond
Faust. It is characteristic of Goethe, and significant
too, that in this poem, as everywhere else, it is
Byron's placing himself above and beyond custom
and usage, law and order, that concerns him, and
that shows him to be more than reconciled with the
defense of Missolunghi.   Goethe has allowed himself to be a trifle misled by his faith in the imbecile stories concerning the deceased.   The real
kernel of Byron's nature was not the kernel for
Goethe.

When the dirge on Euphorion is ended, Helena
returns once more to the lower world, and the entire
episode would be at an end if the chorus, which
remains behind and is now characterised as consisting of the nymphs of trees, mountains, springs,
and vineyards, had not given voice to the concluding
couplets, concerning which it is difficult to decide in
which of them Goethe's new lyric style makes itself
felt most characteristically.   Note, however, especially the amazingly picturesque and musical portrayal by the dryads of the way in which they guide
the sap of plants and struggle with twigs, leaves,
flowers, and fruits:

Wir in dieser tausend Aeste Flüsterzittern, Säuselschweben
Reizen tändelnd, locken leise wurzelauf des Lebens Quellen
Nach den Zweigen, bald mit Blättern, bald mit Blüthen
        überschwenglich
Zieren wir die Flatterhaare frei zu luftigem Gedeihn.

Fällt die Frucht, sogleich versammeln lebenslustig Volk und
    Herden
Sich zum Greifen, sich zum Naschen, eilig kommend, emsig
    drängend,
Und wie vor den ersten Göttern, bückt sich Alles um uns
    her.

The act concerning Helena ends, then, with nature hymns in which Helena and her son are entirely
forgotten; it even disembogues in a wild festival
of Dionysus, in which Silenus and the bacchantian
followers with cloven ram's feet tread morality under foot, drink to excess, and whirl about with muddled senses—just as the Hellas tragedy of antiquity
was followed by a satyr play.

II

The new Faust poem is grouped around the Helena climax. After a beautiful elf-song, and a dignified monologue by the awakening Faust, the details
of which have just been reviewed, the scene opens
before an imperial palace in which Mephisto is court
fool, since his predecessor, after drinking himself to
death, had to be carried off. From the replies of the
courtiers as well as from the emperor's conversation
we derive the impression of a great empire in the
process of dissolution. We feel at any rate that we
have to do with a state that is without currency.
Money is lacking on all sides. A medium of exchange is to be had nowhere. Mephistopheles
makes the point that the empire's soil is full of treasures which were buried in former times out of fear
of the enemy. Asked how they are to be brought
to light, how they are to be realized, he says:

Through the natural ability and intellectual power
of a talented man, of a spiritual leader. In reply
the benighted chancellor remonstrates as follows:

> Natur und Geist—so spricht man nicht zu Christen.
> Deshalb verbrennt man Atheisten,
> Weil solche Reden höchst gefährlich sind.
> Natur ist Sünde, Geist ist Teufel;
> Sie hegen zwischen sich den Zweifel,
> Ihr missgestaltet Zwitterkind.

In the meantime Mephistopheles promises to pro-
cure for the emperor and court just as much money
as they wish. Many contend that his promises are
the effusions of a charlatan, the catch-phrases of a
trickster. But he remains steadfast to his assertion
that the earth has an abundance of riches in hiding.

At this point, and for this reason, the action is
interrupted by a stupendous court carnival the description of which weakens the coherency of the
drama, though it gave Goethe an opportunity to
say a huge number of things that had been on his
mind for years. It opened the way for a discussion
of the varied conditions of life and the numerous
professions by which life is made a reality. He
said all he had to say about gardeners, male and female, who develop the world of flowers. He com-
mented on wood cutters, pulchinellos, niggards, parasites, drunkards, mothers who wish to get rid of
their daughters, a mass of mythological figures,
graces, parcae, furies and so on *ad infinitem*. For
a while Faust and the plot are wholly forgotten.
This is not in the interest either of art or of dramatic economy, especially at this point where the
very exposition of the drama is involved.

Mephistopheles has by no means lost his satiric wit with years. When the court wishes to acquire the treasures of the earth without effort and cannot understand that the grape must first be ripened and then pressed to produce wine, Mephistopheles says:

> Wie sich Verdienst und Glück verketten,
> Das fällt den Thoren niemals ein;
> Wenn sie den Stein der Weisen hätten,
> Der Weise mangelte dem Stein.

The impressionistic force of the style is, without exception, striking and pleasing: Goethe's senses were sharpened with years and the feeling of his sovereignty over the language increased at the same time. He coins new words and expressions in order to reproduce down to the minutest detail the external as well as the internal reality. Thus for example the parasites say:

> Da brät's und prudelt's.
> Da kocht's und strudelt's.
> Der wahre Schmecker,
> Der Tellerlecker,
> Er riecht den Braten,
> Er ahnet Fische.
> Das regt zu Thaten
> An Gönners Tische.

He is as ingenious as he has ever been in his life. What a glorious conceit it is for example that, when the furies are introduced, it turns out that the true furies are beautiful, well formed, friendly, youthful —and none the less malignant, deceitful, passionately backbiting, creating mischief and discontent wherever they go. No better than they is the mas-

culine abuser by profession, Zoilo-Thersites, who
reviles everything that succeeds:

> Doch wo was Rühmliches gelingt,
> Es mich sogleich in Harnisch bringt,
> Das Tiefe hoch, das Hohe tief,
> Das Schiefe grad, das Grade schief,
> Das ganz allein macht mich gesund,
> So will ich's auf dem Erdenrund.

At the carnival the Emperor appears in person as
the great god Pan; we are again moved by the finesse and wonderful power in the aromatic verses
sung by the nymphs in his honor:

> Auch unterm blauen Wölbedach,
> Verhielt er sich beständig wach;
> Doch rieseln ihm die Bäche zu,
> Und Lüftlein wiegen ihn mild in Ruh.
> Und wenn er zu Mittage schläft,
> Sich nicht das Blatt am Zweige regt.
> Gesunder Pflanzen Balsamduft
> Erfüllt die schweigsam stille Luft . . .
> Wenn unerwartet mit Gewalt
> Dann aber seine Stimm' erschallt
> Wie Blitzesknattern, Meergebraus,
> Dann Niemand weiss wo ein noch aus. . . .

Through the aid of Mephisto, Faust now supplies
the Emperor with paper money, approximately as
John Law, in 1716, came to the assistance of the
Regent of France, the Duke of Orleans, with his
banknotes. Mephisto adds a number of witty cyni-
cisms concerning the power that notes bestow, especially on women.

In order that Goethe might abandon all this extraneous and irrelevant discussion and revert to
the real pith, substance, and theme of the poem, it
is necessary to have the Emperor seized with a sud-

den impulse to see Helena and Paris before him as
a spiritual apparition. Faust requests Mephisto to
produce them. The latter replies that the entrance
to the Pagan world can be made possible only by
Faust's visiting *Die Mütter,* stern and lofty goddesses like the Norns, though conceived of as beings
who command the innermost workshop in which
Mother Nature performs her familiar deeds. They
rule over the forms of things and men. Their
thrones stand upon the ground which is beyond time
and place, in a never trodden expanse.

This fancy is surely one of Goethe's most charming and profound. It is, however, such ideas as this
that have given rise to the dolt-like observations
concerning *Faust,* Part II. We are told that it is
altogether incomprehensible. The same was said
of Beethoven's symphonies and Wagner's operas
when they first appeared. The symbolism is in truth
easy to grasp; it is also extremely enjoyable. Note
this alternation of speeches

> *Faust:* Wohin der Weg?
> *Mefistofeles:* Kein Weg! Ins Unbetretene,
>   Nicht zu Betretende; ein Weg ins Unei
>   betene,
>   Nicht zu Erbittende. Bist Du bereit?—
>   Nicht Schlösser sind, nicht Riegel wegzu
>   schieben,
>   Von Einsamkeiten wirst umhergetrieben.
>   Hast Du Begriff von Oed' und Einsamkeit?
> *Faust:* . . . Musst ich nicht mit der Welt ver-
>   kehren?
>   Das Leere lernen, Leeres lehren?—
>   *Sprach ich vernünftig, wie ich's angeschaut,*
>   *Erklang der Widerspruch gedoppelt laut;*
>   *Musst ich sogar vor widerwärt'gen Streichen*
>   *Zur Einsamkeit, zur Wildernis entweichen.*

It is Goethe himself who speaks through Faust—
and he does so with marked distinctness. It seems
to him, and justly so, highly preposterous to ask
him whether he knows the wilderness and solitude
when he never could utter a rational word without
hearing the bellowing of fools against him, until he
finally took refuge in the loneliness of human contempt.

While Faust descends to *die Mütter* the scene is
prepared in the palace for the catóptric images of
Helena and Paris. A Doric temple forms the
scenery; this fact gives an architect, whom Goethe
momentarily wishes to deride, opportunity to emphasize the excellence of Gothic architecture, which
the poet, plainly enough out of politeness to the
Boisserée brothers, allowed in his time to be considered as coördinate. The apparitions appear and
Faust becomes so jealous of Paris and wants to
hinder him so passionately in his abduction of Helena, that the entire performance ends with an explosion.

III

The second act brings us back to Faust's study of
the first part. Mephisto again finds the old mantle
in which he inspired the student with awe, and from
which a chorus of insects now comes forth buzzing
a droll song by way of greeting. It was here that
Goethe had the brilliant idea of having Faust's
former Famulus, the noble Doctor Wagner, become,
during Faust's absence, the first man in the world
of scholarship. He is the diurnal augmenter of
wisdom. Around the lecture platform on which

he shines, there have gathered huge swarms of erudition's devotees. The fame of no man can compete with his. He has even outshone and darkened the name of Faust himself.

It is in this old room that the student from the first part appears as baccalaureus, now grown into an original genius with jubilant conceitedness; he uses phrases from Fichte's philosophy in order to dazzle by his youthful greatness. Here it is that we again find our old Doctor Wagner, the pedant who has now gone in for natural science, and who is on the point of creating a human being by artificial means.

This merry idea Goethe held on to and carried out with energy since just at this time, by a queer coincidence, a namesake of Wagner, Professor J. I. Wagner in Würzburg, had insisted that chemistry simply must succeed in creating a human being through the process of crystalization. The idea, moreover, came from the Middle Ages; during the Renaissance it was championed by Paracelsus, who considered it possible to create human beings without the natural process, through alchemy, somewhat as in our own day F. T. Marinetti has expressed the hope of eventually being able to create "his mechanical son" solely as the fruit of his will. And even during the Middle Ages this delicate human being in the laboratory glass was given the name of Homunculus, the name that Goethe has preserved.

When Homunculus comes to life in the glass flask with the longish neck, his gaze falls at once on Faust who, stupified, has been sleeping since the explosion. As he reads the sleeper's thoughts he begins his personal life with the above quoted monologue, which portrays Leda and the Swan, the ancestors of Helena. Homunculus finds it necessary to divert Faust, and since the latter is already acquainted with the romantic world of ghosts from his trip to the Brocken, this newly born, precocious gentleman suggests that he strike up an acquaintance with the classical world of ghosts by way of contrast.

In his own mind Goethe had quietly decided to work out a parallel between the first and the second part of *Faust,* in so far as this could be done. The witches' sabbath on Walpurgis Night of the first part was to correspond to the classical Walpurgis Night of the second part. Wagner is to remain at home. He still has something to do by way of brooding over the old *pergamenta* that feed his mind. Faust, Mephisto, and Homunculus, the latter of whom floats through the air and guides the others on the way with light from his glass flask, all set out at the same time.

Thessalian sorceresses, griffins, pismires, sphinxes, sirens, nymphs, Chiron the centaur, pygmies, cranes, lamiae, all sorts of fabulous beings meet the travellers as they journey in the dark over the Pharsalian fields. At the song of a siren, which flatters the ear but leaves the heart cold, Goethe was in all probability thinking of Rossini's music which did not correspond to his German taste.

Faust loses himself in great classical reminiscences: As a means of resistance against the song of the sirens, Odysseus had himself bound to the masts of the ship and his ears stopped up. Otherwise Faust is concerned only with Helena; he asks the sphinxes whether they have seen her. Resting on the banks of the Peneios, he sees before him once

more the vision that Homunculus described; the
swan approaches Leda and her hand-maidens. This
is the mystic pairing that resulted in the genesis of
Helena. He also meets Chiron, who had raptur-
ously borne her on the back of his steed when she
fled with her brothers from a band of robbers:

> Da sprang sie ab und streichelte
> Die feuchte Mähne, schmeichelte,
> Und dankte lieblichklug und selbstbewusst.
> Wie war sie reizend! Jung, des Alten Lust!

Goethe once more amuses himself by shattering
all illusions. He has Faust ask: She was only seven
years old? And Chiron replies: I see, *Die Philo-
logen* have deceived you as well as themselves.

We have here a repetition of Mephisto's uncanny
relation to the witches from the first part. The
lamiae give him no peace; nor he them. These old
Greek vampyres are portrayed, incidentally, just
like ultra-modern women. Mephisto characterises
them as follows:

> Man weiss, das Volk taugt aus dem Grunde nichts:
> Geschnürten Leibs, geschminkten Angesichts,
> Nichts haben sie Gesundes zu erwidern,
> Wo man sie anfasst, morsch in allen Gliedern. ..
> Mann weiss, man sieht's, man kann es greifen,
> Und dennoch tanzt man, wenn die Luder pfeifen.

The old philosophers are found here; they have
arisen from the dead. They discuss, as above mentioned, the problem of the genesis of the earth. In
an invocation of Artemis, Anaxagoras has these delightful lines:

> Du Brusterweiternde, im Tiefsten Sinnige,
> Du Ruhigscheinende, Gewaltsam-Innige!

It is annoying to find, as is usually the case in
Goethe's works, the Greek and the Latin names of
the gods so confused, so chaotically arranged. Artemis is called *Diana, Luna, Hekate*. In like fashion sphinxes sing four lines in which the Greek name
for the sun, *Helios*, is paired with the Latin name
for the moon, *Luna*.

In this section Goethe has vigorously asserted,
through Thales as his mouthpiece, the Neptunian
conception of the genesis of the earth. In flowing
verses he has Italian and Lybian snake exorcists
sing the praise of the sea:

> In stillbewusstem Behagen
> Bewahren wir Cypriens Wagen
> Und führen beim Säuseln der Nächte
> Durch liebliches Wellengeflechte
> Unsichtbar dem neuen Geschlechte
> Die liebliche Tochter heran.

Thales, however, as the champion of the theory
that the earth was formed through the rising and
falling of the sea, becomes the leading character
at this juncture. He sings a song of praise to the
water as an element. It sprang from the depths
of Goethe's soul; and it is a happy product of his
genius:

> Heil, heil aufs Neue!
> Wie ich mich blühend freue,
> Vom Schönen, Wahren durchdrungen.
> Alles ist aus dem Wasser entsprungen!
> Alles wird durch das Wasser enthalten!
> Ozean, gönn' uns dein ewiges Walten!
> Wenn du nicht Wolken sendetest,
> Nicht reiche Bäche spendetest,
> Hin und her nicht Flüsse wendetest,
> Die Ströme nicht vollendetest,
> Was wären Gebirge, was Ebnen und Welt?

Following this geological interlude, we have the central act originally entitled Helena. It was the first to be written. It has already been discussed.

IV

The fourth act of the drama is the least interesting. As happened not infrequently in the Middle Ages, an anti-emperor rose up against the real emperor. We become witnesses to a campaign and a defeat during which the magic arts of Faust and Mephisto turn the scales in the favor of the imperial power. The enemy is so completely hallucinated by sorcery that he sees running water on all sides, which makes a firm foothold impossible.

As a reward, Faust demands from the Emperor all the coast land of the empire, and such parts of the land itself as can be wrested from the sea. The Emperor confers titles of distinction on his deserving followers, and grants them positions of trust and honor. But he allows himself to be hopelessly intimidated by the archbishop, who requests and receives penitence and concessions from him because he dared to misuse his power to the extent of liberating a heretic who had already been bound to the stake which, in accordance with an order direct from Rome, he was to set on fire instantly and without mental hesitation. The truth is, we find precious little in this entire political act to arouse human sympathy or chain the reader's interest, whereas an inordinate number of gripping scenes and songs have been fused together in the sublime and singular fifth act.

Faust has become the ruler over a vast stretch

of land situated by the sea, wrested from the sea, as was Holland or Venice, with extensive trade and the wealth of a sea power. He is very old; he has become morose and domineering. Philemon and Baucis, the venerable and innocent old couple, occupy a little home surrounded with linden trees; they obstruct Faust's view and consequently annoy him, somewhat as the mill at Sans Souci irritated Frederick II, or as Naboth's vineyard aroused the avariciousness of King Ahab. Faust has offered the two old people a better home within his realm; but they cling to their own property. Faust then orders Mephisto to dispossess them by force. Mephisto and his servants carry out the order in the rudest sort of fashion They burn the little house, and the old couple, noted for their gentleness and fidelity, are burned with it. Here, as so frequently in Goethe's work, the consequences of a deed, reprehensible and yet *per se* pardonable, become terrifying.

Lynceus, the guardian of the tower, is a witness to the atrocity from his high seat of activity. His monologue belongs to the most beautiful of the lyric parts of the entire tragedy. It begins:

> Zum Sehen geboren,
> Zum Schauen bestellt,
> Dem Thurme geschworen,
> Gefällt mir die Welt.
> Ich blick' in die Ferne,
> Ich seh' in der Näh'
> Den Mond und die Sterne,
> Den Wald und das Reh.

From the ashes of the little house there arise four avenging ghosts, four gray women, in the persons of whom Goethe has condensed romantic terrors. Their names are *Mangel, Schuld, Sorge,* and *Noth.* And *Noth* has a brother whose name is *Tod;* he follows at her heels. The scene between Faust and these four weird creatures is one of the deepest and most emotional, not simply of *Faust* but of poetry as a whole. There is poetically clarified anxiety and depressing knowledge of men in every single line. The fear of old age, torture, and death is expressed magnificently; this it was that Maeterlinck was to vary half a century later and thereby bring fame to his name.

What Faust says and what the four old women say in return embraces the terrifying tragedy of every wretched human life. The uncanniness begins to make itself felt at Faust's very first words:

> Vier sah ich kommen, drei nur gehn;
> Den Sinn der Rede konnt' ich nicht verstehn,
> Es klang so nach, als hiess es—Noth,
> Ein düstres Reimwort folgte—Tod.
> Es tönte hohl, gespensterhaft, gedämpft.

Faust regrets his relation to magic; he would be most happy if he could forget all the words of witchcraft he ever knew. But this point (in which Hermann Türck has seen the leading idea) has for me less interest in comparison with the universally human content of the monologue:

> Wenn auch *ein* Tag uns klar vernünftig lacht,
> In Traumgespinnst verwickelt uns die Nacht!
> Wir kehren froh von junger Flur zurück,
> Ein Vogel krächzt. Was krächzt er? Missgeschick.

Infinitely tragic is the following dialogue between *Sorge* and Faust, which ends by *Sorge's* breathing

into Faust's eyes and blinding him. He feels night
and darkness welling up about him; but his courage
is not crushed. He calls in his servants and sets
them to work; his far-reaching plans must now be
realized. He demands order and industry; he
wishes to hear the sound of hoes and spades. There
is a swamp that must be drained; a dwelling place
must be created for countless men in the future.
And while the Lemures, that is to say, the wretched
shades of the deceased, dig Faust's grave by torchlight in the fore-yard of the palace, Goethe, with
exalted and profound irony, leads him to believe
that the work has been begun on the plan he has
always had in mind, the embankment against the sea,
creating thereby a happy life for generations to
come, in lee and shelter against the storm and protected from the onrush of the ocean. From his lips
there come now the most beautiful truths; and over
them glide at the same time the expression for the
most incurable illusions. He speaks such truths as
this famous one:

> Das ist der Weisheit letzter Schluss:
> Nur dur verdient sich Freiheit und das Leben,
> Der taglich sie erobern muss.

He resigns, in that he confuses the sound of the
spades that are digging his grave with the sound of
the tools that are making fertile a stretch of land,
to the sad illusion that he is preparing a glorious
future. When he, in the anticipation of this, enjoys
the highest moment he shall—by an artificial interpretation of his words—have lost the wager of his
youth with Mephisto, the wager that he himself,
and the readers too, have long since forgotten. He
sinks back while the Lemures catch him and stretch

him out on the earth. His remarks seem more those
of Goethe than of Faust, and in the reading world
they have lost, and not without reason, every trace
of the ironically despairing shadow which the situation casts over them:

> Solch ein Gewimmel möcht' ich sehen,
> Auf freiem Grund mit freiem Volke stehn
> Zum Augenblicke dürft' ich sagen:
> Verweile doch. Du bist so schön.
> *Es kann die Spur von meinen Erdetagen*
> *Nicht in Aeonen untergehn.*

There follows the struggle, after the fashion
of Mediaeval tradition, between the devils and the
angels for the soul of the departed; Goethe has
elaborated it with a deal of energy. He has not
even shuddered from such a disgusting feature as
the depicting of the paederastic lusts that arise in
Mephisto at the sight of the nude angels' bodies;
but in individual strophes of the angels' song, the
metre of which is supposed to recall the angels' song
on that first Easter morning, the song that prevented Faust from committing suicide, are on the
same high level on which the poet moved when a
young man.

While the angels, the clarified Gretchen among
them, scatter roses over Faust's body, and the devils
seek to get possession of his soul, they sing these
beautiful verses:

> Rosen, Ihr blendenden,
> Balsam versendenden!
> Flatternde, schwebende,
> Heimlich belebende
> Zweigleinbeflügelte,
> Knospenentsiegelte,
> Eilet zu blühn!

Frühling entspriesse
Purpur und Grün!
Tragt Paradiese
Dem Ruhenden hin!

We have already seen to what extent the second
part of this sublime creation lacks unity and coherency, though it was written without interruption.
It has in truth not much more unity than the first
part, which was written at odd intervals, as the
spirit moved, and as time allowed. The anxiety
as to whether Faust's soul will be accepted in the
Catholic Heaven has undeniably been thrust into
the background, so far as the reader is concerned,
throughout the long period during which no one
has thought about it, but during which the possibility of an espousal between him as a German from
the period of the Renaissance and Helena as a
Grecian woman of olden days has seemed to be the
kernel of the poem.

Goethe has produced a very strong artistic effect
by reaching back, at the close of the tragedy, to the
very problem that was always presented and solved
in the Mediaeval Mysteries. Posterity has been
struck by the manner in which Goethe's voice seems
to drown out that of Faust in the closing words:

Es kann die Spur von meinen Erdetagen
Nicht in Aeonen untergehn.

And yet it is by no means certain that the words were
not written naïvely and with poetic honesty, and
intended as the expression of the dying Faust's hope.
When we recall other lines written by Goethe that
are equally strong and equally unaffected, lines that
betray a hearty distrust in posterity, one feels a bit

shaky as to the confidence that here seems to be
expressed in the generations that are to come after
us. Incidentally, Goethe wrote also this stanza:

> Nach kurzem Lärm legt Fama sich zur Ruh,
> Vergessen wird der Held so wie der Lotterbube.
> Der grösste König macht die Augen zu,
> Und jeder Hund bepisst gleich seine Grube.

There is a remote possibility, however, that Goethe
conceived of himself as constituting an exception to
the general rule he laid down in these verses.

CHAPTER XXXVII

GOETHE, CUVIER, AND GEOFFROY DE SAINT-HILAIRE—GOETHE AND THE GERMAN PUBLIC—GOETHE AND FRANCE—GOETHE AND ENGLAND

GOETHE'S intellectual interests were just as keen and vigorous after his eightieth year as they had ever been. He followed with real suspense the dispute then being waged between Cuvier and Geoffroy de Saint-Hilaire; he was delighted when it came to an open rupture in the meeting of the French Scientific Society on July 19, 1830, that is, less than two weeks before the outbreak of the July Revolution. The question under discussion had to do with his old, old belief in the mutability, and possibility of development, on the part of all beings and species. The theory had been rejected during his entire life. Now he saw it taken up by Saint-Hilaire and defended in opposition to Cuvier's theory of the finished species, the species that cannot and does not evolve. He lived, therefore, to see his favorite idea come out victorious in scientific debate.

Soret has related the charming anecdote of how Goethe, at the former's visit on August 2, 1830, received him in great excitement with the words: "What do you think! What is the news from Paris! The volcano has broken out!" Soret thought that Goethe was speaking of the political revolution which, in reality, impressed him as being of but quite negligible importance. His mind had really been aroused by the scientific revolution that was then well under way. Soret writes:

Nouvelles inquiétantes de Paris; j'ai un bon coq-à-l'âne avec Goethe à leur sujet; je lui fais visite dans le courant de l'aprè-diner: Eh bien! s'ecrie-t-il, que pensez vous de cette grande affaire? Violà tout en combustion, ce n'est plus une affaire à huis clos, le volcan vient d'éclater!—La chose est terrible, me suis-je mis à répondre; une aussi misérable famille donne bien peu d'espoir, appuyée d'un aussi misérable ministère. On finira par les chasser.

Mais je ne parle pas de ces gens-là, que m'importe! Il s'agit de la grande querelle entre Cuvier et Geoffroy.

By virtue of his spiritual vigilance Goethe overcame the troubles of age, severe attacks of illness, and death which ravaged round about him, as well as the jubilees which belong to the terrors of old age—the fiftieth anniversary of his arrival in Weimar, the fiftieth anniversary of Karl August's reign, and so on. It was this, too, that assuaged the feelings of loneliness after so many friends had departed—his Duke, his son, and the women who had once stood near him. For several years he devoted himself to the completion of *Faust—das Hauptgeschäft,* the appellation under which it at that time alone appeared in his diary. When the work was finished, packed up, and sealed without its occurring to him for a second to publish it, he felt satisfied and at ease; he had received a vacation. He was no longer to write in his diary: "Das Hauptgeschäft bedeutend gefördert." His time was now his own; he could use the days that were left him as he willed. Numerous they were not. July 22, 1831, Goethe wrote in his diary: *Das Hauptgeschäft zu Stande*

gebracht. . . . Alles rein Geschriebene geheftet.
Precisely eight months later, March 22, 1832, he
breathed his last after a week's illness. On the
day of his death he felt so ill that he could not remain in bed; he wished to rest in his easy chair, the
arm chair which even now stands in the little room
in the Goethe house where he sat when he died. His
dead body, according to contemporary testimony,
was surprisingly beautiful.

II

On July 17, 1777, Goethe wrote, with a captiousness that is characteristic of immature minds, this
celebrated little poem to Countess Auguste von
Stolberg:

> Alles geben die Götter, die Unendlichen,
> Ihren Lieblingen ganz;
> Alle Freuden, die unendlichen,
> Alle Schmerzen, die unendlichen,
> Ganz.

Though the thesis seems to have found confirma-
tion in his own life, his familiar words to Eckermann, January 27, 1824, are equally true:

I have always been regarded as having been specially
favored by fortune. I am not inclined to complain of my
lot, or bemoan my career. But in actuality it has been nothing but toil and trouble. I can truly say that in all my
seventy-five years I have not had four weeks in which I was
really happy. It was the incessant turning and lifting of a
stone that had to be lifted and turned once more. . . . The
claims upon my time, within as well as from without, were
far too numerous.

It was not long after Goethe's death that K. von
Conta was speaking of him to his friend Heinrich

Meyer. Conta told Meyer that Goethe was the happiest mortal that ever lived. Meyer denied it stoutly. He insisted that the discomfort which Goethe had been obliged to undergo, at times through his own action, was more than outweighed by the happiness he may have enjoyed. Meyer also made the point that the excess of praise which men occasionally showered upon him motivated the bitterest injustice a man's heart can suffer in that it inspired his opponents to criticism and censure that were all the more caustic.

It would seem that Goethe was not influenced by the painful incidents that befell him in a material and external way; but it only seems so. Silence is rarely the antidote to suffering, and in Goethe's case never. His lips were sealed but his heart was hurt. There is irrefutable truth in Eckermann's statement. Fate was not hostile to Goethe along lines and in fields that are easily described. But as a thinker with an original mind, and a poet with a matchless imagination, he was not the favored child of fortune; his lot cannot be regarded as an enviable one.

What we are pleased to call the public is, all things taken into consideration, a power the stupidity of which can never be fathomed. Goethe's case was unique; his misfortune was without equal. In the first place, his people constituted anything but a united nation. In the second they were so far behind in general development that there was no native standard by which to measure a mental force or an activity such as his. His public was without an organ for free beauty; there was no mouthpiece for liberal art. For centuries the ideal had been

accessible to the public in no form other than the
moral or the moralizing. The apostles of Enlightenment who had been his predecessors, and who had
had their own hard fight with orthodoxy, had never,
even in their poetry, advanced beyond the point
where they disseminated utilitarian truths. The
men of *Sturm und Drang,* who wished to become his
allies, merely revelled in sentimentality, and wielded
their blunt and heavy pens in the cause of common-
places. We have but to think of Lenz. And yet,
his public was quite unable to make an appreciable
distinction between him and them, between a Goethe
and a Lenz.

When therefore voices were raised in older civ-
ilizations, particularly in England, in zealous proc-
lamation of the disjointed, the fragmentary, the
stylistically uncertain elements in Goethe's works,
someone should have had the grace of liberality to
remark that intelligent support on the part of the
general public is one of the prerequisites to creation.
Without it the author feels abandoned by his friends
and surrendered to his foes. He cannot write with
ease and distinction. Feeling absolutely alone, he
gives up his task when only half completed, or even
earlier. He finds it possible to complete it only
through the expenditure of excessive will power
when he knows in advance that it is not going to
meet with a cordial response on the part of those
who did not write it, but who might reasonably be
supposed to read it. Goethe knew that his public
stood on a low level, so low that it could be inspired
only patriotically, only by hearing the nation to
which it by chance belonged praised, preferably at
the expense of other nations. Or it could be moved

only through sentimentality, by reading the stories
of the agonies of love in the hearts of the young.
And there were, truth to tell, only three times in
his life when Goethe had his public solidly with him
and behind him: When he published *Götz,* when
he published *Werther,* and when he published *Hermann und Dorothea.*

The public at that time, as always, was accustomed to look to its leaders to see what it should
think. But on this occasion, for once, the leaders
left the public—and Goethe—in the lurch. Lessing was a stranger to restraint in his malignant
criticism of *Götz* and *Werther.* He was beside
himself with wrath when he read brave Wieland's
epistle in praise of Goethe. Klopstock, who survived Lessing by so many years, invariably treated
Goethe's poetry with ironic or overt contempt. He
had called his *Iphigenie* a *stiff* imitation of the
Greeks; he scorned the theme in *Hermann und Dorothea* on the ground that it was inadequately exalted
for epic treatment. He uttered the most pitiable
witticisms on and against the nine muses who sing
in rustic taverns. Nor did he fail to avail himself
of the opportunity to tell Goethe that it was he who
could not write German. This happened when
Goethe wrote his epigramme against the German
language. Klopstock spake as follows:

Die deutsche Sprache

Goethe, du dauerst mich, dass du mich schreibst? Wenn
    du mich kenntest,
Wäre dir dies nicht Gram. Goethe, du dauerst mich auch!

The friendship between Goethe and Schiller
aroused Klopstock's cordial embitterment. He in-

formed the two gentlemen that they were square-
toes from whose mouths exuded nothing but self-
praise. One epigramme begins:

Afterahmer und Original sind sonst sich was ungleich,
Dennoch gleichen sie sich, *Schüler und Gothe,* die Herrn!
Kaum dass der Eine des Eigenlobs Trompete vom vollen
Mund absetzt, so ergreift sie der Ander' und bläst.

From the very beginning of Goethe's life in Weimar, he was regarded in the German reading world
as dead to literature; he was at any rate forgotten.
In his *Charaktere deutscher Dichter und Prosaisten,*
two volumes, K. A. Küttner, the literary historian,
rejoices to record the fact that "little by little, and
gradually withal, the overwhelming praise that
drunken admirers have lavished upon Goethe is
dying out."

Nor dare we overestimate the satisfaction that
the Court in Weimar could give Goethe, and still
more cautious must we be about the alleged appreciation he enjoyed on the part of its members. Six
months after his arrival, Charlotte von Stein describes, in a letter written in French to the physician Zimmermann, the Ducal family in the following
words:

A ruler who, at odds with himself, discontented with
the world about him, places his very life in jeopardy day
after day, and this despite his naturally weak constitu-
tion; an even sicklier brother; a morose mother; a dis-
gruntled wife. Good creatures all of them, but of harmony in this family—not a trace.

We have already seen what difficulties ensued
from living with Herder. In a letter from Goethe
to Lavater, written in September, 1780, we read:

"Herder continues to make his own life and the lives of those about him bitter." Before he had gone very far on his career, Goethe lost Merck, of whom we read this significant note in his diary of July 13, 1779: "Since he is the only person who thoroughly understands what I do and why I do it, and yet sees everything from a different point of view, a gratifying certainty and assurance arises between us."

Charlotte von Stein's criticisms of Clärchen, the *Römische Elegien,* and *Wilhelm Meister* show that she never had the faintest conception of Goethe's art; that she could not possibly be the ideal public which he persistently tried to find in her. That Christiane could not constitute an ideal audience lies on the surface. So far as she is concerned we did not need, in order to convince ourselves of her lack of ability to appreciate Goethe, the jocose observation which Oehlenschläger alleged to have heard from Goethe's own lips: "Es ist doch wunderlich, die Kleine kann gar kein Gedicht verstehen."

In short, no human being eager for a reputation of sanity, can ever maintain that Goethe enjoyed the appreciation from his fellow citizens that spurs an author on, creates in him a burning desire to write, and enables him to execute the plans his genius has designed. Indeed there were even times when the master, old or young, looked upon Weimar itself with troubled eyes. The question having arisen as to whether his foster-son, Fritz von Stein, should enter the service of Prussia or that of Weimar, Goethe wrote to the boy's mother, his quondam friend: "Anyone who wishes to *live* and see what the world looks like, should stand aghast at the thought of service in a petty state as he would shudder at the sight of *an open grave."* And yet, Karl August was more enlightened than any prince in Germany at that time.

That even Schiller was at first ill calculated to appreciate Goethe's art is proved by his preposterous criticism of Egmont. It was only under the impression of the master's personality as seen at close range, and of his purely personal good-will, that Schiller lifted himself up, as it were, above the level of his own life and that of his century and became the great promoter of Goethe into which he eventually developed. But by his partnership with Schiller, Goethe did anything but incur the favor of the German public. The rising up of the two men against common opponents was explained by that marvelous factor dubbed public opinion in some such fashion as the following: The noble Schiller, who loved the true, the beautiful, and the good, has been led astray by Goethe, as heartless as he is shameless, by Goethe whose immorality even liberal Herder, the friend of his youth, condemned without reserve. (Herder to Knebel, August 5, 1887, concerning *Die Braut von Korinth*: "Priapus as a pagan youth priapises, in this ballad, a cold and heartless corpse into the living warmth of passion.")

That Schiller, after he had finished *Wallenstein*, considered himself in all good faith as Goethe's equal, and ceased looking up to him by way of understanding him, is in no way surprising. His own endowment, which belonged so wholly to the eighteenth century, made it difficult for him to appreciate that in Goethe which not merely extended beyond his century, but was independent of all time.

It was indeed Rahel who led the way toward an understanding of Goethe; she had no misgivings and but few false judgments. Later came Bettina, then the Schlegels. They pointed out the contrast between Goethe's poetry and Schiller's rhetoric. They felt, for a time at least, a really sincere reverence for Goethe. But it was only for a time. At the very beginning of the nineteenth century, their attitude underwent a complete right-about-face. Indifference was followed by hostility. It was the tubercular Novalis who first made the grand discovery that *Wilhelm Meister* is mere prose. His second invention lay in the formula: As a poet Tieck is different from and greater than Goethe. This final break between the author of *Faust* and the rejuvenators of *die wunderbare Märchenwelt* was brought on by Goethe's treatise on Winckelmann. In a letter to Fouqué, A. W. Schlegel called it a "sin against the Holy Ghost." Friedrich Schlegel maintained in all seriousness that Fouqué's *Der Zauberring* was, next to *Don Quixote* (*Wilhelm Meister* and *Die Wahlverwandtschaften* are no longer taken into account), the very best of all novels.

As a sort of Apostles Creed on the part of the Romanticists, the view became more and more general that there was a poet who would some day—the day was not specified—dethrone Goethe and enthrone himself. This poet was Ludwig Tieck. Immermann, the ally of Heine, wrote on November 28, 1831, these glorious words to Tieck: "Methinks the domain of real poetry begins where Goethe (with a few exceptions) stops."

Admiration for Goethe was contrary to the spirit

of a North German on general principles. Without being more moral than the men of other races,
the North German places a high value on, and he
wishes to see portrayed, *moral,* that is to say, bi-
sected beings in whom the intellectual wages a stub-
born war against the sensual. Nothing interests
him less (as is the case with a Northerner in general) than *nature,* nature without dualism, without
the schism between pleasure and duty, nature as an
all-embracing unity. If nature were worshipped
without restraint and with no feeling of shame, what
would the preachers have to preach about? Who
would wish to receive their words of consolation?

In his *Der Fall Wagner,* Nietzsche says: "We
are familiar with Goethe's fate in morally sour, old-
maidenish Germany. Goethe has always been repellent to the Germans; honest admirers he has
found only among Jewesses." We have seen what
Pustkuchen had to say in his *Wanderjahre.* A
little later, Vogler and Köchy wrote the even more
venomous book entitled *Goethe als Mensch und
Schriftsteller.* And when Romanticism was setting
and Liberalism was rising, Goethe became the especial target. To aim at it and hit it was to carry
off the big prize. Wolfgang Menzel was the master
marksman. It is impossible for an individual of
today to realize the weight that was attached at
that time to his history of German literature; there
are two volumes; Tieck is lauded to the skies. But
in this work called *Die deutsche Literatur* (1827),
Goethe is treated with all the contempt known to
envy and born of prejudice. Menzel finds him lacking in morality, in love of country, in love of liberty,
and in religion. Goethe has flattered all the preju-

dices and all the vanities of the age. He has three different brands of personal vanity. He has no poetic *genius;* he does have *talent;* but it is devoid of inner durability; it is a hetæra who has her price for everyone. Goethe has, too, marked "ability to make his readers his accomplices." He loved to swim with the stream and on the surface, like cork. He made himself the servant of every weakness that chanced just then to be in vogue. Under the polished mask of his works there lies concealed a refined lust for sensuous pleasures. His poetry shows the materialism of the modern world in full bloom.

As we have mentioned before, in the discussion of *Die Braut von Korinth,* Menzel catalogued six different types of voluptuousness in Goethe. He went through his works seriatim in order to measure them with his moral-national yardstick. In case it was impossible for him to show up any instances of real immorality, he preferred charges against him on the ground of his lack of originality. *Hermann und Dorothea* was disposed of as a sheer and mere imitation of Voss's *Luise.* In truth, says Menzel, Goethe was original only in *Faust* and *Wilhelm Meister;* and he was original here because he imitated himself. Moreover, he borrowed, as a younger man, from Molière and Beaumarchais. from Shakespeare and from Lessing, whereas his later "iambic tragedies" were merely "the fruits of his contest with Schiller."

And such a book the Germans read! And such a book Heinrich Heine commended! But Heine soon found it convenient to keep poles removed from Menzel. As to Börne's politically well founded though in actuality insane attacks on Goethe, we have already spoken at length in another place (in "Main Currents," vol. VI). Gervinus's moral-political conception of literature led to an idolization of Shakespeare at Goethe's expense. To understand Goethe was not given to Gervinus.

It is highly significant that in every single instance in which Goethe modestly called attention to his limitations, to some inadequate phase of his talents, his opponents leaped at the confessions with uncurbed ecstasy. Incapable themselves of finding defects, or appreciating real merit, they made a great ado out of these statements from the poet himself. And despite the obligatory admiration for Goethe in literary circles, the clerical opposition to him was not disarmed until quite recently; it has indeed not been completely demobilized at this very day. On the hundredth anniversary of his birth, in 1849, everyone was so preoccupied with the revolution and the reaction that the celebration passed by almost unnoticed. Politics at that time swallowed up every other consideration. It was not until after the founding of the German Empire that *Goethe Philologie* gained a firm foothold in Germany. Since then the study of Germany's greatest poet has been developed into a formal system. The homage that is done him has become a service in the temple. It is a matter of consecration or hands off.

III

There was something in Goethe's character that made it impossible for him ever to become universally popular. He was too great, too inaccessable, to be admired with reason by more than the minority. If his renown has spread throughout the entire world, and if it can at this môment be said to be unshakable and indestructible, this does not mean that his works have won such legions of readers as have the novels of Walter Scott or those of the elder Dumas. It merely means that those who know art and appreciate literature in their noblest manifestations have imbued their fellow countrymen with faith in his superiority. Every now and then his incomparable genius is taken to task for this or that. But the charge is invariably weak; it is full of holes and falls apart on being handled. It comes about as the result of just one thing: The skeptic has made unto himself a weapon from his own ignorance and irrationality. Goethe has entered the phalanx of the earth's most excellent minds.

While still living, he was known, and his works were appreciated, by individuals in the majority of the larger, and smaller, literatures, Scandinavia not excepted. A study of Goethe's significance for Denmark has been made in another place ("Samlede Skrifter," vol. I, page 266 ff.: *Goethe og Danmark.*) But from these lesser literatures he never received one single impulse that expanded his soul or enlightened his mind. In order to become world famous, he was obliged to make an impression in France and England. This he succeeded in doing while quite young. But the knowledge of him beyond a little circle was so slight and one-sided that it cannot be said to have been of much value.

It was *Werther*, soon translated into French, that gave Goethe a hearing in France. But even this worked out in such a way that for the next forty

years the French persisted in calling him "the author
of Werther." The expression encompassed their
knowledge of him. By his *Werther* he had made,
along with Rousseau, Young, and Ossian, a lasting
impression on French literature. It was done into
French by Count Schmettau (Aubry), Deyverdun,
Henry de la Bédoyère, Sevelinges, imitated by Nodier, remodelled by Chateaubriand (as *René*), by
Sénancour (as *Obermann*), defended by Madame de
Staël in her book *On Germany,* and copied by Frau
von Krüdener (in *Valérie*). At last it occurred to
the French that Goethe had written a number of
other things besides *Werther*. But his mental plia-
bility confused them for a long time. They were accustomed to find an author at that particular spot
where they had left him. They were always certain never to find Goethe there. When Benjamin
Constant visited Goethe in Weimar, he was astonished to find him utterly indifferent to the attitude
of the public and in no way concerned about the cir-
culation of his own works. Even Constant had an
eye single to the external effect.

The mere name of *Götz von Berlichingen* was,
for men of the old classical school, the sign to laugh.
Even as late as 1825, Auger acted in the French
Academy as though the thing were unpronounceable.
But on some of the leading French Romanticists
the work made an indelible impression. One of
these was Prosper Mérimée. He had turned to
Goethe with deference and confidence. Goethe
abused his trust. He unveiled his *nom de plume;*
he announced him as the author of the *Illyrian Folk-
songs*. Mérimée was vexed; but he was inspired by
scenes from *Götz;* the valiant scenes in his *La Jac-*

quérie show it. Ludovic Vitet also came under the spell of *Götz;* the excellent scenes in his *Les Barricades* prove it.

The younger set who wrote for the *Globe* were introduced to Goethe through Victor Cousin who visited Weimar in 1817 and again in 1825. Also, and especially, by Jean Jacques Ampère, who came to Weimar in 1827, remained there for months, and eventually came to a full appreciation of Goethe's originality.

Hermann und Dorothea, Wilhelm Meister and *Die Wahlverwandtschaften* had been translated as early as 1800, 1802, 1810. The character of Faust was a cryptic puzzle to the French—at first. But *Faust* was again and again translated. Its influence on Edgar Quinet's *Ashasvérus* is unmistakable. *Hermann und Dorothea* was imitated by Victor de Laprade in his *Pernette*. *Werther* was parodied on the French stage, while *Clavigo* was revised and performed time out of mind.

Goethe's lyrics were frequently translated by the Romanticists, each poem many times; the *mot juste* was not easy to find, but the search was pleasing. Charles Nodier even translated the poem on the violet:

> La violette ingénue
> Au fond d'un vallon obscur
> Déployait sur l'herbe émue
> Son frais pavillon d'azur.

Der Fischer was translated several times:

> L'onde frémit, l'onde s'agite,
> Tout près du bord est un pêcheur.
> De ce beau lac le charme excite
> Dans l'âme une molle langueur.

Emile Deschamps laid before Goethe his translation of *Die Braut von Korinth;* it won the poet's approval:

> Un jeune homme d'Athène à Corinthe est venu.
> C'est la première fois. Cependant il espère
> Chez un noble habitant, vieux hôte de son père,
> Entrer comme un ami trop longtemps inconnu.

It was A. Stapfer who gave the best translation of Mignon's song of longing:

> Ne la connais-tu pas, la terre du poète
> La terre du soleil, où le citron mûrit,
> Ou l'orange aux tons d'or dans les feuilles sourit?
> C'est là, maître c'est là qu'il faut mourir et vivre,
> C'est là qu'il faut aller, c'est là qu'il faut me suivre,

Théophile Gautier has even tried to reproduce a few lines of *Wanderers Nachtlied:*

> Pas une feuille qui bouge,
> Pas un seul oiseau chantant.

As an older man Gautier was dominated in general by the idea of Goethe's olympian deportment, as it was then called. His entire collection of *Emaux et Camées* is written in Goethe's spirit, and under the influence of Goethe's *Divan.*

Enthusiasm for Goethe gradually took hold of the thinking and aesthetic youth of France. They outdid each other in their eagerness to show him homage. David d'Angers made a journey to Weimar in order to complete a bust of Goethe. Hector Berlioz sent him the score of his excellent but fantastic work entitled *Eight Scenes from Faust* (in the translation of Nerval). This letter begins as follows:

Dans l'atmosphère de gloire, où vous vivez, si des suf-
frages obscurs ne peuvent vous toucher, du moins j'espère
que vouz pardonnerez à un jeune compositeur qui, le coeur
gonflé et l'imagination enflammée par votre génie, n'a pu
retenir un cri d'admiration.

Though Victor Hugo mentioned "the great Goethe" in his inaugural address on being admitted to
the Academy, as the one at whose death German
thought paled in retirement, Hugo never actually
appreciated Goethe; he found him "cold and egotis-
tical." His brother-in-law, Paul Foucher, published,
on the contrary, a hymn to Goethe, in 1830, that is
replete with passionate admiration. Its concluding
lines run:

> Nos gloires à tes pieds naissent, luttent, s'écroulent;
> Pour leurs flots expirants ton roc est un écueil,
> Ces vagues d'un instant, qui sur sa base roulent,
> Le rendent plus splendide et plus luisant à l'oeil.

The death of Goethe was regarded in France as
the most far-reaching literary event in Europe since
the death of Lord Byron. In Paris, Lesguillon's
Méphistophélès, inspired by *Faust*, was to be performed for the first time just as the news of Goethe's
death arrived. The performance was introduced
by an *Homage to the Spirit of Goethe* (Hommage
aux mânes de Goethe) which began as follows:

> Lorsque nous méditons au theatre, en silence,
> L'oeuvre qu'à votre arrêt nous offrons aujourd'hui,
> Un cri de mort vers nous s'élance:
>   Goethe n'est plus! Goethe! celui
> Qui, depuis soizante ans, de victoire en victoire,
>   Promenant son front radieux
> Toujours jeune et nouveau, se berçait dans la gloire
>   Comme le soleil dans les cieux.

When Auguste Barbier, at that time living in Rome, received the news he united in beautiful verse his homage to Goethe with his homage to the former capital of the world which then lay in ruins.

O Goethe! O grand viellard, prince de Germanie!
Penché sur Rome antique et son mâle génie,
Je ne puis m'empêcher, dans mon chant éploré,
A ce grand nom croulé d'unir ton nom sacré.

Geoffroy de Saint-Hilaire's intimate relation to Goethe in his last years has already been touched upon. In June, 1836, he read a paper before the French Academy on Goethe's scientific works in which he honored him, first and foremost, for his having fixed the hypothesis concerning organic unity.

Among the numerous Frenchmen who were permeated with Goethe's spirit after his death, and who emphasized his superiority over his age, the two greatest have yet to be mentioned. There is Ernest Renan, akin to Goethe by his spiritual adaptability which takes in all history, and his marvelous sense for the primitive and refined ways of feeling. And there is Hippolyte Taine, descended directly from Goethe through his rare powers of understanding, his ability to mould into one natural and mental science, and his practical, enthusiastic, and natural feeling for art and insight into the ways of art.

That Goethe had an ideal public in the newer France is shown by the various translations of *Faust*. There is Stapfer's forceful and Saint Aulaire's less successful renderings, both of the year 1823, the interesting translation of 1828 by Gérard de Nerval which won Goethe's approval, Henri Blaze's which, like the others, partly in verse and partly in prose, was done with assistance from Weimar in the year 1840, Henri Bacharach's prose of 1873, Alexandre Laya's in verse, likewise from 1873, A. Maussenet's, intended as a text-book, in 1879, which tries solely to reproduce the German text, which Maussenet frequently misunderstood, Marc-Monnier's talented but incomplete one of 1875, August Daniel's painstaking and conscientious one of 1881, which is, however, embarrassed by the verse form, Georges Pradez's good metrical one of 1895, and finally the best of all by François Sabatier, published after the translator's death. Sabatier's rank as an artist will be felt by anyone on reading his version of the *Zueignung*:

Mes nouveaux chants ces âmes plus n'entendent
A qui ma voix a dit mes premiers chants;
De tant d'amis se dispersa la bande,
L'écho premier s'est tû depuis longtemps!

Mes plaintes à des inconnus descendent,
Tous leurs bravos pour moi sont un tourment;
Et ceux à qui mes chants avaient su plaire
S'en vont errant, s'ils vivent, sur la terre.

(Fernand Baldensperger: *Goethe en France;* Martha Langkavel: *Die französischen Uebertragungen von Goethe's Faust.*)

IV

By way of picturing the poetic grandeur of Shelley as contrasted with that of the French, we need merely to refer to his translation of the angels' song which opens the prologue to *Faust.*

> The sun makes music as of old
>   Amid the rival spheres of Heaven,
> On its predestined circle rolled
>   With thunder speed; the Angels even
> Drew strength from gazing on its glance,
>   Though none its meaning fathom may;—
> The world's unwithered countenance
> Is bright as at creations day.

This translation dates from the year 1822; it was done consequently just before Shelley's death.

It was not the great English poet, however, but a zealous writer of prose who introduced Goethe as a mental force to the English public; and oddly enough, it was a writer with senses keenly alive to spiritual excellence but woefully lacking in the finer feeling for great poetry. Richard Garnett has well said, apropos of the essay on *Faust* by Thomas Carlyle in the *New Edinburgh Review* of April, 1822, that in a letter by Shelley, written in the same month, there is embodied, in just five lines, more and richer insight into *Faust* than there would have been in five volumes from the hand of Carlyle in the unripe and dyspeptic prose he used in the essay. Carlyle was too impatient; he was too eager to disseminate newly acquired information. The people of Germany have nevertheless always been justly grateful to Carlyle for the work he did by way of making Goethe known in England.

Born December, 1795, he began the study of German in February, 1819. Madame de Staël's book *De l'Allemagne* had attracted his attention to Germany, just as it had attracted the attention of thousands of others. He was on the point of taking up mineralogy, and felt constrained to become ac-

quainted with the ideas of the German mineralogist
Werner in the original. His friend of that time,
Edward Irving, procured him a lexicon; he had a
German grammar sent on from London to Scotland.
As he tells John Murray in a letter written August
4, 1820, he soon had the impression that a new
Heaven and a new Earth had been revealed to him
through his penetration (it was not deep then) into
German literature.

He read Jean Paul whose influence on his style
is most marked. Jean Paul called forth his Scotch
humor and provided his otherwise somewhat monotonous prose with vigorous arabesques. He read
Fichte whose influence is easily discernible in his
fundamental viewpoint according to which the world
of experience is merely a cloak for the divine idea,
and true life consists in placing one's personality
at the service of mankind.

But Carlyle's interest in the spiritual life of Germany soon centred around Goethe, despite the fact
that it would be difficult to find two personalities
more dissimilar. It we except hatred toward chaos,
they had hardly a feeling in common. What Carlyle saw in Goethe was the liberator from the merely
negative and destructive toward which he himself
was at first inclined. He yearned for a great living
model who had found peace after a tremendous
inner struggle. He had found one in Goethe. Years
later he said to Emerson: "He is the only genuine
soul of profound depth and wide range that I have
found in Europe after search through the records
of generations." He also wrote to Goethe himself
the significant words: "I can never forget that
it is you to whom I owe the unspeakably precious

thought that *Ehrfurcht* is possible. Seeing this, I no longer guess and deny; I believe and know."

It was not admiration for Goethe as an artist and a poet that had captivated him. He lacked the feeling for poetry and had a poor ear for verse. His criticisms of Wordsworth, Keats and Shelley, together with the iambic pentameters scattered throughout his translations from German, are incontrovertible witnesses on this point. It was Goethe's personality that charmed him. He said to Sterling: "The existence of this man was for me the message of the evangelists. It ransomed me, I believe, from disaster, inward and outward."

Goethe, who understood everything, was after all quite well aware that Carlyle's attention was not drawn to the purely artistic. One day he remarked (July 25, 1827) to Eckermann that Carlyle, curiously enough, with regard to his criticisms of German writers, "had their spiritual and moral kernels in view; these he regarded as all-important." To Carlyle, poetry was a means of sensualizing the rational. In actuality he clung to the theories from the days of Pope or Lessing.

He published, after considerable interest in Schiller's *History of the Thirty Years War,* a *Life of Schiller.* It is a book of no great consequence. Then he went in for Goethe with all his heart. Though he did not think highly of *Wilhelm Meister,* he translated it into English. In September, 1823, he wrote a letter in which he betrays his Scotch impatience: "Goethe is the greatest genius of the last century and the greatest ass of the last three." But by and by the work and the man won him entirely. He asserts that not for six years has he found so many thoughts in any one book. Shortly after Goethe's death (July, 1832) he wrote his Essay on Goethe for the *Foreign Quarterly*. This was an event in England at that time. There is only one unfortunate thing about it: the essay is a mediocre funeral oration; it is nothing more; from it nothing is to be learned.

But the thick volume of correspondence between Goethe and his apostle across the Channel has not lost its value for the present generation. Carlyle's letters are beautiful because of their profound respect. Those from Goethe do not number more than a dozen; and Eckermann writes at times for his chief. But what Goethe says is deep; his judgments carry weight; they betray vast understanding, and a richness of heart that even a novice can grasp and like. By the mere touch of his spiritual personality, Goethe had initiated Carlyle into life and literature. He won in him, also, a sworn supporter among the English people—a people that is highly developed and noted then, and for a long time before then, for its conservatism.

The beautiful, almost paternal, relation to Byron, evoked by and based on the deferential homage of the otherwise defiant Lord, could not win the hearts of the English to Goethe. Byron had had his own troubles with his countrymen. The misunderstanding between him and them existed even after his death. Emerson's admiration made a lasting impression in North America, though it was not given out until after Goethe's death. His essay entitled *Goethe, or the Writer,* is, truth to tell, irrelevant talk and nothing more. It is immeasurably pretentious and quite void. But the superior, violent and domineering Scotchman, Thomas Carlyle, who would tolerate no opposition and soon acquired the habit of nailing his judgments so fast that they were allowed to stand unquestioned and uncontested, became in the years 1823-1832 the redoubtable mouthpiece of German thought, and especially of Goethe's thought, on British soil. He wrote a score of books, essays and translations. The same man who coined the term *hero-worship* introduced into the Anglo-Saxon world the cultivation of Goethe as a hero. And like a good and trusted general, he won the battle for his emperor.

At Goethe's death, the word *Weltliteratur,* which he himself had coined, had become a reality. And he himself, thanks to the united efforts of others, had become the centre of this *Weltliteratur.*

CHAPTER XXXVIII

THE TREE OF LIFE, AND THE TREE OF KNOWLEDGE

DURING his entire life, Goethe bewildered the reading world through his adeptness at transformation and rejuvenation. First he was Prometheus; then he was the Olympian Zeus. First he was an insurgent; then he was the royal sage. First he was the poet of passion; then he was nature's great, serene interpreter.

There have lived unforgetable personages whose gifts lay exclusively in an extraordinary ability to create life. There have been sculptors such as Donatello, painters such as Rembrandt, Musicians such as Mozart, poets such as Alfred de Musset. They created and handed down to generations after them works that are richly blessed with life, that bubble over with life. The judgments they have passed outside of their own fields, however, do not interest us. Toward the doctrines they homaged we are indifferent. They had an adequate knowledge of the inner and outer world, of man's nature and man's heart. They never theorized on these subjects. Their creations live. That is more than enough. And it is enough for us.

The tree of life is not the tree of knowledge.

And there are minds from which we have received uninterrupted instruction: An astronomer like La-

place who discusses the most difficult problems so
that all men may understand them; a scientist like
Alexander von Humboldt whose wisdom is all-embracing and imparted with delightful clarity; a natural scientist like Charles Darwin, who, with enrapturing modesty, posited an ingenious substitute
for the belief in final causes, and as an explanation
of the origin of species; a historian like Augustin
Thierry who is recondite and yet, despite all romanticism, intelligible, entertaining and informing.
These men have great knowledge and great wisdom.
They have sought and found. But they neither try,
nor are they able, to create characters that live and
move.

The tree of knowledge is not the tree of life.

Goethe is not like the men of either of these two
classes. He has the ability to form characters;
from the clay of art he can create men and
give them life. He has also the gift of the investigator. He explains the cosmos, the genesis of the
earth, the formation of plants, the inner connection
of the skeleton, the true nature of art. He is at
once a fountain of life, and an inexhaustible fountain of knowledge.

In the Eden of art and science he has revealed
to men, the tree of life and the tree of knowledge
are one.

END OF VOLUME TWO

INDEX

489